A COUNTRY MADE BY WAR

A
COUNTRY
MADE BY WAR

*From the Revolution to Vietnam —
the Story of America's Rise to Power*

GEOFFREY
PERRET

VINTAGE BOOKS   A DIVISION OF RANDOM HOUSE, INC.   NEW YORK

To absent friends:
Dr. Gary Francis Cox
and
David Jay Willoughby

First Vintage Books Edition, July 1990

Copyright © 1989 by Geoffrey Perret
Maps Copyright © 1989 by Jean Paul Tremblay

All rights reserved under International and Pan-American
Copyright Conventions. Published in the United States by
Vintage Books, a division of Random House, Inc., New York,
and simultaneously in Canada by Random House of Canada
Limited, Toronto. Originally published, in hardcover,
by Random House, Inc., in 1989.

Library of Congress Cataloging-in-Publication Data
Perret, Geoffrey.
A country made by war : from the Revolution to Vietnam : the story
of America's rise to power / Geoffrey Perret.
p. cm.
Includes bibiographical references (p.
ISBN 0-679-72698-5
1. United States—History, Military. I. Title.
[E181.P55 1990]
306.2'7'0973—dc20   89-40548
CIP

Manufactured in the United States of America
10 9 8 7 6 5 4 3 2 1

CONTENTS

ACKNOWLEDGMENTS

For advice, encouragement and assistance I am indebted to some old friends: in the Bay area, to Al Brewster, Sarah Cirese and Kevin Hughes; in Hawaii, to Chuck and Susan Hurd; in Washington, D.C., to Bob and Carol Hopper; and in England, to Jack Hartley.

In writing this book, as in writing its predecessors, I have relied on the aid of Mrs. Joyce M. Ford and her efficient staff at the General Library of the University of California at Berkeley; and on the staff of the Bancroft Library. I was also helped by Bruce Martin at the Library of Congress; the staffs of the Beverley and Wakefield libraries; the Ministry of Defence library in London; and the friendly librarians of the National War College, at Fort Lesley J. McNair, in Washington.

During a battlefield tour in 1986 I had the good fortune to be able to pick the brains of guides and rangers who were unfailingly knowledgeable and enthusiastic. My thanks go to Ted Alexander and Michael Stuckey, at Antietam; to Stacy Allen, at Vicksburg; to Mike Andrus, at Richmond and Malvern Hill; to Michael Ceniceros, at New Orleans; to David Iglesias, at the Alamo; to Lisa Garvin, at Gettysburg; to Jane Kemble, at Shiloh; to Donald J. Long, at Guilford Courthouse; to Bob McLean, at Cowpens; to Greg Mertz, at Chancellorsville; to John Nissel, at Bull Run; to Gregg Potts at Port Hudson, Louisiana; to Chris Revel, at Kings Mountain; and to Edward Tinney, at Chickamauga. In France, I should like to express my gratitude to the muse of Belleau Wood, Mme. Sabine Verdel.

I am grateful too for the help of Colonel Michael Krause at the National War College, who could not have made a visitor more welcome.

I have also benefited from the willingness of Stephen Ambrose, Ronald Spector and Russell Weigley to take time from their busy schedules and read my book while it was still in manuscript. While not agreeing with all my conclusions they nonetheless provided valuable encouragement and advice.

Finally, I should like to record my enormous good fortune in having for my editor Robert D. Loomis, whose questions, criticisms and comments saved me from error time and again. His awesome erudition, lightly worn, has been both an anchor and a beacon.

INTRODUCTION

In the middle of Belleau Wood the light fades quickly as evening falls. To my right the dank undergrowth stretches away from ground broken by distorted whorllike shapes. The centers are depressed and dark, but the edges are raised and gray, like scar tissue knitting around an old wound. These are the collapsed remains of German rifle pits. Beside them, black and silent, stands a line of elderly artillery pieces, some German, some French.

To my left the woodland rises in a gentle, swiftly darkening slope. And all around are the slender larches, straight, well-spaced trees, many with trunks grooved by bullets, sliced by shrapnel. My attention becomes fixed, though, on the monument.

It is dominated by the muscular back of a man, shown in strong relief. Cast in a creamy bronze, the figure moves away from the viewer, from right to left. From what can be seen of the face comes an impression not of an individual personality but of implacable will. He wears the kettle helmet of World War One. In his strong hands he holds an Enfield rifle with bayonet fixed.

As the shadows deepen, the dark polished stone that holds this bronze relief shades into the middle distance. Gradually the marine seems to come alive, as if he has just emerged unscathed from the rifle pits behind him and is pressing on, deeper into Belleau Wood.

On battlefields around the world stand monuments that are anodyne or peaceful or plain absurd; monuments that are wrapped in longing or regret; monuments that are patriotic, religious or triumphant; and some that are decaying and neglected, as if they marked a secret shame.

The marine who lives in Belleau Wood is unique. He is stripped to the waist, his naked flesh exposed to maiming and violent death, a raw expression of the savagery of hand-to-hand fighting. He is looking to kill or be killed.

Over the years I have visited more than fifty places where Americans have fought their country's wars: Wake Island in the shimmering heat . . . Shiloh in the summer rain . . . the Shuri line when the earth was still lumpy with unexploded ordnance . . . Omaha Beach . . . San Jacinto . . . Inch'ŏn . . . the Little Bighorn . . . the steep forest of the Argonne . . . Gettysburg . . . New Orleans . . . Guam . . . Put-in-Bay . . . Lexington Green. . . . All different, all the same.

Different because each battlefield tells its own story. The same because at all of them the visitor feels the claim they make on us, those men of the monuments. In Belleau Wood as evening darkened the ground where I stood while the sky overhead shone a bright silver and pearl-shaded blue, the breeze down the Valley of the Marne rustled the treetops. *"Rappelez-vous . . . rappelez-vous,"* the leaves seemed to murmur. "Remember . . . remember. . . ."

This book is a military history, resounding to the sound of drum and trumpet. Yet I have raised my sights to look beyond the fields of strife, and placed the nation's nine major wars and other armed conflicts in their truest context, the evolution of American life.

A COUNTRY MADE BY WAR

1

THE INACCURATE FARMERS

HAD IT BEEN left to Major General Thomas Gage, there would have been no fighting. Not yet. He wanted to abandon the city to its rebellious passions. He would have struck down what the colony called the Intolerable Acts that closed the port in reprisal for the Tea Party and quartered his soldiers in citizens' homes. Then he would have sailed back to England. Hard or soft: let them decide. And if they still chose to defy the Crown he would return, with a vengeance, bringing an army of tens of thousands, and crush rebellion to the last contumacious soul in New England.

In London that seemed fantastic. The king was ready to fight for Boston, not give it up. "Blows must decide," he told the prime minister, Lord North. That was the new policy. A large hospital was begun for the flow of casualties expected from Gage's army. The issue was as plain as could be, and always had been: were these people subject to the king's authority or not? In the end it all came down to that. Reason had been tried. Concessions had been tried. Patience had been tried. Time to bring the rebellion to a head. Better to fight a short war now than a long one later. Gage was sent fresh instructions.

There was snow on the ground until April 10 that year. It had been a long, tense, miserable winter. The whole city seemed suspended in ice. Waiting. And then, with all the sudden, blood-racing warmth of the first day of spring in Boston, when the sun appears to burst over the city like a bomb, it came. And with the break in the weather there arrived, on April 14, 1775, the orders from London.

"Force must be repelled with Force," Gage read. He was to go out and round up the rebel leaders. In Boston that seemed fantastic. Most of them were scattered or in hiding. For every one rounded up, another—probably more radical—would take his place. There was no rebel army Gage could bring to battle, no rebel capital he could march on, no rebel treasury he could seize. His sole advantage was that he knew where the rebels hid their arms, but even this was less an advantage than it seemed, because he could not raid the arms caches without the rebels' learning of it in advance. There were no secrets in Boston.

His troops lived close to the people of the city. Scores of his officers and NCOs were lodged in local homes or slept with local women. Some, like Gage himself, had American wives. Neither British nor Americans could conceal much from each other.

If he needed proof of that, it had come in September 1774, when the general sent out two raiding parties to recover gunpowder and cannon that had been diverted from the militia. Many of the rebels were members of the militia and appeared to think that they had every right to arms and ammunition delivered to militia stores. Gage intended to show them just how wrong they were by taking back stores the rebels had diverted.

News of these raids spread through New England like an alarm bell. Rebellious militiamen swarmed toward Boston from as far away as Connecticut. A major clash was narrowly averted, but Gage fortified the land approach to the city, Boston Neck, and acted like a man besieged.

In February 1775 he nearly caught the rebels unawares by sending a raiding party out to Salem, to recover more diverted arms. This time the local militia turned out and dared to bar his troops at the bridge leading into town. To avoid a fight, the search was abandoned. The small army in Boston, 4,000 men in all, lost faith in their commander. They began to call him "Old Woman" Gage. They felt frustrated and hemmed in.

He knew where the main rebel arms cache was held—at Concord, some seventeen miles northwest of Boston. He had a good idea of what was there: hundreds of muskets, some small cannon, barrels of gunpowder, axes, spades, candles, salt, flour, dried beef, medicine chests, tents, wooden spoons, even several casks of wine, along with thousands of cartridges and a pile of cannonballs.

He and the stiff parchment sheets from London agreed on one point: the need for secrecy. He must strike without warning. As earlier raids had shown, the only way to keep the militia from gathering was to maintain surprise. Secrecy was the first essential. The others were strength and speed. He must strike hard, and quickly.

Gage called on the best troops under his command, the 400 light infantry and 400 grenadiers. Light infantry were something fairly new, the bright idea of advanced military theorists. They were tough, wiry, alert men, able to keep up with a horse trotting over open ground; roughly four or five miles an hour. Army horses were chosen for size, not pace: a cavalry charge at full tilt reached twelve miles an hour. The speed of light infantry put them ahead of the army and on its flanks. They could make the historic boast of elite troops, "First to fight."

Grenadiers were the tallest and strongest men in contemporary armies, chosen originally because they could throw a grenade farther than ordinary troops. By 1775 none of them actually carried grenades but they stood out for their height and their strength. They too were the elite of close combat.

Command of this mixed force fell on Lieutenant Colonel Francis Smith, the senior field officer available. It was seniority achieved in the usual way, by plodding service. A grossly fat man, the colonel was as ponderous in thought as in movement. Gage personally wrote out his orders: "You will march with the utmost expedition and secrecy to Concord, where you will seize all the artillery and ammunition you can find. . . ."

Second in command would be Major John Pitcairn, a competent officer well liked by his men, but serving in the Royal Marines. He was a stranger to the infantrymen. Like Smith he too was fat and approaching fifty. A reserve force of 1,000 foot soldiers was put together and assigned to a young brigadier, Hugh, Earl Percy, descendant of Hotspur and heir to the Duke of Northumberland. He was to back up the lightning raid if anything went wrong.

On the afternoon of April 18 Gage put the first part of his plan into action. Patrols on horseback fanned out from Boston to prevent rebel couriers from raising the alarm once the troops moved out of the city. At about the same time, the cache of arms at Concord was being dispersed to towns farther west, or buried shallowly in the furrows of freshly plowed fields. For two days and nights the entire countryside had been waiting.

After the final briefing at army headquarters that evening Lord Percy strolled across Boston Common toward his lodgings to change into uniform. He fell in with a group of men who were clearly excited about something. "The British have marched," gloated one, "but they will miss their aim."

"What aim is that?" asked Percy.

"Why, the cannon at Concord." There were no secrets in Boston.

Percy hurriedly retraced his steps. Everything was compromised, he told Gage. What chance of secrecy now? The general chose to hope for the best. The machinery was already in motion. Besides, simply because his plans were known in the city did not mean the news had spread far. He still had his patrols out covering the roads.

At ten o'clock that Tuesday night, as red-coated NCOs went through the barracks shaking men awake and whispering commands, Paul Revere was being rowed past British warships in the harbor to spread the alarm. The grenadiers and light infantry were soon hurrying to assembly on Boston Common. Then, in whaleboats that moved to the susurration of muffled oars, they crossed Back Bay to disembark in East Cambridge. The boats proved too heavily loaded to run ashore as planned at Lechmere Point. Men bent under sixty-pound packs stepped into marsh water that lapped at their knees. It was midnight.

Paul Revere was at that moment riding into Lexington, ten miles to the west. He had bawled his way through a score of villages and towns: "The Reg'lars are coming!" As he galloped into Lexington, lights blazed in Buckman's tavern. Some of the militia were already out. Rumor, faster than the fleetest horse, had got there before him.

Riding on toward Concord with a courier who had slipped out through Boston Neck past British guards and a doctor who had been up late courting a local girl, Revere was challenged by a patrol. The others escaped into the night while Revere rode blindly into a pasture. Surrounded, he was put under arrest. As the patrol and its prisoner regained the road a gun sounded back in Lexington. The British officer in charge asked what it meant.

"To alarm the country," Revere replied, feeling, perhaps, a certain insolent pride. The patrol took his horse, abandoned their prisoner and rode off eastward at speed, to warn Smith that the rebels were alerted.

It was two in the morning. Smith's force had just left Lechmere Point. He made them wade through a creek rather than let them march, noisily, over a wooden bridge. In the distance they heard alarm guns cracking news of their coming. At about the same time Gage, uneasy ever since Percy's unwelcome news, decided to send the reserve force to support Smith.

The Lexington militia had been turned out once, grown bored and cold, and been allowed to go home or take their ease in the tavern until the British arrived. At four-thirty, as the first pink-gray streak of dawn began lifting the edge of the eastern horizon, a horseman rode hard into town. A minute later drums were beaten. Men came running from their beds, from the tavern, from nearby houses, muskets in hand. They milled about in the near-darkness, some half-dressed, others without ammunition.

The commander of the Lexington militia, Captain John Parker, managed to get the seventy-odd men present formed into two ranks on the Green, in front of the meetinghouse, before the British arrived. The sun gilded the treetops, heralding a bright spring morning. The light infantry, led by Major Pitcairn, swung into view a little before 5 A.M., moving easily and confidently toward the militia under a glittering canopy of slender bayonets. A sense of uneasiness stirred the militia ranks. They were not blocking the road to Concord, but Parker had placed them so they commanded it.

Pitcairn ordered his men into line of battle. The light infantry sent up a cheer and deployed from road column into three ranks. They were aligned in two platoons, each 200 strong and three deep. Pitcairn rode forward with several of his officers, approaching the militia. "Lay down your arms, you damned rebels, and disperse!" No one moved. Behind him the light infantry were shouldering their muskets. Still no one moved. Other officers took up Pitcairn's command. "Lay down your arms! . . . Disperse! . . . Disperse!"

A volley roared from one platoon. Only powder: a warning. Again the command to lay down arms and disperse. The militia were outnumbered more than five to one. They had stood their ground. Honor was satisfied. They would hold on to their arms. Parker gave the order to disperse. And then a British officer shouted, "We will have them!" which might have meant militia muskets, or something else. The second platoon fired. This time with ball. After the volley, the charge; something almost instinctive after years of bayonet drill. The light infantry bowled into the fleeing, stunned militia while Pitcairn, whom they did not know, called in vain for his men to stop.

It was soon over. Eight militiamen were dead, ten more were wounded; Parker was dying. One British soldier had been hit in the leg and Pitcairn's horse had been creased by two bullets.

The light infantry pulled back and re-formed just as Colonel Smith marched up, leading the grenadiers. A volley was fired to celebrate victory over the militia. With fife and drum playing, the column set off for Concord, six miles away. The minutemen there (militia expected to fall out on five minutes' notice) were waiting for them.

At around 7:30 A.M. the confident red column approached the town, passing a small hill on top of which a liberty pole flew a defiant pine-tree Liberty flag. A squad of light infantry wheeled away to pull the pole down. Other troops meanwhile fanned out to search for rebel arms.

The Concord minutemen were gathering on Punkatassett Hill, which overlooked the North Bridge, spanning the Concord River. Two miles beyond the bridge was the farm of Colonel James Barrett, commander of the local militia. Gage had been informed, mistakenly, that the farm held a major arms cache. Three companies of light infantry, about 100 men in all, were sent across the bridge to search the colonel's farm.

The remaining British troops meanwhile made an unsystematic trawl through the town. They found some wooden spoons, five hundred pounds of musket balls, some barrels of flour and two old iron cannon. The musket balls and the flour were dumped in the river, and later retrieved. The trunnions on the cannon were knocked off, but later repaired. The wooden spoons were burned.

Three light infantry companies were detached to hold the North Bridge for the troops who would be returning from Barrett's farm. The militia gathering on Punkatassett Hill noticed smoke coming from half a dozen fires set by British troops in the town, and began moving down the hill, toward the bridge. The militia and the redcoats came face to face.

Uneasy at being outnumbered by two or three to one, the British raised their muskets and fired a volley. It was fired too high. No one was struck by it. A second volley, however, brought down three militiamen.

The British were in a poor position to start a firefight. The narrow bridge and the road to it gave them no room to spread out. Only the leading company of 35 men could fire. The two companies behind were little more than helpless targets. There was a proven tactic for this situation, called street fighting, but in the excitement of the action none of the British officers present seemed to think of using it. The Americans, with ample room to spread out on the hill and fire into the hemmed-in British, opened fire, killing three soldiers and wounding nine.

The light infantry began to pull back from the bridge, only to collide with two grenadier companies led by Colonel Smith coming tardily to their relief.

The militia whooped with jubilation at making British regulars retreat. In festive mood they scattered in various directions, instead of holding the hill and the bridge. The light infantry force sent to search Barrett's farm returned from their fruitless mission unhindered.

It was approaching 11 A.M. Colonel Smith had to make a decision: whether to stay here with his tired troops and hope Lord Percy might come up with the reserve, but at the risk of being cut off by swarms of militia; or whether to put his men back on the road, head for Boston and hope to meet Percy somewhere between here and there, but at the risk of close pursuit by the Patriots.

He could not know that confused orders back in Boston from Gage's headquarters had delayed the reserve's departure from 4 A.M. to 9 A.M. Percy also encountered obstacles on the road from the city, placed there by aroused Patriots.

After dithering for nearly an hour, Smith had his men fall in and marched them toward Lexington. He arrived there at half past two, pursued by militia all the way from Concord. As his men marched into the town from the west, Lord Percy marched in from the east. The reserve formed square. The weary light infantry and grenadiers marched into it, sinking gratefully to the ground. Two six-pounders Percy had brought with him barked intermittently, to keep the militia at bay.

After an hour's rest the British formed up and set off for Boston. All along the road were angry farmers with muskets. They fired at the passing column from behind trees, dry stone walls, fences and barns. They hid in upstairs rooms and fired down. They waited around bends, crouched along riverbanks, lay in wait by bridges, sprang up, and nearly always fired too soon. Others jumped out from their hiding places, shooting point-blank, ready to die rather than miss.

The light infantry fanned out to cover the flanks. More than one farmer, unaware that they were out, died where he crouched, brought down from behind, his musket still primed. In other places the woods hemmed in the road, leaving the flankers no room to do their work. With every mile the British grew more tired while fresh militia, just arrived, rushed into the fight. Enraged and frustrated, British troops attacked homes, pillaged them, killed unarmed civilians, set fires, straggled back toward the column under encumbering loot. In yards and behind trees deadly hand-to-hand struggles left one man dead, another standing, the British using bayonets, Americans knives and hatchets. The British took ten prisoners, the Americans about the same. They were lucky. Surrender had its dangers that day.

At dusk the exhausted column trudged into Charlestown. They counted 65 dead, 180 wounded, and 28 missing, nearly half of them prisoners. American casualties were put at 49 dead, 41 wounded, but this is almost certainly wrong. If the figure on fatalities is right, the wounded should be considerably more. The surviving British, their faces black from tearing open cartridges with their teeth, flung themselves down on the steep slopes of Bunker Hill.

The sun was going down. Here, directly across the water from Boston, they were under the protecting arm of hundreds of guns aboard the warships that crowded the harbor below. Around them, in a vast semicircle, orange flames began winking and dancing in the darkness. The militia, grown to more than 2,000, were not going home.

THE REPUTATION of British troops stood high. Not even news of this disaster and the withdrawal shortly after into Boston affected that, or shook the army's confidence in itself. The steadiness of the king's men under fire had won an empire that reached from Calcutta to Quebec. They were on average shorter than Americans, but in resilience, in the ability to ignore hardship or fatigue there was nothing to choose. The soldiers who fought their way back from Concord, despite the pillaging that was endemic in contemporary armies, put up an impressive combat performance. The light infantry and grenadiers had been on their feet for twenty-four hours. They marched nearly forty miles, with little food, not much rest, and carried nearly a hundred pounds of equipment. Yet after running a gauntlet of heavy fire and countless ambushes they remained a cohesive fighting force, bringing their wounded out with them.

The arch stone of the British army was the infantry regiment. Loyalty ran not to the army as such or to the Crown but to a man's regiment. It had an authorized strength of nearly 500 officers and men but in practice rarely exceeded 400. These were divided among ten companies, of which one was light infantry, another grenadiers. Artillery was organized by battalions, numbering roughly 900 men and 64 guns, and cavalry in regiments of 1,380 men. These were both highly specialized formations and there were few of them.

The standard infantry arm for half a century had been the flintlock musket, and would remain so for half a century to come. The standard British army model, the Brown Bess (nothing to do with Queen Elizabeth I; deriving from the Dutch word for firearm, *bus,* as in blunderbuss), weighed twelve pounds and was four feet nine inches long. A slim triangular bayonet, fitted to the muzzle by a socket, added another fourteen inches overall. It fired a lead bullet three quarters of an inch in diameter and weighing one and a half ounces: a lot of stopping power. The absence of an elevated rear sight was reflected in the British manual of arms—there was no command "Aim!" Men were ordered to "Level muskets!" A "well-leveled" volley, fired on command, was the ultimate in infantry firepower. Pursuit of that was the foundation of infantry tactics in all modern armies.

The regular or standing army was known as "the line." In combat infantry units deployed into a line of battle three ranks deep, as the light infantry had done at Lexington. They were expected to close with an enemy deployed in the same way. Whoever finished their deployment first or managed, while deploying, to outmaneuver the other usually won the firefight. Some maneuvers were designed to turn a flank; others built up one end of a line by thinning out the rest of it. At the beefed-up end there might be enough firepower to blow away part of the enemy line.

To load and fire a flintlock musket involved a dozen actions, from ripping a paper cartridge between the teeth to firing twenty to thirty seconds later. A musket erupted with a stunning roar. The recoil could leave bruises halfway down a man's chest. A tongue of orange flame up to three feet long shot from the muzzle, momentarily lighting up a cloud of choking black smoke.

Trained troops were expected to lay down a steady two rounds a minute. During intense firefights elite units could reach and sustain three rounds a minute. Musket barrels then became so hot that the paper cartridge was likely to explode halfway down the barrel. Men under fire were known to urinate into muskets to cool them down. A little loose powder dropped into the barrel and ignited dried it out. Normal firing resumed.

In rain, snow or drizzle damp flints and wet firing pans often failed. Badly loaded, a flintlock roared harmlessly. In the heat of action it was easy to forget the ramrod before firing and leave it in the barrel. Ramrods, made of brittle iron, fractured easily. Out in the field muskets were easy to break, hard to repair. There were no spare parts, only spare flints. As each one was individually made, so a new part had to be specially produced.

For all its eccentricity and unreliability, the smoothbore flintlock musket was probably the most highly prized infantry weapon in history. Soldiers throughout the world grew deeply attached to them, including Americans. In some parts of Africa, Asia and the Pacific they are still in use, but mainly out of sheer delight in their formidable pyrotechnics.

Their greatest shortcoming was limited effective range. After fifty yards the ball dropped sharply. This made the eighteenth-century battlefield an intimate theater of war. Men closed to a range where the well-leveled volley had maximum effect. Fire discipline—which usually meant allowing the enemy to fire first in order to deliver one's own volley at even closer range—was the hallmark of the best armies.

In this the British were second to none. They had the most compact formations ever seen on the battlefield. The front rank got down on one knee. The men of the second rank stood immediately behind, their left feet placed next to the right feet of the men in front. The men in the third rank had their left feet touching the right feet of the men in the middle. The term for this was expressive: "locking." These formations were so densely packed they tended to make the troops in the front rank fire too low and the two standing ranks fire too high. Once locked, however, they held their ground superbly and as men were hit by enemy fire the ranks could be closed almost instantly. The

British army chose solidarity over accuracy: one flesh in the face of mortal danger.

During the complicated, time-consuming business of reloading, troops were vulnerable to the bayonet charge. A volley followed immediately by a charge was the logical tactic where the forces engaged were at close range, of modest size and sufficiently well-trained to respond quickly. That happened many times in the Revolutionary War.

A line of onrushing, glittering bayonets was the moment of truth for all armies. When men broke and ran it was nearly always from the shock of a bayonet charge. Yet as military surgeons knew, its terrors were mainly psychological. Comparatively few men ever died from a bayonet wound sustained in combat. There are no more than half a dozen vital spots in the human body. Most of them are either deep within it or protected by bone. Either way, they are not easy to strike at with an unwieldy musket and its socket bayonet. Plunged into the fleshy parts of the body, or into the ribs, a bayonet was not usually fatal and nearly always hard to pull out. Experienced troops learned to carry knives and hatchets for close combat once the initial charge had been made or stood. All else failing, muskets were wielded as clubs.

On most battlefields of the late eighteenth century and later, the majority of casualties were accounted for by artillery. The general shortage of field artillery in this war would help keep combat losses fairly low. Infantry weapons were not very effective except in unusual circumstances. The Revolutionary War would produce only one rifle and musket bloodbath, the Battle of Bunker Hill (most of which was fought on an adjoining height, Breed's Hill), but it cast a long shadow.

The British appeared ready to remain in Boston indefinitely while the militia besieging them looked on impotently. No offensive was possible without artillery. The guns the Americans had were too few and too short of powder and cannonballs. Benedict Arnold, a thirty-four-year-old militia captain from Connecticut, knew just where to find guns: at run-down old Fort Ticonderoga, near the southern tip of Lake Champlain. Massachusetts gave him a colonel's commission and authorized him to raise 400 men to go and capture the fort.

New Hampshire was meanwhile sending Ethan Allen and 83 Green Mountain Boys westward on the same mission. Arnold, hearing of this, put spurs to horseflesh and hurried north. He felt he had something like patent rights on this campaign and considered himself in charge.

Allen, contemplating his 83 men to Arnold's one (a servant), disagreed. On May 10 Allen called on the fort commander to surrender, "in the name of the Great Jehovah and the Continental Congress." Ticonderoga fell without a fight. With its outposts it provided American forces with nearly all of their artillery for the first year of the war. In all, 183 cannon, mortars and howitzers were captured, along with 52 tons of cannonballs. Half the guns were of no use, but all the ammunition was.

On May 25 the frigate *Cerberus* dropped anchor in Boston Harbor. It brought three major generals to help the gloomy, anxious Gage: William Howe, John Burgoyne and Henry Clinton. All had served with distinction in the French and Indian (or Seven Years') War. Howe, who had led the advance party that scaled the Heights of Abraham and made possible James Wolfe's attack on Quebec, was regarded as the best field commander in the army. From the moment he set foot ashore he was, in effect if not yet in name, in command of operations at Boston.

Two weeks later fresh troops arrived. With these extra 1,100 men Gage and Howe felt ready to launch an offensive. The American lines stretched in a semicircle ten miles long, from Charlestown, north of the city, to Roxbury, not quite south of it. They were vulnerable to attack at a dozen points, either through Boston Neck or by cross-water assault. Gage and Howe decided to take Dorchester Heights, south of the city, by amphibious attack. Neither side had chosen to occupy it so far from want of men. From the heights the American right wing and center could be caught in a cross fire. Pushed hard, the whole line might collapse. They gave themselves five days to prepare, but within twenty-four hours the Americans knew they were coming.

To counter the threat south of Boston, the Patriots decided to pose a threat north of the city. The militia would fortify Bunker Hill, the highest ground overlooking Boston. Confusion and inexperience led to entrenching at the wrong place, Breed's Hill, over which Bunker Hill loomed four hundred yards to the rear. Breed's Hill was, admittedly, closer to Boston, but that also made it much easier to attack. Which is what happened. At dawn on June 17 HMS *Lively* moored down below became aware of the busy digging above. The man-of-war unleashed a barrage, rattling the city awake. The British attack scheduled for June 18 was in that moment forgotten. The digging on Breed's Hill looked like a threat—and an opportunity.

Clinton wanted to land troops at Charlestown Neck. Tactically the idea was sound. The British could cut the rebels off from behind, cover the Neck with the guns of the fleet, scale Bunker Hill and pour artillery fire down into the entrenchments. More like sport than warfare.

Gage and Howe chose instead to mount a frontal assault, which went against all accepted practice. Entrenchments were charged from the front only as a last resort. Howe had written forcefully on that subject. The whole point of this operation, however, was to teach the rebels a lesson. They were not looked on as real fighting men but a rabble who happened to be armed. This was to be their punishment for daring to attack the British army.

At midday 2,200 men crossed the water in rowboats. The fleet bombarded Charlestown, setting it ablaze, to deny a refuge to fleeing rebels. At three the light infantry and grenadiers began their ascent of Breed's Hill, Howe leading the way. They advanced steadily in two lines instead of in columns. The slope was steep and grassy. It was hard to keep a footing on it under a sixty-pound pack and carrying another thirty pounds or so of musket, water, bayonet and ammunition. Off to the right half a dozen guns provided artillery support. The troops paused several times and fired volleys. There was no return fire.

The Americans waiting for them had loaded with "buck and ball" (one bullet and two pieces of buckshot or a couple of nails) to be sure of hitting something. They were ordered to aim low, to correct the tendency of excited men, then as now, to shoot too high. If they wanted to provide themselves with a sight they could use their left thumbs. The best marksmen were to try to pick off the officers. The main lesson drawn from the fighting in April, though, was that men had fired too soon. Better fire discipline and they might have destroyed the entire column. The British volleys flew overhead. Still they waited.

When the oncoming lines were forty yards away the militia seemed to pop out of the ground. Taking aim as best they could, they poured half a dozen volleys into the slowly advancing line. It halted. Off to the left of the entrenchments was a rail fence held by the militia. If Howe thought it would fall quickly and allow him to enfilade the entrenchments, he was wrong. The fire from there was just as withering. Grenadier companies went down like wheat before the scythe all along the line. In some, nine men out of ten fell back into the long grass dead or wounded.

The treacherous slope became slick with blood. A bayonet charge was impossible. The result was a stand-up firefight, with the British in the open and the Americans under cover. There could be only one outcome. The attack faltered. The British pulled back, re-formed, and rose to the assault once more.

The fight this time was at a range of twenty-five yards and lasted nearly half an hour. Most British volleys hit nothing but the hillside. The return fire, aimed low, sent men sprawling with terrible wounds in abdomen or groin. A few men began to leave, courage or ammunition exhausted. The assault was called off.

Howe could scarcely believe it: rebels beating regulars! Calling on his reserve force, 700 strong, and allowing them to discard their packs, he mounted a third, last and despairing attack. His artillery was repositioned, to advantage. The Patriots, running out of ammunition, fired sporadically. After a brief hand-to-hand fight, they quit their entrenchments. The small force of rebels occupying Bunker Hill gazed down on these events without making a move. The survivors of Breed's Hill made a fighting retreat to Charlestown Neck. American losses were put at 141 dead, 271 wounded, most of them incurred during the retreat.

British casualties were 226 dead, nearly 900 wounded: close to 50 percent. Howe never really got over it. The British army, always conscious of its modest size, had, and would have for centuries to come, a dread of heavy losses. Its strength was quality, not numbers. Howe made no effort to pursue his retreating foe beyond the Neck.

He came down from Breed's Hill spattered with blood. Every one of his staff officers, gathered around him during the battle, had been killed or wounded. He had arrived in Boston eager to fight, despite his Whiggish politics and his sympathy for the American cause. Doubt weighed on him now. That doubt would color his actions for the rest of the war. There would be no other British offensive for fourteen months.

That gave Washington a year in which to build an army.

ALMOST from the moment hard-riding men on foam-flecked horses spread the news of fighting at Lexington and Concord, New England demanded that the Continental Congress take responsibility for the militia host massed around Boston. These colonies could not support a force that swelled to more than fifteen thousand men. The Congress was reluctant to take up the gun, but on June 14 it finally resolved to raise an armed force of its own. It called on the nearest thing the Colonies possessed to skilled soldiers, the riflemen.

Ten companies (six from Pennsylvania, two from Virginia and two from Maryland) were authorized. They were to join the siege at Boston. Next day Congress "adopted" the besieging militia and commissioned George Washington "General of the American Army." When he reached Cambridge on July 2 he found men enough but a shortage of everything else.

A week later the first rifle company arrived: 96 men commanded by Captain Daniel Morgan. They had marched six hundred miles from the backwoods of Virginia in three weeks. Not a man had fallen out. They created a sensation, striding easily into the encampment dressed in hunting shirts (really a long, loose-fitting coat), buckskin leggings, moccasins and round wool hats. On their shirts was stenciled—in a fashion strangely modern—LIBERTY OR DEATH. Each carried a rifle, a tomahawk and a long knife, which he delighted in describing to the curious as "the scalping knife." That sent shivers through the crowd.

Washington's character was crucial to the shape, and possibly the outcome, of the war. He had never commanded any unit bigger than one he could keep his eye on. He had no experience of cavalry or artillery, and never grasped the proper employment of either. During the Seven Years' War his exposure to combat consisted mainly of being a horrified eyewitness to the destruction of Braddock's army in an ambush. He rose to be a colonel of militia through years of dull routine, far removed from the fighting, but he had a deep and abiding interest in military affairs. From his militia experience he had learned how to manage an army on next to nothing.

Congress also found it wise for political balance to enlist southern support for a war being fought mainly by New Englanders by appointing this distinguished Southerner as army commander. New England's pride was appeased meanwhile by appointing the ailing, plodding Artemas Ward, commander of the Massachusetts militia, as the first major general. Nothing was expected from this stout, prematurely aged martyr to gallstones.

Washington was deeply conscious of his want of combat experience, protesting in private as in public that he probably was not up to the task thrust upon him. He asked for Charles Lee to be commissioned second major general. To him and to Congress this was an obvious choice: Lee, veteran of a dozen battlefields, would be his field commander.

The unformed army strung around Boston considered itself lucky. The forty-three-year-old Lee was English-born, American at heart. His military career had begun with a cornet's commission in his father's regiment at age fourteen. He had proven himself a bold commander under fire, an instinctive tactician of remarkable gifts, and a military intellectual versed in four languages. Tall, thin, dressed in patched clothes and curved with a scholar's stoop, Lee never seemed to move without dogs trotting at his heels, or to sit without them climbing over him. A strange man, yet thought a great one. A fierce antimonarchist, he emigrated to America when the conflict appeared certain to end in a fight. The moment the war began he headed for Boston and took command of the American left wing.

Washington faced three immediate challenges: to turn this motley force into something resembling an army, preferably the British one; to keep it supplied; and to avoid major clashes. The last, which worried him most, was the least of his troubles, thanks to Howe's new mood of caution.

Both sides launched raids, to help keep their men alert, and there were the inevitable accidental skirmishes. Washington had his men spend most of their time constructively. They were familiar not only with weapons but, as important, with tools, such as spades, axes, hammers and saws. The ability to build a revetment or erect a shelter or repair a bridge was as useful as being able to shoot straight.

Amid the red-gold brilliance of a New England fall, enlistments in the instant armies the Colonies had separately created in the spring began running out. Washington sought recruits to a new force, the Continental Army. Officers would be appointed by Congress, instead of being elected by the men. The troops would have to provide their own muskets, but they would be the best-paid soldiers in the world. He was authorized to enlist 20,000; he could find barely half that number. The militia kept his force up to strength through that first winter.

His worst shortages were arms and ammunition. He could never be sure of replenishment from his best source—the British army. In the entire country there were perhaps only two hundred gunsmiths. Some of them were Loyalists. Even among those who were not, it took a skilled gunsmith a week to produce one musket, its bayonet and ramrod.

Washington dipped into his precious supply of cannon and gunpowder in the summer of 1775 and fitted out a schooner as a commerce raider. By late fall he had a fleet of eleven privateers at sea, and the Colonies were creating mini-navies of their own. They paid for themselves many times over in the munitions they captured that first year. They helped feed and clothe Washington's army through a bitter winter. Some prizes were floating arsenals, crammed with muskets, bullets and flints. Others carried warming windfalls of rum, potatoes or coal. One, a storeship taken by the *Franklin*, held fifteen hundred barrels of gunpowder.

Thousands of men were eager to join the privateers, and not simply from greed. The Fishery Act of 1774 was another of the Intolerable Acts. It barred nearly all trade from the fishing ports of New England and excluded colonists' boats from the rich cod and whale fishing off Newfoundland. This was intended to make them think twice about rebellion. Life had always been hard in fishing ports, but robbed of their livelihood Marblehead and Gloucester sank into shame: their streets were filled with begging women and children, while their men were idle. The privateers were the fishermen's revenge. The scales tipped. Fear of privation began haunting the British army in Boston.

The city looked like a secure base. So long as the harbor was open it was not really besieged. It was nonetheless a trap. Gage at last realized that, writing bitterly to London, "I wish this cursed place was burned. . . ." Soon afterward he was out of it, leaving behind a force growing uneasy. British troops expected little, but that little mattered. When rations fell, desertions rose.

Food bought for Howe's men was being eaten by Washington's. The basic diet of the British soldier was a pound of meat and a pound of bread a day, supplemented with cheese, butter and dried peas or rice. On special occasions or as a reward for arduous effort rum was authorized. During the winter of 1775–76, however, it became part of the daily ration in Boston. It would remain so for British troops in America for the rest of the war. It was justified on the grounds that the weather was bad (but generally it was not so bad as in Britain) or that the water needed purifying (although British troops had been taking it neat for years). Each man began receiving the present-day equivalent of a bottle of rum a week, supplementing his quart of beer a day. Alcohol was an established antidote to boredom when there was no fighting, to fear when there was. Eighteenth-century armies were not in the habit of fighting sober.

The British in North America had depended heavily on local supplies for decades. In a single day that proven system collapsed. It took the British Treasury nearly a year to admit that was so, but in October and November thirty-six supply ships left British ports to assure the 11,000 soldiers, sailors and marines in Boston a comfortable winter. The ships were laden with hundreds of tons of food, thousands of oxen and sheep. Some of the worst storms of the century blew up in the Atlantic that winter, lashing mountainous seas from the Lizard to Long Island. Most of the ships were sunk. Others were captured, while a few fled south to the West Indies. Only thirteen supply ships reached Boston, and on the long, turbulent crossing most of the food went bad. The livestock, intended to provide meat, was wiped out by disease. Howe's hopes of a rested, well-fed army ready to mount a spring offensive were dashed.

Meanwhile Arnold was trying to capture Canada that winter. He had persuaded Washington it could be done and he was the man who could do it. Canada, "the Fourteenth Colony," was simply irresistible. In American hands it would, in effect, shut the back door to British invasion. Congress sent its own expedition north under Brigadier General Richard Montgomery while Arnold took a thousand men, with Washington's sanction, over river and lake in whaleboats. On November 13 Montreal fell to Montgomery's force in the second *coup de main* of the war. All that remained was Quebec.

Arnold's expedition, much weakened by hardship and bad weather, linked up with Montgomery's. On December 30, 1775, the day before many enlistments expired, they launched a night attack on Quebec in a tremendous snowstorm. It failed. Montgomery was killed; Arnold was brought down with a serious leg wound. What followed is usually described as a siege, but there was in fact almost no choice. The Americans were in no condition to make the long trek home in winter burdened with dozens of wounded men. When the snows melted in the spring and injuries had healed they headed south, to Ticonderoga. Montreal was abandoned. The dream of Fourteen Colonies faded.

As the British army in Boston tried to keep warm, much of the city was vanishing in smoke. Wharves were turned into firewood, so were old ships, so was the Liberty Tree (a pole festooned with patriotic emblems and slogans). Fences went, as did entire buildings. Famous old churches were not spared the bonfire. One was gutted to provide both a fire and a riding school.

Such news made Congress more impatient than ever for the liberation of Boston. Washington twice planned an assault. Twice his council of war talked him out of it. Before the capture of those fifteen hundred barrels of gunpowder in March 1776 his ammunition supply had fallen as low as nine rounds per man. The shortage of powder inspired Franklin to urge a return to the bow and arrow: four rounds a minute, comparable effective range, greater accuracy, no self-blinding cloud of smoke. The idea was rejected. It affronted the modern mind. His other suggestion, to bring back the pike, was adopted by several colonies. Twelve-foot pikes were seen in combat almost to the end of the war.

Through that first winter fifty-five cannon and mortars were being dragged laboriously by ox sled from Fort Ticonderoga. On the night of March 4–5 Dorchester Heights was seized. The guns were hauled onto the high ground and the slopes facing Boston, a quarter of a mile across the water. While Congress had pressed Washington to free the city, it also ordered him not to destroy it. The guns remained silent, but menacing.

Howe worried his way through the winter, watching his supplies fall dangerously low. They were down to a bare six weeks. Strategically, the place to go was New York. Had he been able, he would have gone there in November. Logistically, the place he was forced to go in March was Halifax, Nova Scotia, if only because a supply fleet was scheduled to arrive there in the spring. On March 17 Howe loaded his troops and a thousand Loyalists aboard a fleet of warships and transports that only just met the need. Clearing the harbor as night fell, the ships heeled steadily to port. Behind them jubilant American soldiers raced into the dark city, torches in hand: carnival.

While the Colonies celebrated the liberation of Boston as a great victory, Washington and Lee were trying to decide where the British would strike next. All six of America's principal cities were on the coast. Close to 90 percent of the population lived along the seaboard or along the navigable rivers that flowed into the sea. There was also the chain of rivers and lakes that invited invasion from Canada, reaching all the way down to Manhattan. Every advantage of mobility and surprise was with the British. April 1776 found Lee agonizing that he was "like a dog in a dancing school," not knowing which way to turn.

Howe was at that moment waiting impatiently in Halifax. The supply ships were late. Instead of spending a month before making his descent on New York he was forced to spend three. Before Howe's army could move, the Royal Navy was ready to strike a blow. A fleet under Admiral Peter Parker would take 2,500 soldiers and launch an attack on Charleston, South Carolina. Success was almost certain, and it would remove the southern colonies from the war.

Congress feared as much. While Washington took over the defense of New York, Lee was sent on to Charleston with reinforcements. South Carolina called out its militia. Everything needed to be done. Fortifications were thrown together to cover the harbor mouth. By June half a fort, consisting mainly of double walls of palmetto logs binding sixteen feet of dirt between them, appeared on Sullivans Island. Other bastions were erected within gunshot of the shipping channel. All told, a hundred cannon pointed seaward when, on June 1, the fleet appeared.

The ford that British troops were to cross after being landed proved too deep for them to reach Sullivans Island. Naval gunfire would have to force a passage into Charleston, but contrary winds held up the attack until June 28. By then the fort was finished.

All the while Lee was anxious over the shortage of powder. He enforced the strictest fire discipline on everyone, especially the artillery. As the attack opened three frigates ran aground, unable to bring their guns to bear. Other warships pressed on, sailing into the harbor, broadsides blazing. American gunners held their fire until they could hardly miss. Strong nerves, indeed. The weight of return fire was light but nearly every shot did some damage. British casualties rose to 225 dead and wounded, while the spongy palmetto logs of the ramshackle fort seemed to swallow cannonballs. American fire, striking Parker's flagship, blew off his breeches. The harbor defenses, on the other hand, held—just. As the sun went down the British turned away, leaving one of their frigates, still grounded, ablaze.

THE REVOLUTION had survived its first year of fighting, and more, thanks to the first great surprise of the war: the militia. Without it there might have been no war at all. It was a raid on diverted militia arms that led to the first clash. It was the militia's performance at Bunker Hill that stopped the first British offensive, turning armed rebellion into a war for independence. Yet every account of the militia's role has for more than two centuries been colored by Washington's scorn. He called it "a broken staff."

There is a countervailing myth that would make the angry farmers out to be natural fighters, plow in one hand, firearm in the other. This was true only of the riflemen. By the 1770s more than three fourths of the population lived in long-settled areas. Life for most Americans was easier than it was for most Europeans. There were muskets and gunpowder in many hands thanks to various militia acts dating back to the dangerous days when Indian raids were a constant threat, but training was limited to as little as one day a year. Concord and Lexington showed how far anger exceeded accuracy: no more than one militia bullet in twenty, perhaps as few as one in fifty, found its mark.

As for the riflemen, they had a valuable role to play but they were vulnerable in general engagements. It took a minute to reload a rifle, first hammering the half-ounce bullet, wrapped in its greased patch of linen or buckskin, a foot into the tight .50-caliber barrel with a mallet and an iron rod. It was forced the rest of the way down with a ramrod. In that minute even the toughest rifleman was helpless. Nor would a rifle hold a bayonet, limiting it even further in both attack and defense. There were, if anything, too many riflemen. Some, to their extreme indignation, found muskets being forced on them by commanders desperately short of infantry who could fire volleys and charge.

While the riflemen were looked on with awe for their astonishing marksmanship, anyone describing the militia as a serious military force in 1775 would have been ridiculed. For a generation past, the militia's main role in life was social and ornamental. Membership in it was a sign of respectability. These were men who had responsibilities, and means. When the call to service came they preferred to pay a fine or hire a substitute. Colonial legislatures, including those of Massachusetts and Virginia, began taking vagabonds, even Indians, to meet the quotas decreed by London during the French and Indian War. The British also raised 7,500 volunteers directly among Americans. Some volunteer and militia companies were doubtless up to standard but the vast majority were a mess. British officers claimed they had never seen such filthy camps, such slovenly men or so little discipline.

The disease-prone, slack and scruffy militia of the 1760s was famous, in a way, throughout the British army. One titled general who had served with it assured fellow officers shipping out in 1776 that they would have no trouble suppressing this rabble. "Your American is a very effeminate creature," he said. Lord Percy's attitude was typical of that of many young officers before Concord and Lexington. Colonists were, quite simply, "cowards." What happened that day left him amazed. And Gage wrote back to London after Bunker Hill in complete bewilderment: "In all their Wars against the French they never Shewed so much Conduct Attention and Perseverance."

In effect, the militia had been transformed under his very nose, without his realizing it or the authorities in London being able to imagine it. Such a thing had never happened in the British Empire. Nor would it happen again.

Colonial militia officers held their commissions under the Crown, but when rebellion swept through the Colonies the militia became the ground over which the contest for people's loyalties was fought out in village and town. As is often the case, a comparative handful of extremists made the running, by preaching separation from Britain and taking militia arms to bolster the Patriot cause, while the vast majority hoped that differences with the Crown might somehow be reconciled.

Throughout 1775 and the first half of 1776 most militiamen continued to proclaim allegiance to the Crown. So did the colonial legislatures, as did the Continental Congress. Their quarrel, they insisted, was not with the king but with his foolish ministers who gave him bad advice and with a corrupt Parliament that supported them.

All the while, however, the militia was being purged, as patriotic sentiments rose to a feverish pitch. At least five thousand militiamen were disarmed by their more patriotic colleagues in the first half of 1776 for lack of revolutionary ardor. As the militia was purged politically it was being transformed militarily, into a genuine fighting force. Events at Concord, at Bunker Hill and elsewhere were but a foretaste of a reborn militia, loyal not to a king far away but independence at home.

In some towns men who refused to join the new, anti-British militia were jailed. They could get out only by swearing allegiance to the Revolution. Even then they had to repent as fulsomely as prisoners held in Communist "reeducation camps" of the late twentieth century.

During and after the war there were heated recriminations over the many occasions when militia units took to their heels under British fire or, more often, fled from a bayonet charge. Such episodes provoked shame among Patriots, yet there were Continentals who took to their heels. So did British regulars. When surprised or heavily outnumbered, line units on both sides showed no more inclination to make useless sacrifices of their lives than did the militia. They could also sow panic, as well as reap it. In January 1777 a supply column guarded by 200 British regulars was attacked in the darkness by 30 mounted New Jersey militiamen. The soldiers fled, abandoning dozens of wagons, firing hardly a shot.

The British became increasingly wary about allowing detached units to move very far. *La petite guerre* was a militia specialty, leaving several redcoats killed in an ambush here, half a dozen more wounded in a raid there. In time the casualties inflicted ran into thousands. The militia made it impossible to control the country without occupying it. Not even the entire British army, which would rise to 100,000 men worldwide during this war, was big enough for that. The militia thwarted pacification yet refused to stand in the open and fight. It posed a problem that Howe and his successors never began to solve. British commanders had a far higher opinion of the military value of the militia than Washington ever had.

When popular support for the war declined, it was the militia, by then fully committed to the struggle, who kept the Revolution going. The Continental Army could not be everywhere at once. The militia could be, and was. It found enough recruits to keep the army in existence. It kept the Loyalists under control in most areas. And when the fighting reached its state, its county, its town, it could supplement the Continentals sufficiently to make battle possible.

Militia was roundly damned for its "unreliability," but in an agrarian society that suffered a chronic labor shortage long before the war began there was a sensible reluctance to strip the land of men and put them in the army. To go on fighting, Americans had to go on eating. Nor are men who are fearful for their homes and their crops, and whether their wives and children are starving, ideal troops.

Neither Washington nor Congress ever gave serious thought to the chronic, inherent manpower shortage. It was easier to blame the militia for robbing the army of men.

Such criticism slighted its contribution to the war. In Boston, that first winter, Washington could find only 10,000 men willing to join the Continental Army. To plug the gap he asked Massachusetts for 5,000 militiamen. He got them. He asked New Hampshire for 2,000, and got them.

This set a pattern that lasted throughout the war: the Continental Army short of recruits, Washington calling on the militia to make up the difference. In most cases it did so. In some instances it actually swamped his camps with men. The militia, maligned and misunderstood, was the safety net of the Revolution. So long as it responded to Washington's calls, the war would go on.

Even so, he never saw it that way. Deprecating the militia was a tradition among regulars, and Washington had something of a regular soldier's spirit. He pinned his hopes on the Continentals.

Just how many men served either as militia or Continentals has inspired some ingenious guesswork for more than a century. No one really knows. Because Washington complained often and bitterly about the small size of his army, there has been a kind of retroactive guilt. Every estimate seems lower than the one before. The lowest estimate is roughly 200,000 for Continentals and militia combined.

The military manpower pool was less than it seemed at first glance. The Thirteen Colonies had a total population of 2.5 million men, women and children. Of these, half a million were blacks (mainly slaves). Another half million were Loyalists. Within the remaining 1.5 million were up to 100,000 conscientious objectors and pacifists. Out of a white, non-Loyalist, nonpacifist population there were about 750,000 males (making allowance for the comparatively low proportion of females among immigrants). Of these 750,000, roughly two thirds would be aged sixteen to fifty, but something like 15 percent would be disabled or too ill to bear arms.

This adds up to an able-bodied male population of approximately 425,000. To have mobilized nearly half that number was surely one of the most notable achievements of the Revolution. A mobilization rate of close to 50 percent is one of the highest in the history of warfare.

The experience of Peterborough, New Hampshire, seems fairly typical for a New England town. In 1775 it had a total population of 549, of whom 198 were adult males. Some 170 of these served in the militia or the Continental Army. Only about 50 men served for more than a year, but what is truly remarkable is that virtually every man or youth able to carry a musket on behalf of the Revolution did so.

CONGRESS finally came around to Washington's view that he must have an army enlisted for the duration of the war, but there was no way the states could be forced to provide one. Each insisted on having a say in the raising of regiments within its borders. Each had its own ideas on the conditions of service, the size of enlistment bonuses, the color of uniforms. Most Continentals after the first year had to be "levied"—that is, drafted. Each state appointed conscription officers to find and enroll draftees. Rich men could avoid service by finding paid substitutes.

Although America was prosperous by European standards, there were many people who were not prosperous by any standard. It was such men, lacking property, skills or deep roots, living an insecure existence without facing actual starvation, who were to form the bulk of the Continental Army. There was little to hold them back, much to push them forward—cash bounties, free clothing, the promise of land, the chance for adventure. And despite all legislative efforts to keep them out of military service there were free blacks in nearly every regiment.

Desertion rates always remained high, to the commanding general's despair. At his gloomiest he once wrote that he expected to have half the army out looking for the other half. Most men simply went home. Many felt it was the army that had broken its promise, not they. A year or more might pass before they were paid. Clothing and food were often short, yet they had been told they would have plenty of both. Others deserted only to reenlist and collect another bounty. The punishment if caught was one hundred lashes. This failing, something more severe was introduced: in 1778 a soldier at Fort Ticonderoga was shot for seven enlistments.

Creating this army was heartbreaking work. Washington was moved to say that he would not have taken it on for ten thousand pounds had he known what it would be like. Shortly afterward he raised this to twenty thousand pounds. And then to fifty thousand. It would be some time before he felt any real affection for the Continental Army, or trusted it to stand and fight.

Most of the time it did not even look like an army, to his or anyone else's eyes. When he arrived in Cambridge in July 1775 he had found some men in war paint, others dressed like backwoodsmen, still others resplendent in fancy red uniforms like the British. As cloth became available the one consideration in this cash-short army was price. Bright colors were expensive. This was the first army to dress most of its troops in thrifty greens and browns. The Continentals found themselves in combat camouflage; not that they appreciated it much.

Even when more money and brighter colors became available

there was no uniform uniform. The famous blue and buff was adopted by the line of only two states, New York and New Jersey. The others chose varying combinations of their own. Yet blue was common to them all. It became the color of American infantry, compared with the red of the British and the white of the French. Washington's ambition was to create an army just like the others. It never happened, for already, in small matters as in great, it was different.

On July 9 he had every regiment paraded. To ecstatic cheers and gunfire officers read out the Declaration of Independence. Word was meanwhile spreading of Lee's victory at Charleston. An outburst of patriotic pride, something between feeling pleasantly drunk and running a fever, swept over army and citizenry alike. Never again would support for the Revolution reach such a peak; never again would victory seem so certain as in July 1776.

Even as the noise of these extravagant cannonades faded, the greatest fleet since the Armada was putting to sea. A battle fleet of 52 warships was escorting 427 victuallers and transports that carried an army of 34,000 men: an endless host in white, bright on blue water, rocking westward through high summer's sunshine to end this war.

2

WINTER PATRIOTS

HOWE'S PLANS called for him to seize New York. After that he would advance up the Hudson to link up with another British army, under Sir Guy Carleton, coming down from Canada. A combined land and sea attack was scheduled to capture Newport, Rhode Island. These operations would cut off New England, the heart of the rebellion, from the other colonies. Hemmed in by his and Carleton's armies to the west, with its ports closely blockaded and New York, to the south, in British hands, New England would be strangled into submission.

The first thing was to take New York, and it must fall to him intact if, as he intended, his army was to make winter quarters there when the campaigning season ended. If he tried storming the city the rebels might burn it to the ground. Howe wanted to fight for New York, not in it.

So did Washington. It was "the key to the Continent." Whoever held it would win the war. That conviction was to distort his strategic vision for years, never with worse consequences than now.

The best thing to do with the city was to burn it to the ground and let Howe have the ashes. New York is based on islands. The British had almost complete control of the waters around it.

While tension rose dramatically through that oppressive summer the 20,000 American troops Washington was busily entrenching could not see the British army, but they might gaze upon the fleet that brought it in: a forest of masts that spread all the way to the horizon, sprouting from five hundred dark, menacing hulls. Bright pennants fluttered brilliantly in the breeze for miles. Bronze muzzles gleamed from more than a thousand gunports. No man alive had ever seen such naval power.

It had no effect on Washington or on Congress, which strictly ordered him not to destroy the city. He had no such intention, but later he would blame Congress, and the army, for the ensuing disaster. In August 1776 he was eager to fight, probably too eager. He had commanded the army for more than a year yet still had not led it in battle.

He divided his forces between lower Manhattan and Long Island. Between flowed the East River, which the British were far more likely to control than he was. He had his troops on Long Island entrench on Brooklyn Heights. This was screened to the south and east by a range of low hills known as the Heights of Guan. Heavily wooded, these hills were pierced by four passes. To cover four passes was easy, but to cover the entire range of hills required a cavalry force.

That July just such a force appeared. Some 500 Connecticut farmers, mounted on workhorses, rode up to Washington's headquarters. They carried fowling pieces and risibly, grandiloquently called themselves "Light Dragoons." With a few weeks' training the best half of the men and the best half of the horses could have screened Washington's lines effectively. They could also have kept watch on Howe's troops once they landed on Long Island on August 24. Instead, he sent them home. They were too expensive to maintain, he said, at a time when Long Island was full of forage. In truth, he did not know how to use them. Cavalry was as much a mystery to Washington as seamanship. Meanwhile, General William Heath, attempting to reconnoiter the outskirts of Manhattan, was begging him to find two or three mounted men; in vain.

The covering force along the Heights of Guan consisted of small, isolated detachments. Taking advantage of darkness, Howe on the night of August 26–27 sent 10,000 men and most of his artillery far to the east. By dawn Washington's forces on Long Island had been turned. A British army was marching undetected straight into their rear before the battle even began. What followed came close to a rout.

American troops in the center and on the left wing threw away their muskets and never fired a shot. Others simply hid in the bushes, hoping it would soon be over. Some of the Hessians got out of hand and butchered men who were trying to surrender. With the terror at its height even British women camp followers took prisoners.

As he watched the American survivors fleeing toward Brooklyn Heights and its inviting trenches, Howe ordered his troops to halt. Only one part of his battle plan had gone wrong. An amphibious force coming upriver to land behind the American entrenchments was forced to turn back by contrary winds.

From his position on the high ground Washington had visions of another Bunker Hill, but Howe refused to oblige him. The British were ordered to sling muskets and start to dig "parallels." These were zigzag trenches that, as they advanced, enabled an attacking force to approach a strongpoint without exposing itself. Washington, his fantasies of a second Bunker Hill receding, ferried his army across the East River two nights later.

Howe has been strongly criticized ever since for not exploiting a complete tactical success. When his army began digging in, there were three hours of daylight left. He had thousands of fresh troops available. He possessed the priceless advantage of momentum. Here, say the critics, was the exact moment when the British threw away their best chance of destroying the Continental Army, possibly of capturing Washington, and probably of winning the war.

Most of the Continentals, however, were on the opposite shore, including many of its best regiments. Washington was too good a horseman to be taken easily and there were boats and sailors on the riverside of Brooklyn Heights to row him to safety if necessary. The incoherence of Washington's deployment put total victory out of Howe's reach even had he stormed Brooklyn Heights that golden summer evening.

When the British moved into the abandoned American entrenchments lower Manhattan became untenable. Washington vacillated between leaving the city and fighting for it. Now more than ever was the time to torch New York. Yet once again Congress ordered him not to do it. Scorched earth was out.

Two weeks later, on September 15, Howe bestirred himself once more. Several thousand redcoats and Hessians crunched ashore at Kips Bay, landing just behind the American lines, at what is now the foot of Thirty-fourth Street.

Panic seized Washington's troops. In a towering rage he tried to rally them. The sight of his men fleeing from the enemy was infuriating. He whacked them with his cane, called them cowards, and tried to lead them back into the fight, as bullets ripped the air around him. That day he came as close as he ever would to being captured.

Much of the confusion he raged at was really his own work. Washington had neither prepared his army to stand and fight nor to make an orderly withdrawal if his position was outflanked by a landing in his rear.

His army fled for two miles, until it reached the shelter of Harlem Heights. Behind it British buglers began to play—not the military recall but the hunting call that signaled the end of a chase after foxes or rabbits. The shame of it remained vivid in the memories of some Continentals for the rest of their days.

On the night of September 20, one fourth of New York burned down. Washington credited it to "Providence, or some good honest fellows. . . ."

Howe prepared his next move, to get behind Harlem Heights, by sending his army upriver. His troops landed at Dobbs Ferry on October 12. With thousands of redcoats once again in his rear Washington had to surrender nearly all of Manhattan, yet he still clung to a desperate hope of maintaining an American presence in New York.

On the present-day Washington Heights a huge earthwork had been raised. Apart from a jumble of huts it had no buildings, no barracks. There were no casemates, no stone walls, no well and no spring. Water was got by dropping a bucket into the Hudson 230 feet below. This trap, called Fort Washington, was crammed with nearly 3,000 troops. General Nathanael Greene claimed it could hold out indefinitely. Washington accepted that judgment, but soon began to doubt it. Torn by indecision, he left things as they were.

A similar "strongpoint" arose opposite Fort Washington, on the New Jersey shore, and was named Fort Lee. In the river between the two forts was a line of sunken hulks and dozens of huge iron spikes set into timber frames, to rip the bottoms out of ships. Hardly had these been emplaced, however, when three British warships sailed up the Hudson undisturbed by the forts, the hulks or the spikes.

On November 16 a long cannonade and a furious charge by Hessian mercenaries hired from German princes brought the swift surrender of Fort Washington. American casualties were light. Losses in every other respect were enormous. As much as 100 tons of gunpowder was lost, along with 146 cannon, 2,800 muskets, hundreds of thousands of cartridges, plus the entire 3,000-man garrison. For the small, often trounced Continental Army it was a stunning disaster.

So far the British had never moved far from their ships. Here, though, was the ideal moment to strike hard, swift and deep into the rebellious colonies. Howe's most energetic subordinate, General Lord Charles Cornwallis, made a short and furious assault on Fort Lee. The defenders fled so fast the redcoats found kettles coming to the boil. Beyond lay nothing but flat, open New Jersey, a landscape where there were no heights for the Americans to cling to, no illusory hopes of another Bunker Hill.

The British proceeded to fritter away the advantages won by the capture of the two forts. With nothing in their path they advanced at a rate of less than four miles a day. Howe stopped to round up flour and bake bread. He stopped to inspect potential winter quarters along the coast. Amazingly, this fitful advance became known as "the race across the Jersies."

Entirely on his own initiative Cornwallis one day covered twenty miles. Another day like that and Washington's shuffling, demoralized army of scarecrows would have been cut off, but Howe ordered Cornwallis to halt. And halt he did, for nearly a week. Washington hurried his weary soldiers out of reach.

Howe chose this moment to strip Cornwallis of troops, sending them to Clinton so the long-delayed land and sea assault on Newport could be mounted. The town fell to the British without a shot being fired. To Howe the capture of Newport was worth far more than the destruction of the Continental Army, whose end daily seemed more inevitable.

While Washington was being driven out of New York and pushed across New Jersey, Lee spent the fall up in the Hudson highlands with a blocking force of 2,000 men. Their mission was to hamper the movement south from Canada of Carleton's army. When it became evident that Carleton had been thwarted, for reasons which will be explained later in this chapter, Washington ordered Lee to bring his 2,000 men down to New Jersey.

Lee slowly, reluctantly came south, unhappy to be taken away from what amounted to an independent command. On December 13 he was captured in his dressing gown, while he took breakfast at a tavern in New Brunswick. This news shocked the army and the country. It seemed to be the ultimate straw in a saga of misfortunes, as though fate wore a red coat.

After taking nearly three weeks to cross New Jersey, Howe had Philadelphia in his grasp. He only had to reach out for it. He arrived in mid-December, looked across the Delaware at America's biggest city, and decided this prize could wait. The weather was bitter, snow was falling, and back in New York there was warmth, Tory laughter and the embrace of his mistress.

Washington's bedraggled army huddled on the opposite shore, too sick, too small to fight. Its numbers had fallen to fewer than 4,000 men, and of these desertion and disease were carrying off one hundred a day. A dejected Washington confided to his nephew that unless fresh troops could be found, "The game is pretty near up. . . ."

As he wrote these melancholy sentiments another pen was also busy. Among the fleeing defenders of Fort Lee was the pamphleteer Thomas Paine, whose *Common Sense* had been a powerful force in turning public opinion in favor of complete independence. During the flight across New Jersey he dragged his musket by day, but took up his true weapon by night.

With a drumhead for a desk he began writing *The Crisis:* "These are the times that try men's souls," he began. "The summer soldier and the sunshine patriot will, in this crisis, shrink from the service of his country; but he that stands it Now, deserves the love and thanks of man and woman. Tyranny, like hell, is not easily conquered; yet we have this consolation with us, that the harder the conflict, the more glorious the triumph. . . ."

Lee's division staggered into Philadelphia on December 20, still in shock from their commander's capture. Other units arrived in dribs and drabs. A call for troops brought in 1,500 Pennsylvania militia. On December 23 Washington could muster 6,000 men. That day, as they hunched against the numbing cold, the *Crisis* was read out to them.

It thrilled. It provoked. It lifted men's hearts despite their rags, kindled hope despite defeat and disappointment. It challenged them to rise to its vision and its courage. Summer soldiers? Sunshine patriots? Not they.

THE REVOLUTION did not need a miracle but it did need an army. In just eight days the enlistment of every Continental would expire. If they went so might the war. To hold on to his army Washington had to give them something; something worth more than any bounty, rarer than a new suit of clothes, more encouraging even than free land—a victory. He had no opportunity this time to vacillate, no phantoms to pursue. Like a miser, Washington saved the best that he had for the worst moments. He prepared to put the entire army onto a hostile shore. If the attack failed, he and they were doomed. He wrote out the sign and countersign for Christmas Night: "Victory . . ." ". . . or Death."

For the attack across the Delaware, against the Hessians quartered at Trenton, Washington split his army into three widely separated units. They would not be able to come to one another's support. He had something working in his favor, however. The Hessian commander, Colonel Johann Rall, did not bother posting sentries.

Washington personally led the main assault force. Another division was to act as a blocking force and prevent the Hessians from escaping, while the third and smallest division created a diversion. Almost from the start the plan broke down. Instead of the attack going in before dawn it was three hours late and was made in broad daylight. The blocking and diversionary forces never got across the river. Their commanders looked on the raging, ice-strewn Delaware and decided it was impossible. Only the troops under Washington's eye and will succeeded.

Trenton was a confused affair. Greene's troops charged into town, shouting, "These are the times that try men's souls!" The Americans had wet muskets. The Hessians had dry ones. These too were soon useless in the falling snow. Men stood pulling triggers helplessly at one another. General Henry Knox had foreseen this problem and had ferried eighteen fieldpieces across the river. It was this firepower that devastated the Hessians. Cannon boomed intermittently up and down Trenton's two main streets. Women shrieked, children went into hysterics, and Rall was shot off his horse, mortally pierced by two bullets. In a pocket, neatly folded, was a message warning him of the impending attack, unread.

Thanks to the failure of the blocking force a third of the Hessians escaped. The haul was 948 prisoners, one thousand muskets and rifles, six cannon, enough instruments to equip two military bands, and Washington's first battlefield victory. He had lost just two men, frozen to death on the march.

Four days later he crossed the Delaware into New Jersey again, this time bringing all of his army. He intended to free the entire state in a winter campaign, but already thousands of troops under Cornwallis were moving toward him. They fell on the advancing Americans, scattering them. With the river at his back filling with ice floes and the main highway ahead of him covered by British guns, Washington seemed doomed.

In a ruse straight out of the Bible, campfires burned on while the army tiptoed away into a black winter's night. Then, instead of retreating, he advanced, pushing deeper into New Jersey—the last thing Cornwallis expected. Washington took his men away toward Princeton, down a road the British had left unguarded. Hurrying on, he won a brisk firefight. He set off for New Brunswick. He was within an ace of forcing the British to abandon New Jersey. Men can give only so much. The army ground to a halt, too exhausted to cover the last seventeen miles.

At last he took them into winter quarters, in the hilly, forested area around Morristown. His army was reduced to 4,000 men; shivering, hungry, half naked, poorly armed, virtually untrained; nevertheless, a force in being, and unmolested. Howe's army of 27,000 spent the first six months of 1777 doing little more than consuming their supplies. Early in July Howe loaded most of them aboard transports in New York. They had to wait more than two weeks for favorable winds before clearing the harbor, only to vanish over the horizon. Washington marched and countermarched for weeks, wondering where they had gone, what they intended.

After more than a month at sea Howe finally reappeared. On August 25 his groaning, seasick army tumbled ashore at Head of Elk, some sixty miles south of Philadelphia. They were ten miles farther from the city than they were the day they boarded their transports.

Washington chose to fight for Philadelphia. He had only one thing in his favor—he could decide where the battle would be fought. Apart from that, Howe had the upper hand in everything, including numbers. Washington threw his one advantage away. He deployed his 11,000 men along Brandywine Creek. This put them at the center of a network of roads that Howe was free to exploit.

He deployed 5,000 British troops to keep the Americans occupied while the remaining 10,000 made a wide swing to the west, led by

Cornwallis. Yet again Washington's army would pay for want of a cavalry arm.

The battle, on September 11, was a short, bloody clash that brought the British charging downhill behind the American right wing and center. With the American lines falling apart in complete confusion, Greene's division raced up, covered the withdrawal of the outflanked units and held off the British onslaught until dark. Washington lost a thousand men, dead, wounded, captured or deserted. A defeat, but not a disaster. The army re-formed at Chester in good order.

Howe moved into Philadelphia, his confidence soaring into those reaches where judgment takes flight. He parceled out his forces with no thought for offense or defense. In doing so, he provided Washington with an opportunity; something he searched for as diligently as a pickpocket. A little more than half of Howe's troops were encamped at Germantown. The rest were scattered. Washington began imagining another Trenton—scaled up by ten.

Instead of three columns, this time four. He pictured to himself a great battle of annihilation: Howe's center would be pinned down while both his right and left wings were smashed simultaneously. The troops set off into the darkness in the early hours of October 5, each with a piece of white paper pinned to his hat so the man behind could follow. Mist was already rising.

What Washington had conjured up was a fantasy. The reality was that he had assigned his best troops—raw, poorly trained, badly equipped Continentals—to make a frontal assault on Howe's main force. He then expected the militia—even more poorly trained and equipped—to crush both British flanks. His four columns were marching down roads that were miles apart, with no communication among them. He counted on all four reaching the battlefield at the same time and going straight into action. It was a challenge that would have tested the best soldiers of the century.

All that failure required was for one of the four columns to arrive late. Greene, leading half the entire army, took the wrong road. When he arrived the fighting was well advanced. Six companies of redcoats had taken over a large stone house that dominated the main road. From there they poured a withering fire into American units as they moved up. The column Greene was meant to link up with was busy attacking the stone house.

He nevertheless hurled his division as planned against the British right. His men charged with such élan that some found themselves in the enemy's rear. For a moment the British position was in danger of collapsing. Then, in the morning fog and the choking haze of black powder smoke, another American division approached Greene's units from behind and opened fire. They fired back. Then both divisions broke and ran. The panic spread.

Washington rode in among the fleeing troops, trying to rally them. Those who had been in the thick of the fighting ran past him holding up empty cartridge boxes. Others simply ran past, heads down. He had pushed these men to the very limits of their ability. They had come heartbreakingly close to a victory in the open field that by all normal standards should have been impossible. They retreated from the battlefield at their own pace. The exhausted British made no attempt to pursue.

After Brandywine and Germantown the troops Washington commanded were dispirited if not despairing. They spent their energies looking for shoes and blankets, food and firewood. If there had ever been any illusions about the size of their task, there were none now. They were no match for British regulars in battle. At least, not in the set-piece battles Washington wanted to fight.

For months army records report no offensive action of note. Instead they are filled with accounts of desertion, of drunkenness, of indiscipline. A score of officers were charged with cowardice in recent engagements. Dozens of NCOs were reduced to the ranks. Punishments were daily occurrences—backs laid open under the lash; barefoot, bare-chested men running the gauntlet; captured deserters hanged. At this low ebb life suddenly grew much worse. The army moved into Valley Forge for winter quarters.

It was a compromise, and a bad one. Washington had intended to take the army down to Delaware, where the winter would be less harsh. With a British army in Philadelphia, Pennsylvania insisted he remain. Valley Forge was suggested by one of his best generals, Anthony Wayne, a Pennsylvanian. He could hardly have chosen a worse spot. The countryside for miles around had been stripped bare by both armies. In this ghastly, barren place, officers whispered among themselves, This was finally it: this was where the Continental Army would die.

.   .   .

WE LEFT ARNOLD deep in the Canadian snows early in 1776, after the failed attempt to capture Quebec. Once those snows melted, a British army commanded by Sir Guy Carleton moved south, advancing toward the planned juncture with Howe once the British captured New York. All that stood between Carleton and the Hudson was Arnold's band of survivors.

The broad highway south from Canada through the deep forest was Lake Champlain. Carleton easily took St. John, at the northern end of the lake. Arnold, making camp on the southern shore fifty miles away, began cutting down trees. A naval race began. Through the early summer months of 1776 the tall timber rang to the sounds of ax biting into wood, hammer driving in nail.

The British brought small gunboats over the rapids from the St. Lawrence, knocked larger vessels apart, transported them in pieces and reassembled them by the lake, or built entire warships from the keel up.

Arnold competed by offering five dollars a day in coin, all the food a man could eat, and a cow as a bonus. Skilled workers raced inland from the ports of New England to build him a fleet. Spikes, barrels of nails, bulky hawsers, rolls of canvas, cast anchors and brass guns passed down dappled forest trails before the startled gaze of deer.

Strange fleets arose. Lake Champlain is shallow. The vessels Arnold and Carleton constructed appeared to be warships above the waterline, but were like flat-bottomed scows below. Without a stiff wind from behind they could hardly move.

Arnold won the naval race. On August 24 he sailed onto the lake with eleven instant warships looking for battle. From St. John came only the thud of hammers, the rasp of saws.

It was early October before Carleton painted his ships, ready at last to fight for Lake Champlain. Arnold had meanwhile moved his small fleet to an anchorage near Valcour Island, from where he could intercept any British fleet sailing south from St. John. By now his force had grown to fifteen vessels.

Simply by building a fleet Arnold had delayed Carleton by three months. When battle was eventually joined it was October 11. Arnold's fleet lost the battle, but that did not matter. Once Carleton had won, he took his army back to Canada to sit out the winter, which was already fast approaching.

This faraway fight in the wilderness, witnessed by few, was

mourned throughout the Colonies as another calamitous defeat, but Arnold may have saved the Revolution by keeping Carleton from going south to link up with Howe.

The idea of cutting off New England continued to exercise British minds. A more enterprising figure than Carleton was found, Burgoyne. In the spring of 1777 he headed south from Canada, with an even bigger army, to accomplish the mission. His destination was Albany. A second British army, coming up from New York, would meet him there.

The first serious obstacle in Burgoyne's path was Fort Ticonderoga. Its American defenders watched in helpless fascination on the first anniversary of the Declaration of Independence as British military engineers swung cannon from tree to tree up the side of Sugar Loaf Hill, overlooking the fort. Once emplaced on the summit, on July 6, they pointed straight down into it. Ticonderoga's defenders left what had turned into a deathtrap so hurriedly they did not have time to burn its stores.

Burgoyne scented victory, but he was not rushing to grasp it. He ordered his army to travel light, then set off with thirty wagons filled with his personal effects. He dragged a vast artillery train—138 cannon plus siege guns. In the terrain he was traversing there was nowhere he could deploy so much artillery. And trailing in the dust of his army were up to two thousand women, with several hundred children.

Part of the grand design was to secure the Mohawk Valley, the tribal heartland of the Six Nations. The valley was the highway that led from the Hudson to the West. The British, always short of troops, sought to bring the Six Nations into the war. That might provide thousands of fresh warriors.

The key to the Mohawk Valley was Fort Stanwix, which covered the forest road that wound from Oswego to Albany. In the spring of 1777 the fort was a ruin. Hardly had it been shored up before it was besieged by hundreds of Indians and Tories. In July some 800 New York militia under Brigadier General Nicholas Herkimer marched to its relief. They walked into an ambush. With desperate courage and coolness they fought their attackers to a standstill.

A second relief force set out, led by Arnold. As resourceful as ever, he sent a sometimes crazy, sometimes sane German named Hon Yost Schuyler on ahead, dressed in a coat riddled with bullet holes. The Indians welcomed Hon Yost, believing that madmen were favored by the Great Spirit. Hon Yost showed the besiegers of Fort Stanwix his coat. He made them imagine his miraculous escape from the army led by the feared Arnold. How many soldiers? Hon Yost raised an arm, extended a finger. He drew a great circle, pointing to the leaves of the trees—thousands. The Indians fell on the rum supply, got drunk, then ran off screaming into the woods. The siege collapsed. The British pulled back to Oswego.

Burgoyne, who had paused for three weeks, set off once more for Albany. During a period of twenty-four days he covered less than a mile a day. Ahead of him were hundreds of American axmen felling trees across the trail and shattering bridges. Creeks were diverted to create instant swamps. Even so, he never showed any urgency on the long crawl south.

With Burgoyne were hundreds of Brunswick dragoons, lacking horses, stifling in heavy woolen uniforms, weighed down with twelve-pound hip boots and dragging huge broadswords. An expedition was sent off to raid the Connecticut Valley for horses. Enjoined to swiftness and silence, it took a band. In command was Lieutenant Colonel Frederick Baum, with orders to win over the inhabitants. Baum spoke hardly a word of English.

Burgoyne assured him the area was overwhelmingly Tory at heart. This encouraging news came straight from one of the region's biggest landowners, who had earlier found it wise to take refuge in Canada. The fact that he dared not return home without an army went unremarked. Baum and his curious force of 650 light infantry, dragoons, Indians, Tory militia and German bandsmen crashed boldly through the woods, heading for Bennington.

Arrived, they spread themselves confidently over the landscape, while nearly a thousand American militia set a trap under their complacent gaze. The Indians amused themselves cutting the throats of cattle and taking their bells. When the shooting started they ran jangling into the undergrowth. The rest of Baum's force took heavy losses before surrendering. A second expedition tried to come to its support, only to run into stiff opposition. It was saved from destruction by darkness and a shortage of American ammunition.

Burgoyne began to have doubts. He pressed on anyway. His army trudged toward its destination while its supplies went more sensibly down rivers and lakes. His Indians were meanwhile bringing out the New England militia.

Two of them had captured a young woman moving through the forest in a wedding dress. She was on her way to meet her fiancé, a Loyalist officer in Burgoyne's army. In a fight over which of them should have her, the Indians murdered Jane McCrea. They proceeded in their frustration to mutilate her corpse. Burgoyne chose to pardon them rather than risk losing his Indians. Cleverly publicized, the murder and mutilation of Jane McCrea aroused the fury of thousands of militiamen, ready to fight to the death in defense of white women.

In the midst of these events Horatio Gates arrived to take command of the forces disputing Burgoyne's advance. On September 19 the British tried to storm the American lines at Freeman's Farm, near Bemis Heights. Arnold led counterattacks that drove the British back, but he fiercely resented Gates's authority, feeling that by rights he should have command of this army.

Burgoyne was preparing to renew the offensive when word arrived that Clinton was about to set off from New York and drive up the Hudson River valley to join him. He decided to await Clinton's arrival.

A British army 4,000 strong marched from New York to West Point. From there Clinton sent Burgoyne an encouraging message: "*Nous y voici* [We are here] and nothing between us but Gates. . . ." After which Clinton became apprehensive. Instead of pushing on to Albany as planned he returned to New York, to collect more troops.

The message to Burgoyne was, in time-honored fashion, enclosed in a silver bullet. The captured messenger, in time-honored fashion, swallowed it. In time-honored fashion he was forced to vomit it up. In time-honored fashion he was shot.

Behind Burgoyne the New England militia cut all his communications with Canada. American riflemen perched in the tops of trees like carrion crow picked off his officers. Foraging parties left camp never to reappear. His field hospital was full. Supplies were fast running out and, with them, time.

On October 7 Burgoyne launched his second assault on Freeman's Farm. He was convinced that there was a high hill to the left of the American position. He had done no reconnaissance to find it. He was chasing after another Ticonderoga. What existed in reality was a low hill. On it was the strongest part of the American defenses. The British threw themselves at it, suffered heavy losses, then were routed as Arnold led out a fierce counterattack. Burgoyne fell back to Saratoga, to discover he was cut off. After a week of rain he asked for terms.

Gates demanded unconditional surrender. Next day he heard that General Sir Henry Clinton had captured the Hudson highlands, which was true, and was heading for Albany, which was not. Gates's negotiating position collapsed. He allowed Burgoyne to dictate his own terms. The result was a "convention," not a "capitulation." Less a surrender, that is, than a contract. Instead of becoming prisoners of war British troops would be more like guests of the American government. The Canadian regiments would return to Canada unmolested. Burgoyne could keep his baggage train. British and German troops would travel to Boston, at American expense, and await British ships to return them to England. They were pledged not to fight Americans again. On October 17 they grounded their arms.

Congress smelled a rat. So did Washington. During the Seven Years' War, he remembered, a British army had surrendered under similar terms. After a brief pause it returned to the war, on a flimsy excuse. Congress got in its own flimsy excuse first, unaware that Howe was secretly planning to bring Burgoyne's troops to New York, by way of the West Indies.

Military honor was frequently observed on a small scale in the eighteenth century; violated or evaded on a large one, where it might influence the outcome of a battle, a campaign or a war. Comparatively few of the 6,000 men of the Convention Army ever saw Europe again. They were moved around, from Boston to Virginia, then to Pennsylvania, steadily deserting to take up a new life among their former enemies.

THE NEWS from Saratoga that Burgoyne had surrendered ought to have fired up the entire Continental Army. Instead, it created scarcely a ripple. When Washington took his men into winter quarters in December 1777, faith in him was falling like a stone. Brandywine had been an amateurish shambles. At Germantown the chance of victory had been squandered. Philadelphia had been taken by the British. Gates, on the other hand, had beaten Burgoyne, captured an entire British army and probably brought France into the war. Within Congress there was a fruitless attempt to promote Gates over Washington. This venture, known as the Conway Cabal, broke, as all such moves were certain to break, on the rock of loyalty: the officer corps would win or lose with Washington at its head and no one else.

He had no personal or political ambitions. The men who served under him knew that. He spoke often of honor yet shunned any flirtation with grandeur or glory. He avoided melodrama, histrionics and bad taste. The style he brought to war was that of sound estate management.

In later revolutions civilian politicians were invariably terrified of producing a military dictator. The French dreaded a new Cromwell, the Russians a Bonaparte. Congress had few qualms about granting Washington dictatorial powers. There was no danger he would abuse them. That was not his way. He hardly ever employed them, and then apologetically. He was entitled to take anything from anyone, order people shot without trial, hold citizens in prison without telling them why, take the army wherever he wished and impose censorship. If anything his powers were greater than those of a Cromwell or a Bonaparte. He was a manager, however, not a tyrant. "I am not fond of stretching my powers," he wrote, and it was true. Not even the urging of Congress to have the army live off the land had any effect. A well-managed army did not live by looting.

For every day that he commanded troops in the field he spent several weeks as the military bureaucrat. He had to employ three secretaries to keep up with his correspondence. The torrent of paper work he produced was as banal as could be: the stuff that army clerks are made of—wagons, horses, clothing, blankets, expenses, punishments, new recruits, pay arrears, bullet molds and wayward bayonets.

Much of it was forced on him by circumstances. The eighteenth-century commander did not have a staff but a "family," some of them there by right, the rest as a sign of personal favor. It was with his military family around him that a general discussed his plans and problems and to whom he turned—often hopelessly—for expert advice.

Washington also had to deal with Congress. It liked to remind him of who was really in charge by ignoring him when major appointments were made. Congressional committees appeared regularly at army headquarters, to go through his paper work, advise on strategy, inspect the troops and unearth faults, real or imagined. By the time the war ended it resembled remarkably the system of political commissars attached to the French Revolutionary Army and, later, the Red Army.

Like all truly great men Washington was a man of his time yet also able to transcend it. No intellectual, he nonetheless absorbed the Enlightenment's faith in education and progress. He tinkered and invented and took up scientific agriculture. His greatest ambition after the war was to found a national university. He brought both his experience in managing two large estates to running the army and the Enlightenment's habit of treating all human institutions as machinery in search of perfection.

These went far to redeem his failures as a soldier; something this touchiest of men would never have admitted. There is no record of him ever confessing to a mistake. Greene rated him an appalling tactician but loved him as a great patriot. Alexander Hamilton, his favorite aide, worshiped him this side of idolatry while believing he had no military abilities whatever. Neither, however, could imagine anyone else commanding the army.

It was decidedly a creation in his image. He ordered "vice and immorality of every kind discouraged." Gambling was sternly forbidden. Physical exercise was promoted. No opportunity for self-improvement was let slide. The password "Industry" called forth "Wealth." "Neatness" was answered with "Gentility," and "Inoculation" was followed by "Health." During the winter of 1776–77 at Morristown he had the entire army inoculated against smallpox even though it would be convalescent for weeks and the British were a day's march away. He wanted his soldiers to be devout. There was worship every Sunday, followed by roll call. Money and shipping were scarce but twenty thousand Bibles were imported in 1778 for the troops.

There was no other army in the eighteenth century like it: religious, inoculated and forbidden gambling. It would have been inconceivable under officer aristocrats. It amounted to good management along strikingly modern lines. No twentieth-century army would be permitted half the dissipation expected of professional soldiers in the eighteenth and nineteenth centuries when drunkenness and ruinous gambling, the flaunting of mistresses and bejeweled orders were as much the accoutrements of the officer class as old titles and bad debts. The sobriety and modesty, the interest in character and morals that Washington's army brought to warfare helped create the American military tradition and augured a new style.

It had, for example, no corps of camp followers. The British army never moved without them. Some of the women were married to soldiers. Others combined various functions—part laundress, part trollop; part seamstress, part mistress. And tramping in *their* dust came a swarm of children. When an army surrendered or a fortress was taken, the children went into captivity with the troops. Whenever Howe or Burgoyne, Clinton or Cornwallis set off on campaign there was always this other column, of worn-out women, backs bent under heavy loads, with scruffy children trotting alongside, all trying to keep up with the men.

The Continental Army had some camp followers but so few they rarely appear in contemporary accounts. What usually happened was that once the army was entrenched or encamped, the local tarts sought out the soldiers. When the army moved on, it left behind a number of pregnant women and a hospital filled with men suffering from venereal disease. Not even Washington could turn soldiers into saints.

Nor, before Valley Forge, did he have much faith in them. They had broken so many times. Their perseverance under their present ordeal moved him as it moved nearly everyone who saw it. And his insistence on sharing their privations set an example never forgotten.

There was only one good thing about that winter—it was one of the mildest on record. What made Valley Forge so wretched was not the cold but hunger, disease and the choking smoke of green-wood fires in the soldiers' huts. There were men who had not been paid for a year. Others shivered dressed in little more than a torn blanket while reflecting on the promise when they enlisted to provide them with clothes. On at least three distinct occasions there was simply no food of any kind to be distributed. The want of fresh vegetables encouraged deficiency diseases.

All this in an agricultural country which had just enjoyed good harvests. There was plenty of beef in Connecticut and pork in New Jersey. There were warehouses filled with cloth in Boston. In New York State there were surpluses of wheat, barley and rye. There was also plenty of greed, profiteering and meanness. And there was the appalling neglect of roads and wheeled transport in a country that was overwhelmingly rural. There was no national economy; just hundreds of local economies—as provincial a country as any in that age. The only way to supply the army properly would have been to build up a large and effective transportation arm. No one even suggested it. When the army's quartermaster general resigned in November 1777 Congress could not be bothered to appoint a replacement for three months. Those were the worst months at Valley Forge.

The appointment was thrust on Nathanael Greene. He protested, "Nobody ever heard of a quarter master in History." The QM in an eighteenth-century army was both its chief supply officer and its chief administrative officer, yet he was also expected to command a division in the field. That was what Greene inherited, handling supplies one day, men under fire the next.

There was nothing he could do, though, about the epidemics sweeping through the army that winter. To say that American military medicine was rudimentary would be to praise it. An American soldier got far better medical treatment from British army doctors than he would ever get from his own. And despite Washington's precautions of the previous winter there was an outbreak of smallpox. Worse was the outbreak of "putrid fever"—typhus. As many as 2,500 men—one third of the army—died of disease at Valley Forge.

In March 1778 Charles Lee returned to the army, released in exchange for a captured British general. Congress wanted him back so badly it had halted all prisoner exchanges until Lee was freed. He arrived back at Washington's headquarters in typical fashion, followed by dogs and bursting with ideas. He was eager to reorganize the army. He intended to train it for guerrilla warfare. His imprisonment had given him time to think hard about the kind of warfare best suited to American geography, temperament and means. Fighting with a poor imitation of a European army would never bring victory, and he could cite a long string of defeats to prove it.

Lee's hour had passed. The training of the army had been entrusted a few weeks earlier to "the Baron Steuben, Lieut. Gen. in the King of Prussia's Service, whom he attended in all his campaigns, being his Aid de Camp, quartermaster Genl. etc." The hyperbole came courtesy of Steuben's sponsor, Ben Franklin.

The baron was a peasant's son. He had indeed served the great Frederick, but as an obscure captain. The title he flaunted was as phony as the huge paste star he wore on his chest. Not that it mattered. The Continentals loved him because he saw them as real soldiers, but of a new type. As he believed in them, so they believed in him. He was also a born performer and Steuben's greatest role was leadership.

He introduced three essential reforms. First, he put officers in charge of training their men. This improved the military skills of both parties and strengthened the bonds between them. Second, he standard-ized formations and drill, throwing out the mishmash of texts borrowed from European armies. Finally, he got the Continentals to march in columns of fours. Before Valley Forge they had moved in a long, shambling line, like Indians. No army could fight well if the head of the formation got into action long before the tail came up. Steuben made the Continentals fight like an army, not like a horde.

Spring weather brought an end to the worst of the epidemics. Greene managed to get supplies moving once more. And the French, impressed by the near victory at Germantown and the surrender of Burgoyne, had come openly into the war.

At the beginning of May a grand review celebrated the new alliance. Artillery boomed out three 13-gun salutes. Then the troops fired a *feu de joie,* a complicated, well-coordinated demonstration of musketry. Perfectly executed, it was the mark of well-trained soldiers.

Howe spent the month of May handing over his command to Clinton, a man already packing his bags and longing for New York. On June 18 Clinton quit Philadelphia. He had an army of 11,000 men to move and a baggage train that stretched for ten miles. Up to 1,000 Loyalists joined this long, slow, vulnerable column. Here was a gift looking for a taker.

Lee pushed the orthodox solution: harass it, raid the weak points by night and day until it broke up into pieces, which could in turn be crushed by the main body of the Continental Army. Yet again, Washington could not make up his mind. One day he wanted a set-piece battle, the next he agreed with Lee, and the day after that he wanted neither. The solution he finally offered was a compromise: an attack against one flank only, and the rear.

Lee considered it useless and hopeless and said he would have nothing to do with it. After the attacking force was built up from an initial 1,500 men to one numbering 5,000, he changed his mind. With 5,000 men a man might accomplish something. This entire episode, however, represented less planning than groping, a desire to do something but a fear of attempting too much.

The rear of the British column was attacked near Monmouth, New Jersey. Anticipating trouble, Clinton had assigned half his army to serve as rear guard. Lee's troops ran into stiff resistance. He pulled back to re-form.

On both sides fresh units were hurriedly brought up and thrown into the fight. Night and exhaustion fell on both armies. What Washington had done first to Howe, then to Cornwallis, so Clinton now

did to him. The British stole away in the night. The Americans were
left with possession of the field, but little else.

Monmouth was the longest battle of the war. It showed that the
army that came out of the ordeal at Valley Forge could trade blow
for blow with British and German regulars. It was the last pitched
battle fought in the northern theater of war. It was also Washington's
greatest missed opportunity.

That long, slow column might have been whittled away to destruction. If so, it would have been Saratoga all over again, but on
twice the scale. In its aftermath New York might possibly have fallen,
instead of remaining in British hands for seven years. And with a
French fleet about to arrive in American waters Washington would
have had a good chance of holding on to the city.

It is possible that the loss of an army of 11,000 men would have forced the British government to abandon the war, which was already unpopular in Parliament. Instead, Clinton reached Sandy Hook. A large fleet of transports was waiting there to carry him and his army to New York. He had brought his troops out of the lion's mouth. That was victory enough.

LORD GEORGE GERMAIN had succeeded the ineffectual Lord Dartmouth as colonial secretary in the summer of 1775. Since then this robust, hearty figure—the type George III trusted—had run the war from London with an optimism that was breathtaking. No matter how badly matters went he was never discouraged; he was like a man who possesses secret knowledge. Not that that was the reason. The well that never ran dry was a talent for wishful thinking.

From the beginning he had visions of sending his regulars and mercenaries inland from the seaboard while entire Indian tribes rose up and massacred white communities along the western frontier. The rebellion would thus perish caught between two fires. Using the Indians was indispensable to Germain's strategic vision.

A few Indians had found their way into militia companies during the days of British rule. Some remained even after the Revolution began. Congress authorized the employment of Indians as auxiliaries and scouts. Washington disliked the practice. In 1777 he ended all recruiting of Indians despite his permanent manpower crisis. Like Congress, he would have preferred them to remain neutral. The British, on the other hand, were keen to recruit them. And not individually but by entire tribes and confederations of tribes; much as Germain imagined them.

These tribes had a population of 120,000 or more, providing him with up to 30,000 warriors. In return, the tribes demanded not only "presents" but also the right to pillage white settlements, rape the women and torture the men. Some British commanders equivocated, others turned a blind eye. And within the whooping, shrieking Indian war parties of this and later wars there were, hidden under paint and feathers, more than a few white men. From their belts hung human scalps. They had squaws. They worshiped Indian gods. One, the nephew of the governor of Canada, led the advance guard of Indians when Burgoyne's army moved south.

Congress spared no effort to win the neutrality of the tribes.

Washington invited their chiefs to review the Continental Army and honored them with 13-gun salutes. British efforts to bribe the Indians into fighting succeeded. American efforts to draw them into neutrality failed. The real losers would be neither the British nor the Americans but the Indians.

Their own methods were used against them by the frontiersmen. The Indians had sown the wind, for a pittance. Riflemen gladly volunteered to track them down. The sheer hair-raising danger had its own appeal. The hunter pitted his woodcraft, his cunning, his aim in a grim contest where at the end one man lived, one man died: the ultimate blood sport.

The attack on Charleston in July 1776 was part of an attempt to realize Germain's vision. As the British assaulted the city the Cherokees, their allegiance purchased in advance, launched a campaign of terror inland. The militia was already tied down along the coast awaiting the British. Dozens of settlements and plantations were destroyed. Crops were burned, women were raped, children were tortured to death simply to pile on the horror.

Once the attack on Charleston was repulsed the militia launched a campaign from what is now northern Alabama to the mountains of present-day West Virginia. Over an area the size of the British Isles, militia and riflemen tracked down and destroyed as many as 4,000 Indian warriors and their Loyalist allies. The Cherokees and the tribes related to them were utterly crushed. Only the urgent surrender of much of their territory stopped complete annihilation.

These had been one of the most highly developed of all Indian nations. With their destruction the land beyond the Alleghenies came under American control. And the militiamen who surged into the mountains to fight found, descending on the other side, a wide, inviting land. By 1777 a great migration was under way to settle horizons the Indians had surrendered.

One of the most remote parts of the United States was the Wyoming Valley, in northeastern Pennsylvania, far from any theater of war. In the spring of 1778 Loyalists and Indians launched a campaign of terror along the valley because it was overwhelmingly Patriot. Tories living there had been forced to flee. Four hundred Loyalists and a similar number of Indians overran most of the outposts built to defend it. Several hundred Patriot militiamen gathered, unwisely left their fort to fight in the open and were overwhelmed by superior numbers. Few escaped with their lives. The Indians took 227 scalps. The entire valley was laid waste. More than one thousand homes were burned down, along with mills, forges and granaries. The men were driven into the swamps, where they died of starvation. The women were taken by the Indians as white slaves.

Meanwhile the fate of Kentucky, then claimed by Virginia, was in the balance. An expedition sent to secure it in 1777 ran into so many Shawnees it was forced to cower inside forts instead. Among these expeditionaries was a twenty-three-year-old surveyor named George Rogers Clark. The young man was gifted with a cool head and a strategist's vision.

To secure Kentucky, Clark reasoned, it would be better to strike far beyond it. He decided to capture Illinois. Once that fell, the British grip would be weakened not only along the lower Ohio but through-out the entire West. The British might then be driven back to their only secure base in the Old Northwest, Detroit. Most Indian tribes presently fighting the colonists could be cut off from British support and forced to drop out of the war.

Clark led a small band of Virginia militia and adventurous French-men across hundreds of miles of Indian territory in the spring of 1778. On July 4 he captured the British post at Kaskaskia, Illinois.

The British commander at Niagara, Lieutenant Colonel Henry Hamilton, descended on the British post at Vincennes, Indiana, to mount a counterattack. He never got the chance. Clark captured Vincennes, and Hamilton, in one of the most brilliant small operations of the war. The capture of Hamilton was a cause for rejoicing. His name among the Indians was "The Hair Buyer."

Washington long wanted to put a stop to Indian raids on the frontiers. Not until 1779 could he spare the troops for it. He detached 3,000 men to serve under Major General John Sullivan in pacifying upper New York, where white settlements were suffering indescribable atrocities. This was the one time in the Revolutionary War when Continentals fought as avengers.

They fell on the Six Nations, showing no more mercy than the Indians had shown. Some forty-one Indian towns and villages were razed. Near what is present-day Elmira the Indians and their Loyalist militia allies attempted to ambush Sullivan's army. The trap was unmasked in time. The Indians were not beaten but crushed. The pursuit of the defeated was relentless. Nearly all able-bodied men among the warlike Iroquois were killed.

What remained of the Six Nations huddled in the woods. This too had been among the most highly developed of all American Indian societies. For the pleasure of taking scalps and drinking gin they had lost everything—their lands, their homes, their way of life. The British did little to help them. When winter came disease and starvation reaped a second harvest of the defeated.

Despite this the raids on frontier settlements continued. Sullivan's hopes of pressing on to Niagara, from where the Indians and the Loyalist militia were directed, came to nothing. Nor had Clark's dazzling success really made the Old Northwest secure. From Detroit and Niagara the British might supply Loyalist militia and Indian warriors until the crack of doom. The entry "Scalping Knives" continued to appear on the British army's budget.

In the end the Indians contributed almost nothing to fighting strength and much to British problems. Once bribed, they expected an endless flow of presents. They also expected to be fed and clothed, preferring the white man's food and clothing to their own. Long before the war ended, British commanders counted the Indians a great liability.

The Indians had made a terrible mistake: they chose the losing side. It would be a long time before Americans forgot that the Indians had made war on them not to protect their tribal lands, not to preserve their unique way of life, but for felt hats from London, muskets and vermilion paint.

WASHINGTON marveled that both armies were back where they had started from two years before. They were going to remain in their present positions as if frozen in time for the next three years. Clinton was not strong enough to break out from New York, Washington not strong enough to break in. Operations consisted of raids to keep up morale.

It might have remained like that indefinitely had not Germain imagined the South was full of Loyalists only waiting to rise up and strike a blow for the Empire. This phantom army had been sought first in Boston, later in New York, then in Philadelphia. It never materialized; neither would it go away. No one believed it existed more fervently than Germain.

In the course of the war some 20,000 Loyalists did enlist either in the British army or its Tory militia. Germain's vision was not smoke without fire, but it was mostly smoke. The vast majority of Loyalists *were* waiting—and seeing.

From the moment Clinton reached New York he found himself under pressure from London to direct his attention south. With deep misgivings he sent 3,500 men to test the defenses of Savannah. Georgia was a temptingly soft target: the most recently settled state; the most isolated state; the least populated state—and half of them slaves. In December 1778 Savannah fell into British hands. With it went Georgia.

An American army led by Benjamin Lincoln tried to regain the city in September 1779. The assault had every chance of success. A French fleet attacking from seaward was opposed only by armed brigs. On land the Americans had a two-to-one advantage. What saved Savannah was treachery. The plan of attack was betrayed. The British prepared a huge killing ground. Hundreds of American and French soldiers were killed or wounded before reaching the city's main defenses. Lincoln retired to Charleston, South Carolina.

Charleston became the chief objective of British strategy in the next year. It was besieged for four months. The fortress on Sullivans Island had been allowed to crumble away after 1776. The city was also as vulnerable as ever to attack from the landside.

The slowness of the buildup to the assault was fatal—not to the British but to the Americans. Lincoln, energetically raising strongpoints, had so much time to admire his handiwork he became convinced he had created an impregnable fortress. When the British drew near, he unhesitatingly withdrew the entire American army in South Carolina into the town. With the city cut off by land and blockaded by sea, it was in a precarious position.

On May 7 Sullivans Island fell. British artillery smashed down Charleston's outer defenses. Lincoln was forced to surrender. What he surrendered was eight American generals, 6,000 soldiers, seamen and militia, 300 guns, five ships, and the city. It was one of the greatest disasters in American military history.

It was capped by the massacre shortly afterward by Banastre Tarleton and his Tory dragoons of 400 Continentals marching toward

Charleston. Tarleton was a born cavalryman. He had enjoyed his first taste of military glory as a young cornet of horse at the capture of Charles Lee. This slaughter of men attempting to surrender made him the most hated and feared of all Loyalist commanders.

Congress turned to yesterday's hero, Horatio Gates, without consulting Washington. Some of the army's best units—line regiments from Maryland and Delaware under Johann de Kalb—were already heading south. Gates, however, pinned his deepest hopes on the thousands of militia from Virginia and North Carolina who turned out. After Saratoga militia was ever his preference.

He proposed to negate the loss of Charleston by taking the British base at Camden, in the center of South Carolina. From there he might contest British control over most of the state. He took his army by a route where there were virtually no supplies. It moved sluggishly, taking two weeks to travel 120 miles. In those two weeks Cornwallis assembled an army to beat him. Nor did Gates pay any notice to his biggest weakness, the lack of cavalry. Without a counter to Tarleton's Tory dragoons no American army in the South could ever succeed.

When the Battle of Camden opened on August 16, 1780, Gates expected another Freeman's Farm. A cavalry charge threw his forward units into confusion. The British light infantry rushed in behind the horsemen, putting his militia to flight. The Continentals were cut down from every side. It was soon over. Camden was the most crushing battlefield success the British won in the war. Americans were pursued through the surrounding swamps and woods. Tarleton's dragoons chased them for twenty miles. Gates fled mounted on what was said to be the fleetest horse in the army.

Cornwallis moved toward North Carolina, intending to sweep across it all the way to Virginia. The war in the South looked as good as lost.

Covering his left flank as he advanced was one of the most remarkable figures in British uniform, Major Patrick Ferguson, a thirty-six-year-old Scot who had commanded troops since the age of fifteen. Ferguson was a rarity: a British officer who believed in the rifle. He had invented one. Had the British army adopted it they might have won the war. It was one hundred years ahead of its time. Ferguson's rifle was breech-loaded, fired a pointed bullet and was accurate to five hundred yards, was impervious to rain and had a rate of fire of six rounds a minute. It failed because it was too radical.

Riding a splendid white charger and with two mistresses in tow, Ferguson led 950 Tory militia along the eastern slopes of the Alleghenies, challenging "all the Rebels out of Hell" to do their worst. Local farmers and overmountain men from the reverse slopes—proud and prickly types mounted on sturdy ponies—swarmed toward him. At Kings Mountain, South Carolina, on October 7 Ferguson got the fight he was asking for.

His Tory militia volleyed and charged. The Americans hid behind boulders and trees, taking aim carefully. Ferguson was shot off his charger, killed by a rifle bullet. His militia were cut down even as they surrendered. A dozen of the survivors were hanged after a show trial, to discourage other Tories.

News of Ferguson's destruction reached Cornwallis at a time when he was ill in bed. While he recovered, so did American forces in the southern theater of war. Washington sent Greene south to take command.

The army entrusted to him consisted of 1,500 hungry, beaten, ragged men. His military chest consisted of a battered and empty box. Nor had Greene the flair for leadership that raises men's spirits. Like Washington's, his mentor, his gifts were organizational and managerial. With these, and the help of men such as Steuben and Daniel Morgan, he was about to perform military prodigies.

He wasted no time correcting the fatal flaw: he built up a strong mounted arm. Like a belated convert, he proselytized other commanders: "Enlarge your cavalry, or you are ruined."

The challenge he faced was enormous, and the consequences of failure too appalling to think about. He had to avoid defeat but somehow keep the British occupied. Yet if he could make them chase him and not be caught, he might hope to wear them down until one day he was as strong as they, or they as weak as he.

The key to his strategy was out of his hands. What he needed was a resolute but impetuous opponent. Cornwallis was the perfect foil.

In the most daring strategic decision of the war Greene split his small army in two. It was the most imaginative piece of generalship the Continental Army ever knew. It defied all theory and practice. It was known to be little short of madness to divide an inferior force in the face of a superior one. Cornwallis was astounded. Tarleton put it down to ignorance. Yet it posed a problem for the British. If Cornwallis wanted to hold what he had taken and also pursue Greene to destruction, he would have to do as Greene had done. He split his own force into three—one to hold, two to chase.

Tarleton was given 1,000 men and sent off after Morgan, who had taken command of half Greene's army. Cornwallis, with 3,000 men, set off hoping to find Greene, and the other half.

On January 16, 1781, Tarleton caught up with Morgan at a watering place for cattle on the border between North and South Carolina, almost in the shadow of Kings Mountain. The place where Morgan chose to fight, Hannah's Cowpens, was absurd. There was a river at his back and both his flanks hung in midair, waiting to be turned. Morgan fought here and now because he was not a man for running. And Tarleton made no attempt to turn either flank because he was not a man for maneuvering. He was a straight-ahead fighter.

Nonetheless, Morgan gave thought to his problems. His solution turned the conventional wisdom inside out. He put his weakest units, the militia, in front of his strongest. Half of these militia were sharpshooters, assigned to pick off officers and NCOs long before they were in musket range. After two volleys his militia was to pull back, to be rallied, re-formed and act as a reserve. This meticulous preparation paid off with a double envelopment. When the militia returned to the fight it crushed one of Tarleton's flanks while William Washington's cavalry crushed the other. Virtually the entire British force was killed or captured. Tarleton's Legion, the British trump card in the South, had been wiped out. Tarleton narrowly escaped to fight another day.

Cowpens was a flawless gem but on so small a scale it hardly deserves to be called a battle. Its consequences were enormous: it made Greene's strategy work. Cornwallis was already on the road. He burned his wagons, got rid of his rum, put two men on every horse he could find, and set off after Morgan. Taking a day to burn his baggage train, he gave Morgan time to escape. And when news of this act of self-destruction reached Greene he is said to have rejoiced, "Then he is ours!"

Both halves of Greene's army linked up. There followed a thrilling chase across North Carolina to the Dan River, on the border of Virginia. The British reached it only to see the last of Greene's troops getting out of boats on the opposite side. A nice piece of stage management.

Reinforcements were waiting. Virginia sent 400 Continentals and 1,700 militia. Rifle companies steadily marched in. Cavalry rode up.

Greene at last had an army, if a small one. The only thing to do with it was use it. He recrossed the Dan, looking for Cornwallis.

On March 14 he made camp at Guilford Courthouse. With 4,200 men Greene could finally afford to fight. Cornwallis with 1,900 could not. He would do so anyway. His army was almost out of supplies. Either they fought here and won or they made a two-hundred-mile retreat to the sea, with an army twice as big and just as mobile on their backs. Clinton, being Clinton, would have opted for retreat. Cornwallis, being Cornwallis, chose to fight his way out of trouble.

Guilford Courthouse was the best battle he ever handled. His troops began the day with nothing to eat, marched twelve miles at forced-march pace, then threw themselves without hesitation into combat against an enemy who had them outnumbered more than two to one. They attacked with such determination they forced the Americans back. With the issue still in doubt grapeshot was unintentionally fired into the packed mass of American and British troops by British gunners. The less disciplined American units pulled out. Cornwallis's bloodied survivors pressed on and captured American guns. Greene withdrew in good order, and not very far.

The victorious British sank to their knees. One fourth of their small army was dead or wounded. Greene's losses were comparatively slight. Two days later Cornwallis led his men away, on an anxious, starving trek to Wilmington. The general who originally set out with a splendid force of 3,000 well-trained troops in pursuit of Greene staggered into Wilmington at the head of 700 sticklike figures the color of dust.

Greene harried the retreating column part of the way, before veering off toward South Carolina. He deliberately left the way open for Cornwallis to collect reinforcements at Wilmington and then move north, into Virginia. It was bait. Cornwallis took it whole. He had lost all his earlier eagerness to fight Greene. In Virginia he chased after a small American army led by the Marquis de Lafayette, without catching it.

When Greene advanced into South Carolina the British commander there, Lord Rawdon, defeated him at Hobkirk's Hill, near Camden. Greene's losses were light, and Rawdon's were heavy. The British fell back, toward Charleston.

Greene then laid siege to the British outpost at Ninety Six, but was beaten off. All this while the interior of South Carolina was changing

REVOLUTIONARY WAR: The South

0   100 Miles   ✷ Battle site

hands. Partisan bands rose like mushrooms after rain. The presence of an American army in the state transformed the war there. The partisans rose up not only to ambush British troops but to wage the pitiless war of neighbor against neighbor.

On September 8 Greene fought his last battle, at Eutaw Springs. His men had never been more impoverished. Continentals advanced into combat naked except for swathes of Spanish moss tied around their shoulders to keep their cartridge boxes from galling and to cushion the musket's kick. With the fight almost won, they ate and drank victory away. When the enemy's lines were breached hundreds of starving Continentals fell on British supply wagons. British cavalry quickly formed up and counterattacked the drunken pillagers.

Eutaw Springs was the hardest battle of the war on land: hand to hand, sword to sword, knife to knife. Greene lost one fourth of his troops to death or serious wounds. He pulled back, but British losses were nearly 50 percent. The victors retreated all the way to Charleston. The British had no desire to beat Greene again. He charged too high a price.

The state governments of South Carolina and Georgia were reestablished. In losing all of his battles, Greene had freed the South. The British hold was broken for good. They clung to a handful of ports, depending for survival on the Royal Navy's getting through to them. There was no hope, thought or inclination ever again to move beyond the comforting sight of sails and blue water.

THE WAR would be decided in the end where the British were strongest, at sea. The Royal Navy's supremacy turned out to be largely one of numbers, not of control. No one really commanded the sea in this war. At least 80 percent of American ships putting to sea reached their destinations. The sea-lanes were open most of the time to most ships of whatever nationality. The western Atlantic, free of the kind of choke points the British commanded in the eastern Atlantic, such as the Channel, was a vast and watery no-man's-land.

Almost at the start of the war Congress created a Continental Navy. Orders were placed for construction of 13 frigates. By the time the war ended, the Continental Navy had sent more than 50 ships to sea. The 13 state navies floated another 40 ships or thereabouts. Although these 90-odd vessels were no match for the hundreds of British warships plowing the ocean there were some ferocious ship-to-ship encounters.

The famous battle between the *Bonhomme Richard* and the *Serapis* in British home waters was the bloodiest fight of the war at sea. Half the men on each side were killed or wounded. None of the naval engagements had much evident influence on the final outcome, and before the war ended every one of the original thirteen frigates had been captured, scuttled or sunk. Even so, the foundations of an American naval tradition had been created.

French intervention posed the kind of direct threat to Britain that kept British admirals awake at night in sweaty suspense. In 1779 a joint Franco-Spanish fleet stood poised to land an army of 50,000 men on the beaches of southern England. The French admiral in command lost his nerve when the time for irrevocable decision arrived. A storm blew up. The combined fleet scattered to avoid it. After that scare, however, the Royal Navy kept a large fleet in home waters and lost some of its earlier gambling spirit.

The biggest menace to British shipping came from American privateers. They captured nearly eight hundred British ships. They were denounced then and ever after for robbing the infant American navy of men and naval material but it may be wondered whether the Continental Navy would have done any better with them.

Besides the privateers were ships carrying letters of marque. These were a breed unto themselves: armed merchantmen peacefully going about their trade but licensed, should the opportunity present itself, to capture some less well armed merchantman flying the enemy's flag. They did not go looking for prizes but if one hove into view . . .

If the sea offered potential rewards these were amply made up for by the risks. The majority of American prisoners in British hands consisted of seamen, and most were confined in the holds of rotting hulks in New York Harbor. Each morning began with the cry "Rebels, turn out your dead!" A hundred corpses a day were dumped in shallow graves in the surrounding marshes. The wretches crammed into the hulks were meant to suffer at least enough to make them take the easy way out and swear the loyal oath. The policy failed. Only a few men broke.

The main theme of American war propaganda was the abominable maltreatment of American prisoners. Frightfulness called forth frightfulness. After three years of unheeded protests, American prison hulks were established in which British prisoners might die of starvation and disease. There were also the abandoned copper mines of Connecticut, where Tories caught in British uniform were left to rot in total darkness and squalor.

Imprisonment was a killer. Of the roughly 25,000 Americans who perished in the Revolutionary War some 6,500 were killed in action. An estimated 10,000 died of cold, disease, hunger or wounds. The remaining 8,500 were prisoners, the victims of deliberate neglect, dying in unspeakable filth and undeserved obscurity.

· · ·

THE ACTIVITIES of the privateers in Long Island Sound filled Clinton with dread. He was terrified they might fall on one of the supply fleets from England and starve his army into submission. Fear for his supplies kept him tied to New York, agonizing aloud over all the terrible things that could happen.

Cornwallis, by comparison, craved fighting and movement. In April 1781 he set off from Wilmington, plunging deep into Virginia in pursuit of Lafayette. Ostensibly under Clinton's command, Cornwallis simply ignored him. It was he, not Clinton, who enjoyed the favor of Germain.

That same spring of 1781 found Washington still besieging New York. He remained obsessed with "the key to the Continent." Without the city he could see no end to the war.

After the British had abandoned Newport in 1779 a French fleet had brought a French army in. After which the Royal Navy returned and blockaded the French fleet. Another French fleet, under Admiral de Grasse, was scheduled to sail from the West Indies in the spring of 1781 and break the Newport blockade.

Washington planned to have the 6,000-man French army march south meanwhile and link up with the 8,000 troops besieging New York. Together the two armies would make an all-out attack to capture the city.

They stood no chance of success. Clinton had 15,000 well-armed, entrenched regulars and hundreds of artillery pieces. His army was dug in behind broad, swiftly flowing rivers that were completely controlled by British warships. Every time Washington made a probing attack it was smashed to pieces.

Reluctantly, after endless hours of discussion, he was finally persuaded that any assault on New York would fail. Washington was almost desperate for action. He had been staring at the defenses of New York for three years. For inaction he far exceeded the sluggish Howe and came a close second to the cautious Clinton. To keep the war going he needed to fight, and soon.

At this juncture news arrived that demanded swift decision and prompt action. De Grasse was embarking 3,000 French troops in the West Indies and sailing with twenty-nine warships, heading not for Newport after all but for the Chesapeake, where Cornwallis was trying to catch Lafayette. Within twenty-four hours a letter was being galloped to Lafayette: at all costs he must keep Cornwallis in Virginia. Washington was coming south as fast as he could.

He left behind a bewildered Clinton. It was two days before he grasped that Washington was heading for Virginia with 8,000 men.

In an attempt to leave nothing uncovered the British had scattered their naval strength from Canada to the West Indies. When a British fleet intercepted De Grasse off the Chesapeake on September 5 its admiral was dismayed to find that the Frenchman had him outnumbered and outgunned. After a perfunctory exchange of gunfire the British turned away, heading back to New York. When De Grasse blockaded the Chesapeake, Cornwallis was in the bag.

He was at the end of a peninsula, with water almost everywhere he looked. He dug in, expecting Clinton to send or bring an army to his relief. On the landward side of the peninsula American and French troops moved steadily closer, digging trenches toward his lines. When they were close enough, they brought up artillery.

Under Henry Knox this had been built up into the best-disciplined, most highly trained branch of the army. Knox's gunners smashed down the defenses Cornwallis had built around Yorktown.

With supplies dwindling fast and an epidemic raging among his troops, Cornwallis began a night evacuation by rowing boats over to Gloucester, on the opposite shore. A storm blew up, scattering his boats. There was no escape. On the fourth anniversary of the surrender at Saratoga he scribbled a brief note to Washington, asking for terms. That same day Clinton set sail from New York to come to his rescue with twenty-five warships and 7,000 men.

Six thousand British and German soldiers staggered out to surrender at Yorktown. They were drunk. Tears ran down their cheeks as, cursing, they dropped their muskets and lurched into captivity.

In the early hours of October 22 a lieutenant colonel in the Continental Army galloped into Philadelphia seeking the sleeping president of the Congress, Thomas McKean. The watchman who guided him to McKean's house returned to his patrol, crying, "Past three o'clock . . . and Cornwallis is taken!"

3

CHRYSALIS

THERE WERE still 22,000 British and German troops on American soil. Washington spent the winter preparing to resist a fresh British offensive when the 1782 campaigning season opened. Like previous winters it was a period of hunger, shortages, skirmishes and raids. When peace rumors began spreading, he dismissed them as a British plot aimed at making him disband the army. He would not be tricked.

What spring brought was not a new offensive but news, hard news, that the king wanted an end to the war. Peace really was at hand. Washington remained with the army, still unwilling to disband, because now there were rumors of a revolt. The Continental Army had to be handled like an unexploded bomb and carefully defused.

While the peace talks went their slow and measured way, the bulk of the army was assembled at Newburgh, New York. Anonymous pamphlets were circulating that suggested men with muskets and bayonets had it in their power to wring redress of their grievances from even the most unwilling politician. The attempt to manipulate the legitimate complaints of the soldiers, and the efforts to head off a revolt, marked the beginning of a political struggle that would eventuate in the Constitution.

On April 11, 1783, Congress received confirmation that a peace treaty had been agreed upon at Versailles. Washington was ordered to cease all hostilities one week hence. With a better sense of history than Congress had shown, he added an extra day. The Revolutionary War ended on April 19—eight years almost to the hour since those first musket shots at Lexington.

Never were there so many struggles in one: a civil war, a war of national liberation, a guerrilla war, a class conflict, a global war, a domestic rebellion, a war of outposts and a war of unlimited goals. The British decided it had been a war they could never win. Americans disagreed, claiming the odds against *their* winning made victory as good as a miracle.

Nothing was predetermined. Either side could have won, either side might have lost. Both made tactical and strategic blunders.

Why did the Americans win? The British preferred to dwell on the difficulties of the terrain: rugged and full of woods in the North, broken up by pestilential swamps and treacherous creeks in the South. The French agreed with them. The Americans could be defeated; the country—never. That was the view in any sophisticated European eye. And sophisticates, like everyone else, see largely what they expect to see. Europeans had heard how awesomely rugged the country was before they ever clapped eyes on its long-populated shores.

This terrible terrain in its virginal state had not prevented white men from taking huge areas from the Indians; nor had it stopped the British from driving out the French; nor would it stop the Americans from driving out the British and Spanish; nor, in the War of 1812, was it going to deter the British from launching a three-pronged offensive from the St. Lawrence to the Gulf of Mexico. With the exception of Burgoyne's wilderness campaign—which failed mainly through bungling—major British operations were conducted in long-settled areas, where there were roads not much worse than those in many parts of Britain or France, and much of the woodland had been cut back and cleared for farming.

What undermined the British was not the terrain but the slowness with which they moved over it. In Canada, which the British crawled through, they covered ten miles a day. In the campaign against the Indians of upper New York the Continentals made as much as forty miles a day. Despite being burdened with artillery and baggage carts, a sizable force marching from Tioga to Easton in Pennsylvania in 1779 covered 156 miles in eight days through country that was mountainous and heavily forested. Without such impedimenta American troops thought nothing of marching twenty-five miles a day.

The British, by contrast, were slow not because they were operating in America but because that was part of their style. Burgoyne's baggage train achieved a certain fame but it was typical. In Howe's army of 1776 there were ten wagons to carry the soldiers' tents, and twelve to carry the regimental silverware and tablecloths.

The result was a kind of military anomaly: dozens of battles but hardly any pursuit. There was none after clashes where British losses were light and the Americans ran. Except for Camden there was not a single attempt to destroy an American army, even though Howe always insisted that that was his way to end the rebellion. Private Joseph Plumb Martin retreated from a dozen lost battles, including Brandywine and Germantown, yet never hurried his steps: "I had no more fear of their overtaking me than I should have of an army of lobsters doing it, unless it were there [sic] horsemen. . . ." There were few of those about.

Fortunately for Martin and his fellow Continentals the British army had forgotten the proper uses of cavalry. When the war began, it had 7,000 cavalrymen; they outnumbered the artillery by three to one. They were used for ceremonial and for cowing the unarmed, turbulent lower classes on both sides of the Irish Sea. The British had a global empire, yet in April 1775 there was not a single British cavalryman outside the British Isles.

Howe had no more idea of what to do with cavalry than Washington. To him they were a nuisance, a drain on his supplies. When London sent him 400 dragoons he sent half of them straight back, for want of forage. His troops were meanwhile building a brewery in New York. There was no effort to use the vast acreage of Loyalist Long Island to provide forage for a cavalry force. The main thing was to make sure there was enough beer.

The idea that the country was little more than a tangle of trees led to its being described as "unsuitable" for cavalry anyway. As later events would show, mounted men operated with deadly effectiveness in the forests of the frontier. The militiamen who destroyed Ferguson's troops at Kings Mountain were horsemen. In the areas where the main armies operated there was a lot less wood than some might suppose. There were bitter quarrels among Continentals over the shortage of wood for fires. "I thought that different regiments were upon the point of cutting each other's throats for a few standing locusts," Washington remarked.

Woods were not the great barrier to cavalry. Nor was cost. Greene conjured up cavalry as he conjured up much else, out of thin air. The chief obstacle was want of imagination. Both sides suffered from neglecting cavalry. It was a shortage that led to generals—including that superb horseman Washington—doing their own scouting to discover the enemy's movements. With two cavalry troops, comprising some 450 hard-riding, well-armed dragoons, harassing the British, Clinton would never have escaped at Monmouth. It took his baggage train a week to cover forty miles. "Had we possessed a more powerful body of cavalry in the field," lamented the *New York Journal,* "there is no doubt the success would have been much more complete." Indeed, there is no doubt. Of the two, however, it was the British army that paid the heavier price for this neglect, because it was the slower army of the two.

The neglect of cavalry was blamed, like ultimate American victory, on want of supplies. And there were indeed occasions when British troops suffered hunger. Their deprivation hardly compared, all the same, with the suffering of the Continentals. Congress decreed that the army should have a feast at Thanksgiving in 1777. The feast consisted, Joseph Plumb Martin recalled, of half a gill of rice per man and a tablespoon of vinegar. At Morristown during the terrible winter of 1779 men roasted what was left of their shoes, sucked on nails, gnawed bark from twigs.

It was no accident that the Continental Army reached its peak strength of 30,000 men in the fall of 1777. After Valley Forge it never again topped 20,000. The entire country knew that Continentals were nearly always hungry, could barely cover their backs and had no real medical services. Joining up meant more than the slight risk of death in battle—it meant the absolute certainty of hunger. A soldier's life is always hard but this went beyond hardship.

In 1780 Congress abandoned all pretense of supplying the army, dumping the entire responsibility on the thirteen states. Starvation in winter quarters had already demoralized the troops. With Congress more or less abandoning them, men turned mutinous. In 1781 both the Pennsylvania line and the New Jersey line revolted. The chief grievance was hunger. Had supply determined the outcome of the war the British would have won it.

What lost it for them was a lack of nerve and imagination. British officers felt unable to risk heavy losses. Compared to its worldwide commitments Britain had a tiny population. Habitual caution was beginning to undermine major offensive operations on land. That cautiousness became part of the British army's way of making war. The flair of a Wolfe could find scope only in small operations.

The caution of Howe and Clinton was perfectly suited to American needs and abilities. It allowed American troops to learn how to fight, how to survive, how to cooperate. By moving ponderously, by groping half-blind for want of patrols, by waiting for the phantom army of Loyalists to appear, by squandering months of good weather in idleness, the British provided Continentals and militia with the best training school in the world.

Casualties were low. Battle, thought many soldiers, was safer than winter quarters. Nearly all the fights following Bunker Hill were low-intensity combat with fairly modest figures for killed and wounded; low also in absolute numbers. As Lafayette later described the war to Napoleon, "The greatest issues in the universe were there decided by skirmishes. . . ." It was deaths from neglect in captivity that made this an unusually costly war. Roughly one eighth of combatants perished. The vast majority of these fatalities lacked the dramatic impact of death upon the field. What impinged on public awareness was the low level of combat casualties. This could only have nourished the high level of commitment the Revolution called for.

American victory was more than the sum of British failures. There was Washington; still only a man. The apparent miracle of success led to his being cried to the skies as a peerless tactician, a genius of strategy. Everything turned out all right so he must have planned it that way.

The United States won largely because of Washington and despite his ineptitude both as a field commander and as a strategist. It won because he created an army and kept it in being. For long stretches the war seemed to swirl around him as he beavered away at his correspondence. He never lost sight of at least half the great truth: no army, no Revolution. He may or may not have guessed at the other half: no Washington, no army.

He did not win by taking a cool, long-term view. He might write of the need to avoid general actions, but it never stopped him ignoring all that when the blood rushed to his head. The thin-lipped, unsmiling Washington was no more master of his temperament than most men.

That same temperament made him touchy. A breath of criticism was resented as an aspersion on his honor. And where honor was concerned he had no patience at all. There was a layer of granite beneath that fierce concern for honor, a toughness of spirit that the war turned to stone. The harder the going, the more determined he became to see it through to final victory. Just as Washington would not admit a mistake, so he would not admit defeat. By some cosmic chemistry he was at his best when the war was at its worst.

There was also the militia—ragged, often poorly organized and badly led, but in its own way something to count on even in the most desperate times. The militia gave an added social and political dimension to the war, one that shaped not only the way it was fought but what its consequences would be for the new nation that was being created.

French money, French ships, French arms and French troops were also essential to the outcome. There could have been no victory without them. Joint Franco-American military operations invariably failed—except at Yorktown. Infusions of French gold, or gunpowder, or muskets came nonetheless at the moments when they were needed most.

By dangling the prospect of recovering Gibraltar before Spanish eyes the French brought Spain into the war. This distracted the British on a worldwide scale, forcing them to spread their limited military and naval resources from Canada to the Mediterranean. At some point something would have to give. The British held on to Gibraltar—and lost America.

WITH THE WAR over and won there were no parades, no outpourings of gratitude. The men of the Continental Army simply made their way home as best they could, penniless as usual, in rags, ditto, begging for food at farmhouses along the way. All they had to show for what they had done was a free musket.

Americans had wanted to win because they were virtuous and the British were wicked. As they discovered, virtue did not win battles. Troops won battles. Yet they had been raised to believe armies could never be trusted. These Continentals, trudging down the dirt roads, were both an embarrassment and a source of pride. That heritage of mixed feelings would be handed down to generations yet unborn.

There were other, more martial echoes, destined to reverberate through other wars. America had been a testing ground for advanced military ideas, much as Spain would be in the 1930s. For twenty years bright young officers had argued that the future lay with light infantry, in the same way that naval flyers around 1925 would feel that destiny called. Charles Lee considered the gauntlet of fire the British had to run from Concord to Charlestown an illumination so dazzling it showed beyond all doubt that Americans were born light infantrymen. Properly trained and led, they could whittle any European army to extinction. It would be a tragic waste to turn them into volley fodder. Washington disagreed. To show how much he disagreed he even abolished the army's elite corps, the 2,000-strong light infantry. When the war ended, the Continental Army looked like and was organized like the army of a minor European state.

It had nevertheless worked a revolution in warfare. Its loose two-rank deployment, screened by a cloud of sharpshooting skirmishers, had been adopted by its enemies. The British formation of three ranks closely interlocked had been transformed into "the thin red line" of two. The inaccuracy of musket fire, accepted by European armies for more than a century, no longer was. The British and French had not bothered with target practice. A sheer waste of time and good powder, they said. After all, it took a man's weight in bullets to kill a soldier in battle. Fighting in America changed that. By 1783 marksmanship was prized. Target shooting became part of every infantryman's training in most armies. The basis of close combat was shifting, from cold steel to aimed fire.

The British would have gladly fought the entire war at bayonet point. Closing with the bayonet was the epitome of a soldier's courage and skill. And everyone knew that the only answer to a bayonet was another bayonet. Everyone, that is, but the Southerners.

They had no use for a bayonet except perhaps to spit-roast a chicken. They put their trust in firepower; usually aimed, but they put in buckshot pellets with each musket ball or cut their bullets so they would fragment in flight, determined to hit something. The effect of these techniques on closely packed ranks was devastating.

These men got maximum performance out of a musket. They loaded carefully, aimed calmly. What a British regular could do at forty yards they could do at one hundred. There were also rifles in the hands of thousands of Southerners. At Kings Mountain and elsewhere riflemen shot British units to pieces. Where riflemen had time to reload, aimed fire won. At Kings Mountain they even rode out a bayonet charge, bringing it down with crushing fire from both flanks. For the first time in history infantry firepower alone defeated musket volleys and a bayonet charge.

Such lessons were too important to be ignored. Even while the war was being fought, Henry Knox was lobbying Congress to create a military academy. Hardly had the fighting died away before Washington renewed the plea, "to preserve the knowledge which has been acquired thro' a long and arduous service." War was "the Military Art," something some men could teach and others learn. The country's existence might one day hang by the thread of that art. The amateur soldier was not enough. The army, to be a real army, must be educated.

In his "Sentiments on a Peace Establishment" submitted to Congress at the end of the war, Washington tried to make the best of his "broken staff" but his feelings about them had not changed much. The organizer of armies, the manager of men was bound to take a dim view of militia: it represented a certain untidiness, a lack of reliability, a dispersion of scarce resources. He was prepared to tolerate it, though, provided it was taken in hand. So he recommended militia, but properly trained, properly armed, properly led. There was no way of getting rid of it, anyway. The states would not have considered it. It was give-and-take: he would take the militia (much improved, of course) and in return he hoped it would give the country an army. A mere 2,600 men was all he asked, to guard the frontier and the borders with Canada and Florida. A small army—but a permanent one.

Every officer the Continental Congress consulted on the issue gave the same advice. The America that emerged from the chrysalis of the Revolution was set free in a world where republics were few, monarchies many; set free in an age when conflicts between states commonly ended in war; set free at a time when the spiral of violence was picking up, not winding down; set free as terrorism, conspiracy and fear were wiping the "smile of reason" off the face of the Enlightenment. To these officers a nation without an army was a nation without a hope.

Troops were needed even now, along the new frontier. The peace treaty awarded the infant United States a vast inland empire. In their chastened mood after Yorktown the British washed their hands of the Old Northwest, destined to provide five states—Michigan, Ohio, Illinois, Wisconsin and Indiana. Wild and sprawling, it would serve

as a buffer zone between the Americans and Canada. Along this peril-
ous frontier, said army veterans, only regulars could perform the vital
task of "awing the savages."

Washington resigned his commission. The army disbanded. Eighty
soldiers remained as caretakers to protect leftover military stores. This
famous, piquant detail was rich in irony for a country owing its
existence to a war.

A M E R I C A was free, but with an aching need no one had foreseen, a
yearning for blood ties. All history had produced but three such bonds
that unite an entire society. Humanity venerated them in ritual, literature and art. The trinity of blood relationships was monarchy, theology and antiquity. Americans had just thrown all three aside. They had
no king, no national church and as the newest nation on earth no
antiquity whatever.

The shared sacrifice of war became that blood relationship. No part
of American society came so close to living out the ideals the Revolution proclaimed as the Continentals and militia.

No monarch, no religion, no long history in this land bound
Americans to one another. What did was the commingling of their
blood, shared sacrifice, a memory of danger. Politically the strongest
tie among the states was an image: troops from here, troops from there,
standing shoulder to shoulder, life to life, death to death, in black
powder smoke along the musket line.

The human clay of combat was fairly modest stuff. A fourth or
so were foreign-born, usually from cities. The native-born came from
the land. Both were drawn mainly from the poorest class of whites:
newly freed servants (freed, that is, from indentures), former convicts,
day laborers, sons of poor farmers. Joining the army had been a fresh
start. It offered employment, after a fashion.

Slave owners never lacked for substitutes to send to the militia or
the army. One way and another some 5,000 blacks fought in the
Revolution. When the slave owners tried to reclaim their property at
the end of the war they were rebuffed. Their slaves were transformed
by service into free men. And hundreds of runaway slaves had been
enrolled by desperate recruiters as "free Negroes." Now they were.

Service with blacks and the sight of cruelty to black slaves turned
many Continentals against slavery. Black soldiers were respected not

only for their courage but as survivalists. Many seemed to endure the rigors of military life better than white soldiers.

The Revolution brought into existence societies for abolition. The first antislavery society anywhere met in Philadelphia on April 14, 1775, five days before Lexington. Throughout the eight years of the war there was no selling or importing of slaves.

A heightened awareness marked the whole Revolutionary generation. The attempt to raise an army of eighty-eight battalions—roughly 45,000 men—had failed, but it had brought the war home to towns and villages everywhere. Life fell into an endless round of town meetings as each struggled to find its share of recruits, then to buy salt beef and clothing, then to find muskets and bayonets. To make sure people came to town meetings and did their part in supporting the war, those who stayed away were threatened with being drafted first. This was no mass mobilization yet it had much the same politicizing effect as the famous *levée en masse* of the French Revolution.

The army worked its own transformation on the men sent or recruited. For the first time they had to shave regularly. They were expected to brush their clothes and keep their hair clean. They were taught to keep their surroundings tidy. No matter what rags they were dressed in they were told to look smart. For the first time in the nation's history American men were made to consider their appearance. Most took it to heart, despite a want of means. When Sullivan's army returned from its Indian campaign its 3,000 men looked like beggars. In each man's cap, however, there was a sprig of evergreen and his hair was white with a liberal application of flour. The people who turned out to greet them were grateful, but convulsed with laughter.

Republican simplicity before long induced American men to give up wigs and powder altogether. A true Patriot showed off his own hair—or the lack of it.

For many of the discharged Continentals the transition back to civilian life was hard. They were restless. Men who would never have traveled more than ten miles from their homes without the war had marched and marveled through half a dozen states. It was their Grand Tour.

Land in the West was awarded veterans in hundred-acre tracts. Some sold their claims for cash. Others went to see what it was like out on the frontier.

The opening of the West to settlement was one of the chief

consequences of the war. The British government had closed it off in 1763, and in 1772 Gage had ordered Americans who had moved beyond the mountains "to quit those countries instantly and without delay." The war changed all that. By the time it ended there were 25,000 settlers living on the western slopes and foothills of the Alleghenies. With peace, a stream became a river.

The disbanded soldiers, men used to hardship and weapons, were ideal settlers in a wild free zone where they might have to fight for their lives. To open up the inland empire called for a first wave of a type not easy to find in the generally peaceful, usually comfortable society of colonial America. The war had raised up a new breed, then set them loose over the land.

The frontier brought a thrusting, impatient, democratic element into American life, built on the war's upheavals. Many a notable had found that to hold on to political power or to command men in arms meant bowing to the leveling wind the war unleashed.

Colonel Thomas Randolph of Virginia, for example, was entertaining a captured British officer in 1781. Three men in work clothes arrived, took off their boots, spat in half a dozen directions and joined in the conversation. After they left, Randolph tried to explain to the amazed Englishman that it was all the fault of the war: no man who had borne arms for the Revolution looked on any other man as his superior. "Each of those men considers himself, in every respect, my equal." He shrugged. What could he do?

Knox founded an order, the Society of the Cincinnati, for the officers of the Continental Army. Its membership was hereditary, passed on to their sons. It was denounced as an attempt at aristocracy. Washington joined it as its president, reformed it, stopped wearing its enameled eagle on a ribbon and dropped out. The Cincinnati withered away.

The war produced a society that was far from classless, but one far less class-bound than the one that preceded it. There was no universal suffrage for many years to come, but the franchise was rapidly spreading. As the right to vote spread, the social status of hundreds of thousands of families was raised overnight. The settled, stable social organization of Colonial times perished in the Revolution, never to reappear.

Whole new strata had come into existence, such as a debtor class. For decades to come there would be fierce agitation for a return to paper money, and plenty of it. Currency became a great dividing line, like slavery, cutting deep across both society and government.

The whole world of markets and speculation we take for granted first appeared in America during and because of the war. In the 1780s there were seven kinds of U.S. securities. The states accounted for roughly seventy more. Nearly all could be traced back to war debts.

Revolutionary inflation created a new business class. Ordinary peddlers became rich in two or three years. Skilled craftsmen abandoned their trades in search of business adventure. Goods were scarce, money plentiful: the profiteer's vision of heaven. The entire shoe supply of North Carolina, for example, was bought up by a Maryland syndicate in 1777. The price of shoes in North Carolina tripled. Then tripled again. Never had there been so many chances to make a fortune.

The speculative enterprise was privateering. A sturdy ship and a bold captain could bring home a fortune. Some twenty thousand men were at sea lusting for riches before the war ended. To profit, though, you did not have to master seasickness; you did not even have to gaze on the heaving bosom of the ocean, nor yet on the little brown vessel that carried your hopes. Shares in privateers were traded like securities on the stock exchange. There were hot tips, inside information, bull markets and bears. The army was filled with soldiers wondering how "their" privateer was doing.

All the while the country was awash with paper money. The Continental Congress printed it. So did all the states. So did the Loyalists, printing counterfeit continentals and giving them away.

How much real hardship this inflation imposed is impossible to say. On those with low fixed incomes it probably caused considerable suffering, but 90 percent of the population did not have fixed incomes. Among those who did were the soldiers.

The country as a whole, however, actually prospered. In areas that were fought over there was devastation. Elsewhere, rural America was flourishing. There was an abundance of food. The Continental Army did not see much of it. The French army lacked for nothing. They simply had to appear, with a war chest filled with gold, and everything that could be eaten or drunk was pressed on them, in huge quantities. At times the French found it embarrassing. They held back from buying so there might be something for the Continentals to have.

There was also illicit trade between the British and Americans. In some areas local committees of safety made that dangerous. In the cities, where anonymity was easier to come by, it made fortunes. The millions of pounds in gold and silver that made its way into circulation in pursuit of scarce supplies generated a boom in dozens of cities and towns.

The only people who seemed to miss out in all this happy intercourse were the Continentals. The moment the poor, bedraggled army came into view the price of everything went up as though these penniless men were eccentric princes in disguise. Time and again officers had to restrain their men from hanging a merchant or two.

Government orders also boosted prosperity. The decision to build thirteen frigates was the biggest construction project of any kind up to then mounted in America. By the time the war ended, Congress and the states had built close to one hundred ships, bringing employment and profit to half a dozen ports. Not even Puritan Boston missed this particular boat. When the Prince de Broglie visited it in 1782 he was astonished at the "downright magnificence" of upper-class homes.

America had gone into the war an economically underdeveloped country; not by accident. Before the Declaration of Independence it was bound hand and foot to London's banks and England's laws. The Colonies were to provide raw materials. Britain provided the goods. A long list of regulations was enforced to make this policy stick. It stuck—in American throats.

There was the law of 1750 that banned the Colonies from manufacturing steel: an absolute bar on the emerging Industrial Revolution. Nor could any American erect a rolling or a plating mill. No hatter could take on more than two apprentices; he might get above himself and end up with a hat factory. And so it went. The country that went to war with Britain was an agricultural one, lacking nearly all the features of what was then a modern economy. It did not even have a bank. The first, the Bank of North America, came into existence in 1780, to provide funding for the army's supplies.

An infant arms industry was developed. Its cannon tended to blow up or fire short. Its gunpowder tended to fizz or burn without exploding. Typical products of infant industries. Springfield Armory in Massachusetts was created by Congress on Knox's advice in 1778. The location was chosen with an aim to keep arms production far from British reach. Gun-making was concentrated in Maryland for much the same reason. Congress got the states to exempt arms makers from taxation. What was needed was their products, not their taxes. Some privileges are as old as the republic.

Across the entire range of emerging technologies the war awoke the American gift for making things, or making them better. Wartime vulnerability remained in folk memory, troubled the minds of officials, worried old soldiers. The country was in a hurry to develop—not so it could eat but so it could fight.

THE 80-MAN FORCE of caretakers lasted exactly one day, from June 2, 1784, to June 3. Twenty-four hours after disbanding the last regiment of the Continental Army, the Confederation Congress "recommended" that New York, Connecticut, New Jersey and Pennsylvania raise 700 militia to serve under the secretary of war's direction for one year.

The Confederation and the states both saw the wild lands to the west as their only hope of paying off their war debts. That meant sending in surveyors to map out the land; sending in negotiators to talk to the Indians; sending in settlers, including women and children. All three—surveyors, negotiators, families—would need protection.

Two years after the war ended, settlements still burned brightly along the Ohio, to the sound of screams. Far from being "awed" by American troops, the Indians despised them. It took a third of the Confederation army—200 regulars, in 1786—just to guard the Geographer of the United States as he mapped along the western Pennsylvania border. By this time the 700 militia provided by the states had been replaced by regulars, enlisted for three years.

Not only were the Indians unimpressed, so were the settlers. They launched their own punitive raids, without waiting for the army to do it. The Confederation Congress looked on with a sense of helplessness. The U.S. Army took 40 percent of its meager budget, yet Henry Knox, the secretary at war, had to ban offensive operations for want of money.

At the end of August 1786 a mob 1,500 strong ransacked the courthouse at Northampton, Massachusetts. Over the next six weeks farmers and townspeople, heavily in debt and impoverished still further by the postwar slump, took out their frustration by attacking courthouses throughout the western half of the state. Local militia were called out. They failed to turn up, or else stood by and watched their neighbors get on with it. Sent for, the militia of eastern Massachusetts were less neighborly. So was a volunteer cavalry regiment, hurriedly enlisted. An assault on Springfield Armory in January 1787 to seize arms was easily repulsed. The rebellion, led by a former army captain, Daniel Shays, petered out with the rebels fleeing through the woods into Vermont.

The Confederation Congress had acted quickly. Its hostility to military forces vanished literally overnight. It found the troops. It found the will. It found the money. Too late. A tremor of fear shook down the Articles of Confederation. Indian attacks. Rebellion. What next?

Once the snows had melted, men throughout the land got into saddles, into carriages, and made their way purposefully toward Philadelphia. Each had instructions from his state to revise the Articles. All ignored their limited powers, junking the Articles without regret, like trash.

They acted swiftly, surely, like men who knew what they were doing. And they did. They had been warming up for years. The arguments that were brayed in taverns, brought fists down on dinner tables, set red-faced men shouting face to face in legislative halls, over who had won the war—regulars or militia—rehearsed the struggle for the Constitution.

Nearly one delegate in three had, somewhere, a fading commission in the Continental Army. Others, perhaps one in five, had served on a congressional committee helping to run the war and though civilians had sympathized with the army's feelings; shared something of the veterans' resentment over the shabby treatment—the hunger, the nakedness, the lack of pay, the martyrdom of serving not one good master but fourteen bad ones. Delegates such as these had charged their wartime glasses many a night to "A hoop to the barrel!" and "Cement to the union!"

Washington, presiding over the convention, felt as they did, voted as they did. In politics he was last among theorists, first among Federalists.

For many of the delegates army service had been their entrée into public life. With peace it had become the foundation of a political career. They had not fought, as they recalled, for this state or that. They were among the first people to have a clear, wide vision of the nation as a whole. They felt themselves to be the first, maybe the only, real Americans: their loyalties were undivided.

Washington was their first advantage; youth was their second. On average the Federalists were twelve years younger than their Antifederalist opponents, who swore by states' rights and militia battle honors—Lexington, Bunker Hill, Saratoga, Cowpens.

Through the muggy heat of late spring and early summer they argued, never more fiercely than over regulars and militia. Clause by clause, vote by vote, the Antifederalists were driven back. What emerged was a fighting document.

The Constitution created a national government with four great powers: war, taxation, commerce and control of western lands. The first and last of these amounted to much the same thing. No one had any illusions: control of western lands meant fighting the Indians and driving out the British. The boundary out there was vague; a peacemaker's gesture over maps that had blanks. And the mood in London had changed. As the Confederation stumbled, British hopes rose of rolling back borders too generously conceded.

Taxation was meant to meet two urgent needs: pay off the war debts and discharge current expenditure. The main item in this was and would be the cost of armed forces. Federalists saw war no matter which way they turned. Commerce was a guarantee of armed conflict. Nations competed hotly for markets, for the carrying trade, for fisheries. American ships and seamen were already being seized by Barbary pirates. Britain, France and Spain were making angry noises about American economic rivalry. Promoting commerce meant promoting defense.

At all four corners of the Constitution stood a man in arms.

The rock on which the convention was most likely to founder was the problem of a standing army. The Federalists tackled it head-on. When the original draft came up for consideration with a clause giving Congress the power to "raise armies," this was amended to "raise and support armies": no time limit, no implication of crisis measures, no hint of emergency. These were going to be permanent, peacetime forces.

To appease a public opinion raised to look on a standing army as a standing evil, a two-year rule was adopted for military appropriations. Every two years the legislative branch would have a chance to review military affairs. This, though, was little more than a gesture. No one believed for a moment that the legislature would cut off the money and put the army out of business again; not even for a day.

Elbridge Gerry, a leading Antifederalist, tried to impose another kind of limit: let the size of the army be set at 2,000 to 3,000 men. Washington stirred in the chair from which he presided, whispering loudly enough to those near him that he could be heard clear across the room. Ostensibly—and literally—above the debate, here he felt provoked beyond endurance: if the American army was going to be held down, he grumbled, America's enemies would have to agree to do the same. Gerry's motion failed. No limit was placed on the size of American forces. Even James Madison, eloquent on the wickedness of militarism, accepted the need for armies now: "If they be necessary, the calamity must be submitted to."

Nothing was done about reforming the militia. The states clung to it as tenaciously as ever, convinced that without the militia they would soon wither away. Having forces of their own was the chief expression of state sovereignty. Here was another rock. Splitting control of the militia was the only way to avoid it. The president was put in nominal control of them, as commander in chief.

This was a gigantic leap in the dark. In Britain the king was captain general of both the army and navy. As a rule, he tended to politics and diplomacy and handed over his military responsibilities to a commander in chief. The Constitution combined the two roles in the presidency.

Had it not been for the fact that the country's preeminent soldier was certain to be its first president it is unlikely this would have been done. Some delegates expected and intended that the president as commander in chief would lead American forces into battle, much as Washington had done during the war.

The Constitutional Convention provided all the authority needed to maintain military forces and to use them as desired against foreign foes and domestic disorder. The military provisions are the spine of the Constitution. Its fundamental assumption is that in the end, when all other means fail, government relies on force.

The Declaration of Independence condemned standing armies. So did nearly every state constitution. The United States Constitution makes no criticism of standing armies. Nor does it make any explicit assertion of civilian authority over the military. Some Antifederalists went to their graves convinced that far from being freedom's charter it was a militarist's text, written from start to finish by men who had never outgrown their old uniforms. Men who, in a phrase, believed that power grew out of the barrel of a Charleville Model 1763 musket.

The document provided for armies and fleets under federal control. Each state was assured "a republican form of Government," which meant that the federal government could intervene with force to prevent anarchy or monarchy. It guaranteed to protect the states against "foreign invasion . . . against domestic violence." Local militia could be raised by the national government "to execute the laws of the Union, enforce treaties, suppress insurrections, and repel invasions."

The Constitution does not provide for civilian control. It provides for civilian supremacy; not the same thing. Civilian control, to be more than a pious hope, needs a clear and effective means of expression. The Constitution does not offer one. It splits military powers in half a dozen directions. The president is commander in chief, but only Congress may declare war. The president is commander in chief, but he has control of the states' forces only under limited circumstances. The president is commander in chief, but there is no machinery provided for him to direct military operations.

The military could not, in theory, overthrow the government and claim the sanction of the Constitution. Nor could it subvert the Constitution on behalf of the government. Such barriers, however, provided small comfort to men like Elbridge Gerry.

The standing army the Constitution created was no threat to liberty. Steuben tried to reassure the undecided. All armies, he said, reflect the society that creates them. Even though there would be strong-willed generals in future years who would face down their commander in chief; even though there would be generals who were involved in partisan politics against their commander in chief; there would never be any serious threat to democratic freedoms from the military.

4

HAMMER
AND ANVIL

IN A STARK AGE, stark choices. The new government, filled with soldiers, issued from a war, was the hammer by design, never the anvil. Throughout the eight years of Washington's presidency the country felt it was fighting for its life. Even in periods of peace it breathed an atmosphere of war. Big as the United States was it seemed to be hemmed in, by the British in the Old Northwest, by the Spanish in the Old Southwest, by Indians along every frontier.

Land-hungry settlers were pressing over the mountains or floating down the Ohio on huge rafts that provided the lumber for first cabins. Indian bands, thirsting for justice and loot, fell on them. Roughly twenty white people were scalped every month in 1790, or carried off to a fate unknown but easily imagined.

Knox, once more secretary of war, found little to choose between the ignorance and savagery of frontiersman and Indian. Both were beyond reason. Both lusted for revenge over any slight, imagined or real. Both were pitiless once the smell of blood reached their nostrils. The land they fought over was not in doubt, though. "The Indians, being the prior occupants, possess the right of soil," he advised Washington. The United States was in an odd position: it held sovereignty to the lands north of the Ohio but not title. "It cannot be taken from them unless by their free consent," Knox added, "or by the right of conquest in a just war."

Here was the first great challenge to the presidency and to the Constitution. The government decided to try civilizing the Indians: they could have free tools and free instruction if only they chose to become farmers. If they sold their lands, however, there could be only one buyer—the government. And, just in case the depredations continued, Congress gave Washington authority to make war on the Indians at his discretion.

He pursued a negotiated settlement while simultaneously making military preparations. To pressure the Indians of Ohio into more peaceful ways, a punitive expedition was formed under a Continental Army veteran, Josiah Harmar. Leading 400 regulars and 1,100 militia, he moved northward from Fort Washington, site of present-day Cincinnati. A second, smaller force meanwhile moved north from Fort Knox, more than one hundred miles to the west; two armies, too far apart to support each other.

Harmar's expedition was a ragamuffin affair, fleshed out with men who signed short-term enlistments to get free transportation out to the frontier. They were settlers, not soldiers. The aim was to strike a hard, swift blow against renegade Shawnee, Cherokee and Wabash. That called for one invasion force, not two; mounted, not on foot.

Harmar's advance guard strolled into an ambush. The militia ran. The regulars stood their ground and were cut to pieces. Harmar's main force attacked feebly, was counterattacked and took serious losses. At his court-martial Harmar claimed that avoiding annihilation was a triumph. The court agreed. The expedition from Fort Knox had meanwhile floundered around harmlessly in the wilderness, returning unscathed.

Out of this fiasco in the fall of 1790 came a doubling in the size of the regular army, and "levies" were authorized. These were men raised by short-term enlistment but under regular army discipline. A compromise, that is, between regulars and common militia. Such volunteers were to provide the bulk of American wartime forces for more than a century to come. For the moment they were no more than a desperate makeshift. Their first taste of battle would be a massacre.

Arthur St. Clair was governor of the Northwest Territory, major general in the Continental Army, former president of the Continental Congress: the very model of the modern soldier-politician. When he took the field to avenge Harmar's defeat, however, he was an echo of the man he had been. He was fifty-seven—a gouty, nervous, tired fifty-seven. Nor did his army impress: short of arms, short of training, short of discipline, short of horses, short of spirit, short of hope.

St. Clair needed Indians or frontiersmen to act as guides through the forest. He could find neither. He set off in August 1791 with much of the campaign season already behind him, moving slowly, stopping to build forts. His army found itself looking at a winter campaign in summer clothing. He pressed on anyway, through the sleet of Ohio's November, wrapped in flannels, carried on a litter.

Every precaution was spurned. Reliable intelligence reports were not passed on. Patrols were not sent out. Nor were the troops held in the ranks after reveille until visibility had lifted to three hundred yards: an essential measure against a foe who preferred to attack in the murk before dawn. St. Clair's men were huddled around campfires, cooking breakfast, when the Indians struck.

Eight bullets went through St. Clair's clothing. One clipped his white hair. He emerged without a wound. His second-in-command, a famous Indian fighter named Richard Butler, was less lucky. He dropped dead. The Indians fell on the still-warm body, cut open his chest and ate his heart. In the woods round about, the militia were still running—not fast enough. Two thirds of St. Clair's army of 1,400 were killed, wounded or taken prisoner. It was the greatest victory Indians ever achieved over American arms.

This bloody fiasco reopened old arguments, old wounds. The states said regulars could not fight. Washington said militia would not fight. The real question, though, was whether the United States would have to abandon hope of turning sovereignty into title in the Old Northwest. The British were now happily arming the Indians and holding on to their old forts there.

Congress gave the administration nearly all it asked for: authority for 5,100 regulars, three-year enlistments, a free hand. The army was rebuilt and reorganized, along lines proposed by Steuben, into the Legion of the United States. This was divided in turn into four sub-Legions, each an army in miniature, with its own cavalry and artillery, under a brigadier general. Each sub-Legion was meant to be strong enough to fight its own battle long enough for another one to come to its support.

The Legion never reached its authorized strength, but when it came into existence, early in 1792, it transformed American forces by making them fit to fight.

With the Indian war in the balance something had to be done about the militia. Washington, Knox, Hamilton and Steuben all pressed Congress to create a national militia. They won the argument, lost the vote. Most congressmen simply dared not give the federal government so fearsome a stick with which to cow their states. Serious hope of reform had always hung by a single frayed thread: a national militia, trained to a high standard, providing the army with a genuine ready reserve. Once that thread finally parted, all hope of reform crashed to the ground.

The Uniform Militia Act of March 1792 created a vast paper army, fully equipped with paper muskets, paper spontoons and paper supplies. It made all "free able-bodied white male citizens" aged eighteen through forty-five members of the militia. It was politico-military nostalgia become law; a fond glance backward to the Antifederalists' youth—to the pre-Revolution militia. The new dispensation was like the old one: no standard formations, no uniform training, no real penalties for noncompliance.

Once Congress had given Washington what he asked for—thousands of regulars to fight the Indians—the other side of the bargain was to leave the militia alone. Two months after the Uniform Militia Act became law, Congress passed the Calling Forth Act. This limited the president's powers to intervene in civil strife.

None of which obscured the fact that Washington now had all the authority he needed to raise armies, make war. What the administration needed to justify what it had done—tripling the defense budget, so it accounted for nearly half of all public spending—was a victory. For that it looked, reluctantly, to Anthony Wayne, commander of the Legion: a bold martinet, vain, touchy, feared by his troops, disliked by his officers, held in no high regard by the commander in chief.

Missionaries, interpreters and negotiators meanwhile roamed the Old Northwest carrying twenty thousand dollars in cash and boxes filled with silver objects to try talking the Indians into peace. These were only sweeteners. Hundreds of thousands of dollars was available for treaties that ceded tribal land.

The Indians were torn. Some wanted war, whatever the cost. Others sought peace, whatever the price. Both sides were alarmed at the signs of war readiness throughout 1793: military supply trains . . . new forts . . . improved roads . . . columns of troops. . . .

While negotiations dragged on, Wayne used the time gained. His army was trained to operate in all weather, kept clean and healthy, brought to accept military discipline, honed to something that reflected his own edge. By the spring of 1794, when talks with the Indians broke down after they narrowly voted to continue the war, he led a force that was impatient to fight. Wayne set off down the trail that St. Clair had followed to disaster, leading 2,000 regulars and 1,500 volunteers, most of them mounted riflemen.

At the site of the massacre he cleared away the rotten human remains, buried them with care and built a fort called Recovery. The Indians circled it. At dawn on June 30 they attacked. In a desperate twenty-four-hour fight they were beaten off, at heavy cost on both sides.

With the American claim on the Old Northwest seeming about to collapse, the British built a fort on the Maumee, called Fort Miami, where Toledo now stands. Wayne was ordered to remove this unwanted presence on American soil. With his rear securely based on Fort Recovery he headed north.

The Indians, more than 1,000 strong and reinforced by Canadian militia, prepared to contest his advance. Four miles south of Fort Miami a tornado had sliced through the forest some years before, leaving a tangled mass of fallen timbers: instant fortifications. Here the Indians prepared to fight. Wayne's cavalry screen uncovered the trap.

Without pausing for reflection he moved to attack. His mounted volunteers fanned out into the woods, turned the right flank, jumped the storm-strewn trunks on their sturdy mountain ponies, crashing furiously among startled Indians. Wayne's infantry meanwhile volleyed and charged through the undergrowth in a frontal assault, storming over the defenses, thrusting bayonets seeking out the foe. Terrified braves broke, running from a strong defensive position. Infantry hunted them through the woods. Cavalry chased them to the walls of Fort Miami. The British, afraid it would be their turn next, slammed the gates on their allies.

Indian losses were comparatively slight, yet some of their best warrior chiefs lay slain. Wayne moved on into Indian country unopposed. Bereft of leadership, smarting over betrayal by the Canadians and British who had armed and encouraged them, impotent to stop the Legion's relentless advance, the Indians lost heart. They lapsed into the fatal passivity that marks absolute defeat. The next year they formally ceded to Wayne half of Ohio and much of Indiana. The British finally pulled back into Canada.

By then the frontier had brought another alarm. While the Constitution was being ratified Jefferson and Hamilton had made a pact. Normally they were political foes. Jefferson pushed the merits of state government, while Hamilton believed that only a strong national government would do. As a patriotic Virginian, Jefferson was keen to locate the capital of the new nation in the South. Hamilton did not much care where it went so long as the federal government was decidedly stronger than the states.

The deal they made was that Hamilton would support putting the capital along the Potomac, while Jefferson supported Hamilton's plan to have the federal government take over the states' war debts. That financial burden would create the need for a major increase in the financial powers of the government and make clear its ascendancy over the states.

To raise the money needed to pay off those debts, Congress passed an excise tax on liquor, whether imported or domestic. Almost from the moment that legislation took effect in 1791 excise collectors were attacked.

Confusion over a stray shot fired one day in July 1794 while a militia muster was being held led to hotheaded militiamen attacking the home of the collector for western Pennsylvania. His estate was overrun, his house burned down. Without intending it, thousands of people found themselves in open rebellion against federal authority. A similar crisis had wrecked the Confederation. The Constitution was poised on a razor's edge.

Washington called on four states to raise 15,000 militia while he sent a commission to parley with the "White Indians" out west. The commissioners came bearing promise of pardon in exchange for a loyalty oath.

There was resistance to Washington's call for militia. A draft had to be imposed, but that produced antidraft riots in Maryland, Virginia and Pennsylvania. Liberty poles went up. So did tension. Then came the dramatic news of Wayne's victory at Fallen Timbers. The would-be rebels woke to find there was a conquering army at their backs, while thousands of militia were preparing to cross the Alleghenies. The spirit of resistance guttered out.

All the same, the machinery was in gear. Washington spent two

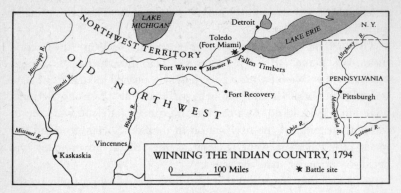

WINNING THE INDIAN COUNTRY, 1794

0 _____ 100 Miles   ✴ Battle site

weeks reviewing the assembling militia host, raising morale sky-high. "Light Horse Harry" Lee led them out, with Hamilton, in uniform, at his side. They advanced to douse a fire already extinguished. Up to two thousand people fled before them—into Indian country or the deep woods, toward Spanish territory or up into Canada. Just two people were convicted, out of dozens who stood trial. Condemned for treason, when their real crime was riot; sentenced to hang, only to be pardoned.

A tragicomic episode, but rich in consequences. The Whiskey Rebellion was a solid-gold gift to the Federalists, coming as their hold on government faltered. The year had been roiled with rumors of war—with Britain, with Spain, between Americans—and of yet another defeat by the Indians. All those terrors were suddenly banished.

The Whiskey Rebellion army took 13,000 men over the mountains. A lot of them never came back. It was a new world out there, with plenty of cheap land for the asking; land abandoned by the thousands who fled rather than face Lee's army. Pittsburgh, a dreary frontier village of nine hundred people in 1794, was little more than a clearing in the woods. Along came an army: thousands of men with money in their breeches and energy to burn. Everything that could be eaten, drunk, slept with or built with brought a high price. Within five years the village would be a thriving industrial town. Forges pounded heavy metal on the outer rim of the civilized world— "sonorous metal, blowing martial sounds."

INDEPENDENCE meant being free to suffer a hostage crisis. With Crown restraints broken, American ships sailed freely into all the world's oceans, but without the protection of the Royal Navy. Protection, that is, against the corsairs of the North African shore whose favorite naval maneuver was to come alongside and drop their great lateen yards across the victim's rail. Instantly pirates would swarm across, pistols stuck in their belts, cutlasses clenched between their teeth, leaving their hands free for climbing.

In July 1785 Algerian pirates scooped up two American ships, taking twenty-one Americans and a Spanish woman passenger into captivity. The ransom demanded was $2,800 per head. The Confederation Congress cried poverty, the press cried vengeance, congregations prayed, years passed.

In 1793 a peace agreement between Algeria and Portugal unlocked the Straits of Gibraltar to the pirates. They swarmed into the Atlantic, hunting rich, unprotected American ships. Eleven were taken that summer. More than one hundred Americans found themselves in Algerian harems and quarries.

Despite the expense of the Indian war Congress voted in March 1794 for six frigates (three 38s, three 44s). As a concession to antimilitary sentiment the program was to be dropped if the hostage crisis was resolved. Construction was a fitful business, yoked to hopes of peace and fears of war. As these rose or fell, so construction slowed, halted or speeded up.

A settlement was reached in 1795 with the dey of Algiers. It called for a ransom of $642,000 and a large annual tribute in naval stores— "powder, lead, iron, bullets, bombshells, bomb stones, masts, poles, yards, anchor chains, cables, sailcloth, tar . . . and other necessities." Construction of the warships stopped.

The prisoners had still not been released. When the dey grew restless over slow payment, though, he was promised a bonus: a brand-new 36-gun frigate. Launched with a wincing lack of sensitivity on July 4, 1797, it was called the *Crescent*. The prisoners—those who had survived or had not gone crazy—were released. The magnificent *Crescent* meanwhile made Bashaw Yusuf Karamanli murderously envious.

Of the three potentates of the Barbary States (the dey of Algiers, the bey of Tunis and the bashaw of Tripoli) he was by far the least powerful and easily the greatest pest. Karamanli had usurped the throne by murdering one brother and banishing the other, who happened to be the rightful heir. In buying off trouble with one cutthroat the United States stored up trouble for itself with another—the bashaw.

The generous payoff to resolve the Algerian hostage crisis made the United States the principal armorer of the pirates for years to come. Given the desperate state of the warship program it seemed to have little choice.

The project was entrusted to Knox, who had a thin man's hustle in a fat man's body. He made his own talent search, turning up a pair of Quakers who were fascinated with warship design, Joshua Humphreys and Josiah Fox.

The most sophisticated, complex and expensive artifact of an advanced eighteenth-century society was a fighting ship. It represented high technology to a degree that nothing else approached. Fox dreamed of faster warships. Humphreys dreamed of more powerful warships. They took advantage of sloppy drafting in the construction bill to design a supership: a bigger, stabler, more heavily armed gun platform than anything Congress expected yet still within the act, if only just. Humphreys added a second tier of guns and sheathed his hulls in copper to produce the most advanced weapons system afloat.

The effort to build six high-tech frigates (plus a seventh, the *Crescent*) was simply beyond the country's resources. The three 38-gun frigates had to be dropped to finish the 44s. These had been estimated at $100,000 each and eighteen months. In the end they took four years and were considered either a scandal or a joke. The cost of each rose above $300,000, more than the British spent on a 74-gun ship of the line. Long delays, upgraded specifications, temperamental state-of-the-art designers, pork-barrel politics, huge cost overruns: the stereotypical defense project of the late twentieth century. Yet the three 44s (*Constitution, President* and *United States*) worked. Even a generation later they could outsail and outfight any frigate on any sea.

They looked certain to see action the moment their hulls touched the water. Under Jay's Treaty, signed following Wayne's victory at Fallen Timbers, the British finally agreed to quit the Old Northwest. The United States in return would close its ports to French privateers. The Directory, the French revolutionary government, retaliated at what they saw as a typical plot by the British and Americans to injure honest France. Their corsairs fell on American shipping, even along the American coast.

In the fall of 1797 American emissaries in Paris tried to discuss the matter. The French demanded a bribe and promise of a cheap government loan just to talk. Having established itself as a soft touch for pirates, that was as much as the United States could have expected.

Because the United States had set itself up for humiliation, the reaction, when it came, was as furious as only wounded pride could make it. The Federalists had been struggling for years to promote naval construction. In 1797 they lacked the votes. In 1798 they had them. The Navy Department was created, putting it on a par with the army, including a seat in the Cabinet. The three 38-gun frigates were resurrected. Money was voted to build twelve sloops of war. The president was authorized to accept warships as gifts and to rent them if necessary. Seaports from Canada to Georgia raised huge sums by subscription to provide fighting sail. And as the three superfrigates got ready to put to sea the U.S. Marine Corps was created, to put men in the tops.

Congress also authorized the government to arm American merchantmen. More than one thousand were in time armed at federal expense, with anything up to thirty guns. Casting so many cannon poured money into the infant arms industry. So did an act to promote foundries. It had appeared in the Senate in 1797, a small bill with even smaller chances. In 1798, scaled up ninefold, it passed with ease. The federal government thus found itself committed to create gun foundries and armories. To please Washington, the largest was placed in Virginia, at Harpers Ferry.

For all this passionate voting and spending, gun-casting and defiance, there was no war declared on France. The government was split between war Federalists and peace Federalists. The only thing they agreed on was the need for a navy. War Federalists wanted to use it to attack the French. Peace Federalists wanted to use it to prevent French attacks. Government policy was quasi-peace, quasi-war. What it gave the nation was a "one-sixteenth ocean navy"—able to operate out to the edge of the continental shelf.

Under the first navy secretary, Benjamin Stoddert (a Continental Army veteran, wounded at Brandywine) American captains were under strict orders. If they encountered an armed French ship, they were to take it or sink it. Unarmed ships were to be left alone. There were not many of those.

Over the next three years one French frigate was sunk, another captured; 111 privateers were seized, four destroyed. Some 70 American merchant ships were recaptured. The French stopped talking bribes and cheap loans. Peace was at hand.

All this time Yusuf "War is My Business" Karamanli was losing patience, however. The bashaw was given to feeling bitter whenever he thought—as he often did—of the brand-new frigate, plus two smaller warships, and the mountain of naval stores being heaped on the dey of Algiers. He demanded a warship too and set a deadline.

As the quasi-war with France drew to a close a squadron of three frigates and two sloops was formed in May 1801 and dispatched to impress the ridiculous bashaw with his impotence. A wasted gesture. Exactly one week earlier he had sent a party of axmen to cut down the flagpole in front of the American consulate in Tripoli. In a country where tall pines or fir never grew this was an act pregnant with meaning. It was a declaration of war.

The bashaw was counting on the reputation of the new president, Jefferson, as a pacifist and appeaser. He had grievously misjudged his man. Jefferson was one of the few in government who had argued back in 1785, during the first hostage crisis, that it was better to fight pirates than pay them. With the Tripolitan War on his hands he had his chance to do it.

The war got off to a dispiriting start. The naval commodore sent to take charge of the blockade was Richard Morris, who believed in proceeding cautiously. So cautiously that he not only allowed the bashaw's trade to continue uninterrupted but, when necessary, helped it to do so. That was too much reasonableness even for Jefferson. In 1804 Edward Preble arrived to impose a blockade: a real one.

One of his frigates, the 38-gun *Philadelphia,* had the misfortune—brought on by dubious handling—to run onto a shoal off Tripoli Harbor. Even the attempt to scuttle her was botched. Her crew of 309 officers and men became prisoners of an exultant bashaw. His sailors refloated the *Philadelphia,* taking her within shelter of the harbor's guns. News of this humiliation stunned the country like the news of Pearl Harbor would. Virtually the entire American navy was soon heading east for the Mediterranean.

Preble did not wait for it to arrive. He scoured the yards of Sicily and Malta to build or buy gunboats and bomb ketches. He also planned to use a captured Tripolitan ship, the *Mastico,* to carry a raiding party into Tripoli Harbor, under Stephen Decatur.

The raiders managed to board the *Philadelphia,* overpower the Tripolitan crew, set her ablaze and escape without losing a single man.

As the flames reached the guns, all double-shotted, she fired two broadsides: one out to sea, the other into the town.

Five times Preble sailed his squadron in to bombard Tripoli: wooden ships versus stone forts. In these artillery duels his gunners far outclassed the Tripolitans ("Turks," to Americans), winning every one. His bomb ketches lobbed hundreds of shells over the high walls. The bashaw cowered in his bombproof shelter under the harem, waiting for the Americans to run out of ammunition or zeal; which they did. Lacking troops to go ashore and take the town, all that Preble was doing amounted to convict labor—turning big rocks into little ones.

The Tripolitan War nonetheless made the navy. It was a nursery of talent. The young officers under Preble included Oliver Hazard Perry, James Lawrence, David Porter, Thomas Macdonough, and Isaac Hull, as well as Decatur. And they were ambitious in the right direction: if they could not have a big navy, then the best. Everything that could be practiced, was: hand-to-hand fighting, gunnery, navigation, sailing. After which it was practiced all over again. It seemed the most natural thing to do during the long confinement in Tripoli for the officers of the *Philadelphia* to turn prison into school: which was better, carronade or long gun? weather gauge or lee gauge? small ship with many guns or big ship with fewer? round shot or bar shot? And so on, *ad nauseam,* caught up in connoisseur's dilemmas.

American naval officers thought long and hard about what they were doing. The navy, like the country itself, was an effort of will, sustained only by grinding effort suffused with romantic visions. These men had none of the comforting worldliness of European navies, where a boy of nine could go to sea as a junior officer, his tiny foot ready to fly nimbly up the ladder of promotion.

Preble had successfully blockaded the Tripolitan coast and carried the war to the bashaw. He was recalled anyway. Jefferson was embarrassed and apologetic. Congress insisted on running the navy as much as he did. What was meant by "commander in chief" was still far from certain. Preble's recall was but one result of that confusion.

Another, more promising attack was about to be made on the bashaw under the leadership of William Eaton, the American consul at Tunis. At sixteen he had joined the Continental Army as a camp dishwasher. By Yorktown he was a sergeant. Eaton later served in the Legion under Wayne, whom he idolized. His plan was to restore the true bashaw, Hamet Karamanli, to the throne of Tripoli, in place of the wicked brother.

Eaton won over Hamet, assembled a force of 10 Americans (including eight marines), an Englishman, 38 Greek mercenaries, an interpreter, 350 Arabs and a "chief of staff" named Leitensdorfer who had been through four religions, five armies, several prisons, spoke half a dozen languages and would one day be custodian of the Capitol. Because Bashaw Hamet was afraid of the sea they approached Tripoli on foot, across four hundred miles of desert, early in 1805. Despite treachery, hardship and daily threats of mutiny or death Eaton's motley band reached the city of Derna, the second largest in the bashaw's sandy state. With reckless courage they wrested it from a much larger defending force that lacked their determination to win.

The loss of Derna frightened Bashaw Yusuf into releasing the prisoners from the *Philadelphia* and putting up a new flagpole. It was not only the loss of Derna, however, that unnerved him. He was a diligent reader of the American press. Then as now the media had a role to play. What the bashaw read was news that Congress had voted a war appropriation of more than $500,000 a year, renewable indefinitely. The Tripolitan War was remarkably popular once American forces seized the upper hand. What the bashaw was being promised was war without end.

Peace came as a terrible shock to Eaton. Hamet was not only abandoned by the treaty the United States signed, but by a secret clause the bashaw was allowed to hold his brother's wife and children hostage for another four years. This odious concession was kept secret even from the president; another indication of how vague his powers still were. By the time Jefferson learned of it there was little he could do to help the betrayed, trusting Hamet Karamanli, whose memory lives on.

Several times he had been protected by Lieutenant Presley O'Bannon and his seven marines. Hamet's parting gift was a sword with a Mameluke hilt. That hilt is the pattern of the sword carried by marine officers; a reminder still of the Corps's first great exploit, the crossing of the desert of Barca by a lieutenant and seven men in 1805.

IN THE INDUSTRIAL REVOLUTION that was remaking Europe and the world, the most important manufacture was textiles;

the most advanced machinery was steam engines, gleaming, hissing and hot. Neither textiles nor steam, however, made people think of interchangeable parts. There were straws in the wind, all the same, cast up by war: In the 1770s the inspector general of French artillery, Jean Baptiste de Gribeauval, had standardized production of the major components of gun carriages. In the 1780s a French gunsmith, Honoré Blanc, had experimented with mass-production techniques for muskets. And in the 1790s the Royal Navy's shipyards mass-produced up to 100,000 wooden pulley blocks each year. These initiatives ran into the sands, however, in the face of strong craft attachment to traditional methods.

America was different. It had one manufacturing need that dwarfed all the rest. There was a frontier to defend at every point of the compass—against the British, against the French, against the Spanish, against the Indians, and overseas there were pirates holding Americans hostage. The country needed arms, in quantity, quickly. How long might national independence survive weapons dependence? The only venture the federal government had even attempted into public ownership was the two armories, at Harpers Ferry and Springfield. They seemed doomed to produce more frustration than weapons, which they turned out in small batches, of dubious quality, slowly.

In 1798, with American frigates trading round shot with French frigates, Congress did the only thing it could: it threw money all over the problem. It voted $800,000 for arms, thrusting a fortune onto a cabinet that had no idea what to buy with it. Where were arms to be got? As John Adams and his cabinet agonized, a letter arrived, as unexpected as divine intervention. Eli Whitney was offering to produce ten thousand stand of arms (a musket, complete with bayonet, wiper and screwdriver) for the only slightly-above-average price of $13.40 per stand. Delivery in twenty-eight months.

The government's purveyor of supplies said, politely, it was impossible. No one stopped to listen. All the established ways of doing government business were ignored. In twelve days Whitney had a contract and an advance of five thousand dollars. Which was all that he had—there was no land, no building, no supply of raw materials. Everything had to be created from a green field site in New Haven. All he really had was a vision. Whitney had never made a firearm; probably never even handled one.

What had led him to this desperate gamble with his health, reputation and happiness was the failure of his cotton-gin business. The gin had made other men rich; not him, not yet. He was as desperate in his way as the government in its.

The standard rate of musket production was one per armorer per week. Revolutionary fervor in France was about to create a factory that turned out five thousand a week—with five thousand workers. A bid from a single producer to provide one thousand stand of arms was ambitious enough. Whitney was conjuring up a new order of magnitude.

He worked himself to nervous collapse in a heroic struggle to create machine tools; undeniably primitive, but the first true machine tools in history. These in turn were to produce another machine, one with precision-engineered moving parts: a musket. Only a new technology could solve America's arms shortage. It was for him to create one, if he could.

When the time came for him to deliver the promised first batch of muskets, he begged for an extension. Oliver Wolcott, the treasury secretary, granted it gladly, one Yale man to another, but Wolcott also saw exactly what Whitney was aiming at. The gain of a new technology was as important as the muskets themselves, maybe more so. Whitney was given more time, more money. The purveyor had been right. After twenty-eight months Whitney had not produced a single firearm, but on the New Haven site, nearing completion, was arising the basis of American industrial growth in the new century.

On New Year's Day 1801 he rode into Washington, bringing in his luggage a collection of musket locks broken into dozens of pieces. Several days later cabinet members and congressmen were invited to gather around a table in the well of the House, pick up the pieces, make a lock for themselves, then fit it to a musket and pull the trigger. It was the most important weapons demonstration before the atomic bomb.

Looking on, fascinated, was the president-elect. Thomas Jefferson was easily won over to any new technology. Whitney asked for an extra ten thousand dollars in advance. He was given thirty thousand dollars instead. Arms purchasing was shifted from the Treasury, which never liked spending money, to the War Department, which never objected to the practice.

Through the Whitney musket contract the federal government put itself on a path of promoting arms manufacturers and inventors that runs right through today and into tomorrow morning. When Congress voted $800,000 for arms without knowing what it would be spent on, it foreshadowed the first Reagan administration. The money was provided so generously in both cases that much of it went unspent.

At one crucial juncture, when Whitney's contract seemed under threat for nonperformance, he was able to call on ten of the most distinguished figures in New England to put up a bond. And as he fell even further behind he vowed, "I shall produce some good arms and introduce some *real improvements.* . . ." The arms contractor's promise ever since: the weapons may be a little late but think how much better they will be! Cost overruns, failure to meet specifications, powerful friends at court, missed deliveries—a pattern was emerging.

Early in 1809, more than a decade after signing the contract, Whitney delivered the ten-thousandth stand of arms. They were not the best muskets in the world, but better than those from the government armories. He had paid off his debts and was now sole owner of a large manufactory filled to the walls with the first generation of machine tools. There was nothing like it anywhere else. He had promised to create a new technology, and he delivered.

The nascent American arms industry led where the rest of manufacturing followed. Far from being left behind by the Industrial Revolution the United States, in a single decade and thanks largely to one man, had suddenly burst into the front rank.

THE PERFECT COMPLEMENT to Whitney was Robert Fulton. They were even the same age, both born in 1765. Much like Whitney, Fulton was less an inventor than an entrepreneur of invention. Fulton had half a dozen beginnings—painter, writer, showman, canal promoter. His greatest achievement, however, was to imagine the future of warfare. Out of that luxuriant talent for wondering came the modern submarine, the mine, the patrol torpedo boat, the torpedo itself, a revolution in troop transport and the steam warship. He counted all his other ventures as froth compared to this. So did that other visionary with pacifist leanings, Jefferson.

The entrepreneur lives the life of his times. Fulton, arriving in England to become a painter, stayed on to throw himself into canals, the leading technological challenge of the early 1790s. Moving on to France in 1798 to promote canals, he immediately abandoned them for something of more pressing interest to the French in the year of the Egyptian campaign. On one side of the Channel he was all canal engineering; on the other, all engines of war.

Fulton's romantic temperament made him think he could create a weapon so deadly, so terrible it would make war harder, not easier; a romantic's deterrent. The only real threat to his own country, he was convinced, came from the great battle fleets of Britain and France. Develop a submarine and those fleets would be useless. His forerunner, David Bushnell, had built an egg-shaped submersible, the *Turtle,* during the Revolutionary War. Two attempts to sink British ships in New York Harbor had failed, one of them spectacularly.

Fulton designed a state-of-the-art submarine, offering it to Napoleon as the answer to all his problems: sink the British. Called the *Nautilus,* it carried a three-man crew, remained submerged for hours and had the basic submarine shape—a large underwater cigar; a corona. The shape, like the name, lives on.

Fulton blew up a sloop with it (by swinging into its path a contact mine attached to a cable). Yet even now his restless spirit was moving on, shifting from the submarine, which he considered a problem solved, to exploring and perfecting new types of contact mines. Napoleon also diverted his attention, with a project for the invasion of England.

Fulton was convinced that he knew just the answer—steamboats. He was familiar with the work of the tragic John Fitch, who had a working steamboat carrying passengers on the Potomac in 1786. Fulton drew up proposals for a huge steam fleet that would carry a French army swiftly across the Channel to the beaches of Kent.

It took Napoleon a year to make up his mind. All at once he grasped what Fulton was offering. A fleet of steam-powered troop transports, he exulted, "could change the face of the world." Too late. Fulton was no man to linger. Napoleon had let slip not one chance but three—submarines to attack British ships, mines to shut British ports, steamboats to carry an invasion army.

Fulton had gone back to England. The Royal Navy's spies had followed his submarine experiments with a keen, vested interest. He went onto the king's payroll. Then, at Trafalgar in October 1805, the Royal Navy sank the French and Spanish fleets in the preferred, traditional way. Fulton finally came home.

Throughout his twenty years abroad he had been pursuing plans that he expected would make him rich and his country safe. America could not afford to built huge fleets to slug it out with the British and French. There was only one answer: create a new technology. That was what all his naval warfare projects were aimed at.

Returning in 1806, he was soon busy rerunning his weapons experiments. Any technical innovation was followed eagerly in the White House. Jefferson and Fulton both loathed big navies; both deplored arms races; both sought deterrents. Peace through technology. Jefferson thought the submarine was the answer. No, said Fulton, mines. Yet all his efforts to convince the navy failed. He was still setting off mines and torpedoes to prove he was right when the next war began.

Meanwhile he had played a key role in arming his country. Shortly after arriving in France he had met a young Frenchman who shared his own fascination with the technologies of war, Éleuthère Irénée du Pont de Nemours. What was America like? asked the Frenchman. Fulton must have painted it in a seductive light. In 1800 Du Pont arrived in the United States.

He brought with him a head crammed with useful knowledge. Du Pont had once been a chemist at the French government's biggest powder works. He knew the best techniques for refining saltpeter and sulfur, combining them with willow wood charcoal, and pressing, graining and polishing the mixture to produce excellent black powder.

Since the Revolution the United States had been almost as short of gunpowder as it had been during the war. Demand far outstripped supply. Du Pont, freshly arrived, went to buy some powder, went into shock at the high price, low quality. Riches beckoned.

He brought skilled workers and vital machinery from France. He discussed his plans with Jefferson. In 1802 along the Brandywine, of Revolutionary fame, he opened his first powder works. Quality was high, prices low. He developed a near-monopoly in supplying the government. In return America would find itself virtually self-sufficient in gunpowder when the next war began.

THE EIGHT YEARS of Jefferson's presidency tell a story, the story of how a man who was a lifelong skeptic about reconciling military power with democratic habits was brought, finally, to a grudging kind of belief. His own party, the Democratic-Republicans, had won the

White House in 1800 only because the Federalists still suffered from their internal wrangling during the quasi-war with France. Having arrived at the presidency as the chief beneficiary of the fallout from that struggle, he had soon found himself fighting a war, trying to create an arms industry, sending out soldiers to establish his country's claim to a vast inland empire and, by a staggering stroke of irony, becoming the founding father of West Point.

In 1803 Napoleon sold Louisiana to the United States. Just how large this new territory was, or what it contained, was uncertain; like France's right to sell it. Originally sold to France by Spain, the Spanish claimed a treaty right to buy it back. Wasting little time to establish ownership, Jefferson sent out his private secretary, Meriwether Lewis, a captain in the 1st Infantry, to explore the new territory. With Lewis went First Lieutenant William Clark, younger brother of George Rogers Clark.

Neither Spain nor France had ever tried to govern the lands west of the Mississippi or north of the Missouri. All that could be seen of civilization out there was the occasional Union flag flying above some British trading post in a forest clearing or on the wind-scrubbed prairie. In 1807, a year after the return of Lewis and Clark, a second expedition set out, under First Lieutenant Zebulon Pike, also 1st Infantry.

The national debate over a standing army was meanwhile dying down to little more than a grumble. One of the more remarkable twists and turns in American political history was that virtually all the military programs urged by the Federalists in the 1780s were being brought to fruition by men such as Jefferson who had spent decades opposing them.

In his first inaugural address he had spelled out the military policy the new administration would pursue. It would be based on "a well-disciplined militia, our best reliance in peace and for the first moments of war, till regulars may relieve them." In praise of the militia, a compliment for the standing army.

In one generation it had made the breakthrough, from being described as a standing threat to being accepted as a symbol of stability and unity. The values it represented—discipline, commitment—had a strong appeal in a country still trying to find itself. The obvious weakness of the 1792 Militia Act also served as a permanent reminder that if the federal government wanted a strong, reliable force available, it had better create one itself.

In 1803, $1.5 million was voted to provide the militia with muskets. At present many were armed with sticks or kitchen knives. Nothing was done about the shortage of military supplies or the absence of anything that resembled military training. The main use of the militia in the North was to provide troops for ceremonial occasions; in the South, slave patrols.

Even had all other defects been overcome, the militia could not have handled military engineering or artillery. Yet no army could fight without them. In the midst of the Revolutionary War, Knox had tried to get a military academy created. The legacy of the militia system was that American soldiers had to struggle for education (the highest expression of which was engineering) and firepower (the highest expression of which was artillery). As a result artillery and engineering became the central pillars of American military faith.

In 1794 a school had been set up at West Point to produce engineers and artillerists. After eight years the results were more than disappointing. In 1802 Jefferson acted, creating the Corps of Engineers, something separate from the artillery. A typical Jeffersonian touch. Artillerists merely blew up things (and people) but engineers were builders; virtually scientists. The Corps of Engineers was to be based at West Point. The army's chief engineer would also be superintendent of a military academy to be created there.

Here was a Jeffersonian vision of redemption; of something positively good being wrung by human ingenuity from something intrinsically bad. That vision was to make an academy of the army, yet one somehow slightly outside it.

Nothing in the Constitution authorized the creation of such an academy. Its establishment was a necessity beating a nicety, even though Jefferson was normally a stickler for the small print.

Even so, this was his best chance to reform higher education: an institution that would teach modern languages, not dead ones, offering instruction in technology, not theology. From the creation of Harvard in 1636 up to the Civil War, the main role of American colleges would be to produce lawyers and preachers. For more than half a century West Point pioneered in the modernization of American education.

Its top graduates went into the Corps of Engineers. Because nearly all the military engineers of the Revolution were French, the practice had grown up of exempting engineering officers from commanding troops. The war was long over, however, and military tradition held that when officers of various branches were gathered together the ranking officer commanded all, whatever his branch.

Jefferson would not hear of it. His engineers were too precious an asset to the nation to be frittered away on purely military pursuits. He made them virtually civilians in uniform. Engineers did not command troops and no officer from another branch, except the general to whose army they were assigned, could command them.

Meanwhile the Tripolitan War was drawing to a close and hostilities were breaking out again between Britain and France. Jefferson's last two years in office were dominated by the prospect of war with one or the other, possibly both.

Since 1792 the country's foreign trade had grown by 500 percent. A ship might easily pay for itself in two voyages. Some did it in one. Shipyards and ports were awash with money. In 1807 customs duties alone paid all federal expenses that year. Then the curtain dropped on this happy scene.

That July a British warship, the *Leopard,* stopped the 38-gun frigate *Chesapeake,* fired three broadsides into her and took off four men, one of them a British deserter. Three American sailors had been killed, a score wounded. At war with France once more, Royal Navy captains were going through intercepted ships like the shades of wrath. If they found men to impress, that was good. If they found a deserter, that was better. Dragged back aboard a Royal Navy ship and hanged from one of His Britannic Majesty's yardarms, the poor fellow's dead body made a deep impression.

Jefferson's response to the attack on the *Chesapeake* was to win passage of the Embargo Act, cutting off virtually all trade between Britain and the United States. It assumed, in that evergreen phrase, "they need us more than we need them." This time they didn't. Britain was hardly touched, but thriving ports like Boston and Philadelphia were crippled.

The *Chesapeake* affair completed Jefferson's tortuous conversion to the need for a larger military establishment. His own faith was pinned to a fleet of gunboats, to be manned by coastal militia. He had been impressed by the use Preble had made of similar craft to attack Tripoli. Nicknamed "Jeffs" in mock tribute, some 176 were built; shallow-draft vessels that rolled too much to provide a decent gun platform. When-ever their main armament was fired, it threatened to capsize the boat. The president, however, was enormously proud of his Jeffs, convinced he had solved the problem of American coastal defense for decades to come.

In the last week of his presidency Congress repealed the Embargo Act, replacing it with the Non-Intercourse Act. This prophylactic measure allowed some trade with Britain. This too failed to provide security for American ships and seamen. It was replaced in 1810 by Macon's Bill Number 2. Trade with Britain and France was restored, but if one of them recognized the rights of neutral shipping the United States would forthwith cease to trade with the one that did not. Napoleon tricked Madison, Jefferson's successor, into thinking France had suspended the Berlin Decrees. It was then allowed to trade with America, while Britain was barred.

In the midst of this legal merry-go-round a Royal Navy sloop of war, *Lille Belt* (invariably referred to as *Little Belt*), unwisely traded shots with the frigate *President,* on May 16, 1811, in yet another hunt for deserters to hang. From that moment on, pressure on Congress to declare war became irresistible. Irresistible not simply because Ameri-cans were incensed at British high-handedness on the high seas but also because there was an Indian war coming to a head in the Old North-west. There too His Britannic Majesty George III was thought to be doing the Devil's own work. Again.

The vagueness of the boundary settlement that ended the Revolu-tionary War was—like many such settlements—a written guarantee of trouble. After Jay's Treaty the British had evacuated their old forts. For a decade they were quiescent, much like the Indians. And then, as their former allies began to recover from the shock of Fallen Timbers, their old interest in the Old Northwest quickened once more.

The sparks that ignited the Indian revival came from two Shawnee brothers, Tecumseh and Tenskwatawa ("The Prophet"). The one, a noble savage; the other, a savage savage. The good guy was handsome; the bad guy was an ugly, born-again, one-eyed fanatic, with a grubby bit of cloth jammed into an empty socket.

Legends grew up around Tecumseh; the brave, the farsighted, the inspiring, the humane. He was hailed by white people as a fine fellow because he was not like other Indians: the one Indian who would *not* scalp you. Yet among the tribes The Prophet was the greater man.

Tecumseh had taken part in the St. Clair massacre. He had fought among the beaten and betrayed at Fallen Timbers. His refusal to accept the Treaty of Greenville won him a following among some of the young warriors, but all around him once-proud tribes were, in their agony, turning into collections of drunks. Among the inebriated was his brother. Until the day, that is, when a vision was vouchsafed him. That day Tenskwatawa became The Prophet. It was much like the revelation claimed by his Seneca contemporary Handsome Lake, in which the Great Spirit enjoined him to lead a holy war against witches and whiskey.

While Tecumseh traveled back and forth over a vast arc between Florida and the Great Lakes trying to sell a different vision—of a huge Indian confederation to hold back the white man—whole tribes were traveling to The Prophet. Prophet's Town, a settlement of several thousand believers, grew up in his name, at the mouth of the Tippecanoe, in northern Indiana.

The growth of a large Indian settlement in this area was more of a threat to white ambitions than Tecumseh's imagined confederacy. In 1809 the governor of Indiana Territory, William Henry Harrison, had parleyed with the chiefs of four major tribes but excluded the Shawnees. They, said Harrison, were merely nomads, without rights to the land. He got the invited chiefs drunk, got them to sign away three million acres, got them to take next to nothing for it. This was good land. The government planned to sell it for six dollars an acre. In Washington and all along the frontier Harrison's coup was reckoned great statesmanship.

The Indians were outraged. As tensions rose British agents offered flattery and muskets. They imagined they could turn Tecumseh and The Prophet on and off like a faucet. By the time they discovered they could not, the frontier was in flames.

Madison had no more control over Harrison than the British had over the Indians. By 1811 the governor and the brothers were moving toward a showdown, protesting peaceful intentions every step of the way.

Bent on "awing the savages," Harrison assembled an army of 1,200 men, including 400 regulars, and moved north from Vincennes. He made camp near Prophet's Town, both threatening and inviting attack. This veteran of Wayne's Legion so bungled the affair that the Indians struck with very little warning just before dawn on November 7, 1811.

The regulars held steady, averting a defeat. Harrison managed to rally the militia. A charge was made as the Indians began to run out of ammunition and darkness. In exchange for 61 dead and more than 100 wounded, Harrison had inflicted unknown casualties on the Indians, but two days later he razed Prophet's Town.

As the settlement burned, Tenskwatawa's glory as a miracle worker turned to ashes. Broken by this disaster, he wandered off to the fastnesses of Canada, to an obscure life, a little-remarked death. For Tecumseh also Tippecanoe was a catastrophe. The struggle had been renewed long before the Indians were ready.

Tribes were rising all along the frontier. Tecumseh could not stop them. Far from being the ultimate Indian leader of white legend, he was a minor war chief caught up in great events. Neither villain nor hero, Tecumseh was a victim to his own mercurial temperament and to the cheap flattery of white men who would give him a red major general's uniform and use him to the end.

Tippecanoe had not brought security to the frontier. What it had brought was fury. Indians, laughing at the propaganda that made the battle a victory for Harrison, fell in murderous rage on a hundred white settlements. The victor himself turned his home into a fortress, built an escape tunnel and sent his wife and children back to Kentucky.

The country moved relentlessly toward war. Madison asked for the regular army to be brought up to its authorized strength of 10,000. Congress replied by raising its strength to 35,000. He asked for power to raise 10,000 volunteers. Congress gave him power for 50,000.

Attempts to expand the navy failed. A proposal to build twelve ships of the line and twenty-four frigates was voted down. This would have increased the navy's fighting power dramatically, but far from enough to threaten British naval supremacy. It would therefore be a waste of scarce money and trained manpower. Bizarre as it seemed not to enlarge the navy on the brink of war, it may in this instance have been wise. The naval challenge ahead would be found not on the oceans but on the lakes.

New England vigorously opposed the slide into war, supported by pockets of resistance in other parts of the country. All those who lived by trade felt threatened. Even so, on June 1 Madison sent a war resolution to Congress.

It covered five points: impressment, Royal Navy operations in American waters, blockades, the corrupt British traffic in licenses to pass through the blockades, and Indian raids along the frontier. Congress went into secret session. It emerged on June 18 with a declaration of war. Five days later the British finally took the threat of hostilities seriously. They lifted the Orders in Council under which 917 American ships had been seized since 1803, some 7,000 American seamen impressed and dozens of unlucky British deserters hanged.

They had calculated everything the past few years—American internal divisions, the Indian threat, the size of navies, the disparity of treasuries—and nearly got it right. The one thing they had fatally underrated was national pride. Mood counts for much when nations choose to fight. And already an American army was moving toward Canada, with orders to invade.

5

AMERICA'S FIRST LIMITED WAR

IT DID NOT take a Napoleon to figure out how to conquer Canada. All that was necessary was to capture three strongpoints in the east: the city of Montreal, the fortress of Quebec and, for insurance, the naval anchorage at Halifax, Nova Scotia. Anyone who held all three had the entire huge country in his hand. The rest of Canada, lying to the west of Montreal, would be cut off from British aid and intervention.

As supplies ran out, all the British military posts stretching one thousand miles west along the line of the Great Lakes and the border with the United States would wither on the vine.

Unfortunately there was no American army ready to invade eastern Canada when the war began. The only army poised to strike was in the wrong place, in the west, assembling at Dayton, Ohio. The resistance of New England to the impending war meant there would be no army available in the east until months after hostilities opened. Madison's ace, an army poised to strike the first blow, was six hundred miles from where it was really needed.

It was thus aimed at an objective of no great importance, the small outpost at Detroit, inhabited mainly by Indians and French trappers. The army was commanded by an elderly, avuncular hero of the Revolution, William Hull, a man who had lost the aggressive spirit of youth. The old soldier set off northward on June 15, knowing a declaration of war might come any day.

Hull's army consisted mainly of volunteers recruited in Kentucky and Ohio. These states pullulated with men eager to fight the Indians and the British, whom they blamed and damned for every settler murdered in the Mississippi Valley.

Bad as American preparations were for the impending struggle, the British were confident theirs were incomparably worse. Much of the population of Canada had French ancestry and no love of George III. More than that, many border towns and villages were filled with American settlers attracted by cheap land in areas free from Indian attacks. They had no love of George III either.

Canadians of British stock were comparatively few and not many of them were eager to fight for a country that was a century or more from independence. Most preferred to wait and see how the American invasion turned out before risking their necks. If Canada was going to be saved the governor-general, Sir George Prevost, knew it would have to be saved by British regulars and the king's Indian allies.

Prevost's regulars were the ordinary cannon fodder of the British army. Nearly all the best regiments and the most able officers were with Wellington, fighting French armies in Portugal and Spain. Prevost's ace was the Indians.

By a tremendous stroke of luck news of the declaration of war reached Canada before it reached Hull, ruining all hope of a surprise attack by American forces. It was the Indians instead who struck the first blow. A band of Chippewas captured Fort Michilimackinac, the American outpost at the northwestern extremity of Lake Huron.

Hull advanced from Dayton to Detroit as planned, but in a state of growing alarm. His supply lines vanished into the forest behind him, snaking two hundred miles down narrow trails to Ohio. From Detroit he crossed the Detroit River over to Canada, intending to attack Fort Malden, but only his regulars and volunteers went with him.

His militia was convinced, like the militia everywhere, that under the Constitution it had no military, legal or moral obligation to set one foot outside the United States. This territorial shyness made any invasion of Canada likely to fail, but no one cared to dwell on that.

While Hull tried to work up the nerve to attack Fort Malden, word was spreading through the forest like wildfire that Michilimackinac had fallen to the Indians. The conquest of this remote spot brought out the tribes as nothing else could. Tecumseh had won few followers before this coup but here was a sign: the Great Father was going to win the war. The redcoats were true warriors, the Americans fought like women. The tribes began puffing on the war pipe.

Hull took fright. Abandoning all thought of attacking Fort Malden, he crossed back over to Detroit and informed the secretary of war, William Eustis, "the entire northern hive of Indians [is] swarming in every direction," but mainly in his.

A few hundred British regulars, led by the able and daring Major General Isaac Brock, crossed the Detroit River hard on Hull's heels. Well aware of his talents as a soldier, Brock felt aggrieved at being forced to squander them in Canada instead of displaying them to best effect against Napoleon. Joined outside Detroit by Tecumseh and 1,000 braves, Brock sent messages to Hull promising torture, massacre and "a war of extermination" if the Americans chose to fight. Considering the fate of hundreds of Americans who fell into Indian hands in the course of this war, these were no idle threats.

Hull suffered a nervous collapse. Torture and massacre were not war as he knew it. And he was particularly vulnerable to terror: his son was with him, so was his daughter, and so were his two infant granddaughters. He slumped glassy-eyed in corners, tobacco juice dribbling into his white beard, worriedly rubbing his face until it turned brown, agonizing over images of indescribable horror.

Twice he sent out detachments to bring in the supply train coming up from Ohio. Both attempts failed. A third effort, made by 350 mounted riflemen, succeeded in finding the train. They were returning with it as Hull reached a despairing nadir, with the likely assistance of narcotics and rum.

Even now Brock was moving toward the fort, but walking unwittingly into a trap. Cannon loaded to the muzzle with grapeshot covered his approach. The returning force of mounted riflemen was approaching his rear. And on the walls of the fort he was preparing to storm were 1,000 Americans ready to fight. At one moment Brock was facing annihilation, the next he was staring at a white flag. Hull had surrendered.

It was the biggest capitulation between the Revolution and Bataan. Hull gave up 2,000 men, a large quantity of stores and a reputation for courage. Brock, disliking Canada, despising Canadians, became their national hero to this day.

The war went on. Two armies were assembling in upper New York, one to attack across the Niagara River, the other to make an attack on Montreal. The Niagara offensive was entrusted to a New York political figure, one of the richest men in the state, Stephen van Rensselaer. He commanded 3,000 militia, 2,000 regulars and a fleet of eighty boats. His orders were to seize Queenston Heights, overlooking the Niagara River from the Canadian side.

Rensselaer had a sound plan. He would launch a diversionary attack on Fort George, seven miles north of the heights, to pin down the bulk of British forces in the area. Then he would make the main assault. Rensselaer, however, was a politician first and a soldier second. He scrapped the diversionary attack because it seemed too complicated for his militia to handle, and he whittled the main assault down to a thirteen-boat affair because that was assigned to his regulars and it might succeed. If so, he did not want more regulars than absolutely necessary to be covered in glory. The militia would be jealous and there were no votes in that.

In a bold night attack the heights were seized, thanks largely to the daring of diminutive Captain John E. Wool, of the 13th Infantry Regiment. All that complete success needed now was reinforcement.

British units led by Brock hurried down from Fort George to make a counterattack. From the opposite shore Rensselaer's militiamen watched in horrified fascination as the bridgehead was wiped out. They would not cross, nor were the boatmen willing to take them over had they wanted to go.

Some 250 Americans were killed or wounded and 900 were taken prisoner. British losses would have been considered trifling had it not been for Brock's death, leading a charge to capture a cannon.

Despite this setback, the main blow had yet to fall, although winter was fast approaching. Montreal remained the great objective. This glittering prize was assigned to a figure out of history, Major General Henry Dearborn, veteran of Bunker Hill, the man who had led Washington's army to Yorktown, and for eight years Jefferson's secretary of war. Alas, by 1812 he was only a kindly, fat, tired old man. His troops despised him and called him "Granny."

As Dearborn's army assembled that summer Sir George Prevost was preparing to bar the way north with an army of his own, but he was no soldier. Half-Swiss by birth, half-pacifist by inclination, Prevost was a career diplomat. He liked the quiet life, abhorred war, lived by reason. He suggested a truce to Granny, which Granny gladly agreed to. Live and let live. They pledged not to attack each other.

This unauthorized bit of peacemaking infuriated the Madison government. Dearborn was ordered to stop being a nice guy and attack, but by now the skies were dark with clouds pregnant with snow. Dearborn took 6,000 men up Lake Champlain. He got his men within sight of the Canadian border. His militia didn't like the look of it. International boundaries invariably made militiamen start frothing at the mouth. After a token crossing by his advance guard and some minor skirmishing for honor's sake, Dearborn marched his 6,000 back to Plattsburgh, campaigning done.

A second attempt was meanwhile being made to cross the Niagara frontier. In place of the wounded and captive Rensselaer, the army there had been entrusted to yet another political general, a congressman known as Alexander "Apocalypse" Smyth. Years before, Smyth had written an exegesis on the Book of Revelation, hence the nickname. As he prepared to cross into Canada in November 1812 it was revealed to him that war is dangerous.

He shrank back once. He shrank back twice. His army disbanded in joy at going home and in disgust at their commander. The troops riddled his tent with musket fire while a terrified Apocalypse hugged Mother Earth.

A NEW ARMY was raised in the west. The loss of Detroit could not cool the fierce passions of Kentucky. When volunteers were called for, two men stepped forward to claim every place. Two men who were so eager to fight they would beat each other bloody to see which of them got to sign up. That was how the volunteers chose their officers, too—let them fight it out. The blood-smeared man who was left standing became a lieutenant.

In Kentucky this was no war, this was a crusade, with Harrison their Richard the Lion Heart. After Tippecanoe they would follow no other commander as they followed him. The regular army general sent out to replace the disgraced Hull was James Winchester. As he and the Kentuckians sized each other up it became evident they loathed him and he feared them. He needed a bodyguard day and night. This army trusted Harrison and no one else.

Madison intended for it to recapture Detroit. Harrison intended for it to crush the Indians. Begging winter woolens throughout the Northwest, he launched a winter campaign, at almost the hour that Napoleon quit Moscow.

The Army of the Northwest, as it was called, moved north from the Ohio River toward the Maumee. Mounted riflemen fanned out over a sixty-mile front. They were to search out and destroy any Indian threat to the advancing army's van or flanks. No distinction was drawn among tribes that were neutral, tribes that were friendly and tribes that were allied with the British.

Desperate to prove that he too was a great leader, Winchester drove deep into the forest, far ahead of Harrison. Snow was thick on the ground, but he decided to go to the aid of an American force that was attacking a Canadian settlement, Frenchtown, on the river Raisin. Frenchtown fell to Winchester and his troops moved into it.

On January 22, 1813, the British and Indians counterattacked. It was a fight in which troops preferred death to surrender. Americans knew that the British would allow the Indians to torture them as a reward. Far better to sell their lives for top dollar. It was their bad luck that Winchester was captured. With the battle still raging and the issue in doubt he ordered them over distraught shouts of "No!" to surrender. He insisted. The British commander, Colonel Henry Procter, had promised there would be no torture, no massacre.

Just as Tecumseh found it convenient on occasion to be elsewhere, leaving prisoners to the mercies of their Indian guards, so did Procter. The British troops vanished during the night. Over the following three days the Indians stabbed, burned, tomahawked and scalped Americans at their leisure, including the wounded.

As screams rent the snow-laden forest the Army of the Northwest ceased to be a fighting force. The few regulars who survived were scattered in pockets, their regiments destroyed. Harrison's motley crusaders hung on grimly in the snow, unable to do much more than shiver. The American hold on the Old Northwest was never more precarious, as though Anthony Wayne had never drawn breath.

THE BRITISH, Canadians and Indians had overcome every handicap. American superiority in manpower was as nothing compared to inferiority in leadership. What military talents the United States possessed during the first year of fighting were nearly all at sea.

Not that the navy was without problems. The navy secretary, Paul Hamilton, was an alcoholic. By noon each day the secretarial head could be found on the secretarial desk; because, as a congressman informed the House, of "the free use of stimulant potation."

When the war began, the navy could pit ten frigates, two sloops, six brigs and its gunboats against the more than six hundred warships of the Royal Navy. The famous Jeffs, however, were doomed to disappoint. Gun for gun they were more expensive to maintain than ships of the line yet their military value was virtually nil. They were the least bang for a buck in American history.

Thinking on naval strategy was sharply divided. The commander of the northern squadron, John Rodgers, wanted to sail in force and carry the war to British waters. Decatur, commanding the southern squadron, wanted to spread out and raid British commerce. The lack of an agreed strategy left aggressive naval officers free to seek battle, alone or together. They soon found it.

Within an hour of hearing that war had been declared Rodgers put his ships to sea. This decisive action forced British captains to steer clear of the American coast for fear of finding Rodgers bearing down on them from the seaward horizon and cutting off their escape. Most American ports were thereby left uncovered. That enabled the American merchant fleet to sail home unmolested after the war began.

On August 19, three days after Hull's surrender in Detroit, the frigate *Constitution* destroyed the British frigate *Guerrière* in the first American victory of the war. Her captain was another Hull, Isaac, nephew to the general.

In the fall Decatur won a remarkable victory over the frigate *Macedonian*. His own ship was the heavy-sailing *United States*. By taking the lee gauge, he allowed the enemy to attack. Decatur's crack crew worked the guns so rapidly the oncoming British thought the *United States* had caught fire. By the time the *Macedonian* had closed to one hundred yards she was so badly cut up her captain surrendered.

There were five single-ship engagements in 1812: three frigate versus frigate, one sloop versus sloop, one brig versus brig. The American ships won all five. The Admiralty issued secret instructions that Royal Navy captains were to avoid future single-ship actions.

The prison school tradition lived on. American crews fired their guns every week to perfect their broadsides. A British crew might spend a year at sea without hearing the big guns thunder. American gunners held target practice, usually firing at empty casks dumped overboard. They took aim as carefully as American soldiers did on land.

Afloat or ashore, the British generally preferred to trust to "luck and pluck," not practice. One of the few Royal Navy captains who was a training zealot was Philip Broke, commanding the frigate *Shannon*. In the spring of 1813 he waited off Boston, hoping to engage the frigate *Chesapeake*.

In May she got a new captain, James Lawrence, a man eager to settle scores with the British. After he had been aboard only ten days he suffered a rush of blood to the head. He sortied from the harbor. His crew had been aboard the ship for even less time than he. They hardly knew one another, the *Chesapeake* or the captain.

Broke, on the other hand, had been training his crew seven years for this battle. The *Shannon* poured a devastating fire into the *Chesapeake* the moment she came in range. Lawrence was mortally wounded. With his dying breath he gasped, "Don't give up the ship. Fight her till she sinks."

His crew was overwhelmed in hand-to-hand combat, then trapped belowdecks. The *Chesapeake* was captured. She did not surrender. The hand that pulled down her colors was British. And in that moment the brief chapter of American glory at sea in the War of 1812 came to a close.

From the summer of 1813 on, the Royal Navy imposed a tight blockade. American frigates were bottled up in port, with few exceptions, and destined to remain there. Only the privateers remained free to roam. During the war they took two thousand prizes.

For nearly two years America's proud 44s and 38s rotted quietly away, the same as the Jeffs, and no more able to break out than the gunboats.

EUSTIS resigned as secretary of war shortly after the war began. His successor was John Armstrong, author of several pamphlets that had sought to spread mutinous sentiments at Newburgh in the closing days of the Revolutionary War. A Philadelphia merchant, William Jones, was brought in to replace the stupefied Paul Hamilton. Jones described the Navy Department as "chaos."

With the onset of spring the administration's thoughts turned once more to invading Canada. Prevost had established the main British base at Kingston, a small town at the head of Lake Ontario, where the St. Lawrence begins its journey to the sea.

Armstrong pressed Dearborn to attack it, but Dearborn refused, convinced there were 8,000 British troops there. There were in fact fewer than 1,000. The country was desperate for a military success on land, as Armstrong reminded the old hero. So Dearborn offered to make a raid on York, more than one hundred miles west of Kingston and the site of present-day Toronto. The military importance of York was close to zero, but to Granny's fading eyesight it looked a safe bet for a successful attack.

On the night of April 26 Brigadier General Zebulon Pike led 1,800 men across the lake, took York by storm and lost his life when a powder magazine exploded. The few small, drab public buildings were burned down by American troops, but the retreating British were responsible for a more important piece of arson: they torched a thirty-gun frigate that was nearly finished, and a hoard of naval stores painfully accumulated over months went onto the pyre.

Encouraged by the raid on York, Dearborn mounted an attack on Fort George. Leading the first wave was a lawyer turned professional soldier, Colonel Winfield Scott. This successful landing on a hostile shore was the first important feat of arms in what was going to be a brilliant military career.

It was a success that owed much to another promising officer, Master Commandant Oliver Hazard Perry, who rowed from ship to ship in an open boat under heavy British fire to direct naval gunfire in support of Scott's troops. Scott captured the fort and prepared to pursue the fleeing British defenders with a body of dragoons. Granny took fright and stopped him. Pursuit involved risks. The best chance of destroying or capturing Prevost's small force of British regulars was thereby fumbled away.

THE TIMIDITY of Prevost and Dearborn was shared by their respective naval commanders in the struggle for control of Lake Ontario, Commodore Sir James Yeo and Commodore Isaac Chauncey. Yeo was famous in the Royal Navy for losing a frigate through poor seamanship. Chauncey had proven his fighting ability in the Tripolitan War, but ten years later he was a pear-shaped middle-aged man whose nerve had gone the way of his waistline.

A naval race began. Both commodores built furiously. As one or the other gained a temporary advantage he would sail out as if eager to fight. His adversary stayed in port, building an even bigger ship, until he had the advantage, and then the other would withdraw to build a bigger ship still. By default the struggle for command of the lakes shifted westward, to what was generally considered the secondary theater of war, Lake Erie.

The remnants of the Army of the Northwest had survived the winter in Fort Meigs, on the banks of the Maumee. When the snow melted, Proctor and Tecumseh attacked the fort. If it fell, the Americans would be pushed out of the Old Northwest. Tecumseh's promised Indian Confederation could then be realized. The Indians could almost taste it, the sweetness of revenge. Fort Meigs stood on Fallen Timbers.

The defenders held on to the fort. The cry "Remember the Raisin!" brought thousands more volunteers from Kentucky. Armstrong sent Harrison 2,500 regulars. Through the steam heat of August men rode and marched to gather hopefully at the Maumee rapids. They were forced to wait, however, on the fortunes of a green-timber fleet, held together with pegs, being built by the twenty-seven-year-old Perry at Presque Isle, where Erie, Pennsylvania, now stands.

Sent to see what he could do on Lake Erie, he first needed to collect seamen, soldiers and oxen. By brute muscle power five small vessels were hauled up the Niagara rapids and floated onto Lake Erie. Then he sailed them down to Presque Isle.

There he faced a second challenge to muscle power: two new brigs, each displacing 480 tons, were being built behind a sandbar that drew a minimum of four feet of water. It was an unusual place to try building ships, but it benefited from its access to Pittsburgh, 150 miles inland. The frontier village of Whiskey Rebellion days had turned into a booming industrial town.

From Pittsburgh Perry brought anchors and anvils, hawsers, galley stoves, a mountain of round shot, tools and skilled workers who knew how to use them. Leading away from Pittsburgh, all the way back to Philadelphia and its naval shipyard, was a military road. Down that road came guns, shipwrights, bolts of canvas, wagonloads of Du Pont's powder.

Perry's adversary for control of Lake Erie was the lavishly scarred, one-armed Captain Robert Heriot Barclay, R.N. He too was struggling to build up a fleet, on the opposite shore of the lake. Barclay's flagship would be the *Detroit,* pierced for twenty guns and by far the biggest ship on Lake Erie once her bottom got wet. Other than that, Barclay was at a severe disadvantage.

Much of what he needed to outfit his fleet had gone up that April night in York, burned by British soldiers. His supply line ran more than seven hundred miles to Halifax, and from there to England. And everything that came down it—men, money, guns—first passed through Yeo's hands. Barclay got whatever the commodore didn't. That proved to be little. To arm the *Detroit* he had to strip the ramparts of the British base at Amherstburg of their guns; some of them were more than a century old.

Perry could at least choose his weapons. He opted for carronades. These were half the length and weight of a long gun of the same bore. They were fairly ineffective at ranges beyond 350 yards. Within that range they were devastating. Perry put his faith in maximizing his firepower, arming his fleet with thirty-nine carronades (all of them 32-pounders) and fifteen long guns.

There remained the problem of the sandbar across the harbor mouth at Presque Isle. The two new brigs *Lawrence* and *Niagara* had the firepower of sloops of war. If he could somehow get both over the bar he would have little to fear from the *Detroit.* On the other hand, if Barclay blockaded Presque Isle, he would never get them over the bar and Lake Erie would be controlled by the British until the end of the war.

On July 20 his worst fears seemed realized. Five of Barclay's ships appeared off Presque Isle. Perry spent anxious nights worrying that raiding parties were about to land and turn his splendid brigs to ashes. Barclay was no Decatur. He was content to kept the brigs under observation. Then, on July 31, he sailed away. Many have since tried to guess why but no one knows.

Once Perry was certain Barclay's departure was no ruse the brigs were disarmed. Anything that could be taken off, was. Huge sunken tanks were lashed to the hull of the *Lawrence.* After sweating, grunting hours stuck on the bar, she was finally wrestled onto the lake on August 2. Her guns were taken out to her in boats.

Rearmed, the *Lawrence* stood guard as the *Niagara* was pushed and pulled over the bar. Just as she floated free on the morning of

August 5 sails appeared from the north. Barclay was back, but too late.

The ships were built. They were armed. And where were the men to sail them? Perry's relationship with Chauncey was as bad as Barclay's was with Yeo, and for much the same reason. Exasperated at what he saw as Chauncey's refusal to help, Perry sent in his resignation from the navy, but before anything could be done about it the men he needed arrived. Overjoyed, he gave the officer who brought them, Captain Jesse D. Elliott, command of the *Niagara* and the pick of the seamen.

Elliott was not exactly overflowing with gratitude. He nursed a festering grievance. He believed that the American naval command on Lake Erie had been promised to him.

For three weeks Perry trained his crews while Barclay struggled to finish the *Detroit*. By September the Americans were ready to fight. Perry took his ten ships to an anchorage off Put-in-Bay, in the Bass Islands, near Amherstburg, where Barclay's fleet was based.

With summer drawing to a close Procter's troops and Tecumseh's Indians were on short rations. To bring supplies to them now that there was an American fleet on the lake, the British had to win control of it. The choice was starve, quit or fight. Barclay, who had left an arm at Trafalgar, spread canvas on the evening of September 9.

At that hour Perry's captains were gathered in his cabin. If Barclay did not come out to fight next day, he told them, he would sail into Amherstburg and attack. To each of his captains he assigned an enemy vessel by name and instructed him to destroy it. From a trunk he brought out a dark-blue flag, nine feet wide and eight feet high. Stitched on it in white letters big enough to be seen at several hundred yards was half a legend: DON'T GIVE UP THE SHIP. They knew the rest by heart.

At first light next morning six ships appeared: Barclay. As anchors were hoisted, ropes paid out, Perry's sailors raised their eyes. High in a cerulean sky an eagle soared on outstretched wings.

The wind, however, was behind the British, giving them the choice of fighting at long range, if they wanted it. Barclay's ships carried sixty-three cannon, most of them long guns. Perry, however, had no interest in a duel at long range. He wanted a battle of annihilation; had trained for it, had armed for it. He must get in close, to use those carronades.

Luck, the wind, shifted, filling Perry's sails. He drove his fleet straight at the British line, the huge blue flag whipping in the breeze. That dark oriflamme, with its air of naïveté and courage, the homespun and the inspired, was his sole conspicuous gesture. Perry stood on his quarterdeck in a common sailor's jacket and hat.

Robbed of the weather gauge, Barclay changed his tactics. He would try to sink Perry's flagship. Barclay concentrated the fire of the *Detroit,* the seventeen-gun *Queen Charlotte* and the thirteen-gun *Lady Prevost* on the *Lawrence.* If the flagship was destroyed quickly the rest of the American fleet might become demoralized and disorganized. Besides, the *Lawrence* alone carried one third of Perry's total firepower.

Barclay had some unexpected help when he changed tactics. Elliott, commanding the *Niagara,* hung back, instead of attacking his assigned target, the *Queen Charlotte.*

The *Lawrence* bore the burden of the battle supported by two small schooners. Sand had been spread liberally on her decks to prevent men from slipping on that greasy substance, blood. After an hour even the sand was slippery. Blood dripped into the tiny wardroom where the wounded and dying were crammed. Five cannonballs passed through over their heads. From a shattered closet came the howling of Perry's spaniel, half mad with terror on a pile of broken plates.

Every minute or so another broadside slammed into the ship. Splinters ripped the air like knives. Above- and belowdecks were the bodies of men fallen into grotesque attitudes, some limbless, others cut in two by solid shot. Perry, spattered with blood and grimy with smoke, was untouched.

For two hours the *Lawrence* fought three ships that carried twice as many guns as she. When her armament was down to a single gun, Perry, aided by the chaplain and purser, loaded and fired it for the last time. All appeared lost. Amid the torn ropes, the smashed planking, the overturned guns, the heaped bodies, the severed limbs, something remained intact, however—a boat.

Pulling off his blue nankeen jacket, Perry dressed in the gorgeousness of rank, hauled down the big blue flag, found his brother, still alive, and with four seamen who shared his luck lowered the boat. Draping the oriflamme over one arm, Perry abandoned ship.

Through a hail of musket fire and grapeshot the sailors pulled him toward the *Niagara,* half a mile away, her long guns barking listlessly. When the rowing sailors reached it they raised oars that were whittled half away by flying lead. The boat was holed and shipping water fast. Perry was still unharmed. Elliott turned pale, blurting out fatuously, "How goes the day?" to a commander who had just lost his flagship.

Elliott was sent off in a rowing boat to hail the smaller ships of the fleet through a speaking trumpet and order them to close in on the British. Perry hoisted his flag on the *Niagara,* brought her around and with a stiff breeze in his sails plowed through the British line. Double-shooting his guns, with his starboard battery he raked the *Queen Charlotte* and the *Detroit,* which had become tangled and lay almost immobile on the water. His port battery put a broadside into the badly damaged *Lady Prevost.* The gallant *Lawrence* had fought all three British ships to a standstill. All that was required was for the unscathed *Niagara* to apply the coup de grâce.

As the *Niagara* swung around, the *Detroit* looked like a ghost ship, without a human being in sight. There was a bear lapping up blood and brains . . . and on the taffrail, a pike . . . being waved . . . and something tied to the blade! A white handkerchief shone in the battle smoke.

Superior firepower, superior preparation, half-forgotten whiskey rebels, inspiring leadership, and luck had brought victory. Above all, luck. Enough luck to spare Perry when two men out of three aboard the *Lawrence* were being killed or wounded. Enough luck to triumph over the cowardice or sulking of Elliott.

Congress struck two gold medals to celebrate and reward Perry's victory. One went to Perry, the other to Elliott. It was the only time a second-in-command shared equal honors with a victorious superior, but Elliott was a close friend of Speaker of the House Henry Clay. And Perry, the most chivalrous of men, made no protest. As he reminded his indignant officers, who damned Elliott for the rest of their lives, it was good naval advice to shield a coward rather than let the enemy know there was one in the fleet.

In the moment of victory Perry had whipped off his round hat, seated himself on an overturned cannon and, using the hat as an impromptu desk, scribbled a message from the deck of the *Niagara* to Harrison: "We have met the enemy and they are ours: Two Ships, two Brigs, one Schooner and one Sloop."

. . .

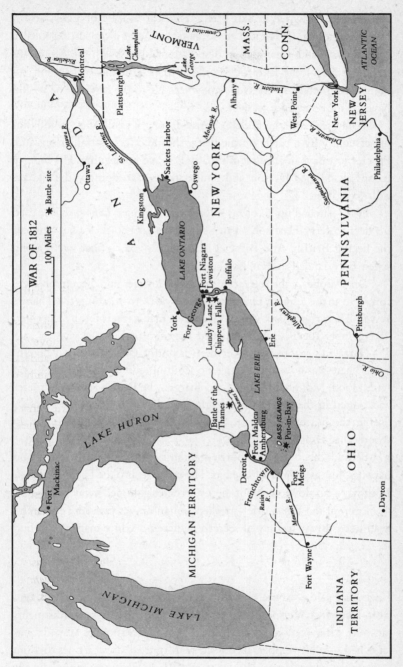

WAR OF 1812

0   100 Miles   ∗ Battle site

AS BLACK powder smoke lifted from the waters of Lake Erie it revealed Procter (promoted to brigadier general after his exploits in Frenchtown) and Tecumseh in desperate trouble. With the Americans in command of the lake they could land behind the British and cut them off. Procter's safety was somewhere far to the east, but he would have to move fast to grasp it.

Tecumseh and the Indians refused to go east. They could not understand why a battle on the water should affect a conflict on land. Procter lost days in argument. Finally he gave up arguing. His hungry troops abandoned Detroit and Amherstburg. Grudgingly the Indians followed after.

Perry patched up all of his ships save the ruined *Lawrence*. He used his fleet to ferry Harrison's army across the lake so they could cut off the fleeing British. And Perry, a man who loved combat, went along when they landed as Harrison's aide.

On October 5 the retreating forces of Procter and Tecumseh were forced to make a stand, ninety miles east of Detroit, along the Thames River. Their right flank was covered by a marsh, their left by the river. "Remember the Raisin!" screamed the men of Kentucky.

Harrison's troops threw themselves on the enemy with a vengeful fury. There was no maneuvering, no scouting, just a lust to repay blood with blood. Mounted Kentuckians charged the British regulars Procter had posted in the open, on the right flank. After sending the redcoats fleeing the horsemen charged into the Indians placed on the left, in woods that fringed the marsh.

Behind the horsemen hurried infantry armed with musket and bayonet, just as eager for revenge. The redcoats broke. The braves fled. Both were cut down without mercy. Procter galloped away to the east.

Deep in the forest grief-stricken Indian braves carried Tecumseh's dead body away, to bury it secretly, where no white man would find it.

FOR SEVERAL MONTHS American forces held the upper hand from Detroit to Vermont, but Harrison had to fall back as enlistments ran out. After prolonged dithering a second invasion of Canada was launched—in November. Its objective, Montreal. Two armies totaling 11,000 men under James Wilkinson and Wade Hampton moved up the valley of the St. Lawrence, confidence dropping with the temperature. Hampton withdrew after a minor skirmish with a much smaller force. Wilkinson, possibly the greatest rogue ever to wear an American uniform, ran into slightly stiffer opposition. He was equally glad of an excuse to pull out. Both these elderly incompetents were soon out of the army. A new crop of generals was being harvested; almost a different breed of men. They were young and they were bold.

One of them, Major General Jacob Brown, took over the northern army from Wilkinson. He moved into army headquarters at Sacketts Harbor but left Winfield Scott, now a brigadier general, at Buffalo to train it. This was work that Scott loved. He was, like Knox, a scholar-soldier. His baggage train always included a wagon loaded with books. Already he owned a library of military history, biographies of Great Captains, manuals on drill, handbooks on tactics. He read four languages and seemed interested in everything, including metaphysics and poetry. What he learned, he was delighted to teach. For half a century any officer with his head in books represented "the Scott tradition." At Buffalo he trained his men ten hours a day, seven days a week, for three months. By July 1814 the United States had one of the best-trained small armies in the world.

Brown used it to launch the third and final invasion of Canada. He crossed the Niagara frontier. At Chippewa Falls on July 5 his main body collided with a British army under Major General Phineas Riall. Scott had dressed his troops in the only uniforms locally available, the gray of the New York militia. As his brigade came on, deploying coolly and smartly under British artillery fire, Riall was astonished. "Those are regulars, by God!" Like British regulars, was what he meant.

The American artillery was meanwhile pounding the British guns, winning the duel. After which they turned their attention on the British infantry, raking it with a hail of canister. The red ranks began to buckle under the deadly storm. Scott's brigade charged. The British pulled back into prepared entrenchments. Rain fell. Night fell. Both armies were back where they had been twenty-four hours earlier. The battle was a tactical standoff.

Three weeks later, still on the Canadian side of the river, Brown detached Scott with 1,200 men, including artillery and dragoons, to move north. There was a report, erroneous it proved, of a British counterinvasion crossing into the United States. Scott ran into Riall's army, its earlier losses more than made good. Riall had 3,500 men at Lundy's Lane.

Outnumbered three to one, Scott instantly did two things typical of his fighting style: he moved to attack, while sending one of his best officers to lead a battalion through a deep wood on his left to look for a way into the British rear. Riall's position was based on possession of a low hill. On a pleasant summer's evening Scott launched a frontal assault on it. The battalion moving through the woods captured Riall.

Lundy's Lane was fought as dusk shaded into darkness: combat by musket flashes at twenty paces. From 10 P.M. to midnight both sides battled at a desperate pitch. As fresh units came up, hurried northward by Brown, they were hurled straight in. They charged blindly into a struggle where men fought hand to hand; where the man you killed was as likely to be friend as foe. Scott took a bullet in the shoulder, Brown a bullet in the thigh. Around midnight both armies simply gave up the fight; sheer exhaustion. Losses to each ran to 800 to 900 killed or wounded. Of those engaged, American losses were 45 percent, British 30 percent.

Scott was hailed as the victor, with a congressional gold medal to prove it. When the first snowflake fell and enlistments began expiring, the American army returned to American soil.

THE strategic initiative had passed months before to the British. Slow to take the war seriously and distracted by the more portentous struggle to bring down Napoleon, it was not until the spring of 1814 that they took up what they considered the war-winning weapon: the combined strike over land and water. Combined operations were the epitome of the military art. What was in prospect was advanced warfare against a backward country. It could hardly fail. No one could fault their ambition. They struck from Canada to the Gulf. The Chesapeake took the first blow.

Baltimore was the fourth-largest city in the country and the third-richest. Its privateers had taken or destroyed more than five hundred British ships. In no American city was the war more popular. Strategically, economically and politically it came top of any target list for British attack.

The British admiral in charge of the naval operation, Alexander Cochrane, was more than willing to strike: his brother had been killed by American troops at Yorktown. The British general in charge of land operations, Major General Robert Ross, was a gifted soldier, but given only 4,000 men instead of the 15,000 originally promised.

The Royal Navy had no trouble establishing itself in the Chesapeake. The gunboat flotilla at Alexandria under Master Commandant Joshua Barney was quickly bottled up. Ross's army was landed and most of it set off for Washington. Still little more than a swamp with prospects, it had no military importance whatever. Cochrane's hatred for Americans tended to dim his judgment.

The national capital was virtually undefended. Armstrong could not imagine why anyone would bother to attack it. No one thinking clearly would. Madison had a feeling, or possibly just a bad case of nerves. He ordered Armstrong to raise defenses. The secretary of war did what he was used to doing and ignored him. Only at the eleventh hour was an effort made, although "effort" may put it too high.

Ross advanced on Washington without cavalry, artillery or intelligence: half armed, half blind. He moved for five days down narrow roads through thickly wooded country. No ambush was sprung. No one even dropped a tree across his path. At Bladensburg, six miles northeast of Washington, he got his first sight of American resistance, an army of 6,000 men, mainly militia, including twenty guns and 400 cavalry.

The president too was there, a brace of borrowed dueling pistols at his waist, ready to do his constitutional duty. Madison would be a real commander in chief, another Washington, leading his troops in the field, sharing their dangers, inspiring their morale. The air suddenly came alive with an unnerving oddity: smoke, flame, a terrifying roar— Congreve rockets. The artillery banged away. Musketry rattled. As the confusion of combat descended, Madison saw the Constitution in a fresh light. "Come," he suggested to the Cabinet, gathered there on horseback to offer advice on the spot, "let us go and leave it to the commanding general."

Only Barney's 350 sailors and some 78 Marines performed creditably. They charged the British, cutlasses raised, shouting, "Board 'em!" All around the militia were running so fast most British troops never saw action that day; so fast few Americans were taken prisoner; so fast the event passed into legend as "the Bladensburg Races."

Ross's lightning strike, culminating in the burning of Washington in reprisal for the burning of York, was one of the finest combined operations of the nineteenth century. His men marched twenty-five miles in a day, fought and won a battle, and captured the enemy's capital. This brilliant military feat was a political disaster. Putting the torch to public buildings—using hundreds of books as kindling— outraged educated opinion in England. It also fired American determination to continue the war.

Armstrong was finally dismissed. He was replaced by James Monroe, a man who was literally a fighter. He carried a Hessian bullet in his body, a little something from Trenton, 1776.

The Royal Navy spent eleven days looting Alexandria. That gave Baltimore eleven days in which to build up its defenses. All eleven were put to good use. When Ross's army went ashore again there were 13,000 militia waiting for them. The question was, Would they fight any better than those at Bladensburg? Ross would never find out. He was killed by an American marksman on the outskirts of the city.

Cochrane meanwhile sent in his bomb ships. These were nearly half as wide as they were long, to provide a stable gun platform. They fired ten-inch and thirteen-inch mortar shells. The fuses were hit-or-miss; mostly miss. When a shell exploded on target it had a stunning impact—two hundred pounds of gunpowder. It was far more likely, though, to explode in midair. Cochrane had five bomb ships, able between them to pump out 250 rounds an hour. Enough, properly handled, to flatten any port in the world. He made only one mistake. Fearful of losing any of his bomb ships to Fort McHenry's guns, he kept them at maximum range, two and a half miles. Cutting the fuses to fit that distance was virtually impossible. He provided the people of Baltimore with the greatest fireworks display they would ever see, and the country with a national anthem. With the American militia refusing to panic and provide the British with another cheap victory, Cochrane pulled out of the Chesapeake. As he sailed away, the second blow was about to be launched, an invasion from Canada.

With Napoleon removed to Elba the British were shipping a thousand men a month to Prevost. By September 1814 he had built up an invasion force of 10,000 men. He moved down the western side of Lake Champlain; objective, New York. Once the city fell all of New England, hating the war, was expected to be ready for a separate peace. The upstart Union might then fall apart.

Cautious as ever, Prevost intended to take control of Lake Champlain. While he advanced on Plattsburgh by land, Captain George

Downie was to destroy the American squadron anchored in Platts-burgh Bay. There the Brown brothers—Adam and Noah—had set new records for building warships, exceeding even their heroic labors for Perry on Lake Erie. In command of this fresh-water navy was Captain Thomas Macdonough, one of Preble's Boys. As a midshipman he had one night boarded the *Philadelphia* in Tripoli Harbor and helped set her ablaze.

Like Perry he based his fleet on firepower. When battle came on September 11 he had fourteen vessels to Downie's fifteen. He conceded a 30-percent difference in total tonnage, a 15-percent difference in size of crews, and could pit only seventy-three guns to Downie's eighty-seven. Yet the smaller, lighter fleet had a 15-percent advantage in the weight of metal thrown, and Downie had nothing that approached Macdonough's fifty-pound columbiad or his forty-two-pound car-ronades. All that Macdonough needed was for Downie to come in close to where his ships were anchored.

The American army based at Plattsburgh had been sent west, to the unthreatened Niagara frontier, even as Prevost was descending from the north. Plattsburgh was lightly defended. Even so, Prevost would not order an assault. He preferred instead to nag Downie into making an attack.

The British fleet did exactly that, believing that once the action began on the lake the army would storm the redoubts and turn the shore batteries on the anchored American ships below. The sailors guessed wrong. Sir George was almost paralyzed with fear. His intelligence service had intercepted a letter that referred to 20,000 militia gathering in his rear. Shades of Burgoyne! The letter was fake but Prevost's terror was genuine.

On the lake Macdonough handled his ships with consummate skill. Downie was killed early on. His seamen pressed home their attacks with exemplary courage, but that brought them under the hammer-blows of the American carronades. The coup de grâce came when Macdonough's two biggest vessels, the twenty-six-gun *Saratoga* and the twenty-gun *Eagle,* were turned around and opened up with their intact port batteries. White flags fluttered like moths. That was good enough for Prevost. He scurried back to Canada. As for Macdonough, he shared Perry's luck: not a scratch.

The third British blow, however, and by far the biggest, had yet to fall.

. . .

BOTH before and after the war began, Tecumseh visited the Indians of the South, performing magic tricks, conjuring up visions of his Indian Confederation, promising victory over the Long Knives, swearing that the British, whose uniform he wore, would put a gun into every warrior's hands and food into his children's bellies. Some of the Upper Creeks of northern Georgia and Alabama followed him back to Canada, there to fight on the river Raisin and enjoy the ecstasies of massacre. On their way home they murdered some white settlers for good measure.

Out of that wanton deed flowed a fatally confused sequence of events that left the Creeks at war with the white man and each other. On August 30, 1813, they assaulted Fort Mims, forty miles north of Mobile. It was guarded by seventy Louisiana militia who dispensed with precautions such as closing the main gate. The Indians overran it. No fort of its size ever before or again fell to Indians. Roughly 300 people, mainly women and children, were butchered.

All over the Southwest Territory men came running, a pony in one hand, a weapon in the other. Moving faster than the rest was the commander of the West Tennessee militia, Andrew Jackson, half dead from a recent shooting scrape. Madison loathed him but in this crisis could hardly do without him.

The chief military asset of the Creeks was that it was hard to penetrate the swamps and forests of their sacred Hickory Ground in central Alabama. The militia forces from Mississippi and Georgia gave up when supplies and enlistments ran out. Not Jackson. He hung on, starving off the land. He munched acorns, hanged a young militiaman to encourage the others, and pursued the Creeks wherever they went.

At Tallasahatchee on November 3 a force of 1,000 mounted riflemen under his protégé John Coffee attacked 200 Red Stick braves.* The militia had every advantage—numbers, firepower, surprise. "We shot them down like dogs," said one of them, Davy Crockett.

Six days later, near Talladega, the Creeks tried to ambush the main body, under Jackson. The trap was unmasked. Only poor coordination

---

*Tecumseh had given his Creek followers bundles of red sticks. After the appearance of an expected comet they were to throw away one stick each day. When they ran out of sticks, they would all rise together.

between infantry and cavalry prevented the Indians from being wiped out. On the ground lay 299 dead braves.

On March 27, 1814, at Horseshoe Bend on the Tallapoosa River, the Red Sticks made their last stand. Across a loop in the river they raised a log breastwork three hundred yards long. The fight that ensued was the biggest battle ever between Indians and white men. Some 1,000 Creeks tried to hold off an army of 3,000. Coffee's men crossed the river, attacking from the rear, while Jackson's infantry stormed the breastwork from the front. More than half the Red Stick warriors perished, to Jackson's 49 killed in action.

For years British and Spanish agents had been arming the Indians of the South, telling them repeatedly that Americans were the enemy of the red man, encouraging them to be hostile yet urging them not to make war. When the war eventually came, both the British and the Spanish were slow to turn their earlier promises of help into arms deliveries. By the time they were ready to arm the Indians, it was really too late to achieve anything, because by then the braves were defeated and demoralized.

In August 1814, Jackson forced them—including even friendly tribes—to give up 22 million acres of land. The Jeffersonian policy of assimilation was dead. Across the South came a single cry: Removal! The farther the better.

The surviving Creek war chiefs and their remaining followers fled to Spanish West Florida. The governor there had sent messages of congratulations to the Red Sticks after the Fort Mims massacre.

AFTER pulling out of the Chesapeake, Admiral Cochrane had sailed to Jamaica, to collect more troops and more warships for the most ambitious operation of the war. Probing the Gulf for a secure base of operations, the Royal Navy tried the defenses of Fort Bowyer, dominating Mobile Bay. Jackson's gunners beat them off. The British lost a frigate. Their attention shifted to Pensacola.

So did Jackson's. With no authority whatever, as he readily acknowledged, he set off for Pensacola in late October. The town fell to him almost without a fight.

Messages meanwhile arrived from Monroe telling Jackson the British were about to invade at New Orleans. He was not entirely convinced even though his own spies had for months been telling him the same thing. Leaving a strong force at Mobile, he hurried west, reaching New Orleans on December 1. Cochrane was ready to sail from Jamaica with a fleet of fifty warships, more than one thousand guns, and transports crammed with infantry. Jackson had thrown him off schedule, forced him to operate from an anchorage instead of a port and denied him allies ashore. Half of the battle was won.

There were at least seven routes into the city. None of them was easy. The fleet anchored in the Gulf, fifty miles away. Sweating British sailors in pulling boats ferried the troops in by way of Lake Borgne. The Jeffs saw action at last. Five of them under Lieutenant Thomas ap Catesby Jones offered an hour of hopeless resistance.

The army was put onto solid ground nine miles below the city on December 23. That very night Jackson attacked. His losses in killed and wounded nearly equaled the enemy's, 213 to 228, but this chaotic fight in darkness gave him a tactical and psychological ascendancy.

He pulled his troops back behind an old millrace known as the Rodriguez Canal, seven miles below New Orleans. Thirty feet behind it he began raising a mud rampart, Line Jackson. It would stretch from the Mississippi on his right to a swamp half a mile away on his left.

The British were meanwhile greeting their new commander, sent to replace Ross, Lieutenant General Sir Edward Pakenham, Wellington's brother-in-law. Only thirty-six, he had scaled the ladder of promotion by bold frontal attacks at Salamanca and the Battle of the Pyrénées.

On the last day of the year his troops moved forward, crouching in the reeds and grass, ready to rush Line Jackson the moment it was breached by British guns on New Year's morning. In the artillery duel that ensued the British had more and heavier guns, but it was like a cannoneer's version of Bunker Hill, with the British out in the open and the Americans entrenched. When the British gunners lost the duel their infantry crept away.

Jackson too had problems. The city's merchants and politicians were a nuisance. He put the city under martial law, shut down the legislature, suspended habeas corpus. All of which was illegal.

Line Jackson was rising each day while his defenses on the west side of the river went neglected. There a handful of underarmed men was strung out over the landscape, both flanks hanging in midair. It was a position begging to be taken. From it the British could have enfiladed Jackson's position, making it untenable. Pakenham committed himself instead to making a costly, frontal assault. Salamanca again. He had 9,600 men, with more on the way, to Jackson's 5,200.

By the morning of January 8 the mud wall was, on average, five feet high, but for much of its length it could easily be pierced by round shot. An advance redoubt was built in front of it, near the river, to draw off some British fire.

When the two main British columns attacked at dawn on the eighth they took the wrong line of advance, thereby exposing a flank and heading for the wrong part of the rampart. These were not, with few exceptions, battle-hardened, battle-wise Peninsular regiments. They were mainly ordinary line units with modest combat experience. Wellington refused to let his best troops be wasted on a war he judged unwinnable.

The British needlessly complicated the assault by making fascines, huge bundles of sugarcane, to fill the canal and heavy ladders of green wood to scale the wall. The men of the 44th Regiment, assigned to carry the fascines and ladders, advanced reluctantly, feeling they might as well have bull's-eyes painted on their chests.

The 44th broke up into small groups while waiting for the divisional column they were supposed to follow come within musket range of Line Jackson and provide covering fire while they made a dash for the canal. Instead, the column simply disintegrated before their eyes, far short of its goal. The 44th's colonel, however, provided the scapegoat for defeat.

Even the best regiments could not have advanced over five hundred yards of open ground against such heavy fire. Jackson had four ranks of riflemen laying down a burst of aimed fire every fifteen seconds. His artillery was even more effective. When the 93rd Highlanders charged, Pakenham sent them the wrong way, exposing their left flank to a naval thirty-two-pounder filled to the muzzle with musket balls. It fired and more than 200 men went down: dozens dead, scores grievously wounded, the rest clinging to the ground in a paralysis of fear.

Pakenham lost his life. So did two of his three division commanders. There was some success. The advance redoubt by the river fell to the British. Rushing on, they crossed the ditch without fascines, scaled the wall without ladders. Then they had to fall back because the Highlanders, instead of being sent to reinforce success, had been sent to reinforce failure. On the other side of the river the Americans were at that moment being routed, just as the main assault was called off.

Along Line Jackson, American losses were six killed and seven wounded. On the west bank they were seven killed and 51 wounded. Total British losses came to more than 2,000.

Reports have it that the Battle of New Orleans was a sterile victory; that it came after the war ended. The truth is more interesting than that. A peace agreement had been reached at Ghent, Belgium, on Christmas Eve. Even so, the British had great expectations. The invasion of the Gulf Coast was a project drawn up by the Cabinet. A delaying tactic—and, if need be, an out—was therefore built into the peace agreement on British insistence: instead of ending as soon as possible the war would continue until ratifications had been exchanged—in Washington. There was no truce, no cease-fire, no suspension of hostilities. They had bought eight more weeks or so for Pakenham to deliver. Special instructions were sent, ordering him to continue fighting. Fresh regiments were shipped out. The war was still on, by their choice.

Britain had never acknowledged the legality of the Louisiana Purchase. Spain claimed Louisiana, the lower Mississippi and the entire Gulf Coast. The Treaty of Ghent was carefully worded so that nothing could be interpreted as British recognition of Jefferson's deal with Napoleon. Had Pakenham won at New Orleans the British could have insisted on keeping Louisiana by right of conquest. More likely they would have handed it back to Spain but retained bases along the Gulf and the right to navigate the Mississippi.

Development of the South and West required American access to the Gulf. Jackson's victory assured that, while turning a disputed title to one third of the United States into unchallenged possession.

Had Pakenham won, the United States would also have given up the Creek lands. Under Article 9 of the peace treaty Indian allies of the British were to have their lands restored as they existed in 1811. In June 1815 Monroe explicitly ordered Jackson to hand the 22 million acres back. He refused. The Indians protested to London. They protested to Washington. It made no difference. They were removed. Had the battle gone the other way it would have been Jackson who suffered removal.

A new country had emerged: assertive, ambitious, stiff-necked. Jackson embodied it above all men. For thirty years after the War of

Independence the United States had looked longingly across the Atlantic; partly habit, partly need. It lacked the wealth of talent, the encrustations of culture, the deep pockets needed to stand aloof. By 1815 that had changed. A fierce nationalism was born, defying Europe, defying the world. Symbol and ritual came into their patriotic own. The Declaration of Independence was rediscovered, to be declaimed by men with lumps in their throats to audiences with lumps in theirs. Huge flags like the one that may or may not have flown above Fort McHenry broke out everywhere. A national anthem arose, long before Congress bothered to make it official. Political ceremony merged with religious feelings and attitudes of worship. Those Enlightenment men, the Founding Fathers, would probably have found much of it distasteful.

Both political parties were scrap waiting to be cannibalized. The Federalists because they had, from their New England heartland, opposed the war; the Jeffersonian Republicans because the war had nourished everything they loathed—a strong military, a strong government, booming cities, high taxes, finance capitalism. The agricultural arcadia of Jeffersonian fancy was doomed to extinction. America had turned into a country of markets and cities, restlessness and rapid change. There was hardly a corner of American life in 1815 that did not give off a whiff of gunpowder.

The struggle for arms had succeeded. Through three years of war and a tight blockade the United States produced all the rifles and muskets, cannon and gunpowder, it needed; even if there was—still!— a shortage of bayonets. Americans learned to live without European luxuries while inward investment raised production heroically. Manufacturing grew as much in three years as it had done in twenty. The war put the United States on the road to getting rich. Before, its highest hope was a crude self-sufficiency.

In the Northwest and the South there was the kind of security that brought in floods of settlers. Both regions were already awash with government money to pay and supply armies. The threat of Indian buffer states, under foreign control, vanished forever.

In the twentieth century, an age of Anglo-American alliances, a belief would flourish that after 1815 the United States prospered behind the bulwarks of the Royal Navy, that Britain had shielded the New World from European predators. In fact, the European state most capable of posing a threat to the United States was Great Britain. And when the French tried to conquer Mexico in the 1860s, posing a direct challenge to American security, that British "bulwark" was then no-where to be seen.

The United States was left alone not as a fortunate beneficiary of British defense policy but because Americans had inflicted the biggest defeats on land and sea suffered up to that time by British forces. There was no desire left to fight Americans again. Ahead stretched decades of war scares: along the Gulf, along the Canadian border, in Latin America, in Hawaii. On every occasion the British backed off. They made war all over the globe after 1815 but treated the United States like a European power.

There remained one unfinished piece of business. The dey of Algiers had entered the war on the side of the British. It looked a safe bet, piracy under the protection of British warships. With ratifications exchanged, peace made, Madison sent Decatur with a powerful force of frigates and sloops to give the dey the benefit of the navy's wartime experience. It did not take long.

6

NATURAL
FRONTIERS

FROM MICHILIMACKINAC to the Gulf, Indians refused to believe the war was over, refused to believe a treaty had been signed, refused to believe the British had abandoned them. Indian attacks continued in some areas almost to the end of 1815. Only irrefutable reports of the Battle of New Orleans convinced them it really was over, that the British had gone and, this time, were not coming back. With that the fight went out of nearly every tribe.

Jackson's defiance of Monroe over Article 9 got removal under way. As the Indians departed, Spanish Florida came under irresistible pressure. In 1818 Jackson invaded it. Next year Spain sold what it could not hold.

By 1825 Jackson had forced the Indians to give up lands the size of Western Europe: 75 percent of Florida, 75 percent of Alabama, nearly 30 percent of Tennessee, 20 percent of Georgia, 20 percent of Mississippi, one tenth of Kentucky, one tenth of North Carolina. A new realm was born—the Cotton Kingdom.

For a decade he was the government's chief negotiator with the tribes. Some balked as he pressured them to sell their lands. At times like that the long, stricken face would flush. Would they rather settle this matter some other way? he would ask. The Indians were ready to grant Jackson anything rather than fight him again.

As they parleyed over land, so they were forced to discuss removal.

By the time of his election to the presidency in 1828 the Indians had sold or surrendered nearly all their lands east of the Mississippi. Still the pressure for removal grew.

The army managed it with a fair degree of humanity and skill, and more than a little distaste and reluctance. Only the Seminoles, joined by Creeks and runaway slaves, offered much resistance. They moved into the swamps of Florida. The army tried to root them out, without much success, after the Spanish departed.

The Second Seminole War began in 1835, turning into probably the most exasperating campaign the army ever fought. By 1843 nearly 5,000 Seminoles had been removed. Several hundred had been killed. An estimated 300 remained. The United States unilaterally declared peace rather than continue chasing so few around so much.

The other important removal war was against the Sauks of northern Illinois and southern Wisconsin, and their chief, Black Hawk. For most of his life he resented bitterly the treaty imposed on his tribe by Harrison in 1804 that took most of their ancestral lands. In 1812 he had gladly allied himself with the British.

In the 1820s white settlers began crowding into northern Illinois. Rather than fight, most tribes crossed the Mississippi. Black Hawk held out, always hoping for British arms to reappear. They never arrived. His "British Band" finally agreed to cross the great river. "I touched the goose quill to this treaty," he later acknowledged, "determined to live in peace."

In 1831 they left. The harvests on the other side of the river were poor. The Sauks became embroiled in fighting with other tribes already established there. In 1832 they crossed back into Illinois, some 2,000 strong.

Days later several hundred soldiers arrived, sent to put a stop to the intertribal violence. Behind them hundreds of militia were coming up. Black Hawk tried to surrender. The militia, convinced his white flag was a trick, opened fire. His braves counterattacked, routing the militia. Other militia units panicked on hearing the news, evaporating like dew. Among those who chose not to flee was militia captain Abraham Lincoln.

A new volunteer army was raised. Black Hawk made a second attempt to surrender. This too failed: the army had no Winnebago interpreter to cope with a Winnebago messenger sent by a Sauk chief.

Militiamen, eagerly pressing around, got the idea that the fierce-sounding syllables that fell on their ears were a death threat.

At the Bad Axe River, on the western border of Wisconsin, the British Band was run to earth, cut to pieces. At least 150 men, women and children were killed. The numbed survivors were herded across the Mississippi.

For a time it seemed that the Cherokees of Georgia might fight. Scott and Wool, sent to force them out, felt deeply ashamed. Faced with the prospect of fighting regulars, the Cherokees, clinging to the last shreds of dignity a desperate situation allowed, offered to remove themselves, with no military escort. As the winter of 1837 drew near they set off. Some thirteen thousand took the "Trail of Tears" that led west to Oklahoma. Many perished of hunger and exposure.

Much of the time the Indians posed less of a military challenge than the terrain. To control the Indians the Army needed better roads, even if it had to build them. The wretchedness of American roads had wrecked almost every offensive operation in the War of 1812. The worst disasters had grown out of the often impassable roads between the Ohio River and Detroit.

That surprised no one, but the states and territories had long pleaded poverty and the Constitution seemed to bar the federal government from even thinking about going into the road business. Wartime humiliation cast a fresh light on the document. Hardly was the Treaty of Ghent ratified before the army had road gangs at work. Soldiers earned an extra fifteen cents a day cutting and grading roads to Detroit, Niagara, Plattsburgh and New Orleans.

Having cut roads, they built forts, securing the frontier and transforming it. Any difference between soldiering and pioneering escaped the naked eye. Captain Zachary Taylor wrote home indignantly in 1820, "The ax, the pick, saw and trowel has become more the implement of the American soldier than the cannon, musket or sword."

Another soldier, the Duke of Württemberg, traveling through the West later in that same decade, was astonished at the economic busyness of what was described as forts. They were really industrial and trading centers, bringing in raw materials, turning it into useful products—rugs, pottery, furniture, milled flour—and distributing these to settlers and troops. They also served as primitive motels, putting up long-distance travelers.

The army found it next to impossible to abandon forts once finished; civilians found them too useful. Their military role often came second, if anywhere. The inspector general, visiting Fort Leavenworth in 1833, reported back in disgust, "Defenses it has none." The managerial, not to say commercial, style of the American military was not to every soldier's taste.

Yet it was an essential response to the country's rocketing rise to power. There was nothing to waste; not time, not money, not people. Anything that could serve both military and commercial needs did not have to argue its way. It happened.

As the roads snaked west, as the forts arose, people were drawn toward them as inevitably as iron filings toward magnetized metal. By 1845 the only government many Americans knew was provided by uniforms. The army represented what law and order there was. Forts and soldiers were the only security they trusted; and that with their lives.

The Pony Express, the telegraph and the railroads would all go down routes explored, cleared and defended by the army. Along these would grow villages, then towns, eventually cities. Like DNA the military roads and forts contained the pattern of future development long before that development could be seen. From the Alleghenies to the Pacific nearly every twentieth-century city grows out of a fort.

The men assigned there felled the trees, burned or pulled out the stumps and broke the soil. One protested feelingly in 1838, "I enlisted to avoid work, and here I am, compelled to perform three or four times the amount of labor I did before." And by his sweat the frontier advanced, pressing on the Indians again.

Removal turned out to be no more than a breathing space. A short one at that. There was well-meaning talk in the 1830s of a permanent Indian frontier: all the Indians on one side, all the whites on the other—forever. Here was one idea whose time would never come. As the Indians crossed the great river, so did white men, for pelts, for land, for gold, for adventure.

And the army faced yet another challenge—all that space. For half a century cavalry had seemed too aristocratic for people to accept, too expensive for Congress to finance. The fiasco of the Black Hawk war, when soldiers on foot tried chasing Indians on ponies, changed that. In March 1833 a regiment of dragoons was authorized.

Soldiers could now move onto the Great Plains. The dragoons

would ride on patrols as long as three thousand miles each summer. It was low-tech deterrence. They made an obvious, magnificent show; they were meant to. These expeditions, though, were but scratches on the arid surface. There were as many as 25,000 braves out there to some 500 dragoons.

In the early years the stunning heat was the greater threat, killing off all but the fittest. They had to travel light, adjust quickly. They cooked their meals over dried buffalo chips. Opinion was divided. Some troops thought the smell ruined anyone's appetite; others that the smoke gave a certain piquancy to boring old salt pork or beef jerky.

In the course of a five-year enlistment a dragoon could expect to see combat only once, but he looked on the mounted Plains Indians as the best light cavalry in the world, which may or may not have been true. They were superb horsemen, used their weapons with consummate skill, were aggressive and courageous and took every advantage the terrain yielded.

It was never difficult, however, to take them by surprise once found. They spurned such light cavalry basics as picket duty. They were really accomplished raiders, not soldiers, highly effective against the poorly organized or badly armed; much like Cossacks. Like Cossacks too they were no match for a properly trained cavalry force.

With few exceptions Indians did not make war. They raided. Their numbers were so small that the white man's way of warfare—men standing in the open, slaughtering each other until the dead covered the earth—seemed crazy. In turn, the army found Indian-fighting one frustration after another. However Hollywood tells it, the Long Knives just were not very good at it. It took at least ten soldiers to wage a successful campaign against one Indian; figures on a par with the guerrilla wars of this century, in which regulars have often thrashed around bemused. When combat did occur it was more or less by accident, as one side stumbled on the other.

For each such encounter there were months of dull patrolling toward daunting horizons. And once battle was joined, it was soon over. The moment Indians could pull out of close combat, they were usually off.

The overpowering advantage the soldier had was his arms. The Indians were nearly always one weapons technology behind and they never handled artillery. The twelve-pound mountain howitzer, models

1840 and 1841, has as good a claim as any to the title "the gun that won the West." Time and again a single howitzer firing canister saved heavily outnumbered troops from annihilation. Indians were rightly terrified of a weapon that could kill twenty men at half a mile. On its "prairie carriage" the mountain howitzer could go almost everywhere a man went, and did.

The Indian-fighting army became, in effect if not intention, the service school for both infantry and cavalry. It was also so small, so close-knit that a dragoon on a single enlistment could meet and serve under sixty officers and NCOs destined for generals' stars.

On paper the army's training system provided every new recruit with thorough instruction in his arm. Manpower shortages on the frontier shredded the paper. Men were hurried west, to where half the army was based, to learn on the job. They became soldiers by soldiering. So did their officers. At West Point they learned much about Napoleon, nothing about Indians.

The small regular army between 1815 and the Civil War learned quickly. It probably had a higher proportion of educated and talented men than any other military force in the world. Many of them were immigrants eager to establish themselves in American life; educated men seeking a fresh start. For half a century the army did what the schools would later do—turn immigrants into Americans. Besides, most of them were too old to go to school.

The harshness of army discipline drove many to desert, roughly one man in four in a typical year. The rawhide whip used for flogging in the American army would cut a man to ribbons, unlike the cat used by the British. Facing such a flogging, who would not think of deserting? American officers also thought nothing of hitting enlisted men. Without the class structure of an old-established culture behind them they felt a need to assert their authority and prove their toughness.

Even so, there was tremendous pride among those who stuck it out, officers and men alike, especially in the dragoons. They were, said Samuel Chamberlain, the Don Juan of the Mexican War, "Far superior in materials to any other arm of the service. In our Squadron were broken down Lawyers, Actors and men of the world, Soldiers who had served under Napoleon, French Cuirassiers, Hungarian Hussars, and Irishmen who had left the Queen's service to swear allegiance to Uncle Sam."

To remote posts they brought pianos and books, string quartets and monthly debates, warm gold and bright silver. There were amateur dramatics, correspondence courses, newspapers; always newspapers. And all of these helped tame the frontier. The West was won with guns and brains: education and firepower.

The Indians had no answer to the implacable instruments of peace, this relentless tide of the white man's culture sustained by its cherished artifacts. What could bows and arrows, trade muskets and hatchets do against the life-nurturing totems of a civilized existence?

Each year the army held treaty-signing festivals out on the Plains. Chiefs in opéra-bouffe uniforms gravely waited for their ornate medals and good-conduct certificates. Near the treaty table boxes and bales packed with store goods vomited their treasures under the sun. Christmas in the wrong season. All the chiefs had to do was sign.

After which the presents were handed out, white men and red feasted to stupefaction, waged sham battles for each other's amusement and were, briefly, like brothers. There was an intimacy, genuinely felt in such moments, that still did not bar mutual cruelty. There was the bond, even so, as there always is, between the men who fight.

And as sand was brushed over the treaties to blot up the ink of temporary peace, other men elsewhere were taking up other pens, more ink, to fill in the blank spaces that troubled maps. Exploring the interiors of the great continents was one of the higher intellectual adventures of the nineteenth century. It created interest, ambitions, devotions, perils and sacrifices our age has forgotten. It made people proud to be human. It was seen, felt, to be a war against ignorance. In the forefront of that stood, among others, the Corps of Topographical Engineers.

Formed as an independent command in 1838, but with roots running back to the Continental Army, they led the way in opening the trans-Mississippi West to settlement. The surveys they made, their missions of exploration, the careful compilations of data on weather, on flora and fauna, on Indian tribes, on geology and landscape all promoted the growth of a federal-scientific complex that made ever tighter the military-industrial relationship. The huge quantities of material brought back also turned the Smithsonian from an enigmatic bequest from a man who had never even seen the United States into one of the world's leading museums and centers of science.

The excitement of discovery was personified by John C. Frémont, a topographical engineer. Under the patronage of his powerful father-in-law, Senator Thomas Hart Benton of Missouri, the young lieutenant set off in 1842 to explore the approaches to Oregon, to arouse national interest in the Pacific Northwest and to make the British think of leaving. The handsome, dapper Frémont gave Manifest Destiny a pleasing, human face.

Jessie Frémont, ambitious wife and senator's daughter, wrote up her husband's accounts of his travels in a luminous prose that, read around oil lamps and smoky hearths, set pulses racing, inspired thoughts of moving west. Deep into this century there were old men who could recall vividly those visionary nights when they first heard or read Frémont's account of what he had found "out there" in 1842.

Next year he set off for Oregon once again. A nation held its breath. More than ever he went his own way, this time taking a mountain howitzer with him. His military superiors were outraged. The Topographical Engineers had their Jeffersonian image to consider: savants first, soldiers second. They addressed scientific conferences, wrote learned papers, did not handle guns. The singular travels of that howitzer were to make it virtually a figure in its own right, sketched and painted a dozen times, referred to often in the literature of western exploration.

From Oregon Frémont moved south, into California. There were few there to greet him: some 15,000 Americans and Mexicans, living in small, scattered communities, and roughly 24,000 Indians. His descriptions of the richness of the soil, the healthiness of the climate and the awesomeness of the scenery aroused every emotion from avarice to mystical revery.

It was California's first and greatest publicity coup, from which it has not recovered yet. Born in hyperbole, California was manifestly destined to remain there. After Frémont's report Americans lusted for the place.

IN THESE YEARS as the regular army strove to excel, the state (or common) militia continued the peacetime tradition of rotting away. The once-a-year muster turned into a local joke. Young men in whose breasts a martial spirit stirred had to look elsewhere, to the volunteer militia companies. These gladly took up the burden of military amateurism, whose latest battle honor read "New Orleans."

The dynamism of most volunteer companies was youthful high spirits looking for somewhere to happen. They soon grew bored with learning how to march in ranks, to deploy from column into line and back again, to present arms smartly or to carry a sword without tripping over it. They began adding extra steps, extra movements, extra flair. After the breakthrough, the deluge.

There came cheerleading, the exaggerated countermarching of brass bands, fanatical training in the service of unbridled enthusiasm. The most obvious characteristics of modern college athletics run in a pure stream from the brash, energetic volunteer companies of the 1830s and 1840s. There was a spirit too expansive to be contained in a uniform. Bursting its brass buttons, it spilled into the world around it, creating a passion for boxing and rowing, footraces and football, and inspiring new sports to emerge from old ones.

Some volunteer companies had long been part of the social elite. They dressed in gorgeous finery, preened self-adoringly, held parades, balls and dinners, unabashedly put up posters praising their dash and good looks and brought to civic occasions that splash of bravura color that gray city politicians feel a growing burg needs. They were an essential part of city life, rattling down rutted streets pulling little cannon behind or clattering into city squares, sabers wickedly shining. Whatever was the latest military fashion, they followed it: light infantry, guard cavalry, riflemen in the 1820s; dragoons, lancers or zouaves a generation later.

In eastern cities membership in the older companies was screened for social standing and ready money. Farther west a more democratic ethos prevailed. Companies made up mainly of Irish or Germans were formed, taking names such as "The Invincibles, "The Avengers" or "The Snake Hunters."

In Boston, New York, Philadelphia, New Orleans and elsewhere the fire companies, some volunteer companies and the strong-arm gangs run by ward bosses formed one seamless, rowdy web. More than one fire turned into a political riot; more than one volunteer muster turned into a vigilante outing that ended in someone sticky with tar, tumbled in feathers.

Not even the flourishing volunteer militia could mop up all the craving for brass and glory. Dozens of military schools opened for business. Many were college-preparatory. Others, like the Virginia

Military Institute and the Citadel, were modeled on West Point, hoping to send their graduates into the army as officers.

The demand for these schools and academies did not come from the army. It came from a society that both adored and distrusted the military. For every family that found war unspeakably sordid there was another trying to get Johnny into uniform. There were untold numbers of people who were torn both ways. Lincoln was one of them. He participated gleefully in the antimilitary demonstrations that regularly set Springfield rocking with laughter. Yet he went off to serve in a sorry scrape like the Black Hawk war.

After 1815 the standing army was no longer an important issue in American life. Only in Congress did it rumble on, kept alive mainly by congressmen from Kentucky, still remembering the Raisin and trying to prove that they, as volunteers, had won the war.

The army, limited to roughly 8,000 officers and men, continued the long pursuit of betterment in its own way. Forever conscious that soldiers are never popular in long periods of peace, it kept its head down, and studied. In 1819 Winfield Scott drew up the first general regulations of any army: seventy-five pages of small print, laying down rules on almost everything a soldier might need to know: dress, salutes, weapons maintenance, prisoners of war, drill, marching, honors, arrest procedures, military etiquette, relations with sutlers and so on. He was possibly the only officer anywhere who had given serious thought not to some military subjects but to all military subjects.

The summit of Scott's hopes for an educated army was West Point. Not a graduate, he worshiped regardless. It had become the intellectual beacon Jefferson envisaged. Its top graduates became engineers. Then, more likely than not, they would find themselves on detached duty for long periods to supervise the construction of canals and railroads for private companies. The army's best talents were not squandered on the army.

George Ticknor, the reforming president of Harvard, and Horace Mann both sat on the West Point board of visitors and took part in examinations. They pronounced the graduating cadets the best-educated students in the country. Large numbers of West Pointers were hired to teach at Harvard, Yale and Columbia. The academy was long misunderstood because the entrance exam was fairly easy. Graduating was not.

While Harvard looked to Germany, West Point looked to France.

It was filled with French instructors, French texts, French ideas. French was the language of both science and advanced military thought. France, however, offered its army a full range of service schools. West Point, by contrast, felt forced to teach everything: mathematics, engineering, languages, small-unit tactics, drill, a smattering of the arts and humanities. Newly minted officers emerged as men who could do it all—command artillery, lead infantry, ride at the head of cavalry. Some really did all three.

Congress adamantly refused to pay for postgraduate schools of the type common in France, Britain and Prussia. For decades it drove the navy wild by refusing it an academy of its own. Subterfuge was the answer. In 1845 George Bancroft, the secretary of the navy, ardent bibliophile and serious scholar, found himself briefly the acting secretary of war. He promptly gave the navy the use of Fort Severn at Annapolis, installed several dozen midshipmen and instructors while Congress was out of session, and when it returned offered a clear choice: pay for the new academy or put it out of business. It paid up.

Annapolis, its first instructors drawn mainly from West Point, refused like it to be a mere technical institution. Both academies were wedded to an utterly unique conviction that what made an officer fit to lead men into combat was education, in the same way that that was what made a doctor fit to cut into other people's flesh, or a lawyer fit to plead a case in court. No military school in the world had so clear and consistent a view of an officer being the special product of professional education as these two. Even the admired French still trusted more to *cran* than to trained intelligence.

West Point's emphasis on engineering meant that the artillerists, themselves founding members, were slighted. They argued for, and in 1824 got, a service school, at Fortress Monroe, Virginia. To it came every artillery regiment at regular intervals to practice its booming business. This was a concession, though, not a precedent.

Young officers took up their commissions with intellectual appetites that West Point had whetted but the army could not satisfy. Ulysses Grant, graduating in 1843, was typical. He had every intention of resigning once he had served his obligatory year. What West Point offered to most of those who went there was an education, not a military career. Within ten years of graduation most were out of the army, not simply to make more money but to enter professions where there was a better chance of intellectual advancement. Far more became college professors and college presidents than went to work for fat salaries on the railroads.

West Point was periodically attacked as a place aristocratic and privileged, but there was never any serious threat of Congress closing it down. It became as integral a part of the upper class as Harvard or Yale, as the roster of any graduating class showed. And in graduating classes elsewhere there was an echo of West Point, in the class rings its students wore.

The country's feelings about the army were both mixed and strong. Americans were fascinated by martial exploits, as every history textbook showed. Yet the regulars got no credit for the army's victories. Under the myth of the militia any ordinary citizen could claim that for himself. For people to realize how professional the army had become would take another war.

TEXAS was a desert. There was hardly anyone there in 1812. Spain claimed it. Under the Louisiana Purchase, so did the United States. Only after the Battle of New Orleans did it matter much what lay between the Sabine and the Rio Grande, but Monroe sought to soothe Spanish pride and speed up the acquisition of Florida by waiving the American claim to Texas. This enraged the Southwest. Instead of making Americans draw back from the Sabine, they poured across it.

By 1832 there were at least twenty thousand white settlers in Texas. That year Mexico was wracked by civil war. Having cast off Spanish rule, the Mexicans found themselves much like the Americans after the Revolution, hotly divided between those who wanted a strong central government and those who wanted power to remain with the states.

By 1835 the Centralists, under General Antonio López de Santa Anna, had won the war. In the lightly populated areas far from Mexico City, however, the struggle went on. In Texas, Americans and Mexicans alike resisted Centralist rule.

In December that year the garrison at San Antonio was forced to surrender. Two months later Santa Anna marched over the West Texas plain with 8,000 men, formed into two armies. The largest, under his personal command, besieged more than 200 Americans in the fortified church of the Alamo, in San Antonio. After thirteen days of siege and battle it fell, on March 6. Not one of the 187 men defending the Alamo survived. More than a dozen women and children were captured, but they were spared. Thwarted from wreaking vengeance on live male prisoners, Santa Anna had the bodies of the dead Americans stacked like cordwood, then burned, like trash.

The second Mexican army, some 2,000 men under General José Urrea, advanced on Goliad, where 300 armed settlers had gathered. They surrendered to him. Santa Anna ordered him to murder them, to the last man.

Other American settlers meanwhile voted for an assembly, wrote a constitution, borrowed one million dollars and created an army under one of Jackson's protégés, Sam Houston. Santa Anna pursued Houston's ragtag force nearly five hundred miles, toward the Sabine. To move faster, the Mexican general left behind his main body and, leading 900 mounted troops, tried to cut off the Americans at the river crossing of Lynch Ferry, near San Jacinto. Houston beat him to it by three hours.

Santa Anna decided to rest his tired force and await reinforcements. Five hundred men came up. Thousands more were expected in a few days. The Mexicans settled down in an area covered with trees and tall grass. They posted no pickets, sent out no patrols. Santa Anna had never lost a fight.

On April 21, as the Mexican camp settled into a refreshing siesta, Houston's 800 men struck even though seriously outnumbered. Rising out of the tall grass with "Remember the Alamo! Remember Goliad!" on their lips, they charged. Two small guns shredded the waking Mexicans as they attempted to form a line. Santa Anna jumped on a horse and departed at speed. The men he left behind were less lucky.

Casualty figures sometimes tell their own story. These certainly did: the Texans suffered six dead, 24 wounded—the Mexicans, 630 dead, 208 wounded. Santa Anna was later captured, dressed in a private's uniform, but spared for a general's fate, because he like Houston was a Freemason.

As head of the Mexican army he ordered the 7,000 Mexican soldiers in Texas to withdraw beyond the Rio Grande. As head of the Mexican government he recognized the independence of Texas, with its boundary along the Rio Grande. As a man of honor he swore personally that he would never fight the Texans again.

In the ten years that followed this debacle the Mexican government resembled a revolving door. In their more assertive moods fleeting coalitions—sometimes mainly Federalist, sometimes mainly

Centralist—claimed all of Texas to the Sabine. On other occasions they claimed only the land between the Rio Grande and the Nueces. By implication, on yet other occasions, they accepted both its independence and the Rio Grande boundary.

The question of just how Mexican was Texas intruded year by year into American politics. From the moment they won their independence the Americans of Texas wanted to give it up. They wanted annexation, security, American troops. In the South and West the passion for expansion ran high. In the North and East it ran less high, but for those who could be bothered to look, it was never hard to find. What gave the annexation question a bitter, unyielding character was slavery.

Mexico, under Centralists and Federalists alike, banned it. Yet in East Texas, along the Louisiana border, there were, undeniably, slaves. The other 90 percent of Texas was completely unsuited to slave labor, but once the idea took hold that annexation was part of a plot to spread slavery nothing would get that conviction out of people's minds.

Because the slavery issue made annexation a threat to national unity no one attempted it until 1844. On his way out of office President John Tyler negotiated a treaty of annexation. The Senate refused to ratify it. In the last days of his presidency, Tyler made a final attempt— annexation by joint resolution of both houses of Congress. The resolution was passed, but there was no provision in the Constitution for territorial expansion in this way. On the face of it the resolution was illegal, but that was left for the incoming president, James Polk, to deal with. He was an emphatically outspoken annexationist.

By this time Mexico owed millions of dollars to Americans, plus millions more to people who were not. The French tried to collect theirs by bombardment, shooting up Veracruz. Santa Anna, in charge of the defenses, lost a leg. Meanwhile, much less dramatically, American negotiators worked out a repayment schedule with the Mexican government. After eight months the payments ceased.

To simple minds the solution was obvious: let Mexico unequivocally accept the independence of Texas and let the U.S. government assume the debts owed to American citizens. Simple. And a lot cheaper than a war.

Polk, a Tennessee lawyer who seemed to have emerged from nowhere, was another Jacksonian protégé. This sickly man was willing himself to live for just four more years in the cause of expansion. He was after Texas, California and a settlement of the Oregon boundary dispute with Britain. Here was a land hunger to match an emperor's. The one thing he did not want was to fight for any of it. During the first two years of his presidency there was no serious increase in the army or navy's size.

On July 4, 1845, Texas voted to relinquish independence, take annexation. Mexico had repeatedly said that this would mean war. Polk made one last attempt at negotiation. It failed. American troops were ordered to move from Louisiana to the Rio Grande. Polk knew just the man to command them.

Jackson had advised him months before, "If we ever get into a war, General Taylor is the man. . . ." Back in 1812 the first American brevet (or honorary rank) had been awarded to him* for the defense of Fort Harrison, Indiana, against an assault led by Tecumseh. Zachary Taylor had also taken Black Hawk's surrender and earned a brevet brigadier generalship pursuing Seminoles over half of Florida.

He was a born, if limited, fighter: stolid, unimaginative, unbudgeable on the defensive, little sureness of touch in attack, simply bang, bang, bang! Straight ahead, hit hard, keep going. No maneuvering, no theory. Everything done by instinct, with the common touch. Lots of experience, strong nerves, a fine contempt for show. Nearly always in civilian clothes; rumpled old ones. During the Mexican War he was found wearing uniform twice; once by mistake. Troops adored Taylor, especially volunteers. As he moved his "Army of Observation," some 4,000 strong, across Texas in March 1846, he called for three-month men. They swarmed toward him.

Mexican politicians and army officers eagerly awaited his coming. They savored the prospect of war with the United States. Anyone could see the loss of Texas had been a fluke, an aberration. If only Santa Anna had not made the elementary mistake of separating himself from the bulk of his army! Here, though, was the sought-for chance to put that right.

Mexico's armed forces were four times as big as those of the United States and, its officers boasted, twice as good. They had been fighting

---

*The brevet system defies all understanding. Brevets were used to recognize gallantry before decorations became widespread, but the standard definition—"rank higher than an officer's pay"—is wrong. Many a West Point graduate spent a year or more as a brevet second lieutenant, waiting for a place in a regiment. Meanwhile he received a second lieutenant's pay.

for twenty years. They would also have the advantage of interior lines, home ground and strong fortifications if the Americans were foolish enough to invade. And, to anticipate, when the French tried to conquer Mexico in the 1860s, their army of 30,000 was completely destroyed. Mexicans could and would fight.

They also counted on political opposition to the war to undermine Polk's efforts to wage it. Britain and France were eager to see the growing United States humbled. They seemed willing to help Mexico with money and arms. Mexican confidence was based on good foundations.

From Corpus Christi at the mouth of the Nueces, Taylor moved along the Gulf coast to Point Isabel, at the mouth of the Rio Grande. At a bend in the river, opposite Matamoros, his engineers raised a nine-foot-high pentagon. He named it Fort Brown. Each night the bands of the opposing armies serenaded each other. The Mexicans usually won. Out of the darkness American soldiers emerged on the Mexican side of the river, dripping wet, sometimes stark naked, wondering whether it was true about the señoritas.

On April 23, 1846, Mexico declared war on the United States. That this was called "a defensive war" is neither here nor there. The justification for nearly every war is self-defense. Two days later, complying with an order sent by the minister of war on April 4, 1,600 Mexican cavalry ambushed Captain Seth B. Thornton and 63 dragoons at a *rancho* on the Texan side of the Rio Grande. Sixteen Americans were killed. Of the survivors all except one man were captured.

Polk was assailed in Congress and the country for fighting an undeclared war. Before the Thornton ambush he had given Congress a choice between voting money to support Taylor's army down by the Rio Grande or letting it be wiped out for want of food and ammunition. Not much of a choice. After the 16 dragoons had been killed he was able to say, "American blood has been shed on American soil . . ." and get a declaration of war. What neither he nor Congress nor the country knew was that Mexico had already declared war on them.

After the ambush of Thornton's dragoons the commander of Mexican forces along the Rio Grande, General Mariano Arista, boastfully proclaimed, "I had the pleasure of being the first to start this war." He proceeded to take his army across the river to attack Taylor's advance base, Fort Brown. For Mexico it was bright confident morning still.

Taylor had left the fort a short time before, to fetch supplies from

Point Isabel. The fort held out. Taylor returned, knowing that at Palo Alto the Mexicans held the road. A mile from the Mexican army the Americans, outnumbered three to one, came to a halt, formed line of battle and waited for the inevitable attack.

Drawn up in front of them was a small-scale *Grande Armée*. The Mexicans based their striking power on a large cavalry arm, filling it with the sons of the governing class, while infantry ranks were filled with Indian conscripts. They were meant to bring to battle something like Murat's cavalry reserve—the unstoppable force.

The Mexicans had Gribeauval artillery too; some pieces were nearly eighty years old. All they could fire was round shot. Heavily encrusted with rococo metalwork, they would have looked terrific in a military museum.

After Waterloo, where Napoleon had mishandled his artillery and Wellington got less than full use from his but still won, the long arm was generally neglected. In the United States, however, where the gunners alone had a service school, it attracted some of the best young officers in the army. One of them, Major Samuel Ringgold, organized "flying artillery."

These guns were technically six-pounders, cast from bronze, slung between oversize wheels, pulled by a six-horse team that the gunners rode into battle. For eight years Ringgold drilled both men and horses until, by 1846, they were razor-sharp. Each of his four-gun batteries could fire six times a minute for as long as the ammunition held out.

At Palo Alto, Taylor had two 18-pounders pulled by oxen, several mountain howitzers and three batteries of flying artillery to slug it out with the Mexican gunners in the first hour of battle. The 18s and the howitzers outranged the Mexicans, shattering their museum artillery, leaving dead and wounded gunners around them. After a duel that cost the Americans nothing but sweat and powder the Mexican cavalry charged: more than 1,000 lancers, pennants fluttering in a magnificent, obsolete show.

Taylor's infantry formed square. The flying artillery burst a torrent of grape over the oncoming horsemen. At fifty yards the infantry opened fire, emptying dozens of saddles. The lancers pulled back, re-formed, charged again. With the same result. Only now the grass was on fire, set ablaze by burning wads from the busy guns.

Hostilities were suspended for one hour, while the smoke cleared away. Taylor advanced part of his army, the Mexicans part of theirs.

Through the thinning haze came the Mexican infantry, but in columns, not lines: a perfectly unmissable target for infantry and artillery alike.

Flying artillery, galloping here in support, there in support, wherever crisis threatened, came as a revelation to Lieutenant Ulysses S. Grant, in combat for the first time. Instant, overwhelming firepower: that was how battles were won. And despising the war, seeing nothing in it but a campaign of conquest to spread slavery, accusing himself of moral cowardice for not resigning his commission, he felt proud all the same to be a part of this army; an army that could fight as well as this against such heavy odds. In his *Memoirs,* after he had seen many armies in battle, he would write, "A better army, man for man, probably never faced an enemy."

The Mexicans pulled back. Darkness fell. American losses were five dead (including Ringgold, shot through both thighs, remembered in the name of a dozen small towns) and 43 wounded. Mexican casualties ran into the hundreds.

Amazed and demoralized by the revealed power of the first truly mobile artillery, firing grape and canister in the open field, Arista pulled back seven miles, to Resaca de la Palma. There a four-foot-deep channel carved by the great river offered one of nature's entrenchments for his men and what remained of his guns. With their heads down, not even the flying artillery could do them much harm there.

Taylor came up, still outnumbered nearly three to one. This time he attacked. An infantry charge captured the few remaining Mexican guns. A counterattack by the lancers was beaten off by American dragoons. An infantry assault overran the Mexican right, ending in hand-to-hand fighting in ditches and among the chaparral. As the Mexicans pulled out, the flying artillery galloped up, to cut them down with canister. Scores, perhaps hundreds drowned in terror as they flung themselves into the Rio Grande. American losses came to 150. Mexican casualties may have reached 1,000.

Taylor moved into the Mexican border town of Matamoros, vacated by Arista's defeated army. While his victorious troops disported themselves, Taylor, his aggressive instincts roused by battle, tried to decide what to do next.

President Polk was trying to buy a peace. The man offering to sell it to him was Santa Anna, living in luxurious disgrace in Cuba. Jackson had always said time and money would solve the problem of Texas.

Polk hoped eagerly the old man was right, that what had worked with Spain would work with Spain's heirs.

Two million dollars was the opening price: for back pay to the Mexican army, for the grease of goodwill, for the sundries of sellout. After that, of course, land cessions would cost millions more; tens of millions more. First, both men agreed, the fighting must stop. Santa Anna, claiming to be horrified by bloodshed, promised to stop it.

The American fleet blockading the Mexican Gulf coast was ordered to let Santa Anna through. He returned to Mexico a little grayer but with the old appetites as keen as ever, for opulence, for opium, for teen-age girls, for glory. This ardent Bonapartist who had modeled his country's army on the *Grande Armée* was also the world's leading collector of Napoleonic memorabilia. When modesty lapsed, he referred to himself as "the Napoleon of the West."

In the event, Polk did not raise his two million dollars. The bill failed to win passage in August 1846. With that, the last hope of a peaceful settlement ended. It was a slender chance at best, for Santa Anna arrived in a country so desperate for a savior that former sins were forgiven, if not forgotten.

In these early months of the war there was no American strategy. After six weeks in Matamoros Taylor advanced on Monterrey, more than one hundred miles from the Rio Grande, simply because Arista had gone there to try rallying the Mexican army. He reached it just in time for most of his three-month volunteers to arrive, turn around and go home. Another call went out for volunteer militia, this time twelve-month men. The response was overwhelming. In some areas ten men disputed every place.

After the ambush of Thornton's dragoons Taylor sent for the Texas Rangers. He needed people who knew the country and were used to fighting Mexicans to keep his lengthening line of communications open. The Rangers' exploits in scouting and stamping out the guerrilla threat in Mexico made them famous throughout the world.

Monterrey was a fortress built by nature and improved on by man. Behind it ran a river, the Santa Catarina. Two steep hills guarded the western approaches. The approach from the north and east was dominated by a massive stone fort, the Citadel. The houses were loopholed for musketry; their flat roofs had parapets offering cover to marksmen; the streets were easy to barricade. The cathedral had been turned into an ammunition dump and some 7,000 men and forty guns, under a new general, Pedro de Ampudia, were well dug-in before Taylor's army appeared out of the desert on September 19.

Two days later his best divisional commander, William Jenkins Worth, attacked from the west, scaling the two fortified hills in an enthusiastic assault. The rest of the army meanwhile made a diversion to the north and east. Worth's attack was flawless; his losses were 32. The diversion grew, for want of clear instructions and firm control, into a full-scale effort over well-prepared killing ground in front of the Citadel. The fort fell, but mainly by a stroke of luck and at a cost of 394 dead and wounded.

Next day both armies rested. On September 23 the Americans fought their way into the town: street fighting all the way—close, intense, terrifying. Night fell on two tired, cold, hungry armies. So did heavy rain. Each held roughly half the town; each was as good as fought out. Ampudia cracked first. He asked for terms. Taylor demanded unconditional surrender, before granting an armistice for a minimum of eight weeks. The Mexicans were allowed to retain their side arms, their personal baggage and six artillery pieces, with ammunition, to fight off attacks by the Kiowas and Comanches.

Such generosity outraged Taylor's soldiers. Polk scribbled hotly in his diary that the general had no authority to grant armistices, and sent explicit, firm instructions that Taylor was to remain right where he was and not go chasing Mexican armies around Mexico. With firm views of his own on civilian control, Taylor marched on, to Saltillo, twenty-five miles down the road.

Back in Washington, Scott looked on Taylor's movements with mixed feelings—pride in the success of American arms, irritation at the failure to turn victories into peace. As general-in-chief, Scott ordered him to remain in Saltillo. It was evident by now that only the capture of Mexico City would end the war, and a campaign like that was probably beyond Taylor's generalship.

His pride wounded, Taylor ignored Scott's order and set off for Victoria, 150 miles south of Saltillo. At Victoria he assembled an army of 5,500 men, and secured nothing but supply problems for himself.

Polk was looking for a short war. That mean quick, total victories. Taylor had failed him, and developed political ambitions. "To conquer a peace," as he put it, Polk was forced, with evident loathing, to turn to Scott. It was not only that Scott was a Whig but was, the president informed his diary, "a visionary . . . of scientific views." He read too much. For a time Polk had a plan to make Senator Benton a lieutenant general. He had never commanded an army, but what of that? Congress declined to share the presidential fantasy. Scott it would have to be.

A project was drawn up to land an army under Scott at Veracruz, march it inland and capture Mexico City. Attempting to reach the capital from the north was out of the question: too much desert to cross. Instructions were sent to Taylor to release most of his regulars and some of his better volunteers to join the invasion force. A list of the units involved fell into Mexican hands. The logical assumption made ever since is that this list reached Santa Anna, who was at that moment creating a new Mexican army—the Army of Liberation. And as Taylor gravitated back toward Saltillo, with little interest in the war now that the baton had passed to Scott, that new army was coming after him.

It was the biggest decision Santa Anna ever had to make, and he got it wrong. Taylor was no threat to Mexico City. Scott was. To have created a new army of 20,000 men was an achievement, but half of it was absolutely green. By waiting seven or eight weeks for Scott, Santa Anna would have had time to train them. If the landing had been defeated there would have been no chance of the Americans conquering a peace, in which case Taylor's army would have nothing to do but quit Mexico.

When Taylor reached La Encantada, roughly twenty miles south of Saltillo, he linked up with his second-in-command, John Wool. Their combined forces came to 4,800 men. He was all for fighting there; he usually was, wherever it happened to be. Wool, after a furious argument in which, to his deep shame, he actually blasphemed, got the army pulled back more than ten miles to a better place. There was a ranch called San Juan de la Buena Vista, six miles from Saltillo, at a place called La Angostura, or The Narrows.

Seventeen Texas Rangers meanwhile located Santa Anna's army, rode into its encampment, counted the fires, from that estimated its strength exactly, rode out again in the morning and reported to Taylor. Santa Anna, in a vain hope of taking Taylor's retreating army by surprise, marched his main force forty-five miles in less than twenty-four hours; no time to eat, almost none to rest.

At Buena Vista the road ran between steep mountain ranges. On the American right the mountainside came almost to the road, ending in a maze of deep gullies. To the left were three long ravines with steep sides at right angles to the road, running back two miles or more to the foot of the other range of mountains. Imagine a hand, the fingers slightly apart: the spaces represent the ravines, the fingers (pointing toward the road) are the long narrow plateaus on which Wool posted the bulk of the army and most of its fifteen guns. Lacking maneuver room, the Mexicans found it impossible to get more than half of their army into battle at the same time. And Wool blocked the narrow road with wagonloads of boulders.

Santa Anna would rather have fought almost anywhere else but here, yet he dared not pull back for fear of losing his army. Half of his cavalry, some 2,500 horsemen under General Juan Miñon, rode off to make a wide circling movement and threaten Saltillo, where Taylor was. Other Mexican units worked their way around the American left and into the foothills of the mountains there.

On February 23 Santa Anna launched a massive assault against the American left center, sending infantry divisions down into the ravines. As they emerged, the American artillery cut them down with canister and grape. At times the gunners scooped up handfuls of stones at their feet and threw them in with the ammunition. Grape and canister used close-in like this were the machine guns of the Mexican War. When this ammunition began to run low the gunners double-shotted their pieces with a single charge of powder. The solid shot, colliding in the barrel, shattered, spraying metal in a wide arc.

The pressure on the American left center almost broke it. A few guns alone made it possible to pull back and re-form the American line. Farther left, by the mountains, the Mexicans got the upper hand. Taylor hurried out from Saltillo with fresh troops. Jefferson Davis, one of those West Pointers who had resigned his commission, recently elected to command the Mississippi Rifles, brought his men at the double. They made quite a sight in their uniforms of black slouch hats, white duck pants and red shirts hanging out. A Gilbert and Sullivan regiment. They advanced to link up with the 3rd Indiana while, to their front, more than 2,000 Mexican lancers in blue uniforms with red facings prepared to charge.

Regulars would have formed square. Volunteers had trouble forming a decent line. So they made a V instead; wide, inviting, opening toward the foe. The Mexicans worked up to a trot but just when they should have picked up to a gallop, they slowed to a walk. This V was the most peculiar thing any cavalry officer had seen. They were deep inside it, trying to decide what it meant.

That was when the Mississippians forming one leg and the Hoosiers forming the other shouldered their rifles and opened fire. Their cross fire riddled the bemused lancers. Horses plunged to their knees. Riders fell to earth under a cloud of bright plumes. Davis's troops rushed forward, drawing eighteen-inch bowie knives, to fall on the Mexicans, hacking and thrusting.

Narrowly, narrowly, every attack was beaten back. Miñon's cavalry was driven off on the outskirts of Saltillo. Desperate hand-to-hand fighting roiled the ravines. A furious brief storm broke, to be followed by a dazzling rainbow. A ruse with a white flag extricated the trapped Mexican lancers. Once they were free, the rest of their army pulled back. By nightfall only the fitful booming of artillery expressed hostile intent.

Nearly 700 of Taylor's men, roughly 15 percent of his army, were dead or wounded. Another thousand or so were scattered far and wide, with no intention of fighting again. Wool advised Taylor to pull back. Advice wasted. The remaining Americans slept on their arms through the long, bitter coldness of a February night in the mountains. When morning broke, they rose to give battle again. Santa Anna was gone. His campfires still glowed. Round about were nearly 2,000 dead or wounded Mexicans. Thousands more had deserted him. Wool and Taylor then did something extraordinary. They burst into tears and fell into each other's arms.

Even after Buena Vista opinion was split. Credit for the good moves here and elsewhere was generally given to Taylor's officers; he was credited only with the costly mistakes. Worth expressed the opinion of many of his officers when he called the army in northern Mexico "a huge body without a head." No imagination, no brains. In most armies simply winning against four-to-one odds might have been considered enough. This one—permeated by the spirit of Scott, West Point and professional pride—expected something better than victory alone.

Such criticism cut little ice with the volunteers. Taylor was exactly the kind of general they were happy to fight for. Getting men to fight well is among the greatest challenges of military leadership. Few of the troops at Buena Vista had ever been in battle before. Drawing such a performance from raw units was good generalship in itself, however clumsy his tactics may have been.

For the Mexicans, so confident about going to war, it was never bright morning again. The Mexican army spent the rest of the war on the defensive. The hopes of foreign aid vanished. Had Santa Anna won, it would probably have been a Mexican Saratoga.

In ten months Taylor's army altered forever Mexico's idea of itself and the world's idea of Mexico. Mexican pride never recovered. It was not only militarily that Mexico was forced onto the defensive. Henceforth Mexican nationalism and anti-Americanism would amount to much the same thing. Anyone who doubts that need only visit the Museum of Intervention in Mexico City, which thrives to this day. Most of the exhibits date from 1846 to 1847.

For Taylor the war was over. Nothing short of death could prevent him from succeeding Polk. Winning a peace was now up to Scott.

IN OCTOBER 1842 the commander of the Pacific Squadron, Commodore Thomas ap Catesby Jones, of Lake Borgne gunboat fame, acting on a rumor of war, sailed into Monterey, forced the Mexican garrison to surrender, ran up the American flag and claimed California for the United States. The rumor was false. The flag was run back down. Jones took a red-faced retirement.

Spanish rule in Mexico had left a heritage of shaky foundations. It was rule based almost entirely on the conquest of the Indian population. In time it was overthrown because it was chaotic, ineffective and despotic. Soon, though, exactly the same arguments were raised by the American and Mexican settlers of California, New Mexico and Texas against Mexican rule. There was still no public opinion that government appealed to nor was there any mechanism for peaceful political change.

In 1836, following the Centralist victory in the civil war, the Mexican population of California revolted. The army sent to chastise them was forced to withdraw. They revolted yet again, in 1845. No one ruled California, least of all the Mexican government.

That same year also saw the start of Frémont's third expedition. This time he had instructions to explore the Southwest, where maps were abysmal and tensions rising. Entirely on his inclination he took the men and equipment provided by the army and set off for the Pacific Northwest.

From Oregon he moved south into California again, expecting that the next news he heard might be that war had begun. Frémont thrust himself to the center of events on no authority but his craving for fame.

He arrived in California as a revolt of American settlers broke out at Sonoma in June 1846, two months after war was declared. Fifty armed men ran up some homemade heraldry: a brown patch that, if you squinted at it, might pass for a grizzly bear, a stripe made from a bit of bright ribbon, and the Lone Star of Texas. Under this flag they skirmished with a small force of Mexican troops, driving them off. Placing himself at the head of the Bear Flag rebels, Frémont led them on to occupy the empty fort at the village of San Francisco.

Meanwhile Commodore John Sloat, commanding the eight ships of the Pacific Squadron, took Monterey without a fight and without orders. He sailed up the coast to join Frémont at San Francisco but his health was fading rapidly. He was soon replaced by Robert Stockton, a vain, energetic officer with a towering temper and a heart set on glory.

With northern California secure Stockton set about taking the rest of the state. He put a small garrison into Santa Barbara. At San Pedro he landed 360 men armed with whatever they could lay their hands on—pistols, cutlasses, boarding pikes—and four small artillery pieces.

By the end of August 1846 he had started a newspaper, organized a school system and scheduled elections. Everything seemed under control, and all without bloodshed. Heading toward him was Brigadier General Stephen Watts Kearny.

Shortly after the war began, Kearny, the commander of the 1st Dragoons, left Fort Leavenworth, leading out the "Army of the West"—some 1,700 men plus sixteen guns. His orders were to capture New Mexico. Once it fell to him, he was to proceed to California and take command there.

The eighty thousand people of New Mexico had grown dependent on American trade. There was therefore little willingness to fight. Three thousand Mexican troops assembled by the governor occupied a strong defensive position along Kearny's line of march but pulled out when combat seemed imminent.

Once Kearny reached the village of Las Vegas, he climbed onto a rooftop to offer something no Spanish or Mexican governor had ever promised: protection against the fierce Kiowas and Comanches. There was rejoicing, although it would take thirty years to make good the promise. As the excitement died down, Kearny raised his right hand and proceeded to administer a loyalty oath en masse.

When he got to Santa Fe, he wrote a constitution for New Mexico with the help of two lawyers, Private Willard Hall and Colonel Alexander W. Doniphan. Much of it governs the state to this day even though Congress later decided Kearny had no power to make laws (or confer citizenship).

Having conquered an area the size of France without firing a shot, he split up his army. Doniphan led the 900 men of the Missouri Mounted Volunteers south, hoping to link up with Wool. They never did, but their journey to Reynosa on the Gulf coast and back to Missouri was one of the most remarkable feats of the war. From hearth to hearth they covered five thousand miles in a year, fought two battles against heavy odds, and won both, and in those twelve months were never paid or supplied by the government.

Colonel Philip St. George Cooke was entrusted with the 400-man Mormon Battalion. The Mormon leaders had welcomed the war. It meant that Zion would be part of America, not Mexico. It also meant they could enroll young Mormons in the army and with their U.S. government paychecks finance the creation of Zion, somewhere out in the desert. Brigham Young personally blessed them, swearing as a prophet that none would die at the enemy's hand: in their special Mormon underwear no bullet could harm them.

The Mormon Battalion was not a combat unit. It was a supply train, sent to cut a road to San Diego. With a secure, year-round road linking it to the east, California gained would become California defended. Down that road there soon would follow tens of thousands of settlers and gold seekers, to be followed by the overland mail and, in time, the Southern Pacific.

Kearny left 300 men to hold New Mexico. Taking 100 dragoons and two howitzers, he headed west to join Stockton. On December 6, 1846, at an Indian village named San Pascual, forty miles southeast of Los Angeles, his troops saw action at last.

They collided with a Mexican force led by Andres Pico, brother of Pio Pico, the last Mexican governor of California. The Americans charged. They had no plan. There was simply a wild rush at the enemy,

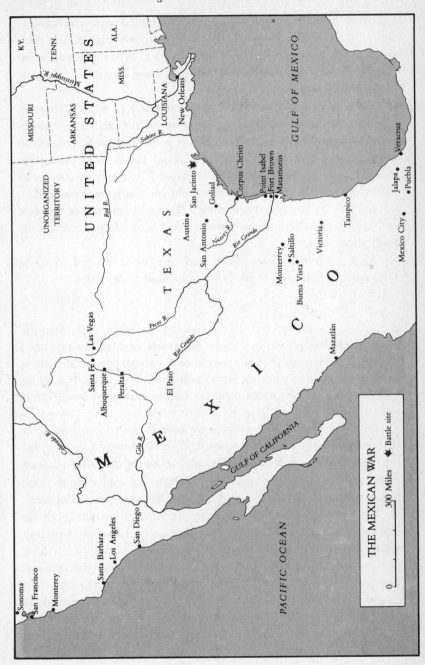

THE MEXICAN WAR

★ Battle site

0   300 Miles

led by the horsemen in front. The Mexicans pulled back. The momentum of the charging dragoons carried them on, leaving the main body behind. The Mexicans suddenly turned about. What followed was a hand-to-hand fight in which 18 Americans and two Mexicans were killed to no purpose.

On January 8, 1847, at San Juan Capistrano, Kearny and Stockton, leading a heterogeneous force of dragoons, sailors and marines, prepared to fight the last battle for California. A Mexican force took up position at a crossing of the San Gabriel River. The Americans charged, shouting, "Remember New Orleans!" It was thirty-two years to the day. The Mexicans ran. The fight for California was over.

On January 19 a revolt broke out in Taos, challenging the conquest of New Mexico. Within three weeks it had been stamped out and the ringleaders hanged.

Mexican rule between Texas and the Pacific proved to be as substantial as cobwebs. Gestures brought most of it down.

AS TAYLOR moved out of the limelight another larger-than-life figure, Scott, sailed into it. Despite brave talk of Mexican privateers challenging shipping, the Gulf proved an American lake for the whole of the war. The fleet carrying Scott's army to Tampico, and from there to Veracruz, faced no threat from the enemy during the whole of its long voyage.

Like Washington, he expected his officers not to get drunk, not to gamble and not to chase women. Unlike Washington, he expected them to be men of high culture. He had years before dismissed a captain from the messroom, apologizing to a visitor, "I am ashamed to think that a member of my staff should confuse Dryden with Shakespeare."

His style of action, his towering appearance, but above all his character had an appeal among his fellow officers that no American soldier after him ever quite matched. Grant was but one of hundreds of West Point cadets who, having seen him, became Scott men for life. The admiration was mutual. He adored the cadets.

Scott also identified himself with the professional interests of junior officers. As the artillery developed into the most modern branch of the service, he wrote the manual (just as he had written the infantry manual), with typical thoroughness. He covered everything, down to the position of a gunner's fingernails while loading and firing.

For a long time he was a presidential troubleshooter. When war looked imminent with Britain in 1837 after Canadian militia attacked an American steamship, killing one man and destroying the boat, Scott was sent to defuse the crisis.

Yet it was the vagaries of politics more than his undoubted abilities as a general and a diplomat that put him in charge of the Veracruz expedition. There was no keeping party politics out of the war: Polk foisted eight generals on the army straight from civilian life; "deserving Democrats" all. Especially Gideon J. Pillow, the president's former law partner, known to the troops as "Polk's Spy" and, once the bullets flew, someone who cowered.

This landing was the most ambitious operation of its kind before the Second World War. It had Scott's fingerprints all over it. He conjured up specially constructed landing craft, or "surf boats." They were built in sets of three, roughly forty feet long, twelve feet wide and pointed at both ends. Like Russian dolls one would fit inside another, and a third inside that. They were towed in formation behind the troop transports. Off the coast of Veracruz they were combat-loaded with men and supplies: what went in last came out first. Crews of sailors rowed them toward the beach in midafternoon, March 9, 1847.

None of which surprised the Mexicans. Scott's plan of campaign had been entertaining the newspaper readers of both countries while he was at sea. Fortunately for the invasion force Santa Anna's army had been shattered at Buena Vista, and in Mexico City a revolt was currently under way. No one was in control of government or defense.

Scott's vulnerable first wave of 2,600 men crunched ashore unopposed as the sun went down. Half a dozen guns and a few hundred lancers bursting from behind the dunes might have stopped them, but from Veracruz, four miles up the beach and garrisoned by 4,400 soldiers, there came—nothing.

The city was defended on the landside by nine forts. Looming over the harbor was the massive stone fortress of San Juan de Ulúa. Veracruz was the most heavily fortified spot in the Western Hemisphere. Scott had to take it. He put all his bets on firepower.

Lundy's Lane had had a sobering effect on him. It left him with a loathing of frontal assaults. At Veracruz he borrowed extra guns and gunners from the navy. A shell was lobbed into the city every twenty seconds around the clock. After eighteen days and nights of this relentless pounding, it surrendered. American casualties were less than 100. He could now move inland, as Cortés had done in 1519, taking the road Cortés's men had cut to Mexico City.

The campaign he waged over the next five months was pre-Napoleonic in its reasonableness of means and objectives. He was not interested in battles of annihilation. Better to avoid humiliating the Mexicans and stirring the country into a fight for national survival. He attended Catholic masses. Troops were ordered to respect priests and churches. Deep in a Catholic country he dreaded anything that might set off a guerrilla war as the French had done in Spain and, sixteen years on from this war, would do in Mexico.

He had complete confidence in his regulars. The problem was what he called "the wild volunteers." They swaggered in the names they gave themselves: "Killers" or "Gunmen." They dressed up in fancy uniforms of green and white or some other easy-to-shoot-at combination. Some wore three-cornered hats and hip boots of red morocco. Some dressed like Continentals, others like Napoleon's Old Guard. Anything but like a regular, Model 1847.

They fought, but mostly they died. In Taylor's army disease carried off so many the birds along the Rio Grande were reportedly warbling the dead march. One of the rising young stars with Scott, a captain of engineers named George B. McClellan, loathed volunteers: "I have seen more suffering here than I could have imagined to exist. They literally die like dogs. . . ." Among the regulars there was something like proper hygiene, and the discipline to enforce it. Even so, that did not stop many of them from coming down with the ailment most common to Americans in Mexico. One band of sufferers organized themselves as the 1st Diarrhea Rangers.

The rubber man of the century, Santa Anna, bounced back yet again. By the end of March 1847 he had traveled a thousand miles or more, formed a new government, raised money to pay the army and buy supplies, and prepared to oppose Scott's advance at a place called Cerro Gordo, fifty miles from the coast. It looked like Buena Vista all over again, but this time with Santa Anna victorious: a narrow road, dropping sharply away on one side while steep mountains rose on the other. He put artillery on the overlooking peaks. Twelve thousand infantry dug in along the road and around the gun positions. This time he waited; let the Yanquis attack.

Another rising star of the engineers, Captain Robert E. Lee, who was in effect Scott's chief of staff, blazed a precarious trail into the Mexican rear. Artillery—twenty-four-pounders, that is—was taken apart and dragged up slopes and along a scratch of a trail that a goat might have shunned. It was a feat to rank with Napoleon's getting guns over the Great St. Bernard Pass in winter.

On April 18 the Mexicans, attacked in front and rear almost at the same time, panicked. They pulled out so quickly that only 3,000 fell into American hands. The rest vanished into the mountains. Santa Anna's estate nearby was turned over for souvenirs. The 4th Illinois came away flourishing a wooden leg: Santa Anna's spare! It went on display in the state capitol at Springfield until the 1920s. Imitations circulated as freely as splinters of the True Cross in the Middle Ages. Scott's jubilant army swung down the road singing lustily, "The *Leg* I Left Behind Me. . . ."

From the next town, Jalapa, Scott sent back 3,000 volunteers whose enlistments were soon to expire. After moving farther inland, to Puebla, he awaited reinforcements. By August his strength had risen to 14,000 men.

Taking 10,000, he set off once more, this time cutting regular links with the base at Veracruz. To bring his army back he must take Mexico City and force the government to sue for peace. Between him and the sea he held nothing but Puebla. The small garrison there was besieged for weeks.

No fresh infusions of troops and supplies could reach him, but messages still got through. He used Texas Rangers as couriers and hired Mexican bandits to suppress the guerrilla threat. "Woe to the unfortunate soldier who straggled behind," wrote Sam Chamberlain. "He was lassoed, stripped naked, and dragged through clumps of cactus . . . then, his privates cut off and crammed in his mouth, he was left to die. . . . Such were the daily acts of the Guerillars."

In and around Mexico City some 30,000 Mexican soldiers prepared to fight Scott's army. The city looked impregnable. Rising above the marshes left by huge lakes, it was almost an island. Long stone causeways reached out from it over the swampy land, each one of them easy to block. The army must get onto the causeways, but the approaches to these were made narrow and difficult by what remained of the lakes.

Scott, refusing frontal assaults, outflanked one position after another until he reached the vast, forbidding lava bed called the Pedregal to the southeast of Mexico City. Here the egregious Pillow (he had disobeyed orders at Cerro Gordo and taken his men the wrong way, getting them badly shot up) blundered again. Chasing the shadow of personal glory, he put his division between two Mexican armies. He escaped with help from a regular, Persifor Smith, and Santa Anna, who pulled one Mexican army back. Smith sent part of his division into the rear of the remaining army, at Contreras, and they charged at first light on August 20. The battle that ensued is usually described as lasting seventeen minutes. The actual fighting was over in five.

The drug called invincibility—delicious, dangerous—rushed the army on, after fleeing Mexicans, toward the hamlet of Churubusco. Scott, exultant, cried, "Make haste, my sons!" Waiting for them was a convent filled with Mexican militia behind thick walls and a bridge-head where a blocking force was dug in with artillery. The pursuit flowed on, a torrent of emotion. No one stopped to ask if it was taking the right road.

Scott had briefly lost control at Cerro Gordo and on the Pedregal. At the Churubusco bridgehead he nearly lost the war.

Two frontal assaults failed, at daunting cost. The units that fell back were among the best infantry companies in the army. Like the step back of the Imperial Guard at Waterloo it spread fear among other troops. Happily Scott was still Scott. Already there were other units turning the position, to threaten it from behind. As some Mexicans faced about to deal with them, a third assault overran the convent and the bridgehead in a hand-to-hand fight.

Scott had missed his best chance of winning the war. Using the good open roads available, he could have placed himself between the city and Santa Anna's disorganized, demoralized army, forcing them to fight in the open or surrender. Instead, the Americans had taken 1,000 casualties to cross a stream.

Santa Anna asked for an armistice. Scott granted it. It lasted sixteen days. The Mexicans used it to pull back toward the city and build formidable defenses on the causeways and under the city walls. That done, they declared the armistice over.

On September 8 the advance on the city was renewed. Scott's objective was the Molino del Rey, or King's Mill, where, report said, church bells were being recast as cannon. Worth, entrusted with the assault, dispensed with the scheduled artillery bombardment.

The mill was a fortress, not because it was a gun foundry but because it was a major grain store for the city. Worth's troops, formed in column as per the book, ran straight into a Mexican division concealed in a ditch and supported by four guns. This had to be cleared before the main structure, the Casa Mata, could be attacked. At a cost of 706 dead and wounded Worth won the most hollow victory of the war.

Less than a mile away loomed the hill of Chapultepec. Crowning it was a summer palace, since transformed into the Mexican military academy. Despite its losses the army was eager to press on and take it. Not Scott. Not after Churubusco, not after this empty mill. He called a halt.

Five days later Chapultepec was shaken by a furious cannonade. The assault that followed still met a wall of bullets and flame, yet the fighting was over in ninety minutes. Pillow was bruised in the foot by a spent ball, which he described as being "at the very Cannon's mouth, where I was cut down."

From Chapultepec Scott's plan was for the army to move north at once, then make the final assault on the city from due west, along the San Cosme causeway. One of his mustang (*i.e.*, political) generals, John Quitman of Mississippi, had other ideas; much, admittedly, like Pillow's ideas. It seemed to Quitman that other people were grabbing undeservedly large slices of glory pie.

Up the Belén causeway he dashed, making his own assault, from the southwest, to jubilant shouts of "Quitman's division to the city!" At the gateway, or *garita,* where the causeway reached the walls, the Mexicans fought his troops to a standstill. Every member of his staff was killed or wounded. The Americans huddled in knots, almost out of ammunition.

It was Worth's division, coming down the San Cosme causeway, that got into the city. As street fighting raged below, Lieutenant Grant got a mountain howitzer up into a church belfry. He began lobbing shells into surrounding plazas and streets.

That night Santa Anna pulled out of Mexico City, knowing he could not hold it another day. Scott had won. At noon he galloped into the plaza in front of the great cathedral, escorted by dragoons and looking the epitome of the conquering general. Yet it was with Nicholas Trist of the Department of State that Mexico now had to deal.

Trist was a man who wore a face as somber as his name. At first Scott had resented his presence with the army, regarding him as yet another of Polk's spies. On the long march from the coast, however, the two men become close friends.

As a graduate of West Point and a fluent Spanish speaker, Trist was ideally qualified for his mission, yet even before he reached Mexico City the president fired him. No one kept the sickly, cantankerous Polk happy for long. With peace within reach, Trist ignored the message telling him to return to Washington at once. Vested with no authority whatever, he negotiated the peace his friend Scott had won. The Senate in time ratified the treaty. The president showed his gratitude by forcing Trist out of the State Department.

Scott's career was virtually over. Polk shelved him. The general found it more congenial to live in New York, instead of in Washington, and to spend up to half of each year abroad. He remained general-in-chief, while commanding next to nothing in fact.

MEXICO introduced American soldiers to the mustache, the *cigaritto* and chewing gum. It was the first steamboat war, the first telegraph war, and it saw the first widespread use of anesthetics, thanks to army doctors. And a new breed of scribbler emerged from the conflict, the modern war correspondent, sending eyewitness dispatches from the front lines by wire.

For a small war it had been inordinately expensive in lives lost. Some 1,700 men were killed in action or died of wounds. The wounded in action came to 4,100. What made it expensive was the 11,000 who died of disease in a war in which 116,000 men served, making a death toll of 11 percent.

Scott's campaign was one of the most brilliant in all military history. He made mistakes. On four occasions he lost effective control over his army. No one, it must be said, could have controlled egomaniacs like Quitman and Pillow, who were thrust on him by the president. Grant really had the last word when he said of Mexico, "Scott's successes are the answer to all criticisms."

The war was the proving ground of the professionals, yet it also showed that volunteers could and would fight well, something no one expected from the common militia. It gave the regulars a glimpse of the future: large numbers of men could be recruited in wartime, trained by professional soldiers and led forward under fire.

As the future beckoned, an old favorite waved farewell. The

smoothbore musket's day was ending, after two hundred years. The Mexican War was fought mainly with artillery and bayonets. It was the last conflict in which the smoothbore musket was the standard infantry weapon. It was too inaccurate for a modern fire and movement army.

Among older officers such as Taylor the first article of faith was what it had always been: in the assault, give 'em Old Betsy. Younger officers such as Grant, though, had grasped the point made by the artillery. Firepower was greater than courage. It was no longer a tool of warfare; it was *the* tool of warfare.

The country's territory had increased by a third, but the immediate benefits were hard to see, except perhaps for the gold of California, coming glittering into the light in 1848. Even while the war was on, people hurried west in hopes of finding something out there. Despite the sand, despite the risk of having one's scalp lifted by the Apaches or the Comanches, it was where the action was, the place to be.

Resistance to Manifest Destiny destroyed the popularity of the Whig party. Opposition to the Mexican War killed it off.

Slavery was not the main itch behind Manifest Destiny, nor was greedy land-grabbing, even though expressions of both were easy to find. The vast majority of people owned no slaves. Nor would any but a minority profit economically from the Mexican conquests.

Expansionism sprang from that most compelling of human desires, the search for security. For centuries nation-states had sought to satisfy that need through "natural frontiers." Mountain chains, broad rivers, oceans and seas were part of a territorial imperative that governed the lives of nations. In some parts of the world it governs them still.

The United States had felt profoundly insecure ever since the Revolution. That changed once it held the Pacific Coast on its western flank and possessed a boundary in the Southwest marked by the Rio Grande and burning deserts. In acquiring nearly half of Mexico it also eliminated a possible future rival for supremacy in North America.

No American government, Whig or Democratic, could ignore the craving for security. And once the shooting stopped and the ink was dry on the peace treaty, the arguments over expansion stopped. Not even the fiercest Whig critics of the war argued that what had been won from Mexico ought to be given back.

What remained was a rising tide of anger over slavery. The new territories were unsuited to it, but the slavery debate now dominated

American life and poisoned its politics. "Poisoned" not because the issue didn't matter—it did—but the spirit of compromise and moderation was dead or dying.

In France there are signs at the railroad crossings that caution motorists, UN TRAIN PEUT EN CACHER UN AUTRE, "One train may be hiding another one." The Mexican War was like that. Behind it another conflict—much bigger, much deadlier—was thundering down the track.

7

TRIPLE
REVOLUTION

NEW MILITARY ROADS snaked across the open land-
scapes of the West. Down them—vanishing in winter in rivers
of mud, disappearing in summer in choking clouds of dust—went
settlers and gold hunters. More than fifty forts arose: one day towns,
someday cities.

Government spending turned the wilderness into a cash economy.
The army spread fertilizing money all over the land. In Texas military
surveyors and work crews made the rivers deep and navigable far into
the heart of the state, linking the southwestern acquisitions with the
waters of the Gulf and, beyond them, the world. New rivers and roads,
new bridges and dams, new forts and canals built up the power of the
federal government, promoted feelings of nationalism, trained hundreds of army officers and NCOs in fighting, in engineering, in leadership.

In the 1850s the army doubled in size. Its strength rose to 16,000
officers and men. Too little, all the same, to meet the military challenge
of the new frontier. Some of the infantry climbed onto mules, to
Scott's disgust, as cut-price cavalry. The experiment failed. So did an
attempt to tame the Southwest with camels. In 1855 the dragoons were
enlarged and that same year two cavalry regiments were created.

The Indian-fighting army discovered its own way to destroy an
enemy who preferred raiding to battle and hid in huge, empty places:

reprisals. Entire tribes found themselves held responsible for the marauding of a few impetuous braves. It was crude. It was unfair. It worked, for a time.

Soldiers too could start wars. In 1854 a second lieutenant fresh from West Point used artillery on a Brulé Sioux encampment in an attempt to arrest just one brave. The result was an Indian war along the North Platte River. The officer sent to take charge, Colonel William S. Harney, arrived in 1855 with his strategy already formed: "By God, I'm for battle—no peace!" He trampled all over the Indian Bureau as furiously as he crushed the hapless Sioux.

In 1856 another attempt to arrest wayward braves set off yet another war, this time with the Cheyennes, considered the most amenable of all Plains tribes. The newly formed 1st Cavalry scattered a large force of war-painted warriors on the only occasion there was ever anything like a Hollywood-style clash, with mounted Long Knives and Indians charging each other. Before the great collision came, it was the Indians ("finest light cavalry in the world") who broke, pulling up hard on their ponies before turning to flee.

That same year the Rogue River War brought the destruction of hostile Indians along the California-Oregon border. This wretched affair was conducted mainly by volunteer militia, under orders from the governor of California to take no prisoners.

Militia atrocities led to the Yakima Indians declaring war on the United States in a desperate attempt to keep white marauders out of the Oregon Cascades. In 1858 the Yakimas brought to battle a sizable force of regulars armed with the brand-new 1855 Model .58-caliber rifled musket. Out in the remote Pacific Northwest, amid scenery that took men's breath away, the firepower revolution underwent its baptism by combat, at this, the little-known Battle of Four Lakes.

More than 1,000 Yakimas closed confidently on 500 soldiers. The infantrymen coolly began cutting down Indians at half a mile. The Yakimas, well organized, well led, and well armed with smoothbore muskets, never got close enough to shoot. They fell in heaps beneath towering trees, dead, dying and maimed, puzzled and helpless. Not a single solder was harmed.

The Indians tried again, at the Battle of Spokane Plain. It was even worse for them the second time. Mountain howitzers added to the long-range carnage of rifled musketfire. The war was over, the Yakimas broken, the Pacific Northwest secure.

. . .

THESE WERE the kind of tumultuous times when the unthinkable becomes thinkable. Slavery was wrecking the country's political life as surely as cotton had distorted the development of the South, making it aggressive and insecure. Southern economic and political institutions hung by the thread of a single crop; a crop that others could grow, a crop for which there was already a search for substitutes.

The South, unable to manage either transition or decline, was by 1860 talking only to itself as it sought to defend the indefensible, slavery; to deny the undeniable, union. As always, rising passions made mighty the single-issue fanatic: in the North, a John Brown; in the South, an Edmund Ruffin. Both had the hairiness of Old Testament prophets. Both possessed Old Testament imaginations, steeped red in visions of blood.

In October 1859 Colonel Robert E. Lee, on leave at his Arlington home to tend his invalid wife, was summoned to suppress the seizure of Harpers Ferry. John Brown and a handful of followers had tried to capture the arsenal, intending to arm a huge slave revolt. The first person they killed in the name of racial liberation was a free black man.

Lee, commanding 90 marines, retook Harpers Ferry. Brown was badly cut in the head by a dress sword but still fit to hang. From the gallows he prophesied what was by now widely assumed to be inevitable, civil war.

Northerners had little love for blacks but they abominated slavery. As Southerners turned the defense of bondage into threats to secede, the North, responding in the same spirit, turned the denunciation of slavery into a militant nationalism.

It was all too much for James Buchanan, elected president in 1856 as something of a soft option. He was so overwhelmed that, not knowing which way to turn, he hammered together an intellectual box, crawled in and threw away the key.

First he convinced himself that no state had the right to secede. That done, he convinced himself that he had no right to stop them if they chose to depart. Buchanan was a president the South could accept.

Abraham Lincoln, however, could not be accepted for a day or an hour. Elected in November 1860 with only 40 percent of the popular vote, he felt he had not a right but a duty to hold the Union together.

The crystalline clarity of his goal and the steely strength of his will were the foundation of all that followed.

A month after his election, South Carolina passed the Ordinance of Secession. Five other states swiftly followed them out, while a dozen more wavered, debated, jabbed wet fingers in the rising wind. As the country held its breath in unbearable suspense, something moved.

Still guarding Charleston was Fort Moultrie, that ramshackle edifice of Revolutionary times. Over the years sand had piled against its walls, enabling curious cows to scale the ramparts of a major fort. Major Robert Anderson, in command of the harbor defenses, moved his men out to unfinished Fort Sumter days after the Ordinance passed. There he and his soldiers would be entirely surrounded by water. An outraged South Carolina cried out that this move was a wickedly provocative act.

Fort Sumter had its merits but adequate supplies were not among them. In January 1861 Scott tried to come to Anderson's aid by sending a civilian steamboat, the *Star of the West,* from New York to Fort Sumter. The ship was crammed with food and military stores while belowdecks 200 regulars crouched out of sight.

As the *Star of the West* attempted to enter Charleston harbor Confederate gunners fired warning shots. The big guns of Fort Sumter remained silent. Anderson had not been informed that anyone would try to aid him. He looked on, bemused, as the mystery ship turned away.

Lincoln in his inaugural address in March hoped out loud that war might even now be averted. He reassured Southerners, "The government will not assail you. You can have no conflict without being yourselves the aggressors."

The seceding states, risen to eleven, were in no mood to turn back. They had created a congress. It had drafted a constitution. That had not occupied it for long; most of it was taken almost verbatim from that fighting document, the U.S. Constitution. The only major changes were a guarantee of slavery and a limit on the Confederate presidency of a single six-year term.

The president of the Confederate States of America was Jefferson Davis; not popularly elected but chosen by the Confederate Congress meeting in Montgomery, Alabama. Confederates saw in Davis martial qualities that he gloried in possessing. A West Pointer, a hero wounded in the foot at Buena Vista (and often in pain and depressed as a result), secretary of war under Franklin Pierce, chairman of the U.S. Senate Military Affairs Committee, he was another of the many figures of the age who measured his height by Napoleon's shadow. Few of those who chose him at Montgomery even knew him, and no man knew him well; only a woman could claim that, his wife, Varina.

In February 1861 the Confederate Congress voted to create an army of 100,000 volunteers enlisted for a year. By mid-April nearly 70,000 had been enrolled and armed. The South felt able to fight. The North felt able to hope.

Scott prepared a report for the new president. The South, he informed Lincoln, could be conquered, provided the Union found a young and talented general (a "Wolfe, a Desaix or a Hoche") and raised an army of 300,000 long-term, well-trained troops. The task of conquest would take three years. The cost would run into hundreds of millions of dollars. From the outset Lincoln knew the scale of the struggle ahead.

Still hoping, he essayed a cautious opening move. On April 6 the governor of South Carolina was informed that fresh food supplies were being sent to Anderson. The Confederate government was thrown into confusion. Not Davis. He ordered that the fort be seized.

Brigadier General Pierre Gustave Toutant Beauregard, a swarthy Creole who had served brilliantly in the artillery during the Mexican War, politely requested Anderson, his former gunnery instructor at West Point, to surrender. Anderson refused, with equal courtesy.

Shortly before dawn on April 12 the Confederate batteries at Charleston opened up. The famous "Fire Eater," Edmund Ruffin, a sixty-seven-year-old agricultural expert with a mane of white hair that flowed over his shoulders, was credited with firing the first shot. True, he yanked on the lanyard of the first columbiad that fired but already mortar shells were making bright arcs in the lightening sky.

The people of Charleston climbed onto their roofs. Doorways were crowded, windows were open and jammed. There had been no spectacle to match it since Fort McHenry, or perhaps since Bunker Hill. Through forty hours the bombardment thundered on. At the battered fort there were fires everywhere, threatening to blow up the magazine.

Anderson ran out of material to make powder bags and keep his guns working. His food supply was down to some dubious "rusty" pork. He at last offered to surrender. Surprised, the Confederates accepted. No one had been killed. Beauregard, looking around his conquest, remarked that he could have held it with his staff.

The South had won its cheapest victory. And its most expensive.

EAST OF the Mississippi the army had less than 4,000 men. Many were commanded by officers soon to be measured for Confederate gray. No one as yet saw that while 300 of the 1,100 army officers would resign to serve the South, nearly every enlisted man and NCO would remain true to his oath.

The great prize, Washington, half expected to wake one morning to find itself taken, either by assault from without or a coup from within. That danger troubled Lincoln like pressure on a nerve. Twenty-four hours after Fort Sumter fell he summoned 75,000 volunteer militia. They were to serve for the traditional militia term, three months: a stopgap to save a capital, not an army to win a war.

Within days the District filled with men in arms. States ebulliently exceeded their quotas. Nearly 93,000 troops were provided; enough to hold Washington, Fort Monroe and secession-minded Maryland; enough to do what they were meant to do.

Nevertheless Harpers Ferry fell, on April 18. As 3,000 Confederates marched on it the handful of Union troops guarding the armory set fires everywhere. Rifles and muskets, their stocks broken, were thrown into the flames. In the intense heat barrels warped. All around, in the musket factory and the rifle works, stood much of the world's most advanced arms-making machinery; unharmed, unconsidered. Dismantled and shipped to Richmond, it armed Confederate soldiers throughout the war.

Lincoln proclaimed a blockade of Southern coasts and ports. He grasped the importance of the sea to the Confederacy long before the Confederates did. In an hour he had reversed an American policy on freedom of the seas nearly seventy years old.

On May 3 he doubled the size of the navy, increased the size of the regular army to 22,000 men and called for 42,000 volunteers to serve for three years. He tapped the high tide of patriotism long before it began to ebb. He showed how big he expected the war to be not in the numbers he called for but in the numbers he accepted. After 42,000 volunteers had been enrolled no one shut the door. In all, some

230,000 volunteers were taken under this May 3 call. They were to prove the bedrock on which all Union armies were created.

Lincoln had no clear constitutional authority to do this or to increase the size of the regular army and navy. He spent millions of dollars without congressional authority, in open disregard of the Constitution. Nor had he any qualms about suspending habeas corpus.

In this apocalyptic hour Lincoln had penetrated the secret of the Constitution: far from tying the hands of the president, it gave him, in time of war, all the powers he would need.

Yet that secret, so obvious to him, might be less so to Congress, ever jealous of its own place. He chose to let events do their educational work. Instead of calling Congress back quickly in the hour of crisis he told it, in effect, not to hurry. He did not want it back until July 4. By which time congressmen found the country had acquired the biggest army in its history and was on the verge of a mighty battle, on which everything might hang.

Eventually Congress and the Supreme Court would acquiesce in all that Lincoln had done. They would confer authority retrospectively that they might never have been so ready to grant before the event. The life-or-death struggle seemed to justify his reading of the Constitution's deepest meaning, or at least made denying it fatal.

There was by July 1861 a desire for battle. The officers of both armies had breathed the same spirit all their professional lives—the spirit of the offensive. After Mexico it could hardly be otherwise, with them or the nation at large. In these early days everyone—soldiers, politicians, ordinary people—saw vividly the shape the Civil War would take: two armies would march out, clash in a stupendous fight in the open field; the winning army would then march on to take the other's capital and conquer a peace. Just like Mexico.

The old general-in-chief knew better. So did another voracious reader and deep thinker, William Tecumseh Sherman. So, it is likely, did Lincoln. When news arrived early in July that Confederates were massing at Manassas Junction, an important railroad center in northern Virginia, Scott was deeply unimpressed. The enemy were only twenty-five miles away, he advised the president, but in no condition to attack. He rather wished they would try it. It would be easy to defeat them.

Lincoln and the Cabinet had their gaze fixed on a broader horizon than mere numbers, firepower, mobility, tactics. What they were looking at was public opinion. The country bellowed for battle. So did the ninety-day militia. If this phony war went on much longer, public support might collapse. The instant army he had summoned might not amount to much in the eyes of men like Scott, he conceded, but the rebels would not be any better.

The president exuded the spirit of the offensive deeply for a peaceable man. He knew what he wanted—a Napoleon, someone eager and able to destroy the enemy in the open field. The search for his Napoleon would take Lincoln several years. For now, the most Napoleonic figure in an American uniform was Irvin McDowell, recently a major but rocketed up in the hour of need to a shoulder-strap star. McDowell spoke French fluently, had lived for years in France to study French methods of warfare, and cultivated a resemblance to Napoleon III. He had served creditably in Mexico but had never commanded even a company in battle. Suddenly he was entrusted with an army of 35,000 men and told to go out and fight.

On July 16 he set off, cautiously, from Alexandria. He moved slowly toward Manassas, fearful of "masked batteries"—camouflaged artillery. that is—reported to be the Confederates' most devastating weapon. A second Union army, this one 16,000 strong, was operating fifty miles west of him, under Robert Patterson. It had retaken Harpers Ferry and was assigned to pin down a Confederate army of 12,000 men in the Shenandoah Valley under Joseph E. Johnston. Patterson was expected to prevent Johnston from either threatening Washington or reinforcing the Confederates at Manassas Junction.

At and around the railroad center Beauregard had assembled 22,000 men, whom he called "The Army of the Potomac." He was outnumbered by McDowell, as Johnston was outnumbered by Patterson. Yet Beauregard and Johnston held the east–west railroad line. They could use it to come to each other's support within hours. McDowell and Patterson, lacking a rail link, were two days apart.

As McDowell's army crawled over the peaceful hills of northern Virginia toward him, Beauregard grew anxious. Like McDowell he had never commanded an army before. He had the advantage, though, of knowing McDowell's strength and line of advance, thanks to Southern spies and Northern newspapers. He sent an urgent telegram to Davis, demanding reinforcements. These could only come from Johnston and the army in the Shenandoah Valley.

Patterson, receiving messages from Scott, under whom he had led a division in Mexico, was unsure whether he was expected to attack Johnston's army or merely to keep it pinned down by threatening attack. Unable to decide, he did neither.

McDowell's troops were meanwhile having a good time. There were the usual spells typical of all armies known as "hurry up and wait." The sun almost directly overhead at noon bathed men in rivulets of sweat beneath coarse woolen uniforms. They marched only five miles a day, with frequent stops to pick the plump ripe blackberries that beckoned as they passed.

They had set off with three days' cooked rations in every knapsack. Unused to army ways, they gobbled them up in two. A day was spent in the woods cooking, to replenish food supplies. That day Johnston began putting regiments aboard trains and sending them east to Beauregard.

McDowell wondered hard and long about just what the rebels somewhere ahead might be doing. The eight companies of cavalry in his army were never asked to go out and see. They simply tagged along with the other enthusiastic gourmands, their faces streaked purple with blackberry juice.

What they would have found was Beauregard moving into position along Bull Run. This is a narrow fast-flowing stream with steep banks that runs north and east around Manassas. By the afternoon of July 20 the Confederates were strung out over a frontage of twelve miles. Although in a strong defensive position he planned to leave it the next day, to launch a frontal attack on an army bigger than his own.

McDowell struck first. His plan was based on two strong feints against Beauregard's right while an ambitious turning movement enveloped the Confederate left. Scott again; Mexico again. The arrangements for units to get into position was complex but manageable. His plan would probably have worked had it been given to Scott's army of 1847. For the troops McDowell led in 1861 it was simply too difficult.

As Sunday, July 21, dawned the roads out of Washington were crowded with excited picnickers heading, like veterans, toward the sound of the guns. Silk ribbons, bright smiles, hampers of champagne; war as romance, for the last time. Lincoln was on his way to church, to pray.

McDowell's feints were launched hours late and unconvincingly.

They only aroused the Confederates in time to discover the turning movement and strip their right flank and center to block it.

All battles are confused; this one was confusion squared. On the Union side men wore the fancy outfits of volunteer militia or some other gaudy confection meant to bring glory to their state. Confederates were also uniform only in the absence of uniform. Many arrived for battle in their everyday work clothes. Beauregard and Johnston appeared, still dressed as officers in the United States Army.

Men scurried about the battlefield, some in panic, some trying to obey bewildering orders, some trying to obtain orders, even bewildering ones. Nothing seemed to have been thought out in advance, not even obvious concerns such as ammunition supplies. Colonel Ambrose Burnside reported to McDowell that his brigade had fought so magnificently it was out of cartridges. Flustered, McDowell allowed him to pull his men out of the battle, as the fighting came to a crescendo, never to return.

The weight of federal numbers began to tell on the Confederate left flank, pushing the rebels off the crest of the dominating height, Henry House Hill. In the dwelling that gave this eminence its name lay an elderly invalid widow, Mrs. Judith Henry. Federal artillery was turned on Confederates using her home for cover. Mrs. Henry became the first civilian fatality of the war.

Confederate units milled about in terrified confusion on the reverse slope of the hill. Other troops, falling back from Bull Run, were shaken by shells exploding in the trees over their heads. Brigadier General Thomas J. Jackson's brigade arrived at the double from the right center where it had been posted. The Confederate position below Henry House seemed about to collapse. Jackson's troops formed line of battle halfway up the hill.

"It was at this moment," according to Beauregard, "that General Bee used the famous expression, 'Look at Jackson's brigade! It stands there like a stone wall!'—a name that soon passed from the brigade to its immortal commander." Barnard Bee, about to be killed, rallied his men behind Jackson's.

The Federals, however, had planted artillery on the crest of the hill. McDowell, like Taylor in Mexico, had run his guns in front of his infantry. Two Union batteries now dominated the field, threatening the entire Confederate center. One hundred yards away, where two woods came together at the base of Henry House Hill, a regiment dressed in blue emerged from the foliage.

The battery of Captain Charles Griffin loaded canister, preparing to cut them down. Up rode McDowell's artillery chief, Major William F. Barry. Those men, Barry said, are coming to your support. Never, replied Griffin—they are Confederates. The argument was settled after the men in blue were rallied, listened to a rousing speech from their colonel, advanced to within seventy yards, loaded their muskets, took aim and let loose a volley that cut down every gunner and every artillery horse on the top of the hill. With a rush and a yell the Confederates gained the high ground.

Union attempts to get it back failed. All the while fresh Confederate regiments were being brought in from other parts of the field. Then came something unheard of: reinforcements by train. Two thousand men from the Shenandoah Valley pulled into Manassas Junction aboard flatcars, jumped off and marched straight into the fight.

McDowell had regiments of his own in reserve, three and a half miles away, at Centreville. They were commanded by Colonel Dixon S. Miles. He spent the day threatening to fall off his horse, wearing two hats and so drunk he could not give orders under either one.

At 4 P.M. the Union army began pulling out, unable to dislodge the Confederates from Henry House Hill and under growing pressure on the right flank. No one was any longer in command control on either side. The Federals were not so much defeated as disheartened by the constant flow of rebel reinforcements and the absence of their own reserve.

Losses were almost equal: 1,500 dead and wounded on the Union side to 1,900 Confederate killed and wounded. For raw troops it was a sanguinary beginning. Never had so much blood been shed on American soil. Neither side had demonstrated much skill. McDowell and Beauregard had both failed to get much more than half their troops into action.

Southern victory, such as it was, came after the battle was over, when panic routed the picnickers and sightseers who had never imagined seeing federal forces retreat under fire. Along the approaches to the stone bridge a few shells burst in the air, fired by jubilant Confederate gunners. A single shell struck a wagon on the narrow bridge. A flash, a bang, a puff of smoke and instantly it was crammed with rearing horses, screaming people, overturned carriages. Terror, feeding on itself, rounded out a day of heat and chaos. Its spoors were borne on the wind the twenty-five miles back to Washington, over the chain bridge and along the broad avenues.

Davis ordered a rapid, vigorous pursuit. Beauregard spelled out four reasons why it could not be: lack of food, lack of arms, lack of ammunition, lack of transportation. Days when a jittery capital might have fallen to a bold thrust passed. Shattered nerves mended. Only the embarrassment remained.

Militarily, First Bull Run was a stalemate. Politically, it was one of the great defensive victories of the war. It turned the Confederacy from an assertion into a reality. The best chance to destroy it quickly and cheaply was gone.

BULL RUN, Harpers Ferry and the loss of Norfolk Navy Yard, with its twelve hundred cannon and a mountain of gunpowder, worked to Lincoln's advantage. He reached the White House as others had, and do to this day, to preside over a system of government that nurtured timeservers, vested interests, stubborn bad habits and willful old men.

The Confederate government under Davis had its problems, but being brand-new it had something of a blank slate to work on. To fight the war, Lincoln quickly realized, constitutional authority was not going to be enough. He needed an aroused public opinion, preferably sharpened to an edge by a sense of danger. The panic unleashed by Bull Run was, when it simmered down, worth any act of Congress.

When the senators and representatives returned on July 4 he asked them to give him "at least 400,000 men." Rising to the urgent hour, Congress gave him authority to raise half a million volunteers, to be enlisted for three years. With the 230,000 three-year men from his May 3 call the United States had, or would have in the months ahead, as many as 770,000 men under arms: 22,000 regulars, 18,000 sailors and 730,000 three-year volunteers.

The secretary of war, Simon Cameron, proved to be uniquely handicapped to oversee the mobilization and organization of armies— he had no interest in military affairs. Of the mistakes Lincoln made on coming to office this appointment was probably the worst.

In his choice of Gideon Welles to be secretary of the navy, however, he could not have been luckier. The pugnacious Welles comes down to us as something of a monochrome figure of fun, staring wide-eyed from his century into ours from under one of the most badly fitting hairpieces captured by glass-plate photography. He proved to be one of the most gifted public servants in the republic's history. Under him a navy that had been allowed to rot away became a major instrument of victory.

Lincoln would have been happy to retain Scott, but the old hero was ever a realist once the shooting started. He was too infirm at seventy-three to exercise command. Old wounds from Lundy's Lane and Mexico sapped his strength, as did his enormous bulk. Besides, his strategic advice had been rejected.

Scott's idea was to raise big armies, train them thoroughly, drive down the Mississippi, take Vicksburg and press on to Mobile. Meanwhile, the upper South would be occupied by Union forces and all the Confederate ports would be closely blockaded. He looked to grinding down the South instead of trying to bleed it to death in huge battles. His plan would take three years. That made it unacceptable. Lincoln and the country wanted quick victories.

Whether they got them would depend partly on who led their armies. Scott's own choice of successor was Robert E. Lee, whom he had looked on ever since Mexico as his star pupil. On April 18, the day Harpers Ferry went up in smoke, Lee was offered field command of the Union army being raised under the call for volunteer militia. Half expecting, half fearing news at any moment that Virginia had seceded, he turned it down. The general, himself a Virginian, was dismayed. "Lee," he told him, "you have made the greatest mistake of your life."

Scott's second choice was "Old Brains," Henry Halleck, a West Pointer who had resigned his commission to go into mining and banking. Halleck was the best-read soldier in the country, after Scott. A third possibility was McClellan, who had also resigned his commission to pursue a lucrative career building and running railroads. He was exceptionally bright and the Scott tradition always meant rapid ascent for scholar-soldiers, but he was still only thirty-four.

The younger man was, by August 1861, the people's choice. While the Confederates were humiliating Union forces close to Washington, out in the mountains of western Virginia federal armies so defeated their foes that the region was not only held for the Union but would in time enter it as a new state, West Virginia. For this McClellan, back in uniform as a major general of volunteers, got the credit.

Barrel-chested and short, he had been reared as a child prodigy. West Point waived its entrance requirements to recruit him. He never doubted his gifts or his destiny. To the people around him he could be the most thoughtful, modest and approachable of men. Only one thing could ruin him—success.

In reward for western Virginia the press crowned him "the Young Napoleon." He began issuing proclamations about what he had done and what he was going to do. These were McClellanite versions of the bulletins of the *Grande Armée,* full of rodomontade and self-infatuation. The eagerly scanned photographs of the young general showed a stern expression, a flourishing moustache and a spade beard: Napoleon III. His right hand was stuck into his partially unbuttoned tunic while his left hand was tucked behind his back: Napoleon I.

All of which would have meant nothing had he a spark of military genius, something as rare as the ability to paint great pictures or compose great music. That spark was the one thing the gods withheld. The victories in western Virginia were won by his brigadiers. They had fought the battles while McClellan sent a string of exhortatory telegrams from Cincinnati. And when they had won he disparaged their tactics. There was only so much glory to go round.

This performance convinced Scott that McClellan would not do. He hung on as general-in-chief, trying to ensure the succession for Halleck. On August 8 he received a letter from McClellan, recently brought to Washington to organize the flood of three-year volunteers into *the* Army of the Potomac. The capital, McClellan informed him, was in "imminent danger" from 100,000 Confederates. It might fall at any moment.

Scott judged this warning so ridiculous it had to be part of an intrigue to panic the government and undermine confidence in himself. He was too old, too tired for such games. He offered his resignation. Lincoln urged him to remain. The old soldier was adamant but not until November, when the "imminent danger" had evaporated into the mists from whence it came, was Scott finally allowed to depart.

McClellan was named general-in-chief. He assured Lincoln blandly, "I can do it all," but before he could fight he must organize.

IN THE three months between Lincoln's call for volunteer militia and McClellan's arrival in Washington, American military forces increased by 2,700 percent. It was the biggest mobilization in terms of time and scale the country would ever manage. It was more impressive in some ways than any mobilization since.

Manpower was the most obvious advantage the North possessed: 3.8 million white males aged eighteen to forty-five, compared to the South's 1.1 million. The Confederacy, however, possessed a huge labor force of slaves attached to its armies, freeing its soldiers to fight. The South also had hopes of recruiting many of the 500,000 men of military age in Maryland, Missouri and Kentucky, where secessionist sentiment was strong. Lincoln struggled throughout the conflict to keep those states, and their manpower, out of the war, fearing which way they would go if freely allowed to take sides.

The North appeared to have more than enough men to defeat the South. In the end the disparity in manpower would play an important part, but for the first two years of the war it meant comparatively little. The South had begun to raise armies earlier. Union officers familiar with Confederate military preparations when the war began credited the enemy with a six-month lead.

Scott had refused to break up the regular army and distribute its officers and NCOs among the hundreds of volunteer regiments being formed. McClellan chose to do the same. The regular army remained intact for the entire war while a vast force of volunteers emerged, overshadowing it: amateur soldiers under amateur officers. The Union was fortunate that hundreds of West Point officers who had resigned their commissions returned, as did hundreds of volunteer officers who had served in Mexico.

As the three-year men poured in, an estimated 20 percent proved too unhealthy or too cowardly for the army to do anything with them. Medical examinations were such a parody that adventurous women had no difficulty enlisting in federal infantry units. Every camp found itself amply provided with syphilitics and tuberculotics. Despairing noncoms tried to make marching material out of men with varicose veins, flat feet and hernias. The camps themselves were pestilential. It was not quite as bad as Mexico had been; conditions had improved to the merely appalling. Officers elected by the men were as ignorant as ever of basic hygiene. Four Union soldiers would die of sickness for every one killed by the enemy. More would perish from diarrhea alone than from Confederate bullets.

For many thousands the Union army provided their introduction to cleanliness, beginning with regular washing and underwear. A common sight by the quartermaster's store was young men holding up their first pair of drawers, gawping in amazement, wondering what they were for.

The poor physical condition of so many offers an idea of the nation's health in the 1860s. These volunteers were drawn from the fittest portion of the population and from the most prosperous, best-educated part of the country. It is doubtful that even half would have been accepted by the modern army.

The rich North lavished on its sons unprecedented abundance. The supply system broke down at times under cornucopia overload. Some regiments knew periods of hunger, while somewhere to the rear a frustrated QM was trying to round up wagons and mules or get control of a train.

The daily food allowance of the Union soldier was nearly twice that of his French counterpart and more generous than anything a British private had to face. There was so much it seems some men could not eat all of their rations.

The wastefulness of federal soldiers was one of the first things foreign observers noticed. Along the line of march of a Union army was enough abandoned clothing, food and arms to take care of thousands of Confederates.

Even so, not everything could be had. Before 1861 Americans almost invariably put milk in their coffee. North and South, soldiers had to learn to manage without fresh milk. The new taste, black coffee, displaced the old.

The Union provided its troops with essence of coffee, desiccated potatoes and dried vegetables. The men hated them all, telling each other wild stories about what modern convenience foods did to the human body.

Salt fat pork was the principal meat ration, supplemented by the real dietary mainstay, "army bread," better known as hardtack. A biscuit roughly three inches square and half an inch thick, it acquired an almost legendary character among soldiers. Some kept a few samples as war souvenirs and decades later proudly reported they were still intact and as hard as pieces of oak.

Many were consumed fried in bacon fat. Those that were weevil-riddled were best consumed, connoisseurs suggested, in the dark. The most popular way to devour hardtack, though, was to crumble it—

sometimes with the aid of a blunt instrument—into coffee. Milk out, hardtack in.

THE PATRIOTIC FERVOR that brought men forward on both sides in the first year of the war ran at flood tide. It was not hard to find one hundred men and be commissioned their captain, or to find one thousand for a regiment and be made their colonel. The war came during an economic recession in the North. A private's pay of thirteen dollars a month plus a bounty of fifty dollars or more may have been a powerful recruiting aid, especially among immigrants. And there is no doubt that many thousands served in the Union army. The colonel of one regiment learned to give commands in seven languages. The foreign-born, however, were considerably underrepresented in the Union army. Not that Confederates would have believed it. They complained feelingly that the North was as good as hiring foreigners, spoiling what ought to be a fair fight between Americans.

In the first year of the war men joined both armies because they wanted adventure, they wanted to take part in historic events, they wanted to show themselves as brave as their friends and neighbors, but above all they wanted to fight for their country. The modern state, even one as new and untried as the Confederacy, could draw upon the deepest veins of patriotic sentiment.

As men arrived at Union camps they came bowed down with gifts pressed on them by loving friends and anxious relatives: a revolver, an ample supply of ammunition for it, an eighteen-inch "Arkansaw toothpick," or bowie knife, a Bible and a ten-pound piece of steel body armor to be strapped to the chest before going into battle. Discipline, they found, was haphazard, much like the system of military justice. Desertion rates were high.

After the first year many of the worst officers and the more turbulent men were weeded out. The privilege of electing officers was ended. Discipline and hygiene both improved.

The Union army that emerged was a far different body from Washington's Continentals. Among the soldiers of 1861–62 there was widespread profanity and drinking; gambling flourished; God was mocked. There was the usual wartime suspension of gentilities. Every city had its flourishing demimonde.

Washington took the prize in the North, Richmond in the South.

Each had stiff competition. In Memphis, New Orleans, Chicago, Boston and New York entire streets were crowded with heavily rouged prostitutes and brothels catering to all tastes and sexes. Soldiers had ample opportunity to partake of "horizontal refreshments" if they were anywhere near a city. If they were not, all was not lost. A soldier stationed in Virginia later in the war was far from any town when he wrote to a friend in New Hampshire, "We cannot get anything here but fucking and that is plenty."

As McClellan labored to turn these thousands of volunteers into an army, he displayed all his reputed talents for organizing. He thought clearly, delegated responsibilities well and showed a genuine interest in his fledgling soldiers. They marched in from every point of the compass, the pride of a city or state, the first of this, the second of that. He took the raw material of youthful high spirits and turned it into unit pride; he took the joy of camaraderie and turned it into unit solidarity. It was a quick way to lose oneself, to part with youth, but it meant that once the froth of patriotic sentiment had been blown away by a blast of gunfire something good and true would remain: men would go on fighting out of loyalty to one another. That was something all army commanders had to achieve but no one did it better than McClellan.

He was no remote figure. As the Army of the Potomac—the main Union army, created for the main theater of war—took shape he was often among the troops, showing himself (and such entrances; like those of a conqueror) and at the same time showing that he had his eye on them. He treated indiscipline sternly yet his direct, friendly manner belied the pompous little man frozen in those formal photographs. After six months as general-in-chief he had an army ready to follow him anywhere and fight its heart out.

McClellan's organization was less than perfect. Among the flaws that would cost him heavily was a neglect of cavalry. He scattered it throughout the Army of the Potomac. When it tried to act together as a unit in 1862 it would fail. With Scott he shared an inability to imagine any major role for cavalry on the battlefield. Look what a few guns had done to those thousands of Mexican lancers.

The structure of the Union army was basically French. There were to be 1,046 men to a regiment, three regiments to a brigade, three brigades to a division, and any number of divisions to an army. This structure was later modified; but whatever arrangements were made on

paper, combat knocked all figures into cocked hats. There were brigades known to contain the remnants of ten regiments, and "regiments" with fewer than fifty men present for duty.

AS THE North sought to mobilize large armies, so did the South. By
March 1862, when federal land forces reached 637,000, the Confederacy had raised and armed (after a fashion) 401,000 men.

Southern soldiers—electing their officers long after the practice
stopped in the North, choosing which orders they would obey, ever
resistant to discipline—were much like the militia of the Revolutionary War. There was the same combination of individual commitment
and collective disorder. They refused to accept the possibility that
anyone else might say when they were free to return home. And once
having "been to see the elephant" (combat: the greatest show on
Earth), they wasted little time about it, especially after a Confederate
victory.

Coming from the part of the country where life was harder may
have inured them to the rigors of life in the field; on the other hand,
it may have undermined their health and lowered their resistance to
disease. They were invariably said to be better fighting material because
they had more experience with firearms. As far as the evidence goes,
however, the Union soldier appears to have been a better shot than
Johnny Reb. Confederates had the fault common to inexperienced
marksmen: they shot too high.

The chief advantage the South possessed in the first year or two
of the war was better organization. Not having a regular army to
preserve, the Confederacy simply distributed its experienced officers
and NCOs among all its regiments. As Grant put it, "the whole loaf
was leavened." Each regiment thus contained a handful of people who
knew how to train troops, how to organize and how to lead them.
They understood small-unit tactics. They were familiar with military
terms and ideas. And what they knew they could impart rapidly and
directly to others, as well as setting an example of how soldiers behaved
under fire.

Confederates were alert to the value of cavalry. They used it
effectively to screen their own movements and to uncover those of the
enemy. There is a myth that Southerners were raised in the saddle while
poor Northerners knew only how to walk. There were in fact five

million horses in the North. Even if only one in twenty-five was actually ridden and the rest pulled carts and carriages, that still meant there was a large pool of riders from which the Union might have created a powerful cavalry force in the first year of fighting.

Davis, Lee, Albert Sidney Johnston, Earl Van Dorn, John Bell Hood and a dozen other Confederates who would rise to high command had served in the dragoons or cavalry out west. They knew the importance of horse soldiers. They also knew how their cavalry would fight—dismounted. That was how they had fought, and defeated, Indians.

The Achilles' heel of rebel armies was supply. The South lacked a vigorous internal trade. Nearly all of its trade was overseas. That left it poor in markets, roads, trading centers and management skills. For most of the war there was plenty of food in the South, yet no Confederate soldier known to history was spared hunger for weeks at a time. Some states made matters worse by refusing to supply any troops but their own, instead of contributing to a pool on which all might draw. Supply parochialism was one more echo from the Revolutionary past.

During the first year of war spontaneous private contributions bridged the gap between what the troops needed and what the CSA could provide. After that, there was little left to give.

That first year also exhausted the South's enthusiasm for war. By March 1862 the tide of volunteers had fallen to a trickle, just as the first regiments enlisted were due for release. On April 16, 1862, the Confederacy—that sworn foe of strong centralized government—began conscription. The term was set at three years but there was a wide range of exemptions, notably for owners of at least twenty slaves. Comparatively few men were drafted. Conscription bore a stigma. The flow of volunteers picked up again. This time they signed on for the duration.

The camp life that awaited them was different from that in the North. Confederates gambled and drank just as eagerly as Federals but they were also more religious. Union armies created neat tent cities and slept under canvas. Southrons slept in the woods, under trees.

Both armies shared a passion for music. These may have been the most musical soldiers in history. There was band music everywhere and singing from dawn until long after dark, on the road, in camp, even in action.

There was not all that much that separated these men; so little it will always seem strange they could have fought each other so hard. Expressions of deep hatred were rare. Examples of easy, laughing fraternization were common. Yet they not only killed each other freely, many threw away their own lives in the effort to take another man's.

We will never know, but it may be that brother fought brother *because* they had so much in common. There was always a touchiness, a bristling underside to the friendliness of the nineteenth-century American character. Refusing to be told what to do was a man's birthright. So was the raised fist at the first hint of an imperious tone.

With that touchiness went a common fear of rejection. Friendliness always springs from more than love of mankind. There is no rejection, though, like that within families. The thunder of the guns masked a shriek of pain, a cry of unspeakable hurt, as people north and south rejected each other. Anguish there was, desperate for expression, finding it when the legal and political arguments ran out in the smoking barrels of guns.

It was around these primal emotions that young men formed armies, took up their weapons. It was not the least part of these tragic events, of greatness flawed, that the arms they handled so eagerly like exciting new toys were a technological revolution come to flower. Harvesting it was going to cost 600,000 their lives. Almost no one, certainly not they, had any idea what the new firearms would do.

THE U.S. government found a successor to Eli Whitney in John H. Hall, holder of the first patent for a breech-loading rifle. The Ordnance Bureau had glimpsed the possibility of weapons made from interchangeable parts; weapons that could be repaired in the field. One glimpse was enough. Hall was installed at Harpers Ferry in 1819 with the entire town at his disposal. A famous factory, the Rifle Works, was built for him.

During twenty years deadlines were set only to be ignored. Costs overran. Hall's rifle and a breech-loading carbine both proved too fragile to meet specifications. The promise of cheaper weapons was never kept. It made no difference. Nothing could shake the faith of the Ordnance Bureau.

The army did not want only weapons that were easier to repair.

It also wanted weapons that were better made, more reliable, more accurate, more powerful. The pursuit of firepower became, decade by decade, a driving, energizing force. In time the search for firepower would become, in its potential consequences, as momentous as the search for fire.

By 1840 the government had created six more arsenals, thereby spreading the creed of machine tools and interchangeable parts over much of the country. Dozens of workmen trained at Springfield, Harpers Ferry and Whitneyville were headhunted for their leading-edge skills. Some rose to become powerful industrialists.

By the 1840s there was complete interchangeability of parts. The pieces made at one arsenal fitted with those made a thousand miles away at another. Machine tools had emerged from the primitive stage of Whitney's day to become sophisticated instruments of production.

Around such parts, such tools, Springfield, Whitneyville and a score of related businesses along the Connecticut Valley evolved into a precedent. Here in this corner of New England was the first genuine example of technological convergence, the forerunner of Route 128 outside present-day Boston, or California's Silicon Valley. Roughly 80 percent of the American arms industry was located in the Connecticut Valley. Around that industrial base arose a congeries of high-tech businesses that both competed and cooperated, creating ever newer businesses, ever newer technologies.

This was where Samuel Colt grew up; born in Hartford, in the shadow of the Whitney legend, haunted since childhood by talk of "the impossible gun"—one that would fire five or six times without reloading. It was an idea that had taunted and baffled gunsmiths for three hundred years.

The solution came to Colt while he was still in his teens, during a year spent as a seaman, watching the spokes of a helmsman's wheel coming successively into line with a clutch. The clutch could be set to stop the wheel at any spoke. Colt whittled a model revolver from wood and, back on shore, tried to make one from metal.

What made his inspiration practical was the creation of the percussion cap by the Reverend Joshua Shaw of Philadelphia around 1815. An expendable copper cap filled with fulminate of mercury when struck by a hammer would ignite a cartridge; no need any longer for flints and powder pans.

Colt's first attempt to cash in on his idea was a complete failure.

He was reduced to becoming little more than a minor employee of his business partners. Like Fulton before him he had the quintessential American gift, promotion. For a time he had run a laughing-gas show. What he had learned of hype he put into his revolver. Failed again. The Ordnance Bureau tested his invention and turned it down flat.

In the decade leading up to the Mexican War fate seemed to hold a grudge against Colt. In the decade after, he seemed its adopted son. In the hands of Texas Rangers and army officers during that war his revolvers became famous. With his flair for publicity he made it appear that victory owed as much to Colt as to Scott.

The revolver helped break the Indian hold over the Southwest and flooded it with settlers, nearly all of them armed. Then came the Gold Rush. How could any prospector hope to hang onto his claim without an equalizer? And there were the Mormons, setting off to erect a theocracy in the desert. Like other people heading west they preferred to skimp on rations before six-shooters. They clung to them as if to life itself.

As the Civil War drew near, demand for Colt's revolvers soared into the stratosphere. Abolitionists had to have them. So did the slavers. "Bloody" Kansas got that way largely with revolvers.

What Colt had done was create the perfect dual-technology product. The six-shooter was just as useful, just as much in demand among civilians in peacetime as among soldiers in wartime. He had also achieved a leap in magnitude, increasing an individual's firepower by a factor of three or four.

And he had democratized it. In 1845 there were comparatively few Americans who owned a musket or a rifle, as any militia muster comically showed. Nor in settled areas far from the frontier did there seem much point in having a rusty musket hanging around the house gathering dust. By 1900, however, handguns would be everywhere; personal protection in cities grown dangerous.

Colt's invention had other historic consequences. In 1848 he offered to produce ten thousand revolvers for the War Department at twenty-five dollars each. During the Mexican War, by comparison, he had sold two thousand at twenty-eight dollars each. He was damned as a scoundrel, a wicked profiteer, a man who brazenly took advantage of his country in wartime and now had as good as admitted it!

It was a long time before spluttering congressmen and incensed editorialists grasped the point Colt was making. What he spread before

their bemused gaze was something new—economies of scale. He ush-
ered in a revolution in the development of capitalism. Colt was the
first manufacturer to offer a lower unit price to attract a larger volume
of business. Before him the unit price for one item was the same as
for a million.

Colt was among the first men to see the entire globe as a market.
In this case, a market for arms. Seeing it that way, he helped turn it
into one. In the 1850s government representatives from a score of
countries traveled to Hartford to talk prices and stopping power. And
he repaid the compliment, going to see them. For a decade he was the
first transatlantic commuter, constantly getting on and off ships. He
was utterly impartial. He was as happy to sell arms to revolutionaries
such as Garibaldi as to reactionaries such as the Hapsburgs. During the
Crimean War he profitably helped outfit both sides.

He also knew how to create strong customer loyalty. Among his
earliest foreign buyers were the Fenians. In the 1980s the weapon of
choice among the IRA is the Colt Armalite rifle.

Colt's emblem, the stallion rampant with a spear between its teeth,
was well known for a century in places where the Stars and Stripes
was never seen. Even more than the flag it represented American
technology, American power.

When the Great Exhibition of 1851 brought the world's leading
achievements in science and engineering to London, three gold medals
were awarded. Two went to Americans: one to Colt for his revolvers
and one to a Vermont producer of rifles made, like Colt's revolvers,
entirely from interchangeable parts. The British soon had a committee
on its way to learn how such weapons were made.

They hired the master armorer from Harpers Ferry, contracted for
the services of a revolver designer named Oliver Jones, bought up
American machine tools and brought in American mechanics. Around
all of these they established the Royal Small Arms Factory at Enfield.

In time they came to realize that "the American system" they—
and others—were so eager to emulate meant more than arms. It
promised to transform all their manufacturing industries, generating
prodigious wealth; more than enough wealth to buy advanced weapons. It was their introduction to the world of dual technologies.

There was not a single important element in the American system
that did not derive from an arms contract. As the money rolled in,
invention rolled out—the engine lathe, the milling machine and others

important in the history of technology. These in turn created new industries, flooding the Victorian world with cheap products. Singer's sewing machine was producing cheap clothing in the 1850s. McCormick's reaper was producing cheap food. Cheap rolling stock was producing cheap transportation. And the well was far from dry. While the Confederacy was forced to exempt cobblers from the draft in 1862 to get its soldiers shod, that same year Lyman Blake invented machinery that turned out millions of excellent cheap shoes for Union soldiers.

Singer, McCormick and Blake stood in direct line of descent from Whitney, Hall and Colt. The results appeared on every Civil War battlefield—in the arms men carried, in the uniforms they wore, in the food in their stomachs, in the shoes on their feet. At the same time, they appeared in every American home, small triumphs of dual technology.

By 1861 Colt's Hartford plant was the biggest small-arms factory in the world. He ruthlessly stamped out anything that smacked of craftsmanship. A worker's efforts were reduced to a few simple operations and one or two parts. Colt pioneered in many directions.

On hearing the news that Fort Sumter had fallen he instantly drew up plans for expansion. He expected the Union army to grow to one million men. The war, said Colt, would last four years.

He already had a repeating rifle in production. It fired five rounds and was basically a Colt revolver with a shoulder stock and a long barrel. The Ordnance Bureau rejected it.

There were more than a dozen repeating rifles and carbines presently on offer but all had serious defects. The man who solved all the problems was a young Quaker named Christopher Spencer. He had learned his trade under Colt. In 1860 the twenty-six-year-old Spencer had taken out a patent on a repeating carbine. It contained a tubular, spring-loaded magazine in the stock holding seven .52-caliber all-metal rimfire cartridges. These were loaded into the chamber by working a lever that formed the trigger guard.

Spencer's carbine provided sustained fire of fifteen rounds a minute. It was accurate to six hundred yards. It represented the maturing of various technologies in a single weapon: metallic cartridge cases, magazines, breech-loading and repeating action. The Ordnance Bureau turned it down.

Its new chief was sixty-seven-year-old Colonel James Wolfe Ripley. Never an easy man, he had been threatened with a hanging early in his military career by President Andrew Jackson, driven to fury by the young officer's love of red tape. For years Ripley struggled to standardize the army's firearms. The .58-caliber Model 1855 rifled musket was intended to achieve exactly that: all subsequent shoulder arms were expected to be .58 caliber. Then along came Spencer offering a state-of-the-art .52-caliber arm.

He had, moreover, no plant, no work force, no money. All he had were patents, prototypes and persistence. Spencer managed to see Lincoln, to place a repeating carbine in those strong, capable hands. The president preferred to conduct his own weapons tests on waste ground near the White House. Ripley was overruled. In December 1861 he was ordered to give Spencer a contract for ten thousand carbines.

Of all the organizational and administrative tasks the Union army faced during the first eighteen months of the war, putting weapons in the hands of troops was the most difficult. Yet the Ordnance Bureau was consistently discriminated against. Both the War Department and Congress appeared to despise it, utterly blind to its central role in transforming American industry.

Throughout the first half of the war it alone of army service departments was held to its prewar size. Others doubled, tripled, quadrupled, in budgets and manpower. As late as November 1862 Ripley's domain was about the same size it had been during the Mexican War.

To be assigned there was more or less the end of an officer's career. His chances of promotion dropped to the lowest in the army. Nor were its enlisted men and NCOs treated any better. They alone in the entire United States Army were not allowed enlistment or reenlistment bonuses. No one ever sought to explain why or to justify it. Ordnance was starved of manpower, money and recognition even in wartime, even at the height of the firepower revolution it had done so much to create. If its performance was at times less than brilliant it had less to be brilliant with.

Ripley and other ordnance officers had seen a long succession of breechloaders fail: they leaked fire, or their loading mechanism was too complicated, or they were too fragile, or they missed fire. They cost twice as much to make as muzzle-loaders of the same caliber and three times as long to manufacture. The cost of Spencer's ten thousand unproven carbines, for example, represented the loss of thirty thousand proven muzzle-loaded rifled muskets. Resistance to breechloaders gave rise to a legend of Ordnance Bureau resistance to innovation. That is all it was, legend.

Throughout the Civil War the master armorer at Springfield worked at perfecting the world's first safe, reliable center-fire metal cartridge. The result was the bottlenecked round that infantrymen all over the world have handled down to the present day. Around it nearly all breech-loading small arms and automatic weapons were designed for more than a century.

Ripley's gunsmiths were meanwhile devising a technique for converting muzzle-loaded rifled muskets into breechloaders. It was a technique destined to be copied around the globe.

The Ordnance Bureau was also receptive to foreign innovations. Back in 1847 an inspector at the school of musketry at Vincennes, Capitaine Minié, had developed (or was credited with developing; the matter is in dispute) a new kind of musket ball. In the base of the standard lead item he placed a small iron cup. This was driven by the exploding charge into the ball, making it expand and travel snugly down the barrel. Put grooves in that barrel and the musket acquired the range and accuracy of a rifle.

Minié's idea had the simplicity of true brilliance, but sometimes the piece of iron simply shot through the lead ball, leaving the infantryman with a problem. The assistant master armorer at Harpers Ferry, James Burton, got rid of the cup. Instead, he made an elongated, sharply pointed bullet with a deep hollow cavity in its base. The thin walls of the hollow base expanded when the charge ignited, fitting the lead to the rifling.

The Burton bullet was more accurate, more reliable and had a higher muzzle velocity than the Minié ball. That was what American soldiers fired all through the Civil War, hundreds of millions of Burton bullets, only they called them by the name of an overtaken technology, "Minny balls."

At the start of the war the federal armories held 35,000 rifled muskets. Mainly what they contained were 370,000 old-fashioned .69-caliber smoothbore muskets and about 50,000 rifles and carbines of varying quality. One fourth of the armories' holdings were seized by secessionist officers. More serious was the loss of the machinery at Harpers Ferry. It cost the Union half its rifled arms capacity. The

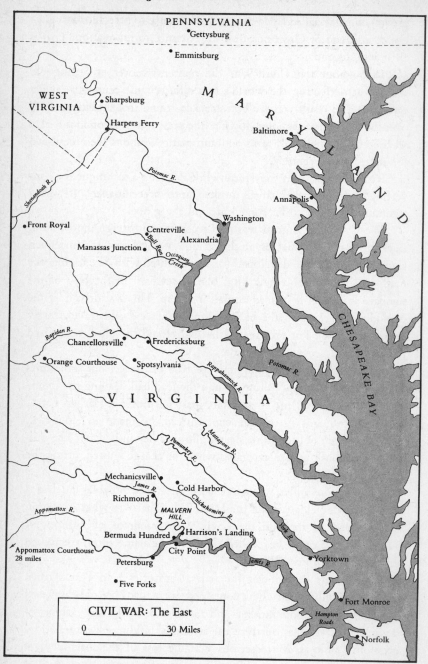

PENNSYLVANIA
•Gettysburg

•Emmitsburg

M A R Y L A N D

WEST
VIRGINIA
•Sharpsburg

Harpers Ferry•

Baltimore•

Potomac R.

Shenandoah R.

Annapolis•

•Front Royal

Centreville•
Washington•

Alexandria•

Manassas Junction•
Bull Run
Occoquan Creek

CHESAPEAKE BAY

Rapidan R.
Chancellorsville•
•Fredericksburg

•Orange Courthouse
Spotsylvania•

Rappahannock R.
Potomac R.

V I R G I N I A

Mattapony R.

Pamunkey R.

Mechanicsville•
James R.
•Cold Harbor

Richmond•
Chickahominy R.

MALVERN HILL △

Bermuda Hundred
Harrison's Landing•

Appomattox R.

Appomattox Courthouse
28 miles

City Point•

York R.

•Petersburg
James R.
•Yorktown

•Five Forks

Fort Monroe•

CIVIL WAR: The East

0   30 Miles

Hampton Roads

•Norfolk

North was forced to buy hundreds of thousands of foreign weapons based on American technology, notably rifled muskets from Enfield.

Although it never seemed fast enough—and never would in the frenzied atmosphere of wartime—the expansion of arms production in the first two years of war was astonishing. Northern arms producers were turning out fifty thousand shoulder arms per year when the war began. Two years later they produced more than that each month. It was an unparalleled achievement in economic history, for these weapons were not old technology. They were the newest technology, produced to the highest standards known.

American weapons were so nicely finished and so agreeable to handle that European arms—equally serviceable, equally deadly—were scorned as being obviously inferior. They neither looked nor felt as good.

From McClellan down to buck private the Union army clamored for breechloaders and repeaters. Special units, such as sharpshooters, were created simply to get hold of them. State governors made fervent pleas to friends in Washington on behalf of favored regiments. The soldier who got his hands on a twelve-shot Henry repeating rifle felt invulnerable, a warrior king.

No one had to force breechloaders on the men in the field. By 1862 virtually every soldier in the Union army wanted one. Lincoln was also convinced. During the first year he ordered Ripley to buy 37,000 breech-loading rifles and 36,000 breech-loading carbines. The issue was, in effect, settled over the ordnance chief's head. The real delays came from the manufacturers. Spencer would take eighteen months to fill his contract for 10,000 muskets. That was typical even of those with smaller contracts to fill.

Nevertheless, a triple revolution had come to the battlefield: in range, in accuracy, in rate of fire. All three had made a leap in magnitude at the same historic moment. War itself had been remade.

8

GENERAL
ABRAHAM
LINCOLN

THE YEAR 1862 began well for the Union: Lincoln fired
Cameron. The new secretary of war was Edwin McMasters Stanton, a short and stocky, fiercely bearded Democrat who had served as
Buchanan's attorney general. Private griefs had turned him into an
impatient, angry man whose one solace was religion, whose sole recreation was to pick up a wicker basket and go shopping. At forty-seven
Stanton looked like an Old Testament prophet in wire-rimmed specta-
cles, breathing fire and brimstone on a sinful, rebellious South.

The War Department that he took over was known in District
patois as "the lunatic asylum." The unprecedented mobilization it had
achieved was like a towering monument surrounded by confusion and
chaos. The Union had fielded huge armies but the other things that
mattered—strategy, leadership, ideas—were wanting.

When Stanton took charge, the War Department had more than
500,000 troops drawing rations and pay, yet there was little action and
few plans for action. McClellan seemed in no hurry to go south.

Organizing and training dragged on, wearing out Lincoln's patience. On January 27 he issued President's War Order Number 1,
commanding a "general movement" of all Union forces to be made
on February 22, Washington's Birthday. On February 1 he followed
up by specifically directing the Army of the Potomac to advance on
Richmond, by way of Centreville and Manassas, where Joe Johnston

and 40,000 Confederates were passing the winter insolently close to Washington and untroubled by Union forces.

McClellan managed to buy more time by portraying Centreville and Manassas as areas of tremendous Confederate strength, full of well-camouflaged artillery and up to 80,000 strongly entrenched Confederate troops. His chief source of military intelligence was a private eye from Chicago, Allan Pinkerton. In effect, he subcontracted the intelligence task to a civilian who knew less about the gathering and interpretation of military information than he did.

Pinkerton naturally sought to be cautious in his novel assignment, which meant he played safe by overestimating Confederate forces. McClellan in turn cautiously added a margin for error on top of Pinkerton's estimates. At the same time, he consistently underestimated the size of his own army. The upshot was a false view of reality that constantly threatened to paralyze McClellan's will. The Union could never have provided him with an army big enough to conquer his fears.

Pushed and prodded by Lincoln, he finally started south on March 9, the day after Johnston pulled out of Centreville and Manassas. The formidable entrenchments proved to be imaginary, the powerful artillery turned out to be painted logs.

Lincoln relieved Little Mac of the burden of being general-in-chief to allow him to devote all of his energies to commanding the Army of the Potomac in the field. The president wanted the army to continue its advance all the way to Richmond. McClellan disagreed strongly. Better, he insisted, to take the army by sea to Fort Monroe, at the tip of the Yorktown peninsula. The fortress was in the steady hands of John Wool. Using that as a base, McClellan would land on the peninsula and drive west the seventy miles to Richmond. When the Army of the Potomac embarked, Stanton shut down the recruiting offices. After all, the war would soon be over.

When McClellan landed on the peninsula on April 4 he found a line of entrenchments across it. These were lightly held, amounting to a bluff. Patrols revealed as much, yet McClellan was taking no chances. He decided to besiege Yorktown. It took a month to ship siege artillery down to him. As the big guns prepared to blast the little town sky-high, Joe Johnston pulled out.

McClellan began edging cautiously toward Richmond against the heavily outnumbered and overwhelmingly outgunned Confederates left to keep his army under observation. By May 24 his leading regiments were within sight of Richmond's church spires. It had taken seven weeks to move seventy miles.

Part of the plan for the conquest of Richmond was to send a second Union army from Washington, under McDowell. It would advance overland, converging on Richmond from the north as McClellan attacked from the east. The Confederate army defending the capital of the rebellion would be caught between them and crushed.

As McClellan began deploying around Richmond, however, word came that McDowell's army had been sent to the Shenandoah Valley instead, in an ambitious attempt to trap a Confederate army of 17,000 commanded by Stonewall Jackson.

This change of plans seemed to leave McClellan flummoxed. He proceeded to deploy the Army of the Potomac as though McDowell might appear from the north at any moment. He put 65,000 men north of the treacherous, swampy Chickahominy River, and his remaining 40,000 troops south of it.

Joe Johnston's reaction to the news that McDowell had headed for the Valley was to heave a sigh of relief and launch an attack on the Union forces south of the Chickahominy, on May 31. The assault was poorly handled and Johnston was seriously wounded. Davis named Lee to take command of all Confederate forces in Virginia.

This was not a popular appointment. Lee had been involved in the loss of western Virginia. Sent to defend South Carolina and Georgia, he entrenched so zealously his soldiers dubbed him "The King of Spades."

Including the men serving with Jackson, the forces he took command of numbered 90,000 men. McClellan's and McDowell's armies totaled 145,000. This disparity seemed only to inspire him. Lee was an avid Bonapartist and a devout disciple of Scott's. In all that he did in the Civil War there were echoes of Mexico. His style of command, his audacity, his belief in reconnaissance and military intelligence, his hands-off approach once battle was joined all harkened back to Scott and those twenty months of tropical splendor.

Lee proved himself the master deceiver on a dozen battlefields. He began by snowing his own. He titled his new command the Army of Northern Virginia. It was a showman's touch, because northern Virginia was then, and would remain, mainly under Union control.

Lee's cavalry was entrusted to the dashing and colorful J.E.B.

Stuart, a modern chevalier *sans peur et sans reproche*. He sent this latter-day knight in an ostrich-plumed hat on a ride around McClellan's divided army. Most such cavalry excursions were joyrides, not military operations in any serious sense. This one proved invaluable. Stuart reported back that there were 30,000 boys in blue still north of the Chickahominy, wide open to attack.

By this time Jackson's army had returned from the Valley, but to be sure of having a crushing superiority in numbers when he attacked north of the Chickahominy, Lee stripped the forces defending Richmond against the main body of the Army of the Potomac. He left 25,000 Confederates facing 75,000 Federals. One strong attack by McClellan and either Richmond would fall or the bulk of the Confederate army would be trapped on the wrong side of the river and open to destruction. Either way, victory beckoned.

Lee had known McClellan in Mexico and had the measure of his opponent. Even now Little Mac was thinking of withdrawing. There was no evident need for a backward step. His troops were protected by entrenchments and strong breastworks. Another Union army, under a promising young major general named John Pope, had been created and was coming south, to converge on Richmond in line with the original plan.

Withdrawing an army split as his was involved hair-raising risks. Yet McClellan preferred those to the risks of battle. When the Confederates attacked his troops north of the Chickahominy on June 26 and again on June 27, he took fright. Nothing would stop him now from pulling out.

He got away successfully largely because the erratic Jackson failed to seize the chance to trap nearly half the Army of the Potomac as it tried to cross White Oak Swamp. Jackson and his famous fast-moving infantry, who reveled in the name of "foot cavalry," had only to move. Instead, they spent twelve crucial hours building a bridge they did not need.

Lee himself showed an uncertain touch. McClellan's withdrawal down to the James River took a week, and there was a battle every day. Yet Lee failed to win even one of the Seven Days' Battles, though he held the initiative throughout.

When the Federals reached a bluff known as Malvern Hill on the approaches to the river, the Confederates blundered into what could have been an irreparable disaster. The Union army's artillery reserve, commanded by Colonel Henry J. Hunt, took up position with one hundred guns. His gunners had wide fields of fire in nearly every direction. Lee launched his troops in futile frontal assaults against this massed artillery. His losses were enormous, his army demoralized. Had McClellan counterattacked then, he might well have continued all the way into Richmond. Instead, he crawled on, to hole up at Harrison's Landing on the James, from where the Union navy could quickly take him home.

LINCOLN did everything to win the war short of getting into a uniform. Before dawn most mornings he strode across the White House lawn toward the telegraph office in the War Department. He arrived early to read through the night's dispatches without having to disturb the general-in-chief. There were four critical months, from April through August 1862, when he was virtually his own general-in-chief, trying to direct the operations of sixteen Union armies from the telegraph office.

There were telegrams from Lincoln time-stamped "4 A.M." His field commanders soon learned to sense that brooding presence. The president was there, at the other end of the line, sitting on a hard chair next to some Morse code wizard, open for business when they awoke. When battles raged he spent entire days and nights in the telegraph office, standing over the cipher clerks, reading letter by letter as they decoded.

Lincoln sent up to a dozen telegrams a day to his generals: pithy, direct, urgent instructions, whose meaning was clear. He wrote them out himself, rarely making a correction, hardly ever having second thoughts. During calm spells he could still be found in the telegraph office, listening to the chatter of the clerks, occasionally stepping outside to have a word with Stanton, or sitting by a large window writing out a speech or granting a pardon or corresponding with a citizen.

He not only directed operations, he reorganized the Army of the Potomac. When the war began there were not ten people in the entire country who had the rare but essential experience of handling units bigger than a regiment. The search for men capable of handling divisions, corps and armies took up much valuable time for both Lincoln and Davis.

The president repeatedly urged McClellan to organize his army into corps, the better to manage it. The general repeatedly resisted. In the end Lincoln simply ordered it done, creating four corps (formally known as *Corps d'Armée*—the French influence was still strong. It was also why Union soldiers dressed in blue, like the French). The president personally selected the corps commanders. Three divisions were to be assigned to each corps, and two or more corps would form an army.

This clash of wills was typical of Lincoln's relationship with McClellan. It was invariably the aging president and not the young general who welcomed new ideas. McClellan openly despised his commander in chief. Not that Lincoln cared, saying he would gladly hold McClellan's horse if that might help win the war.

When the Army of the Potomac set off on the Peninsular campaign it was left for the president to organize the defenses of the capital, something the general had overlooked in the excitement of departure. Lincoln granted the Young Napoleon a free hand to fight the campaign. All he asked in return was success. Even so, McClellan deeply resented that almost palpable presence at the other end of the telegraph wire, looking over his shoulder as if he too were a cipher clerk.

The diversion of McDowell's army to the Shenandoah Valley just as McClellan reached the outskirts of Richmond did not help either. The attempt to trap Jackson failed, at the cost of scrapping a basically sound plan for destroying Johnston's army by converging columns. At one point Jackson with 17,000 men was tying down 50,000 Union troops commanded by McDowell and Nathaniel Banks. Meanwhile the change in plans undermined McClellan's shaky confidence in himself. And he was no man to improvise a strategy under pressure. The 50,000 troops chasing Jackson would have been better employed heading for Richmond.

Whether McClellan would have put them to good use is uncertain. He was forever complaining about being short of men, yet he never managed to get as much as two thirds of his army into battle. His usual figure was about 50 percent. Again and again telegrams tapped down the line urging the general, almost begging him, to please use *all* of the army the taxpayers provided.

More than any other wartime president, Lincoln embodied the nation's faith that it would win through by technology. Almost any inventor with a new weapon to demonstrate could get in to see him. Armed strangers were constantly going in and out of the White House.

Congress revised the patent laws to encourage new weapons technologies. The search for war-winning arms never stopped. In the end, they appeared.

Lincoln shared the tinkering itch of an inventive age. The patent office a few blocks away held his original design for lifting boats over shoals. The only lecture he ever gave was called "Discoveries and Inventions."

During the war he was offered a crude forerunner of napalm, flamethrowers and artillery shells filled with chlorine gas. Despite promising experiments nothing came of these. His eagerness at being present at weapons experiments on one occasion nearly cost him his life.

Arms were a subject he knew as well as most experts. At the end of 1861 he ordered the Ordnance Bureau to buy the world's first machine gun. It was hopper-loaded with .58-caliber paper cartridges and was worked with a crank. Several of the ten that were ordered saw service in the Peninsular campaign, but the results were poor, probably because they produced a huge, choking and blinding cloud of smoke. That also made them excellent targets for Confederate artillery.

Lincoln promoted the formation of the Balloon Corps, under the splendiferously named Thaddeus Sobieski Coulincourt Lowe. The young aeronaut went off to the peninsula, where the mere sight of one of his balloons hovering above the tree line was enough to slow the Confederate army to an apprehensive crawl. Lowe, however, did not hold a commission. The Union army was unsure of what to do with this civilian, if anything. Lowe eventually quit in disgust.

Lincoln's management of the war inspired the famous journalist who became assistant secretary of war, Charles Dana, to call him "the greatest general we had." All the same, in 1862 Lincoln was still learning by doing, and not completely sure yet of just what strategies would work. The one thing certain was that the war must be won.

The failure to trap Jackson led him to amalgamate several of the smaller armies operating in Virginia. The new command, called the Army of Virginia, was entrusted to John Pope.

Lincoln needed a general-in-chief to coordinate the operations of McDowell, presently defending Washington, with those of Pope, who was occupying north-central Virginia, and with those of McClellan, down by the James River.

The president made a secret visit to West Point, to consult with Scott. The old hero had retired to the academy, where he was surrounded by adoring cadets. Scott urged Lincoln to send for Halleck, who was serving out west. This recommendation was seconded by Dennis Hart Mahan, the most influential professor at West Point and the nation's leading authority on the military art. Halleck was summoned east, to assumed the vacant post of general-in-chief.

He was to prove a profound disappointment. This general, on whom Lincoln pinned his highest hopes, was, he told his secretary, John Hay, "only a first-rate clerk." Halleck was full of advice, history, precedents and analogies, but the responsibility of making tough decisions made his scholar's soul squirm. He ambled with a professorial stoop. His bulging, rheumy eyes inspired rumors that he was an opium addict. He was forty-seven in 1862 but looked seventy-four. Halleck had no manners to speak of and when people spoke to him had an infuriating habit of looking away and scratching his elbows.

The question Lincoln wanted an answer to from his new general-in-chief was, What should be done about the Army of the Potomac? It was crammed into a small area around Harrison's Landing, unable to train or maneuver, and so tightly packed the risk of epidemics was high.

Halleck lectured the president so comprehensively on the dangers run by divided forces that Lincoln ordered an evacuation. McClellan protested, rightly, that Washington was making a terrible mistake.

The army ought to have been ordered instead to improve its position. It could have been maintained by the James indefinitely, posing a threat to Richmond that Lee could never have taken his eyes away from. It would be two years before another federal army was so close to the Confederate capital, and then only after paying a high price to get there. What the Army of the Potomac needed in August 1862 was not a new location but a new commander.

LEE HAD organized the best military intelligence system of the war. Even before McClellan's troops began reembarking he sent Jackson north, to maul Pope's provocatively named Army of Virginia. And once most of the Army of the Potomac was steaming over the horizon, Lee too was on the move, heading north at top speed. He intended to destroy Pope's army before McClellan could disembark his troops and redeploy.

Virginia, however, is cut by numerous east–west rivers and streams, offering good lines of defense to commanders who know how to make the most of them. Pope showed his skill by frustrating Lee's attempts to cross the Rapidan River for an entire week.

During that week, though, Jackson was left free to roam. He took his foot cavalry north, to Manassas. That railhead had been turned into a supply valhalla for all the Union forces operating in Virginia. The starving, ragged Confederates fell on it like piranhas. There was too much to eat, too much to wear, too much to carry away. The bonfire the rebels created burned for days.

This daring stroke nevertheless left Jackson deep in enemy territory. McClellan and the tens of thousands of troops in and around Washington had only to make a swift descent on Manassas, using the hundreds of trains available, to trap Jackson. It was the North's misfortune that McClellan hated Pope so much, seeing in him a potential rival, that the trains and troops put in motion to cut off Jackson were halted at Alexandria.

Here was Halleck's first great challenge as general-in-chief, and he blew it. He lacked the strength of character to intervene and order McClellan to push on down to Manassas and stop wasting time. Lincoln looked on in mental anguish, unwilling to overrule his new general-in-chief.

Pope raced north from the Rapidan, looking for Jackson, intending to crush him before Lee could bring up the main Confederate body. The foot cavalry kept its cool, going to ground in woods near Bull Run, dropping out of sight as if spirited away. By the time Pope eventually found them Lee was not far away. They were also in a strong position, along an unfinished railroad grade. It was as good as a rampart. Pope's frontal attacks on it achieved nothing, and as night fell Lee arrived on the scene.

In the morning the battle resumed, over almost exactly the same ground as First Bull Run. Pope launched another attack on Jackson's troops, under the mistaken impression they were retreating. And then the Confederate main body, under James Longstreet, suddenly appeared on his left front. Pope had assumed Longstreet was somewhere far to the west. The Confederates began to overwhelm Pope's left. He disengaged coolly, bringing his army out of danger in good fighting order.

That did not stop panic from gripping the capital. All the money in the Treasury was shipped to New York. McClellan ordered the chain bridge over the Potomac demolished. Some steadier hand and cooler head, probably Lincoln's, countermanded the order.

Second Bull Run was a defeat, not a disaster. Pope was banished to the wilds of Minnesota anyway. His army was merged into the Army of the Potomac. And Lee moved on, advancing triumphantly toward Maryland.

As the Confederates pressed deeper into the North, Jackson was sent west to seize Harpers Ferry, thereby covering Lee's left flank. By massing a dozen guns on the heights overlooking the town the Confederates forced the surrender of Dixon S. Miles and 12,000 Federals.

The 40,000 men of the Army of Northern Virginia who advanced into Maryland with Lee were buoyed up by the thought that they were coming as liberators, on a mission to free secessionists who were being held down by the force of Union arms. They were in fact invading the wrong part of the state. Western Maryland was filled with prosperous German farmers, who despised Southern poverty, Southern slavery, Southern soldiery. They slammed their doors shut in the face of Lee's starving, tattered troops, among whom many were barefoot (and thereby excused from combat).

The loss of a copy of Lee's orders to his corps commanders for the northern campaign gave McClellan the greatest intelligence windfall of the war, and possibly the century. It enabled him bring 85,000 men to Sharpsburg, five miles north of Harpers Ferry, in time to check Lee's advance. On September 17 the Confederates formed line of battle along Antietam Creek.

The countryside was deeply undulating. To Lee's practiced eye as a topographical engineer it was ideal for defense. McClellan attacked, but piecemeal. He never had more than 20,000 men in action at a time. The Federals struck Lee's left shortly after dawn, driving it back. Around noon McClellan attacked the center, wrecking it at dreadful cost to both armies. In the afternoon he launched an assault with Ambrose Burnside's corps against the Confederate right. Just as Burnside got across the creek and in position to crush Lee's right flank, up from Harpers Ferry pounded the 2,000 men of A. P. Hill's Light Division. They rode out the last Union attack as evening fell.

It was the deadliest day of a very bloody war. Union dead were 2,000, wounded 9,500. Confederate losses were estimated at 2,700 killed, 9,000 wounded. The Army of Northern Virginia was shoeless, ravenous and fought-out. Said E. Porter Alexander, Lee's artillery chief, "The end of the Confederacy was in sight."

Lee remained on the battlefield all next day, like a general who was ready, possibly more than ready, to fight again. McClellan, who had a reserve of 30,000 men who had seen no action except as spectators, lacked the nerve to attack again. What little confidence he had was spent. When Lee pulled out he departed unharried, unhurried.

Yet with him went the last, best and possibly only hope of the Confederacy—foreign recognition. That prize was never so close as after McClellan evacuated Harrison's Landing and Pope was beaten at Second Bull Run.

Since the Revolution, Britain and France had longed to see the American experiment fail, to see it break up, with the states going their separate ways. That way it would never be a rival for world power. In the summer of 1862 they were sorely tempted to help disintegration along. As they tried to talk each other into recognizing the Confederacy, Secretary of State William Seward sent them an unambiguous, unyielding message: recognition of the Confederate States would mean war with the United States.

The South tried to force Europe's hand by imposing a cotton embargo shortly after the war began. Yet there had been huge cotton crops in recent years. A glut of the stuff filled European warehouses. Britain and France had also begun to depend on cheap American food to feed their fast-growing urban populations. It was easier to do without the South's cotton than to risk the loss of Northern corn, wheat and canned meat.

Only battlefield victories, the dazzling stepping-stones to a Confederacy that would last into the twentieth century, could have brought European intervention to the aid of the South. However badly McClellan performed at Antietam, the battle showed that Lee, for all his tactical genius and inspiring character, lacked the manpower and the firepower to win ultimate independence for the Confederate States of America.

Lincoln seized the psychological moment and pulled off the propaganda masterstroke of the war. Five days after Antietam he announced his intention to declare the independence of Southern slaves at the New Year. With that he turned the war for the Union into a moral crusade, to the indignation of federal soldiers, few of whom cared a fig for blacks or worried one bit about slavery. What they were fighting for was the Union.

Lincoln's timing revealed the politician beneath the crusader's cloak. So did the way he presented the Emancipation Proclamation when it was promulgated on January 1, 1863. He unveiled it not as a great leap forward in justice but as a military necessity. The freeing of Southern slaves was promoted as if it were a battle plan, designed to undermine Southern resistance while raising Union army spirits high.

The president had done something else that was even more likely to discourage the Confederates while helping the boys in blue—he had gotten rid of McClellan. The Army of the Potomac ambled after Lee following the Battle of Antietam as if on a fall stroll. One week after the November 1862 elections, Lincoln sacked Little Mac, replacing him with Burnside.

The army that Burnside took over numbered 120,000 men. It was lavishly equipped, well trained and experienced, but this was not an ideal time to open a campaign in Virginia. The rivers were high, broad and fast-flowing, overbrimming with the rains of late fall.

His intention was to drive south, cross the Rappahannock quickly, then strike at the Army of Northern Virginia before Lee could dig in for the winter around the strategically important town of Fredericksburg. For the best part of a week Burnside maneuvered so adeptly Lee was bewildered, but delay in shipping him the pontoons he requested to cross the river wiped out the advantages won by his rapid advance and maneuvering. By the time Burnside reached Fredericksburg, Lee had half the Army of Northern Virginia securely dug in on Marye's Heights, the steep, high ground that dominates both the town and the river.

Burnside pushed across the Rappahannock, captured the lower town and on December 13 launched six frontal assaults on the heights. Federal dead fell three deep in places, to no avail. South of the town a diversionary attack got across the river at little cost and drove the Confederates out of their defenses, but went unsupported. Burnside had suffered 12,650 casualties for nothing. That thought nearly drove him mad.

He pulled out of Fredericksburg like a man dazed and close to a nervous breakdown. For days he led the Army of the Potomac like a lost tribe through pouring rain, looking for another place to cross the raging Rappahannock. Derided by his sodden troops as "the Mud March," this futile trek undermined the army's confidence and forced Lincoln to relieve him.

Despite profound misgivings, the president gave the command to Joseph Hooker. The man looked magnificent astride a spirited horse, with the prospect of battle lustering his eye. Known throughout the army as "Fighting Joe"—a moniker he loathed—Hooker began well.

He revived morale after it sank into the mud of the Rappahannock by giving every corps a distinctive unit patch. The idea of a unit patch began with one of the Army of the Potomac's division commanders, Philip Kearny. Under Hooker unit patches spread throughout Union armies, and from those patches much modern military heraldry has evolved.

His fellow generals rated Hooker highly, but only as a division or corps commander, where he could watch his entire force in action. Lincoln had elevated him to his level of incompetence. As if suspecting as much, the president gave Hooker plenty of unsolicited advice.

There were directions on strategy: "Lee's army, and not Richmond, is your true objective point." He told him how to fight Lee: "In your next battle *put in all your men*." He told him where to fight Lee: "If he comes toward the upper Potomac, follow on his flank."

Once the roads dried out and the rivers fell, in April 1863, Hooker pulled off one of the best feats of maneuvering the war produced. By rapid marching and clever feints at various fords he managed to to cross the Rappahannock undetected and put three entire army corps in the rear of Lee's positions at Fredericksburg without the Confederates realizing he was there. At which point he received word that Lee was pulling out of the town and coming toward him. Hooker simply froze in his tracks.

His nerve gone, he waited for the rest of his army to cross the river and join him around a house known as Chancellorsville. The area he found himself in was so densely forested it had few roads and few dwellings. It was known to local people as "The Wilderness."

Lee withdrew from Fredericksburg, leaving only a small covering force to defend the town and protect his rear as he headed west, toward Chancellorsville. Compared to the 73,000 Federals Hooker had brought over the Rappahannock, Lee was heading toward him with only 43,000 men. Even so, the Confederates intended to attack.

Lee detached Jackson with more than half the army to make a long detour around the Union right wing. Throughout an entire day a modest Confederate force faced down a federal army three times its size while Jackson got into position to attack. It was late afternoon when Jackson's troops burst from the woods, some half naked, their clothes left in strips on the closely packed trees and bushes of The Wilderness.

Hurling themselves on Union troops who were busy preparing supper, the Confederates nearly broke the Union right. Darkness was falling fast. The attack petered out. Jackson rode ahead of his lines, to make the kind of command reconnaissance he had often made. He may well have been planning a night attack. We shall never know. In the fast-gathering darkness he was mortally wounded by his own troops, who mistook him and his aides for Union soldiers.

After two more days of inconclusive clashes the Battle of Chancellorsville sputtered to a close. The Confederates were too used up to launch more attacks and the Federals too leaderless. Once more the Army of the Potomac marched away in good order while behind them Lee's army was gasping and hurting, on the brink of collapse. Each side had taken roughly 12,000 casualties.

In late June, Hooker, resenting stories circulating in the army that the War Department would never trust him to fight a battle again, sent Lincoln a telegram that amounted to "Back me, or sack me." Next day Lincoln sacked him, probably to Hooker's immense relief. The new commander of the Army of the Potomac was George G. Meade.

As he took over, Lee was on the move once more, heading north once more.

LEE's objectives when he set off for Pennsylvania are debatable. The campaign arose from various concerns—a long-running disagreement with Davis over strategy, a wish to help relieve some of the pressure Grant was applying against Vicksburg, the need to deny the Army of the Potomac the initiative. His attempts to justify the march north were so vague they left his two ablest corps commanders, Longstreet and D. H. Hill, bewildered and depressed. Hill felt he heard in the beating drums of his regiments as they advanced "the death knell of the doomed Confederacy."

Yet a rare spirit lifted the marchers' hearts, a feeling of power, even invincibility. After Fredericksburg, after Chancellorsville, they had the bluebellies on the run. Now they would finish them off. Behind their bloodred battle flags 75,000 Confederates pounded down the dusty roads of summer, heads high, with toothbrushes stuck in frayed buttonholes like roses.

By June 24 Lee had his army across the Potomac. Richard S. Ewell's corps was advancing rapidly across southern Pennsylvania. Yet although these developments sent a shock through the North, Lee seemed unsure of what he was doing. Orders along the line of march were vague and muddled. Stuart, on whom the army depended heavily for scouting enemy movements, rode off toward the east when it was intended that he should go west.

For once it was the boys in blue who knew hour by hour where the Johnny Rebs were, and in what strength, while Lee could only guess what Meade's army was doing and which way it was headed.

Although much of Washington was frantic with worry, Lincoln saw the Confederate advance for what it really was: "A raid into Pennsylvania . . . [and] the best opportunity we have had since the war began." To seize that opportunity he had to rely on Meade.

The general described all battles as "gambles." And now, raised to command an entire army, Meade never felt lucky.

On June 30 A. P. Hill's divisions were closing from the west on Gettysburg, from which roads and railway lines radiated like spokes from a wheel. Ewell's corps was descending on the town from the north. That same day Meade was scouting defensive possibilities twenty miles southeast, along Big Pipe Creek.

Next day a Confederate infantry division moved briskly toward Gettysburg, spurred by a rumor of shoes. Awaiting them were 3,000 dismounted cavalry under Brigadier General John Buford, supported by an artillery battery. While every fourth man held horses' reins the rest used their breech-loading carbines to hold off more than 7,000 Confederates for two hours. Time for John Reynolds, commanding I Corps, to come to their aid.

Neither Lee nor Meade wanted to fight at Gettysburg. The issue was settled by Buford and Reynolds, Ewell and Hill. Confederates surged into the town throughout the afternoon of July 1, forcing the Federals out.

They fell back on the low hills and ridges strung in an arc south of Gettysburg. That night, as more Union divisions marched in, axes sang in the darkness. While behind the Confederate line slaves could be heard calling out their masters' names as they sought them, dead or alive, thousands of Union soldiers were cutting down trees. They collected railroad ties, dismantled stone walls, rebuilt them somewhere more helpful, dug trenches, caught fitful sleep.

As dawn broke on July 2 Meade, who had arrived around midnight, found most of his 91,000 men behind strong defenses. These ran from Culp's Hill, which covered the right rear of his position, to Cemetery Hill, at its northern end, then south from that along Cemetery Ridge toward the eminence of Little Round Top: a convex line that stretched three miles.

The bow shape made it possible to reinforce any point along it quickly and helped protect the rear. At the same time the upper portion was, in effect, a salient, thus vulnerable to fire from two directions. The Federals were fortunate: Confederate gunners failed to see the prospect before them.

The chief Union advantage was holding a position based on a ridge. The Confederates could spring no surprises. They had to cross open ground swept by artillery and rifled musket fire.

Lee's plan for July 2 was to turn Meade's left, near Little Round Top. From there Longstreet's troops would push north, rolling up the line.

At 1 P.M. as both armies waited in rising anticipation for the attack all knew was coming, an entire Union corps advanced. Daniel Sickles, a mustang general from New York, did not like the look of the high ground to his front. The enemy might plant artillery on it. Without securing Meade's approval or informing the units to his right or left, he moved III Corps forward half a mile. He had created a large triangular salient to the right front of Little Round Top, leaving it exposed.

Longstreet smashed one of his flanks. Hill smashed the other. The III Corps seemed about to collapse. Sickles lost a leg and was removed from the field. Regiments from I and XII Corps pushed forward to cover the men of III Corps streaming back from the road where Sickles had taken them.

Longstreet's troops charged exultantly toward the base of Little Round Top, occupied only by a Union signal detachment that was about to pull out. The Confederates collided with one hundred sharpshooters armed with breechloaders. Their fire was so intense Confederates flung themselves among the rocks and bushes, reporting back they were fighting at least two Union regiments. For forty minutes Longstreet's advance halted.

In that space Meade sent his chief engineer, Gouverneur K. Warren, to inspect his left wing. Warren saw at a glance that Little Round Top was the key to the Union position. Enemy artillery placed here would enfilade Meade's line. He asked a nearby battery to fire a single round into the treetops opposite. There was a flash of golden light: the sun, reflecting on thousands of bayonets and gun barrels as Confederates, massing under cover in the woods to attack the hill, turned to follow that shell's flight. "Thrilled and appalled," said Warren, he sent for an infantry division.

Five minutes after it arrived, Hood's Texans stormed up the boulder-broken slope. They were successfully driven back in merciless hand-to-hand struggles. When the sun set on July 2 the Union left was stronger than it had been when it rose, but only just.

That night Meade called a council of war. During the morning he had ordered plans be drawn up for a retreat. The events of the day seem to have encouraged his resolve. The unanimous decision was to remain in position, to see what another day might bring. It brought legend.

Lee decided to break the Union center. Longstreet, looking over the twelve hundred yards of open ground between the woods of Seminary Ridge, where his corps was posted, and the rising ground of Cemetery Ridge, protested. It was impossible, unthinkable, against modern guns and rifled muskets.

Lee had only one fresh division left, commanded by George S. Pickett, holder of last place in the West Point class of '46, the class of McClellan and Stonewall Jackson. Pickett, with his perfumed curly hair falling romantically to his shoulders, was to lead out his three intact brigades and what remained of eight others. In all, roughly 12,000 men.

Stuart had returned the previous day, during the fight for Little Round Top, with jaded horses and exhausted men. Lee now ordered him to make a wide circuit, to hit Meade's center from the rear while Pickett struck it from in front.

From 1 P.M. until shortly after 2 P.M. Confederate and Union artillery dueled across the open ground. A Confederate band offered a medley of waltzes and polkas. Federal fire suddenly slackened: Hunt was saving his long-range ammunition for Pickett. Confederate gunners, misunderstanding, were jubilant.

They mistakenly thought they had won a great victory over Union artillerists. Cutting their fuses too long, firing too high, hampered by poor ammunition, they had achieved nothing beyond killing some artillery horses.

Pickett finished writing a letter to his fiancée, rose and saluted Longstreet. "Shall I advance, General?" Longstreet looked away. Too choked with despair to utter a word, he nodded stiffly from horseback.

A gray wave half a mile long broke from the dark-green woods; row upon row, men trampled the high grass of summer, behind forty-three fluttering flags. The wave flowed across the open fields. Hunt's gunners blew holes in it. The gaps closed up. The gray tide flowed over the fence along the Emmitsburg road. Three hundred yards from the federal guns men calmly dressed ranks by the roadside. Bodies and limbs flew through the air. Six Union guns manhandled onto Little Round Top enfiladed the advancing line, making it sway, forcing it to bunch up in the center. It flowed on. Its famous last classman stayed behind, in a farmhouse near the road.

Two miles to the east Stuart was headed off by 3,600 Union horsemen led by another academy last classman, George Armstrong Custer.

All this while Lee was seated on the stump of a tree, watching the gray line move away from him. Throughout that afternoon he sent one message, received one report. He passed his epic hour alone, rising at times to watch the action through his field glass.

At last the gray line broke upon its destined shore, around a grove of trees near the center of the Union line. For the last one hundred yards rifled musket fire, aimed steadily and low, harvested men like death's own scythe. Twelve-pounder Napoleons,* double-shotted with canister, boomed like gigantic shotguns.

The handful of Confederates who planted red standards on Ceme-

*See page 237.

tery Ridge were killed, taken prisoner or driven back. Lee, advancing from his tree stump, consoled General Cadmus Marcellus Wilcox, close to tears beneath a ragged straw hat as he mourned the extinction of his brigade: "This has all been *my* fault, General." And as darkness fell he would groan, "Too bad! *Too bad!* Oh! TOO BAD!"

Meade had missed the moment. He came riding up the reverse slope of Cemetery Ridge, face white and drawn. "How is it going here?"

"I believe, General, the enemy is repulsed," said Captain Frank Haskell of the 6th Wisconsin.

"What! Is the assault already repulsed?"

"It is, sir."

"Thank God!" Then, hat in hand, too restrained to wave it, Meade shouted, "Hoorah!"

His losses for the three days were one fourth of his army; Lee's amounted to one third of his. Innocent of History's judgment that they had lost the fight, Lee's troops remained in position all day on July 4. That night, as heavy rain drowned out the sound of retreating feet, they started on the weary march home.

Meade launched no counterstroke. Ten days later, as Lee escaped back into Virginia, Lincoln collapsed onto the couch in Gideon Welles's office. "There is bad faith somewhere! What does it mean, Mr. Welles? Great God!" He lay there, too depressed to move.

West of the Alleghenies, Union and Confederate armies were fighting what was almost a separate war. When 1862 began and Lincoln issued his War Order Number 1 there were 85,000 Confederates defending a front that stretched from Arkansas to the Cumberland Gap. They were commanded by Albert Sidney Johnston, a man of such imposing military talents that federal agents had tried to capture him shortly after Fort Sumter, while he was still a civilian, rather than allow him to join the Confederate cause. Like Lee, he had made his reputation in the Mexican War.

On January 19, 1862, an enterprising Union commander, Brigadier General George H. Thomas, mounted an attack on the Confederate division holding Mill Springs, Kentucky. Thomas's victory dented what amounted to Johnston's right wing.

Two weeks later Ulysses S. Grant, returned to uniform as a colonel of volunteers and recently promoted brigadier general, led a force of

18,000 Federals on a fleet of steamboats down the Tennessee River in western Kentucky to attack Fort Henry. This "strongpoint" had been erected the previous summer, when the river was low. In the February rains the waters rose rapidly. Seven Union gunboats moved in to engage the fort. Water was lapping the defenders' ankles. It soon rose to their waists. The magazine was about to drown.

As most of the garrison pulled out, a fort surrendered to a fleet. There was no need for the infantry assault, formed up in columns, waiting orders to attack. With the fall of Fort Henry on February 11, Johnston's center was dented.

Grant rapidly moved on, toward Fort Donelson, on the Cumberland River, only twelve miles away, to which the Fort Henry garrison had fled. This time when the gunboats closed in on the fort they were forced to withdraw under heavy fire. In command at Fort Donelson was Gideon Pillow, also returned to uniform; a fact that gave Grant enormous confidence.

The Union army set siege in bitter cold, over snow-flecked ground. Each morning saw burial parties make their rounds, collecting pickets from trees and trenches where hypothermia had drawn them into everlasting sleep. As the siege works advanced, the Confederates tried to break out. For several hours they had an open road south. Grant, arriving in haste, soon shut it.

Pillow escaped in the night on a raft, abandoning his men to their fate. Nathan Bedford Forrest was the last to get away, leading his cavalry regiment through freezing water that reached their saddles. And it was here that Grant's personal legend began, in his offering the fort's remaining defenders "No terms except unconditional and immediate surrender." On February 16 the fort and its 11,500 Confederates were in his hands.

Johnston's center was now shattered. Forced to pull back, he gave up Nashville without a struggle to Don Carlos Buell and the Army of the Ohio. Meanwhile Grant was virtually under arrest. Halleck, stationed in St. Louis and trying to coordinate the operations of three Union armies in the west, was busily exchanging telegrams with McClellan about court-martialing Grant for insubordination.

Grant had a reputation in the army as a man who had resigned his commission in 1854 to avoid being thrown out as a drunk; a man who had then failed as a farmer, failed in real estate and failed in the leather business. If military careers were limited to the saintly and the infallible, however, there were hardly enough officers left to command a platoon. The real problem was that Grant went his own way.

The swift descent on Fort Donelson, for example, was not even discussed with Halleck. Grant did it on his own responsibility, reading the situation on the ground as requiring it once Fort Henry fell. It was characteristic. When the Confederates had seized Columbus, Kentucky, while federal forces nearby hung back, reluctant to invade a neutral state and possibly force it into the enemy camp, Grant acted alone. On September 6, 1861, he had seized Paducah, Kentucky, just thirty-six hours after Columbus had fallen. His commanding general at that time was Frémont. Grant did not bother to tell him what he was doing until he had done it. He counted on events to vindicate him. They did. Kentucky stayed neutral. And by this movement he had begun, without realizing it, the push south he was destined to lead.

For all his great learning Halleck had a serious blind spot, and Grant's genius was it. The more impressive the little general's victories, the more strenuously Halleck tried to shunt him off into oblivion. It may have had nothing to do with jealousy or foolishness; simply sheer incomprehension. Grant's kind of generalship did not appear in any of the books Halleck read. And all he knew of war he drew from books. Only Lincoln's intervention saved Grant in February 1862, and would do again. It showed that this Kentucky-born president who lived in central Illinois had his eye on an Ohio-born general who lived in northern Illinois. Although they had never met they had friends in common.

Restored to command once again, Grant moved his Army of the Tennessee down the Tennessee River toward Mississippi and the railroad hub of Corinth. On the advice of Sherman, who was commanding a division in his army, he placed his 43,000 troops at Pittsburg Landing, once busy with boats loading cotton but long since bypassed once the railroads reached western Tennessee. Halleck ordered him to wait there until joined by Buell and the 20,000 men of the Army of the Ohio.

To Johnston and his second-in-command, the ubiquitous Beauregard, it was obvious they must defeat Grant before Buell arrived. Gathering troops from all over the South, they brought their strength at Corinth to 41,000 men. The inexperience of these troops and their officers, the ruggedness of the terrain and the poor communications of an impoverished army slowed them to a crawl. It took three days to cover the last twenty-three miles—a delay that allowed Buell's van to reach the Tennessee River. At daybreak on April 6 the Confederates attacked Grant's army as it lay scattered around a log church with a biblical name, Shiloh.

The Confederates achieved a psychological surprise and, to some degree, a tactical one: Union regiments got into line of battle, but half undressed and half asleep. The terrain worked to federal advantage. There were many places where troops under pressure could fall back and make a stand. And the Confederates, trying to deploy a large army off of what amounted to a pair of cart tracks, were unable to concentrate their full weight at any one point.

Both armies were green: the kind of raw levies that, officers said, would "either fight like the devil or run like hell." Which is what happened. While thousands skulked, other thousands fought with fatal courage. For years afterward Shiloh was described as being utterly chaotic. It was, rather, the great curtain raiser on modern battles. Gone were linear tactics. Each regiment, each company found itself fighting its own war as, within units, did each soldier. Troops were milling in the hollows, crawling under bushes, crouching behind trees, only to be formed into fresh combinations under commanders hardly any of them knew, ignoring the boundaries between regiments and divisions. Men found themselves fighting with up to half a dozen units—or fragments of units—as the battle wore on.

Albert Sidney Johnston did a colonel's work, rallying first this regiment, then that, and leading them in charge after charge. When he remounted his horse around 2 P.M. he was shot in the leg. His left boot filled with blood. A tourniquet might have saved him. He ignored the fact that he was bleeding to death.

A Union division at the center of the line turned a hollow near a slight crest into a natural fortification. The Confederates put most of their efforts into reducing this position, instead of sealing it off and moving around it. When its 2,000 survivors finally surrendered late in the day a new Union line had been formed, artillery massed to defend it, and Buell's troops were crossing the river.

The Confederates had pushed the Federals back nearly two miles. Next day Grant and Buell regained all the lost ground in three hours. There was no pursuit. Grant would later claim that he lacked the heart to order men exhausted by two days of fighting and mired in pouring rain to give chase. Most of Buell's army had seen no fighting, nor had several of Grant's divisions. More than 5,000 fresh cavalry were on hand. The battered Confederate army limped away, unhindered, toward Corinth.

In the North, Shiloh was greeted not only as the first great battle of the war but also as the first great Union victory. Despite the losses it was celebrated exuberantly. Union casualties were 1,754 killed in action, 8,508 wounded. Confederate losses were 1,723 killed, 8,012 wounded. The South too hailed Shiloh as a victory. It was a stalemate; a bloody one.

Halleck's response was the same as after Fort Donelson: he tried to shelve Grant. This time, though, he left St. Louis and came to take command in person. The troops noticed the change at once. Halleck made them dig in. He advanced toward Corinth at one or two miles a day, entrenching each night.

Instead of fighting for the town, Beauregard pulled out. Halleck then dispersed his army, unsure of where to go next. Grant argued for a descent on Vicksburg, but was more or less banished to occupation duty in western Tennessee. Buell was sent to hold central Tennessee and watch over Kentucky. Halleck was content to remain where he was, to sit it out in Corinth if it took all summer. In mid-July came the call to go east and become general-in-chief. Only by that turn of fate would Grant get a second chance.

The defense of Corinth was handed over to William S. Rosecrans. He soon had a fight on his hands, because Earl Van Dorn and 21,000 Confederates attempted to retake the town. The well-entrenched federal defenders inflicted 5,000 casualties, suffered 3,000, and beat off the attack.

Rosecrans's performance was less than brilliant. As the shattered Confederates pulled out, he was too disorganized mentally to use his half-dozen fresh regiments to make a pursuit. The successful defense of Corinth nonetheless made him a coming man in the Union army.

Shortly afterward, in September 1862, as Lee advanced into Maryland, another Confederate army, under Braxton Bragg, advanced into Kentucky from Chattanooga. Buell's Army of the Ohio was expected to stop Bragg's invasion. Instead, Buell fell back nearly one hundred miles. Like his good friend and mentor Halleck, he was in his element at headquarters but in the field had no love of fighting. Pushed hard by Washington, he turned around and went looking for Bragg.

Bragg was meanwhile dismayed as he led his 30,000 troops deep into Kentucky. His army too felt it was on a mission of liberation to free downtrodden, captive secessionists. As it advanced, however, Bragg had serious doubts. He had never seen such fat cattle. "The people here are too rich to fight," he complained.

October 8 found him busy stage-managing the swearing-in of a secesh governor at Frankfort. The sound of artillery fire interrupted the ceremony. His troops and some of Buell's collided near Perryville and began fighting. When he realized Buell had a 50-percent advantage in manpower, Bragg abandoned his half-sworn governor and fence-straddling Kentucky. Buell's failure to chase after Bragg cost him his command. He was replaced by Rosecrans.

This appointment was another case of elevating a man to his level of incompetence. Dana, who was a shrewd judge of character, called him "mazed and dazy." The general was a recent convert to the Catholic faith and liked to keep his staff up till dawn discussing theology. His temperament was mercurial, his judgment too emotional, his orders ambiguous and sometimes incoherent.

At Christmas 1862 Rosecrans caught up with Bragg at Murfreesboro, twenty-five miles southeast of Nashville. The Confederates were deployed in strong positions along both sides of the shallow Stones River. When Rosecrans hesitated to attack, Bragg struck, on New Year's Eve.

The Union right was forced back and nearly enveloped, but Rosecrans rose to the challenge, showed inspiring courage and rode out the storm. After two days of further skirmishing and hopeless attacks by both sides, Bragg retreated. He had lost nearly one third of his 38,000 men. Rosecrans had lost one fourth of his 47,000.

FROM the moment Halleck went east and Grant resumed command of the 65,000 men of the Army of the Tennessee, he knew exactly what he should do with them—take Vicksburg. In April 1862 the Union navy had forced its way up the mouth of the Mississippi, forced a passage past the forts below New Orleans, and pressed on to capture the Crescent City. At a blow the navy had taken one of the South's main industrial centers, in one of the most remarkable achievements of the war. In the summer two attempts were made to capture Vicksburg by the navy. A fleet of powerful gunboats came down from

Memphis to force the town to surrender, only to be compelled to withdraw by artillery posted on the bluffs overlooking the river.

Vicksburg was protected by nature like few places on earth: by the serpentine Mississippi below and by the swampy land all around. Elsewhere, rivers and streams were highways and roads. Here, among steaming forests and malarial bayous, they were barriers. Armies needed firm hard ground to march along, to put their guns upon, to fight upon. What high ground there was, the Confederates held. The terrain was worth an army to John Pemberton, the Confederate commander at Vicksburg.

Grant attempted to storm it from the river, sending Sherman with four divisions to land at Chickasaw Bluffs during the last days of December 1862. Sherman pushed his men right up to the Confederate lines under a withering cross fire. He lost 208 killed, 1,005 wounded, and had nothing to show for it. Confederate losses totaled 197. Sherman withdrew, utterly frustrated.

Grant's plan to move overland and attack Vicksburg from the north also suffered a setback. The huge supply base he created at Holly Springs near the Tennessee-Mississippi border was raided by Earl Van Dorn. Millions of dollars' worth of supplies was looted or incinerated. Hundreds of Federals were taken prisoner, among them Mrs. Grant.

These were depressing days for the Union army. Morale fell like a stone in the winter of 1862–63. Second Bull Run, Lee's escape from Antietam, the heavy losses at Stones River, the slaughter at Marye's Heights, the bonfire at Holly Springs, the total defeat at Chickasaw Bluffs and the degrading Mud March made officers speak softly, their thoughts turning gray with the winter's gloom. Yet in the bright dancing flames of Holly Springs, Grant was vouchsafed a revelation. Van Dorn's raid was cheered across the South as gilded success. If so, it cost dearly.

In April 1863 Grant sent a music teacher, Brigadier General Benjamin Grierson, on a raid that cut a wide swath of alarm through the length of Mississippi. Grierson's 1,000 horsemen drew off all of Pemberton's cavalry and some of his infantry. Grant meantime moved 40,000 men down the Mississippi, landing them nearly fifty miles below the town.

Once safely ashore he cut loose from his base on the river, to march east and north, heading for Jackson—the state capital and Vicksburg's main rail link. From Jackson he intended to move due west, heading back toward the river, to attack Vicksburg in effect from the rear. He was doing much as Scott had done in 1847 when he cut himself off from Veracruz to advance on Mexico City.

All thanks to Holly Springs. A mountain of supplies had gone up in flames yet not one soldier went hungry. The countryside was so rich his army could live off it without forcing the people to starve. That came as a revelation to former quartermaster Grant. When his army cut itself loose from its base on the Mississippi his troops carried five days' rations. Their wagons carried nothing but ammunition and engineering equipment.

Pemberton parceled out his forces in his attempt to stop Grant's inexorable, rapid advance. As a result, Confederate superiority of numbers was thrown away. In the space of three weeks Grant fought five battles, winning all five.

The biggest, at Champion Hill on May 16, saw 20,000 Confederates defending the crest of a line of low hills against 33,000 Federals. After each side had suffered roughly 2,200 casualties, Pemberton pulled out, his troops racing the nine miles back to Vicksburg and its welcoming entrenchments. Six days later Grant tried to take the town by storm. He failed, with heavy losses.

Grant settled down to a siege, begging heavy guns from the navy. He had 32s and 42s and 10-inch columbiads as well as the army's 13-inch mortars to batter the Confederate lines. There would be no bombardments to match these until World War One. What Grant really counted on, however, was hunger and despair.

Lincoln knew the Mississippi well. He could see it in his mind, could understand the problems Grant faced. As the siege dragged on he sent a message: this campaign would rank, he said, "as one of the most brilliant in the world," even if it failed.

By the end of June, Pemberton's men were living on one biscuit and one ounce of bacon per day. They boiled grass and weeds for make-believe soup.

Pemberton hoarded nearly fifty tons of food and forty thousand artillery rounds, planning to ride out Grant's ultimate, all-out assault. When he realized that there was not going to be a gigantic battle, that Grant would starve him out however long it took, Pemberton asked for talks. On July 4, the day after the grand climacteric at Gettysburg, Vicksburg fell to Grant.

News that the town had fallen broke the siege of Port Hudson, ninety miles farther south, where Nathaniel Banks and a Union army had been wallowing in Mississippi mud for months. By August 1863 the entire mighty river was in Lincoln's hands. And this, urged Grant, was the time for a federal assault on Mobile, which would cut the deep South in two. Stanton and Halleck turned him down, because the upper South was not yet secure.

Even now they were prodding Rosecrans to attack. For six months he and Bragg hardly moved. When Rosecrans finally advanced in August 1863 Bragg fell back all the way to Chattanooga, almost taking himself out of Tennessee, and on September 9 he gave up the city to advancing Federals.

As blue regiments marched into Chattanooga in triumph, Longstreet's corps was arriving by train on the outskirts, shipped west hurriedly from Virginia. With these reinforcements Bragg's strength rose to 66,000 men. Now he felt strong enough to fight a battle.

So did Rosecrans. He was sending telegrams to clergymen all over the country, demanding their prayers in the impending fight.

It began along Chickamauga Creek, five miles southeast of Chattanooga, in woods so deep they resembled a jungle. On September 19 some of Bragg's cavalry clashed with George H. Thomas's corps. After a day of bitter, close combat, Thomas ordered his four divisions to raise breastworks across their front. There was an ample supply of fallen trees. At first light next day Thomas's troops stood to arms behind log walls four or five feet high.

With this strong position firmly established in the center of his line, Rosecrans proceeded to snatch defeat from the tight jaws of victory. Bragg attacked as expected, but Rosecrans chose this moment to order an entire Union division out of the battle line. The order made no sense and cried out for clarification. Instead, the division commander it was addressed to obeyed it, possibly to make a fool of the unpopular, erratic "Rosy."

Longstreet's jubilant corps of veterans poured through the gap, ready to sweep all before them. Then they crashed against the wooden rampart that Thomas had raised. Even without artillery support Thomas's men could hold their ground indefinitely. A dozen Confederate attacks broke against those crude logs.

Thomas and the army's reserve corps, under Gordon Granger, provided the cover needed for Rosecrans to pull his army out and hurry it back toward Chattanooga. Nathan Bedford Forrest had his cavalry mounted, ready to pursue the fleeing Federals, eager to pursue them. Yet that other unpopular and erratic general, Bragg, refused to give the word.

Falling shadows swallowed up a battlefield where as much blood was spilled as at Antietam. Chickamauga was the last Confederate offensive victory, and Rosecrans's last battle.

Following the fall of Vicksburg, Grant had been raised to command nearly all Union forces west of the Alleghenies. He fired Rosecrans and replaced him with Thomas. Then he went to take a look at Chattanooga in person.

What he found was an army that was not exactly besieged but one that felt and acted like one anyway. Rosecrans had pulled back so frantically he had even yielded the high ground overlooking the town.

Grant's first step was to open a secure line of supplies, proving to the troops they were not cut off. Bragg was meanwhile quarreling with Longstreet. In the prewar army Bragg had the reputation of being the most argumentative man alive. The upshot of this quarrel was that Longstreet and his 18,000 men went back to Virginia.

Longstreet's departure, battle losses and a high rate of desertion thinned out the Confederates considerably. On the high ground there was just one rifle to every ten feet of front, and thanks to an entrenching error the troops on Lookout Mountain had obscured fields of fire.

On November 24, with the mountain swathed in fog, Grant attacked. Confederate resistance was light. Next day, the lowest line of Confederate entrenchments was struck at both ends in a double envelopment, completely overrunning them. Then, without any orders to press on, Union army regiments simply raced up the slope in an impetuous rush, giddy with victory.

As the Federals charged the ridge a confused order to a Mississippi regiment created unexpected movement. That produced panic among the thinned-out Confederates left behind. After firing a few wild shots they jumped out of their rifle pits and scampered over the hill.

IT WAS a miserable autumn for Meade. He trailed after Lee following Gettysburg like a man burdened with a chore. There was no urgency, no daring. He was a plodder, and his troops knew it only too well, mocking him in a song that made fun of all the commanders of the Army of the Potomac to the tune of "When Johnny Comes

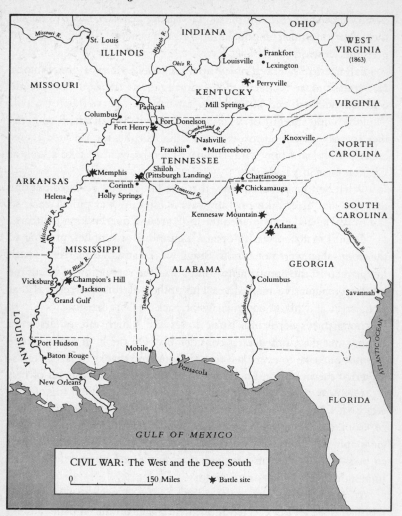

CIVIL WAR: The West and the Deep South

0 _____ 150 Miles   ★ Battle site

Marching Home." The verses dedicated to him began, "Then came
General Meade, a slow old plug/ For he let Lee away after Gettysburg."

He showed a strong disinclination to tangle with the Army of
Northern Virginia. In October 1863 Lee appeared about to attack
Meade's army south of the Rappahannock. Meade rapidly recrossed it,
to put a river between himself and the foe he was ostensibly chasing
after. All battles were gambles and he didn't like the odds on offer.

After all, Lee had 55,000 men, to his own 90,000. He continued falling back. Lee continued advancing.

Lincoln was beside himself with disgust and rage. Why didn't the general attack? Washington was in no danger. It was protected by 21,000 men, one thousand guns and a girdle of strong forts. Lincoln declared publicly that if Meade attacked Lee and was defeated the blame would fall wholly on his, the president's shoulders, for urging him to fight. It made no difference. Meade simply couldn't bring himself to be aggressive.

Lee advanced as far as Centreville before falling back. He was "pursued" once again, by Meade. It was a military quadrille that looked as if it would go on forever.

Lincoln had never given up his search for a Napoleon; a master of victory in the open field, a destroyer of armies, a lord of war. Shortly before Gettysburg he burst out in frustration to Gideon Welles, "We cannot help beating them, if we have the man. How much in military matters depends on one mastermind." After Vicksburg, after Chattanooga, the man had emerged. Lincoln knew it. Congress knew it. The North knew it. That pessimist Longstreet knew it, and warned his fellow generals in gray.

Congress revived the rank of lieutenant general. In February 1864 Lincoln conferred it on Grant, for one purpose: to prepare him for the fight, almost a showdown, with Lee. The Union, about to send forth its champion, clothed him in dazzling raiment—the habiliments of Washington.

It was to be a struggle between two divergent military traditions, embodied in very different men. The son of Light Horse Harry Lee had grown up with military talk, military ideals, military heroes. Grant was prodded forward by his father, an ambitious tanner and real estate speculator who became the richest man in town but thriftily sent his son to West Point when he reached college age.

Grant had no wish to go there and, arrived, had one wish—to leave. From the moment he received his commission his strongest desire was to resign it. Left to follow his own inclinations, he might have been happier as a pacifist than as an officer. He disliked uniforms, found the small world of the military irksome, fled from military music and deplored the celebration of military victories. The sight of blood made him feel faint. Dead men made him turn away. The screams of the wounded were torture to his nerves.

He nevertheless loved his country deeply; even when it was wrong, as he saw it, in fighting Mexico. He was also intellectually certain that "War is progressive, because all the instruments and elements of war are progressive." At frightful cost it dragged the human race forward.

Lee was also a deeply emotional man. Love of his native Virginia, and loyalty to family and friends, proved more compelling than his devotion to the United States. Nearly everyone goes through life with some competing loyalties, but few have ever had to face the kind of choice the war forced on men like Robert E. Lee. When he chose to fight for the Confederacy, Scott counted that a serious loss to the Union. Yet he may have been wrong.

A federal victory under the generalship of Lee would have left the country with a different military heritage, and probably an outdated one. Grant expressed and understood far more deeply the emerging shape of modern warfare.

There is a brief sketch of him that could never have been applied to Lee, dating from April 1864, as Grant prepared to take the field in Virginia: "He keeps his own counsel, padlocks his mouth. . . . Among men he is nowise noticeable. There is no glitter or parade about him. To me he seems but an earnest business man."

He had, in truth, a manager's temperament, an executive's outlook. A stream of telegrams poured from his headquarters. They were concise, they were to the point, they created trust. Sherman was not alone in advancing toward battle confidently, buoyed up by the certain knowledge that Grant was thinking of him at that moment and if anything went wrong would come to his aid, in Sherman's words, "if alive."

As the very model of a modern general, Grant kept himself well informed on technical matters, whether they involved logistics, ordnance or military engineering. Officers assigned to these branches of the army worked all the more effectively for knowing that what they did would be noticed by Grant.

To some degree he simply embodied the bureaucratic, organizational culture of the North at its most energetic and progressive. All Union armies produced paper mountains. By comparison there were few orders and written messages flowing from the headquarters of Confederate armies. Northern officers descended in a straight line from Washington to Scott. That was a tradition Grant both inherited and added to. He was sensitive despite himself to the romantic, idealistic elements of the military art, yet a part of him forever remained the quartermaster and the storekeeper, who saw the war starkly in terms of numbers, logistics and money.

The most obvious difference between his style of command and Lee's was in their orders. There was, and is, what might be termed the elder Von Moltke's First Law of Operations: "Any order that can be misunderstood will be misunderstood."

Grant's orders were pithy but clear, cutting those risks to a minimum. He developed a literary style that made his the best of the thousands of Civil War memoirs and the most admired general's memoirs since Caesar's.

Lee's orders tended to be polite and vague. His style was to issue directives that were long on courtesy but short on specifics. His corps commanders were allowed almost complete autonomy, leaving them free to cooperate with one another as much or as little as they pleased.

In practice this meant that whenever the Army of Northern Virginia gave battle the morning was spent with generals and colonels milling about the headquarters tent trying to agree on a plan, while couriers sped off in a dozen directions on fast horses. Sometime around midafternoon the attack began. If it succeeded, as it often did, it led absolutely nowhere, because by then darkness was falling. Night came many times to the relief of Union armies.

Grant's staff was described by Dana as "a curious mixture of the good, bad and indifferent . . . a mosaic of accidental elements and family friends." Even so, it was far in advance of the "system" Lee had to rely on.

When Grant became general-in-chief he took charge of seventeen army commands and 533,000 men scattered over a continent. He promptly simplified this unwieldy accretion. As a good manager would, he made it more manageable. He created a new position, chief of staff, and put Halleck in it, to provide administrative direction to all Union ground forces. Then, in his private's blouse that glittered with a lieutenant general's stars, he set off for the showdown with Lee.

9

MODERN
TIMES

HALF-FORGOTTEN when the war began was *Fulton the First,* precursor of the steam warship. Fulton had finished her in haste during the winter of 1814, hoping to spare New York from Washington's fiery fate. The War of 1812 ended just as she entered service. Ironclad and double-hulled, armed with a few gigantic guns, she was the most powerful ship afloat and decades ahead of her time. She was lost in a fire at Brooklyn Navy Yard in 1829.

The U.S. Navy of 1861 was a force *Fulton the First* could have demolished. It consisted of twenty-three wooden vessels devoted to showing the flag. This was no mere thimblerigging. In 1853 Commodore Matthew Perry had taken a squadron of ships painted dramatically black to Japan. The flag had been shown so impressively that Japan hastily abandoned its feudal isolation to embrace Western naval guns, and the industries that produced them.

When Lincoln decreed a blockade of Southern ports following Fort Sumter there was little to blockade with. Conversely, the South had even less with which to challenge a blockade had the North been able to impose one. A naval race began to beg, build, borrow or buy anything that floated. The Confederates seized Norfolk Navy Yard. This provided a few ships but the biggest windfall was the mountain of guns, powder and shot. Without this ordnance it may be doubted whether Southern armies would have been able to fight in 1861.

In the 1840s and 1850s Britain and France developed armor-plated, steam-driven ships, carrying guns that fired shells that exploded after penetration. Such shell guns could sink any wooden ship within minutes. The United States, with its all-wooden fleet, had fallen a generation behind in naval technology.

The South, unable to produce even such essentials as marine engines, rose to the naval challenge, showing the kind of ingenuity Northerners liked to preface with "Yankee." When Norfolk Navy Yard fell, one of its newest steam frigates, the USS *Merrimac,* was burned and scuttled. The fire went out at the waterline. Confederate engineers raised the wreck. On her wooden hull they erected a huge superstructure resembling the roof of a Dutch barn, but made of metal and pierced for guns. They were equally forward-looking below. The previous half-century had produced five important naval innovations: steam engines, shell guns, screw propellers, rifled ordnance and armor plate. The *Merrimac* had all five.

Informed by Union spies of these developments, Welles ordered the construction of a ship that could match her, the *Monitor.* Built at New York Navy Yard in the winter of 1862, she carried two guns, both of them ten-inch columbiads, set in a revolving turret. With only eighteen inches of freeboard she looked about to sink; often she was. Slow, ungainly, a poor seakeeper, the *Monitor* was towed out of New York Harbor on March 6, 1862.

The *Merrimac* won this particular naval race. On March 8, while the *Monitor* was off the Delaware coast in danger of going down, the *Merrimac* was smashing up the federal squadron in Hampton Roads, off Fort Monroe. She destroyed one Union frigate, captured another and ran a third aground.

Next morning the *Monitor* arrived. For nearly four hours floating iron slugged it out. All around bobbed the bodies of Union seamen drowned the previous day. The wood-piercing shells of the *Merrimac* bounced off the *Monitor*'s turret. The cast-iron round shot of the *Monitor*'s guns caromed like billiard balls off the *Merrimac*'s sloping superstructure. Check . . . and check. No one was killed. Neither vessel suffered serious damage.

Some of the worst hours Lincoln ever spent were those that dragged between reports that the *Merrimac* was at sea and news that the *Monitor* had fought her to a standstill. Even then, the *Merrimac* preyed on his nerves for weeks. McClellan's advance up the Yorktown peninsula in May 1862 finally ended the suspense. She drew so much water she could not be moved up the James River to safety. She was blown up and scuttled by her grieving crew.

The *Monitor* did not survive her by much. On December 29, 1862, she foundered in a gale off Cape Hatteras. Rarely have such famous ships had such brief careers, yet in a few hours on a single gray March day they had closed a generation gap in naval warfare.

The next year, 1863, Confederate sailors tried to break the blockade of Charleston by using contact mines and a submarine. Neither the mines nor the craft succeeded, but in 1864 a more advanced model of the submarine, the CSS *Hunley,* sank a sloop of war, the USS *Housatonic,* off Fort Sumter. The *Hunley* used a "spar torpedo," a contact mine fixed to the end of a long pole. She never returned from this, the first successful submarine attack in naval history.

The U.S. Navy devoted most of its men and ships to the blockade, yet more than 80 percent of everything shipped to the Confederacy got through. In some respects blockade running was the most successful of all Confederate operations. Anything the South wanted could be shipped in: more than a million firearms, hundreds of thousands of Bibles, tons of chloroform and morphine. Luxuries such as perfume arrived in large quantities. It was late 1864 before all the major Southern ports were closed; most fell to advancing Union armies. By then, however, the South had industrialized to a point at which it no longer needed to import manufactured goods.

The Union blockade had little effect on the outcome of the war, but on western rivers naval operations played a vital part. Beyond the Alleghenies it was the rivers, not the railroads, that kept Grant's fire-and-movement armies advancing. A Union commander supported by river gunboats and supplied by steamboats had a good chance of success. A single steamboat would carry the five hundred tons of supplies needed to keep a Union army of 40,000 men in the field for three days.

Army and navy cooperation on the rivers set an unsurpassed example of interservice harmony. It had been the soldiers, though, who were behind the creation of the powerful river gunboats. Armor-clad with iron plates and railroad rails, mounting thirteen heavy guns, they were almost a secret weapon sprung on unsuspecting Confederates in the spring of 1862. The Confederacy never found an effective answer to them.

On the other hand, the Union never found an effective answer to Southern commerce raiders. Few in number, famous in effect, they fell on Northern shipping in every quarter of the globe. Deficient in seamen and a naval tradition, the Confederacy manned its raiders with hired foreign sailors. Some 257 Northern ships (nearly all under sail, instead of steam) were taken or destroyed. Another 700 were prudently transferred to foreign flags. It took half a century before the American merchant marine grew back to its prewar size.

The most successful of the raiders was the nine-hundred-ton British-built *Alabama,* commanded by Raphael Semmes. This hero of the Mexican War had managed to get assigned to Scott's staff even though he was a naval officer, and he marched all the way to Mexico City. Semmes was a fine character, full of high principles and flowery speeches. After the war he became a professor of moral philosophy. Taking command of the *Alabama* at Birkenhead, England, in August 1862, he found her "a perfect sailing ship and a perfect steamer." Semmes set off on an odyssey that would last two years and carry him around the world. His prizes ran to at least sixty; he himself lost track of the number.

He set his aim high from the start. Unarmed liners were bringing millions of dollars in gold from California to New York every month, around South America. In December 1862 Semmes was lying off the coast of Cuba with steamship timetables, New York newspapers and larcenous hopes. On Sunday, December 7, a steamer, the *Ariel,* appeared. As he ran up the Stars and Bars melodramatic shrieks carried over the water.

What Semmes had stopped was a *west*bound steamer, taking five hundred women and children to California. He sent over his most handsome young lieutenant to calm them. The officer returned with hardly a gold button on his coat. The women of the *Ariel,* once calmed, got out their scissors and snipped off his buttons for souvenirs. This encounter was their golden opportunity, not the Confederacy's. The *Ariel* sailed on. After this, and because of it, the federal government ordered future gold shipments be made overland.

The section of Union shipping hit hardest by Confederate raiders was neither the liners nor ordinary cargo vessels; it was the whaling fleet. One tenth of all whalers were sunk by Confederates during the war.

For generations New Bedford and Nantucket had prospered on

whale oil, burning in tens of millions of lamps. As it became scarce and expensive, something as novel as could be came into demand—petroleum. With the help of the Confederate navy it went from being a smelly curiosity in 1859, sold mainly as a patent medicine, to being a thriving modern industry in 1865, brightening Northern homes. In those same six years New Bedford and Nantucket made the transit from riches to rags.

The *Alabama* circled the globe, pulling into Cherbourg in June 1864. Three days later the USS *Kearsarge* appeared at the harbor mouth. Semmes knew her captain, John Winslow, well. Once they had been messmates and roommates.

In armament, in displacement, in size of crew, there seemed little to choose when the *Alabama* came out to fight on June 19. In a brief engagement superior Union naval guns and gun handling were decisive.

After the war ended, the United States demanded compensation from Britain for the damage the *Alabama* had wrought. The claim was ultimately settled by international arbitration. The peaceful resolution of such a bitter dispute between two proud and powerful nations was and remains a landmark event in the development of international law. The moral philosopher had not sailed in vain.

CAREER SOLDIERS took it for granted that artillery would dominate the Civil War battlefield. Mexico again, but more so. Guns were now twice as powerful. Effective ranges had doubled; an improvement largely wasted for want of an indirect fire system. Gunners could still fire only at what they could see. After a few rounds that was not very much.

The Napoleonic technique of massing guns, running them forward and crushing the center of the enemy's line had brought victory in Mexico, but was to prove prohibitively expensive only fifteen years later. Taylor had been able to push his guns to within three hundred yards of Mexican armies: still out of smoothbore musket range. When McDowell did that at Henry House Hill his gunners were blown off it by rifled musket fire. In this war the artillery could not get much closer to the enemy than half a mile and unlimber safely in the open field. Far from dominating the battlefield, Civil War artillery found itself struggling to secure a place on it.

Lee, however, was a close student of Napoleon and retained the old belief in massed fire. The principle was sound, it simply needed adapting to altered conditions. With half as many guns as the Army of the Potomac his artillery outperformed it on occasion, especially at Chancellorsville.

In armies on both sides the field artillery's weapon of choice was the twelve-pounder Napoleon. This gun was made of brass or iron. For aesthetic reasons, gunners preferred the brass version: it gave off a pleasing ring, like a well-cast bell. It got its name from a story that it had been designed by Napoleon III, but this seems unlikely.

Supplementing it was the three-inch rifle, a gun that fired a ten-pound shell more than three miles. It was not effective against oncoming infantry, but against a big, immobile target, such as an enemy battery, it could be devastating; something Confederate gunners discovered at Antietam, the hard way. Lee's nephew, Fitzhugh Lee, described the battle in two words—"artillery hell." As a rule, however, rifled artillery did not achieve much, for want of high-quality ammunition. Every major battlefield was littered with three-inch shells that had traveled far but not exploded. They also lacked the penetration and power to destroy log breastworks or to make trenches untenable.

In the duels between opposing batteries the Confederates usually came off second best. Often they had to save precious ammunition for an infantry assault they were certain was coming. On other occasions they lost duels because they aimed too high, as they did at Gettysburg. Union artillery, once in action, hardly stopped firing; ammo-rich, and it showed.

Federal artillery superiority was achieved largely despite the War Department, which persistently denied it money, manpower and recognition. For most of the Civil War the Union artillery was forced to scrounge men where it could and beg for the horses the cavalry had worn out.

Old Brains had little idea how artillery should be used or organized. Halleck was to prove the heaviest cross that Henry Hunt, the artillery chief of the Army of the Potomac, had to bear. Hunt's branch of the service was denied field-grade officers, brevets for gallantry and a coherent structure. Artillery came bottom of the replacement scheme in the Union army.

Hunt was one of those who rated McClellan above all other generals as a creator of armies, because Little Mac had allowed him to organize an artillery reserve. These were guns not assigned to serve with the infantry or cavalry but placed under Hunt's direct control. In the spring of 1862 the War Department ordered it broken up, but Hunt reorganized it again, in time for Malvern Hill, as McClellan withdrew toward Harrison's Landing on the James River. On that day, July 1, 1862, McClellan reaped his reward for listening to Hunt: the artillery reserve saved his army. Three months later it was again abolished.

In the summer of 1863 the artillery of the Army of the Potomac had four hundred guns and 9,500 officers and men. It could boast exactly one general, Hunt, and only five other officers above the rank of captain. There were no artillery staffs. For much of the war, when the guns went into action no one troubled to organize their firepower for maximum effect. Instead, a typical battery was likely to find itself assigned to supporting an infantry brigade. Infantry officers then posted the battery, simply telling its gunners to fire straight ahead at any enemy they could see.

Artillery arrangements were much the same in most Confederate armies, the principal exceptions being the armies of Johnston and Lee. The brigade-battery combination was a legacy of the Mexican War. Many officers reverted to it more or less from habit.

Even officers who had served with the artillery at times failed to grasp the importance of concentrated fire directed onto carefully selected targets. Hooker was one of them and the mishandling of his artillery played a key part in his defeat at Chancellorsville.

Conversely, artillery properly employed was a battle winner. At Perryville it was guns posted on the high ground that made the biggest difference to the outcome. Buell got less than half his army into the fight but as long as his artillery continued to pound the Confederates hard he was content to defend. Bragg's attack was one huge infantry assault, without maneuvering or diversions; a harbinger of Gettysburg.

On July 3, 1863, Hunt's gunners virtually destroyed Pickett's advance. Years later Hunt set off one of the biggest arguments of the nineteenth century by claiming that his gunners alone could have killed or wounded every Confederate who advanced beyond the Emmitsburg road had infantry generals not interfered with the artillery.

At the opening of the battle more than half the Union artillery was organized into brigades, each one attached to an infantry corps. These "brigades" were commanded by captains, and one by a lieutenant. They were really artillery battalions. Hunt nonetheless hoped this organization would produce massed fires.

Once battle was joined, however, the firepower of the artillery brigades was—inevitably!—parceled out, with many batteries being assigned to infantry divisions, and down to infantry brigades. Yet, ironically, it was just such a brigade-battery combination that saved Little Round Top.

Hunt's attempt to create a more modern structure paid off, all the same. It was the ammunition train of the recently reformed artillery reserve (with nearly a third of the army's guns) that on the night of July 2 replenished the caissons of the batteries that had spent the day assigned to various infantry units. Without that ammunition reserve the Confederates might well have won the artillery duel on July 3 and been able to advance in support of Pickett's charge in sufficient strength to enable it to succeed.

Once the battle was over, Halleck again abolished the artillery reserve. Months later, remarked Hunt dryly, "It reconstituted itself without orders . . . through the necessities of the army." The artillery had found its new leading role: supporting infantry that was well entrenched and awaiting attack.

THAT CAVALRY survived on the modern battlefield seemed amazing. All theory and practice were against it. Like the artilleryman the cavalryman was looking for a place of his own in modern warfare.

The firepower revolution made traditional cavalry tactics impossible. The role of shock force was denied it. Massed horsemen riding across open ground would be cut to ribbons; had been cut to ribbons, in Mexico. The U.S. Army had absorbed that lesson, long before European armies were aware of it.

In this war the cavalry did nearly all its fighting on foot. They were really mounted riflemen or dismounted dragoons. It became a boast among cavalrymen on both sides that they were *not* traditional cavalry.

The principal arm in close combat was no longer the saber but the Colt revolver. Horsemen kept their sabers but rarely drew them, even more rarely did any damage with them. What the modern cavalryman wanted was firepower.

In 1863 Sharps carbines and other repeaters began to appear by the thousands each month. The Union cavalry at last gained an ascendancy over Southern horsemen. Ostrich feathers were fine but a seven-shot repeating breechloader was better. Confederate cavalry had a fatal disadvantage: they were still armed with muzzle-loaders. It must have been nightmarish trying to reload one in the saddle under fire.

During the last two years of the war Union horsemen had the mobility of cavalry combined with more firepower than any equivalent force of infantry. It was this revolution in cavalry firepower that enabled John Buford to hold off an entire Confederate infantry division at Gettysburg long enough for Reynolds's corps to come up. It was not Meade or Lee who chose Gettysburg as a good place to fight—it was Buford. His four-hour stand against superior numbers was a contribution to eventual Union victory that no mere cavalry raid could have matched.

The new faith in firepower led cavalry commanders almost from the start of the war to demand horse artillery: the flying batteries lived on. Whenever Union cavalry clashed with Confederate cavalry it was more likely to lead to a duel between the horse artillery batteries than a hand-to-hand fight between horsemen plying their sabers and firing their revolvers.

No army commander—not Lee, not Grant—managed to keep his cavalry on a short rein. They went their own way, often at the wrong moment. At Stones River, Bragg's cavalry rode away on a raid. For three days he tried in vain to get it back, while the battle roared on.

On each side the infantry both hated and envied the cavalry. The eternal glamour of the chevalier, but especially his absence in critical moments, infuriated the foot soldier. There was a story going around in the Union army that General John Logan was offering a reward for a dead cavalryman, blue or gray—he was curious to see what one looked like.

As Grant prepared to lead the Army of the Potomac south in 1864 he appointed the thirty-three-year-old Philip Sheridan to command the newly created Cavalry Corps. Given the responsibilities that this new formation would have to shoulder, it amounted to an army command. Sheridan's youth made Halleck and Lincoln skeptical that he was up to it, but Grant had no doubts about his protégé. At Missionary Ridge and elsewhere he had shown aggressive leadership combined with good organization.

Horse soldiers had been parceled out in every direction, as mounted escorts for infantry generals, as pickets and patrols, as orderlies and messengers. When one corps commander refused to give up his imposing mounted escort, he got a taste of Sheridan's famous short temper: "I have been placed in command of the cavalry of this army and, by God, I want it *all*!" He got it: 12,000 horsemen, organized in three divisions, with more firepower in its repeating carbines than Napoleon commanded in the half-million muskets of the *Grande Armée* when he invaded Russia.

A s Meade and Grant led the Army of the Potomac toward the Rapidan at the end of April 1864 there were two headquarters, two staffs. If this seemed a contradiction of sensible management, as many officers claimed, an absolute guarantee of confusion, it certainly was. Yet Grant and Lincoln alike believed this splendid instrument of war had never been fought to its offensive limits. Grant went with it to make sure this time it would be. That, of course, did nothing to make him popular with the Army of the Potomac. Officers and men alike resented his presence, jeered at his reputation; he may have been great shakes out west, but he hadn't ever fought Bobby Lee.

Conscious of this lack of trust and respect, he lost his former daring. Grant wanted to turn Lee's left, breaking the Army of Northern Virginia's rail and road links to the south and west. That ran the risk of letting Lee's right swing around and get behind him, to threaten Grant's own communications. With a western army he would have taken that chance.

Instead, he felt constrained to move almost in a direct line toward Richmond, through The Wilderness; over ground where, twelve months before, Hooker had met his Chancellorsville. As the 101,000 men of the Army of the Potomac pushed through in the first week of May, bleached skulls grinned up at them.

This was Lee's preferred battleground. He knew it well. Grant did not know it at all. Nor, judging from the maps, did cartographers. The slightly sinister fecundity, the "roads" that proved to be cart tracks, the density of the trees and undergrowth deprived Grant of a nearly two-to-one advantage in manpower and the benefits of Hunt's superb artillery arm. In these thickets, corps and division had no meaning. Battles here were going to be firefights between platoons and companies. And with lines of sight and fields of fire so reduced, Lee's entire army might conceivably be put into action against almost any part of Grant's.

On May 4 the Federals crossed the Rapidan. Grant's unwonted caution made him pause. Ahead stretched ten miles of open road that would take him to Spotsylvania—clear of The Wilderness—but he did not know it. Having created the Cavalry Corps, Grant and Sheridan threw away its first great opportunity. It was not being used for scouting ahead, nor was it covering the flanks of the army as it advanced. Nor was a large body of horsemen ready to be sent ahead to seize important objectives, such as Spotsylvania. It was strung out for seventy miles behind Grant, guarding supply trains. With two entire infantry corps safely across the river by noon, he halted, waiting for the trains to come up. He was doing just what Lee wanted him to do, right where Lee wanted him to do it.

During the next twenty-four hours Confederate units hurried into The Wilderness, after being spread far and wide in recent months to improve their chances of eating regularly. As at Gettysburg, battle was brought on by combative subordinates, in a ragged, piecemeal fashion. Lee's battle management in some of these 1864 engagements was as faulty as Grant's. Neither commander was on his best form in their opening encounters. The fighting raged for three days, setting much of The Wilderness on fire. Thousands of men were burned to death.

To Confederate surprise and dismay Grant, after burying his dead and sending back his wounded, refused to acknowledge defeat. He pressed on, hacking his way toward Spotsylvania by sheer will and superior numbers. During a lull in the fighting on May 8 Meade worried aloud about his trains. Sheridan was disgusted. He did not look forward to a summer nursing wagonloads of hardtack. "If I am permitted to cut loose from this army," he announced, "I'll draw Stuart after me, and I'll whip him, too." Grant let him go.

The force Sheridan led out was immense: in column of fours, well closed up, it stretched thirteen miles. For sixteen days Sheridan swung it in a circuit around Lee's rear. The Confederate cavalry was defeated four times. Stuart was killed. Hundreds of Union prisoners were freed. Sheridan penetrated the outer defenses of Richmond before turning back. In the meantime the army was fighting some of the bloodiest engagements of the war, around tiny Spotsylvania Courthouse.

Some of the firefights were so intense men claimed to have fired more than four hundred rounds in a single assault. Trees up to eighteen inches in diameter were cut down entirely by small-arms fire. And when the sun went down each night, out came Confederate salvage parties, gleaning the terrain for valuable lead. Never did they find it in such abundance as here, retrieving up to sixty tons a night. This was point-blank war. Grant dissolved the artillery reserve and sent back half his guns, hoping to press on faster. Lee took the opposite approach, forcing guns into the deep woods, squeezing them among the trees, up mountain trails, across swamps. Log breastworks or entrenchments hurriedly scooped out with bayonets, tin cups, plates, bare hands, anything, were expensive to take. With a few guns to support them the Confederates put the price through the roof.

Grant all the time kept hammering at Lee's army, kept trying to turn its right flank. Lee continued to frustrate him, steadily extending the right, shortening the left; moving, that is, southeast, toward Richmond.

By the end of May the two armies had reached Cold Harbor, a crossroads fifteen miles east of the Confederate capital. For three days, May 31 to June 2, each side tried to dislodge the other. Badly written orders from Grant's headquarters and poor communications led to delays that enabled Lee to create strong entrenchments, supported by artillery, in time to meet the main attack, scheduled for June 3.

On the evening of June 2 Colonel Horace Porter of Grant's staff came across the men of Winfield Scott Hancock's corps sitting on the ground calmly writing their names and home addresses on slips of paper, then pinning these to the backs of their coats: making identification of their dead bodies and shipping them home easier. One young veteran wrote out the last entry in his diary: "June 3. Cold Harbor. I was killed."

The advance next morning lasted eight minutes. Three corps attacked but advanced on diverging lines, across a swamp no one had reconnoitered and into enfilading fire from Confederate artillery. Cold Harbor was a victory for Lee's gunners. Without them the Union assault, for all its flaws, might have overwhelmed his trenches from sheer weight of numbers. After twenty minutes the Federals were pulled back, but forward movement had stopped ten to twelve minutes earlier. There were 7,000 Union killed and wounded on the field. For the rest of his life, said Grant, "I always regretted the last assault on

Cold Harbor." Those twenty minutes more than anything else created the legend of "Butcher" Grant.

It was an attack containing so many elementary mistakes it hints strongly at the psychological toll the campaign had taken on him since crossing the Rapidan. Grant became so frustrated he forgot to handle an army properly, even how to concentrate his forces before an attack. A photograph taken of him about this time shows a tragic, intense figure whose dulled eyes, downcast, are fixed on images no man should ever see.

He gave up trying to outflank Lee. Disengaging deftly with some of his old flair, he shifted the army south to the James River, and moved toward Petersburg, ten miles south of Richmond. For several days Lee could only guess where he had gone. Petersburg was almost undefended, yet through it ran every railroad line but one that supplied the Confederate capital and the Army of Northern Virginia.

The town might already have been in Union hands. On May 5 the Army of the James had landed unopposed at City Point and Bermuda Hundred under Major General Benjamin Butler. Grant had instructed him, "Richmond is to be your objective point." By this direct threat to the heart of the Confederacy he hoped to draw off part of Lee's army from The Wilderness and Spotsylvania. On disembarking, Butler had immediately entrenched his 15,000 men, posing a direct threat to no one. Thanks to this inertia Lee did not have to worry about Butler. Nor did Petersburg, four miles to the south of his entrenchments, open, undefended and incuriously unreconnoitered. At the end of May, Butler finally moved, shuffling north, toward Richmond.

Grant, disengaging from Cold Harbor, sent XVIII Corps south by water to reinforce Butler. On landing, these troops approached Petersburg, opened a mile-wide breach in its unmanned outer lines, and entrenched themselves. What might be termed the Cold Harbor syndrome afflicted the Army of the Potomac for the rest of the war. "We believe in Grant," men joked, "but we believe a deal more in Lee and the Army of Northern Virginia." So XVIII Corps dug in, expecting Hancock's II Corps to join them; after which they would probe Petersburg's defenses. Hancock, however, was unaware of what was happening. The order to him to link up with XVIII Corps and attack Petersburg was routed through Meade's HQ and it vanished. A second chance to take the town was lost.

Petersburg's defenses were commanded by Beauregard, but he had few men, few guns and little ammunition with which to resist a Union attack. He had managed to dig roughly ten miles of crude trenches and build a few unimpressive forts. For most of their length, however, the trenches were unmanned. Beauregard concentrated his guns and manpower in half a dozen places, covering no more than two miles of trenches, and hoped. On June 18 Meade launched a direct assault on Beauregard's defenses. He had chosen to attack the only section that was strongly defended. Meade suffered a mini–Cold Harbor. To his right and left were open roads and unmanned positions. Unreconnoitered too.

Three times Petersburg might have been taken at little cost. All three chances were muffed. Grant was now faced with the one strategy the president had rejected since the war began; the one strategy Grant had tacitly promised never to adopt: Richmond besieged. If he was to escape from the last resort of trench warfare, Grant had only one card left to play, Sheridan's Cavalry Corps. And this was the ideal time to play it.

For three years the South had used the Shenandoah Valley as an invasion route to the North. To Union commanders, on the other hand, it had little military value because its southern end led to nowhere that mattered much in federal strategy. Then, in the first week of July 1864, Lee sent Jubal Early on a raid from the Valley; a raid that took Confederate cavalry to the outer suburbs of Washington and forced Grant to ship VI Corps at high speed back to the District. Neither Early nor Lee believed for a moment that Washington could be captured, but the raid's embarrassment factor was high. Lincoln began wondering pointedly whether something ought to be done about the Shenandoah.

During this anxious time Grant was outside Petersburg, studying maps, tearing his string gloves to shreds, furiously smoking his usual twenty cigars a day, and trying to decide what to do next. As his line of entrenchments extended to the west he could break every one of Richmond's rail links except for the Virginia Central, and yet . . . if he could seize the southern end of the Shenandoah Valley it might be possible to push a force south to Staunton and break that remaining railroad line! That might then force Lee to come out from his entrenchments, fight a huge battle in the open and decide the issue quickly. No siege.

His chosen instrument for conquering the Valley was Sheridan.

The little hero was personally brave and led from the front. His troops adored their five-foot, four-inch leader's bravura style. Responsibility for one of the most important operations of the war, however, made him cautious. So did Early, a born cavalry leader and a natural soldier. In the late summer and fall of 1864 he repeatedly intimidated Sheridan, whose force had been increased to 48,000 men by the assignment of large numbers of infantry. Early commanded barely 18,000 men yet forced Sheridan into hurried retreats and prolonged inactivity.

With his reputation sinking faster than Confederate money, Sheridan reported to Halleck, "I have thought it best to be prudent," but he had not been sent to the Valley to be prudent. In mid-September Grant had to go in person to encourage him to take a few risks.

Even this did not work. It was not Sheridan who attacked Early but the heavily outnumbered Early who attacked him, twice. On each occasion superior federal numbers finally brought victory for Sheridan, but only after coming within a hairsbreadth of defeat. Those two victories nonetheless gave the Union control of the Shenandoah. They had also so unnerved Sheridan he failed to press south as expected, to where Early, around Staunton, was guarding the Virginia Central line.

Grant moved into a small wooden house built for him at City Point. The siege Lincoln had dreaded and argued against for more than three years was all Grant could offer him now.

WHILE the Army of the Potomac fought its way across Virginia, Sherman was advancing on Atlanta. Opposing him was Joe Johnston, whose method of coping with superior federal numbers and firepower was an elastic defense—falling back where the terrain favored Sherman, digging in where it favored him. Sherman and Grant admired the artistry of Johnston's tactics, but they were too sophisticated for Davis to follow. He fired Johnston, replacing him with the hard-charging John Bell Hood. Said Sherman, "I was pleased with this change." For his method of advance Hood was the ideal opponent.

Sherman had perfected the strategic offensive based on the tactical defensive. He moved forward rapidly to seize ground that was important to the enemy and turned it into a strongpoint the Confederates felt they had to get back. When their attack on it failed, which it usually did, Sherman moved rapidly to take the next position while they were still demoralized by their recent expensive failure. And so on across most of Georgia.

His was a generalship that rose from skill to artistry even though Sherman was little more than a so-so combat commander. He never got all his troops into battle. He never won a battle outright and never destroyed a Confederate army. At Kennesaw Mountain, in June 1864, he suffered his own Cold Harbor, with a futile frontal assault that left 3,000 Union dead and wounded in two murderous hours.

Grant instructed Sherman to destroy Hood's army, after which Atlanta would inevitably fall to him. Instead, Sherman headed for Atlanta and maneuvered Hood out of it. On September 2 Union regiments paraded through its streets. By taking Atlanta against Grant's orders Sherman was trying to secure Lincoln's reelection. A week earlier Admiral David Glasgow Farragut had won a naval battle at Mobile Bay in an operation also designed to help the president at the polls that fall.

Sherman, Farragut and many others, including Lincoln, were fearful that the North had grown weary of the war. They expected the election to be hair-raisingly close. They were wrong. Most Northerners were ready to see the war through to victory. Lincoln's 55 percent of the popular vote in November 1864 to the 45 percent for his Democratic opponent, George McClellan, is one of larger margins of victory in presidential elections. In the electoral college it was a landslide: 212–21. In Congress, the Republicans achieved the most one-sided House and Senate the country has ever seen. Barring a battlefield disaster, Lincoln's reelection was safe.

Sherman dawdled in Atlanta for a month, resisting instructions from Grant to chase after Hood. He finally did as he was ordered, soon lost interest in it, gave up trying to convince Grant and Halleck that he ought to march to Savannah, and set off for it anyway. He sent a message to George Thomas in Nashville that it was for him, and the Army of the Cumberland, to do something about Hood.

Every professional soldier but one admired Thomas. Dana, a civilian, was equally impressed: "He had more of the character of Washington than any man I knew." Grant was almost alone in disliking him. That may have been because Halleck had made it clear in 1862 that he considered Thomas the better general. Nor did the open admiration of the assistant secretary of war for Thomas help much in the late fall of 1864 when Grant's inertia in the trenches around Petersburg was bringing barbed telegrams from Stanton.

Thomas had a gift of inestimable worth: he could see clearly the battle to come. It was that gift that enabled him to hold the ground at Chickamauga. Grant turned Thomas's knack for careful preparation into accusations that he was dreadfully slow. Thomas only prepared carefully in order to fight more effectively. After the war ended, the government tried to offer Thomas the third star he deserved; a star Grant had denied him. Thomas turned it down: honor delayed was honor denied.

Hood's army of 39,000 men advanced into Tennessee in November 1864. Thomas assigned John Schofield, with 34,000 Federals, to delay Hood's approach while Nashville's defenses were strengthened. On November 15 Schofield was dug in at Franklin, fifteen miles south of Nashville. Hood launched a massive frontal assault. The attacks went on for five hours, until night fell. Confederate losses were 6,250, to the Federals' 2,300, yet Schofield fell back, toward Nashville.

Grant burned up the wires with demands that Thomas move out of the city and attack Hood. Thomas was willing to do so, but wanted to get all his cavalry mounted first. Then, as he prepared to attack, a sleet storm blew up. Grant, fuming, wrote three separate orders removing Thomas from command. Lincoln suspended the first, confident Thomas knew exactly what he was doing. The second, to be delivered by hand, was held up by the appalling weather. The third was delayed because the telegraph operator who was to transmit it was convinced the president did not want Thomas removed. As the operator wrestled with his conscience late in the afternoon of December 14, the machinery in the telegraph office began clicking. Thomas had attacked.

His battle plan hearkened back to Frederick the Great's oblique order of battle, where one wing or the center of an attacking army is weakened as it advances to make the other wing overwhelmingly strong. It was too clever for Hood. And the care Thomas took with his cavalry paid off. In the very moment of victory he unleashed a vigorous pursuit of the defeated Confederates. Thomas pulled off what no other army commander achieved in the Civil War—the battle of annihilation. Hounded to destruction, surrendering gladly, Hood's army ceased to exist.

Grant spent the winter waiting for the spring. He intended to extend his lines west, then north, cutting all Richmond's rail links. He still had hopes of forcing Lee to come out and fight. The scale of Confederate surrenders and desertions that winter raised another possibility—collapse. The South was running out of men to fill its armies. One way or another the war must surely end in 1865.

On March 25 the Confederates tried to break out. Union counterattacks held the line. To stop Lee getting the jump on him, Grant sent Sheridan farther west. On March 31 Confederates under Pickett clashed with Sheridan's mixed force of cavalry, infantry and artillery at Five Forks, only to be badly mauled when Warren arrived with V Corps.

Two days later federal attacks breached the Confederate trenches. During the night of April 2 Lee abandoned Petersburg, following the Appomattox River west, toward Amelia Courthouse. There he expected to find supplies and rally his army. Thousands of men simply drifted away along the line of march. After two harrowing days and nights Lee reached Amelia Courthouse. No supplies. Dazed, his remaining troops pressed on, drawn by the hope there was something to eat on the western horizon.

What was there was Sheridan. The pursuit of Lee's army was a classic of its kind, with cavalry harassing the leading units, slowing down the retreat, while infantry pressed hard from behind. Union gunners made their contribution by unlimbering to fire shells that exploded over retreating wagon trains. The mules would go mad. A single terrified six-mule team could block a road long enough for federal infantry to come up and capture everything behind it.

On the morning of April 9, at Appomattox Courthouse, Lee's starving army made a last attempt to break the enclosing ring by attacking Sheridan's cavalry. Once more the firepower of Union horsemen allowed them to ride out an infantry attack, while two Union infantry corps raced eleven miles to link up with them. Blue ribbons spread over the landscape. So much blue. It was hopeless. The fighting stopped.

The grandest house at Appomattox was occupied by Mr. Wilmer McLean. He had brought his family there after his house at Bull Run was damaged by Union artillery in the first major battle of the war. Somehow the fighting followed him almost to the end. Defeated Confederate generals unpacked their effects from the wagon train and mounted the steps of Mr. McLean's house in crisp new uniforms and brilliantly polished boots. The victors followed them in. In their shabby stained blue and worn-down muddy boots, they looked like the vanquished. Lee wore a red silk sash and carried a sword encrusted with precious stones. Grant appeared in his private's blouse.

Fighting would splutter along for some weeks, but in effect the war was over. Grant wasted little time returning to Washington, to save the taxpayers' money. The war was costing four million dollars a day. He was the "earnest businessman" even in the hour of rejoicing.

Once Lee and his generals had left the McLean house, Sheridan offered twenty dollars in gold for the table at which Lee had signed the surrender, hoisted it on his back and set off to present it to the belle of the Cavalry Corps, Libby Bacon Custer. Behind him, a bemused Mr. McLean was entertaining bids for everything else in the room. That was the way the war ended—not with a bang but an auction.

THE MILITARY SIGNIFICANCE of the Civil War was missed for fifty years. So much about it was new that it bewildered more than informed. No one had really foreseen what the firepower revolution would do, although a few officers had tried to anticipate it. Two of the most popular manuals of the war were William Hardee's *Tactics,* in two volumes, and Scott's *Tactics,* in three. After a day of drilling the enlisted men, officers and NCOs would gather in the yellow light of kerosene lamps and study them intently.

Both Hardee and Scott responded to the challenge of the rifled musket by trying to hurry troops along. They increased the speed at which infantry crossed open ground. Changes in formation were now made while units in line or column were still in motion; always before, they had halted first. Innovations like these reflected the greater alertness expected from troops and the quicker wits expected of officers. Yet little had been done about the size and density of deployed formations. For that, the Union paid dearly.

It was Confederates, closer in spirit and outlook to the army and militia of the Revolution, who coped better. They fought in loose, not to say ragged, formations. Such was their style; it owed little to theory. Close-order formations, on the other hand, were the natural style of the more tightly managed Union army.

Some of the impression of Confederate military superiority arose from this contrast in fighting styles, for while it helped hold down losses on one side, it magnified them on the other. When Confederate regiments were drawn up in big, unmissable formations—as at Gettysburg—they too took heavy losses and had nothing to show in return.

Federal officers proved loath to throw their tactical manuals aside. Down in the bayous of Louisiana in 1863 Union regiments were forming line of battle and advancing shoulder to shoulder through slimy water to constant cries of "Close up! Close up those gaps!" And on countless other fields were other men in blue advancing thus through woods, across rail fences, into ditches, splashing across winding streams, before halting at point-blank range to recover their parade-ground magnificence before making the charge.

There was also a costly disdain for entrenchments; another legacy from Mexico. American soldiers had defeated well-entrenched Mexicans at Monterrey, Cerro Gordo, Molino del Rey, Churubusco and Chapultepec. American officers were convinced their men could storm any entrenchment on Earth. The war was half over before they acknowledged how profoundly matters had changed: one man with a rifled musket behind a wall or in a ditch could hold off at least three attackers, however brave they were.

European military observers noted such developments with a keen professional interest. In their splendid uniforms, with their courtly manners and charming accents, they brightened the social life of army camps on both sides. Some observed battle so closely they appeared to be participants on occasion. Yet the lesson drawn by European armies was that this war had nothing to teach them; it was merely a gigantic melee—"war," they decided, "conducted by amateurs." It would be the twentieth century before the modernity of the Civil War was understood.

What gave it a clumsy amateurish air was an eagerness to fight that yielded meager results, time after time. There were sixty major battles. In only one, Nashville, was an army destroyed. Grant and Lee, Lincoln and Davis labored to create fire-and-movement armies. Armies, that is, which were designed, trained and equipped to pin down the enemy with fire and, having immobilized him, to move to attack his flanks or rear. They were not interested in producing armies of occupation, siege armies, armies of mutual attrition, or armies for show. They were seeking decision on the battlefield, yet almost never found it, despite the great talents of men such as Grant and Lee, Thomas and Jackson.

At the end of most battles one side advanced, the other retreated. Southern withdrawals were likely to owe more to logistics than to anything else. Northern advances were usually so hesitant they could hardly be described as the forward movement of conquerors. For all the bloodshed, the courage and the military skill on both sides there was no Austerlitz, no Waterloo. And yet it was possible for modern forces with modern arms to win decisive battles. The Prussians crushed the Austrians in 1866 and the French in 1870 in lightning campaigns.

In fifty-five of the sixty major battles of the Civil War the generals commanding the armies engaged were West Point graduates. In the remaining five the army on at least one side was commanded by a West Pointer. All of these generals, and nearly all of their corps commanders, were former students of Dennis Hart Mahan.

The revered professor of "Military Art and Engineering" was the nation's leading authority on warfare. He worshiped the memory of Napoleon. West Point's intellectual elite gathered at the Napoleon Club, presided over by Mahan. There, under maps showing the Emperor's campaigns, the brightest students, such as McClellan and Halleck, gathered to discuss the finer points of military history.

Not surprisingly, the writings of senior officers who served in the Civil War are filled with references to Napoleon's battles, life, tactics and troops. Not only did they have Napoleon at the back of their minds, so did Lincoln and Davis.

Civil War generals were seeking to fight much as Napoleon had fought, yet they did so without anything resembling the centerpiece of the *Grande Armée,* the Imperial Guard. American democracy ruled out aristocratic guards regiments, which were common in European armies. The Guard contained Napoleon's best infantry, his best cavalry and his best artillery. It was recruited from men who were veterans of at least five campaigns. It was a force apart from the rest of the army and served as Napoleon's reserve.

In the writings of Mahan and his star pupil, Henry Halleck, there was no direct reference to the Imperial Guard. Accordingly, there was perfunctory discussion of the creation, training and handling of reserves. Here was the great blank page in the education of American generals.

One of the essential functions of a reserve force was pursuit. "Without cavalry," Napoleon declared, "battles have no result." What he had in mind was a strong cavalry reserve, such as the Imperial Guard cavalry. It was Thomas's cavalry force, commanded by James Harrison, that destroyed Hood's army after it was beaten. Sheridan's pursuit of Lee all the way to Appomattox was war in the Napoleonic style.

Yet these were lessons that had to be relearned, because Mahan and Halleck were pursuit pessimists. "A retreating force can always retreat faster than a pursuing one can advance," said Don Carlos Buell in defense of his failure to pursue Bragg after the Battle of Perryville. That was what he had been taught at West Point.

The failure to create and form an elite into a reserve combined with pursuit pessimism to make the Civil War unique in the dozens of indecisive battles that were fought. In the whole of Western military history there was nothing like it, before or since, including other civil wars, where brother fought brother, like fought like.

The sum total of these inconclusive battles was nevertheless victory for the Union. There was, and is, a widespread conviction that it was a victory won off the battlefield. Hardly a Southerner alive believes the Confederacy lost for want of martial virtues. Their belief was expressed shortly after the war ended by Senator Benjamin Hill of Georgia, who put it in the form of a four-word obituary: "Died of state's rights."

A higher level of Southern nationalism would probably not have made much difference, however. Finnish and Polish nationalism has always been strong but not enough to save them from the Russians. National sentiment may make a difference in guerrilla wars, but Lee declined to fight that way.

What the Confederacy broke against was a pair of battlefield problems to which it had no solutions, and a more cohesive national sentiment was not going to provide answers either. The war was won for the North by superior manpower and firepower. The South was bled and battered into submission. Nearly every Confederate soldier recognized that.

For most of the war the "present for duty" figures gave Northern armies a 2.5-to-1 advantage over Confederate armies. Yet by the time battle was joined that seemingly insuperable advantage of 150 percent had shrunk to a mere 35 percent because Union supremacy was not brought to bear in combat.

Tens of thousands of federal troops were like IX Corps—Grant's reserve in the Army of the Potomac—assigned to guarding railroad tracks. Still others were tied down occupying areas recently captured.

And many were guarding the huge supply trains that followed Union armies in the field.

An advantage of 35 percent was enough to ensure that most of the sixty battles counted as Union victories, but that margin was not enough to make Union generals feel confident enough to take risks against a courageous foe.

To the end the South had abundant crops and idle factories. What it ran out of first was not food, or arms, or raw materials. What it ran out of was men——men to harvest the crops, men to make the factories hum, men to carry the arms into battle. By resorting to trench warfare the Confederates were able to prolong the agony by six months or so. Rifled muskets and entrenchments (which Confederates called "ditches") could offset much of the Union superiority in manpower. By 1865, however, that superiority had risen to four to one.

That January there were 621,000 Federals under arms, to 155,000 Confederates. The toll of deaths, wounds, prisoners and paroles was too high for the South to keep its armies manned. And as hope of victory faded even more men went home, while no one on the Union side wanted to miss out on the finish.

Not only did Lincoln's armies have a fourfold advantage in manpower, they had, partly thanks to his intervention, an even greater supremacy in shoulder arms. By 1865 as many as seventy thousand repeating carbines and rifles were in the hands of Union troops, mainly among the cavalry. Thousands more were flowing off production lines every week. Repeating arms doubled small-arms firepower in Union armies. The total federal firepower advantage was roughly eight to one in the closing months of the war.

Against such disparities in manpower and firepower not even "ditches" sufficed. Lee's lines and forts around Petersburg were simply overwhelmed. Union faith in the firepower revolution produced by Hall, Colt and Spencer finally triumphed.

NEARLY 600,000 men, most of them young and spirited, had lost their lives. Heartbreak clouded the lives of millions who mourned them. Yet in the minds of men such as Grant, the nation had gained from the war. It had brought a rush toward modernity. His was a faith in progress, in redemption through suffering and in America's boundless future that was shared by millions, including many Southerners.

Such beliefs formed a seamless web that bound past, present and unborn generations; a web that held the nation fast in peace and war and through the blood just spilled animated once again a blood relationship that made free Americans a nation unlike any other.

The most obvious and immediate beneficiaries of the war were the blacks. It had not been fought to end slavery, but from the first shots fired at Fort Sumter it was clear that a Northern victory would bring that result. And blacks had fought and died for their freedom. Nearly 180,000 served in the Union army. Another 20,000 served in the Union navy. In all, blacks accounted for 10 percent of Northern armed forces.

The other great beneficiary was the federal government. Every constitutional amendment before 1861 sought to restrict Washington's powers. The Thirteenth Amendment both freed all slaves and set a pattern for expanding federal authority, at the expense of the states.

The war also broke a legislative logjam that had held up needed reforms since the Mexican War. Southern states, with their strict constructionist view of the Constitution and deep suspicion of federal power, had blocked a wide range of liberal measures. Once the eleven states of the Confederacy seceded, Congress passed the Homestead Act, giving away federal land to families willing to work it. It was a measure that quickly populated much of the West.

The Pacific Railroad Act gave federal land to the railroads, which soon thrust shining ribbons of steel down the trails the settlers followed. The Department of Agriculture was created, to the incalculable benefit of millions of farmers down to the present day. The National Bank Act was passed, to the lasting benefit of commerce.

Above all, there was the Morrill Act. This gave federal land to the states to help them finance higher education. The result was more than fifty small but valuable colleges, a few well-known universities such as Penn State and Michigan State, and some world-class institutions such as the Massachusetts Institute of Technology and Cornell.

The war slowed the growth of some parts of the economy and speeded up others. The most enduring heritage of Lincoln's war finance measures is carried in every American's wallet or purse, the greenback. Congress also introduced a progressive income tax, stamp taxes, excise taxes, and a value-added tax. One Northern family in four ended the war holding U.S. war bonds. This one fourth of the population that owned government stock formed the bedrock of the new middle class.

In its depth and broad reach it marked the advent of a mature capitalist society and economy.

For the defeated South the war was a psychological and economic catastrophe that future generations were condemned to bear. The abolition of slavery could not save it from a tormented political heritage and a sense of political isolation.

The traditional economy of the South lay in ruins. It would be thirty years or more before Southern living standards recovered to their 1860 level. Even so, the heroic effort to create war industries formed the basis of the eventual industrialization of the South. Bit by bit the region was brought back into the Union and entered hesitantly into the modern world.

Lincoln and Davis set aside days of "national fasting, humiliation and prayer" when the war was going badly for their soldiers. On October 3, 1863, however, the president declared a day of thanksgiving instead. It would be a day to thank God for the success of Union armies: for Gettysburg, for Vicksburg, for the fall of Knoxville, Tennessee; for these signs of ultimate victory.

Thanksgiving Day had been celebrated for more than a century in New England and Pennsylvania. It was a movable feast, a religious harvest festival transplanted from the British Isles. It was intended to celebrate and give thanks for that year's crops.

Lincoln's proclamation turned this regional religious occasion into a great national festival of rejoicing, fixing it then and forever on the last Thursday in November. And there it remains, no longer a movable feast, thoroughly secularized, with hardly any mention of crops. Few now recall that it was meant to give thanks for the triumph of Union arms. It has been transmuted into America's favorite holiday, an occasion when blood ties are refreshed through the celebration of family life, within the context of a national family's rejoicing.

10

IMPERIAL
CRUMBS

THE PLOT to kill Lincoln in April 1865 was intended to
avenge the beaten South. A murderous logic drove the conspira-
tors on to encompass the deaths of his cabinet, but all that achieved
was a failed attempt on Secretary of State William H. Seward in his
home, while Lincoln was mortally wounded at Ford's Theater.

Like a man inspired by a deep need for revenge, Edwin Stanton
directed the hunt for John Wilkes Booth; a hunt that ended in the
assassin's death, either by his own hand or at those of the soldiers who
cornered him in a barn. Booth's co-conspirators were tried by a military court organized by Stanton and wielding dubious fatal powers.
Four of the accused, including a woman, were hanged.

Had Stanton's wrath run its course unchecked, Lee and Davis
would have joined the plotters on the gallows. Grant, with a better
sense of both history and justice, stopped him. There was to be only
one trial for "war crimes," that of the commander of Andersonville,
the sprawling prisoner-of-war camp in Georgia where skeletal
doomed guards had gazed dully under a blistering sun on skeletal
doomed Federals. The camp commandant, Henry Wirz, died much
as he had spent his years as a Swiss Confederate—baffled, angry and
helpless.

Reconstructing the Union was a task taken up by many hands.
That would have been so even had Lincoln lived. Never entirely free

to manage the war as he wished, he would have been no freer to manage the peace.

His successor, Vice-President Andrew Johnson, was a Tennessee Democrat who had opted for unionism and republicanism. He sought to effect Lincoln's policy of Reconstruction by amnesty and loyalty oath. Even before the guns fell silent the machinery for creating new governments in the eleven states of the Confederacy was in operation. Six months after the war all but Texas had new or amended constitutions. All these phoenix states passed laws against blacks. They also raised former Confederate politicians to high office. Only now did a spirit of revenge take hold in the North, which felt its blood sacrifice mocked, its generosity abused. And Johnson, with perfectly bad timing, chose this embittered hour to present himself as an unreconstructed president after all. Congress sought to enlarge the powers of the Freedmen's Bureau, a War Department agency created to succor liberated slaves in areas under military rule. Johnson vetoed the bill. Congress passed a Civil Rights Act to achieve the same ends. He vetoed that too. He was, he said, "against the Africanization of half the United States."

Out of this conflict between the president, Congress and an angrily divided people came the most fundamental change to the Constitution since the original Bill of Rights, the Fourteenth Amendment. This flatly barred state government from denying anyone "life, liberty, or property, without due process of law; nor . . . anyone within its jurisdiction the equal protection of the laws." The historic relationship between federal and state power was hereby reversed.

Defiant still, ten of the former Confederate states refused to ratify the Fourteenth Amendment. To the rest of the country that amounted to rejecting Reconstruction. Congress turned to the army to impose it; something Stanton had never doubted was necessary. Northern voters too now favored a conqueror's peace. In the fall of 1866 they elected a Congress that was firmly under the control of Radical Republicans, zealots who promised the rebels the smack of firm government. Presidential reconstruction of the mild Lincolnian variety was over.

Long before the war ended the army had been responsible for running large parts of the former Confederacy, usually through pro-Union civilians in the conquered areas. Soldiers in blue were providing food, clothing, housing and medical care to hundreds of thousands of freed slaves and war-destituted whites.

Such efforts merged effortlessly into the benign reconstruction that characterized Johnson's first year as president. Defiance, however, was exhausting the army's patience. When the mood in Congress changed, the army was of much the same mind. Reconstruction became essentially an operation run by soldiers and congressmen. The president was steadily frozen out.

In May 1866 he tried to regain some measure of control over the military occupation by sending Grant on a mission to Mexico to force the French to leave. Grant angrily departed a cabinet meeting at which Johnson told him to go to Mexico and the attorney general gave an on-the-spot ruling that the order was legal. "No power on earth can compel me," said Grant as he stormed out, and none did.

Johnson was meanwhile trying to get Sherman to agree to become "acting secretary of war," in a cherished hope of getting rid of Stanton. That also failed.

In March 1867 the newly elected Congress had barely convened before it passed the Military Reconstruction Act, giving the army sweeping powers over every aspect of Southern life; the Command of the Army Act, which made it impossible for Johnson to remove Grant; and the Tenure of Civil Office Act, which was meant to make it impossible for him to fire Stanton.

The Reconstruction Act divided the former Confederacy into five military districts, each under a major general. Famous figures such as Thomas, Sheridan and Meade found themselves controlling the destinies of the Southern ruling class. Army officers were empowered to arrest civilians for crimes petty and grand. They appointed town marshals and mayors. They decided who was eligible to vote and who was not. They removed elected officials from office, sometimes almost on a whim. Sheridan removed the governor of Texas on the grounds that he was "an impediment," installing a political rival in the man's place.

The second and third Reconstruction Acts only added to these powers, while placing the army ever further from Johnson's control. Army officers upheld and overturned court convictions, raised or reduced court sentences. Hundreds of cases were handled by military commissions, where civilian defendants found themselves being judged by men in blue uniforms and gold buttons. Many a former Confederate protested bitterly, to the amusement of the court, "This ain't constitutional!"

Johnson never lost hope of getting rid of Stanton. His efforts to involve Grant in this grand design led, however, to a quarrel with Grant. From this falling-out Grant emerged in the popular mind as a kind of plaster saint fallen among conniving politicians. The country's revenge was going to be the replacing of Johnson by Grant at the earliest opportunity.

In February 1868 Johnson persuaded Major General Lorenzo Thomas, the elderly, white-haired adjutant general, to accept appointment as secretary of war. On the morning he prepared to take up his new post, Stanton had him arrested. Once released but still in shock, Thomas was then treated to whiskey and a little chat with the *real* secretary of war.

Congress began impeachment proceedings against Johnson for "high crimes and misdemeanors." That is, for violating the Tenure of Civil Office Act. The attempt to remove Stanton provided the Radical Republicans with the excuse they sought to cast out Johnson. The law they had drafted, however, would not fit the case. In their wrath they had been careless. The Tenure of Civil Office Act barred Johnson from removing his cabinet appointees without congressional approval once the Senate had confirmed them. Stanton was not his appointee—he was Lincoln's. For three months, while impeachment proceedings ground on, Stanton savored Johnson's discomfiture. Before the acquitted Johnson could fire him, he quit.

The army struggled on with Reconstruction, organizing voter registration drives, arranging elections, installing officials, but never imposing the conqueror's peace on a prostrate South that Radical Republicans were hoping for.

Conditions varied widely, not to say wildly, from state to state and county to county; so did the form and degree of resistance. Few directives from Washington offered clear instructions that could be universally applied. Much of the time army officers were either in doubt about what they were supposed to do or worried about their powers to do it. Much Signal Corps telegraph traffic consisted of the question "What shall I do?" going one way, and the answer "Use your own judgment" going the other.

Reconstruction inevitably dragged the army much deeper into

politics than it wished to go. Nonetheless, its fundamental integrity allowed it to restore civilian government throughout the former Confederacy when there was no other agency that could. People trusted the army to be honest and fair about it. The country therefore accepted the result.

In its other major task, protecting the recently freed blacks, it was less successful. Organizations such as the Ku Klux Klan and the Knights of the White Camellia came into existence. White terrorism virtually nullified the rights guaranteed blacks by the Fourteenth Amendment. There was little the army could do in towns where more than a thousand people, including children, might gather to watch a black man tortured to death but not one of them would talk.

When the military occupation began, optimistic Northerners expected it to produce a new South, one where racial harmony, clean government, economic prosperity and social stability ruled. Few army officers had any illusions about what government by major generals might achieve. Sherman spoke for them all when he wrote to his senator brother in September 1865: "No matter what change we may desire in the feelings and thoughts of people South, we cannot accomplish it by force."

In 1871 the last state to establish a reconstructed government, Georgia, did so. The army's active role in courts and elections came to an end. In 1877, as part of the deal to resolve the disputed presidential election of 1876, Rutherford B. Hayes, a former Union general, formally brought the occupation to a close. The army's attention, however, had long since shifted elsewhere—to the Sea of Grass.

LINCOLN had cultivated the West, creating six new territories: Colorado, Nevada, Arizona, Idaho, Montana and Dakota. He needed western votes, few and scattered though they were, to remain in office, to pursue the war, to save the Union. He needed western gold to pay Union armies, western silver to buy them guns. By his will and his need Nevada—rich in ore, poor in population—made the transit to statehood in just three years. Mining-rich California was exempted from the draft. What the West wanted most, though, was neither quick statehood nor exemption from the Civil War; it wanted the Indian suppressed.

While brother fought brother there had been no end to fighting on the Plains. In 1862 the Santee Sioux, herded onto a reservation along the Minnesota River, were facing starvation at the onset of winter. Indian agency warehouses bulged with food. The tribe's annuity was for some reason delayed. The annuity was due under a treaty. It was, quite literally, the price of peace. Each year when it arrived, it was used to buy food out of the warehouses. One government department was settling accounts with another government department.

The Indians were not overly impressed with the niceties of book-keeping while children went hungry. The warehouses were seized. Twenty agency employees and contractors were killed. The corpse of a white official who had jeered that the Indians could eat grass was found with grass in his mouth. Fed and exultant, Sioux braves poured off the reservation, drunk on the delirium of revenge. Across Minnesota hundreds of white settlers were murdered.

Troops under John Pope put down the uprising. At Mankato that winter thirty-eight Santees, tried and convicted of murder, were hanged in a mass execution. Much of western Minnesota remained unpopulated for another generation.

In 1864 a dispute over a cow led to trouble with the Cheyennes of Colorado. Indian raids that summer took the lives of more than two hundred settlers and travelers. A volunteer regiment composed largely of Denver's barroom sweepings and alley rats was formed under pious but martial John Chivington. "A crazy preacher," scoffed one acquaintance, "who thinks he's Napoleon."

A Cheyenne chief named Black Kettle meanwhile gathered 600 to 700 followers at Sand Creek, to arrange a peaceful surrender. When Chivington's force began deploying on a nearby bluff the chief ran up a white flag alongside the Stars and Stripes he habitually flew over his tent. Chivington was meanwhile telling his volunteers what their duty was: "Kill and scalp all, big or little; nits make lice."

In the massacre that followed as many as 200 Indians perished, most of them women and children. Denver acclaimed its heroes. The army and the administration were less enthusiastic. Chivington hurriedly resigned his commission to avoid the certainty of a court-martial and the shadow of the penitentiary. Congress made what amends it could by paying compensation.

With the Civil War over the regular strength of the army was set at 57,000. This was more than twice its prewar size and due less to the demands of Reconstruction than to the need to secure the West for the tens of thousands who crossed the Mississippi each month to make claims to free land under the Homestead Act.

The West had to be secured too for the railroads. Sherman, becoming commander of the Division of the Mississippi, considered building the transcontinental railroad more important than Reconstruction. "The Civil War trained the men who built that great national highway," he proudly reported. "General Dodge could call on any body of men to 'fall in,' 'deploy as skirmishers,' and fight the marauding Indians just as they had learned to fight the rebels down in Atlanta." He loved to inspect new stretches of track. As he rode down the rails cheers rippled along the line. Excited shouts of recognition—"It's Uncle Billy!"—rose to greet him from sunburnt section hands, straightening up, hammer in hand. Wasn't this a change, he would joke with them, from *twisting* rails? In 1869 the great artery was finished, with the driving of the golden spike at Promontory, Utah.

Throughout Reconstruction twice as many troops were on the Plains than occupying the South. No one denied there was "an Indian problem," yet to the East, swiftly forgetting its own Indian wars, the answer was simple: more reservations. Soldiers had their doubts, but after Sand Creek the army sought peace without fighting. Grant above all wanted a fresh beginning.

Following his election to the presidency in 1868, Grant tried to reform the notoriously corrupt Indian Bureau. Religious worthies, especially Quakers, were appointed Indian agents. He created a board of peace commissioners to resolve Indian grievances: no more full warehouses and delayed annuities. Sherman, succeeding Halleck as chief of staff, tried to keep volunteers out of Indian conflicts: no more Sand Creeks.

Grant's "Peace Policy" treated Indians like children. They were no longer to be held responsible for their actions. Indians could spend the winter on the reservation eating government rations, sleeping wrapped in government blankets and collecting government arms and ammunition. When spring came, the war paint went on and the braves went off, to raid, to rape, to kill and mutilate the hated settlers, but also to claim the pride of manhood in their time-honored way.

For all the goodwill among sensible and sensitive spirits on both sides, the Peace Policy was doomed. Out on the Plains two cultures had come into a contact neither could break. And both were cultures where the warrior ethos was central to their history and beliefs.

Consider the most numerous of the Plains tribes, the Sioux. These were not a people of the Plains by timeless tradition. They had been driven there from the lakes and forests of Minnesota by the Chippewas in a long war during the early 1800s. In turn, the Sioux defeated the Crows in a war to see who would get the best hunting grounds along the Powder River. Tribal lands on the Plains were not fixed. They depended instead on the number of warriors a tribe could send out each year. This varied greatly, with the rise and fall of epidemics. Indian lands were not something immemorial handed down by the Great Spirit. They were an expression of military power. The losers in a tribal war were not offered, in a fraternal spirit, a share of the best lands. They were forced out, to fend as best they could on the worst lands remaining. If they starved, tough luck. White settlers amounted to a new tribe entering an ancient struggle.

As the Peace Policy broke down, the army was exasperated by the peculiar rules it imposed. When Indians left the reservation each spring the soldiers were sent for. A campaign was mounted. If it succeeded, the marauders would gallop back to the reservation, where troops could not go. The reservation was a sanctuary. It infuriated soldiers to see Indian braves swagger past them with freshly dried scalps, sometimes trailing long feminine braids, swaying from their belts, and to be unable to do anything. All the same, many soldiers felt a certain sympathy for the Indian. White warrior and red shared much in common.

Just as Indians were despised, so were soldiers. It came as a shock to many a recruit signing on after Appomattox to discover that he had not joined the feted, admired Union army, with its ice cream socials, first-name terms between officers and men, and the attentions of dewy-eyed female admirers. This was the *regular* army—scorned, hard-bitten, isolated and tough. Many found life on the Plains unendurable, just as Indians did, and like them sought refuge in drunken oblivion or suicide.

Army rations were inadequate, even when regularly supplied. Boxes marked "Bacon" would, opened, prove to be filled with rocks. Moldy food was so common men simply brushed off the greener parts and chowed down. Corruption scandals involving army rations were nearly as frequent as those involving rations for Indians.

Conditions in military prisons were claimed to be better than those at frontier forts. Most posts were really villages consisting of crude huts thrown together by men suffering, most of them, from VD, cholera, dysentery, scurvy, or something just as unpleasant. Troops called their barracks "the government workhouse." In many places the squalor in which Indians lived was not much worse than what prevailed at the nearest fort.

Alike they suffered the attentions of swindling traders. Little of the money paid the Plains tribes for land cessions ever crossed an Indian palm. Even before the ink was dry on treaties that sold kingdoms for as little as a nickel an acre, traders appeared waving what they claimed were receipts for goods provided the Indians on credit. Every soldier meanwhile had tales to tell of crooked sutlers who robbed the boys in blue.

Soldiers were close to Indians in more direct ways. Fort Stevenson was considered the best posting along the Missouri River, for example, because it was overrun with squaws and there was, said one trooper, "plenty of time to make love."

Nearly every army officer who expressed an opinion on the subject blamed Indian wars on crooks and incompetents in the Indian Bureau. To these, however, one should also add the time-honored slowness of bureaucracy and the traditional parsimony of Congress. Soldiers got used to going months, even a year, without pay; to missed deliveries of hardtack and bacon; to petty injustice and arbitrary authority. When food or money promised to Indians did not arrive, for whatever reason, there was not soldierly resignation but tribal indignation. It did not take much indignation to start braves raiding again.

Soldier and brave were sacrifices offered up by two of the most sharply different and, in the context of the time and place, irreconcilable cultures. Both came from societies used to fighting over land. There were, on both sides, people who preferred reason to violence, but there were no two more democratic societies on Earth. The elders of neither could curb their young men for long, and the popular culture of both glorified brave deeds of war. Chivington's volunteers were no more under Lincoln's control than were young braves under Indian chiefs. Clashes were as inevitable as was the ultimate outcome.

The Indians of the southern Plains were among the first to be subdued. Winfield Scott Hancock had won enduring fame as commander of the II Corps at Gettysburg but had no experience of Indian warfare. He was sent to overawe the southern Cheyennes, the Oglala Sioux and the Arapahoes into good behavior, after the war ended.

Instead, he provoked them into taking to the warpath. Sheridan, when not reconstructing Texas, took over direction of the war Hancock had begun.

He and Sherman believed in fighting Indians with the thoroughness they had perfected in the Civil War. Neither gave much thought to public relations. Sheridan was credited with saying, "The only good Indian is a dead Indian"; something he may have believed but always denied. In the aftermath of bloody Indian raids Sherman spoke angrily about "exterminating" all Indians. To a later day that has sometimes made him appear a frontier gauleiter. He possessed an excitable nature and a lurid imagination. These came out in eyebrow-raising utterances, as when he predicted the Civil War would last one hundred years.

Sheridan made his major campaigns when the Indians were least alert and most vulnerable, in the middle of winter. His chief instrument was Custer, at the head of the 7th Cavalry.

Across southern Kansas, Oklahoma and the Panhandle hostile and friendly Indians alike were subjected to merciless attacks and constant pressure, intense hunger and repeated humiliation. Custer, known to his men as "Hard Ass" for his ability to stay in the saddle once a trail was struck, drove his troops hard. The 7th had the highest desertion rate in the army.

The most successful Indian fighter, however, was not Custer but George Crook. He was the most knowledgeable student of Indian ways the army ever possessed. Indians themselves were convinced that anyone who understood them so well must be part Indian. Crook, an 1852 graduate of West Point, was an idiosyncratic figure, with a close-cropped head and huge forked beard, riding a mule instead of a horse, dressed in a canvas hunting suit and a pith helmet, pursuing an ascetic life—no smoking, no swearing, no alcohol, no coffee—among men who were anything but ascetic. He had two interests only. One was hunting. The other was adding to a scrapbook that grew fat year by year with newspaper clippings that related his exploits.

In 1866–67 he defeated the Paiutes and Snakes of Idaho and northern Nevada in a winter campaign, overcoming unimaginably harsh conditions to do so. Thereafter miners poured into Nevada and a torrent of silver poured out.

In 1871 he was sent to Arizona, in response to heartfelt pleas from the territory's politicians. The enemy he faced was the Apaches; braves who could cover seventy-five miles a day in the desert, traveling stark-naked in temperatures that reached 120 degrees. Soldiers who attempted such feats went mad or died from sunstroke. No Indians were feared like the Apaches. Some two hundred settlers a year lost their lives to Apache raiders in a struggle that went back to the days of Cortés.

Crook dispensed with the wagon trains that slowed down other commanders. He relied instead on mules, carefully selected, under tough civilian mule skinners. There was nowhere left to hide for the Apaches. Wherever they went Crook, his troops and his mules would follow. No trail was abandoned once found.

Crook's other innovation was to organize Indians not only as scouts but as combatants. He hired them to fight other Indians. He often used one tribe to fight another. Nobody fought a hostile Indian more effectively than an Indian brave on the government payroll. Crook was unique in risking his men's lives on the loyalty of Indians in combat, and winning.

Most soldiers on the Plains never saw action. Those who served under Crook in the early 1870s saw action on average every eleven days. By April 1873 he had pacified the Apaches. He had concluded, he noted in his report, a military campaign that had begun more than three hundred years before, under the conquistadores.

The pacification of the southern Plains was completed in 1874 with a campaign directed by Ranald Mackenzie along the Red River and its major tributaries. With something of the drive and intelligence of Crook he cowed the Kiowas, Comanches, southern Cheyennes, Arapahoes and other warlike tribes into submission. This was a campaign based on converging columns. Its success was to have unforeseeable results shortly after, on the northern Plains.

There the Sioux were still basking in the treacherous rays of a false dawn. They had succeeded some years earlier in stopping the army's advance along the Bozeman Trail, into Montana. Sioux warriors inflicted a series of defeats on the soldiers. The most famous was the destruction to the last man of a detachment of 80 cavalry under Captain William J. Fetterman almost within sight of Fort Phil Kearny, in northern Wyoming, in December 1866. In 1868 the forts along the Bozeman Trail were abandoned. By the Treaty of Fort Laramie that year the Sioux were promised peace, schools and the preservation of their hunting grounds from white intruders. In return, they agreed to live on reservations that covered most of what is now South Dakota. This was one war the Indians won.

In 1874, however, Sheridan, elevated to command the Division of the Missouri, sent Custer into the Black Hills to scout possible sites for a fort. The Black Hills were clearly on the Sioux reservation, yet there were precedents; there were forts, that is, on other reservations. Custer returned proclaiming the discovery of something more interesting than a potential construction site—gold, "even among the roots of the grass." A wild exaggeration, of course, but that was always the Custer style. Prospectors flooded into the Black Hills. The army, under orders from the commanding general, Sherman, forced them out, until there were so many prospectors it simply gave up.

A government commission arrived in 1875 to negotiate mining rights to the Black Hills. The Sioux were mystified. Did the white man want to *borrow* the land? Promises of royalties mystified them even further. Offered six million dollars to sell the Black Hills outright, they rejected it outright. The commission returned empty-handed, recommending that the government take the area under eminent domain and make a compulsory purchase. An ultimatum was made that winter for all Sioux to report to the reservation. The Indians were too scattered and poorly organized to comply. They were then deemed to be at war with the United States. Early in the Centennial Year, 1876, the army moved in.

Sioux streamed off the reservation to join bands under medicine men like Sitting Bull and warrior chiefs like Crazy Horse, bands that had never been agency Indians. Thousands of northern Cheyennes joined them.

As the tribes gathered in southeastern Montana the army mounted a campaign of converging columns: Brigadier General John Gibbon would advance from the west, Major General Alfred H. Terry would approach from the east, and Crook, sent to the Black Hills in 1875 to throw the prospectors out, would move up from the south. The Indians' sole chance was to defeat the oncoming columns separately; which they did, if largely by chance.

On June 17 along Rosebud Creek, Crazy Horse led more than 2,000 braves in a rearguard action to save a big Indian village from Crook's troops, some 1,100 strong. It was a hard-fought encounter in which Crazy Horse enjoyed superior firepower and manpower. That gave Crook pause. He chose to wait where he was for three weeks, demanding reinforcements.

Custer and the 7th Cavalry, operating ahead of Terry's main body, found the Indians eight days later, this time encamped along the Little Bighorn. His original intention was to go to ground and wait for Terry before attacking. Fearing, wrongly, that he had been seen by Sioux scouts, he attacked without delay. Dividing his 560 men three ways, he defeated himself.

Major Marcus Reno with 180 men attacked the southern end of the village. Captain Frederick Benteen and 160 men were sent off on a wild-goose chase in search of more Indians. Custer chose to take the rest of his command and strike the center of the village; something that to accomplish would require crossing a river four feet deep and flowing fast virtually at the entrance to Indian tepees. Not that Custer was aware of this; he made no reconnaissance.

Reno dismounted his men, and thereby saved them but got the reputation of a coward. Custer threw his men's lives away, and became a folk hero. The attack was a clumsy affair, with no attempt to coordinate Reno's action with Custer's.

Custer appeared in plain sight of the village around 3:30 P.M. Thousands of Indians swarmed across the Little Bighorn. Among them were "squaw men"—whites who had chosen Indian wives, Indian lives. Hundreds of braves carried twelve-shot Henry repeating rifles. Hundreds more brought repeating Winchesters.

The troopers were armed with single-shot Springfield carbines whose extractors had a habit of snagging the expended cartridge in the breech and jamming. Custer's men were outgunned on a scale of three to one. Finding the battle lost and capture inevitable, some men by pairs put their Model 1872 Army Colts—the famous "Peacemaker"— to each other's heads and on a count of three, in the last act of friendship either ever knew, blew each other's brains out.

Around 5:30 P.M. it was all over. By this time Benteen had quit his footling mission and joined Reno. Entrenched, their men held off Indian attacks without difficulty. Thirty-six hours later the Indians pulled out in a hurry, when Terry appeared. It was not the fabled cavalry they feared but lowly infantry, for they brought with them "the gun that shoots twice"—mountain howitzers.

Terry and Crook organized a fall campaign, aiming to trap the

Sioux between two converging columns. This time the Indians eluded them by splitting into two columns themselves, one heading south toward the Black Hills, the other going north, into Canada. To the dismay of his troops, Crook pressed on despite the early onset of winter, starvation rations and played-out horses. Then, in late November, in blizzards and snowdrifts his cavalry, under Ranald Mackenzie, found and destroyed a large Cheyenne village. This utterly demoralized the Cheyennes, the most-admired warriors of all the Plains tribes. They went over to the white man. This in turn demoralized the Sioux.

They were doomed anyway. Even without gold in the Black Hills their hunting grounds were going to be opened up for construction of the Northern Pacific Railroad. Meanwhile the buffalo were fast disappearing, slaughtered indiscriminately by Indian and white man alike. Their unique way of life depended almost entirely on the huge, dim-witted beast.

The construction of two forts in the Yellowstone Valley in 1877 marked the end of Sioux military power. Crazy Horse gave himself up that summer. Four years later Sitting Bull returned from Canada, to surrender his rifle and draw government rations.

There were still armed clashes, but rarely and on an ever-diminishing scale. Serious fighting had ended. Indian tribes, their spirits broken by too many lost wars, eked out an existence as best they could. The women of the Paiutes, for example, earned a little cash for the tribe by posing for pornography that was peddled to travelers along the shining rails of the transcontinental.

In 1887 the Dawes Act was passed. This formally made Indians wards of the government, making official the policy of treating them like children. The act gave a plot of land to most reservation Indians. They were to become small farmers. Here was a wheel turned full circle in a century: the post-Revolutionary Jeffersonian ideal of turning red men into whites. Few Indians wanted to be farmers. By 1920 the plots assigned to most of them had been sold off to white families eager to work the land. Indians instead made jewelry, consoled themselves with dreams or, putting themselves in bottles, threw their lives away.

SINCE THE Revolution the main—at times almost the only—reason the army was preserved was to fight Indians. That challenge drew to a close in the 1870s. At the same time there was a powerful mood in the country, one that grew strongly once the Civil War ended, that Americans would never have to fight again. The United States had seen its last war. First, America had no enemies strong enough to attack it. Second, modern weapons were so awesomely destructive it was inconceivable that anyone would use them again. War was on its way out. And the fate of the army seemed to prove it: by the late 1870s it was back to its pre–Civil War size.

Pacifistic beliefs held by millions of their countrymen made the military feel more isolated than ever from the ordinary citizen. As the army and navy turned in upon themselves, the sense of specialness grew. The commitment to service did not weaken but deepened. Military men thought harder than ever about who and what they were. That intense self-scrutiny and in-family discussion provided an intellectual climate in which innovative professionalism matured quickly.

The poor combat performance of many units in the Indian campaigns was an embarrassment that had to be remedied. The army began holding war games. Marksmanship competitions revived the sharpshooting tradition.

The Franco-Prussian War of 1870 had broken the old French ascendancy in military fashion. The spiked helmet (or pickelhaube) of the Prussians displaced the kepi. Adorned with big brass eagles and flowing horsehair plumes, the spiked helmet was adopted by the cavalry and the artillery in 1872 and by the infantry in 1881. Uniforms were cut better and trimmed with ornate piping and facings. Gone were the plain and shapeless garments of the Civil War. By the 1880s officers had acquired cords, tassels and epaulets. In full dress they positively dripped gold buttons and braid.

Yet what survived longest from the peacock era was something simple and useful. The webbed equipment of troops throughout the world in the twentieth century derives from the woven cartridge belt devised by Captain Anson Mills in campaigns against the Sioux. The War Department adopted his woven belt in 1881 to replace the cartridge box, that cumbersome item soldiers had cursed almost since they first took up firearms.

These changes in uniforms and accouterments were only external manifestations of a profound internal debate whose presiding genius was Sherman. For nearly twenty years after the Civil War it was the restless, imaginative Sherman who transformed the army. For many years after that the challenge was taken up by the young officers whose talents he had encouraged and whose careers he had advanced; with one tragic exception—Emory Upton.

Graduating from West Point in 1861, Upton had commanded cavalry, artillery and infantry in the Civil War, rising to a brevet major general's stars. He was the only officer on either side who solved the problem of assaulting entrenchments held by men armed with rifled muskets. He put what he had learned into a new handbook on tactics, which was formally adopted by the army in 1869. His chief innovation was the four-man team: highly trained, working together to take advantage of whatever cover the terrain provided, relying more on speed, surprise, teamwork and concealment than on firepower versus firepower. Upton's four-man team was the precursor of the modern infantry squad.

In 1875 Sherman dispatched him on a one-year world tour to study foreign armies. The one that made the deepest impression was that of the recently victorious Prussians. The Prussian army, with its general staff, three years of universal conscription, a large ready reserve, its excellent service schools, its ability to combine quantity with quality, left him dazzled. It seemed all an army should be.

The War Department declined to fund publication of his report, *The Armies of Asia and Europe.* Upton had to publish it himself. Its call for Prussian-style arms fell flat. And not even Upton dared suggest that the United States adopt the bedrock of the Prussian system, universal peacetime conscription. Neither could he conjure up any real need for a mass army of the European type. Invasion from Mexico? From Canada? From Spain by way of Cuba? Impossible, all three. His thesis, that America needed to create the rudiments of a mass army, lacked conviction. Lacking conviction, it was easily ignored.

He turned to writing a critical account of his profession since the Revolutionary War, *The Military Policy of the United States.* He stopped his narrative, however, at the end of 1862, in a fit of deep pessimism. He doubted that anyone would publish it, and feared that if they did his career would be ruined. The influence of this unfinished work was nonetheless enormous. It circulated in manuscript within the army for decades, before belated publication in 1903.

Upton's thesis this time was that the United States had never faced military challenges squarely. Instead, it had resorted to makeshifts; mainly to military amateurism—to politically appointed officers, hopeless common militia and poorly trained short-term volunteers.

Meanwhile the regulars were starved of money, modern weapons, schooling and justice. The result of so much amateurism was unpreparedness in every war, forcing the country to expend life and treasure on a prodigal scale to secure victory. The Uptonian unpreparedness theory has dominated American military history for the past one hundred years.

Tormented by blinding headaches, dogged by doubts that his infantry tactics would work in future wars, demoralized by reflections that nearly all the great captains had won their greatest battles by the age of forty, Upton gazed on San Francisco Bay's beauty for the last time, one day in 1881, wrote out his resignation from the army, took out his Colt .45 revolver, and shot himself in the head. He was forty-two years old.

He departed just as army reforms were getting into full stride. The artillery was equipped with breech-loading steel guns. The magazine rifle was adopted. Smokeless powder was introduced for both small arms and artillery. Only the thriftiness of Congress slowed the pace at which modern arms were acquired. Meanwhile new service schools were created, something long desired, long denied: schools for the Signal Corps, for the engineers, for field artillery and cavalry combined, for cavalry and infantry combined, and for the new hospital corps. An army medical school was opened recognizing the unique demands of military medicine.

In time would come the Army War College and the Naval War College. Neither would be an institution where intellectuals were likely to feel at home. Even so, both war colleges were propelled by a faith among American army and navy officers that advanced education was essential to a proper military career.

There was nothing new about this hunger for military professionalism. It was a struggle that went back to the days of Sylvanus Thayer, and before that to the prison school in Tripoli. The reforms of the 1880s and 1890s were the sudden blossoming of flowers long since planted. The paradoxical result was that an army that appeared to be passing through its dark ages, its very existence in doubt, was at the same time enjoying its renaissance.

WHEN THE Civil War ended, the navy returned to its old love, canvas. In 1869 a general order made it official: all naval vessels were to have "full sail power." The next year David Dixon Porter succeeded Farragut as admiral of the navy. Porter disliked steam despite its having proved its value on vessels he had commanded in action. The young innovator turned middle-aged conservative neglected steam, armor and modern guns. What naval strategy there was consisted of echoes—of commerce raiders like Gustavus Fox, echoes even of the Jeffs. The navy continued to build monitors, but they were useful only as floating batteries. Millions were poured each year into huge gun emplacements around American ports. This policy of passive coastal defense was adopted by both the army and the navy for want of anything better. It was one of those rare instances where both services formed one harmonious whole. It did not reflect thought, however, but the absence of thought.

Successive administrations were content to let the navy wallow in benign, money-saving neglect until, in the 1880s, the climate changed. First Garfield, then Arthur, then Cleveland appointed navy secretaries who proved to be champions of naval reform. All three secretaries were chosen for political reasons; it was chance more than anything else that made them believers in a modern navy. Beginning in 1883 Congress responded to their lead by authorizing construction of modern steel ships, notably "protected" cruisers,* but including two battleships, the *Texas* and the *Maine*.

Once more American industry had fallen behind in advanced naval technologies. As a result, the "New Navy" found itself with slow ships, poor guns and underpowered engines. Legislation was passed in 1886 requiring American naval vessels to be made entirely from domestic materials. This stopped ship builders from relying on foreign suppliers, whose governments invariably refused to allow the export of the most advanced technologies. The law made it profitable for American ship builders to develop the most modern naval technologies for themselves. By the mid-1890s American naval vessels were of world class. Meantime, another big business lobby had been created, one devoted not simply to the New Navy but to a big navy.

It was a lobby that had already borne fruit, in the Navy Act of 1890. This bill ended the traditional American policy of passive coastal defense. It authorized construction of three "sea-going coastline bat-

---

*A protected ship had an armor-plated deck. An armored ship had not only an armored deck but armor plate along its sides as well.

tleships," but with a range of five thousand miles they could command the sea-lanes more than one thousand miles out from American shores. The days when American naval strategy in wartime consisted of commerce raiding and blockade running were over. A new strategy was needed for a new day. Many helped provide it, but only one was remembered—Alfred Thayer Mahan.

The son of Dennis Hart Mahan, he had chosen the Naval Academy despite being a poor sailor. Away from West Point he could make a life of his own, yet the navy soon irritated and bored him. He was afraid of the sea, he discovered, and spent much of his career pulling every string he could lay his hands on to avoid service afloat. Appointment to the Naval War College at Newport, Rhode Island, in 1886 came at a critical juncture in his career. For the aloof, scholarly Captain Mahan, teaching the lessons of naval history to eager young officers was the ideal billet.

He had already published his first book, *The Gulf and Inland Waters,* in 1883. This offered a sailor's view of the Civil War, in which the blockade defeated the Confederacy and the navy saved the Union, with a little help from Grant and Sherman. In his Naval War College lectures he turned to an even loftier theme, the role of naval power in the rise and fall of great nations.

His insights were offered to a wider audience in a manuscript, *The Influence of Sea Power upon History.* Alas, each time he sent it to a publisher, the publisher sent it back. It seemed too narrow, too dull, too technical, too badly written to appeal to anyone but naval officers. With the desperation that writers know too well, he swiftly concocted a ninety-page introduction, called "Discussion of the Elements of Sea Power." This did the trick. His manuscript was accepted.

The introduction amounted to a fervent plea for an expanded merchant marine and a powerful modern navy. Mahan fixed his eye firmly on the Caribbean. He imagined it becoming to the rise of American naval power what the English Channel had been to the Royal Navy. The Zeitgeist was with him. When the book appeared in 1890 most reviewers concentrated on the "Elements" and skipped the 450 pages of turgidly written narrative history.

Mahan's central thesis was fundamentally flawed. Britain had been able to exert its power on waters all over the globe by controlling just five choke points: the English Channel, the North Sea, the Straits of Gibraltar, the Red Sea and, after 1869, the Suez Canal. The bulk of world trade and communications passed through these five "narrow seas." By dominating them the British had risen to wealth and power beyond anything their small population and limited domestic resources offered. Mahan struggled, with some ingenuity, to produce a range of analogies between the geographical position of the United States and that of the British Isles. Without exception his analogies were false or fanciful. The awkward truth was that there were no such choke points within American waters or even near them.

If Mahan's strategic conceptions were shaky, they were no more so than his ideas on naval tactics. These were taken largely from Baron Henri Jomini. They were based on land warfare, on the maneuvers, that is, of the infantry and cavalry of the *Grande Armée:* Mahan offered the world Napoleon afloat. The debt to his and Papa's mentor was cheerily acknowledged: Mahan's favorite dog answered to "Jomini!"

He believed he had unearthed the eternal principles of warfare; elements so vital that no development in propulsion, armor or guns could ever affect them. For all his frosty exterior he was at heart a romantic, struggling to apply the outlook of the Age of Sail to the new Age of Steam. He was entranced by billowing white canvas; repelled by hissing, pounding, hot metal.

The centerpiece of Mahan's mental universe was the battle fleet, a mighty force of capital ships going forth to wrest command of the sea from the foe. His reward for that vision was to be hailed as the great teacher by all who sought big navies—Theodore Roosevelt, the British Admiralty, the German kaiser. Like most fame it was won less by being right than by filling a need.

Mahan was all of a piece with powerful currents shaping public opinion and intellectual fashion in the frenetically Gay Nineties. The economic boom of Civil War and Reconstruction had doubled American incomes in the 1860s and made the United States the world's leading industrial power. In the 1870s a thrusting, unified Germany was transformed into the leading economic power of Europe. Britain and France, troubled by the usual self-doubts of those on the way down, flaunted with a desperate ostentation all the mummery of imperial might. Germany and the United States, troubled by the usual self-doubts of the nouveaux riches, were meanwhile seduced by the prospect of putting on a similar show.

No one seriously wanted to take on the responsibilities of large, and largely troublesome, empires. A few glittering crumbs would do, to demonstrate one's arrival in the big time. Japan was currently in much the same mood, for much the same reason.

Two speeches from two veterans of the Civil War showed how much opinion had changed. In 1880 Sherman had made his most famous utterance to a rain-sodden gathering of five thousand members of the main Union army veterans' organization, the Grand Army of the Republic, at Columbus, Ohio. On the fringes of the crowd were hundreds of awestruck teen-age boys. As he closed his speech, he addressed them: "There is many a boy here today who looks on war as all glory, but, boys, it is all hell. You can bear this warning voice to generations yet to come."

Fifteen years later, the great jurist Oliver Wendell Holmes spoke to the Harvard graduating class of 1895. In recent years the thrice-wounded Holmes had begun cultivating a military mustache and observing battle anniversaries, and now he descried a meaning in his experiences that had formerly eluded him. "War, when you are at it, is horrible and dull," he declared. "It is only when time has passed that you see that its message was divine."

Such sentiments these days set racing the pulses of a generation of young men who had missed out on battle, but whose fathers and uncles had not: men such as Theodore Roosevelt and Brooks Adams in the United States, Friedrich Nietzsche in Germany. Very different men, yet they wrote and spoke of war as among the noblest human ventures; as nature's way of culling the weak and worthless from the strong and courageous; humanity's way of improving the breed. Millions disagreed with them, but the tide—in sentiment, in national ambitions, in the rise and fall of economies, in population structures—was with them.

In 1897 William McKinley, the last Civil War veteran to occupy the White House, took office. Unlike Holmes, he did not discover anything divine in war. The sights he had seen haunted him still. For his secretary of the navy he chose one of the luminaries of the Peace Society, the elderly John D. Long. For assistant secretary of the navy he chose the pugnacious Theodore Roosevelt. A balanced team.

Barely had he got his feet under the desk before Roosevelt delivered a sensational speech to the Naval War College. His theme was Uptonian, the dangers of unpreparedness. It was an address informed from beginning to end, however, by a passionate creed: "No triumph of peace is quite so great as the supreme triumphs of war." That rang like an alarm bell, for there was little doubt what it was—a fresh call to arms; if not today, tomorrow.

IT WAS a war that began in sweetness and light: sugarcane, growing under a tropical sun. Cuba had a one-crop economy and the new imperialism called for conquering world markets while defending those at home. In the mid-1890s Congress raised tariffs accordingly. Almost the first commodity to suffer was Cuban sugar. Their wretched lot made much worse, Cuban peasants rose again, as they had in the past, against their Spanish masters. And once again Spain poured troops into the island to suppress the revolt.

The Spanish army did not consist of the bloodthirsty villains described in Cuban propaganda or the pages of Joseph Pulitzer's *World* and William Randolph Hearst's *Journal,* two New York newspapers locked in a circulation war and peddling atrocity hard. Most of the suffering in Cuba was the result of Spanish inefficiency.

The strategy was to reconcentrate the rural population in garrison towns, where it could be simultaneously watched and protected. The cleared areas were then systematically devastated, in a drive to starve out the guerrillas. Starvation indeed took hold, but among the *reconcentrados.* Guerrillas can nearly always find food. As many as one hundred thousand Cubans in the reconcentration camps died of hunger, neglect or disease.

McKinley was deeply distressed. When a fund for Cuban relief was opened in 1897 he made an anonymous five-thousand-dollar contribution. He pressed Spain to use more humane methods, with some success. Madrid offered the island autonomy but had no intention of relinquishing it peacefully.

Congress had passed a resolution declaring American neutrality and demanding Cuban independence before McKinley took office. This was one foreign policy question in which Congress, not the White House, made the running. All through 1897 the new president vacillated and agonized.

When rioting shook Havana at the end of that year the U.S. consul there grew anxious for the safety of Americans in Cuba. To reassure them, he asked for a battleship to pay a courtesy call.

The Spanish did not want any American warship to visit Havana at such a tense time but dared not say so. The Americans were so touchy these days. The Spanish resigned themselves to having this unwanted courtesy thrust on them. The battleship *Maine* duly arrived. As naval courtesy visits go this one seemed likely to drag on forever. After six weeks the *Maine* was still in Havana Harbor.

On the evening of February 15, 1898, she was ripped apart by an explosion. Of her 354 officers and men some 266 perished. Spain expressed shock and sorrow, proffered condolences, tended the injured, deeded part of Havana's finest cemetery in perpetuity to the United States as a resting place for the *Maine*'s dead, and suggested a joint U.S.-Spanish inquiry into the disaster. This was rejected.

While a U.S. Navy court of inquiry sat, "Remember the Maine!" was brayed from soapboxes, was emblazoned on peppermint lozenges dissolving in the mouths of children, was sounded Sunday mornings from pulpit and pew, was sung in vaudeville theaters to tacky martial tunes, appeared on downtown streets in rows of store windows and bobbed along on badges pinned to ten million lapels. "Remember!" was only a polite word for "Avenge!"

The governor of Texas sent his Rangers to stand guard on the border, to hurl back any invasion launched by "Spanish sympathizers." At a Broadway theater where a comedy, *The Bride Elect,* was showing, performances of a song called "Unleash the Dogs of War!" nightly unleashed a tempest of excitement. There was no escaping it. Even the journal of sober-minded New England literati, *Atlantic Monthly,* succumbed, putting Old Glory on its cover.

Meanwhile both houses of Congress voted unanimously to give McKinley fifty million dollars to be spent on the army and navy in any way he chose. On March 17, Senator Redfield Proctor, recently returned from Cuba, gave a thirty-minute speech on the Senate floor describing what he had seen. What mattered was less the facts he related, which were well known, than the way he presented them. As he portrayed it, war with Spain over Cuba would be morality made real, something sublime, beyond party or country. Proctor turned Spanish villainy into a casus belli.

After five weeks the navy inquiry reported, finding "the *Maine* was destroyed by the explosion of a submarine mine" setting off the forward magazine. The possibility of accident was ruled out.* Public opinion took "external explosion" in the navy report as a euphemism for "Spanish attack."

The Spanish naval inquiry attributed the explosion to a mishap aboard ship. Had it been caused externally by a mine or torpedo, there would have been a geyser of water rising high in the air when it went off. No one reported seeing a geyser. The waters of the harbor would have been covered with dead fish in the morning. No one reported that either.

The administration demanded indemnity for the *Maine* and independence for Cuba. As McKinley waited for Madrid's reply, it dawned on him that the country was sliding into a war, and he could not prevent it. He became haggard, depressed and jumpy. In the dead watches of the night he was tormented by visions no words can describe. His one refuge was a drugged simulacrum of sleep that left him, when day broke, exhausted and weeping.

On April 9 he had Spain's reply: no independence for Cuba. On April 11, McKinley asked Congress for authority to intervene in aid of the Cuban rebels. Eight days later he had it. On April 21 the navy began to blockade Cuban ports. On April 25, Congress formally declared war. Americans rejoiced, as crusaders going forth to halt the oppression of the poor and weak. Spain's mood was resignation to fate: better defeat in war than grovel before the bellicose Yanquis.

Only with the country on the brink of hostilities was the strength of the regulars raised from 28,000 to 66,000. McKinley was authorized, after war was declared, to raise 216,500 volunteers. There was no need for half so many troops; nor much chance of avoiding them.

The common militia had all but disappeared, supplanted by volunteer militia, which most states had taken to calling, grandly, "The National Guard." Its legal standing was shaky. An all-volunteer force on two- or three-year enlistments, this was hardly the militia mentioned in the Constitution. Its chief activity in the decades following

---

*In 1976 the navy's leading experts on damage control concluded that the *Maine* was sunk by an internal explosion, probably caused by a fire in a coal bunker touching off ammunition in an adjacent store. The 1898 court of inquiry took no evidence from technical experts.

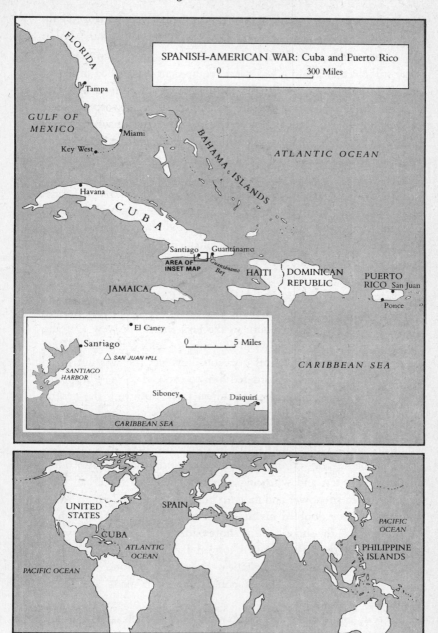

the Civil War was intervening in the violent labor disputes arising from the country's breakneck industrial growth.

Many of the old militia traditions lived on, all the same: officers were still elected, training was a lark, equipment was ruined or left to rot, there were few support units. With strong roots in local and state politics, the Guard was a pressure group McKinley and his secretary of war, Russell A. Alger (a former cavalry brigade commander under Custer), could not ignore. The War Department enrolled the volunteers for two years' federal service, then tried to keep them out of harm's way.

McKinley, Alger and the commanding general, Nelson A. Miles, were not sure at first that even a large force of regulars would be needed. In the first few weeks the navy and the Cuban *insurrectos* seemed as if they might win the war unaided. Nor was victory slow to appear. It was produced by the most dapper figure ever to don navy whites, George Dewey, on May 1.

With the aid of powerful friends—Roosevelt and Proctor— Dewey had taken command of the Asiatic squadron only six months earlier. Having served in youth in the fleet that took New Orleans, he had a habit in maturity, when in doubt, of asking himself, "What would Farragut do?" On this occasion, however, he was left in no doubt. A cable from Long ordered him to proceed to the Philippines and destroy the Spanish naval squadron there. Quitting the neutral waters of Hong Kong, he painted his buff ships gray and sailed for Manila, six hundred miles away. With him went a chow dog for company and a rabbit's foot, stroked often, for good luck.

The Spanish admiral, Patricio Montojo, commanded an assortment of elderly cruisers and wheezing gunboats. Dewey's force had three times as much firepower and modern guns with superior range. Montojo might have doubled his firepower by fighting close enough to Manila to have the support of its shore batteries. To spare the civilian population of the city he sailed instead farther down Manila Bay. Montojo took his ships into shallow waters so that once they were sunk, surviving Spanish sailors could climb the masts and escape drowning.

Throughout the morning of May 1 Dewey's vessels sailed back and forth, edging steadily closer to the Spanish line of battle, raining on it a hail of exploding shells. The day was as hot and humid as a sauna. Under battened-down hatches American sailors fought on blindly, dressed only in their underpants and shoes. Above was the commodore, in starched whites and incongruity: unable to find his uniform hat, he wore a checked golf cap for the occasion. A gentleman did not go into combat bareheaded.

Dewey's only other anxiety all day was his supply of shells. The squadron's ammunition bunkers were only half full when the battle started, and of six thousand rounds fired by Dewey's gunners they scored only 142 hits. It was enough. Montojo lost seven ships, 161 men killed, another 210 wounded. The American loss came to nine men wounded and splinter damage.

Dewey's attack had removed a potential threat to his force and provided his squadron with a secure base. Neutral ports such as Hong Kong were closed to him. He had no choice about remaining in the Philippines, yet without troops he could not take and hold Manila. He commandeered the Spanish naval base at Cavite, ten miles south of the city, and waited for Washington to send him an army.

Brilliant though the Battle of Manila Bay was, the theater of decision was going to be Cuba, and by May the navy had Havana closely blockaded. Rejecting Mahan's teaching and preaching, both the American and Spanish Atlantic fleets had been split into two: a flying squadron to guard home waters and a Caribbean squadron to operate off Cuba.

The U.S. Navy's flying squadron was at Hampton Roads, Virginia, under Commodore Winfield Scott Schley, to reassure the panicky cities of the East Coast, which hourly expected to be raided. The Caribbean squadron, under Captain William Sampson, was covering both Havana and San Juan, Puerto Rico. The Spanish Caribbean squadron, under Admiral Pascual Cervera y Topete, was somewhere at sea.

The Spanish army in Cuba faced an uncertain future. It had devastated the countryside too successfully for its own good. It was forced to depend on imported food, right down to the fodder for horses. Spanish garrisons were easy for the *insurrectos* to besiege. An effective blockade of all Cuban ports would in time force the army to surrender, although that might take the rest of the year.

Miles and Alger had sent Major General William Shafter to Tampa, the closest major American port to Cuba, to build up an invasion force. It seemed unlikely that it would be needed for months, if ever. The agreed strategy—agreed to by McKinley—was for a fall invasion, after the yellow fever season had passed; assuming the war was not over by then.

Cervera sailed into tropical waters, only to find Havana was closed to him. So was San Juan. He took his squadron into Santiago de Cuba, on the southeastern coast of the island, four hundred miles from Havana, on May 19. Naval intelligence quickly and accurately located him. Schley, steaming toward Cuba at high speed, refused to believe it. For nearly a week he blockaded an empty port. Cervera was meanwhile urging Madrid to let him return home: dividing the Spanish fleet was going to allow the Americans to defeat it piecemeal. He finally secured permission. Too late. Schley had come back to take a closer look at Santiago, seen the Spanish ships and blockaded the harbor. Days later Sampson joined Schley.

A message from Sampson on June 7 that with 10,000 men he could take Santiago overturned the agreed strategy. Miles and Shafter were ordered to launch an invasion with whatever was at hand down in Tampa. Next day Shafter embarked 17,000 men of V Corps: two infantry divisions, a division of dismounted cavalry and an independent brigade. The dismounted cavalry was commanded by grizzled old Joseph Wheeler, the former Confederate cavalier. The war was an important act of national reconciliation.

Shafter had no time for journalists. They in turned mocked his three hundred pounds, but the fat man held the Medal of Honor and had proved to be an aggressive commander in various Indian campaigns. His departure was delayed a week by reports of a Spanish fleet off Key West. During that hiatus a marine battalion landed at Guantánamo Bay, forty miles east of Santiago, to secure a foul-weather anchorage for Sampson's fleet and to carve out a coaling station. Spanish attacks were beaten off so decisively they used up what little offensive spirit Spanish commanders possessed. The navy and Marine Corps hold Guantánamo to this day.

Santiago is at the head of a narrow bay. The navy wanted the army to take the forts at the harbor mouth so they could enter the bay and attack Cervera's squadron. Shafter chose instead to land fifteen miles to the east, at Daiquirí, move inland and attack the city.

The V Corps splashed ashore unmolested on June 22. Two days later a second beachhead was established, at Siboney, six miles closer to Santiago. Second Infantry Division, under Henry W. Lawton, advanced to protect the invasion beaches while Shafter got his supplies unloaded.

With Wheeler was the 1st U.S. Volunteer Cavalry, better known as the Rough Riders. This was democracy gone to war: Ivy League athletes as officers, cowboys as troopers. Their colonel, Leonard Wood, was a regular, but one completely outshone by his second-in-command, Theodore Roosevelt. Wood and Roosevelt were close friends, and the colonel knew when to defer to an influential politician. Wheeler, Roosevelt and the Rough Riders were all desperate to distinguish themselves. One midnight they got around Lawton's right flank and went stumbling through the bushes toward what reports said was a Spanish position. The Spaniards were about to pull out but paused to set up an ambush for whoever was thrashing around out there. The Rough Riders walked into it, taking 16 dead and 52 wounded in what amounted to a publicity stunt that backfired.

Receiving news that a Spanish relief column was heading for Santiago, Shafter gathered up every man who could carry a rifle and threw virtually his entire force into an attack on the city's outer defenses on July 1. He wasted no time and formed no reserve, except for unwisely holding back half of his available artillery. Only two light batteries saw action.

Shafter himself was out of the fight, too sick with malaria and gout to direct it. His plan was poorly conceived. The best divisional commander, Lawton, was dispatched to a fortified village called El Caney, nearly four miles northeast of Santiago. The village was held by 550 Spaniards and a stone blockhouse. The fight for El Caney was a bloody and unnecessary affair. All that was needed was a blocking force of several hundred men to isolate it. Most of Lawton's 6,600 troops would have been better employed in the main assault, the attack on the San Juan Heights, to the east of Santiago.

The bulk of V Corps moved toward the town down a narrow road, coming under well-aimed Spanish fire long before reaching the heights. The 71st New York, one of the Guard's "crack" outfits, panicked and broke. An officer of the 13th Infantry found them "in this prostrate formation for the purpose of avoiding exposure to bullets." Finding a trail running parallel to the road, V Corps spread out and continued its advance.

The main objective was San Juan Hill, roughly at the center of a line of low hills and giving its name to the whole. On the crest of San

Juan Hill was a blockhouse. To control the heights it would have to be taken. The Spanish had made the task easier by scattering their 10,500 troops far and wide. The defenders, moreover, were thoroughly demoralized.

The Americans attacking San Juan Hill had an advantage of at least ten to one. This advantage in numbers would have compensated easily for the lack of artillery support had it not been for the lack of leadership in the attack. Well-aimed Spanish rifle fire from above kept men crouching in the tall grass for three hours, taking needless losses while waiting for someone to take command of the situation. There was neither advance nor retreat, only a growing casualty list.

Many of the troops had not eaten for twenty-four hours and the temperature rose to 100 degrees. Heat and hunger dulled the wits of junior officers, it seemed, and the absence of firm direction from Shafter left inexperienced field-grade officers in suspense.

Around the middle of the afternoon a battery of three Gatling guns was brought into action by Lieutenant John B. Parker. The drumfire of lead beating on their blockhouse and sweeping their rifle pits unnerved the Spanish defenders. Some jumped out, running for the reverse slope and the safety of the town at its base. This inspiring sight brought American troops rising from the tall grass and moving forward in long, ragged lines.

The Rough Riders panted on foot up Kettle Hill, roughly six hundred yards from San Juan Hill, behind the 10th Cavalry. This position had to be taken because the Spaniards entrenched on the crest could enfilade the line of troops assaulting the San Juan Hill blockhouse. Here too rifle fire from above had halted the advance for hours, leaving dead men sprawled in the grass, but once the black cavalrymen resumed their attack they swept on without a pause. On Kettle Hill five black cavalry troopers won the Medal of Honor.

From the press, however, the country got the impression that the Rough Riders had borne the brunt of the fighting. A military legend was born of men in dusty brown charging up San Juan Hill on horseback, contemptuous of the wall of lead thrown up by awestruck Spaniards, sweeping irresistibly to victory and, with throat-catching panache, winning the Spanish-American War.

This exciting image conveniently buried an uncomfortable truth. The best combat performance that day came from the Gatling gun battery and from the 9th and 10th cavalries—black regiments both.

The superiority of the white warrior over all men of darker hue was a central tenet in the imperialist's faith. Between Appomattox and the San Juan Heights black soldiers had earned an enviable fighting record. Like a shutter coming down that suddenly changed. Soon they would be denigrated as constitutional cowards. It would take more than fifty years before black soldiers were able to overcome a stigma that took root in false accounts from Cuba.*

Shafter's V Corps had suffered 216 killed, 1,318 wounded; a six-to-one ratio of wounded to dead that reflected the shortage of Spanish artillery. Losses of 10 percent in one day were as much as Shafter thought the country would tolerate. Worn down by illness, heat and disappointment, he wanted to pull back five miles. The former major, McKinley, refused to allow it.

Shafter settled down to negotiate Santiago's surrender, knowing it must come; just as surely as he knew reinforcements were on the way for his starving, louse-scratching soldiers. Already, though, the yellow fever cases had started.

On July 3, in an assertion of Spanish honor forced on him by his political superiors, Cervera sortied from Santiago Bay, beneath a forest of red-and-gold flags that cried to the sky four centuries of imperial splendor. His ships came out one at a time, steaming down the twisting narrow channel at six knots. Nearly a mile out to sea they paused, to avoid a shoal and drop their pilots. If this was defiance it was prudently conducted.

Of all days, Sampson had chosen this one to go and confer with Shafter. He was off Siboney, in riding boots and spurs, when the action began. By the time he rejoined the fleet the shooting was virtually over.

The Spanish squadron consisted of four armored cruisers and six torpedo boat destroyers (a name soon to be shortened to destroyers). The newest and fastest of the cruisers, the *Cristóbal Colón*, was still without her main battery.

Sampson had left the fleet in the charge of Schley. Its standing orders were for all seven battleships and armored cruisers, drawn up in a *U* shape outside the harbor mouth, to make a converging charge if Cervera came out. It was a plan whose sole merit was simplicity.

*There was no segregation in the navy before the 1890s. As the United States became an imperial power, it became almost impossible for blacks to join the navy.

Rushing forward, guns blazing, American ships were soon in danger of sinking one another. Schley, aboard the *Brooklyn,* was obliged to make a half-circle, and nearly collided with the *Texas.* In the confusion the Spanish might have escaped had they scattered. Instead, they formed line of battle, steaming westward, hugging the coast, being sunk, run aground or surrendered one by one as they went. It was another one-sided victory for the navy, but marred this time by an unseemly wrangle between Sampson and Schley as to whose was the glory.

Two weeks later Miles arrived with reinforcements for V Corps. The army prepared to assault the town. The pretense of negotiating surrender terms came to a swift end, although as balm to Spanish pride the United States paid for shipping the surrendered troops home.

Miles moved on to invade Puerto Rico. His operation against the 8,000 Spanish regulars there was one of converging columns, fighting them as if they were Indians who had gone off the reservation. The price of victory was four killed, 40 wounded in action. The only problem he reported to Alger was a shortage of American flags for a jubilant Puerto Rican populace to wave as they greeted their liberators.

The army and navy still expected to fight for Havana in the fall. It remained the center of Spanish power in the Caribbean, guarded by more than 30,000 troops. Spain also had plenty of ships despite recent losses. What it did not have, however, was the will to fight on. Late in July Madrid put out feelers for peace terms. A swift settlement and the Philippines might yet be saved for Spain.

There too an insurrection had broken out several years earlier against Spanish rule. The Filipinos rose up against the brutality and near-slavery it imposed on them, but what they hated even more was the filched wealth and arrogance of the Spanish monks who had taken most of the best lands for their orders. The revolt was suppressed by garroting, mass executions and terror, plus an attempt to buy off the leaders with a promise of $850,000 and future reforms. These revolutionary commanders, among them Emilio Aguinaldo, took ship for Hong Kong. Once they were there, the Spanish government shrugged off the promised reforms and found excuses for not paying most of the money. Dewey brought Aguinaldo back from Hong Kong in order to establish contact with the insurgents.

The second-ranking officer in the army, Major General Wesley Merritt, assembled a Philippines expedition at San Francisco in May, following news of Dewey's victory. Even before the month was out, Merritt's advance guard was on its way, pausing only to scoop up Guam. The 60 Spanish soldiers there did not know there was a war on until summoned to surrender; which they did. On July 25 Merritt himself reached the Philippines, in some confusion about what McKinley and Alger expected him to do. Was he simply to capture Manila? Or to take the entire archipelago?

As American units arrived their officers had to negotiate with Aguinaldo, whose forces now had Manila effectively besieged. They had to talk the *insurrectos* into allowing American troops to take up places in the encircling line so they might launch an attack on the city. Aguinaldo had a cabinet as well as an army. The existence of the Republic of the Philippines had been proclaimed. It had a flag, but the United States did not recognize it. Aguinaldo's hope was that by allowing the Americans to share in the conquest of Manila recognition would follow.

The Spanish authorities in Manila were terrified the insurgents would take the city and do to them what they had done for three centuries to Filipinos. With the aid of the Belgian consul a mock battle was planned, in which the Americans would appear to fight for the city, the Spanish would—for honor's sake—appear to defend it, and the *insurrectos* would be frozen out. The attack was made on August 13. Many of the troops on both sides and their company officers were unaware the fight was fixed.

In the confusion six Americans and 49 Spaniards were killed. The *insurrectos* broke through and captured part of the city. The Spanish-American War was already over. It had effectively ended more than twenty-four hours earlier, with the signing of an armistice, but it would take three days for the news to reach Manila. Back in May Dewey had suggested to the Spanish captain general that the telegraph cable to Hong Kong should be available to them both, so they could remain in contact with their respective governments. In an assertion of Spanish honor, the captain general disagreed. Dewey then cut the cable, denying it to them both.

Spain protested angrily over the capture of Manila after an armistice was agreed, but unless it wanted to refight the war it was not going to recover the city. On the basis of holding the Cavite naval base and roughly three fourths of Manila the United States demanded the whole of the Philippines—and got it.

Secretary of State John Hay pronounced it "a splendid little war" in a letter to Roosevelt. Casualty lists were short. Only 379 servicemen were killed or died of wounds. A further 5,049 died of disease, mainly in volunteers' camps. It was the most popular war the country had fought and a hard one to get into. The regulars virtually monopolized the action. More than 200,000 volunteers went home feeling cheated and their friends in Congress berated the War Department as though it had lost the war instead of winning it.

Even so, the gains were historic and undeniable. After twenty-five years of vacillation and debate, Hawaii had been annexed. The feverish emotions of wartime had achieved something decades of calm deliberation had failed to resolve. Guam and Puerto Rico were acquired as little more than colonies. Cuba was under American protection. In the Pacific and the Caribbean the United States had become a force to be reckoned with. Since the Civil War it had been an economic giant and a political pygmy. No longer. It stood on the stage of world affairs as one of the great military powers.

11

PLANETARY
SOLDIERS

FRESH-FACED, corn-fed lads, not much different from fathers who had once ridden with Custer or marched with Lee, signed up by the tens of thousands for Cuba. Staying on for the Philippines, many soon grew used to army life and made it their own. This, though, was not the "Old Army," the guardian of inner frontiers. These men were America's first planetary soldiers, making its presence felt in the world in ways more dramatic and direct than anything in the subtle currents of trade or diplomacy. For untold millions of the world's people the first American they ever saw wore a uniform.

The new American role sprang from the Philippines. It was a tar baby: once picked up, it proved impossible to put down. Congress argued and the president prayed until, he claimed, divine intervention informed him that God wanted the United States to hold on to the islands and civilize them.

More convincing—if still open to argument—were three other justifications he advanced. First, American blood having been shed for the Philippines it was unthinkable to hand them back to Spain. Second, the United States could hardly let them fall into the hands of its commercial rivals such as Germany and Japan. And finally, the Filipinos had no experience of self-government. To leave them in their present state would mean abandoning them to anarchy and intertribal wars, out of which would come tyranny even worse than Spanish rule.

While the Senate debated the Treaty of Paris which would both end the war with Spain and inaugurate American rule in the Philippines the American army in Manila was under siege from thousands of Aguinaldo's followers. On the night of February 4, 1899, an American patrol clashed with an insurgent patrol. Shots were fired, leaving two Filipinos dead.

Neither Aguinaldo nor his senior officers had expected a fight but as news spread that two Filipinos had been killed gunfire erupted along a ten-mile front. Probing attacks were launched against American positions.

At daybreak the army took the offensive. Supported by naval gunfire from ships anchored in the bay, the infantry swept over Filipino entrenchments with irresistible élan. American losses totaled 300 but the insurgent death toll was at least 1,000. The siege was broken.

On February 6 the Senate ratified the controversial Treaty of Paris by a single vote. The outbreak of fighting was credited with getting it through but recent scholarship has shown this was not so.

The military governor of the Philippines, Major General Elwell S. Otis, was also accused by anti-imperialists and Filipinos of provoking a clash. There is no hard evidence either way, but if Otis did set out to start a fight it would have been completely out of character. He fought the Insurrection so cautiously he made himself the most despised commander in the army.

A Harvard-educated lawyer turned soldier, Otis directed the pursuit of Aguinaldo's troops across Luzon without ever leaving his desk at Malacanang Palace. Obsessed with detail, reluctant to delegate and slow to decide, he was self-contained, occupying a bubble of optimism that nothing could penetrate.

In the six months before the insurgency started he sent a stream of cables to Washington, assuring the president that the Filipinos would welcome American rule. Not even the outbreak of fighting shook his rose-tinted view of Philippine realities.

Among the troops life looked a lot less rosy. As they pursued retreating insurgents they faced some hard choices. If they plunged into the paddies they were instantly immobilized, but if they took to the roads raised high above the paddies, they made themselves unmissable targets.

Away from the paddies, the roads were not much better; traces, scratches on the landscape. They turned to mud when it rained, and it rained most days. The hot, humid climate sapped the strength even of the iron men.

It was the horse cavalry, for the last time in an American war, that provided mobile striking power. The main complaint of the infantry was not the vile food, the terrible weather or the aggressive insect life but the lack of combat. Cavalrymen, fighting on foot, mounted on big fast horses shipped in from San Francisco, made no such complaints. They harried Aguinaldo's troops into the mountains and jungle.

Otis's field commanders wanted to fight the war with fast-moving, compact columns given a license to roam. Otis preferred to organize huge, slow infantry formations which lurched through the paddies on timetables he had drawn up without even inspecting the terrain. Woe betide the officer who decided to alter his route or speed up his march.

The insurgency might have grown completely out of control had Otis not had the help of two gifted soldiers, Henry W. Lawton and Arthur MacArthur. When Otis insisted he needed no more troops, that the 40,000 he already had would be enough for the job, Lawton let his friends in the War Department know it would take up to 100,000 men to suppress the Insurrection. Acting on Lawton's word instead of Otis's, it raised twenty-five regiments of U.S. Volunteers for service in the Philippines. They had no state apron strings, no political officers, but they also never acquired the discipline of regulars. Their fearsome aggressiveness was what the army prized.

Lawton pressed for the creation of a battalion of Macabebe scouts. Descended from Mexicans imported into the Philippines in the eighteenth century by the Spanish, the Macabebes had a traditional hatred of the Tagalogs, the largest Filipino tribe. Lawton knew something about using one tribe to fight another: he was the man who had captured Geronimo. Otis rejected the proposal to raise the Macabebe scouts. Once more Lawton's friends in Washington overruled Otis.

A year after the Insurrection began there were more than 70,000 soldiers, sailors and marines fighting in the Philippines. Four hundred military posts held down conquered territory. The army fought the war not with rifles only but with new bridges and hard roads, with schools and textbooks, with vaccination programs and public health campaigns, with telephones and sixteen thousand miles of telegraph wire.

The Progressives who were at the forefront of the reform move-

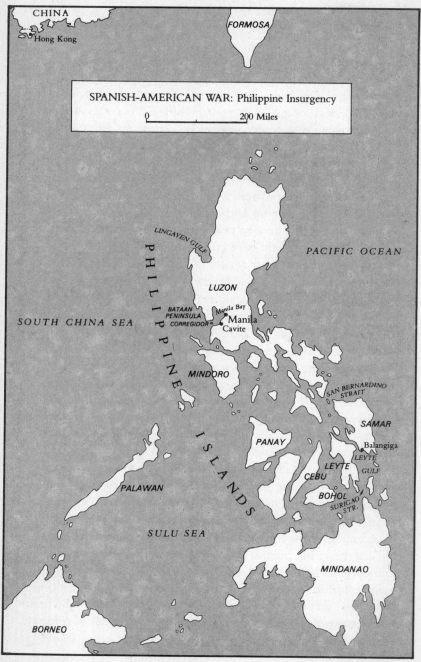

SPANISH–AMERICAN WAR: Philippine Insurgency

0   200 Miles

CHINA

Hong Kong

FORMOSA

PACIFIC OCEAN

LINGAYEN GULF

LUZON

SOUTH CHINA SEA

BATAAN
PENINSULA
CORREGIDOR

Manila Bay

Manila

Cavite

MINDORO

SAN BERNARDINO
STRAIT

SAMAR

Balangiga

PANAY

LEYTE

CEBU

LEYTE
GULF

BOHOL

PALAWAN

SURIGAO
STR.

SULU SEA

MINDANAO

BORNEO

PHILIPPINE ISLANDS

ment in the United States at the start of the new century had counterparts in the army and navy. Junior officers especially were drawn from the kind of homes that produced the young idealists who were trying to clean up city government back home. In the Philippines young military Progressives brought the same high-mindedness to pacification. Land reform was launched. Crushing taxes on the peasants were repealed. Bribery virtually disappeared. The foundations of effective civil government were created.

For a year Aguinaldo's army tried to hold back the advancing Americans. His forces paid a high price for attempting to stand and fight. Insurgent losses inspired Otis to declare in May 1900, "The war in the Philippines is over." He was completely wrong. Mauled but tenacious insurgent units had simply scattered into the mountains and jungle. From there they waged a bitter guerrilla war, much of it directed against fellow Filipinos, accused of collaboration. As terrorism rose, so did American casualties. On both sides former restraints broke down.

American excesses, mostly the work of frustrated volunteers, caused an outcry in the press. The most popular form of interrogation was the "water cure," in which more than a gallon of water was forced down a prisoner's throat. His sore, distended stomach·was then stood or kneeled on until the water gushed out. At which point the whole terrifying and painful business started again, until he decided to talk. It was torture. There was no denying that, yet it could not compare to what the Filipinos did to each other, or the captured Americans who were staked out, groins split open and their bowels smeared with jam to attract ravenous ants.

With the war reported won and the basis of civil government created, federal judge William Howard Taft was installed as governor in the summer of 1900. Otis returned home, leaving military operations to MacArthur, who had a flair for leadership and a flinty intellectual integrity.

MacArthur had no illusions about what the war was like out in the villages: "The presidentes and other officials act openly in behalf of the Americans and secretly in behalf of the insurgents and, paradoxical as it may seem, with considerable apparent solicitude for the interests of both." Like the military Progressives, he believed the war would never be won until the occupation was made acceptable to the Filipinos.

He fought the guerrillas with amnesties, with rewards for surrendered weapons, with improved military intelligence, and with 75,000 soldiers. He also had the services of 6,000 Filipino scouts whom Taft insisted he employ despite army doubts about their loyalty. MacArthur stepped up peaceful pacification measures while bearing harder than ever on the insurgents. Thousands of suspected accomplices were rounded up. Hundreds were deported to remote islands. Scores tried for involvement in attacks on Americans were convicted and hanged. All the while fresh arms became even harder to obtain, thanks to the navy's aggressive patrolling.

The guerrillas pinned great hopes on the candidacy of William Jennings Bryan in the 1900 election. Bryan committed himself to Philippine independence. The continuing Insurrection was the main issue in the contest. McKinley seemed to find it all very embarrassing, but Roosevelt, as his running mate, offered what amounted to a promise of victory. When Bryan lost, the guerrillas paid the inevitable price of inflated hopes defeated.

Early the next year Colonel Frederick Funston, a muscular five-foot, five-inch redhead who had fought with the *insurrectos* in Cuba before the United States declared war on Spain, devised and led a clever operation to capture Aguinaldo. This enterprise was blessed with the luck its daring deserved. Aguinaldo was taken alive. In time he swore allegiance to the United States. Funston was rewarded with the Medal of Honor and a commission as brigadier general in the regular army. In just three years he had reached a rank few West Point graduates ever achieved.

Even after the capture of Aguinaldo the insurgency rumbled along. As it spluttered out on Luzon, it flared up on Mindanao and Samar. Mindanao, the second-largest island in the archipelago, was occupied by the Moros, a tribe of fierce Muslim warriors.* The more infidels a Moro killed, the more houris there would be waiting to welcome him to his harem when he reached paradise. The fighting

---

*In 1902 the Colt factory at Hartford began producing a .38-caliber semiautomatic pistol for the army and navy, but officers in the Philippines were clamoring for something that would stop a Moro dead in his tracks. Even with a couple of .38 bullets in him a Moro could still take a slice out of someone with his bolo. The Ordnance Bureau consulted the nation's leading gun designer, John M. Browning. He designed a .45-caliber bullet, then built a gun around it. The final result was the Colt .45 automatic pistol, military issue since 1911.

tradition of the Moros was renowned, along with other Muslim traditions such as polygamy and slavery.

Army and navy officers preferred overawing the Moro chiefs by
putting on demonstrations of high-school science and naval gunnery,
rather than fighting it out in the jungle. Many chiefs, gratifyingly
impressed by modern wonders such as electricity, proved tractable, but
there was much agitation back on Main Street when it was learned that
upright, God-fearing Americans were making allies of slave-owning,
Islamic polygamists.

Samar provided a different kind of shock. C Company, 9th Infantry, was lured into an ambush in the fishing town of Balangiga. When
it was over, 45 men were dead, many only after gruesome torture, and
26 survivors had fled. The ambush of C Company shook the country
as profoundly as Custer's defeat had done a generation before.

A marine battalion under Major Littleton Waller was assigned to
pacify Samar. Waller received his instruction from an army officer,
Brigadier General Jacob Smith, who told him, "Burn all and kill all.
The more you burn and kill, the more you will please me." Waller
was ordered to take no prisoners and to kill every male above ten years
of age.

This was ranting and Waller ignored it. Press stories on the "rape"
of Samar nonetheless brought about the court-martial of Waller, who
was acquitted, and of Smith, who was convicted and forced out of the
army.

Trouble broke out in remote areas for years to come but on July
4, 1902, President Theodore Roosevelt declared the Philippine Insurrection over. Some 4,200 Americans had been killed in action, to only
2,800 wounded. The casualty figures revealed the kind of struggle it
had been. More men fell in ones and twos, murdered in back alleys,
in flyblown village bars, and in the arms of smiling girls, than fell in
open combat. Up to 16,000 guerrillas were killed. As many as 100,000
noncombatants perished from hunger and disease in war-ravaged areas.

Among the dead was Lawton, the American soldier the insurgents
feared most. A Filipino marksman shot him dead in December 1900
while Lawton was rallying troops to make an attack. Like MacArthur
he had the kind of open mind that was crucial to fighting this kind
of war. He once said of the insurgents, "Taking into account the
disadvantages they have to fight against in arms, equipment and military discipline, they are the bravest men I have ever seen."

This was a war that divided America more than any other between Appomattox and Vietnam, yet it was quickly forgotten, except in the army. Nearly every combat unit saw action in the Philippines. So did virtually the entire officer corps. It was the army's most important school of application and, in a sense, the Insurrection saved the army. Since the Revolutionary War it had been the Indian threat that kept the army in existence. With the Indians destroyed as a military threat the regular army needed a new role. Like the nation at large, it found one in the Philippines. With bayonet and entrenching tool the United States was carving out a place for itself in the world. And from this one small war would flow a century of consequences.

The War Department's performance in the Spanish-American War was strongly criticized in Congress and the press despite the fact that the army had won quickly, at small cost and decisively. McKinley offered his own judgment by retaining Alger as secretary of war, but in August 1899 Alger's maneuvers to win a Senate seat caused difficulties within the Republican Party. McKinley asked him to go. His replacement was a New York lawyer, Elihu Root, who had no knowledge of or apparent interest in military affairs.

Once again the crucial factor was the Philippines. Whatever their merits, the islands did not fit the Constitution. Nor did the Constitution, however it was stretched, fit the Philippines. What the Founding Fathers had in mind for American expansion was territories which, once organized, could become states. No one imagined the Philippines becoming a state of the Union. Root was one of the best lawyers around. McKinley wanted him in Washington to provide high-level advice on how to square the governing of colonies abroad with domestic government under the Constitution.

Root arrived at a time when the War Department was ripe for reform. Alger had begun some needed changes but lacked the energy to push them through. Settling into his new office, Root began reading the works of Emory Upton. Here was an intellectual framework, he found, that dealt with fundamental issues. He had Upton's *The Military Policy of the United States* edited and published, then sent free copies to newspaper editors to enlist them in the struggle for army reform.

As a newly minted Uptonian, Root was glad to get rid of the 1792 Uniform Militia Act. In its place came the 1903 Dick Act, a piece of legislation written mainly by the National Guard Association. Charles Dick was a congressman from Ohio and a major general in the Guard.

The new law made federal money available to the Guard, in exchange for which the army was allowed to impose higher standards of training and make inspections to see that they were met. The heart of the Dick Act, however, was an explicit commitment by the federal government that the National Guard would be called "in advance of any volunteer force."

With its elected officers and its lack of support units, the Guard to Root was no more than the old militia—"state troops for state purposes." Yet the Dick Act was something he could live with. In a time of emergency he expected that the National Guard would be used to man the huge and largely useless coastal fortifications the army had built near all the major ports during its search for a new role as the Indian wars drew to a close. Bedding it down in all that concrete would keep it out of trouble, while the better-educated officers and more alert NCOs could be recruited into fresh regiments of U.S. Volunteers like those that defeated Aguinaldo.

Root could also live with the Dick Act because it did not interfere with his more important reforms, which were concentrated on army education. He placed education above reorganization on his list of priorities. During the 1890s the service schools had been allowed to run down. Root revitalized those that already existed, and added new ones. Attendance at the right schools became essential to a successful military career.

He established the Army Staff College at Fort Leavenworth, where promising lieutenants and captains were to be trained as staff officers. A military revolution was under way as the new century began. The name of the revolution was "doctrine," and "indoctrination" was far from being something undesirable. It was fervently desired by those young officers as they pored over German military textbooks and studied maps of the forested, mountainous terrain of northeastern France. It was there that the Prussian army, with its general staff and first-generation staff officers, defeated the French in 1870 and rang up the curtain on the modern management of warfare.

The population explosion of the nineteenth century provided a manpower pool that transformed military thought. The size of armies was so great it made them seem almost unmanageable. The Union had difficulty coordinating the operations of 600,000 men, but only a generation later France was preparing to put three million men in the field, and Germany planned for four million. Simply getting half such numbers into action would be an achievement. Getting more than one hundred divisions—roughly 1.5 million men—to function coherently in the inevitable confusion of combat looked like asking for a miracle.

The answer worked out by the German General Staff, and adopted by most other armies, was doctrine. This meant something more than the traditional "principles of war" beloved by the Mahans, father and son. Doctrine was a way of thinking about military problems, a mind-set that was acquired through intense study. Those who acquired it were "indoctrinated"—generally speaking, they would think alike.

Doctrine strove to bring a higher level of organization to combat. Its aim was to formulate standard solutions to predictable tactical problems, such as crossing a river under fire or making a reconnaissance in force. The solutions inevitably reflected each nation's own military resources and traditions, so doctrine was not the same everywhere.

Indoctrination was one of those simple yet brilliant ideas that changed the world. It allowed German armies to deploy confidently and quickly over huge fronts, with little continuous contact between advancing units because, in effect, its battalion staffs, its regiments and its divisions all carried the same mental picture of what they were expected to do, whether the resistance was strong or weak, the terrain flat or hilly, the weather good or bad.

Doctrine tried to anticipate every situation, while recognizing that in war no two situations are alike in every detail. It offered possible solutions to almost every problem. Its prime teaching tool was the war game, with maps and pins, or the sand table, with toy soldiers and flags.

In most situations, doctrine in the German army stressed envelopment: attacking, that is, the enemy's flanks and, where possible, turning his position. From a division down to a platoon German doctrine sought rapid movement and strong attacks. It was clear and coherent, providing a firm foundation for the education of officers and the training of troops. It was also entirely in keeping with army strategy at the highest level.

French doctrine was by comparison muddled. France had a smaller manpower pool to draw on, yet French generals, lusting to avenge the defeat of 1870, wanted to be just as aggressive as the Germans once war began. The wide gap between what the French army wanted to do and the realities of manpower inferiority undermined both strategy and doctrine. France was caught between a strategy that was essentially defensive and military doctrine that was essentially offensive.

The ideal of indoctrination was in all armies nonetheless the same. On a day when the maps proved false, when the telegraph line to higher headquarters was down and shells were falling all around, staff officers assigned to brigades, regiments and battalions would make sure the army still had a brain directing operations in the field; even amid seeming chaos it would fight on like an army, not like a horde.

No modern army could hope to manage a modern war without a general staff. Creating one was another Uptonian cause taken up by Root. The opportunity came in 1902, when Nelson Miles retired. A born soldier, Miles also dabbled in politics too much for the good of his reputation. The post of commanding general was abolished, as a kind of belated revenge on the man. Root filled the resulting vacuum with a chief of staff, in charge of a general staff made up of forty-four officers.

In European armies the chief of staff was usually more powerful than the minister of war. There was no danger of that here. The General Staff that Congress created was a shadow of the European ones. Even so, it finally gave the army a planning arm, located in the War College that Root had created, a place where majors and colonels went to round out their education for high command. At the Army Staff College meanwhile captains and lieutenants were learning about doctrine, while mulling over strange place names such as Metz and Sedan.

DURING the Spanish-American War the battleship *Oregon* spent sixty-eight days on a thirteen-thousand-mile voyage from Seattle to Hampton Roads around South America. After more than two months of steaming she arrived ready to fight. The *Oregon*'s epic voyage thrilled a nation, while making it mutter, "Never again!"

Since the defeat of Mexico in 1848 there had been two seaboards to defend. To some the answer was two fleets. To others it was a divided fleet linked by a canal across the Isthmus of Panama. A better answer than these was two fleets *plus* a canal. Which is how it worked out.

Almost from the moment Theodore Roosevelt succeeded the murdered McKinley he was determined to build a canal. The French, under Ferdinand de Lesseps, had already attempted it, and failed. De Lesseps had built the Suez Canal but that was a mere ditch cut into the

Egyptian sand. An Isthmian canal meant constructing more than thirty massive locks in a jungle rife with disease, especially yellow fever.

Panama itself was in 1902 simply the northernmost province of Colombia. That year Roosevelt secured agreement to build a canal across the Isthmus, but the Colombian government dragged its feet over ratifying the treaty.

Roosevelt and his secretary of state, John Hay, proceeded by hints and asides to inspire a revolution in Panama, financed by people who had a stake in the canal project. On the appointed day, November 3, 1903, the revolution was launched. Three American warships and a battalion of marines steamed off the Colombian coast, ready to intervene. The coup turned out to be bloodless and successful. The new government secured instant recognition from Washington as an independent state. In turn, it ceded a strip of land that cut the new country in two. Roosevelt was so pleased he bragged openly, "I took Panama."

This time the canal was built. Under a brilliant army doctor, Colonel William C. Gorgas, yellow fever was defeated. Under an army engineer, Colonel George Goethals, the locks were constructed. In 1914 the Panama Canal was opened to traffic. Roosevelt had long since left the White House, but this was the leading achievement of his presidency.

The Atlantic and Pacific fleets could now reinforce each other quickly. The canal would also claim an important slice of the world's trade. In effect, a new choke point had appeared on the map—a choke point under American control.

In the passions aroused by the Spanish-American War anything involving the sea was good for money. Congress rained dollars all over the navy. As president, Roosevelt kept the party going. By 1905 the United States had built or was building a total of twenty-eight battleships and twelve armored cruisers. With a single bound, it seemed, the country had become the world's third naval power, behind Britain and France.

Roosevelt's promotion of big ships was pure Mahanism, reflecting the Mahanite obsession with the battle fleet. Other types, such as destroyers and support ships, were neglected. The result was a navy that was nearly all teeth and little tail.

Nor was anyone quite sure just what this mighty force was intended for. There was no clear statement of naval policy; not from the president, and certainly not from the navy, which was denied a general staff even after the army had secured one. There was much heated debate over gunnery, but almost none on the navy's likely wartime targets; much over the size of the fleet, little over where it would operate during hostilities. The United States had entered the great naval arms race not with a naval policy but with a construction policy.

The demand for modern steel ships and mountains of armor plate brought a technological revolution in the American steel industry. Armor plate was high technology, hedged about with secrecy and whispers. From the Civil War until 1941 there ran a deadly competition between the gun makers and the plate makers. In the end the gun makers won, but along the way the American steel industry became the richest and most advanced in the world, in an age when steel production was a symbol both of a nation's technology and its virility.

As ships became heavily armored, interest revived in the submarine, because the most vulnerable spot now was well below the waterline, where the armor belt stopped. The loss of an experimental submarine, the *Intelligent Whale*, in 1872 had taken the lives of 39 officers and men and dampened the navy's interest for a generation. In the late 1890s, however, John P. Holland, an Irish immigrant with a hatred of all things British, had begun trials of a boat that he hoped would one day lead to Britain's decline by threatening her command of the sea. In Paterson, New Jersey, Holland made submarines.

His design was based on an internal combustion engine for surface cruising, electric motors powered by storage batteries for undersea operations. Holland's boats fixed the design and operating principles for submarines in two world wars. And his ambitions were realized: he did help undermine British power. His invention twice nearly brought Britain to its knees. In the early 1900s Holland was producing submarines that had a range of one thousand five hundred miles, with a speed of seven knots on the surface, six knots underwater. Armed with self-propelled, or in the expression of the time "automobile," torpedoes they could attack even the most powerful warships afloat.

The battleship nonetheless remained the pride of the fleet, steadily equipped with more and more big-caliber guns. No one doubted its powers of devastation, if only it could hit its targets. Off Santiago and at Manila Bay victory had been won but no one praised the navy's shooting. Up to 98 percent of all shells fired struck nothing but water.

A gifted young naval officer, Bradley A. Fiske, had spent much of the 1890s trying to interest the navy in telescopic sights to improve naval gunnery; to no avail. Another reform-minded young officer, William S. Sims, was so disgusted with the navy's marksmanship that in 1901 he risked his career by writing to the new president about it. Roosevelt was already acquainted with the lieutenant's prose.

Sims had graduated at Annapolis in 1882, a cadet of no evident promise. Seven years later he managed to arrange a year off to improve his French. Arriving in Paris in 1889, he moved into an artist's *pension,* an experience art lovers since can only envy, while wondering what kind of sailor this was. His fluent French led to his being posted back to Paris, as naval attaché, in 1897. His prolific, interesting reports from there caught the eye of the new assistant secretary of the navy, Roosevelt. The next year Sims organized an espionage operation from his Paris base that kept Washington well informed on whatever naval secrets the Spanish were hoping to keep.

Roosevelt's response to Sims's letter damning naval gunnery was to ask him to keep on writing. A year later, Sims was appointed inspector of target practice. Sims was at last able to impose telescopic sights on the navy, along with an elevating wheel that made it possible to keep the sight fixed on a moving target.

Throughout 1902 a naval lieutenant named Homer Poundstone devoted all his spare time designing an all-big-gun ship that his friend Sims called the USS *SkeerdoNuthin'.* The navy looked at the design and said no. Other navies had tried them—the French, the Russians, the Germans—but gunnery still was not good enough for any capital ship to scrap the numerous small, quick-firing guns that it carried as a defense against small aggressive craft such as torpedo boats. Battleships were armed with four guns of big caliber, usually about twelve inches, and dozens of smaller guns from eight inches down.

Around 1903 a Royal Navy officer, Percy Scott, devised a system called "director fire." A gunnery officer posted one hundred feet above the waterline controlled all the guns, bringing them to bear on a target together and firing them all at once by means of an electrical circuit. This was the advent of fire control. With a salvo of shells falling into a fairly small space, the chances of hitting the target increased at least 300 percent.

Scott's director system was not perfected until 1910 but even before then he so improved naval gunnery that the Admiralty commissioned an all-big-gun ship, the HMS *Dreadnought.* Laid down in the deepest secrecy, she was finished in eighteen months instead of the usual four years. Only one outsider was let in on the secret: Scott's close friend and fellow gunnery zealot William Sims. Late on Christmas Eve 1905 Sims, dressed in civilian clothes and muffled to the eyes to hide his distinctive beard, was smuggled aboard the unfinished *Dreadnought* by a Royal Navy officer.

When she put to sea in 1906 she carried no secondary armament, only ten big guns, all twelve-inch caliber. The *Dreadnought* had more than twice the firepower of any ship afloat. From the moment her bottom got wet she put all other navies at least three years behind in the race. She did not, however, as the myth has it, make all other warships obsolete. Dozens of pre-*Dreadnought* battleships performed valuably in wartime a decade later.

Roosevelt took alarm at the sudden gap in naval technology that had opened up. In the greatest political fight of his presidency he tried to step up the construction program to four all-big-gun battleships a year. He lost. Congress stuck with the two-a-year program. When he left office in March 1909 there was a fleet of sixteen battleships in the Atlantic and eight armored cruisers in the Pacific, with more of both on the ways. His more pacifically inclined successor, William Howard Taft, deplored the naval arms race, as did Taft's successor in 1913, Woodrow Wilson, yet neither felt able to opt out.

The Atlantic and Pacific fleets continued to grow. Colonies did not make a world power, but colonies and a powerful navy did.

THE MASS ARMIES he had seen arising in Europe had troubled Upton. Increasingly they troubled his successors. They were the most important new development in land warfare yet the United States had nothing like them. The only answer to one mass army seemed to be another one.

American technology offered a different solution: firepower. For all practical purposes the man who succeeded Colt was Richard Jordan Gatling. Born in North Carolina, he moved to technically more promising Indiana. Throughout the Civil War he tried with little success to sell his gun to the Ordnance Bureau. It was operated by a handcrank which rotated six barrels past a firing pin. It took a big bullet, one-inch caliber, and fired at a rate of 150 rounds a minute. The war ended before he produced a genuinely effective weapon, but once he did it was adopted by armies around the world, with one important exception—France.

National pride led Napoleon III to reject it. The French army instead adopted the Montigny *mitrailleuse,* which weighed two tons and was difficult to operate.* Napoleon III had such faith in it, though, that he declared war on Prussia in 1870 and confidently waited for the *mitrailleuse* to destroy Von Moltke's onrushing armies. Instead, the superb Prussian field artillery stayed out of range and picked it off.

Automatic weapons really belonged with the infantry but as long as they were bulky and hard to move the infantry did not want them. Nor did the cavalry. Custer refused to take three Gatlings with him as he moved toward the Little Bighorn. Something better was needed.

The man who provided it was Hiram Maxim. In the years following the Civil War the national love of tinkering and invention turned to electricity. The most successful of these electrical entrepreneur-inventors was Thomas Alva Edison, but for a time Maxim was not far behind. Like Whitney and Colt, however, he became embroiled in patent disputes. In the midst of these he encountered a fellow American in Vienna. "Hang your electricity and chemistry!" his friend exclaimed. "If you want to make a pile of money, invent something that will enable these Europeans to cut each others' throats with greater facility."

In 1884 Maxim demonstrated the first truly automatic machine gun: no hand-cranking. He used the force of the recoil to operate the cartridge-ejection mechanism, reload the gun and fire it. All the human effort involved was in holding down the trigger.

By 1900 there were dozens of machine-gun designs based on Maxim's patents. The army used machine guns in the Philippines, but with poor results. It was not a weapon likely to succeed in a war where the enemy was rarely seen. The first real test came in the Russo-Japanese War of 1904–05. There it ruled the battlefield. The Russians used Maxims. The Japanese used the lighter Hotchkiss weapon, produced by the French factory set up by Benjamin B. Hotchkiss, onetime master mechanic at Colt's Hartford plant.

---

*It was not a repeating arm but an improved artillery piece that fired 172 grapeshot, or musket balls, at a time. Under test conditions it was awesome; in the heat of action, however, it was too complicated.

European armies ignored the machine gun's battlefield success. They lacked the traditional American faith in firepower. The few officers who shared it were looked on as eccentrics. All armies acquired machine guns but in modest numbers, just in case they proved handy.

Although fairly small the U.S. Army was, comparatively, the best equipped of all. By 1914 it had roughly one thousand automatic weapons for an army of 95,000 men. Some were Maxims but the vast majority were the Benét-Mercié Model 1909. It was not, properly speaking, a machine gun but an automatic rifle mounted on a tripod.* The Benét-Mercié was known in France as the Hotchkiss Portative (or portable). It had a knack of performing well in weapons tests and failing completely in action. Troops loved it in peacetime because it was light, hated it in wartime because it was useless.

The army itself possessed one of the finest machine-gun inventors in the world, Isaac Newton Lewis. Graduating at West Point in 1884 and commissioned in the coast artillery, Lewis had an original mind. Going into partnership with a Buffalo arms company in 1910, he produced a gun that weighed only twenty-five pounds yet fired at a rate of 750 rounds a minute. In June 1912 he persuaded two army aviators at College Park, Maryland, to mount a Lewis gun on a Wright aircraft and make strafing passes at a cheesecloth target. They riddled it.

Lewis turned the airplane into a weapon of war. His machine-gun design was so sound that it equipped fighter aircraft in combat air forces for the next thirty years. The Ordnance Bureau tried it out and turned it down. The British tried it out and adopted it at once, building a new factory to produce it in quantity, to arm both aircraft and infantry.

In August 1914 the war that Europe had been arming for erupted. On the very eve of the conflict the French abandoned their plan to stand on the defensive along their line of frontier forts, while preparing a massive counterattack to be launched as the German advance lost momentum. Instead, they adopted a strategy of all-out offensive, even though they had an army smaller than Germany's.

*Machine guns were capable of sustained, accurate fire up to 500 yards. Automatic rifles were much lighter and designed for short bursts of fire accurate up to 250 yards. Such distinctions were not widely appreciated before 1914, and all automatic weapons were likely to be called machine guns whatever their performance.

The Germans too abandoned the plan that all their doctrine pointed to. The great Von Moltke's nephew had succeeded his uncle as chief of the general staff. The massive envelopment that formed the basis of German war plans was designed to sweep across Belgium and across northwest France, then swing around to the south of Paris, driving what remained of the French army toward Switzerland and Lorraine. The younger Von Moltke found this too daring for his cautious nature. He weakened the German right wing and bolstered the left. The blow when delivered lacked the necessary weight for the role assigned it.

Instead of passing south of Paris, the German right wing bunched up and gravitated toward the center. And in these early days of doctrine, the system broke down. There were too many troops, too many units, deployed over too wide a front. When a gap appeared between two German armies north of Paris, the hard-pressed French and British delivered a sharp counterstroke that stopped the German offensive along the river Marne. After which both sides entrenched, from Switzerland to the English Channel.

The real victor was the machine gun. It was firepower that wrecked the mass armies of Europe; in the guns made by Krupp for the German army, based on Maxim's patents; in the guns made by Vickers for the British, based on the same patents; in the guns made by Hotchkiss for the French armies of Joffre and Foch; and in the Lewis guns that, chattering above, sent entire divisions into the ditch. America was not yet in the war but its technology ruled it from Day One.

WORLD WAR ONE offered a conundrum. The United States appeared to be in no danger. Yet as a global power could it remain aloof indefinitely without its influence in the world being seriously, perhaps permanently, reduced?

The wish to stay out of Europe's wars was ultimately irreconcilable with the longing to be a world player. Few, however, were able to confront that squarely; certainly not the president. Woodrow Wilson called forthrightly for neutrality "in word and deed." His secretary of state, Bryan, got the secretary of the navy, Josephus Daniels, to have some old naval swords melted down. Recast as miniature plowshares, they were presented to diplomats of the warring powers.

For nearly a year the essential issue was avoided. Then, in the summer of 1915, Britain and France began running out of money and foreign assets convertible into cash. The cost of financial neutrality was spelled out by the Treasury: a severe recession, possibly a depression. Already thousands of factories depended on war orders from the Allies; so did several hundred thousand jobs. Money neutrality would have ended Wilson's influence over Congress as the recession deepened. It would have wrecked his hopes of reelection in 1916. The banks would not grant the Allies the huge loans they were asking for without a lead from the Treasury. Wilson swallowed hard, nodded firmly, and the loans were made. Yet even now the president continued preaching a neutralist's creed.

It was not only money that went to the Allies but arms and ammunition too. Surely, protested Bryan, *this* was not neutral? Surely, replied the professor-president, it was. The crunch came for the Great Commoner and great pacifist in May 1915 after a German submarine sank the British liner *Lusitania* off the southern Irish coast. More than 120 American lives were lost—along with 4,200 crates of ammunition. Strong notes of protest were sent to Berlin. To Bryan this was cynicism and hypocrisy dressed up in the garb of humanitarianism and principle. He said so, was ignored, and resigned.

As the war spread, bringing in neutrals such as Italy and Japan, the War College Division, entrusted with drawing up war plans, began preparing for the worst. Its inexperienced planners lived in a fantasy world where Germany, unable to threaten Britain by putting a single division across the Channel, was projected as shipping more than one million men across the Atlantic and entrenching them from Washington to Erie, Pennsylvania. This was summarized as "a commonplace military operation ridiculously easy of accomplishment."

One day in August 1915 the president read in the Baltimore *Sun* that the army was working on war plans. "Trembling and white with rage," according to an eyewitness, he threatened to fire the entire General Staff and ship the culprits out of Washington. It was not understood by the president that making war plans was part of what the army was supposed to do.

Wilson was equally disgusted at the "Plattsburg camps" that drew thousands of college students and youngish businessmen that summer into spending their vacations drilling under army officers, sleeping under brown pyramid tents and peeling potatoes under regular NCOs.

The camps were closer to Boy Scouting than military training, in both what they did and the uplifting atmosphere in which they did it.

By 1916 the novelty of drilling and peeling was wearing thin and something more martial was the latest cry: universal military training. The army encouraged this, just as it encouraged the camps, while taking neither of them seriously. To give military training to every male eighteen to forty-five years old would be absurd; the army did not want the physically fit but mentally backward, or the bright but physically disabled. There would have to be selection. And that was what the army really wanted, conscription. For the present, though, the best it could do was encourage the growing interest in the nation's military posture. As a War Department memorandum put it, universal military training "is a happier phrase than compulsory military service."

Wilson's secretary of war, Lindley Garrison, proposed to create a "Continental Army" of 140,000 regulars and 400,000 reservists; regular reservists, that is, with no state connections. The army already had more than 100,000 regulars, but only 16 regular reservists. Garrison's bill was an attempt to create a ready reserve, trained to regular standards by regular officers. The National Guard Association counterattacked with a bill of its own. Wilson, his mind increasingly on reelection, found it wise not to back his secretary of war. Garrison, and the assistant secretary, Henry Breckinridge, resigned in disgust in February 1916.

One month later his successor was sworn in: tiny, youthful Newton D. Baker, the Progressive mayor of Cleveland, a man whose nose hardly showed over the top of his desk, and a member of various peace organizations. It seemed one of Wilson's more whimsical decisions; at the very least an attempt to dampen the ardor of preparedness rising like steam in the War Department. The first thing the press—and the army—wanted to know was whether the stories were true: was the new secretary of war a pacifist? So much so, said Baker, "that I would fight for peace."

Only hours before Baker took office 1,500 Mexican raiders under Pancho Villa had ridden into Columbus, New Mexico, home of the 13th Cavalry Regiment. By rights they were no match for regulars, but these were regulars armed with Benét-Mercié automatic weapons that jammed, misfired or proved impossible to reload. Villa's raiders killed eight soldiers and nine civilians, wounded at least 40 other people, shot up the town and returned untroubled across the border.

The army quickly got a punitive expedition under way, led by Brigadier General John J. Pershing. Eighteen years before, he had led a troop of black cavalrymen up Kettle Hill ahead of the Rough Riders. Theodore Roosevelt was so deeply impressed by Pershing's coolness and competence under fire that when he became president he jumped him from a captain's bars to a general's star over the heads of 884 officers senior to him.

Villa's raid was a military emergency such as the National Guard had been preparing for since the Dick Act was passed. The administration played its part, calling out the entire 130,000-man Guard. Only half showed up. Roughly one in four failed the army physical. Guard companies were the size of army platoons; Guard regiments were smaller than army battalions. The one thing it had no shortage of was officers.

Some 50,000 national guardsmen spent the summer and early fall of 1916 on the Mexican border while Pershing chased after Villa, possibly with little intention of catching him. This taste of soldiering was enough to threaten the destruction of the National Guard: 84 percent said they would refuse to reenlist under the recently passed National Defense Act, which had been written mainly by the NGA.

The new law created the Reserve Officers Training Corps, basing it on the sixty-eight land-grant colleges created by the Morrill Act. The army would provide instructors for the ROTC. In time the ROTC was expected to produce thousands of junior officers for the Guard, whose strength was scheduled to rise over five years to a total of 440,000. Over the same period the army would double in size, to 234,000. The core of the 1916 National Defense Act was a clause that made the Guard a component of the army; in effect, federalizing it and making it the army's reserve, whether the regulars liked it or not.

The navy fared better. Wilson had a certain partiality for it. Born in Georgia, reared in Virginia, he had heard the usual horror stories about damn Yankees in blue. There were no horror stories about Union sailors. As the 1916 presidential election came into sight Wilson sprinted from the rear of the preparedness parade to the front. On a nationwide speaking tour in February 1916 he began speaking of the red lines in the flag as being "lines of blood, nobly and unselfishly shed." And in St. Louis he called for the United States to acquire "the greatest navy in the world." The Navy Act passed six months later authorized 10 new battleships, six battle cruisers, 10 light cruisers, 50 destroyers and 67 submarines.

In the fall he campaigned for reelection under the slogan "He kept us out of war," but this was thought up by some obscure Democratic party functionary and launched without Wilson's being aware of it. Once that was done he could not repudiate it. The appeal of this slogan may be judged by the fact that he came as close as a man can to losing the presidency and still hold on to it.

For all his belated conversion to preparedness, Wilson failed to promote American rearmament, while taking steps that made intervention in the war ever more likely. If the United States remained strictly neutral in word and deed, Germany would win. In that event the British and French navies—or sizable parts of them—might fall into German hands. Germany would acquire a claim on their colonies around the world, including the Caribbean. A victorious Germany controlling all of Europe's great shipyards would inspire massive, not to say frantic, rearmament.

Alternatively, the United States would at some point enter the war. That too spelled massive rearmament. Either way, the country's most precious military asset, time, had been wasted. It took up to five years to build a battleship, two years to convert the economy from civilian to military production, and at least twelve months to raise and train an infantry division.

The continuing flow of trade with the Allies brought the risk of intervention every time a ship went down with the loss of American life. After prolonged hesitation, Germany decided the risk was affordable. On January 9, 1917, the German naval staff assured the kaiser that a submarine offensive would win the war quickly. Admiral Henning von Holtzendorff promised him, "England will lie flat on the ground before a single American soldier sets foot on the Continent."

Wilson's response to unrestricted submarine warfare was to break diplomatic relations with Germany. An armed-ships bill was presented to Congress, to provide naval guns and trained gunners to the merchant fleet. Congressional pacifists, neutralists and pro-Germans tried filibustering the bill to death, but the British sprang a propaganda coup. Some weeks before, they had intercepted and decoded a German cable addressed to the Mexican government. It promised Mexico that if, in the event of war between the United States and Germany, Mexico allied itself with the German cause, then a victorious Germany would reward it by returning all of the territories lost in 1848. The British had sat on this cable, waiting for the right moment. And this was it. The filibuster failed, the Armed Ships Bill was passed. The U-boats continued sinking American ships. There was no way out now.

On the evening of April 2 Wilson asked Congress for a declaration of war. He received the greatest ovation of his life. He returned to the White House through cheering crowds, told his secretary, Joseph Tumulty, that he had never believed in neutrality, then put his head on the cabinet table and rained hot tears onto its lustrous surface.

12

A LEARNING ARMY

FROM street corner platforms drowning in bunting Four Minute Men bellowed four-minute speeches to excited crowds, shouting the patriotic virtues of Liberty bonds. At ball games, in movie theaters or wherever else "Oh-oh, say can you see . . ." rose in the air, throats were tight and faces shone with deep emotion. It looked and sounded like a country enthusiastically at war, but that was only on the surface.

Military men were relieved that the waiting was over. Many had felt embarrassed by Wilson's assertion two years before that their country was "too proud to fight." That was a stain on American honor they were eager to erase. Such men had few doubts about the rightness of intervention. Nor did the natural world players like Theodore Roosevelt, nearly blind in one eye, stooped by bad health, yet eager to go to war once again. And there were millions of people who never saw themselves as being martial or bellicose who simply believed this was a war for humanity and civilization.

There were millions of others, though, who were at least half convinced the country had been duped by British propaganda. There were also those who blamed intervention on Wall Street's eagerness to make war loans and ensure it did not lose its money. They were typified by a young second lieutenant at Fort Sam Houston, outside San Antonio. He was willing to die for his country but he refused to listen to patriotic speeches. "J. P. Morgan caused this war," he insisted. "We are a bunch of collectors, that's what we are."

Shortly before the declaration of war the army began planning an American expeditionary force, to be commanded by Frederick Funston. When he died suddenly, the assignment went to Pershing, in recognition of his handling of the pursuit of Villa.

Utterly unlike "Fighting Fred," Pershing was a cautious, stoical man. He was aloof and remote to all but a very small circle of friends. No one called him "Papa" Pershing or "Uncle" Jack. He would organize the AEF but would never inspire it, never thrill it, never win its heart. He possessed an objective, duty-haunted mind and a character as straight as his back.

Pershing radiated a sense of cold competence, yet even his impassivity had its limits as he moved among the shades of great soldiers. Arriving in Paris in June 1917 with a small, untried staff and enough sergeants and riflemen to form a couple of platoons, he went to visit Napoleon's red porphyry tomb at Les Invalides. The *gardien* offered him the Emperor's sword to hold. Overwhelmed, he leaned forward instead, kissing it reverently. He was unworthy, his gesture suggested, of holding Napoleon's sword until he too had led victorious armies in battle.

Wilson had few ideas on how the war ought to be fought except to suggest that the navy would cooperate with the British at sea and the army with the French on land. This left it for the French to decide where to place the AEF. Never trusting the Anglo-Saxons when they got together, they put Pershing as far from the British as possible, out in Lorraine and the Vosges Mountains of northeastern France.

This was the quiet sector of the western front. The terrain was so rugged over much of it that no one bothered to make more than an occasional probing attack, mainly to keep up morale. In many villages between the opposing lines life went on normally, under the gaze of the opposing armies.

Pershing's staff officers thrilled as they traveled down the Paris–Metz highway. Along this road Napoleon had fought the brilliant Campaign of France in 1814. It was in this part of France that Von Moltke had fought with comparable skill in 1870. And long before that it was here, along the Valley of the Marne, that Roman legions under Caesar had marched to fight the Franks. Pershing established AEF headquarters at Chaumont, inspired by the thought that in the château he occupied the kings of Britain and Prussia once met with the emperors of Russia and Austria to decide Napoleon's fate.

Not far away was the birthplace of Joan of Arc. Pershing and his staff officers visited Domrémy more than once, to sit by the wall, under the tree where she first heard voices calling her to save France.

With AEF headquarters established it remained for the War Department to provide it with millions of men. The only possible source was conscription. A draft law was soon passed that created the Selective Service System, with a manpower pool of 24 million men aged eighteen to forty-five to draw on. Of these, some 2.8 million were eventually drafted. A further 250,000 ran away, changed their names or otherwise simply failed to show up. The fateful letter began, "Greetings, Your neighbors have selected you. . . ." Your neighbors had, in fact, been closely guided by the army in making their selection, although some boards could not resist the temptation to get rid of the town's misfits and halfwits by getting them into khaki.

The idea of setting up thousands of local, citizen-run draft boards came from Newton Baker. It brought community involvement in a hair-shirt operation and spared the army a chore that would have made it unpopular.

The main effect of the Civil War draft had been to send men into the army as volunteers. One major effect of the World War One draft was to send men into marriage; volunteers of a different kind. Of those who did not disappear around the corner or into the marriage bed, roughly one man in four was accepted for military service; another one in four was found defective but fit for partial military service. The remaining 50 percent were not strong enough, tall enough or bright enough for the army to do anything with them. Draftees were not average Americans. They were above-average Americans. Yet only 4 percent had a high school diploma. Most had never gone beyond grade school.

To lead these 2.8 million, plus the 1.4 million who enlisted as regulars or as national guardsmen, the army had to find at least 200,000 officers. Thousands of regular NCOs were given commissions. There were 1,100 commissions for graduates of the Plattsburg camps. The Reserve Officers Training Corps provided tens of thousands more. Yet it was far from enough. In something like desperation the army seized on the intelligence tests invented by a Frenchman in 1905 to identify subnormal children and had them modified to identify potential officer candidates among the millions of draftees and volunteers.* The success of this program spread intelligence and aptitude testing into schools, colleges and business.

As the AEF took shape, Pershing faced the traditional problem of American commanders, a total absence of men who had commanded large formations in combat, a problem compounded by the size of an American division. Known as a square division, it contained two infantry brigades, an artillery brigade and three machine-gun battalions. In all, it held 1,000 officers and 27,000 NCOs and enlisted men. It was twice as big as a British, French or German division, but it could be operated, or so it was hoped, by a staff of similar size, thus making the few trained staff officers in the AEF go twice as far.

Regular army divisions were numbered from 1 to 25. Numbers 26 to 42 were reserved for National Guard divisions, but Guard units were so understrength half the men in most Guard divisions were draftees. Divisions numbered 43 and above were composed mainly of draftees, with a leavening of regulars.

One of Baker's aides, Major Douglas MacArthur (son of Arthur MacArthur), inspired the formation of the famous 42nd Division. Composed of Guard units drawn from twenty-six states and the District of Columbia, it formed, in MacArthur's phrase, "a rainbow division." Before the war ended he had the satisfaction of commanding it, if fleetingly.

Pershing held the Old Army view that it took at least a year to make a real soldier. He was criticized by Peyton C. March, who became chief of staff in 1918, for *over*training his men. March claimed, with some justice, that modern recruits and draftees were bright enough and fit enough to become competent infantrymen in six months. What he overlooked was that a division could not learn to function as a unit in less than a year.

Only the Marine Corps sent Pershing fully trained men—40,000 of them, and every one a qualified marksmen. He proceeded to waste this valuable force by having most of the marines guard docks and

*The first recorded intelligence test had much the same purpose. The Old Testament describes Gideon being swamped with volunteers for his army. Taking them to the river, he singled out those who drank with cupped hands and rejected those who simply put their mouths in the flowing water. The men with cupped hands showed greater alertness, being less likely to be taken by surprise and in a better position to defend themselves.

stores. Many of the soldiers sent to the AEF reached France after two months' training in the United States during which they never handled a rifle, fixed a bayonet or learned how to put on a gas mask. All they appeared to have mastered was community singing.

The French and British provided American units with instruction in the trench warfare techniques of the western front. After which Pershing had them retrained in open warfare, fearing they might have lost their fighting spirit. Allied and German troops had virtually abandoned the rifle. They fought with machine guns, trench mortars, hand grenades, automatic rifles and one-pounder guns fired at point-blank range. Rifles and bayonets were a last, almost pathetic resort.

Reports were common of men chasing each other around the battlefields of northern France fighting it out in grenade-throwing duels and never firing a shot. Pershing was affronted by such behavior. He clung to the old faith in the highly trained marksman, moving forward to close with the enemy armed with his rifle, his bayonet and an aggressive spirit. There was a certain nobility to that image that appealed deeply to his professional soldier's mind. It was that image that lay behind his entire conception of how he would train the AEF and how it would fight.

Training went deep with him. Before going to West Point he had been a schoolteacher. Pershing had returned to West Point as an instructor in tactics. He later spent four happy years teaching military science and history at the University of Nebraska to officer candidates. For all the high standards of the draft there were 121,000 illiterates in the AEF. There were also 50,000 former teachers. Need and remedy existed side by side. Pershing set up schools for everyone, from unlettered privates to ambitious light colonels. There were dozens of technical schools and what amounted to grade schools for adults. There was an AEF university at Beaune and a general staff college at Langres, twenty-five miles south of Chaumont. Some 250,000 men received AEF schooling. From this beginning the military emerged as one of the major educational institutions, often succeeding where others have failed.

The relationship between Pershing and March was famously bad. March felt he was left with most of the headaches while Pershing was left with most of the glory. When he took over as chief of staff, March arrived at the War Department late at night, fresh from France, where he had commanded the AEF's artillery. He found a single officer on duty and the corridors piled high with sacks of unopened mail.

March labored heroically and effectively to help the AEF, an effort in which he had Baker's unstinting support. The secretary of war won the lasting esteem of the army by reinterpreting the law to mean that the chief of staff did have authority after all over the bureaus. On any plain reading of the words he appeared to have no such thing. Baker instantly turned the General Staff into the planning and coordinating arm that Root had intended and Upton foreseen.

Pershing meanwhile created an independent American army out of whatever March and Baker were able to send him. The British and French were completely opposed to such an army's existence. The best use for doughboys,* they protested, was as replenishments for their own tired and understrength divisions.

Wilson was not interested in the question one way or the other. At times Pershing felt he labored almost alone to save the AEF from abolition. The Allies† treated it as a tiresome assertion of the Yankee ego. By taking nearly half the AEF across the Atlantic the British helped ensure that nearly half Pershing's troops served with them or the French. These divisions were shipped from the United States to Britain, then by Channel steamer to France. To move them across northern France from the Channel ports to the American sector would create logistical problems the AEF preferred to avoid. Doughboys never really warmed to the English or understood the French. They felt at home though with the storm troops of the Allied armies, the Australians. The fight for American independence distracted Pershing almost to the end of the war.

Similarly, his strategic outlook conflicted with those of his allies. By the fall of 1917 the British and French had adopted a strategy of attrition, even though they lacked the manpower for it. Pershing, who alone had the manpower, rejected it. One day, he preached, the stalemate on the western front would somehow be broken. The Allied

---

*There is a belief that "doughboy" goes back to the Mexican War, when American regiments pounding down the roads of the Southwest got covered with white adobe dust. Why this term should be revived in France, a country notoriously lacking in adobe dust, is a mystery.

†Strictly speaking, the United States was not an Allied Power: it was never a party to the relevant treaties.

armies would have to get out of their trenches and move forward in the open to fight a war of maneuver.

He failed to convince the British and French. He failed to persuade March. He even failed to persuade his own staff. For one thing, he was not the most articulate man in the army. For another, he could not explain exactly how men advancing in the open were going to break through deep defenses based on barbed wire, machine guns, gas, trenches and massed artillery fire.

Even so, the AEF was something the Allies had to take seriously as, month by month, it became a real army; an army that was decidedly Pershing's creation. Its arrival on the western front could not have been timed more dramatically had it fallen out of the clouds in a stunning theatrical coup.

In the summer of 1916 the British had launched an offensive in Flanders that traded blood for mud, and gained little even of that. Mention of the Somme to this day makes Englishmen sober.

That summer the Russians too launched a major offensive. They hurt the Austrians badly but themselves even more. The czar's armies lost one million men. Morale collapsed. In that spiritual vacuum Soviet propaganda found a soil more fertile than anything Lenin and Trotsky might have produced in a millennium of tilling. In March 1917 bread riots broke out in St. Petersburg. The czarist regime was toppled. The army ceased fighting. Russia was virtually out of the war.

In that same spring of 1917 the French hurled half their army at strong, deep German defenses in the rolling hills of Champagne. French divisions broke like eggs thrown at a wall. Survivors mutinied against the sheer stupidity of an offensive that took 200,000 lives without the least chance of success.

That fall an Austrian and German offensive in northern Italy broke the Italian army around Caporetto. One more such battle and Italy would be knocked out of the war.

It was against this background of defeat, paralysis and despair that the doughboys came to France. Half trained, gangling, awestruck, they were pitied by their British and French instructors yet cheered rapturously by British and French crowds as victory's men.

CROSSING the Atlantic was a journey through the looking glass: on one side, Americans were proud citizens of the richest, most productive nation on earth; on the other, they were beggars in uniform, dependent on their allies for arms. Even humble items like revolvers and pistols were so scarce American officers crammed their holsters with toilet paper to suggest a menace they did not possess. The army itself was partly to blame.

After the supply shambles of the War of 1812 the army and navy won control over military procurement, a power they have to this day. Within the budgets provided by Congress they decide which weapons and other equipment to buy. For all other major armies and navies those decisions are made by politicians. In 1917, however, the army and navy bureaus rushed out thousands of contracts within weeks of American entry in the war, without any coordination at all. Bureaus such as Ordnance and Quartermaster competed frantically with each other for scarce labor, plant and materials. By the end of 1917 all this produced was confusion and bottlenecks.

The War Industries Board set up in July was intended to match what the military needed with what industry could provide. With the nation at war there was no time to be lost, yet the WIB spent most of its energies for the first nine months of its existence simply on staying alive. It lacked the expert knowledge and the political authority to do what needed to be done.

Reorganized in March 1918 under Bernard Baruch, a wizard of high finance, it began reporting directly to Wilson. Its existence was finally secure. It took responsibility for the manufacture of thirty thousand different products. In the drive to convert to war production and to save raw materials it made millions of people feel they were a vital part of the war effort. Baruch especially caught the public imagination, radiating youthful energy with mature good sense. Even so, the results of the WIB's labors were meager. Under the most favorable circumstances it would have taken about two years to convert the economy to full war production. Too much time was lost before and after the United States entered the war for its industrial power to arm the AEF as it went into battle. And for all the favorable publicity Baruch and the WIB received, the army and navy were left in charge of their own procurement. The country and Congress simply did not trust big business and its friends in government to avoid corruption. Military men were held to be honest even if they were not always wise.

Production failure at home meant that not a single American-made

75-millimeter field gun or 155-millimeter howitzer—the main weapons of the artillery—reached the front. Even something as obvious as boots for the infantry proved a challenge too great for the War Department and the WIB. The footwear issued to doughboys fell apart after a few weeks' hard wear.

Billy Mitchell of the AEF Air Service made a study of flying outfits before sending his requirements to Washington. He asked for flying coats made of waterproof gabardine lined with Belgian hare, with Australian opossum fur collars. He knew they were warm, dry, comfortable, and available in Europe. The War Department and its domestic suppliers chose to provide instead American-made coats of heavy canvas, lined with dog skins that stank from lack of curing and topped with collars of dirty billy-goat hair that raised boils on the neck.

The AEF was desperate for tanks. Not a single American tank was produced, despite Pershing's pleas. He had to beg the British and French to sell him some of theirs. The army bought from the French 3,100 75-millimeter guns, 1,200 heavy howitzers, 9,600 Hotchkiss machine guns, 40,000 Chauchat automatic rifles, millions of artillery shells, mortar rounds and hand grenades. Only 194 American aircraft—none of them combat types—reached the front. This was small beer compared to the 4,800 French planes that American pilots flew.

Intervention did have the effect of shaking the Ordnance Bureau out of its machine gun bewilderment. It finally saw the merits of the Lewis gun.* It also took another look at the weapons offered by the country's most prolific gun designer, John M. Browning. His designs included the famous Winchester rifles and the Colt .45 automatic pistol. The Ordnance Bureau had rejected his .30-caliber machine gun in favor of the Benét-Mercié. On belated second thoughts it accepted it, and an automatic rifle, familiarly known as the BAR. It also accepted his .50-caliber machine gun. The BAR became the infantryman's weapon of choice for nearly forty years and Browning machine guns were nothing less than superb. Pershing put limits on their use so the Germans would not capture them and discover their secrets.

While the AEF was short of weapons to the end of the war, some

---

*Lewis received more than one million dollars in royalties from the Treasury during the war. He sent the money back, refusing to profit from the defense of his country.

items reached France in overabundance. Pershing had to beg the War Department in the spring of 1918 to send him no more shipments of "bath bricks, bookcases, bathtubs, cabinets for blank forms, cuspidors, office desks, floor wax, hose except fire hose, stepladders, lawn mowers, refrigerators, safes except iron field safes, settees, sickles, stools, and window shades."

An American army was a prodigious consumer of supplies. An infantry division needed 700 tons a day from the United States, plus another 150 tons purchased locally. There was such a shortage of unloading facilities at French ports, however, that some supplies went to France, returned to the United States, and crossed the Atlantic for a third time before being unloaded. The AEF found it had to create its own port operations, its own railroad and its own telephone service to get anything done quickly; sometimes, at all.

Pershing was forced to assign some of his best officers, including his former chief of staff, Major General James Harbord, to sorting out the supply shambles. The situation behind the front was so bad it often threatened to paralyze the AEF. The most valuable civilians employed by the government were not the dollar-a-year businessmen who flocked to Washington but the railroad executives and AT&T managers who went to France to help with Pershing's logistics. They had endless squabbles with middle-ranking French officials, whose love of forms and procedure was second only to the French love of eating. The immature bureaucracy of the AEF found itself outmatched by the mature bureaucracy of the centralized state.

Short of half its authorized truck strength and one third its authorized manpower, Harbord's Service of Supply performed prodigies of unsung labor, yet the supply challenge was too great. It was never really overcome. Besides, it was a problem that did not have its roots in France, so it was unfair to expect the SOS to solve it.

The greatest logistics effort went not into shipping supplies but into shipping men. The principal achievement of the "Bridge to France" was getting two million soldiers across the Atlantic. The shipping of nearly everything else was chaotic.

THE NAVY in April 1917 was far from being in the high state of readiness that modern navies were expected to maintain even in prolonged periods of peace. It was seriously undermanned. The high standards of gunnery achieved under Sims had slipped so badly the gunnery trophy went unawarded in 1916. Maintenance was poor in much of the fleet. The U.S. Navy went to war in no shape for battle.

It was an extraordinary situation for a country that since 1901 had been committed to building a navy second only to Great Britain's. The outbreak of war had only raised American naval ambitions. The prospect of a Germany that held all Europe by the throat and possessed all the great European shipyards was disturbing. A victorious Germany, moreover, might force a country such as Denmark to hand over its foreign possessions, including the Danish West Indies. That would provide Germany with a naval base in the Caribbean. To preclude that happening, Denmark was pressured into selling those islands (the present-day Virgin Islands) to the United States for 25 million dollars.

Wilson and the navy meanwhile enunciated a new naval policy—a navy "Second to None." That was the goal of the Navy Act of 1916, but this growing naval force was organized much like the modest navy of 1898. It had a general board, but this was no substitute for a general staff. The board could only offer advice, if asked. It did not make plans.

Navy Secretary Daniels was suspicious of anyone who wore a uniform. As a good Progressive he viewed all military men as closet militarists. Navy officers in turn disliked him, for his dithering and his simplistic views, and for the stunning neglect of the navy in time of war. In 1915 he reluctantly allowed the creation of the post of chief of naval operations, but made sure it did not amount to much. He denied his CNO the kind of authority Baker gave to March.

Wilson and Daniels's mutual aversion to genuine preparedness only stored up trouble for the future. All through 1915–16 the shipbuilding industry boomed, grown rich and busy on foreign and domestic orders. When in late 1916 Daniels finally bestirred himself and went to the shipyards with the Navy Act's construction program he was told there was no capacity to spare, and why hadn't he come around sooner? The navy second to none would have to wait.

The best thing Daniels did was to send Sims to England even before the United States declared war. Sims had spent the past three years as president of the Naval War College, where Daniels, who thought he was too clever to be trusted, could forget about him. Sims arrived in England two days after the American declaration of war. He was the "logical man"—fluent in French, outspokenly Anglophile. He found the British on the verge of being starved out of the war.

In January 1917 the Allied Powers had 21.5 million tons of shipping. In the first three months of that year losses exceeded new construction by 2 million tons, and the rate of loss was rising fast from week to week. To prosecute the war at the current level the Allies needed at least 15.5 million tons. By the end of the summer they would be below that.

The hottest secret the Admiralty possessed was its forecast that Britain would leave the war in October. Prime Minister David Lloyd George expected to start evacuating his armies from France as early as August, rather than risk having them trapped there as the western front collapsed. And with Britain gone, France could not long survive.

The only solution Lloyd George could see to the shipping crisis was for Allied ships to be gathered in convoys for mutual protection. Most of his admirals were against it, convinced that would only provide large collections of sitting ducks for the exclusive benefit of U-boat captains. Merchant skippers too were strongly opposed to convoys. They had no experience of steaming together in formation, let alone attempting it at night.

Sims added his weight to the pro-convoy faction in the Royal Navy. He never claimed, as some of his admirers did, that he tipped the balance in the debate but his presence probably had an effect. Adopting the convoy system was not a practical possibility anyway without an adequate destroyer force to provide escorts. Sims's presence and his belief in convoys offered an assurance that American destroyers would soon be on their way. After a trial convoy sent from Britain reached Gibraltar safely, in May 1917, convoys were adopted.

The key to the system was keeping track of the U-boats, by sightings made from aircraft and ships. A submarine had to surface to charge its batteries. It spent more time on the water than under it. U-boat commanders were also a garrulous crew, chattering to one another over their radios without any thought for security.

By tracking the U-boats the Admiralty was able to steer convoys away from them. Inbound convoys were met by half a dozen destroyers four hundred miles west of Land's End. Outbound convoys had a similar destroyer screen through the danger zone. Out in mid-Atlantic submarines rarely operated. By October 1917 the Battle of the Atlantic was won. Convoys were running on a regular schedule. The rate of loss to submarines had fallen to well below the rate of new construction.

The British had also developed the tools needed for hunting down and destroying U-boats: the hydrophone, the depth charge and ASDIC.* The U.S. Navy was so top-heavy with capital ships it initially lacked the large numbers of destroyers and other fast, small ships antisubmarine warfare demanded, but before the war ended a score of future American admirals had chased subs. The convoy system succeeded so comprehensively that only a single troop transport heading for Europe was sunk. Nearly all the men aboard her were saved.

In its eagerness to defeat the submarine, the Navy Department pressed ahead with the North Sea mine barrage. This was a project dear to the heart of the assistant secretary of the navy, Franklin Roosevelt. Sims considered it a waste of time, effort and resources. The barrage finally stretched 240 miles from Scotland to Norway. It cost 40 million dollars and used 73,000 mines. It represented a major advance in mine warfare technology. It was claimed to have destroyed as many as eight submarines. There is no indisputable evidence it sank even one.

Five U.S. battleships were sent to form part of the Royal Navy's Grand Fleet. They joined it as 6th Battle Squadron, ready for the great Mahanite fleet action that would decide command of the seas. Their captains scanned the cold, gray-green horizons of the North Sea in vain. After the inconclusive Battle of Jutland, in May 1916, the German High Seas Fleet never came out again.

THE ARMY subsidized the flying experiments of the scholar-inventor Samuel P. Langley. He put ever larger, more complicated models into the air, leading up to the logical, inevitable culmination, manned flight. In 1903, just two weeks before the Wright brothers' plane flew at Kitty Hawk, Langley's first piloted aircraft was launched from the top of a houseboat moored in the Potomac. It plunged into the river. Hauled out and relaunched, it crashed again. That dampened army interest in planes for a decade.

Enterprising spirits were not deterred. In 1911 Lieutenant Riley E. Scott began experimenting with airplanes in an offensive role. With Lieutenant T. DeWitt Milling he began aerial bombing at College

*A primitive form of sonar but fairly effective against the shallow-diving submarines of the time. It took its name from the Anti-Submarine Detection Indicator Committee, the body of scientists and sailors that developed it.

Park, Maryland. Scott invented the world's first bombsight. It was used in the Balkan Wars of 1912–13. In June 1914 the French held an international bombing competition. Scott won all the prizes. Yet it was the machine gun rather than the bombsight that created war in the air. There would have been bombing raids, no doubt, and aerial reconnaissance, but the fighter—the principal warplane of World War One—would not have existed.

In 1914, however, few people foresaw any serious combat role for aircraft. Army doctrine almost everywhere described the airplane and the balloon as "the eyes of the army." That was why aviation was assigned in the U.S. Army to the Signal Corps. And that was how a young Signal Corps officer, Captain William D. Mitchell, came into contact with it.

Dropping out of college in 1898, Mitchell joined a Wisconsin volunteer regiment as a private. His senator father secured a commission for him and Mitchell stayed on in the army, having discovered a taste for soldiering. He spent two years in the Philippines during the Insurrection, where he fell under the spell of Frederick Funston. Mitchell was affected for the rest of his life by Funston's adventurous spirit and love of new ideas. The young general became the model on which Mitchell would base his own tempestuous career.

When World War One began, Mitchell was a General Staff officer. His first wartime assignment was to revise daily the war maps at the White House and the War Department. Convinced that the United States would have to enter the war, he launched a personal preparedness program: at his own expense he took flying lessons. Arriving in France in May 1917 to study French aviation, Mitchell was the first soldier in an American uniform to come under fire in the war; of which he was always proud.

Other Americans were already fighting in France, but they were in the French army. Dozens of flyers had pestered the French to allow them into the war. At first they were known as the American Squadron, commanded by a French captain, but the name was later changed to the more evocative Lafayette Escadrille. When the United States entered the war 90 of these pilots transferred to the Air Service of the AEF, providing a reserve of talent and experience the Signal Corps needed badly: in April 1917 it could boast 35 pilots and 55 obsolete aircraft.

In July Congress tried to make amends by voting the Air Service

640 million dollars. It was an absurd gesture, but the best it could do. All the money in the world would not produce trained pilots and modern aircraft overnight.

American aviation was so underdeveloped that Pershing had to turn to the British to train his aviation mechanics. Some 15,000 were sent to Britain to gain the necessary skills. Mitchell spoke frankly to the French air minister, Daniel Vincent, about the bungling in the War Department and the WIB that was strangling American plane production. Vincent ordered vastly more planes from French factories than France could provide pilots for, knowing the Americans were going to need them. Until the summer of 1918, though, American pilots had to make do with the French Nieuport, while French squadrons were reequipped with the newer, faster, tougher Spad.

Despite all of which the best American pilots were among the best anywhere. Their highest scorer in aerial combat was Eddie Rickenbacker, who arrived in France as Pershing's driver. From the day he learned to fly Rickenbacker had a stark picture of what was expected of him: "Aerial warfare is nothing less than scientific murder."

He prepared himself in that spirit. And as he soon discovered, there was a lot less chivalry in air fighting than people on the ground imagined. Rickenbacker was a cool, precise technician. He had no illusions about being a knight-errant of the skies sallying forth to offer individual combat. At twenty-seven he was much older than the average rookie fighter pilot. A former champion racing driver, he had the reflexes of the natural athlete and the level head of a business executive. In only a few months, including a long layoff, he shot down 22 enemy aircraft and four balloons. He had to wait, all the same, until 1930 to be awarded the Medal of Honor.

Press and public invested combat flyers with a glamour that outshone all other combatants. Pershing spoke for virtually the whole army, however, when he said he did not see why pilots should be paid 50 percent more than other officers of the same rank. Men in the trenches faced equally great risks, and worse living conditions. Baker agreed with him, but Congress did not. The flying bonus stayed.

As Mitchell himself expressed it, "This was not an interesting war for troops on the ground. There was no marching or maneuvering, no songs, no flying colors and bands playing while going into action. It was just groveling in dirty mud holes. The only interest and romance in this war was in the air."

Even doughboys were affected by it, despite their envy of the airmen. After Theodore Roosevelt's son Quentin was shot down, his crude grave near Soissons became a shrine for soldiers moving up to the front. They dropped to their knees at the foot of it and prayed.

Half the American pilots rounded out their training by flying with a French squadron before being assigned to an American one. They were happy with French instruction but found even French flyers were affected by the defensive mood that prevailed in the trenches below. French squadrons were constantly putting up small patrols to defend their airspace.

To Mitchell this was all wrong. Airplanes were to his mind really weapons of the offensive. He much preferred the tactic practiced by some German commanders who did not waste their pilots' energies on dreary little patrols but launched dozens of planes together on offensive sweeps. Any patrol colliding with one of these 40–60-plane formations was almost sure to be wiped out. That was how Quentin Roosevelt had died. The idea of French pilots that they were "defending" airspace struck Mitchell as a delusion.

His kindred spirit was Hugh Trenchard, commander of the Royal Flying Corps' Independent Air Force. The two men became instant, close and lasting friends. Trenchard was convinced he could bomb Germany so hard that at the very least whole divisions and thousands of guns would have to be pulled back from the front.

This visionary conception of air power was shared by few other flyers. It seemed absurdly ambitious, for one thing, given the technology available, and so far removed from the war on the ground that belief in it required an act of faith.

Most pilots spent most of their time in the air flying observation missions over enemy territory, or trying to stop the enemy from flying observation missions over theirs. There was a little light bombing, the occasional strafing, but the justification for the glamorous, expensive business of combat aviation was that it provided eyes for the armies.

Trenchard's soaring ambitions were humbled, in fact, by the tool he had to work with in 1917–18, the Handley-Page heavy bomber. It flew low and slow: easy meat for German fighters. It was used mainly at night, making nuisance raids on cities under cover of darkness, flown by pilots who had little idea of where they were or what targets they were hitting.

The IAF struck Mitchell like a revelation of things to come. His

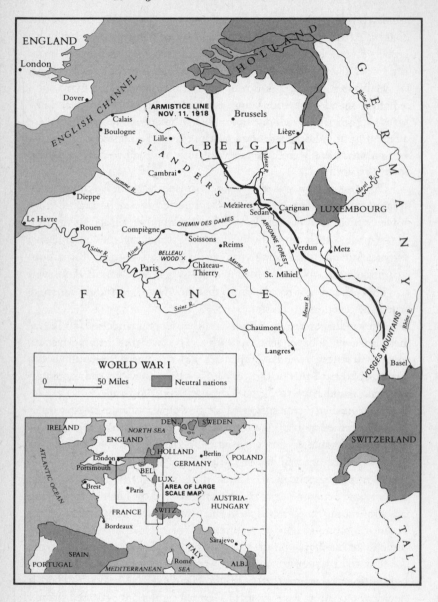

ENGLAND

London

Dover

ENGLISH CHANNEL

Calais
Boulogne

Lille

FLANDERS

Dieppe

Le Havre

Rouen

Somme R.

Compiègne

Paris

Seine R.

Aisne R.

CHEMIN DES DAMES

Soissons

Reims

BELLEAU
WOOD ×

Château-
Thierry

Marne R.

FRANCE

Seine R.

HOLLAND

ARMISTICE LINE
NOV. 11, 1918

Brussels

BELGIUM

Cambrai

Mézières

Sedan

Liège

Meuse R.

Carignan

ARGONNE FOREST

St. Mihiel

Chaumont

Langres

GERMANY

Rhine R.

Mosel R.

LUXEMBOURG

Verdun

Metz

Meuse R.

VOSGES MOUNTAINS

Rhine R.

Basel

SWITZERLAND

ITALY

WORLD WAR I

0   50 Miles

Neutral nations

IRELAND

NORTH SEA

DEN.

SWEDEN

ENGLAND

HOLLAND

Berlin

POLAND

London

Portsmouth

BEL.

GERMANY

ATLANTIC OCEAN

Brest

Paris

LUX.

AREA OF LARGE
SCALE MAP

AUSTRIA-
HUNGARY

FRANCE

SWITZ.

Bordeaux

ITALY

Sarajevo

SPAIN

Rome

ALB.

PORTUGAL

MEDITERRANEAN
SEA

mind whirled with visions of 1,000-bomber raids . . . 2,000-bomber raids . . . 3,000-bomber raids! Victory through air power.

IN EUROPE the tradition of winter quarters and spring campaigns remained the natural rhythm of warfare. Throughout the winter of 1917–18 both sides were racing to build up their manpower on the western front. The Germans hurried back divisions from a defeated Russia, the Allies hurried green troops across the Atlantic. By March 1918 the Germans had a manpower advantage of about 35 percent.

On March 21, the first day of spring, the blow fell. The mastermind of the German army now was Erich Ludendorff; a general whose power was greater than the kaiser's and, in effect, the military dictator of Germany. Ludendorff's spring offensive was designed to crush the Allied left flank, separate the British from the French and reach the Channel ports.

The secret on which it hinged was new tactics. The Germans brought up elite units under cover of darkness, hiding them in woods and houses during the day. Instead of prolonged artillery bombardments there were short ones, with gas first to drive the defenders under cover, followed by high explosive to rip open barbed wire entanglements. The new doctrine did not seek to smash the Allied lines but to penetrate them. Advance units were trained to go across the trenches, to flow around strongpoints and to strike deep in the rear. Behind them other regiments would pour through the gaps they had made.

This technique of deep penetration broke the British Fifth Army apart. The Germans advanced forty miles and inflicted 300,000 casualties. Without meaning to, Ludendorff had vindicated Pershing: open warfare *was* possible on the western front. The Germans broke through, moreover, without tanks.

In the white heat of this crisis, as a gap opened up between the British and French armies, Marshal Ferdinand Foch was named supreme commander. Foch was to exercise strategical direction, while each national commander retained tactical control of his divisions. Pershing hurried to Foch's temporary field headquarters. Rising to the best French he ever achieved, he offered *"Infanterie, artillerie, aviation— tout ce que nous avons est à vous. Disposez-en comme il vous plaira."* All we have is yours. Use it as you will.

Ludendorff was like a chess grand master who has mastered everything but the end game. A brilliant planner of opening and intermediate moves, he was a poor improviser and weak on logistics. As, inevitably, momentum of his spring offensive slowed he made diversionary attacks elsewhere instead of reinforcing success. The British and French had a breathing space. The Channel ports were saved.

The next blow fell in May, against the center of the Allied line. By now the German manpower advantage had all but disappeared as the flow of doughboys reached 8,000 a day. Pershing's intelligence officers saw the assault coming, warning the French on May 26 that the Germans were about to storm the Chemin des Dames. This is a long, east–west ridge a little to the north of Soissons and Rheims. South of the Chemin the land is flat and open almost all the way to Paris. The French saw the Chemin as a mighty wall. The Germans could never take it.

In the early hours of May 27 they took it. By afternoon they had seized the bridges across the river Aisne, which flows south of it. In three days, using the tactics that shattered the British Fifth Army, they covered thirty miles and took 60,000 prisoners. A million people fled Paris. The French government began packing up, to follow them. Yet this offensive too broke down, trickling away in chilly, cobwebbed wine cellars. This was the very heart of Champagne. Conquered *caves* were filled with heavy green bottles. The German army got roaring drunk; too drunk to fight, for several days too drunk to get up. While it sprawled in a stupor the French and Americans were already counterattacking.

Pershing sent the pride of his affections, 1st Infantry Division, into action for the first time, on May 28. The Big Red One suffered 900 casualties fighting for a hillock at Cantigny. It was to be his own demonstration that open warfare tactics would work. The objective was taken, and seven fierce counterattacks beaten off.

Second Division was committed the next week at Belleau Wood, in a struggle for a square mile of trees that could have been bypassed, but it was important to impress on the Germans that the Americans were there to fight. Half the division's infantry strength was made up by the Marine Brigade, consisting of the 5th and 6th Marine regiments. The marines spent most of June clearing Belleau Wood, which proved to be a miniature Verdun: four lines of defense, overlapping fields of machine gun fire, huge boulders, deep ravines and dense vegetation.

The marines attacked day after day, without mortars, hand grenades or signal flares. They had to fight their way from trench to trench, rifle pit to rifle pit, armed with rifle, bayonet and the Chauchat automatic rifle. This pitiful object was hailed by the French as a triumph of Gallic ingenuity: a nation of thrifty peasants had produced a firearm from battlefield scrap. Doughboys claimed it was a triumph of foreign idiocy—a piece of scrap made from old sardine cans. At Belleau Wood the marines fought almost to the end with little of the massive artillery support that all the other armies took for granted.

On 2nd Division's right flank 3rd Division was meanwhile holding the line against the Germans along the Marne, around Château-Thierry, even as French divisions pulled back. By holding and counterattacking the German units that got closest to Paris, the two divisions were forever after convinced they had saved it. Paris was forty miles behind them, however, and a lot can happen in forty miles.

Although short of supplies, the Germans tried to renew the offensive, on July 15. Foch was already preparing a massive counterstroke. Three days later he launched it: a drive against the German left flank, spearheaded by the Big Red One, 2nd Division and an aggressive French colonial division, supported by five hundred tanks. In a three-day battle on the outskirts of Soissons the Germans were beaten back. Other American and French divisions plunged into the German center. By August 6 the Germans were digging in along the Aisne. Paul von Hindenburg, chief of the German Great General Staff, wrote of the Battle of Soissons, "We had lost the initiative to the enemy." The German army never got it back.

On August 8 the British, whom the Germans believed were in poor shape to fight, surprised them with an offensive around Amiens. Hundreds of tanks and armored cars sent the Germans reeling. The greatest shock for Ludendorff and Hindenburg was the demoralization this offensive exposed. The 2nd Guards Division, for example, was one of the elite formations of the German army, yet it fell apart. Thousands of its men fled; others surrendered eagerly.

The discipline that was the bedrock of the German army was legendary. It was an army governed by a strict honor code, and being sent back to civilian life was considered the ultimate punishment. Until the prospect of defeat undermined discipline the honor code by and large remained intact, making unnecessary the kind of prisons and punishments common in Allied armies. It seemed unthinkable that Germans would surrender in droves, yet it was happening.

One of the most successful of Allied campaigns was the propaganda offensive. In the first twelve months following American intervention Allied propaganda demoralized the German people. In the next six months it demoralized the German army. Behind it loomed the lean shadow of Woodrow Wilson, successor in war propaganda to Jefferson and Lincoln.

From the moment he asked Congress for a declaration of war he insisted there was no American hostility toward the German people. The war would be fought to liberate them as much as anyone else from despotic government. Only eight days after the United States entered the war he created the Committee on Public Information. This propaganda agency hammered home American war aims, both here and abroad. Germany on the other hand dared not state her war aims openly.

Wilson's Fourteen Points, enunciated in January 1918 as the basis for peace negotiations, were a propaganda triumph. They were perhaps overly idealistic in the world they envisaged, where the rights of small nations were guaranteed and disputes between all countries would be settled with the aid of an international peace-keeping body; where diplomacy would be open, armaments reduced and the seas free to all. Even so, they had a powerful effect on German opinion. Hitler's propaganda chief, Joseph Goebbels, spent much of the next war worrying about the power of American propaganda as he recalled it from 1918.

That year there were food riots in German cities, strikes in the munitions plants, even strikes against the brutal Treaty of Brest-Litovsk that took from the Russians much of the most fertile land and their raw materials. Meanwhile troops at the front were bombarded with leaflets, while balloons rode the prevailing winds, blowing from west to east, carrying more. Entire regiments became unmanageable. Some refused to return to the front once pulled out of the trenches. Orders to attack were increasingly ignored.

It was in these circumstances, with AEF manpower approaching two million and the Germans too weak and demoralized to launch new offensives, that Pershing felt able in August 1918 to realize his ambition. The American contribution on the western front turned on two compromises: the compromise of 1917, when Pershing was given his own section of the front, albeit far from the sector of decision, in exchange for the promise of millions of fresh men; and the compromise of 1918, when Pershing was allowed to form half his available divisions into the First American Army, while the other half stayed with the British and French.

Pershing chose to command First Army himself. He assigned its first objective: reduction of the St. Mihiel salient, a triangular projection between the rivers Meuse and Moselle. It was thirty miles wide at the base and twenty miles deep. Both faces of the salient were attacked on September 12. The Germans had begun pulling out four days earlier. It collapsed like a pricked balloon.

Pershing's next offensive, launched hard on the heels of this success, was aimed at cutting the Mézières–Sedan–Carignan railroad line. This twenty-five-mile stretch of track was crucial to German lateral communications east of Belgium. To reach it the AEF would have to fight its way through four lines of German defenses, twenty miles deep, north of Verdun. There was no room for maneuver. On the right flank was the deep, twisting valley of the Meuse, and the German defenses were embedded in the mountainous forest of the Argonne.

In the early stages Pershing retained command of First Army, but it was too much to fight a battle and run the whole AEF. He handed First Army over to Hunter Liggett, the fattest man in the army, an accomplished soldier, reader of lyric poetry, former head of the War College, owner of the finest palate ever to survive West Point. Like Custer, Liggett took his personal chef on campaign.

The Argonne Forest was, said Liggett, "a natural fortress beside which the Wilderness in which Grant fought Lee was a park." The main German defensive position, the Hindenburg line, ran along the northern edge of it. Instead of trenches it offered defense based on concrete redoubts—"pillboxes." These were usually T-shaped, with the crossbar facing the expected line of attack and machine guns set in the upright of the T, which both protected the T's flanks and overlapped with the fire from pillboxes on either side. There was no opening at the top or front. Set low in the ground and camouflaged, they were hard to spot and nothing short of a direct hit by a heavy artillery high-explosive shell had any impact. Taking them out one at a time was some of the hardest infantry fighting of the war.

With fresh divisions becoming available, Pershing created Second Army, entrusting it to Robert Lee Bullard. Compared to Liggett,

Bullard was lean and mean. He was outspoken, capable with a few words of cutting anyone down to size, and always spoiling for a fight. With the formation of Second Army, Pershing renewed the momentum of his offensive. Clear at last of the forest, the AEF fought on as Pershing had always said it would, attacking continuously until the objective was reached. The cost was high.

Rifle strength in his two armies fell dramatically. With many of his best divisions still attached to the British and French he had to fill them up with green replacements. The result was predictable. There was an unbroken cordon of MPs, Bullard reported, behind some of his frontline units. Nothing, however, would make Pershing relent. A division commander who failed to press home attacks did not last long.

The Meuse–Argonne offensive opened on a twenty-four-mile front. It continued for six weeks, gaining forty miles. Pershing eventually had more than one million men in action, holding a ninety-mile front. By November 9 the railroad was under direct artillery fire on the outskirts of Sedan, but the French had cut it days before around Mézières.

Farther west, in Flanders, British and French armies had driven the Germans back remorselessly across terrain where the Allied superiority in tanks, artillery, aircraft and manpower made itself felt. Demoralized German divisions evaporated. Others, with a modicum of fighting spirit left, fought delaying actions. Hunger weakened them. So did an influenza epidemic that ravaged all the armies in the closing months of the war. The High Seas Fleet mutinied. A revolt in Berlin toppled the kaiser. Even before that the Germans were seeking an armistice.

Pershing and Foch argued against it. They believed that an Allied demand for unconditional surrender might prolong the war by a few weeks, but it would bring the total collapse of the German army. An armistice was nothing compared to victory. All the politicians could think of, however, was the present moment: why shed more blood tomorrow if we can stop today?

At 11 A.M. on November 11 the guns fell silent, after firing victory salutes. Men gave up a ratlike existence, emerging into the open. It was safe to stand up. Frenchmen drank *vin ordinaire* toasts and swayed to accordions. British Tommies cheerily kicked soccer balls around in the mud. Scots bagpipers keened away. Aussies bellowed "Waltzing Matilda." Germans cheered, shouted *"Kamerad!"* across the lines and wept for joy. Banality and stereotypes, all along the front, except for the doughboys. Compared to the French and British, their gains were modest at best. There seemed little to show for all they had suffered and done. Besides, if the Allies had won, why were the Germans celebrating as if theirs was the victory? Not every doughboy rejoiced when the firing ceased.

Pershing felt no sense of triumph. We should be marching down the Unter den Linden in Berlin, he thought, under our banners and flags, with battle honors streaming in the wind, behind military bands. This will all have to be done over again.

IN A CLEARING in the forest at Compiègne, Foch's gleaming brown-and-brass railway carriage is preserved. The seats where cowed Germans sat and sullenly signed the Armistice are dominated by a portrait of the supreme commander. In the museum next to the carriage the visitor is invited to see the war as the French see it: in a titanic struggle between France and Germany, France won.*

American and British accounts of the First World War offer their own interpretations. Drawing on German memoirs published after the war, they variously prove that it was the Tommy or the doughboy who won.

Doughboys headed for French ports happy to leave such issues to posterity. Their only war aim, some said, was "to come home and out-lie the Grand Army of the Republic."

Maintaining American military tradition, they were avid souvenir hunters. Spiked helmets were favored. Old companions were remembered: countless trench cooties crossed to the New World preserved in a few drops of candle wax. Demand for the Iron Cross was so strong the Germans obligingly continued to manufacture them.

It had taken eighteen months to ship two million men across the Atlantic; March brought them back in half the time. Five hundred towns and cities held victory parades. The doughboys were feted as

*In 1920 a museum was built around the carriage. Twenty years later, after the fall of France, Hitler forced the French to demolish the building and pull the carriage out, so it could be used for France's surrender. After World War Two the carriage was put back and the museum rebuilt. There is no mention at the site that Hitler ever set foot in this carriage, or that it witnessed the French surrender.

heroes and were proud of what they had done, yet many felt cheated of recognition.

Napoleon had decorated men in the field, in front of their comrades, sometimes only hours after the feat of gallantry that had won them their Legion of Honor. The French army of World War One tried to live up to that. Awards were made promptly and generously. They were as freely bestowed on Americans who served with them as on the French. Pershing considered the whole business slightly absurd. Doing one's duty was reward enough for a soldier.

His resistance to decorations caused deep unhappiness throughout the AEF, leaving a residue of bitterness that made the army unpopular for years. All it had in its gift before 1918 was the Medal of Honor and the Certificate of Merit. Congress created the Distinguished Service Medal, mainly for staff officers, and the Distinguished Service Cross for acts of heroism not meriting the Medal of Honor. In 1920 the Silver Star was created for the 5,000 men recommended for the DSC who did not get it. Most awards were made so long after the event, after being sifted by slow-moving committees, they were devalued in the eyes of the men who eventually received them.

It all seemed academic anyway. The country the doughboys returned to in 1919 was convinced of one thing: there would never be another war. Wilson had promised them "the war to end all wars." They believed him.

They also returned to a country where everyday life had been changed in a thousand ways. It was the army, for instance, that got American men to use safety razors and wear wristwatches. It was the war that raised women's hemlines for the first time in fifteen hundred years from the ankle to the knees. In a strange reversal, the shortage of humble cotton and wool promoted the rise of a luxury, silk stockings. And the doughboys set off a perfume panic by sending home, then bringing home millions of small bottles of Paris's finest. A people with a tradition of plain living were suddenly crazy for silks and perfumes. The new narcissism created the beauty parlor. From plastic surgery, developed by wartime surgeons to repair disfiguring wounds, came the facelift. Among men, rampant peacockery broke loose. Revolting against the dull colors and uniformity of the military, they dressed in loud checks, screaming stripes, socks that could be seen a mile away and ties that made their mothers feel faint.

The wartime heritage spread in every direction. The campaigns against vice to protect the health of soldiers had shut down entire red-light districts. The proliferation of venereal disease that had left one fourth of the population with gonorrhea or syphilis was halted. Concern for young men torn from their families had also done more for Prohibition than the temperance movement ever did. State after state went dry to save draftees from drink until, by 1919, it was a certainty the federal government would follow.

Before 1914 there was a sense of malaise. The melting pot was not melting. The free land was gone. The political reforms promised by progressivism were faltering. The country was almost evenly torn between its small-town past and an urban future, between the nineteenth century and the twentieth. The old verities were dead. Preparedness parades, Plattsburg camps, rolling bandages down at the Red Cross, serving on a draft board, preparing meals at the community kitchen, organizing a scrap drive or simply saving food at home all had a revivifying effect on a nation that felt a deep need for some kind of revival.

At the same time, there was less patience than there should have been with those who held apart from the mainstream, challenging it. Wilson had agonized the night he asked Congress to declare war, "Once lead this people into war, they'll forget there ever was such a thing as tolerance." There were hysterical and ludicrous anti-German gestures, often by those who ought to have known better. The federal government, however, did not try to stem the tide—it jumped into it. Hundreds of harmless people were persecuted under the Espionage Act and other wartime legislation for their beliefs. The prosecutions continued even three years after the war ended.

The federal courts proved no refuge. Since the enactment of the Constitution they had never been a haven for the poor, the black, the exploited or the alien. They were conservative and inflexible. The federal judiciary had done almost nothing to extend or defend freedom of speech. It was the embarrassing memory of the persecution of people for their beliefs and the courts' acquiescence in it that brought pressure for change both from within and without. It was the intolerance of World War One that produced the modern federal court system, which steadily extended the protections and opportunities implicit in the Bill of Rights.

There was another subtle but profound change in the relationship between the citizen and the state. After earlier wars there had been pensions of one kind or another, but by and large discharged soldiers were expected to reintegrate themselves into society. The government did not feel obliged to find them a job or provide them with training to get one. That was true after the Armistice too, but when the 1921 recession came there was, for the first time in American history, a feeling that unemployment *was* the government's concern. After all, many of those thrown out of work were former doughboys. For better and worse the modern state, with responsibility for managing the economy and looking after its citizens, had arrived.

13

SUN DAY

THE Treaty of Versailles demanded the impossible—the permanent humiliation of Germany and reparations it could never afford. This vindictive peace was unpopular, yet Wilson campaigned hard to get the treaty ratified. A strong League of Nations with full American participation, he argued, would correct the treaty's flaws. While ratification was being debated in the Senate he was struck down by a massive brain hemorrhage. The statesman whom the people of Europe had hailed as a savior was transformed into a crotchety invalid lost in fantasies of running for a third term.

The Senate was prepared to ratify the treaty, on certain conditions. Wilson would not hear of it. He demanded ratification of the treaty as it stood or nothing. So he got nothing. The United States filled the League with experts, but would never join it. America remained deeply involved in European affairs, but would never admit it. For fifteen years after the Armistice international politics chased after shadows. The world was willing not to notice, because what it clamored for most was being dangled before it—disarmament.

The British, heavily in debt, feared another naval arms race. In 1920 they proposed, and the United States eagerly endorsed, talks between the major naval powers, all victors in the war: the United States, Britain, Japan, France and Italy. When the conference opened in Washington in the fall of 1921, Secretary of State Charles Evans

Hughes struck the keynote by offering to scrap the world's newest fleet. The mighty force of warships authorized by the 1916 Navy Act was nearing completion. Wilson's successor, Harding, was prepared to scrap the lot.

This dramatic offer turned the conference into something like a naval fire sale. Battleships built or under construction were alike shunned as if tainted. Ceilings were imposed on the maximum size of capital ships. A limit was placed on the total tonnage each country would be allowed.

The formula agreed upon gave Britain and the United States equal tonnage in capital ships. For every five tons each of them was allowed, Japan was permitted to build three tons, and France and Italy were granted the right to construct just under two tons. These ratios were thought to provide naval security to all five major powers, and nothing more.

The chief gainers from the Washington Disarmament Conference were the Japanese. Although allowed considerably less capital ship tonnage than Britain or the United States, they could concentrate their naval forces in the western Pacific. The United States had to divide its ships between two large oceans. The British were stretched even thinner, having to cover the Atlantic, the Mediterranean, the Indian Ocean and the waters of the southwestern Pacific around Australia and New Zealand.

Japan's naval position was strong. On entering World War One, Japanese forces had promptly seized the German-owned islands in the Pacific—the Carolines, the Marshalls, the northern Marianas. Its claim to them was upheld at Versailles, over strong protests from Wilson. Having joined the war under its treaty of military alliance with Britain, Japan demanded at the peace conference to be paid off in the coin of military advantage. This left it with a line of island bases that cut across American sea lines of communication with the Philippines.

The Washington Conference looked not only to the battleships and battle cruisers but, looking ahead, counted aircraft carriers as capital ships, and limited them too. It was a farsighted gesture because when the conference met there were only two aircraft carriers in the world, both British.

The failure of the Royal Navy's battle cruisers at Jutland in their assigned mission to locate and pin down the High Seas Fleet led the British to create a new vessel for that role, the aircraft carrier. Before the war ended an airplane—launched from the top of a British cruiser turret—had sunk a ship.

Even without a carrier the United States had built up a naval aviation arm. During the war USN pilots flew tens of thousands of antisubmarine missions. In Rear Admiral Bradley Fiske the navy boasted the inventor of the torpedo plane. It was also five navy flyers, under Lieutenant Commander Albert C. Read, who were the first to fly the Atlantic, in May 1919, with a refueling stop at the Azores.

The visionary William Sims was among the first men to grasp fully the implications of carrier warfare. Had it been in his power all battleship construction would have stopped in 1920. "The battleship is dead," he told a friend.

In the spring of 1922, shortly after the Washington Conference ended, the navy commissioned its first carrier. She was a converted collier, once named *Jupiter* but renamed the *Langley*. She was small and carried ten fragile aircraft. To navy pilots she was the most inspiring, most modern ship in the fleet, even though their only means of communicating with her was to reach down into a crate of homing pigeons, attach a message to a pigeon leg and toss the bird out.

The navy had never operated a ship like her. It was a nonaviator, Captain Chester W. Nimitz, who worked out a way of integrating the *Langley* into surface operations. For centuries warships had sailed in line formations. When steam came they steamed in line formations. When a battle fleet, composed of line after line of heavy warships, had to turn, it was a slow, complicated and dangerous business, with much frantic signaling up and down each line and across all the lines in the formation. And the *Langley* had to turn, to get the wind over her flight deck, every time she wanted to launch her planes.

Nimitz's solution was to put the *Langley* at the center of a circular formation, with her escorts arranged around her in concentric rings. Each time she turned all her escorts turned with her, and all the escorts could see what she was doing. That circular formation became the standard formation for naval task forces down to the present day, in all navies.

In 1927 the *Langley* was joined in the fleet by the carriers *Lexington* and *Saratoga*. These were powerful ships built on the unfinished hulls of two battle cruisers condemned to extinction by the Washington Conference. Each of these carriers displaced 33,000 tons, with 800 feet of flight deck. The United States was still well below its total carrier limit of 135,000 tons.

Naval doctrine continued to describe carriers as "the eyes of the fleet." Their planes were to locate the enemy. Then the battle line—consisting of battleships, with support from heavy cruisers—would close in and do the real fighting. Meanwhile carrier aircraft would patrol high above, providing aerial defense to the battle line as it fought for command of the sea.

Early one Sunday morning in February 1932, while Honolulu dozed and the Pacific Fleet battle line looked magnificent in the rising sun, fighters and bombers raced in from the sea to make a surprise attack on Pearl Harbor. It was only an exercise but the planes from the *Lexington* and *Saratoga* proved in an hour what naval pilots had claimed for a decade: to get full advantage from the carriers naval air power had to be freed from nursemaiding the battleships. After 1932 the strings were loosened, but not cut.

In 1933 the *Ranger* was commissioned. She was not a converted or modified anything but a carrier from inception. Even so, she was small, slow, lacked armor and displaced a mere 13,800 tons; a baby flattop. That same year, as part of the incoming Roosevelt administration's public works program, construction was started on two new carriers, the *Enterprise* and *Yorktown,* plus a score of destroyers and submarines. This was the first new warship construction for five years. Undertaken mainly to reduce unemployment, it nonetheless marked the beginning of American naval rearmament.

The Japanese and Germans were currently repudiating or making end runs around the limits agreed at Washington and elsewhere. Roosevelt asked Congress to build up to the limits. Another carrier was authorized, and seven new battleships were begun, in 1934. Battleship admirals, whom flyers called "the Gun Club," were not going to roll over and play dead.

THE MARINE battalion that landed at Guantánamo Bay, Cuba, in 1898 and wrested enough territory from the Spaniards to create a strong base was something new. For a century the Marine Corps had provided ships' landing parties, able to seize the customshouse of a small, hot country that would not pay its foreign debts. The battalion that made the landing at Guantánamo was something else again, a strong force of combined arms designed to seize and hold an advance base for the fleet.

Despite this success, McKinley suggested to Congress in 1899 that it might like to abolish the marines. Congress replied by doubling the size of the Corps, to 6,000 men. Theodore Roosevelt too would have gladly abolished the marines without trace, merging them forever into the army. This was one of the rare fights the ebullient Theodore lost.

In World War One the marines' strength reached 75,000 and brought them something they had never had before, establishments of their own. For nearly 150 years the Corps was a Man Who Came to Dinner kind of guest at navy yards: unwelcome but immovable. When the war ended, its strength fell to 20,000 but it had places to call "home," at Quantico, Parris Island and San Diego.

The marines were far behind the army and navy in developing professional schools. Shortly before the war they opened an Advance Base School at New London, Connecticut, to develop doctrine for amphibious warfare. Any hopes marine officers cherished that this would close the educational gap were shattered by service in the AEF, where Pershing ran more schools than divisions. They had nothing like it.

When John Archer Lejeune, veteran of Belleau Wood, became commandant in 1920 he created the modern Corps, and mainly through schooling. Lejeune revised marine education from boot camp upward. He personally picked out his best and brightest young officers and sent them on to the army and navy staff colleges. This had the effect of turning them into experts in combined arms. They emerged versed in marine doctrine, army doctrine and navy doctrine, familiar with the other services' planning techniques, weapons and officers. Viewed by the army and navy as fairly small-time operators, marine officers were often more sophisticated students of modern warfare than their counterparts in the other services.

Lejeune promoted another good idea, the Marine Corps Institute. This was a system of correspondence courses that offered a high school education not only to marines but to their dependents as well. A generation later the army, navy and air force would pay the MCI the flattery of outright emulation.

During Lejeune's ten years as commandant a shadow hung over the marines, the blood-bright memory of Gallipoli. That absorbing, horrifying chain of ifs seemed to discredit ambitious amphibious assaults, to rule them out of future wars as too complicated, too risky, too costly. The British and others virtually abolished their marine forces, reducing them to mere ships' landing parties once more. Only the USMC continued to train for amphibious assault on a hostile shore. They studied the Dardanelles campaign in every detail, dissecting it, teasing out every lesson it had to teach, until they knew it almost as if they had been there.

It was education with a purpose. What they wanted to know was not how to get ashore in Turkey in 1915 but how to get onto those Japanese-held islands in the Pacific; islands the Japanese were busily making fortresses while the United States, under the Washington Conference treaty, had forsworn fortifying its own island possessions, except Hawaii.

As early as 1921 some Marine Corps officers foretold a war with Japan that would open with a Japanese surprise attack. They had clear ideas about how the war would be fought and the weapons they would need, many of which still had to be invented. They would need an armored vehicle that was amphibious and able to cross coral reefs. There was nothing remotely like it in the early 1920s. They imagined landing craft and assault ships that carried landing craft. They did not exist either.

Among these farsighted officers the palm went to Lieutenant Colonel Earl Ellis. He foresaw a war in which American forces island-hopped across the Pacific, leading up to an invasion of Okinawa that was far bigger than the Gallipoli landings. In 1923 Ellis visited the Palau Islands, recently mandated to Japan by the League of Nations. He had taken a year's leave and traveled as a civilian. He arrived there alive, and left dead.

As they prepared for a violent future, the marines embraced innovation as the key to getting the most out of their small numbers. Sent to Nicaragua in 1928, when government collapsed in that turbulent land, they became enthusiasts for air power. They built eighteen airfields and used them for close air support, logistics support, medical evacuation and speedy communications.

This, however, simply represented a modernizing of the marines in their established role as "colonial infantry." What they really wanted did not come until 1933, when the Fleet Marine Force was created. This was the culmination of marine ambitions for a generation. They now had the doctrine, the training and much of the equipment to seize and hold territory on a hostile shore, backed up by naval and air support. The Fleet Marine Force was an integral part of the fleet as it too got ready for another war.

In 1938 one of the imagined instruments appeared, the amphibian tractor, shortened to amtrac. It was a lumbering swamp craft when it was first offered to them but they descried within it a chance to cross those coral reefs. Each year now Marine Corps planners worked on an annual problem, such as, The Japanese have taken Guam and fortified it. How do we get it back? Amtracs would help.

One thing they no longer had to worry about was hostility from above. They had a friend in the White House. During his time as assistant secretary of the navy, Franklin Roosevelt's responsibilities had included the marines. As president he took a strong, personal interest in the Corps. Roosevelt liked to open his conversations with the commandant by saying, "We marines. . . ."

WHILE the Meuse–Argonne offensive ground on, Billy Mitchell went to Pershing with a war winner—blitzkrieg. He wanted to turn 1st Division into 1st Parachute Division. Come the spring of 1919, he claimed, the AEF could drop 12,000 airborne troops deep in the German rear from heavy bombers. He described hundreds of fighters and light bombers flying in to provide the airborne with close air support, while German frontline defenses were being attacked by powerful tank formations also backed up by tactical air. He laid out for Pershing's inspection all the elements of blitzkrieg that the world would one day recognize, including dive-bombing that hammered enemy pillboxes and motorized infantry racing through breaches in the enemy's lines. Pershing enthusiastically endorsed these ideas as the basis for his spring offensive.

It was not to be. Mitchell returned home after the Armistice to become assistant chief of the Air Service, where he felt surrounded by unsympathetic superiors. The chief of the Air Service had never flown an airplane. Nor had anyone on the General Staff. The secretary of war had never gone up in an airplane, and showed no inclination to do so.

To his racing mind the air was the whole future of warfare. Combative, articulate, engaging and energetic, he made all discussion of air power turn on his ideas for the next generation, much as Mahan before him had dominated thinking about sea power.

Mitchell saw the airplane dominating war both on land and at sea. For much of the 1920s he fought within the army to make it air-minded, and against the same naval establishment that navy flyers cursed among themselves. To discover whether there just might be anything to claims made by Mitchell and its own pilots that ships were vulnerable to bombing, the navy set up a secret test.

In the fall of 1920, while the nation's attention was fixed on the presidential election, Captain Nimitz supervised attacks on the old battleship *Indiana.* Dummy bombs filled with water drenched her decks. Explosives set off below her to further research into torpedoes and bombs tore the veteran of the Spanish-American War apart. The navy at first denied the test had taken place. When that did not work it denied the test had any significance. Josephus Daniels loyally announced he would be happy to stand bareheaded on the deck of any ship that Billy Mitchell tried to bomb.

A few months later Daniels was out of office. His successor agreed to a joint bombing operation in which army and navy flyers would attack a variety of surrendered German warships, starting with a U-boat and working up to the 27,000-ton battleship *Ostfriesland.* All through July 1921 ships were bombed, studied and bombed again, until they went down.

The *Ostfriesland* was the navy's best hope. She had four skins, to protect her against mines and torpedoes, and was basically a strong steel box divided into one hundred watertight compartments. At Jutland she had shrugged off eighteen hits by heavy shells plus a mine explosion. Fully repaired, she was as buoyant and well armored as any ship afloat.

Mitchell's pilots had little trouble sinking her with two-thousand-pound bombs. The film of her destruction was cheered in movie theaters like another wartime victory, yet the demonstration was so unrealistic it proved nothing.

Two years later Mitchell and his bombers were set loose on two 1906 battlewagons, the *New Jersey* and the *Virginia.* Each sank like a stone.

In 1924 Mitchell got married. Combining air business with pleasure, he traveled to Japan and Hawaii on his honeymoon. On his return he offered a lengthy report on Hawaii's lack of air defenses and on the failure of army-navy cooperation there. He told a Senate committee, "I have never seen anything like it." The senior admiral and the senior general refused to attend the same social functions.

The main thrust of his report, however, was that Japan was becoming a major power in the air and a threat to the United States. He warned of a future war that would open with surprise attacks on Pearl Harbor and the Philippines. Both attacks, he prophesied, would succeed. The General Staff examined his report in detail, and rejected it in detail.

His outspokenness was becoming an embarrassment. In 1925 he was forced out as assistant chief of the Air Service by the secretaries of war and navy getting together in one of the few notable instances of interservice harmony the 1920s produced. He was banished to remote Fort Sam Houston; a brigadier general with a command that by rights belonged to a captain.

If this was intended to force Mitchell to leave the army, it failed, but from San Antonio a man would have to raise his voice very loud to be heard all the way back in Washington. The Mitchell problem appeared to be solved.

The navy was meanwhile experimenting with airships; "battleships of the skies," it called them, even though they were unarmed. The navy had only the vaguest ideas of what it would do with them, but they were a great hit with the public and that made them good publicity for the navy. In September 1926 it sent the giant dirigible *Shenandoah* on a tour of midwestern state fairs. This was the height of the thunderstorm season. Large gas-filled airships were not designed to ride out skies crackling with lightning and raging with high winds. The *Shenandoah* was ripped apart, killing her commander and half of her thirty-man crew.

Mitchell raised his voice loud enough to be heard around the world, damning the War and Navy departments alike for "incompetency, criminal negligence and almost treasonable administration of the national defense," of which the *Shenandoah* disaster was but the latest example. He was begging for a court-martial. For once, he got what he wished.

He was tried by a board of six generals, including his boyhood friend from Milwaukee, Douglas MacArthur. Had he been tried by public opinion and the press, Mitchell would have been acquitted, and he clearly expected to be vindicated despite the extremity of his language. He was tried under the Old Mother Hubbard article of war, Number 96—"conduct prejudicial to good order and discipline." His defense witnesses included Sims, who supported all of Mitchell's arguments for air power and endorsed his criticisms of naval conservatism. Nothing, though, could save Mitchell from being convicted. The furor he had made and the language he used *were* prejudicial to good order and discipline.

The court unanimously found him guilty. Attempts would later be made to suggest that MacArthur had tried to save his old friend but there is no evidence for this and MacArthur was always evasive about it. The sentence imposed was five years' suspension from duty, with the loss of all pay and privileges. Calvin Coolidge reduced this to two and a half years, but it made no difference. Mitchell resigned his commission. Behind him he left a body of true believers who guarded his teachings like a sacred charge. Mitchell departed, Mitchellism flourished.

Out of the army he was freer than ever to preach the doctrine of strategic bombing and make it his own. The true target of air power was the enemy's "vital centers." It was no use trying any longer to destroy his main army in the field. "Armies themselves can be disregarded. . . ." The proper objectives were industrial and communications centers. Mitchell himself did not work out a target list of vital centers. That remained for others to decide. The doctrine of strategic bombing nonetheless became something like a crusade at the Air Corps Tactical School at Maxwell Field, Alabama, in the 1930s where bright Air Corps officers were sent to think about the future of war in the air.

Mitchell's old mentor Hugh Trenchard did not seriously believe that bombing alone could defeat a major power. Nor did the Italian theorist of command of the air, Guilio Douhet. Instead, they saw air power as an indispensable component in the totality of military force. The essence of their argument was that only after command of the air had been won would ground and naval forces be free to make their own contribution to final victory. Mitchell's followers alone believed it possible to bomb a major foe into surrender.

Such views did not endear them to the rest of the army, which saw only one role for aviation—ground support. Throughout the 1930s the Air Corps, as it had become, fought furiously to avoid being tied to the infantry. All it cared about was bombing the enemy's homeland; that was all it cared about even when it had no modern bombers.

In 1934, however, Benjamin Foulois, the head of the Air Corps, convinced the General Staff that a four-engine bomber with a range of five thousand miles would make Alaska and Hawaii virtually invulnerable. Given such a bomber, the Air Corps would sink any invasion force while it was still far out to sea.

A competition was launched for such a bomber. The winner was an all-metal aircraft with armor plate and five gun emplacements, the B-17, although it never achieved the five-thousand-mile range. Its seeming invulnerability inspired its nickname, the Flying Fortress, but being so heavily armored and so filled with guns and ammunition it carried the bombload of a medium bomber. At the same time, it was fast—faster than pursuit aircraft of the mid-1930s. This created a belief among the theorists of the Air Corps that the bomber would always be able to outrun the fighter. As a result, no effort was made to develop long-range fighters to escort it.

The navy meanwhile was forced into the position of arguing that long-range bombers were no threat to warships. In 1937 a B-17 flying in foggy weather found the battleship *Utah* out in the Pacific and dropped practice bombs in its main deck. The navy classified the exercise "Secret." Next year three B-17s found and took photographs of an Italian liner, the *Rex,* 625 miles out from New York. This time the navy got the army chief of staff to issue a ruling that Air Corps operations could not extend more than one hundred miles from the coast.

By this time Foulois was about to retire, to be replaced by a man who had much of Mitchell's outlook and temperament, Henry H. "Hap" Arnold. The new Air Corps chief had learned to fly from the Wright brothers. Just missing action in World War One, he nonetheless made a reputation for himself as a Mitchell man—tempestuous, constantly in hot water, short-tempered, a perfectionist; above all, a believer in strategic bombing.

I N 1919 MacArthur returned from France to become superintendent of West Point. He had a mandate from March to reform the academy. During the war it had become little more than another officers' training school, graduating five classes in two years.

The root problem with West Point and Annapolis was the same. They did not provide a liberal education, nor did they provide a professional education. Officers ended up learning their profession by practicing it, while the best chance to acquire the intellectual and cultural background common to educated people had been wasted.

At thirty-nine MacArthur brought to the task the prestige of being the most decorated soldier of the AEF and the energy of youth. He placed his faith firmly on liberal education ahead of technical training. Many thousands of draftees, he recalled, had been brighter and more learned than their officers and NCOs. And civilian educational standards were shooting up as high school education spread out to reach millions each year. To lead conscript armies of the future a new officer corps would have to arise.

Some of the West Point faculty agreed with him. Most resisted, to little avail. Out went the traditional courses in geology and mineralogy; in came electricity, the internal combustion engine and aerodynamics. There was a new department, teaching government, economics and history. There were classes in psychology, to raise the standard of leadership. There was instruction in foreign affairs, to break down parochial mental walls. Entrance requirements were raised and instructors were forced to adopt the best teaching practices of the Ivy League colleges. MacArthur also instituted intramural athletics; something colleges across the country copied. When he left West Point in 1922 it was well on the way to becoming what he intended it to be.

The army's inevitable man almost from the day he was commissioned, MacArthur became chief of staff in 1930, at the age of fifty. The reforming impulse was as strong as ever. Since 1920 the army had been based on a structure of nine corps—existing mainly on paper—divided into three armies, also on paper. He pushed through a "Four Army Plan" that provided a more ambitious framework, one that anticipated a future wartime army bigger than the 4.2 million men of 1918.

In 1932 unemployed veterans descended on Washington to demand a bonus for their wartime service. Violence flared and the army quelled the trouble. MacArthur pressed on, exceeding his instructions, and destroyed the bonus marchers' camp.

These were hard times for the military, and public relations disasters such as this only made them tougher. When Roosevelt became president in 1933 he received, and seriously considered, a proposal to cut the army's already small budget by 51 percent.

In a stormy confrontation in the Oval Office MacArthur's emotions rose to a melodramatic pitch. "I spoke recklessly," he later admitted, "and said something to the general effect that when we lost the next war, and an American boy, lying in the mud with an enemy bayonet through his belly and an enemy foot on his dying throat, spat out his last curse, I wanted the name not to be MacArthur but Roosevelt."

Leaving the White House, he threw up on the steps, while Secretary of War George Dern rejoiced, "You've saved the army!"

These were tough times not only because of the Depression but because of a powerful resentment against World War One. American involvement seemed at first to have been a mistake, as the Europeans began repudiating their war debts and reviving old quarrels among themselves. By the early 1930s, however, American disappointment found a focus closer to home. In 1934 Congress held hearings under Senator Gerald Nye into the ties between the War and Navy departments and major arms producers such as Du Pont.

There was a heartfelt outcry against the "merchants of death." Arms makers were blamed for getting the war started, then for getting the United States into it. The Nye committee did not make such assertions explicitly, but it dwelt on the close relationships between munitions companies and the military in a way that suggested they were somehow sinister; a conspiracy against peace.

Against this background MacArthur found all his considerable energies being spent on fighting for money, and often losing. To take one example, the army's only armored unit was disbanded as an economy measure. Meanwhile, a breakthrough in tank design was sold to the Russians but ignored in the United States.

In 1935 MacArthur stepped down as chief of staff, but at fifty-five he was too young to retire. He set off for the Philippines, and the promise of promotion to field marshal in command of the Philippine army. The one officer he insisted on taking with him was a workaholic major who labored up to eighteen hours a day for the General Staff, Dwight D. Eisenhower.

When he failed to get to France in 1918 Eisenhower was convinced his career was as good as finished, just three years after graduating from West Point. Instead, it revived dramatically when he was sent to Panama in 1922 to become executive officer to Major General Fox Conner, former chief of operations of the AEF.

For three years Eisenhower had the benefit of an intensive tutorial from one of the most accomplished men in the army. Conner forced him to study past wars and think about the next one. He also told him to team up, if the chance ever came, with another young officer, George C. Marshall, who had served as chief of operations of First Army. "He," said Conner, "is a genius."

Through many long nights, surrounded by the screeching, chattering jungle, the aging general passed on the lessons of the western front to a blond, eager young man who had never been there; and always with one eye on the pupil, another on the war he never doubted was coming. In another twenty years, said Conner, it will start and we will get involved in it. Between now and then the army will go down and down. There will be times when you are tempted to get out. Don't do it. Your country will need you.

The army did go down and down. Eisenhower was tempted to get out. In 1935 he was offered fifteen thousand to twenty thousand dollars a year to become a military correspondent. He turned it down. Instead, and groaning at the diabolical tricks of fate, he went to Manila with MacArthur.

Marshall, whom he had met only twice (when both of them helped Pershing write his memoirs), was meanwhile nursing disappointments of his own. In 1935 he was still only a colonel, the rank he had held at the Armistice. It did not help that he was a graduate of Virginia Military Institute, and not West Point. Few VMI graduates even received commissions. Marshall got his chance because he graduated in 1900, just when the army was expanding to meet the demands of the Philippine Insurrection.

In 1906–08 he spent two happy years as an instructor with the Pennsylvania National Guard, discovering he had a vocation as a teacher. His record as a staff officer in World War One was outstanding, creating his reputation as a planning wizard. He once moved tens of thousands of troops through the rear of frontline divisions in action without creating chaos. And did it at night.

From 1927 to 1932 Marshall ran the Infantry School at Fort Benning, as head of its academic department; the teacher once more. His greatest service was his simplification of tactics, making them easier for the bright young officers who would be dragged from civilian life and forced to learn them in a hurry in the next war.

He challenged and stretched the young professionals who came to Fort Benning as never before in their lives. He would send entire classes out to solve difficult tactical problems equipped with foreign maps, or out-of-date maps, or road maps. When they got used to that, he took their maps away. All of which proved useful, one day, in North Africa or the Solomons.

Marshall pushed them to improvise solutions, whatever the doctrine said. Revealing something of the frustrated intellectual in his nature, he loved the unorthodox approach. Conventional wisdom taught nothing.

In 1933 he left the Infantry School to run the Civilian Conservation Corps camps in the Southeast. The CCC was the main job-creation program of Roosevelt's New Deal. Only the army had the manpower and the experience to handle the millions of young men who joined the CCC to plant trees, to cut fire roads, to build dams and streams, to live in the open air, to sit around campfires at night and feel they had a place in the world. Officers such as Marshall rose gladly to the challenge of the CCC. Here was an unlooked-for chance for regulars to do in peacetime what they would have to do in wartime—train, organize and motivate a mass of civilians. It was a dry run, made more challenging by the absence of army discipline or wartime solidarity.

One of the most striking features of the response to the Depression was the way people looked back to the war for models of national unity and cooperation in a time of crisis. It seemed only natural that the National Recovery Administration, the spearhead of Roosevelt's program, was entrusted to a general, Hugh Johnson. In its parades, its emblems and its oratory the NRA had a quasi-military character. And far from resenting programs like the CCC as an intrusion on their professional concerns, some army officers felt a patriotic duty to help overcome the Depression.

Even so, the army never forgot the main purpose for its existence. The National Guard was made a component of the army and some of the best army officers, such as Marshall, were assigned to Guard units. Marshall spent 1935–36 training the 33rd Division in Chicago; teaching again.

In 1936 he finally got his star. Two years later he became assistant chief of staff. By this time he had a champion more useful to him in the competition for promotion than his long-standing mentor Pershing. A close relationship grew up between him and a former New York social worker, a man in appallingly bad health, yet Roosevelt's closest adviser, Harry Hopkins. With Hopkins's help Marshall reached

the top, becoming chief of staff on September 1, 1939. That day
Conner's prophecy came true.

Even as Marshall was sworn in, German units were over the Polish
border. Tank columns drove east. Ahead of them Stuka dive bombers
blasted Polish positions. It was the way Mitchell had imagined it—
blitzkrieg.

D U R I N G the Munich crisis, a year before the war began, Roosevelt
had sent for Arnold. He told him he wanted to build 10,000 planes and
raise production capacity to 20,000 aircraft a year. What he did not
tell Arnold was that he expected most of the 10,000 planes would
probably go to Britain and France, to help them fight Hitler. And ever
the realist, Roosevelt did not ask Congress for all 10,000 planes at once.
He asked for 3,000 in 1939.

Production that year turned out to be only 2,200, and even when
the war began there were problems getting aircraft to the Allies. Under
the 1937 Neutrality Act sales of war equipment were strictly cash-and-
carry. The British paid for planes in advance, then they were parked
so they straddled the U.S.-Canadian border; after which the British had
to drag them across.

The drive to step up plane production had an invigorating effect
on the Air Corps. In the spring of 1939 Arnold gave the go-ahead to
a new fighter, the twin-engined P-38, and a new bomber, the B-24.
In the fall came approval of a gigantic, revolutionary aircraft, capable
of flying five thousand miles and carrying huge loads, the B-29.

Through the winter of 1939 orders from Britain and France
breathed life into scores of depressed steel and textile towns. The rust
belt suddenly belched fire. The British bought weapons that existed
and weapons that did not. When their Purchasing Commission asked
North American Aviation to build P-40 fighters for them, NAA's
president, James H. Kindleberger, offered something better, something
more likely to cope with the Messerschmitt 109. On a single sheet of
paper he sketched a new fighter. The plane that emerged fifteen months
later was the P-51, and when the British put their Rolls Royce Merlin
engine into it the Mustang *flew*.

While Americans were happy to help arm the British and French
there was as much reluctance to get into this war as the last one, a

reluctance that military officers shared. Just in case, however, they wanted both a belt and galluses—a strong army and a powerful navy.

Such sentiments had plenty of time to crystallize during the six months of phony war between the destruction of Poland (in which Hitler's Soviet partners joined) and the lightning offensives of 1940. The speed at which the Wehrmacht conquered half a dozen countries impressed and terrified. It was safe now for Roosevelt to ask Congress not for 10,000 planes but for 50,000 planes, and get approval for them all.

Congress at last took a serious interest in the state of the army. It was shocked to discover how bare the soldier's cupboard, or foot-locker, was: almost no tanks, nearly all the artillery consisting of World War One French 75s, old Springfield rifles instead of modern Garand semiautomatic M-1s, and so on. Congressmen gasped at what they found, like people who'd had nothing to do with it. The army was swiftly given $2.75 billion for equipment; more than twenty times the entire army budget of 1938. And this was simply a down payment. Military budgets would soon rise to several billion dollars a month.

The strength of the Regular Army was raised to 400,000, but this was clearly not going to be enough. If he started right now, Marshall testified, it would take him two years to raise and train an army the size of the AEF, and to do it would require conscription. In the fall of 1940 a draft law was passed, giving the War Department authority to call up 900,000 men. Meanwhile eighteen National Guard divisions were seeking recruits and unpacking trainloads of new equipment.

No one was better prepared than Marshall to turn millions of civilians into soldiers. It was a subject he had studied intensively for most of his life. He knew what they would respond to and what they would reject, what they could learn quickly and what would take time. Their welfare was never far from his mind. The United Services Organization came into existence as the result of a personal investigation made by the chief of staff, in mufti and unrecognized and alone, in southern towns swamped by the army camps springing up in 1940–41. Recreation facilities such as libraries and playing fields did not exist. All that was available were raddled whores and blind pigs: solace for some perhaps but not for most lonely young men far from home.

Marshall dropped the big square division, replacing it with the triangular division, roughly 15,000 strong, based on three regiments, each in turn being based on three battalions. From running the Infantry

School he knew where to look for his division commanders. Marshall was personally acquainted with hundreds of the most promising captains and majors in the army. Consulting a little black book that he had carefully kept long before he became chief of staff, he accelerated the careers of 150 of his former pupils until he had them right where he wanted them, with stars on their collars. He did the same with fifty of the instructors he had known at Fort Benning. He abolished promotion by seniority and weeded out hundreds of middle-aged colonels from the regulars and the National Guard; some of them were old friends. He brought Eisenhower in from the field to work in his office and promoted George Patton to command the army's first armored corps. The United States Army of World War Two was a George C. Marshall production.

He infused it with a strong spirit of the offensive. Like Black Jack, he believed only open, aggressive, mobile warfare suited the American character. The force he was building would reflect that or fail.

As 1940 drew to a close the British ran out of money and negotiable assets. Roosevelt had a Christmas present for them, Lend Lease. The United States would lend the British whatever arms they needed the way a neighbor would loan his hose to someone whose house was on fire, said Roosevelt. In his last fireside chat of the year he conjured up a vision of what the country must become in 1941, "the Arsenal of Democracy."

Month by month sentiment for entering the war was rising, but it was resisted fiercely every step of the way by isolationist and antiwar pressure groups. In June 1941 Hitler attacked Russia, lifting the threat of invasion of Britain, but U-boats once more raised the specter of starvation. The navy began to help the hard-pressed Royal Navy by hunting down U-boats. In September and October 1941 two destroyers were severely damaged by torpedoes and a third, the *Reuben James,* was sunk. More than one hundred American sailors died.

More than two years had passed since the war began, yet the United States had retained its neutrality while rearming on a historic scale. Between June 1940 and December 1941 military expenditures exceeded those of World War One. Metal was being pounded into weapons as though every day mattered, which it did. The Depression was over. The national defense program ended it, while the New Deal had failed to do much more than pass a limp hand over the gaunt visage of hunger.

Factories sprang up in record time. Raw materials funneled in at one end emerged hours later as a stream of tanks or guns or airplanes. Something like plane pandemonium had followed Roosevelt's call for 50,000 aircraft. North American Aviation and Douglas began putting up plants all over the country without contracts, betting Congress would pay for whatever they produced.

The Air Corps grew mightily. In 1939 it had trained 750 pilots. In 1941, enlisting the help of civilian flying schools, it trained 11,000. To some airmen the time was obviously right to create a separate air force. Since the mid-1930s the Air Corps had undeniably enjoyed a separate identity, and in July 1941 it received what amounted to Roosevelt and Marshall's sanction for strategic bombing if the United States entered the war. The twenty-year battle had been won.

The Air Corps did not have the staff resources, however, to run an independent air force of the size envisaged. All it possessed was pilots, planes and airfields. It was dependent on the rest of the army for logistical support and trained staff officers. It had to settle for becoming the Army Air Forces, a halfway house to independent living.

By the end of 1941 plane production had risen to 1,500 a month, but 70 percent of these were earmarked for Britain or the Soviet Union. Arnold had thousands of trainers and transports but only 1,100 combat aircraft, to his outspoken irritation. Yet the basis of the world's biggest aircraft industry was firmly in place, ready to turn out close to 50,000 planes in 1942.

For all the armed forces this was a fat year. The marines had two divisions in training by summer and by the end of the year Corps strength reached 70,000; almost equal to the peak in World War One. Camps were under construction to receive tens of thousands more in the coming year.

The navy had seven fast carriers in commission, with eleven more under construction. The new carriers were the Essex class, displacing 27,000 tons and carrying 96 aircraft. They would start entering the fleet in 1942. The navy already had 5,000 planes, with 10,000 more to come.

The second Battle of the Atlantic had seen the return of convoys, but now they needed air cover. German Kondor long-range light bombers were flying out to mid-Atlantic from airfields in western France. In 1941 they sank as much tonnage as the U-boats. A dozen baby flattops were begun.

Marshall had in some respects the toughest fight of all, even in the fat year. No one wanted to believe major ground forces would be needed. The navy said they were unnecessary, the British said they did not want them and the Lend Lease lobby said they were consuming resources better used elsewhere. All the country seemed to think mattered was planes and ships.

Even so, the draft law was renewed in October. By December 1941 the army had 1.6 million men, providing thirty-seven divisions in training, with dozens more planned for the year ahead. It was a long way from that September day when Marshall took over the nineteenth-ranked army in the world, behind those of Belgium and Greece.

Roosevelt had proven the Wilsonian theory wrong: it was possible to rearm and retain American neutrality. It was not the booming munitions plants, the busy shipyards and the lively army camps that broke the spell. It was the Japanese.

RELATIONS with Japan had turned sour in 1931 when Japan invaded Manchuria. They became bad in 1937 when Japanese armies moved into China proper, and turned dangerous in the spring of 1940 when Japan took advantage of France's defeat to move ground troops into northern Indochina. The bulk of the Pacific Fleet was shifted from San Diego to Pearl Harbor to signal American displeasure. A few months later Japan joined with Italy and Germany in the Tripartite Pact, making them military allies.

In January 1941 a letter from Navy Secretary Frank Knox to Secretary of War Henry Stimson advised that naval planning officers studying the worsening political situation had concluded, "If war eventuates with Japan, it is believed easily possible that hostilities would be initiated by a surprise attack upon the Fleet or the Naval Base at Pearl Harbor." Surprise attack was the traditional Japanese method of going to war.

By April 1941 army, navy and Air Corps officers, working separately, had anticipated the major elements of any attempt to knock out the Pacific Fleet: it would come on a Sunday morning, the attack would be launched from a position north of Hawaii, it would involve six carriers and up to 400 planes. The chances of such an attack succeeding were considered good.

Placing most of the Pacific Fleet at Pearl was intended to deter the Japanese from further aggressive moves. Stimson argued against it. The only country that was being deterred by this move was the United States, which was deterred from acting more boldly in the Atlantic.

In July 1941 the Japanese got their German ally to lean on the Vichy government of France and open up air and naval bases in Indochina to Japanese aircraft and ships. The United States had already curbed exports of metal to Japan. Roosevelt now cut off all exports of petroleum, including crude oil.* Sanctions were the only effective weapon against Japanese expansionism, so it was thought. They certainly worried the Japanese military. Within two years the Imperial Japanese Navy would be immobilized for want of fuel oil. Even before then, entire industries would be crippled, leaving the army and navy desperately short of vital equipment.

Roosevelt was not trying to provoke the Japanese into war. On the contrary, he was trying to avoid a war in the Pacific in order to concentrate American military strength on the eastern seaboard. As tension grew in the Atlantic that summer, Pacific Fleet units were brought east, through the Panama Canal. Roosevelt was interested in fighting fascism, not the Japanese, who represented a much less serious threat to American security.

He guessed wrong in thinking that sanctions might make the Japanese back down. What they did was shift decisively the balance in a fierce debate within the Japanese military. The army was heavily committed in China and Manchuria, but the Japanese navy was in the best position it could ever hope for to launch an offensive against the Pacific Fleet. In the summer of 1941 it had six small carriers, four fleet carriers, 1,400 combat aircraft and 2,500 pilots, most of them with more than five years' flying experience.

Traditionally Japanese naval strategy had been defensive, looking for victory in a great, all-out battle fought in home waters, much as they had annihilated the Russian fleet at the Battle of Tsushima. In August 1939, Admiral Isoroku Yamamoto became commander of the Combined Fleet, the IJN's largest force of warships and aircraft. Within weeks he rejected this strategy. It was irrelevant to Japan's need to thrust south, to seize the oil and metals, the rice and rubber, of Southeast Asia.

Economic and political realities dictated an offensive strategy, but

---

*The British and Dutch, at American urging, also imposed an oil boycott, thereby making the cutoff of supplies to Japan virtually total.

they called for a man with the daring to pull it off. That man was Yamamoto. He used his enormous prestige to face down the Navy General Staff, who considered what he was proposing almost suicidal—a surprise attack on Pearl Harbor. His intention was to put the Pacific Fleet out of action for a year: one year in which to seize the riches of Southeast Asia and turn them into military might. By the end of that year Japan would be so strong the Americans would prefer to negotiate rather than cross the Pacific to fight her.

Detailed planning of the Pearl Harbor attack was entrusted to Commander Minoru Genda, a Japanese Billy Mitchell, in love with air power and contemptuous of battleships. The biggest technical problem he faced was to perfect a torpedo that would straighten up and run true in less than forty feet of water. A torpedo dropped from a plane would plunge as much as seventy feet deep before straightening up. Driven on by Genda, the Japanese solved the problem by putting small wooden fins on their torpedoes. They straightened up at about thirty-five feet underwater. At Pearl Harbor the main shipping channel was only forty feet deep, so there were no antitorpedo nets across it.

By November 1941 the War Department, the Navy Department, the State Department and the White House were convinced the Japanese were about to attack, somewhere; probably the Philippines. On November 27 a message sent to all Pacific commands warned that war might break out at any moment.

The Pacific Fleet commander, Admiral Husband E. Kimmel, and the army commander on Hawaii, Lieutenant General Walter Short, reacted accordingly. Short gathered all his planes together, so it would be easier to protect them from sabotage. This also made it easier to bomb and strafe them, while making it impossible to get them airborne in a hurry.

Kimmel blundered more luckily. He failed to do what he ought to have done, namely, to mount long-range air patrols, which were a naval responsibility after the army was forced to stop sending its planes more than one hundred miles out over the sea. At the same time, and without meaning to, he frustrated the Genda-Yamamoto plan. He sent the carrier *Lexington* to Midway with marine fighters to strengthen its defenses, and the carrier *Enterprise* went to Wake on a similar errand. His third carrier, the *Saratoga,* was back in San Diego. His fourth carrier, the *Wasp,* had been transferred to the Atlantic. The prime objective of the Pearl Harbor attack was American carriers; the more the better.*

Had Kimmel mounted long-range air patrols he would have known on December 5 or 6 that a Japanese naval force was about to make a surprise attack. It is almost certain he would have taken his fleet to sea and called *Lexington* and *Enterprise* to head toward him at top speed. The Japanese fleet he clashed with would have had an advantage in speed and a strong superiority in planes, both in numbers and performance. Kimmel was doomed to spend the remainder of his long life in regret and remorse, but he may have been a lucky man.

The reason for the confident prediction that war was about to begin was that American cryptanalysts had been reading the main Japanese diplomatic code, named Purple, for more than a year. The window it opened on Japanese intentions was small and opaque, because the most important decisions were being made by the army and navy, and military codes had not yet been broken. On December 6, however, the last big piece in the puzzle, the piece that said the opening attack would come at Pearl Harbor, was in the code breakers' hands. Owing to the backlog of business it was not translated until December 8. That delay also helped save the Pacific Fleet from annihilation in deep water.

At seven fifty-five on Sunday morning, December 7, the first wave streaked in from the north, 189 fighters and bombers, to strafe, to bomb, to drop torpedoes that straightened up with one foot to spare and slammed into battleships lined up in a double row. Twenty minutes after the first wave departed, the second flashed in over the palm trees; another 170 planes. Soon there were no assigned targets undamaged.

In those closing minutes IJN pilots circled, looking for targets of opportunity. They missed the fattest of all, the oil tanks. They expended their remaining ordnance on mess halls and hangars. Lady Luck had kept company with the Japanese right up to seven fifty-five. Once the first torpedo splashed into the water, success ended. The primary objective, the carriers, were missing. Yamamoto would never have mounted such an attack to sink battleships.

*Most of the navy was in the Atlantic, including the majority of the carriers: *Hornet, Wasp, Yorktown, Long Island* and *Ranger*.

The Japanese plan looked comprehensive: six carriers, total surprise, air superiority, all types of bombing—torpedo, dive and high level. Even so, it contained a major flaw. Yamamoto and Genda had left something out; an ironic omission considering that fears over oil had brought the Japanese navy to the brink of war. They gave no thought to the tank farms that ringed Pearl Harbor.

Like the IJN, the Pacific Fleet ran on oil, yet every drop of the stuff had to be brought from the mainland. On Oahu huge tanks containing 4.5 million barrels of oil rose high in the air. Hundreds of miles of pipe, operated by thousands of easily ruptured valves, stood in the open, above ground. Setting the tanks ablaze and bombing the pipelines would have forced the Pacific Fleet to withdraw to the West Coast, and held it there for up to a year. With oil tankers burning daily in the Atlantic there were none to spare anywhere.

Eight battlewagons were sunk or damaged, as were three light cruisers and three destroyers. Aircraft losses—most of them suffered on the ground—were 69 fighters and 85 bombers wrecked and more than 100 damaged. The wrecks were mostly obsolescent types; and 80 percent of the planes damaged, like 80 percent of the ships, could be repaired. Among the wreckage and devastation 2,400 people were dead.

To the north, Genda argued that the task force must stay in the area for several days, to hunt down the carriers. Nearly all of the pilots agreed with him. The task force, however, had been entrusted to one of the admirals who had opposed the operation from the start. It was enough to him to have struck such a blow and lost only 29 aircraft. Besides, he was a battleship admiral and there was one thing all battleship admirals knew: a fleet that had lost its battleships could not fight.

The attack on Pearl Harbor was daring, skillful, courageous. It was also a failure. It did not win the Japanese a free hand for one year. It did not wreck the fast carriers of the Pacific Fleet. All it had achieved was to get the United States into the war; and far from being willing to negotiate a peace with Japan, millions of Americans felt mad enough to swim the Pacific if they had to and kill Japanese with their bare hands.

14

THE
BEST-LAID
PLANS

THE Imperial Japanese Army already had its hands full. Numbering five million men, soon to rise to seven million, up to 80 percent of its manpower was tied down fighting in China, occupying Korea, Manchuria and Formosa, standing ready to seize Soviet territory if the opportunity appeared, and defending Japan. Only one fifth of the Japanese army could be spared for the southern operation. Even after the army increased considerably in size, the bulk of its troops would remain committed far from the main scenes of combat.

Restrained by this manpower shoestring, the Japanese army went south nonetheless fired with an invaluable self-confidence and a boldness that matched the navy's coup at Pearl Harbor. To secure its lines of communication between Japan and Southeast Asia it would have to take the Philippines.

Back in 1935 Congress had promised the islands full independence in 1946. Until then the United States would be responsible for their defense. Few people in Manila or Washington seriously believed the islands could be made secure against Japan, but one of the few was MacArthur. Even after President Manuel Quezon publicly ridiculed his plan to turn the archipelago into a Far Eastern Switzerland, MacArthur pressed on in a blaze of optimism. As tensions rose between the United States and Japan in the fall of 1941, he repeatedly assured the War Department that there would be no Japanese attack before the spring of 1942. By then, he insisted, the Philippines would be impregnable.

His plan to crush the Japanese army on the beaches, wherever and whenever it landed, left the islands, for all practical purposes, defenseless. The invader could strike at thousands of miles of coastline and hundreds of beaches. On hand to defend them were 13,000 American soldiers, 7,000 airmen, and 115,000 Filipinos. MacArthur had exaggerated expectations for what his poorly led, poorly trained, lightly armed Filipino units could do and shared the widespread illusion that the B-17 would sink the Japanese navy.

American naval forces consisted of three cruisers, some aging destroyers and a collection of wheezing gunboats given the impressive title of U.S. Asiatic Fleet. Its commander, Rear Admiral Thomas C. Hart, detested MacArthur, and the feeling was mutual. They made army-navy relations in Hawaii look like a model of brotherly cooperation. Relations were bad also between MacArthur's staff and his air commander, Major General Lewis Brereton.

Word of the attack on Pearl Harbor reached Manila at 0230 local time on December 8. A Japanese air attack launched from airfields on Formosa, four hundred miles to the north, could be expected at daybreak or shortly after. Fog over Formosa held up the attack, giving Brereton time to organize a preemptive strike with the thirty-four B-17s based at Clark Field. Whether they could have achieved anything without fighter cover and without reconnaissance is doubtful, but in the confusion that prevailed in MacArthur's command an attack was not even launched. Nor were the aircraft flown to safety. They were left where they were. When the Japanese struck at 1215 they found Brereton's seventy P-40 fighters on the ground, instead of aloft, along with the B-17s: ripe for destruction.

The thinly spread Japanese ground and naval forces were in no position to make a swift, overwhelming descent on the Philippines, but with air superiority secured they could afford to take their time. Meanwhile Guam fell, on December 10. On Wake the Japanese ran into a minor epic of resistance. The island was defended by a marine defense battalion and a dozen marine pilots. They sank four Japanese cruisers and destroyers, damaged eight more, shot down twenty-one aircraft and inflicted up to 1,000 casualties on the Japanese in the fifteen days it took them to secure the island despite vastly superior numbers and firepower. Marine casualties totaled 81.

The blow MacArthur was waiting for fell on December 22, right where he expected it to fall: on the beaches of Lingayen Gulf, one hundred miles north of Manila.* The Japanese Fourteenth Army under Lieutenant General Masaharu Homma came ashore 45,000 strong. Two days later a second force, in division strength, landed south of Manila, at Lamon Bay. Homma's intention was to fight MacArthur on the open ground of central Luzon and catch him in a huge pincers movement. MacArthur frustrated him by abandoning Manila and pulling back into the Bataan Peninsula.

The withdrawal, conducted by Major General Jonathan Wainwright, was one of the finest delaying actions of the war. Wainwright fell back on five prepared lines of resistance, at each one halting long enough to force the Japanese to deploy for a major attack. Just before the blow landed Wainwright pulled out. All of which bought priceless time for strengthening the defenses of Bataan.

Unfortunately Quezon interfered with efforts to build up food stocks by refusing to allow the army to buy large amounts of food or to ship the small amounts they did buy to Bataan. Neutralist before the invasion, he became defeatist once it was under way. The supply effort was so mismanaged that ten million rounds of ammunition sat in warehouses at Cebu waiting for someone on MacArthur's staff to sign the authorization to move it to Bataan. No one did.

Civilian refugees flooded into the peninsula along with the troops. By mid-January MacArthur's men, sharing the food supply, were on half rations. By mid-February they were on quarter rations, and by March they were down to less than one thousand calories a day. Sharp as the pangs of hunger were, sharper still was the feeling of abandonment. "We are the battling bastards of Bataan," they sang. "No mama, no papa, no Uncle Sam."

The truth was Marshall and Eisenhower were doing all they could to get aid to them. Militarily the Philippines were a lost cause, but American political prestige made it unthinkable to write them off. The effort had to be made to sustain MacArthur even if it proved hopeless. Eisenhower had a fund of ten million dollars in gold and cash to hire what Marshall called "pirates" who would try running the Japanese blockade. In the whole of brawny, swashbuckling Australia there were only six ships with crews willing to risk a highly unpleasant fate at

*Small-scale landings to secure air strips began as early as December 10.

Japanese hands. Three ships turned back far short of their goal, and of the three that got through none would attempt it again.

Eisenhower's hard labor in this discouraging enterprise was the foundation stone of Marshall's lasting trust in him. And while he was spending sixteen hours a day in the hunt for spare parts, risk-running merchant crews and spare ammunition stocks, bases were being developed in Australia from which the long haul back might one day be launched.

MacArthur directed the battle on Bataan from Corregidor, "the Rock," a tadpole-shaped island two and a half miles long in Manila Bay. Deep beneath the Rock's Malinta Hill was Malinta Tunnel: 1,400 feet long, 30 feet wide, with two dozen 400-foot laterals pierced along it. The tunnel housed 11,000 people in comparative comfort and safety; many of them Filipinos, including Quezon. It was in these desperate circumstances that Quezon made MacArthur a rich man, giving him a present of $500,000 (in 1989 values, at least three million dollars). It was not exactly war as taught at West Point. Two years earlier Quezon had tried to give Eisenhower $60,000 for his services to the Philippines. Eisenhower had firmly and politely turned it down.

On February 22, with time clearly running out fast, Roosevelt ordered MacArthur to leave. He had planned to stay to the end, to die in the tunnel with his wife and young son when the Japanese broke in. MacArthur's staff persuaded him to go by arguing that he could do more harm to the enemy alive than he would ever do dead. MacArthur escaped with his family, running the blockade at night in a torpedo boat.

He left his command to Wainwright, who was in an impossible position. A statement from Roosevelt that American forces would remain in the Philippines and fight to the end seemed to rule out surrender, even though the troops on Bataan were so starved they could hardly stand up. The senior officer still on the peninsula resolved the problem. He surrendered, and told Wainwright afterward; an action the president swiftly endorsed.

With Bataan gone, Corregidor could not hold out long. On May 6 the Japanese invaded. Wainwright promptly ran up a white flag.

WITH WHAT amounted to small, improvised ground forces the Imperial Japanese Army reached all its planned objectives in the southern operation. Malaya was conquered not with firepower but with the folding bicycle, providing mobility on the few roads and putting the Japanese into the fortress of Singapore by the undefended back door. Thailand and Burma fell virtually without a fight. The French offered no resistance in Indochina.

After Pearl Harbor, Japanese carriers swept through the southwestern Pacific and into the Indian Ocean like a typhoon, sinking Allied ships all the way to Ceylon. The main prize was not shipping, though, but oil. While the Japanese navy closed in on Java, Chuichi Nagumo's carrier planes bombed Port Darwin, the largest town in northern Australia, to neutralize Allied air and naval power there.

There seemed almost nothing the Japanese could not take if they simply reached out for it. Forgetting earlier planning to carve out a defense perimeter that Japan might just be able to hold with its limited resources, the army and navy pushed farther south and east. The Japanese would later call this euphoric recklessness "victory disease."

For Nimitz, taking over from Kimmel after the Pearl Harbor debacle, Japanese overextension offered opportunities not to be missed. The IJN had an advantage over the Pacific Fleet of roughly two to one in most categories of combat ships. Nimitz's sole advantage was in signals intelligence. By April 1942 his cryptanalysts could read up to one third of any message transmitted in the Japanese naval code, JN 25. Combined with decrypts from Purple and careful monitoring of the volume of radio traffic between one Japanese base and another, this opened a window, if a sometimes smudgy one, on Japanese intentions.

In the grip of victory disease Japanese forces abandoned the principle of advancing only under the cover of land-based air power. In May 1942 they launched an ambitious two-pronged assault against objectives nearly six hundred miles apart—Port Moresby, on the southern coast of New Guinea, and Tulagi, in the southern Solomons. Nimitz sent two carrier task forces, those of the *Lexington* and *Yorktown,* into the Coral Sea to mount a spoiling operation.

Tulagi fell to the Japanese, but on May 7 American carrier planes struck the IJN's Fourth Fleet as it tried to secure the sea-lanes for the invasion force heading toward Port Moresby. A small Japanese carrier was sunk. In turn, the Japanese found the American carriers. The *Lexington* was sunk. The *Yorktown* and two Japanese fast carriers were seriously damaged. The Japanese admiral withdrew, refusing to chal-

lenge Allied land-based air power after losing the use of his two biggest
carriers.

The next major clash would come at Midway, where Yamamoto
sought to do what the Pearl Harbor strike had failed to achieve—gut
the Pacific Fleet's carrier force. His intention was to seize Midway,
some eleven hundred miles north by northwest of Hawaii, with a force
of 5,000 Japanese marines and a four-carrier task force commanded by
Nagumo. The main body, consisting of four more carriers and a
powerful battle line, would be held back, waiting for the Pacific Fleet
to come steaming up from Hawaii at flank speed to try retaking the
island. At which point they would be ambushed, caught between
Nagumo's strike force and Yamamoto's main body.

The Japanese naval staff had a plan of its own, for capturing the
Aleutians. As this offered a role for the army, the army supported the
naval staff. Unable to agree on one plan, the two were stitched together. What had begun as the concentration of Japanese naval power
on a single goal was turned into a complicated, multifaceted dispersion
of forces over a vast area in pursuit of conflicting objectives.

As the Midway-Aleutians operation developed, the code breakers
were piecing parts of it together like a gigantic intellectual jigsaw
puzzle that consisted largely of blank spaces.

Building up a file of partial decrypts and carefully monitoring the
volume of radio traffic passing between enemy ships, planes and shore
bases, code breakers were able to establish the broad outlines, and some
of the details, of many operations still in the planning stage.

Only six months after Pearl Harbor, though, it took a brave man
to bet everything on incomplete code-breaking and intelligence guesswork. It was possible—and Admiral Ernest J. King's staff thought
likely—that the Midway-Aleutians operation was a ruse, intended to
make the Pacific Fleet head north at flank speed. The Japanese navy
would then attack Pearl Harbor all over again but this time land an
invasion force to capture the islands.

Nimitz gambled that the code breakers were right and the doubters
wrong. He would send everything he could scrape up to Midway.

When the *Yorktown* limped into Pearl he went to take a look at
her. The damage reports said it would take up to three months to repair
her, but he needed a minimum of three carriers if he was going to fight
at Midway. Sloshing around in her bowels in a pair of hip boots, he
cast his marine engineering expert's eye over the shattered bulkheads

and popped seams. Three days, he said. That was all it would take to get her patched up and watertight. The *Yorktown* did not have to be perfect to fight.

With the *Yorktown,* the *Enterprise* and the *Hornet* ready for action there was a chance of upsetting Yamamoto's Midway plan. There was a better chance of the opposite, of the IJN gutting the Pacific Fleet.

Shortly after dawn on June 4 Nagumo's carrier planes struck Midway, setting fires and sweeping aside air opposition but doing comparatively little damage. The leader of the attacking aircraft signaled back to the strike force that a second attack would be needed before the landing force hit the beach.

Up to this point Nagumo had made only perfunctory searches for American ships, confident that American carriers were far away and would not appear for several days yet, ready to be bushwhacked. With Genda concurring on the need for a second strike to soften up Midway, he began arming his remaining available planes with antipersonnel and fragmentation bombs. When this was about half completed came a sighting of American carriers. The armament would have to be changed, to torpedoes and armor-piercing bombs. There were fuel lines and bombs all over his carrier decks. He was just where Raymond Spruance wanted him to be.

Spruance was a battleship admiral, a leading light in the Gun Club, but given command of the *Enterprise* and *Hornet* days earlier when William F. Halsey, one of the navy's leading carrier admirals, fell ill. He approached the battle sure that Nagumo would launch two attacks, not one, against Midway. If he could find the Japanese before they found him, and if the *Enterprise* and *Hornet* launched their planes at 0700 instead of at 0900 as planned, they might just catch Nagumo preparing his second strike, with fuel lines and bombs all over his decks. It would be an attack at maximum range for most of Spruance's planes, and beyond range for his Devastator dive bombers to get there and back. The Japanese were found first. At 0700 Spruance launched deckload strikes from his two carriers: 68 dive bombers, 30 torpedo planes, 20 fighters. Ninety minutes later *Yorktown,* coming up from the south in support, launched half of her planes.

Nagumo's four carriers shattered an air strike launched from Midway. They smashed torpedo attacks made by pilots from all three American carriers. All the while, Japanese planes were being rearmed and fueled. Nagumo began turning his carriers into the wind. He was

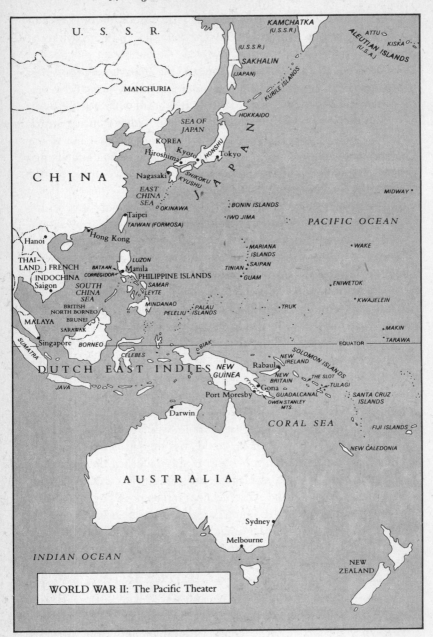

WORLD WAR II: The Pacific Theater

ready to launch. As his ships turned, dive bombers from the *Yorktown* and the *Enterprise* appeared high overhead.

The dive bomber squadrons arrived without seeing one another and at almost exactly the same moment. Had they practiced it for a year they could not have expected such perfection in combat. The Japanese had known they were on their way, from outlying destroyers. They had chosen to pull all of the high-level fighters on combat air patrol down to deck level to attack the torpedo planes.

Able to concentrate on the task in hand, the dive bombers whistled down, taking aim on the huge red circle—"the meatball"—on the yellow decks below. Within five minutes three of Nagumo's four carriers were blazing like bonfires as ruptured fuel lines ignited.

At noon planes from Nagumo's fourth carrier, *Hiryu,* found and crippled the *Yorktown.* Spruance scraped together a force of 24 dive bombers and torpedo planes and sent them off without fighter escort to look for *Hiryu.* They found her as her crew was having dinner and left her sinking. The *Yorktown* could not be salvaged and was eventually sent to the bottom by an American submarine. She seemed a small price to pay for this day's work.

Many Japanese officers wondered how the ambushers could have been ambushed, unless the Americans were reading Japanese codes. From a captured navy ensign who was interrogated and drowned after he had cooperated the IJN had a strong clue that such was indeed the case. Even so, it retained JN 25 to the end of the war. As a result Nimitz was able to set up yet another ambush, in April 1943, to kill Yamamoto on a flight over the South Pacific.

DEFEAT AT Midway ruled out a second seaborne assault on Port Moresby. The Japanese army made its landing at undefended Gona and Buna on the north coast of the Papuan peninsula, which juts from the mass of New Guinea like a tail. The Japanese army intended to march over the Owen Stanley Range by way of the Kokoda Trail and capture Port Moresby from the landward side, much as it had taken Singapore.

The trail was the width of a man's shoulders, and 120 miles long. In a score of places it consisted of swaying rope bridges strung over vertiginous gorges. In other places it rose thirteen thousand feet into mountains that were lost in clouds yet choked with dense, pestilential jungle.

By mid-September the Japanese were only twenty miles from Port Moresby, but they ran out of food. The ramshackle supply system of the IJA had no answer to the Kokoda Trail. Counterattacked by Australian troops, the Japanese retreated into the mountains. MacArthur went after them.

By air-dropping supplies even though up to half were sure to be devoured by the jungle, he got his combined American-Australian army over the Owen Stanleys in force. Closing in on Gona and Buna, his men were too starving and exhausted to do anything but besiege them. The defending Japanese were even hungrier and more demoralized: the living were eating the dead. Suffering losses of 30 percent (11,600 killed and wounded out of a force of 33,000), MacArthur wiped out the Japanese army on the Papuan peninsula.

The Japanese were meanwhile coming under intense pressure in the southeastern Solomons. After taking Tulagi they had swiftly turned it into a seaplane base but it was July before they began construction of an airstrip on the island of Guadalcanal, some fifteen miles away. The Japanese already had the biggest air base in the South Pacific, at Rabaul, 350 miles to the northwest. With a second such base, at the other end of the Solomons, they would have overwhelming air superiority in these waters. That was not something the navy could live with if it intended to operate in the South Pacific.

Admiral Ernest J. King, who was both chief of naval operations and commander in chief, U.S. Fleet, proposed to deny the Japanese use of the airstrip on Guadalcanal. Arnold and much of the army were completely opposed to the project, convinced the navy and marines lacked the muscle to pull it off. They would soon be sending for the AAF and the army to bail them out. Marshall, however, backed King, because there happened to be an instrument ready-made to thwart the Japanese—the 1st Marine Division.

It was already at sea and heading for New Caledonia. The navy was eager to get it into action soon if only to stop MacArthur getting his hands on it for his own pet project, an assault on Rabaul.

On August 7, just one week before the airstrip was expected to become operational, marine paratroops and raiders assaulted Tulagi at dawn. Two hours later 15,000 marines landed on Guadalcanal, five miles west of the airstrip, avoiding opposition.

Here was the first major American landing of the war. It did not represent any great advance on Gallipoli. The 1st Marine Division, reinforced with a regiment from 2nd Marine Division, came ashore in flimsy plywood craft that were towed by deafening speedboats spewing sparks and smoke.

Unloading supplies on the narrow, shallow beach was chaotic, hampered by a shortage of hands while marines amused themselves by shooting down coconuts or going swimming. Of the Japanese there was nary a sign. Within twenty-four hours the unfinished airstrip was in American hands but the beach was so clogged with supplies that unloading had to stop.

Three carriers, under Rear Admiral Frank Jack Fletcher, provided air cover for the beachhead. The marines hoped the carriers might stick around while a naval construction battalion (the SeaBees) finished the airstrip. On the evening of August 8 Fletcher pulled out without warning or permission. In his haste he did not bother to inform the commander of the fleet of transports and supply ships, Rear Admiral Richmond Kelly Turner.

During the early hours of August 9 a Japanese force of cruisers and destroyers came down New Georgia Sound and destroyed the force of American and Australian warships covering the northern approaches to the beachhead. Off Savo Island, the blackened cone of a burned-out volcano, three American heavy cruisers and an Australian cruiser went down. Damage to the Japanese was trifling. More than one thousand American seamen perished. The Battle of Savo Island was the worst defeat at sea in U.S. naval history.

Over the weeks and months that followed, so many ships were sunk (48 in all, split evenly between the U.S. Navy and the Japanese) that the waters off Guadalcanal became known as Ironbottom Sound. The Japanese had a superiority in night fighting that was the fruit of a decade of practice and thought.

In their torpedoes they had developed the ideal weapon for close-in night fighting at sea. A Japanese torpedo was bigger, faster and had more than twice the range of its American equivalent, yet it carried a heavier warhead. Instead of using searchlights to find enemy ships they relied on floatplanes that dropped flares. Night vision among Japanese lookouts was so sharp they could sometimes spot an American ship before its radar could pick up their vessel. They also had the aid of 16-power binoculars. Taking the gun flashes of enemy warships as the aiming point for their torpedoes, Japanese sailors were masters of the night.

As the sun went down on June 4 at Midway, Spruance had prudently retired to the east, while the Japanese tried to find him, hoping to redress in darkness what had been lost by day. Savo Island vindicated Spruance's caution when night fell at Midway.

Turner courageously continued unloading until noon on August 9 before he pulled out. Even so, he took 75 percent of the marines' supplies with him. The SeaBees finished the airstrip by using captured Japanese equipment. Marines meanwhile enjoyed a taste of the Orient, living on abandoned soya sauce, canned crab meat, hard candy, seaweed, sake, Kirin beer and pungent cigarettes.

On August 19 the first marine pilots landed at the airstrip, named Henderson Field in honor of a marine flyer killed at Midway. It was an unprepossessing 2,500-foot dirt strip covered with an Arnold innovation, metal matting, but so long as the marines held it they could hold Guadalcanal.

Most nights Japanese destroyers would rush down New Georgia Sound—nicknamed The Slot—unload men and supplies, bombard Henderson for an hour or two, then hightail it north before dawn and marine aviation found them. The Japanese stood little chance of driving the marines out but pride made it unthinkable to give up. Once ashore American forces could not let go either. When exhaustion and disease threatened to destroy the beachhead, Roosevelt ordered the Joint Chiefs of Staff not to pull out and had Marshall send two army divisions to relieve the hard-pressed marines.

The navy commander in the South Pacific, Vice Admiral Robert Ghormley, was convinced the whole operation was doomed to fail. Nimitz, overcoming a profound distaste for intervening while a battle was on, replaced him, sending for Halsey, recently returned to duty after his illness. Halsey's pugnacity was not an unmixed blessing. On this occasion it soon brought a fight—the two-day Battle of the Santa Cruz Islands, October 26–27—but he was outnumbered in carriers by four to two and the Japanese found him before he found them. He lost the *Hornet* and nearly lost the *Enterprise*.

The one bright spot in this affray was the performance of the new fast battleship (fast enough, that is, to keep up with a fast carrier making thirty knots) *South Dakota*. She shot down 26 Japanese aircraft. The battleship had found a new role, protecting the thin-skinned carriers.

All that fall American and Japanese strength on Guadalcanal was rising, to reach 30,000 on each side. The marines and soldiers had the benefit of defending on interior lines while the Japanese had to attack through thick jungle, with little air and feeble artillery support.

Despite costly failures they refused to quit; not while they owned the sea at night. The navy took it away from them. During a night action on November 12–13 the heavy cruiser *San Francisco* slugged it out with the battleship *Hiei* at three thousand yards. Both ships were wrecked but not sunk. Two American light cruisers and four destroyers went down. At daybreak marine torpedo planes sank the *Hiei*. Later that same day other planes from Henderson shattered her cruiser and destroyer escorts and sank seven of eleven transports loaded with an invasion force of 10,000 Japanese soldiers. The survivors who stumbled ashore were in no shape to fight. The next night the *South Dakota* and her sister ship, the *Washington,* sank the battleship *Kirishima.*

The Japanese began to think the unthinkable. It was now a matter of time before they pulled out from Guadalcanal, when nights were long and the moon was down.

FOLLOWING Pearl Harbor and the German declaration of war on the United States three days later, Churchill wasted no time in heading for Washington with his military advisers. For nearly a month the president and the prime minister discussed ways of defeating the Axis. Their conference's optimistic tenor was expressed in its code name, Arcadia.

To talk with their allies on an equal footing, Marshall and King formed the Joint Chiefs of Staff, modeled on the British Imperial General Staff. They brought in Arnold to represent the air force and a retired former CNO, William D. Leahy, to act as chairman. It then became possible to organize a Combined Chiefs of Staff to run allied military operations.

As planning moved forward with the British, the army and navy found the time and energy to conduct what amounted to their own private world war. Much of it was provoked by the flinty personality of King, a man widely feared within his own service. Eisenhower had a reputation for getting on with almost everyone but he drew the line at the admiral. "One thing that might help win this war is to get someone to shoot King," he wrote in his diary in March 1942.

Major conflicts between the army and navy had to be resolved by the president, but there were some that not even he dared touch, although they had a direct bearing on combat efficiency. King favored a unified command in the Pacific—under Nimitz. Marshall favored a unified command in the Pacific—under MacArthur. Deadlock. There was no unified command.

While the army and navy fought each other, the president and the prime minister were putting on a world-beating demonstration of brotherhood in arms. They were closer to each other than to any of their military chiefs. The Anglophile Roosevelt and the half-American Churchill were almost twins.

Like Churchill, the president had a penchant for making strategy off the top of his head. "With a wave of his cigarette holder," in Marshall's phrase, he would pass a hand over the map, wanting to attack here, there, everywhere, oblivious to terrain, weather or logistics. Secretary of War Henry Stimson protested in vain against "dispersion debauch." Where the War Department dragged its feet, the president was likely to plunge in. American operations in China—consisting of a futile effort to turn Chiang Kai-shek into an ally who would fight the Japanese with the enthusiasm he brought to fighting his own people—were run from the White House. Stimson and Marshall had comparatively little to do with the Chinese puzzle.

American strategic thinking was based on a pre–Pearl Harbor plan known as Rainbow 5. This had anticipated American entry into the war as part of an anti-Axis coalition. It called for the defeat of the strongest power, Germany, first. American forces would attack in Europe while assuming the defensive in the Pacific. Rainbow 5 was accepted as the basic U.S. war plan.

As Marshall's chief planner, Eisenhower accordingly drew up plans for a cross-Channel attack at the earliest moment. The date he fixed was April 1, 1943. He proposed to assault French beaches from Le Havre to Boulogne. He envisaged a force of 48 divisions and 5,800 combat aircraft. He called it Operation Roundup. The year-long logistical buildup for it was Bolero.

Marshall, becoming fearful that the renewed German offensive in the summer of 1942 might put the Red Army on the ropes, had an emergency operation, called Sledgehammer, planned too. Sledgehammer aimed at seizing the Cotentin Peninsula, which juts out from Normandy, with four divisions in the fall of 1942 in a desperate attempt to help keep the Russians fighting.

The British, who would have to provide most of the troops for it, were absolutely and irrevocably opposed to Sledgehammer. Ditto for Roundup. They were also too experienced in the arts of alliance warfare to spoil the honeymoon mood of Arcadia.

The only thing the Americans had got right, in the British view, was to grasp the importance of Germany First, yet that was the one strategy King firmly rejected. So did MacArthur, and so did American public opinion. Tokyo First was the people's choice.

Had the Rainbow 5 strategy of Germany First been scrupulously adhered to in 1942, that would have given Yamamoto and the Japanese navy exactly what they had failed to win at Pearl Harbor—a free hand for at least a year in exploiting the riches of Southeast Asia. The aggressive strategy of King and MacArthur nullified most of the gains the Japanese had won in their initial onslaught.

Mundane reality played at least as great a part as personalities and arguments. There simply was not much the United States could do in 1942 to strike a blow at Hitler. For two years, until the spring of 1944, the main U.S. military effort would have to go into fighting Japan.

Not that the British were themselves in any hurry to get to grips with the might of the Wehrmacht. Churchill and his generals were haunted by memories of the Somme. Recent defeats and humiliations such as Dunkirk made them doubly cautious. The British never lacked courage but Marshall felt they were wanting in aggressiveness, if with good cause. Their strengths were elsewhere, in the vital areas of new military technologies, intelligence and limited operations.

For six months the arguments went on over Roundup. Because the British had not objected when it was first proposed, it was assumed they would go along with it. On discovering, layer by layer, the depth of British hostility many on Marshall's staff felt they'd been had.

Churchill's counterproposal was Torch: a landing in North Africa. The British had been fighting there for nearly two years, to hang onto Egypt. While it was not a true substitute for the second front in Western Europe that Stalin was demanding, it could be presented as an attempt to relieve some of the pressure on the U.S.S.R.

To Eisenhower and Marshall a landing in North Africa made as much sense as a landing on the moon. Germany could not be brought to its knees fifteen hundred miles from Berlin. The British were prepared, however, to nibble at the edges of German power for as long as it took, much as their forebears had done against Napoleon.

They were the world authorities on alliance warfare, while Americans had little experience of it and most of that was unpleasant. Churchill and his advisers knew how to exploit the differences between the army and navy, knew how to play on Roosevelt's sympathies, knew how to argue their case, and never stopped pushing it.

The decision was Roosevelt's and by the time he made it, in July 1942, there seemed little else he could do. Congress and the country expected American troops to get into action on the other side of the Atlantic as soon as possible. It was inconceivable that they should be told to wait another year, for a better opportunity than the one available.

Eisenhower took the blow hard, lamenting melodramatically, "This is the blackest day in history." Adopting Torch meant postponing the cross-Channel attack until 1944 because the resources for Roundup would have to go to North Africa. Roundup may have been too optimistic a plan anyway, as events were to show.

To Marshall, Eisenhower and Arnold, American strategic planning had been undermined by the devious British and that rankled for years. Yet what happened to planning for war in Europe was what was presently happening to strategic planning in the Pacific, where British influence was negligible. On both sides of the globe operations were undertaken in 1942–43 simply because it was possible to mount them while other, bigger operations were not. However logical those bigger operations were, they simply had to wait, but the country was in no mood to wait for perfection. Nor were American generals and admirals. They were chafing to fight.

ONCE Torch had been decided on, the old challenge reappeared, to ship an army over the ocean. The Germans were winning the second Battle of the Atlantic.

Pearl Harbor was as much of a surprise in Berlin as in Washington. When Germany declared war on the United States there were no U-boats off the East Coast. It took a month for Karl Doenitz, commander of the submarine force, to get some of his best crews into position off Cape Cod and Cape Hatteras. The score they rang up was staggering. They sank at least one ship most days, and on some days two or three. The U.S. Navy's antisubmarine warfare (or ASW) force consisted of two dozen antiquated World War One craft. American shipbuilding priorities left the door wide open to Doenitz's skippers as they gleefully squinted into their periscope eyepieces at fat targets. They called this "the happy time."

Their boldness could be breathtaking. Vacationers at Virginia Beach one hot afternoon that summer watched in fascination and horror as two ships were torpedoed a mile offshore in broad daylight. At night lights along the shore silhouetted tankers and freighters for the convenience of U-boats. It did not take a good skipper long to expend his fourteen torpedoes.

In the six months between the end of Arcadia and the approval of Torch nearly 500 ships, totaling 2.5 million tons, were sunk between the Gulf of Mexico and the English Channel by a submarine force so small it could not keep even 12 boats on patrol at a time off the eastern seaboard.

This was a battle the British had been fighting for two years. As in the First World War they relied on convoys for salvation. With the United States in the war, convoy traffic would soon double, and double again, but it would take time to produce escort vessels. King considered unprotected convoys mass suicide at sea. He did not know how right he was: in 1940 the Germans had cracked the British convoy code.

The convoys avoided total annihilation because the German system of decrypting broken codes and distributing the product was inefficient, and because the British had scored a code-breaking success of their own. German military codes were based on a machine called Enigma, which both encoded and decoded radio messages. On the eve of the war Polish intelligence officers had stolen two Enigma machines and given one to the French, the other to the British.

Within a year the British were reading German army and air force signals almost as if they were their own. The German naval code was harder to crack but in February 1941 a U-boat was captured with its Enigma machine intact, making it possible to break the main U-boat code, Hydra.

Two months after the United States entered the war, the Kriegsmarine introduced a new submarine code, called Triton. This setback for Allied intelligence coincided with the U-boat offensive off the East Coast. For the next year the second Battle of the Atlantic ran increasingly in Hitler's favor.

With its traditional tenacity and inventiveness, the Royal Navy fought back hard, but still unaware that its convoy code had been broken. As in World War One, German submariners were a talkative lot. Using a system of high-frequency radio direction finding known as Huff Duff, the British could often calculate a U-boat's position to within forty miles, divert convoys away from the area and send aircraft to look for it. Airborne radar, while still crude, was remarkably successful at pinpointing subs lying on the surface. In 1942 nearly half the U-boats sunk (83 out of 174) were victims of aircraft.

Sonar had improved considerably since World War One, and was now integrated with powerful ASW weaponry. The British had devised Hedgehog, a forward-firing system of twenty-four projectiles. As an ASW vessel broke sonar contact with the U-boat it was tracking, the Hedgehog was fired, dropping twenty-four warheads in a circular pattern one hundred yards wide over the U-boat's location. Hedgehog warheads exploded on contact, making them vastly more dangerous than depth charges, which exploded at preset depths, whether they struck a target or not.

The Germans, however, still held the aces. Not only had they cracked British convoy codes, they had broken some of the operational codes of the Royal Navy and the U.S. Navy in 1939, and these had not been changed. The Germans also demonstrated their own technical ingenuity in this ferocious struggle for mastery of the North Atlantic.

They countered the menace of airborne radar by developing a detector that could pick up the one-meter radio wave it generated in plenty of time for a U-boat to dive. They perfected electric torpedoes that left no visible wake, making evasion virtually impossible. Huge submarines called "milch boats" toured the Atlantic to replenish U-boats with fuel and torpedoes.

Hitler finally glimpsed the obvious: he could win the second Battle of the Atlantic. In the summer of 1942 U-boat construction rose dramatically. In the fall Doenitz began sending out wolf packs of six, ten, even twenty boats to operate together. By the winter of 1942 there were wolf packs all the way from the freezing waters around Iceland down to the balmy Azores.

Up to four ships a day were sunk: more than 500,000 tons of shipping a month. Not even the United States could keep taking losses like that. And still the loss curve was rising.

In the midst of this crisis, the U.S. and British navies were tripping over their own feet. They bickered over ASW priorities, techniques, areas of responsibility and who was best at this or that. The Combined

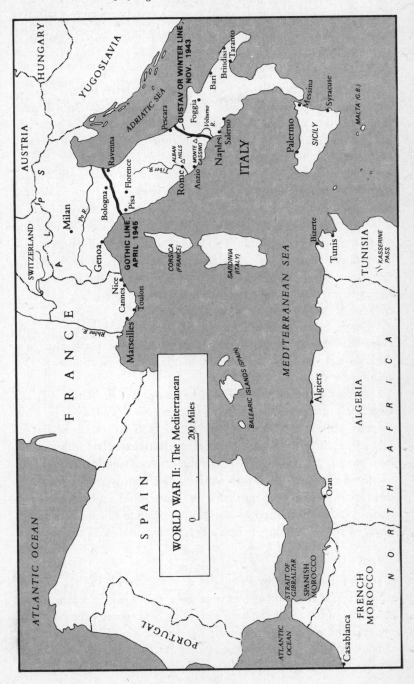

WORLD WAR II: The Mediterranean

0 ___ 200 Miles

Chiefs were forced to step in and impose a reasonable facsimile of Allied unity. King created Tenth Fleet, a purely paper organization with himself in charge, to keep the ASW campaign from going off the rails again.

Toward the end of 1942 American escort carriers began to appear in the battle, providing air cover for convoys and blasting the Kondor out of the sky. The British developed an airborne radar that generated a wave only ten centimeters long. Centimetric radar, fitted aboard a plane that carried a searchlight, was a killer. The last thing many a U-boat crew heard, as they sprawled topside in the middle of the night to stretch cramped muscles, was the sharp whine of a plane swooping low. The last thing they ever saw was a blinding light overhead.

What really turned the battle around, though, was the breaking of Triton, in February 1943. To Doenitz's eternal bewilderment, just as he flooded the Atlantic with U-boats, he lost the fight. Until the last days of a very long life he would blame it on the invention of centimetric radar. It was impossible to believe his codes had been broken.

On the other hand, Allied cryptanalysts became increasingly suspicious that the staggering losses of 1942 had to be partly due to a German code-breaking coup. Early in 1943 Allied naval and convoy codes were changed.

Victory in the signals war told its own story. In March 1943 the Germans had the second Battle of the Atlantic nearly won. In May, Doenitz pulled his U-boats out of the fight. That month he lost 41 submarines. Boats and crews were being lost twice as fast as they could be replaced. The U-boats were on the brink of annihilation.

In time they would return, with various improvements that made them more potent weapons than ever, but the old aggressiveness was gone. A U-boat that attacked was almost certain to be counterattacked. There were no safe targets now. The happy time had gone forever.

ONE OF the ironies of Eisenhower's rapid ascent was that Torch, which he had tried so hard to stop, gave him what he wanted most, command of troops. In the long wrangling over strategy the American officer who got along best with the British was Eisenhower. The famous grin and friendly manner brought him assignment as commander of the Allied Expeditionary Force, with British deputy commanders for ground, air and naval forces who had long years of experience fighting the Germans. The British aimed to shoot Eisenhower into high orbit and while he revolved harmlessly high above they would fight the battles.

With him he took the chief American planner of Torch, Mark Clark, one of the beneficiaries of Marshall's youth movement. At forty-five the tall, vain, strikingly handsome Clark was the youngest major general in the army.

The aim of Torch was to destroy Field Marshall Erwin Rommel's famous *Panzerarmee Afrika* and its Italian allies by the end of the year. The British Eighth Army under General Sir Bernard Montgomery had dealt it a major defeat in October 1942 at El Alamein. With his enemy on the run Montgomery had cautiously stopped to organize his troops for pursuit, thereby giving the Germans time to collect themselves and make a fighting, time-consuming retreat.

The key to Torch was Tunisia, with its vital airfields, ports and roads. If an Allied force could take them and attack east while Monty advanced west from Egypt, the Germans and Italians could be pinned down in Libya and destroyed. The Axis supply crisis that enabled Montgomery to secure a three-to-one advantage at El Alamein made defeat in North Africa certain, yet to all of Rommel's pleas to pull out while it was still possible Hitler turned the deafest ear known to military history.

Torch called for landing three task forces at widely separated beaches on November 8. One would land on the Atlantic coast of Morocco and seize Casablanca. The second would take the valuable naval port of Oran, in Algeria. The third would take Algiers, the second-largest city (after Cairo) in North Africa. There would be no direct assault on Tunisia.

American troops were green and Allied air cover too thin for Marshall to take risks with them in their debut. Landing near Casablanca, however, seemed to the British surprisingly timid for an ally who was usually keen to preach the virtues of aggressiveness to them. The western task force, under Major General George Patton, took 35,000 American troops straight from East Coast ports to the beaches of Morocco. Going ashore under air cover provided by three escort carriers, they ran into some initial resistance from Vichy French forces, but losses were slight.

The center task force, consisting of 39,000 troops under Major

General Lloyd R. Fredendall, captured Oran with comparable ease, after similar token resistance.

The biggest challenge fell on the 10,000 Americans and 23,000 British troops assigned to capture Algiers. They were expected to capture the city, then race three hundred miles east and seize Tunisia before the Germans could move in and secure the main towns, roads and airfields. The French governor of Tunisia was planning to defect to the Allies, with the 15,000 Vichy troops he commanded, provided the Allied forces arrived in sufficient strength to hold the country.

Algiers fell quickly. A cease-fire was arranged in Algeria and Morocco. Most Vichy troops came over to the Allied side. Tunisia might yet be taken too. Eisenhower had a floating reserve, the British 78th Division. If he landed it at Tunis he might beat the Germans to the punch. Unhappily the reserve remained aboard ship. He would take no risks in his debut.

The Germans airlifted paratroopers, light armor and artillery into Bizerte and Tunis from airfields in southern Italy. When American and British forces reached western Tunisia ten days after the landings, they ran straight into dug-in Germans defending the few roads and mountain passes.

For a month they attacked, achieving nothing. Then the rains came down, turning Tunisia into a glue pot. Eisenhower would have to wait at least two months until the rainy season ended before he could mount another offensive.

Rommel beat him to the punch, attacking through the Kasserine Pass in mid-February in an attempt to shatter Fredendall's II Corps. The British operation for decoding and distributing Enigma intercepts was known as Ultra, from ultra-secret. Eisenhower knew from Ultra that an attack was coming, but he and his deputies misjudged where the blow would fall. They deployed their forces in the wrong positions to meet it. The sector that took the force of the attack was the one that was left thinly held.

Fredendall compounded his own problems by having his combat engineers blast a huge hole in the base of a mountain far to the rear, then putting his command post in the hole. When Rommel's desert veterans struck toward the pass, Fredendall instantly lost all effective control of his forces, consisting of the Big Red One and 1st Armored Division.

Rommel captured Kasserine Pass, smashing through Fredendall's units with excessive ease. Three thousand Americans were killed or wounded. Another 4,000 were taken prisoner. The wreckage of 200 American tanks lined the road. Yet what had Rommel achieved? Half his army was stuck on a long, narrow mountain road while the Americans, recovering quickly, were bringing up massive firepower to cut it. Eisenhower had not been sufficiently decisive while the battle raged but he was far from discouraged. The battle had blooded an army that was too lax and complacent for its own good, as he had repeatedly warned. And the Germans now had their head in a noose. Unhappily, Fredendall was too out of touch to realize that in time. Rommel, smelling a trap about to snap shut, pulled back.

Fredendall had to go. Clark, offered II Corps, turned it down, saying it amounted to a demotion. Patton took it, gladly, even though he was already slated for an army command. The difference between Patton's attitude and Clark's did not go unnoticed by Marshall.

Even before Pearl Harbor Patton had been determined to show Marshall how keen he was, fearing the youth movement might hold no place in combat for a balding fifty-five-year-old. He'd driven himself and the tankers he trained like a man possessed. Patton pioneered the use of light aircraft and a new invention, FM radio, to control armored columns on the move. Stunningly foulmouthed in front of troops ("We've gotta save all the fucking for the fighting men . . . we're gonna kill the purple-pissing Japs . . ."), he was among his peers a knowledgeable, sometimes eloquent master of tank warfare.

His devotion to hard training was something the shaken II Corps needed. British instructors were invited to provide lessons in desert fighting. Discipline was tightened up. Recovery was swift, but the botched debut of the supposedly elite Big Red One and 1st Armored Division left an impression many British officers never lost that Americans made poor soldiers. British troops captured in Tunisia were asked by German interrogators what the Americans were like. A shrug, a sigh, perhaps a smile. "Our Italians," they replied.

That seemed all too plausible, given the alacrity with which Americans surrendered. They had been trained to do it. During maneuvers and field problems back home umpires invariably ruled that men who were outnumbered or cut off had to surrender. This underestimated the defensive powers of troops who are willing to dig in and fight. After Tunisia training was revised to make white flags less easy to wave.

While Rommel was trouncing II Corps on the western border of Tunisia, the Eighth Army reached the eastern border. The rains stopped, the land dried out, and Axis forces were caught in a vise. Rommel departed on sick leave, never to return. Behind him he left an army doomed to defeat. Allied command of the Mediterranean had become a stranglehold. German and Italian units were short of fuel, spare parts and ammunition, yet they fought bitterly even so, under able, experienced officers and NCOs.

On the treeless Tunisian landscape Allied infantry and armor were forced to attack with little chance of concealment and only fitful air support. Both the RAF and the AAF disdained the lowly business of supporting ground troops. The airmen saw their role as attacking enemy airfields and dueling in the sky with the glamorous Luftwaffe.

Eisenhower's lack of command experience and his shaky grasp of infantry tactics were brutally exposed as his units inched their way forward. Had it not been for his political support from the British, who found him more responsive to their point of view than any successor might be, he might have shared Fredendall's fate. During the Casablanca conference in January 1943 Marshall dropped the heaviest of hints that Eisenhower could do with some extra help. Eisenhower agreed. The man sent to him was Omar N. Bradley, *the* Marshall protégé.

A former commandant of the Infantry School, he was also, with Marshall's backing, the first member of Ike's own West Point class of 1915 ("the class the stars fell on") to reach brigadier general. Bradley had spent half his army career as an instructor, either in math or in infantry tactics. When journalists described the gangling, homely, bespectacled general as having the air of a schoolteacher, he happily took it as the highest compliment: his adored, deceased father had been just that back in rural Missouri. Sent to North Africa ostensibly as Eisenhower's troubleshooter, he in fact provided Ike with what amounted to a walking encyclopedia on infantry operations.

By May the Axis forces had been driven into the northeastern corner of Tunisia. They had their backs to the sea. Luftwaffe units pulled out in a hurry, flying off to Sicily. Almost out of ammunition, some 238,000 Axis troops (two thirds of them Germans) surrendered. It was a bigger bag of prisoners than the Russians had captured at Stalingrad three months before.

Tunisia had been an embarrassment to the army—and its finishing school.

15

A WORLD
OF SAND

GETTING ASHORE in French North Africa or on Guadalcanal involved risks and casualties, yet these were fairly straightforward amphibious landings. What loomed ahead in 1943 was something much tougher, the first true amphibious assaults. Frontal attacks, that is, on hostile shores, with no room for maneuver, no flanks that could be turned; simply hurling men straight into the teeth of prepared defenses, against an enemy who knew they were coming and had modern firepower to try and stop them.

To carry war to Germany and Japan in this way a new class of ships had to be created. They had bows that opened, allowing a ramp to be lowered, or bows that could be lowered and used as a ramp. They had shallow draft, using seawater as ballast, enabling them to beach at low tide and float off when the waters rose. Such landing ships, and smaller versions known as landing craft, would put men, tanks, trucks, jeeps, artillery and supplies straight onto a beach as if they were being squeezed from a tube.

The Royal Navy began toying with ideas for landing ships shortly after Dunkirk, as it dreamed of returning to the Continent one day. Eight months before Pearl Harbor a British naval officer arrived in Washington with sketches for a "Landing Ship, Tank" and a "Landing Ship, Dock." Would the Americans be so kind as to build a hundred or so under Lend Lease?

These were no small boats. An LSD was built around a massive hold that could be flooded, disgorging up to twenty-five landing craft or amtracs crammed with men and equipment. An LST would carry twenty medium tanks on its upper deck, and a dozen 2½-ton trucks below. At four thousand tons it was the size of a light cruiser.

American shipyards in 1941 were awash with orders for battleships, carriers and Liberty cargo ships. The British request was shelved. Even after Pearl Harbor amphibious assaults seemed a long way off. Construction of landing ships and landing craft was slow to get started.

To decide where to go from Tunisia, Roosevelt and Churchill met at Casablanca in January 1943. Roosevelt declared the Allies would settle for nothing less than unconditional surrender. There would be no repetition of the mistake of 1918. His main purpose, though, was to help keep the Russians fighting, by assuring them the Allies would not do to them as they had done to the Allies in 1917 and make a separate peace with Germany.

Despite this declaration, Roosevelt and Churchill did not intend to apply it strictly to the Italians. They had hopes of persuading Italy to leave the war. To help bring that about they set as their next objective, once Tunisia fell, the conquest of Sicily.

With the first amphibious assaults reaching the planning stage this was the logical moment to press flat out with the construction of landing ships and landing craft. Logic took second place to Doenitz. As Roosevelt and Churchill sat in their wicker chairs—imitation vacationers in Morocco's winter sunshine—the Battle of the Atlantic was reaching its climacteric.

The word went from Casablanca that escort carriers, destroyer escorts and ASW aircraft such as Catalina flying boats had Triple-A priority on scarce labor and raw materials. Landing ships and landing craft would have to wait. That decision, unavoidable when it was made, was to bedevil amphibious assaults almost to the end of the war.

The invasion of Sicily, code name Husky, aimed to put two armies ashore on the southeastern corner of the island on July 10: Seventh Army under Patton and Eighth Army under Montgomery. Together they formed 15th Army Group, commanded by Eisenhower's deputy for ground forces, General Sir Harold Alexander, an amiable Scotch-Irish aristocrat and a soldier of wide experience.

Husky marked the debut of the landing ships and the 2½-ton DUKW, an amphibian truck which could carry supplies straight from a ship at sea to wherever they were needed ashore. Doubling as a landing craft, it could put twenty-five fully armed infantrymen on the beach.

Sicily offered a foretaste of the crushing firepower and unprecedented mobility of Allied armies, but Husky was deeply flawed: the plan ignored all possibility of trapping the Germans and Italians by seizing one side or the other of the Strait of Messina.

The initial assault was opposed by a screen of Italian divisions while behind them German armor massed for a counterstroke. When the Panzers struck on July 11 Seventh Army took the force of the blow, and took it without air cover. The airmen's obsession with hunting the Luftwaffe in its lair might have produced a catastrophe on the beaches had it not been for the zealous intervention of the seamen. Destroyers closed with the shore to act as antitank guns, knocking out Panzers that broke into the beachhead.

Seventh Army's assigned role once established on land was to guard the left flank of Eighth Army; after North Africa, this was as much as the British believed American troops were good for. Patton turned permission to make a reconnaissance to the west into a freebooter's license to roam. Striking out with his armor, he made a three-hundred-mile swing, clearing the southern coast, then the northern coast, while Montgomery doggedly clawed the one hundred miles from his landing beaches toward Messina. Patton beat him to it by three hours, on August 17.

Several times he used landing craft to outflank German lines of defense. A similar determination at higher levels to exploit Allied command of the sea might have forced a major surrender. Instead, some 40,000 Germans and 70,000 Italians escaped across the Strait of Messina, taking with them 10,000 vehicles, 50 tanks, 200 guns and 17,000 tons of supplies.

While the battle for Sicily was being fought, Allied bombers struck the railroad network of Rome in a massive raid, on July 19. Entire streets around the tracks were pulverized. This was the culmination of nearly three years of Italian military disasters. It broke Mussolini's nerve and encouraged the politicians he had browbeaten for a generation to topple him from power. Italy was looking for a way out. The British were eager to help.

Given half a chance, Churchill would have fought almost the whole war in the Mediterranean. The fighting there was on a scale that matched his resources, and from Gibraltar to Suez there were valuable British economic, military and political interests to be retrieved. It was inevitable that they would want to make the three-mile jump from Sicily into Italy. Beyond that, Churchill's old fascination with the Balkans had returned; the fatal fascination which had led a generation earlier to Gallipoli. Now he called them "the soft underbelly of Europe"—the easy way to Berlin.

The JCS saw any Italian campaign as a diversion from the main event, the cross-Channel attack, yet that could not be mounted until spring 1944 and forces in being were there to be used. Grudgingly, they agreed to an Italian campaign, but it was a strictly limited commitment.

Most of Italy, like most of the Balkans, consists of mountains. Eighth Army would land in the south and advance up both narrow coastal plains. Fifth Army, composed of American and British divisions under Mark Clark, would make the amphibious assault, at Salerno, south of Naples—just within range of fighters operating from Sicilian airfields.

On September 8 Italy surrendered but the affair was so badly bungled the Allies got zero military advantage out of it. The Italian army went home. The assault on Salerno next day put American and British forces ashore despite German opposition, but their beachheads, divided by a river, could not link up.

The Germans came down the river valley to exploit that gap, attempting to crush the invasion piecemeal. Eisenhower had a division to spare but lacked the landing craft to put it ashore and plug the breach. As on Sicily, it was the American beachhead that took the onslaught.

In scenes of desperate struggle over three long nights and days paratroopers were dropped straight onto the Salerno beaches. Clark got ready to pull out his headquarters and made plans for evacuation of Fifth Army. Gunners cut their fuses to four tenths of a second: point-blank range. The artillery line held. Green troops fought like veterans. Naval support plastered German positions with 11,000 tons of shells. Air strikes rained down 3,000 tons of bombs. German forward units vanished in roiling smoke.

With Salerno secure and the beachheads linked up, Eisenhower expected to capture Rome by November 1. He was as innocent as Churchill of what mountain fighting was like. Allied armies were still fifty miles short of the Eternal City when the November rains fell. For six weeks the Germans had fought a bitter and bloody delaying action while behind them their engineers constructed one of the strongest defensive positions of the war.

It was a line based on Monte Cassino, a peak which dominates the north–south roads leading to Rome through central Italy. Germany Army Group Southwest was commanded, moreover, by Albert Kesselring, a Luftwaffe general who was a master of ground warfare. Not only did he hold the high ground but in front of it ran swift, deep rivers. More than one division was wrecked trying to cross them. By January 1944 blizzards were sweeping the mountains, freezing American and British soldiers to their blackened slopes.

Desperate to save a campaign that only the British believed in, Churchill wrung enough landing craft from the buildup for the cross-Channel attack to make a second assault, this time striking at Anzio, thirty miles south of Rome—and deep in Kesselring's rear.

The landing, on January 22, was unopposed, but it had not been given a clear objective. Experience would show that the key to success in amphibious assaults nearly always hinged on rapid occupation and exploitation of whatever high ground overlooked a beachhead. In this case it was the Alban Hills—twenty-five miles inland. The commander of the Anzio force, John P. Lucas, did not feel he had enough manpower to hold a position so far away and still defend his beachhead. He consolidated instead. Kesselring seized the hills and contained Anzio.

In mid-February the famous abbey on Monte Cassino was flattened by Allied bombers. Battles are usually contests for the high ground and buildings on it are inevitably targets. War had destroyed the famous abbey three times before. In an edifying demonstration of uncoordinated air support, it was bombed a day earlier than planned, owing to a break in the weather, but no one bothered to inform the ground commanders of the change. Any chance of a breakthrough the bombing might have produced was thrown away.

A month later air power was tried again, this time in the first attempt at "carpet bombing," obliterating the town of Cassino. Ground units advanced so slowly the Germans returned and turned the rubble into strong defenses.

It was the French who held the solution to the Cassino deadlock. They provided four divisions to the Italian campaign, organized in the

Corps Expéditionnaire Français. The CEF consisted mainly of colonial troops, notably the colorful *goumiers* from the Atlas Mountains of Morocco and Algeria. These small dark figures, dressed in what appeared to be brightly striped blankets, went out looking for mules, while machine-minded Americans and British simply cursed at tanks and trucks stuck in the mud.

This was the *goumiers'* kind of terrain, their kind of fighting. There was a tendency, however, both to pity the French and despise them. The commander of the CEF, Alphonse Juin, was personally liked by Clark and Alexander, yet his military advice was not given much weight; not until everything else had been tried, and failed.

In May the French finally got their way. They infiltrated 12,000 well-armed *goumiers,* threatening German communications, outflanking Cassino, spreading near-panic at Kesselring's headquarters. As the German line unraveled Alexander hit it with yet another frontal assault. This time it broke wide open. With the Germans stunned and disorganized the troops in the Anzio beachhead broke out, but instead of moving east quickly and in force to cut off the retreating enemy, Clark ordered most of them north, to capture Rome.

Alexander too came to Kesselring's rescue by putting his advancing armies on a single road. Huge traffic jams built up, Clark celebrated his Roman triumph, and 150,000 Germans escaped. North of Rome they built another formidable barrier, the Gothic line. Nothing was soft in the mountains.

WITH Guadalcanal firmly in American hands, King and Nimitz sold the JCS the riskiest of the strategies available for getting to Japan but, if it worked, the quickest—island hopping. By driving straight across the Central Pacific they aimed to bypass most of the island bases that the Japanese had spent more than a decade fortifying. The techniques they would employ were untried and unproven. Some of the essential equipment they needed did not yet exist.

However, the modern fleet under construction since late 1940 was becoming operational almost as if on cue for the navy's offensive. In 1943 a fast battleship would be commissioned, on average, every two months, a fast carrier every five weeks and an escort carrier every twenty days. Minute study of a Zero captured intact led in just six months to a fighter that would outfly and outfight it, the F6F Hellcat. From November 1942 Hellcat squadrons started joining the fleet.

In broad outline, the navy proposed to use carrier aircraft to win air superiority over the target island while surface ships and submarines isolated it from reinforcement and resupply. Once command of the sea and the air were achieved, the marines would take it with an amphibious assault. Captured or constructed airfields on the island would then provide land-based air cover as the naval and marine units proceeded to their next objective.

The first bypassing operation came in the Aleutians in May 1943. The Japanese had taken Attu and Kiska during the Battle of Midway. The navy bypassed Kiska and attacked Attu, 250 miles farther west. After it fell the Japanese evacuated Kiska without a fight.

In the fall the huge air base at Rabaul was repeatedly attacked by navy and marine aviators. To defend it the Japanese stripped planes and pilots from the Central Pacific. By the time the Central Pacific offensive was unleashed what Japanese flyers needed was a breather, not a battle.

Nimitz wanted Eniwetok, one of the world's biggest atolls, as a fleet anchorage fifteen hundred miles west of Hawaii. To reach it he would launch a two-pronged attack on the Gilbert islands, simultaneously striking Tarawa in the center and Makin in the north.

The force he built up was immense: Fifth Fleet, under Spruance, contained the fast carriers and the battle line; Fifth Amphibious Force, under Richmond Kelly Turner, transported the troops and laid down naval gunfire support; and V Amphibious Corps (mainly marines), under Major General Holland M. Smith, would make the assaults. The short, fat, bald, bespectacled Smith looked an unlikely combat commander, yet his fiery temperament and outspoken ways gave him his well-known nickname, "Howlin' Mad."

Tarawa's defenses were on the main island, Betio. The assault went in on November 20. The first three waves of marines crunched over the outlying reef in one hundred amtracs, but the follow-up waves were in plywood Higgins boats that drew four feet of water. A local oceanographic idiosyncrasy known as "a dodging tide" left less than four feet of water over the reef that day. The follow-up force waded seven hundred yards through chest-high water while being raked with machine-gun fire. The message flashed to the fleet from the beach was

"Issue in doubt." Nightfall found two badly mauled marine regiments clinging to the shoreline by their fingernails.

Next day the tide rose. The regiment being held in reserve was landed. This turned the battle around although there were two days of hard fighting ahead. The 3,000 dead and wounded suffered to take an island half the size of Central Park sent a shock wave through public opinion. It was fortunate that Betio was flat, depriving the defenders of the priceless advantage of high ground. One small hill and the Central Pacific offensive might have opened with a defeat.

Makin, by comparison, was lightly defended, but the task of taking it was assigned to the Army's 27th Division. Its performance won no accolades and during it an escort carrier, the *Liscome Bay,* was sunk, taking 800 sailors to their deaths.

In December Nimitz reached for the atoll of Kwajalein, in the center of the Marshalls. It was within range of four Japanese airfields and most of his senior commanders were against the operation. The small islands of the atoll were swiftly overrun and the Japanese air threat never materialized—the result of all those IJN pilots lost down at Rabaul.

In February 1944 he went for the most northerly atoll in the Marshalls, Eniwetok. Once again the amphibious assault quickly defeated Japanese resistance. It was hard to defend any small flat island, depriving the Japanese of all opportunity to observe or to shoot from high ground.

The attackers were improving their craft from one assault to the next. The advance through the Gilberts and Marshalls enabled them to practice on a regimental and divisional scale what they would soon have to do on a corps and army one. The weight of the assault was growing from island to island. Each beach was hit harder than the last.

Fire-control parties on the beach brought naval gunfire support to pinpoint accuracy. LCIs packing artillery swarmed in the shallows.* Earl Ellis had forecast the need for frogmen who would blow up or clear underwater obstacles, to provide safe channels for the landing craft. In the Marshalls they appeared. The underwater demolition teams were the smallest of the combat elites and by many the most admired. Command ships a mile or so offshore coordinated the assault. Amtracs in rapidly growing numbers brought the first waves in but

---

*Landing Craft, Infantry; capable of putting up to 100 infantry on the beach.

once ashore fought as light tanks. Landing craft with bows and ramps brought in the follow-up force. DUKWs swam in with ammunition, spare parts, rations and fuel, and took out the wounded to LSTs that served as casualty stations. With planes from the escort carriers shuttling to and fro overhead on close support missions this was not so much amphibious as triphibious warfare, concentrating land, sea and air power against fairly small targets.

As the navy and Marine Corps blasted their way across the Central Pacific, MacArthur was moving toward the Philippines in an offensive of his own. For nearly a year he demanded authority to assault Rabaul. King opposed it, as he would oppose anything that threatened to divert resources from Nimitz. Marshall too was opposed, believing it would be better to bypass Rabaul. It could be neutralized instead, with air strikes. This decision saved MacArthur from plunging into a hornet's nest: there were 100,000 Japanese troops at Rabaul (and not the 20,000 he estimated), with 6,000 guns and mortars.

At first dejected and angry, MacArthur soon came around to recognizing the offensive possibilities of bypassing on the heroic scale. In itself it was nothing new in warfare to bypass strongpoints but in the Pacific there was a leap in magnitude that amounted virtually to a change in kind. Open flanks ran for a thousand miles. Enemy strongpoints might be left three hundred miles or more in one's rear.

Such perspectives galvanized MacArthur's offensive outlook, as if he felt challenged to show Marshall and King that if that was how they thought the Japanese should be fought, then he, by God, would show them how a man of genius would do it. Using Buna's airstrip to provide air cover, he began the long haul up the eighteen-hundred-mile northern coast of New Guinea in September 1943.

The Japanese had him heavily outnumbered in men, planes and ships, but he kept moving, never giving them a chance to concentrate against him. What he went for was places where the terrain was suitable for airfields. His method was to land under air cover provided by George Kenney's Fifth Air Force, carve out a strong defense perimeter, build an airstrip, bring in Kenney's planes and use them to cover the next landing.

He depended heavily too on his fleet of LSTs, LCTs and LCIs. They not only brought his infantry ashore but housed his troops for months at a time, provided transportation up and down the New Guinea coast and kept his supplies coming. He had nothing remotely as powerful as Fifth Fleet to secure command of the sea. It was his good fortune that the furious onslaught in the Central Pacific made it impossible any longer for the Japanese to divert planes and ships to his area.

Deception and speed helped bring a string of quick, inexpensive successes that left 100,000 Japanese troops cut off. Some positions, though, could not be bypassed. The commander of the 11,000 Japanese on Biak, Colonel Nayuki Kuzume, knew absolutely that MacArthur was heading his way. Nearly 75 miles off the northwestern coast of New Guinea, Biak had three airfields.

Japanese army doctrine for repelling invasion was to destroy the enemy at the water's edge, when he was most vulnerable. Kuzume took a strictly pragmatic view: the best he could do for Japan was to deny MacArthur use of those airfields as long as possible.

He blasted caves and gun positions into the low hills that dominated them, leaving the beaches—nine miles away—undefended. Sure enough, MacArthur's troops grabbed the airfields on the second day of the assault in May 1944, but nothing could take off or land without being shot to pieces. It was three months before Biak's airfields were in operation again.

By allowing MacArthur to push up from the southwest while Nimitz drove west from Hawaii the JCS had put the Japanese in an untenable position. They might have stopped a single strong thrust but they had no hope of stopping two. This strategy, arrived at mainly by army-navy rivalry, was reminiscent of the old converging columns. As before, it nullified the defender's advantage of fighting on interior lines.

The problem of deciding which islands to take and which to bypass nevertheless provided a subject for endless arguments, then and afterward. Biak was one of the very few exceptions. After taking the Gilberts and Marshalls the navy was determined to assault the Marianas. Marshall and MacArthur could not see why these islands were better targets than a lot of other islands they could think of in the western Pacific. Then Arnold said the AAF would like to have them. There was a new heavy bomber entering service, the B-29 Superfortress. From airfields in the Marianas, said Arnold, he could bomb Japan better than he could from the alternative offered him, Kuomintang territory in China, which the Japanese might overrun.

On June 15 Spruance and Turner closed in on Saipan, bringing 127,000 marines and soldiers and the firepower of more than one hundred warships. The first wave of marines put 8,000 men on the beach in twenty minutes, but Japanese mortar and artillery fire was so intense that was as far as they got. The second wave landed right on top of the first. By nightfall 20,000 men were clinging precariously to a shallow beachhead.

All through the first two days artillery fire took such a toll of gunfire-control and air-control parties that naval support and air strikes were ineffective. On the third day the reserve, 27th Division, had to be landed to save the invasion from failure. With three divisions now ashore (two marine, one army) it was possible to push the Japanese back.

The performance of 27th Division was such that Howlin' Mad asked Spruance to relieve the division commander, Ralph Smith. The removal of an army general by an admiral at the behest of a marine set off one of the epic interservice rows of all time.

Removing Ralph Smith made no difference. The 27th was not simply a National Guard division, but a special case for treatment. Lesley J. McNair was entrusted by Marshall with organizing and training all army ground forces. In the end he simply despaired of the National Guard divisions.

Saipan cost 16,500 casualties and took nearly a month to secure. Japanese losses ran to 30,000 dead and a handful of prisoners, most of them wounded. In a flawless demonstration of combined arms the nearby island of Tinian was snapped up quickly and cheaply.

Guam, that war game problem so often pondered in the 1930s, was recaptured at the end of July in a quick, skillful assault that was preceded by a ten-day bombardment that no war gamer had ever foreseen.

COMMAND of the sea had gained a meaning beyond anything in Mahan's philosophy. It now meant winning command of the air in order to win command of the sea. The carrier was a hybrid, a convergence of technologies, adding the striking power of aircraft to the age-old mobility of the warship, and doing so as fleets converted from coal to oil. The new fuel doubled the range of a ship yet took up less space aboard, making it possible to pack it with greater firepower.

The aircraft carrier was a strange fighting ship: so vulnerable its safety lay in attack. Its skin was only one inch thick. Small projectiles easily pierced its wooden flight deck or set it ablaze. Filled with ammunition and high-octane fuel, it was a huge, gray, floating bomb. Its salvation lay in its speed and mobility, enabling it to close quickly with the enemy air base or carrier that threatened its existence and to strike before being struck.

The Japanese had seen in the carrier a perfect instrument for supplementing the land-based air power of their far-flung island bastions. Strong air forces could thus be projected thousands of miles from Japan without being tied down in any one place. The combination of island bases and carriers made the striking power of the Japanese navy twice as great after the Washington Conference as before it.

The urgency of getting in the first blow led to the neglect in both navies of long-range scouting. Far from being "the eyes of the fleet," carriers were gropers. The performance of American and Japanese search planes in the Coral Sea in 1942 was a mirror-image comedy of errors.

The carrier battles of that year were a learning experience in this novel form of warfare. At times it was the Americans who seemed to need instruction most. At Midway and the Coral Sea their torpedo planes hit nothing. Direction of airborne planes from carrier flight centers was haphazard. Radio discipline among navy pilots was a joke . . . followed by another joke. At Midway no one bothered to tell the attacking pilots where their carriers had moved to while they were gone. Dozens came down in the sea out of gas looking for a deck to land on.

Antiaircraft defenses were poor in the early days, but just before Pearl Harbor Swedish Bofors 40-millimeter guns and Swiss Oerlikon 20-millimeter guns began entering service. A year later they were lavishly installed on carriers and their escorts. The British invention of the cavity magnetron brought a 1,000-percent increase in power that made centimetric radar possible and also increased the range of ships' radar so that incoming aircraft could be detected at 125 miles.

Another British invention, the proximity fuse, arrived in the fleet early in 1944. It exploded a five-inch AA shell close to an attacking aircraft, producing a spray of high-velocity shrapnel. It made dive-bombing and level bombing almost impossible.*

By this time the fast carrier task forces of the Pacific Fleet were surging westward, lessons learned, techniques well practiced. As they advanced toward combat, a fleet of floating gas stations would rendez-vous with them, refueling the fast carriers and the fast battleships at speeds up to twenty-five knots. As the TF moved on, the battleships and carriers in turn fueled the cruisers and destroyers. Submarines would move into the area of the amphibious assault to rescue downed flyers. Once the island was secure the TF would withdraw, to be refueled and replenished once more.

The projection of naval power thousands of miles from American bases was the work of organizations and ideas that did not exist before Pearl Harbor. Many of them were the products of combat experience and would have never come into existence without it. By 1944 ships were staying at sea for nearly a year, yet the men aboard them never went short of anything; well, almost anything. Victory in the Pacific was impossible without this victory in logistics. Had the Japanese enjoyed American-style logistics and American forces been yoked to the Rising Sun variety, Japan might never have been defeated. There was not simply abundance for the navy, it was well-organized abun-dance.

Even such crucial items as planes and pilots seemed to be in overproduction. It cut back sharply on both. What it wanted most was a chance to use the resources it already had. The IJN had avoided a fleet action since the night battles off Guadalcanal eighteen months before. It was the profound wish of King and Nimitz that by striking at the Marianas they would force the Japanese navy to come out and fight. They got what they wanted.

Saipan was the linchpin of the ring of island bases guarding the way to Japan. On June 19, the fourth day of the invasion, with the battle delicately poised, the Mobile Fleet—five battleships, nine carri-ers, 450 planes—thrust across the Philippine Sea to strike at Fifth Fleet. Spruance had seven battleships, 15 carriers and nearly 1,000 aircraft.

---

*The secret of the proximity fuse was to put a radio inside its aerial; in this case, a shell casing. The fuse was a radio tube which emitted a signal. As the signal was reflected back from the target it was picked up by the shell casing and, once a preset proximity was reached, detonated the shell. A British scientist, W.A.S. Butement, invented it but only American industry could mass-produce it in wartime.

The Mobile Fleet's commander, Admiral Jisaburo Ozawa, was counting on 500 land-based planes from Guam to balance the equation.

In an event rare in naval warfare Ozawa, who intended to attack, and Spruance, who intended to defend, deployed in almost identical fashion. As the Mobile Fleet steamed eastward, three of its light carriers and their escorts formed an antiaircraft screen one hundred miles ahead. Spruance meanwhile put his battle line of battleships and cruisers fifteen miles to the west of his carriers to form *his* antiaircraft screen. He expected Ozawa to try to get behind him and attack Turner's transports and destroy the beachhead. Ozawa's plan, however, was to destroy Spruance's carriers. He would use the superior range of his planes to attack them while keeping his own big carriers out of harm's way.

The 500 planes he expected to join the battle from Guam never showed up. U.S. Navy pilots strafed and bombed every airfield in the Marianas and swarmed over everything that got into the air. Before and during the Battle of the Philippine Sea the commander on Guam, Vice Admiral Kakuji Kakuta, continued sending Ozawa reports of huge air attacks being made against Spruance's ships, setting carriers on fire and splashing scores of American planes.

Encouraged and deceived by the fiction that his plan was working magnificently, Ozawa launched four attacks. His pilots were inexperienced and undertrained. They hurled themselves at the battle line, barreling into the wall and roof of steel raised by the Bofors guns, the Oerlikons, the proximity-fused shells. Spruance's carriers, fifteen miles to the east, calmly continued recovering and launching planes. The few Japanese pilots who got past the battle line ran into the AA fire from the carriers' escorts or were pounced on by Hellcats flying combat air patrol. One battleship suffered minor damage. Not one carrier was hit. Twenty-five American planes were brought down, against 383 Japanese.

As this slaughter of Japanese navy pilots ran its course Ozawa's flagship, the biggest carrier in the Japanese fleet, *Taiho,* was hit by a single torpedo from an American submarine, and blew up. The same fate befell *Shokaku.* The oil crisis that had helped push the IJN into war was now killing it. Japanese carriers were forced to travel to Borneo and take unrefined oil straight from the wells. Full of impurities that ruined ships' boilers, this pungent stuff filled carriers with highly volatile fumes that exploded easily.

The Battle of the Philippine Sea was the greatest defensive naval triumph of the war, yet to Spruance's pilots the decision to tie the fleet to the beachhead was a travesty of carrier combat. Fate sent them a consolation strike. In late afternoon came a sighting of the Mobile Fleet, 275 miles distant. With the light already fading and the distance too great for many planes to make the round trip, he cleared his decks.

The attacks were too hurried and too uncoordinated to have maximum effect but another Japanese carrier, the *Hiyo,* was sunk. On the return flight scores of planes ran out of gas and ditched in the night-covered sea. The loss rate on this one mission was 25 percent. When the sun went down on June 19, however, it set inexorably on the Japanese carriers. As a fighting force, the war for them was over.

SIX MONTHS before Pearl Harbor, Arnold's inexperienced air staff drew up their first war plan, basing it on two principles: Germany First and strategic bombing. Roosevelt's acceptance of their ideas crowned the twenty-year struggle to win a strategic mission for air power.

It was a plan that ignored the need for tactical air support. It said nothing about developing long-range fighter escorts. It seemed not to notice the technological superiority of German and Japanese combat aircraft.

The most important element the air planners got right, with a strong nudge from Marshall, was to think on a heroic scale. When the Air Corps had asked in 1940 for an increase from the current three air groups to 54 (roughly 5,000 combat planes, which in turn implied an extra 10,000 trainers, transports and so forth) Marshall's response had been "Why only fifty-four?" He was the first army chief of staff who was neither hostile nor indifferent to the airmen's cause. He grasped better than some of them Mitchell's first principle of air power, the supremacy of numbers.

Air superiority would not be won easily or maintained cheaply. It would have to be fought for anew every day. Without mighty reserves of pilots and planes, sustained combat operations were impossible. Accidents, bad weather, poor maintenance and the infinite variety of human error wrecked more planes and killed more pilots than were ever lost in dogfights. Size was the first thing to get right.

To produce the numbers needed after entering the war, Arnold leased the war-emptied hotels of Miami Beach and turned them into a palmy, white-tiled preflight school holding up to 35,000 aspiring pilots at a time. His instant solution to the maintenance challenge was to order the plane manufacturers to train five AAF mechanics on the factory floor for every bomber delivered. In overcrowded Seattle this meant lodging his trainee mechanics in church basements and local jails, but up at the sharp end it meant that planes like the B-17, designed to fly three missions a month, flew as many as seven.

The Victory Program adopted after Pearl Harbor set a goal of 50,000 aircraft a year. In 1942 that target was as good as met, with 47,800. By the time of the Torch landings the AAF had more combat aircraft (13,000) than the three Axis powers combined (9,500). This numerical superiority within a year of American entry into the war assured Allied domination of the air, yet this was only a beginning. In 1943, 86,000 planes were produced and 83,000 pilots trained, as well as 240,000 ground crew.

The margin of Allied production superiority was crushing. It was 2 to 1 in 1940, 2.5 to 1 in 1941, 3 to 1 in 1942 and 4 to 1 in 1943. The Germans and Japanese managed to close the gap slightly in 1944 but an air battle fought at 3-to-1 odds had much the same result as one fought at 4-to-1.

They also dissipated their advantages in pilot training and combat experience by treating their flyers romantically instead of managerially. A German or Japanese fighter pilot was an elite warrior whom destiny called every day to give battle—until the day he died. American and British pilots were managed like valuable resources and frail human beings. After a while they were pulled out of the front line to become instructors, imparting what they had learned to others, unlike their Axis counterparts who took their knowledge to the grave.

Axis plane producers complacently sat on their technological lead and when they woke up to the fact that they had lost it tried to get it back by turning out entirely new aircraft. The United States and Britain took a different approach, concentrating their research on just three areas: radar, engine power and armament. Nearly all of the combat aircraft of the RAF and the AAF in service when the war ended were based on pre–Pearl Harbor airframes. Their performance, however, had improved tremendously. Improvements were accumulated until there were enough to make it worth stopping the production run and incorporating them into the plane, but nothing was allowed to hold up the aluminum torrent for long.

The Allied triumphs of production, organization and technology were the sure bedrock of air supremacy. All the same, it could only be won by men in the air. That proved as frustrating as anything that happened on the ground or at sea. Eighth Air Force, operating out of bases along the east coast of England, began bombing Germany toward the end of 1942. One third of the bombers Arnold had counted on using were diverted to North Africa. Another third were diverted to help save Guadalcanal. The air offensive against Germany began with none of the sky-blackening masses of the air staff's fond hopes. The results were meager and at Casablanca the British asked for American daylight bombing to be stopped. Better, they said, to have Eighth Air Force meld with the RAF's night-bombing offensive and give it more weight. Roosevelt was inclined to agree. So was the JCS. The commander of Eighth Air Force, Ira C. Eaker, had to outthink and out-argue Churchill to win a reprieve for daylight bombing.

The B-17 was proving a less than ideal instrument. At Midway the Flying Fortresses had dropped 377 bombs and hit not a single Japanese ship. They were so crammed with armor plate, machine guns and ammunition their bombload was not much more than some medium bombers'. The Norden bombsight was supposedly able to drop a bomb into a pickle barrel from twenty thousand feet, yet it was only a fair-weather friend. In the cloudy skies of Europe it proved a constant disappointment. Radar bombsights could pierce the cloud cover but they offered a picture as blurred as a rain-lashed window. Even in clear-weather attacks Eighth Air Force could not drop more than one bomb in five within one thousand feet of a target.

Eaker had to wait nearly a year before he could launch the kind of strike Eighth Air Force was created for. On August 17, 1943, he sent it to attack the ball-bearing plant at Schweinfurt. This was a complicated operation that was upset at the outset by the vagaries of British weather. Five hundred German fighters rose to challenge 376 Fortresses. Dozens of Germans were shot down, but so were 60 bombers. Fifty more were damaged beyond repair and 100 put out of action for weeks. The plant was hit but kept producing. The next big raid, on Stuttgart, saw another one hundred B-17s shot down or totaled. A second raid on Schweinfurt was another costly failure. Daylight bombing without fighter escort meant losses of 20 to 25 percent on every big raid. Not even the United States could afford war at these prices. Arnold's Mitchellian faith was shaken.

Eighth Air Force began shifting over to the British way, area attacks, putting enemy morale, in effect, on the target list. The loss rate and the limitations of B-17s and Norden bombsights pushed it hard in that direction. The first area target was Münster, on October 10, 1943. The bombers' aiming point was the city center.

A practice soon developed of designating a military target such as a railroad yard and hitting that with saturation bombing. Pilots and air staff knew that up to 90 percent of all bombs dropped would not hit the target but were sure to fall on the surrounding area. This nevertheless helped square what might be seen as attacks on civilians with the consciences of airmen and with public opinion back home.

The British needed no such moral fig leaf, having been bombed in their homes by the Germans in two wars. And against Japan, Americans had few qualms about attacking Japanese cities. Area bombing of Japan was seen as due punishment for the attack on Pearl Harbor.

Even area raids took a heavy toll. The AAF turned its attention at last to long-range fighters. The Mustang with a Rolls Royce Merlin engine was its best pure air-superiority machine but lacked range. The answer was to put an 85-gallon fuel tank behind the pilot's seat and fill the wings with fuel, in bulletproof tanks. This increased its range so it could make thousand-mile round trips into southern Germany in the winter of 1943, but it was the arrival of the 108-gallon drop-tank in the spring of 1944 that made the P-51 into the ultimate long-range fighter of the war. With long-range escorts the Fortress loss rate in daylight raids fell to 6 percent, something Eighth Air Force could live with.

With the cross-Channel attack drawing close, a tactical air force was created, under Lewis Brereton, to support it. Eisenhower was meanwhile being forced to choose between two plans for the best use of the heavy bombers in the run up to invasion. One, urged by Carl "Tooey" Spaatz, the commander of U.S. Strategic Air Forces, aimed to destroy German oil facilities. The other, promoted by the British, sought to wreck the railroads of France.

This Transportation Plan, as it was called, was the brainchild of Sir Solly Zuckerman, a former professor of zoology. He had thought up the attack on the marshaling yards around Rome that helped bring

Mussolini's downfall. The same kind of attacks, he argued, would paralyze German movement to the invasion beaches and throw the Wehrmacht into disarray throughout France.

Eisenhower had his doubts about that, but if the Transportation Plan worked it might produce results faster than Spaatz's Oil Plan. British and American bomber generals resisted his choice so stubbornly that Eisenhower threatened to resign unless he got a direct say in the use of strategic air power. He won that battle, only for Spaatz to counterattack by adopting his tactics and threatening to resign if the Oil Plan were shelved. A solution was found: the Transportation Plan was formally accepted but bombing runs were routed so that "stray" bombs fell on oil targets.

Brereton's IX Tactical Air Command meanwhile turned its 700 medium bombers and 1,200 fighter-bombers loose on a bridge-busting and radar-site demolition campaign.

The Luftwaffe rose to defend them all—railheads, refineries, bridges and radar—and was torn apart. In April 1944 it lost 2,500 pilots. In May it lost another 2,500. By June it was flat on its back, short of fuel, almost blind from the loss of radar, a bleeding and demoralized wreck. Absolute air supremacy had been won where it was needed most when it was needed most.

MARSHALL, the great problem solver, had become a problem. Roosevelt was deeply troubled at the idea of letting Marshall leave Washington to command Overlord as the war reached a crescendo. Yet simple justice demanded that a man who had done so much for his country should crown his career by commanding in the main theater of war.

Roosevelt resolved this dilemma as he did with so many others, by handing it over to Marshall. The general had only to say he wanted to be supreme commander in Western Europe—and he wanted it profoundly—for it to be his. He could not bring himself to do it. The president, he said, must decide what was best. He thereby left Roosevelt free to do what King, Arnold, Congress and the press were clamoring for—to leave Marshall where he was, in Washington.

In this way supreme command of Overlord gravitated into Eisenhower's hands. In November 1943 he left the Mediterranean for England. His original intention had been to take Clark with him and hand

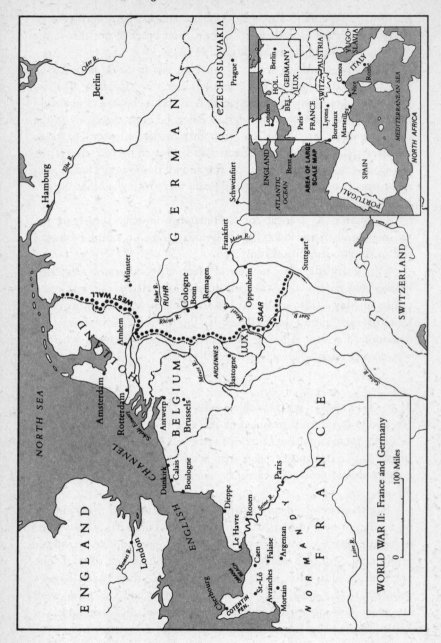

WORLD WAR II: France and Germany

0   100 Miles

over Fifth Army to Bradley. Marshall told him to take Bradley, leave Clark.

The date penciled in for the cross-Channel attack was May 1, 1944, but assault shipping was in such short supply it slipped back to June 1. This made an extra month's production of LSTs and landing craft available, but it meant losing good campaigning weather and giving the Germans more time to guess where the invasion would come.

There were only two serious possibilities: the Pas-de-Calais, facing England across the Strait of Dover, or Normandy, one hundred miles to the west and more than one hundred miles from English shores. Gerd von Rundstedt, the sixty-eight-year-old commander of all German armies in the west, bet on Pas-de-Calais and put Fifteenth Army, his strongest, there. Rommel, given responsibility for coastal defenses, guessed it would be Normandy and devoted his efforts to strengthening forces there instead.

Von Rundstedt had a vision of strong, mobile armor and artillery reserves massing inland and crushing the invaders in a war of maneuver on the plains of northern France. Rommel had only to scan the skies above to see that was a fantasy. The invasion must be stopped at the waterline or it would not be stopped anywhere.

German forces were neither concentrated along the coast as Rommel wished nor massed in large mobile reserves. They were dispersed, in an attempt to keep the two commanders happy, badly deployed to offer one defense or the other. With Hitler, one of history's less successful strategists, looking over their shoulder straps it was a situation rich in opportunities for error.

Advance elements began moving out on June 4, only to be called back after two hours because of the weather. Relaunched while the storm still churned up the Channel, it was hurled through a "weather window"—a break of sixteen hours or so—predicted for June 6. Shortly after midnight American and British paratroopers began dropping into Normandy, to sow confusion behind German lines and to secure both Allied flanks.

The British and Canadians came ashore against light resistance. Even so, they were kept on the short leash of the cautious Montgomery. Back in London he had boasted of thrusting his armor more than thirty miles inland on D-Day. In the event, he dug in halfway to his assigned objective, the city of Caen, eight miles from the coast.

The place where the planners' hopes were most fully realized was at Utah Beach, taken by the 4th Infantry Division. They moved quickly inland on causeways through the surrounding marshes seized by the 101st Airborne Division*. Only ten miles away, at Omaha Beach, everything was meanwhile going horribly wrong.

The assault was based on proven techniques and a few new ideas: heavy bombing of defenses at first light to drive the defenders under cover . . . underwater demolition teams emerging at low tide to blow clear paths through the obstacles and booby traps for the landing craft . . . 32 amphibian tanks swimming in to engage enemy artillery and machine gun positions . . . the first waves of infantry hitting the beach close behind the tanks . . . DUKWs quickly boating in 105-millimeter guns . . . follow-up forces landing to renew the momentum of the assault . . . men swarming up the four draws that snaked their way from the sand to the top of the steep 150-foot cliffs that towered over the one and a half miles of beach.

One essential element was missing: the air and naval bombardment that thundered night and day for a week or more against target beaches in the Pacific. Here, the enemy had to be kept guessing up to the last minute.

No one ever thought it would be easy. Ultra had revealed the presence at Omaha of a strong German division, engaged on anti-invasion exercises. The assault was assigned to the Big Red One, beefed up with two regiments from the 29th Infantry Division.

The bombers came in on schedule but early-morning mist veiled the beach below. To avoid killing UDT frogmen emerging from the dark waters, they delayed releasing their bombs. Nearly 1,300 tons of high explosive fell on cattle grazing behind German positions.

Landing craft began their run in from twelve miles out—twice the distance chosen by the British or by commanders in the Pacific. This two-hour journey in small vessels through rough seas left many men violently seasick. Their energies were drained even further by having to bail with their helmets to keep their craft from foundering.

Of the 32 Sherman amphibian tanks 27 were dropped in water too deep for them. They sank without trace. DUKWs carrying 105-millimeter artillery found the going too rough and capsized. A strong

---

*82nd Airborne Division, dropped farther inland, blocked German forces coming down from Cherbourg and from the western side of the Cotentin peninsula to attack the beachhead.

lateral current along the coast pushed the landing craft far off course. Almost no one hit the beach sector they had trained for.

They arrived to find German gunners mowing down the frogmen. There were few cleared channels onto the beach. Landing craft coxswains circled in bewilderment until a few hardy souls crashed through, or blew up attempting to. German machine gunners trained their sights on the ramps and when they dropped hosed the inside of the craft mercilessly. Heavily burdened men pulled themselves in terror over the side. Hundreds drowned in the shallow water while others stripped themselves and dog-paddled for hours, exposing only eyes and nose, to pass for dead among the dead.

Entire infantry companies disintegrated, putting not even a rifle squad ashore in condition to fight. Those who struggled onto the beach suffered a shock. Where were the bomb craters they had counted on to provide them with cover? Scrambling for the shelter of the seawall—a line of dunes three to four feet high—they had to cross minefields sown the length of the beach.

This was the toughest amphibious assault of the war, probably of all time. It looked, felt and sounded like total disaster. The Germans observing from above jubilantly reported back that they had crushed the invasion here. Local reserves were diverted to counterattack the British instead.

Bradley, commanding First Army, was offshore on the cruiser *Augusta*. As reports came in they pushed him remorselessly to a single conclusion. He was within minutes of canceling the remaining followup forces and pulling the survivors out when word came that it might still be possible to hold the beach. A handful of men had begun moving out.

Old battleships, some going back to Teddy Roosevelt's two-a-year program, were pounding the cliff top with large-caliber projectiles. Plucky destroyer crews came in so close their ships brushed rocks and sand. At unmissable ranges they took on German artillery while here and there small groups of enterprising men made their way up the mined and trip-wired draws.

It was a fight so precariously balanced that when it was over combat historians could name the 47 men who that day plucked victory at Omaha from the jaws of defeat, even though they had to reach in up to the armpit to do it. Casualties at "Bloody Omaha" rivaled those of the three days it took to capture Tarawa.

The beachhead consisted of scattered pockets along the cliff top and in fields full of slaughtered cows, yet it was enough. This triumph sealed the greatest combined-arms operation in history. By the evening of D-Day, when the weather window shut, there were 156,000 Allied troops and 20,000 vehicles in France.

Allied commanders soon discovered they could not break out. The Germans found they could not break in. The five beachheads linked up and as fresh divisions arrived the Allies slugged their way forward while supplies piled up and logistics officers grew old quickly. Without a working port and with the two artificial harbors towed to Normandy wrecked by a storm on June 19, little more than half the supplies intended for the battle could be shipped over. There was no fuel problem—no one was going anywhere. The biggest headache was artillery ammunition: it was never easy to bring cargoes so heavy and bulky over beaches and ammunition was being expended on a scale no one foresaw. The planners had been so anxious about getting forces ashore little thought had been given to what was beyond the beaches, such as the *bocage*.

This was the French term for the hedgerow country that hemmed in half of Bradley's First Army. Some of these hedgerows were up to one thousand years old and twenty feet thick. They turned fields into miniature battlegrounds that gave every advantage to the defender. The roads between the hedgerows had been worn down over centuries. This part of France was one sunken road after another, where tanks got stuck and infantry groped blindly into ambushes. Artillery alone seemed able to blast a way through.

Where the *bocage* ended, the *prairies marécageuses* took over: marshes that swallowed men and beasts. This network of swamps and bogs blocked the other half of First Army. Not even artillery blasts a way through water.

It was the British and Canadians, farther east, who had the dry, open terrain—dry and open all the way to Paris, 120 miles away. Montgomery liked to boast of how he had "drawn" the bulk of German forces onto his sector, but the terrain deserves most of the credit. Rommel and Montgomery settled down to a war of tank attrition that neither could win.

Six weeks after the invasion, the Allies held a beachhead fifty miles wide and only five to fifteen miles deep. For the whole fifty miles there was a convincing simulacrum of deadlock. Trench warfare seemed about to cut deep into marlaceous soil of France once more.

With one vehicle to every five men American units possessed mobility to the nth degree; nobody had to walk. Yet all this mobility was like a coiled spring to which no one seemed able to find the release mechanism. And then the traditional American saviors intervened—firepower and ingenuity.

A technical sergeant began cutting and shaping spiky beach obstacles into what looked like pitchforks for giants and welded them onto the front of Sherman tanks. With the tank's weight, traction and momentum behind it the pitchfork gouged huge chunks out of the *bocage,* opening up the fields of Normandy.

Germans who were once securely dug in had to cope with that plus something terrifying—napalm. Shipped to battlefields on both sides of the world in July 1944, it looked harmless enough: a waxy, granular substance that resembled soap flakes. Mixed with gasoline, it intensified fire and made it stick to whatever it fell on. Napalm was the one weapon that made even the best troops in German and Japanese armies break and run. In Normandy it burned out German positions no matter how deeply entrenched in the *bocage.* To Bradley, who had been forced to ration artillery shells, it came like a gift from the gods of war.

The prospect of deadlock concentrated minds as nothing else did and air support of ground troops suddenly came into its own. When Elwood "Pete" Quesada took over IX Tactical Air Command he treated the men on the ground as his customers. Equipped with dazzling recognition panels and two-way FM radio sets, infantry platoons or tank crews could call in air strikes as needed or ask the fighter-bombers to scout ahead for them.

The final push that released the coiled spring came from the technique that had never worked yet, carpet bombing. It was attempted twice in the British sector to get Montgomery rolling and had failed both times. On July 25 it was tried in the American sector, near St.-Lô. Nearly 2,500 bombers and fighter-bombers dropped 4,200 tons of high explosive on a rectangle covering roughly five square miles. The devastation wiped out an entire Panzer division in the space of ninety minutes. The spring flew open, hurling American armored units out of Normandy, free at last.

Patton's Third Army, activated on August 1, roared across France at unparalleled speed. Other divisions raced through Brittany. Montgomery and the Canadians broke loose. And this, Hitler judged, was the perfect moment to launch a counterstroke. Allied forces were suddenly spread all over the landscape and their lines of communication were vulnerable.

Convinced like his predecessors in World War One that if he could only break through to the Channel coast Allied armies would collapse, Hitler took personal command of the battle. His generals had no faith in it, preferring to fall back gradually on the five river lines between Normandy and the German frontier. The planners of Overlord had expected them to do exactly that, forecasting it would take a full year to fight from Omaha to the Rhine. Hitler gambled away his five strong lines of defense.

Ultra revealed—and doomed—the attack before it began. Just enough strength was devoted to blunting it while the bulk of Allied forces was deployed to attack its flanks. Fighter-bombers armed with armor-piercing rockets swarmed over German tanks. Massed American artillery reached such peaks of coordination and precision it was as devastating as bombing.

Commanders who had served on the eastern front thought they had seen hard fighting but they had never witnessed firepower like this. They wrote home in stunned disbelief, amazed that anything could survive the awesome carnage that broke Hitler's counterattack in Normandy. It ended with Germans fleeing east to escape a closing trap.

The fighting in Normandy cost Von Rundstedt enough men, tanks, guns and vehicles to form seven Panzer divisions plus twelve infantry divisions at full strength. Sent reeling, the Wehrmacht imagined it was fighting an Allied force twice the size it really was. Eisenhower's manpower superiority in France that summer was about 20 percent. The real difference came in air power, firepower, mobility and intelligence.

By August 19 Allied forces had reached the Seine and stood at the gates of Paris, on a line the planners had not expected to reach before October 4. Paris liberated, the armies flowed on, but with every mile they were throwing their mobility away. Some 22 million five-gallon jerricans had been shipped to France. Once drained of their precious gasoline, they were tossed into the bushes or dropped in the ditches, instead of being collected and sent back to the cross-Channel pipeline for refilling.

From Belgium to Lorraine tanks and trucks ran out of gas in September. The heady talk of the war ending by Christmas ran dry too. The great race was over. The Germans dug in along the West Wall—the thousands of pillboxes and the long rows of concrete teeth that snaked over the landscape for mile after mile across the approaches to the Reich.

16

IRRESISTIBLE FORCE

WITH MOST of France secure, Eisenhower shifted Supreme Headquarters Allied Expeditionary Force across the Channel and assumed personal command of the ground battle from Montgomery. First Army was assigned to Courtney Hodges. Bradley was moved up to command the newly created U.S. 12th Army Group.

This meant that Montgomery, now commanding only the British-Canadian 21st Army Group, found himself on a par with Bradley. After the weeks in Normandy as Eisenhower's deputy for Allied ground forces this seemed a demotion, if not an insult. The dimming of his star was unthinkable to the Englishman; and Monty, like Houdini, had made a career out of escaping from restraints. As he boasted to Patton in Sicily, he knew how to deal with orders he disliked—he ignored them.

Small, unprepossessing, with darting eyes, a bristling moustache and a squeaky voice, this Gilbert and Sullivan figure nonetheless held the priceless gift of presence. The effect on the troops he led could be electrifying and a Montgomery briefing often provided a bravura performance from one of the best actors never to go onto the British stage.

He proceeded to turn the whole force of his personality to winning control of the ground war in Western Europe. Holing up in his great prize from the desert, Rommel's wood-paneled trailer, he summoned

Eisenhower to come to him in good weather and bad, in sickness and in health, for lectures on how to run a war. The Ike-Monty battle of wits shaped every important ground action from Paris to Berlin.

Once the British and Canadians had crossed the Seine, Eisenhower tried to speed their progress toward Belgium by giving Montgomery supply priority. This, he hoped, would lead to the swift capture of Antwerp, the largest port on the Continent. Twenty-first Army Group drove forward with an élan that rivaled Patton's. Antwerp fell, with wharves and docks intact, on September 4. Nothing was done, however, to clear the Germans from the banks of the Scheldt Estuary that links the port with the North Sea. This left the Allies with a superb port that was intact but useless; something that did not seem to trouble Montgomery at all.

His 21st Army Group could just about manage on supplies landed at minor Channel ports such as Dieppe and Seine river ports such as Rouen. It was Hodges and First Army, still tied to the beaches of Normandy and the badly damaged port of Cherbourg, four hundred miles away, who really needed Antwerp. By helping Hodges to advance, Montgomery would be promoting Ike's strategy, not his own.

That strategy had been outlined by SHAEF back in May and confirmed after the breakout from Normandy. It is usually described as a broad front advance, but this is misleading. It may be more accurately described as a gasoline-powered revival of that traditional American technique for conquering large areas, the campaign of converging columns. That was the strategic design by which Grant, moving south, and Sherman, moving north, ground the Confederacy down. That was how the West was won from the Indians. It was how the Pacific was being recaptured from the Japanese.

Although SHAEF was an Allied command and the degree of Allied harmony was unprecedented in warfare it was inevitable that Americans would dominate strategy in the closing stages. Fresh American divisions arrived every month, while the British were breaking up some of theirs to keep the rest up to strength. The United States was providing 70 percent of the men and the arms employed by SHAEF. And as Marshall, Eisenhower and Bradley surveyed the options before them the military heritage of their country led them, almost by instinct, to converging columns. The British, who had never operated on a truly large scale on land, did not grasp it, then or later.

Army strength columns, going north of the Ardennes, through

Belgium, would converge on the Ruhr. Other army strength columns, passing south of the Ardennes, through Alsace-Lorraine, would converge on the Saar. Having taken these two major objectives and established themselves firmly on German soil, all of these armies would fan out, converging with Soviet armies advancing into Germany from the east. Such was the broad design.

The Ruhr was an obvious objective because it held the largest concentration of German heavy industry. Although close to the frontier it was doubly protected, by the broad waters of the Rhine and by the strongest defenses of the West Wall. Conquest of the Ruhr was assigned to the British Second Army, moving through northern Belgium, and to the U.S. First Army, advancing through central Belgium.

The dead hand of supply shortages reined in the drive on the Ruhr. Ike's hints to Montgomery about getting Antwerp working were ignored. The one break in the logistical gloom was the fall of Marseilles. Seventh Army, under Alexander Patch, had landed on the beaches of the French Riviera in mid-August. Marseilles was captured in full working order a week later. By the end of September it was handling 40 percent of all supplies shipped from the United States to Europe.

Seventh Army meanwhile drove up the Rhône Valley and along the Saône into northeastern France to support Patton's assault on Germany's second smokestack heartland, the Saar. This was no easier target than the Ruhr. All the main approaches to it pass through the deep valley of the Moselle or wind their way through the Vosges Mountains.

Patton spent the fall of 1944 in the kind of slow, infantry fighting that he loathed. While his Third Army tried to claw its way to the Saar through Lorraine, Seventh Army sought to break in through Alsace.

Montgomery spent the fall offering easy solutions to complex problems. He flatly rejected Eisenhower's strategy. The plans he offered invariably placed 21st Army Group in the forefront, yet he weakened his arguments by shifting his ground almost from day to day. Sometimes Monty wanted to make a swift "knifelike thrust" into the heart of the Reich. At other times this became an advance with "a solid mass" of forty divisions. On some occasions he promised only the lightning capture of the Ruhr, on others it was nothing less than the fall of Berlin.

The upshot of every Montgomery plan was that everything—men, gasoline, armor, artillery, air support—must be assigned to 21st Army Group. As he pressed these views home he was invariably and vehemently critical of Ike, even to his face. The supreme commander had to grab hold of him one day and remind him gently, "Steady, Monty. You can't talk to me like that. I'm your boss."

All the same, Montgomery got his chance. Code-named Market Garden, it was the biggest airborne assault in history.

Marshall and Arnold, both enthusiasts for new ideas and thinkers on the grand scale, had pushed through the creation of an Allied Airborne Army, under Lewis Brereton. Comprising the 82nd and 101st airborne divisions, the British 1st Airborne Division and the Polish Parachute Brigade, it numbered 45,000 men who could be dropped or landed by glider.

Montgomery proposed to use this, the cream of SHAEF's infantry, in an airborne assault that would seize seven bridges in Holland, the last of them spanning the Rhine. While the paratroopers held the bridges the British Second Army was to drive the ninety miles from Antwerp to Arnhem in less than seventy-two hours, linking up all seven bridgeheads as it advanced.

Eisenhower adopted Market Garden unreservedly. Its boldness and imagination seemed odd coming from Montgomery, but also enthralled him. He was no longer the cautious, untried commander of untried troops. Ike had become a high roller. During the breakneck dash across France he held nothing back, despite the risks. At one point his entire infantry replacement pool consisted of a single American soldier. One reason why France was liberated so quickly was his willingness to fight without reserves.

If the Market Garden operation worked as planned the Ruhr would be enveloped, the maze of Dutch canals and rivers leapfrogged and Allied armies would be lodged on the edge of the north German plain. The West Wall and the Rhine would both be outflanked and the road to Berlin dramatically shortened. Had it turned out like that, Montgomery's claims over supplies and strategy would have been virtually irresistible.

The plan failed before the first airborne trooper had shrugged into his parachute harness. Two Panzer divisions moved into the outskirts of Arnhem for rest and refitting after a savage mauling in Normandy. Ultra revealed at least one was there, probably accompanied by the other. Oblique-angle photographs taken by low-flying reconnaissance planes confirmed it, showing the unmistakable outlines of tanks underneath camouflage netting.

Montgomery dismissed the photographs and ignored the Ultra intercepts. This was his big chance; too big to let slip.

The airborne assault went in on September 17. The paratroopers seized all seven bridges. It was British Second Army that fell short, taking a week to reach Arnhem. It then failed to cross the Rhine to relieve a British parachute battalion that was holding at bay the equivalent of an entire Panzer division.

Market Garden created a long, narrow salient deep into Holland. The Germans whittled it down to a stump. One by one the bridgeheads were wiped out. Some 17,000 Allied troops were killed, wounded or captured.

The cost did not stop there. The collapse of Market Garden coincided with the gasoline supply crisis that brought First, Third and Seventh armies to a standstill. They were also desperately short of artillery ammunition. These shortages in the American armies combined with Market Garden's failure to provide the Germans with the respite they needed desperately.

They could now rebuild divisions wrecked in France, raise fresh units and man the West Wall. They deployed everything from tough SS Panzer regiments to "stomach battalions," consisting of men suffering from ulcers, to "ear battalions," where no one could hear properly, to rosy-cheeked Hitler Youth and middle-aged men who limped. In many places the defenders heavily outnumbered the attackers. German arms production was meanwhile reaching its height, pouring out vast quantities of guns and shells. The Germans called it "The Miracle in the West."

It was a miracle that enabled Hitler to launch a strong counterattack despite Allied superiority in mobility and air power. While his enemies bogged down in mud and rain along the West Wall he assembled ten Panzer and twenty infantry divisions north and east of the Ardennes. This high, densely forested plateau covers most of Luxembourg, much of Belgium, and extends into Germany, where it is known as the Eifel. Few good roads traverse it and both the American and German armies used it as a quiet sector where battered divisions could recover without being pulled out of the line.

Allied code breakers discovered Hitler was planning a winter offensive. Reconnaissance flights disclosed a buildup of German armor, including a new *Panzerarmee*. Yet there were so many radio intercepts of German units bewailing gas shortages that a major counterattack seemed impossible. Besides, there was no point in the Germans coming out from their formidably strong defenses to launch an attack that was certain to fail. Only the Allies would gain from that.

It was a view shared completely by Von Rundstedt and other senior German generals, but since an attempt to assassinate him in July Hitler paid less heed than ever to them. Through a drug-induced haze he saw only victory ahead. His Panzers would rip through the Americans with contemptuous ease. After all, these were the "Italians," he had been told, of the Allied side. His armies would drive all the way to Antwerp, which the British expected to have in operation, finally, by the end of November.

Hitler planned to shatter both First Army and Ninth Army, recently brought up from Brittany under William Simpson to add yet another column converging on the Ruhr. With Antwerp in his hands Hitler would have the entire 21st Army Group trapped. The distance his Panzers had to drive to achieve all this was more than one hundred road miles.

The offensive was postponed two weeks, finally opening on December 16, when fog and rain pinned Allied planes to the ground and heavy frost hardened it for German tanks. Three attacking armies drove east, led by more than 1,000 Panzers and 600 self-propelled 75-millimeter assault guns that were, in effect, turretless tanks. They crashed into a thinly stretched line of American divisions: the experienced, battle-hardened 2nd and 4th divisions, the green 99th and 106th divisions, fresh off the boat, and the 28th Division, sent to the Ardennes to rest up from the appalling bloodletting it had recently endured in the Hürtgen Forest. The 28th was a Pennsylvania National Guard outfit but Bradley had reorganized it and trained it before his departure for North Africa. The payoff came in the Ardennes.

Under the German onslaught field hospitals, heavy artillery, truck companies, field kitchens and other units that rightfully belonged to the rear pulled back. This gave rise to a legend of American units breaking and fleeing in panic. Almost without exception, green troops and veterans alike fought off superior numbers with a stubbornness that threw Hitler's attack off the rails before it had traveled a mile. Not a single German division attained its first-day objectives. Some did not reach them for a week.

In the first five days as many as 7,000 Americans were taken prisoner, but nearly half were men surrendered by their regimental commanders when ammunition and rations gave out. Units that chose to break up into small groups filtered back through the woods and lived to fight again.

Until now proximity fuses had been used only over England or the waters of the Pacific, where duds would not fall into enemy hands and reveal the precious secret. In this emergency they were authorized for use by the field artillery. Set to burst fifty feet above the ground, proximity-fused shells blew German infantry formations apart. Mass artillery fire wreaked the same kind of havoc among German armor.

In straight tank-versus-tank engagements the Germans had an edge, mainly because the Sherman's 75-millimeter gun lacked hitting power. With a gasoline engine instead of diesel it also burst into flames easily when hit. Tankers called it "the Ronson." On the other hand, its main rival, the German Panther, was even more combustible and more prone to mechanical breakdown.

At night enemy tanks fired high-velocity flares that blinded American tank crews and silhouetted their machines. American bazooka teams meanwhile stalked German tanks day and night on foot, leaving blackened Panther carcasses all over the Ardennes. Some 1,500 tanks were wrecked in the Battle of the Bulge, with honors roughly even.

When the Germans struck, Eisenhower had no mobile reserve available. The only battle-hardened divisions not already committed were the 82nd and the 101st, recuperating near Reims from their losses in Market Garden. He sent them in open cattle trucks toward Bastogne, on the southern face of the salient the German attack created. Like Gettysburg, this Belgian village derived its importance entirely from the road network that fanned out from it, to threaten the flank of an advancing army. In the race for Bastogne the 101st got there first. The Germans virtually surrounded it but air drops kept the paratroopers supplied through a bitterly cold Christmas.

Three of Patton's armored divisions drove one hundred miles north over snowbound roads to attack the Germans around Bastogne and lift the siege. The weather cleared, allowing IX TAC and XXIX TAC fighter-bombers to swoop with stunning speed and firepower onto road-bound German units. No German got within fifty miles of Antwerp.

In a move that left bruised feelings for decades afterward, Eisenhower attached First and Ninth armies to Montgomery's command at the height of the battle. It was easier to communicate with them that way. Bradley's HQ was too far south and too close to the front for him to direct them effectively, given the wedge the Germans had made in the American line north of him.

Montgomery's contribution proved disappointing. His tactical ideas were out of touch with frontline realities. In effect, Hodges, Simpson and their corps commanders fought their own battle. Few British troops were involved in it and Montgomery refused to commit himself to a counterattack for so long that the chance of cutting the salient off at its base and trapping the Germans inside it was lost.

By New Year's Eve, Hitler's last offensive had collapsed. What remained was a bulge in the Allied lines, forty-five miles deep and thirty miles at the base. First Army, attacking the northern face, and Third Army, attacking the southern face, gave themselves a month to eliminate it. They finished the job with three days to spare, on January 28.

Hitler's winter offensive left deep cracks in the West Wall. His armies lost 100,000 men killed and wounded, plus 250,000 taken prisoner. Every German armored division had been wrecked. Once the Allies crossed the Rhine the Germans would lack the mobile firepower needed to contain them.

As Allied troops approached the legendary river the dazzling lure that drew them on was Berlin. It had fascinated them since the moment they hit the beach in Normandy. The nature of the terrain east of the Rhine, the road network and the alignment of Allied armies made the British Second Army the logical choice for a drive on Berlin. To help speed Montgomery on his way Eisenhower gave him supply priority and reinforced him with twelve American divisions.

Monty spent forever organizing a crossing of the Rhine. On March 7 the 9th Armored Division, of Hodges's First Army, dashed forward and seized the one bridge still intact, a railroad bridge at Remagen, twenty miles south of Bonn. Two weeks later Third Army crossed the Rhine at Oppenheim. These two breakthroughs upset SHAEF's plans and expectations but Eisenhower reinforced success instead of failure, giving Bradley the priority he had earlier given

Montgomery. American armies drove east and south into Germany. Monty was still trying to get across.

Eisenhower would be criticized severely for not racing the Russians to Berlin, but the best chance for doing that was lost by Monty's excessive caution. Ike had also had second thoughts about the value of the prize. Roosevelt, Churchill and Stalin had met at Yalta in February and decided on the fate of postwar Germany. It would be divided into zones of occupation. Berlin would be administered jointly by the Allied powers.

Taking the city would cost an estimated 100,000 casualties. Montgomery lacked the dash and the nerve to seize it, which meant the operation would have to go to Bradley. Yet even if the city fell to American forces, they would have to let the Russians in. There was no political or military advantage there that seemed worth another 100,000 dead and wounded Americans. And if by some miracle Monty found a way to take the city quickly and cheaply . . . well, Eisenhower was no longer in the mood to do him any favors. He had even stopped going to the field marshal's tutorials on strategy in Rommel's fancy trailer.

On April 12 Roosevelt died, almost at the very moment when 2nd Armored Division reached the Elbe—the line where American and Soviet armies had agreed to link up. For the next two weeks American units arrived, only to wait while the Red Army shot its way at point-blank range into the heart of Berlin. The Russians were willing to pay the price, for revenge and in hopes of taking Hitler alive. On April 30 he cheated them by blowing his brains out while in the streets round about Russians broke down doors.

THE DAY would come when the Japanese government would have to explain defeat to the Diet. The main reason we lost, the government would say, was the destruction of our merchant fleet; by mines, by aircraft, but above all by American submarines.

No one had foreseen that, despite years of war gaming and war planning on both sides. In the 1920s and 1930s the United States had signed a variety of treaties that outlawed unrestricted submarine warfare, that evil business which had dragged America into World War One.

U.S. Navy submariners dreamed of attacks on Japanese warships, whose outlines they memorized. Tactics and doctrine breathed not a word about merchant ships: they were off limits. Yet the emotional fury ignited at Pearl Harbor made a bonfire of those treaty commitments and the navy discovered that in the fleet submarine it possessed the ideal weapon to bring the Japanese empire low.

It was bigger, faster and had longer range than the boats of other navies.* Designed with the vast distances of the Pacific in mind, the new submarine began entering the fleet in March 1941. It was handicapped by an obsolescent torpedo that ran on steam, thereby leaving a white wake that could be seen and avoided; carried a modest warhead; and was equipped with a complicated magnetic exploder that did not work, plus a backup contact exploder that did not work either. For eighteen months Japanese merchant ships came home with unexploded torpedoes stuck in their hulls. Only after German electric-driven torpedoes ran up onto East Coast beaches in the summer of 1942 were American "fish" fully modernized. The faults in the exploders were corrected. Almost as important, the Japanese merchant navy code was broken in mid-1943. Losses rose spectacularly thereafter.

American submariners complained bitterly at the time and ever after about the defects of the torpedoes they started the war with. That was a lousy break, but offset by a major break entirely in their favor—the Japanese navy's aversion to ASW. All it could think of was a decisive fleet action, the great, all-out battle. Convoys with escorts would have cut losses but Japanese merchant skippers were utterly opposed to them because they would reduce the number of trips a ship could make and thus reduce profits. The Japanese never mounted a serious ASW effort, to the immense benefit of American submarine crews.

They sank 4.75 million tons of Japanese merchant shipping, plus 200 warships, for a further 550,000 tons. The cost was 52 submarines lost (two of them to American planes). It was this kind of equation— one submarine lost for every 100,000 tons sunk—that had made for the U-boats' happy time. For them it was a temporary phenomenon. For the Pacific Fleet it was the start-to-finish figure of the underseas war.

By the summer of 1944 the fleet submarine dominated the waters

---

*In 1942 it was overtaken in size and range by the five thousand-ton I-boats of the Japanese navy, of which few were built.

below the waves just as completely as the fast carriers dominated the waters above. With the initiative firmly in American hands, the question of where to go next—the Philippines? Taiwan?—brought Roosevelt to Hawaii to hear the arguments in person.

Nimitz wanted no more of the Philippines than a piece of Luzon, for airfields to cover an assault on Taiwan. MacArthur was obsessed with what he considered a sacred obligation to liberate the entire archipelago. Each expected the president to decide, but he left it to the JCS.

They opted for the liberation of the Philippines, starting with a landing on Mindanao in December 1944. Six hundred miles south of Manila, Mindanao was likely to be defended lightly. Once securely ashore, MacArthur could work his way up to Luzon using the tactics perfected in conquering New Guinea.

All of which changed dramatically when Halsey pushed his fast carriers up to the Philippines and launched a series of air raids. His pilots expected to run into hundreds of Japanese planes. Instead, there was hardly a Zero to be seen. Halsey reported back that the Philippines were lightly defended everywhere south of Manila. He urged the invasion timetable be speeded up.

The JCS swiftly concurred, and changed both the timetable and the plan. If, as Halsey's reports suggested, Japanese defenses were strong only on Luzon, MacArthur could land somewhere north of Mindanao. The assault was shifted to the island of Leyte.

When this decision was being made, a marine division and an army division were at sea, heading for the island of Peleliu, in the Palaus. Peleliu had an airfield from which planes could threaten the planned invasion of Mindanao. With the Mindanao operation canceled, there was no need any longer to capture Peleliu.

Nimitz insisted the assault should go ahead anyway. The marines aboard their attack transports were less than forty-eight hours from touchdown on L-Day.* Besides, Peleliu was reported to be held by a small garrison. It wasn't. The cost of taking it was 10,500 American casualties.

---

*After the Normandy and southern France landings the designation D-Day for amphibious assaults was dropped; much like retiring the jersey of a great football player. Henceforth the designation was L-Day, for Landing, even though *L* in the phonetic alphabet was "Love."

The reason why Halsey's pilots had run into so little opposition was that the Japanese carriers were being kept out of harm's way, in the Inland Sea. Their planes and pilots were on Taiwan, from where they could rejoin the carriers when they came south or, if the Philippines were invaded first, could stage on down to airfields on Luzon.

Halsey did not propose to give them that chance. Bringing his carriers up for a straight fight between land-based air power and sea-based air power he unleashed an epic three-day air battle over Taiwan. More than 500 Japanese planes were shot down. Several hundred more were damaged on the ground. The invasion of Leyte could proceed.

MacArthur landed on October 20, with his eye fixed covetously on several nearby airfields. There was no easier invasion in the war: perfect weather, no underwater obstacles, no mines, no beach defenses; just sporadic, inaccurate mortar fire. Four divisions landed that day, at a cost of 49 killed. There were 23,000 Japanese troops on Leyte, but they had pulled back to fixed defenses far inland, out of the range of naval gunfire.

Still seeking the fleet action its officers had talked about for twenty years, the Combined Fleet put to sea once more. Its carriers were without planes and pilots. American submarines had sunk so many oilers the crews of Japanese battleships and cruisers were severely undertrained. The best the Combined Fleet could hope for was to make the Americans pay a high price the day it died. It set sail for Leyte Gulf, to shatter "MacArthur's navy"—his fleet of transports, escort carriers and old battleships commanded by Vice Admiral Thomas C. Kinkaid.

Two strike forces would make the attack. One would pass through San Bernardino Strait and come around the island of Samar, to the north of Leyte Gulf. The other would come through the narrow Surigao Strait, at the southern end of Leyte. Meanwhile the fast carriers and the battle line of Third Fleet would be lured away. The Japanese knew exactly the bait Halsey would go for—their carriers. The planeless force from the Inland Sea was sent south to bedazzle him. It worked. Picking up reports of Japanese carriers one hundred miles north of his position, Halsey took after them in the early hours of October 25, taking the entire battle line. He left not even a rowboat to guard the exit from San Bernardino Strait even though he knew a Japanese force was about to come through.

Surigao Strait was covered. The six battlewagons used for naval gunfire support formed a battle line across it. This was veteran's day: five of these old battleships had been lifted off the mud of Pearl Harbor where Japanese flyers had left them. Among the decoy carriers far to the north was *Zuikaku,* last of the Japanese carriers that made the Pearl Harbor attack.

As the Japanese tried to emerge in column from Surigao Strait they ran into a wall of steel. Each ship as it emerged was the target for the concentrated fire of the six battleships. It was hopeless. After seeing the first ships that tried it wrecked the remainder of the Japanese force turned tail.

The force coming through San Bernardino Strait contained Japan's five fastest battleships (two of them were also the biggest in the world, with 18.1-inch guns), plus nine cruisers and 14 destroyers. Exiting untroubled, it ran into a group of six baby flattops whose assigned role in life was ASW, ground support and antiaircraft fire. Their pilots were not trained for attacking ships or their planes usually armed for combat at sea. Even so, they swarmed over the Japanese warships, making them take evasive action. American destroyers rushed forward to take on battleships and cruisers, damaging some and making others, such as the huge battleship *Yamato,* hang back for fear of torpedoes. There was no coordination and no determination in the Japanese attack. With a ten-to-one advantage in firepower they fought like men who already felt defeated. The Americans took on one-to-ten odds like men who felt invincible. In early afternoon the Japanese pulled out, turning back for San Bernardino Strait before Halsey returned. They had sunk one escort carrier and a destroyer.

The Combined Fleet's losses in and around Leyte Gulf were three battleships, four carriers, six cruisers and 14 destroyers. It would never fight as a fleet again. As the light faded on October 25, however, a new and ominous note was struck: one that effectively announced the death of the Combined Fleet. Japanese planes appeared from airfields inland. Instead of trying to bomb the escort carriers offshore they crashed into them, sinking one, damaging three. The suicide plane—the kami-kaze—had arrived.

In the weeks that followed, MacArthur was frustrated by torrential rains that made his captured airfields unusable. Clearing Leyte proved to be a grueling, wet and bloody affair. At the New Year a second landing was made, this time on the Lingayen beaches of northern Luzon. The invasion force was harried all the way by kamikazes.

MacArthur had 200,000 men plus the aid of thousands of Filipino guerrillas to defeat the 275,000 Japanese troops on Luzon. The Japanese commander was General Tomoyuki Yamashita, the "Tiger of Malaya" and captor of Singapore. His plan was to fight the Americans up in the mountains, not on the central plain of Luzon, which stretches the 120 miles from Lingayen to Manila. It was a strategy that meant abandoning the capital, but it was the best way to buy time.

Local commanders in Manila chose to make a fight of it, on their own initiative. Twenty thousand Japanese troops took up defensive positions in the old Spanish fortifications and the stone-built public buildings. It cost a month of bitter fighting to dig them out. More than 100,000 civilians died in the Battle of Manila, many of them murdered by the Japanese. Their city was one of the most devastated of the war, joining Warsaw and Stalingrad in that unhappy distinction.

MacArthur sent many of his best units south, to retake other islands before he had finished reconquering Luzon. This decision flouted the strategy agreed with the JCS. It prolonged the fighting on Luzon, where Japanese forces in the jungles and mountains threatened his communications. Yamashita was fighting on with 50,000 men when the war ended.

The Philippines campaign marked a watershed in the Pacific war. Once amphibious assaults started putting 100,000-plus ground troops onto the beach they were run by the army. The marines had one last show all their own, called Iwo Jima.

This strange volcanic island six hundred miles off the coast of Japan had a radar station and two airfields crammed with Zeros. When B-29s flew up from Tinian to bomb Tokyo the radar station gave the city two hours' warning and the Zeros mauled the bombers on their way in and on their way out. Arnold wanted Iwo very badly.

The island had once emerged from the sea in a stunning volcanic eruption. In 1945 it was still growing, still steaming. The caves that sheltered its 21,000 picked defenders were like saunas and the whole place stank. *Iwo* is the Japanese word for sulfur. The island smelled like the world capital of rotten eggs.

The marines hit the beach February 19—only it was a beach without sand. Instead, Iwo was fringed with black ash. It had the texture of cigarette ash. Men sank halfway to their knees. Not even amtracs could get a grip on it. The worst thing, though, was not the choking, infuriating ash but the total lack of cover beyond it. The

Japanese, dug into the mountain at the far end of the island, could see everything that moved. It was like advancing across a pool table.

The eight square miles of Iwo Jima had the best-organized defenses the Marine Corps ever faced: hundreds of artillery pieces and mortars, nearly one hundred pillboxes, dozens of blockhouses, gun emplacements with concrete up to five feet thick. Ten miles of tunnels connected hundreds of caves.

It took five weeks of bitter fighting and 90,000 marines to take Iwo. Even with overwhelming superiority in numbers and firepower it cost the marines 6,000 dead and 20,000 wounded.

If the amphibious assault could have been stopped at the water's edge anywhere that place was Iwo Jima. The Japanese commander on Okinawa, General Mitsuru Ushijima, drew the appropriate lesson and decided to fight for his island *off* the beach.

On April 1, 1945, Spruance's Fifth Fleet closed on the west coast beaches of Okinawa, to disgorge an unbroken line of landing craft eight miles long. Ushijima's Thirty-second Army numbered 90,000 men and could be counted on to put up a tremendous fight. Instead, and to their amazement, the soldiers and marines of the U.S. Tenth Army walked ashore standing up, laughing with relief. April Fool on them. The joke didn't last long.

The two marine divisions quickly cleared the northern half of the sixty-eight-mile-long island. The three army divisions heading south, toward the port city of Naha, walked right into the war's premier killing ground. All the hills in southern Okinawa run east to west, giving the defenders one reverse slope after another, one strong line after another, against any attack from the north. In the defense zone dominated by Shuri Hill and Shuri Castle 250,000 Americans and Japanese fought virtually toe-to-toe on a line just five miles long. Entire divisions were crammed into frontages normally held by regiments. Not even the crowded trenches of World War One were as tightly packed with men and weapons as the Shuri line.

The ideal instrument in this twelve-week struggle was the Ronson portable flamethrower. The perfect heavy support weapon was the "Zippo" Sherman, which had made its combat debut on Iwo. From its 75-millimeter gun mount it could spew a terrifying tongue of burning napalm one hundred yards. These Zippo tanks burned out caves, pillboxes, machine gun nests. They spewed liquid fire over the crests of hills to burn out defenders on the other side. They also had an attachment to which a two-hundred-foot flame hose could be fixed, allowing daring infantrymen to squirt napalm into ditches and spider holes where tanks could not go.

Nowhere on southern Okinawa was out of range for naval gunfire. More than 600,000 naval shells from 16 inches to 5 inches slammed into the island. With the Japanese surface fleet virtually eliminated the fast carriers were tied to the beach as never before. Navy and marine flyers provided all the close air support, and they did it while fighting off kamikazes.

There was no doctrine that covered this threat, only desperate improvisation, such as a ring of fifteen radar picket destroyers drawn in a huge arc north of Okinawa, and flying so many CAP missions that pilots were soon burned out.

Kamikaze flyers were poorly trained in ship recognition, so they threw themselves at the first American vessel they saw, usually a picket destroyer. The crew of one erected a sign in exasperation. Under a huge arrow pointing south it announced, "Carriers this way."

The navy had raised damage control to the level of an applied science. Off Okinawa, it reaped the benefits. Many ships were saved that two years earlier would have been sunk. Roughly 2,000 kamikazes were thrown at the navy. It lost only 26 ships, none of them bigger than a destroyer. The loss of 4,900 sailors killed or drowned, however, made this its costliest fight.

Ashore, soldiers and marines were burning and blasting their way ever closer to Naha, but against an enemy who counted each day the battle was prolonged as a minor victory. It was valuable time for strengthening the defenses of the home islands. The commander of Tenth Army, Lieutenant General Simon Bolivar Buckner (son of the commander who surrendered Fort Donelson to Grant), came under strong criticism for his conservative, unimaginative approach. Why crawl forward inch by inch when he had an amphibious reserve, 2nd Marine Division, available to land below Naha and outflank the Shuri defenses? Buckner would not consider it, arguing it would simply produce "another Anzio."

Even after Naha fell, the Japanese fought on, but now they were fast running out of room for retreat. Buckner did not live to see final victory. He was killed by the last enemy artillery salvo fired on Okinawa. Nearly 80,000 Japanese soldiers died, including Ushijima.

American casualties totaled 50,000. Tens of thousands of civilians perished.

It was a bloodbath that made people think hard and long about the impending invasion of the home islands, when Americans would finally come up against a Japanese field army; or rather, two field armies. Each numbered close to one million men. On the basis of taking Iwo and Okinawa, the current cost of killing, disabling or capturing one Japanese soldier was the death or wounding of an American. The invasion was set to go on November 1.

K I N G was utterly opposed to an invasion of Japan. With its merchant fleet sunk and its navy erased from the surface of the sea, it could be starved and blockaded into submission, with carrier air operating as a tactical air force to shoot up everything that moved by road or rail.

Arnold too was against an invasion, but ridiculed the navy's strategy of blockade. It might take years. No one could wait that long. This was a job for strategic air power. It had failed to bomb Germany into defeat, but Japan was a different matter. His faith was pinned less on a theory than on a machine, the B-29 Superfortress. Begun in the fall of 1939, it cost more to develop than the atomic bomb, running up a tab of $2.8 billion.

It dwarfed all other warplanes. Its engines were so big and powerful they overheated and tended to burst into flames. Its early test flights were a succession of spectacular disasters. Yet the AAF had to stay with it: all its hopes for an independent air force rode on the B-29.

The Joint Chiefs gave it special treatment, creating Twentieth Air Force entirely around it. It was a force independent of theater and area commanders, answering directly to Washington, to Arnold himself. Its sole mission was bombing Japan. The man he chose to run it was Curtis LeMay, an abrasive, aggressive figure hated by his flying crews. They could not do anything about that, except to take out their frustrations on the Japanese—just as Arnold intended. Or so AAF pilots believed.

When the B-29s began operational missions, however, in the summer of 1944, they were disappointing. Clear skies are rare over Japan and the B-29's high-tech radar bombsight was inaccurate. High-altitude bomb runs safe from antiaircraft fire and interceptors pushed the bombers up into the jet stream, where 200-mile-per-hour winds propelled them over their targets too fast to hit them. If they dropped down to lower altitudes AA fire and enemy fighters took a heavy toll. When Nagoya was attacked in December 1944 half the seventy-two bombers on the raid failed to return.

After Iwo Jima was captured, the loss rate of B-29s fell sharply and damaged planes used the island as an emergency landing field, but the two main problems remained. First, Japanese industry was widely dispersed. Second, the B-29 could not bomb accurately. LeMay discovered that not one bomb in every hundred dropped landed within half a mile of its target. Twentieth Air Force turned to incendiaries, putting morale at the top of the target list. In the wood and paper cities of Japan the greatest fear, instilled into every Japanese since he learned to speak, was fire.

On the night of March 9–10, 1945, a force of 279 B-29s crammed with incendiaries attacked Tokyo. Since 1942 the Japanese fire service and police had trained every able-bodied adult in fire fighting. There was no neighborhood without its hose and stirrup pump brigade, its ladders, its shovels and its buckets of sand and water. It made not a bit of difference on the night foreseen and feared.

The bombers dropped up to seventy tons of incendiaries per square mile, first creating huge rings of fire, to be filled in by succeeding waves of planes dropping clusters of smaller incendiaries. Thermal currents rose from the fire storm with such force they hurled the bombers two miles overhead up and down like yo-yos. Smoke forced the last bombers to attack blind. Silver B-29s flew back to Tinian as black as ravens, coated with soot.

Behind them raging fires were burning out sixteen square miles of Tokyo. Up to 90,000 people died, more than one million were left homeless. In loss of life and property it was the most devastating attack in the history of war. Follow-up raids burned out another forty square miles and similar area attacks were launched against scores of other cities.

Any hope that putting urban Japan to the torch might halt its war industries was illusory. Serious damage was done, but even more damage had been done by the destruction of the merchant fleet which robbed them of raw materials. Nor did the area attacks break the Japanese will to resist invasion. Arnold needed something more than fire. That something more was already promised him—the atomic bomb.

It was a weapon that began in the mind of a novelist, H. G. Wells, in a book called *The World Set Free,* published in 1914. A bomb like this had to begin in the mind of a fantasist because it was, by definition, impossible. For more than two thousand years *atomos* had meant the smallest constituent of matter: the one thing in nature that could never be split. Revolutionary advances in physics in the 1930s convinced some European scientists that the atom might be splittable after all. The energy released by splitting a large number of atoms at once could produce an almighty explosion.

Refugee and émigré scientists knew when the war began that Hitler had launched a research program to develop such a bomb. Through Albert Einstein they alerted Roosevelt to the dangers, but for nearly two years nothing much was done to produce an American atomic bomb. For one thing, the United States was not yet a world-class producer of basic science. Its best young scientists went abroad to complete their education, to Germany, Britain and France. It was not the ideal place to seek researchers for the most advanced work. For another, federal officials were reluctant to commit themselves, and their careers, to a way-out idea being pushed by foreigners with funny names and thick accents.

It was the British who saw production of the bomb as a race between democracy and disaster. By the summer of 1940 they had worked out the principles of a bomb based on uranium. One year later a government committee reported to Churchill that a more powerful bomb based on plutonium was possible, that atomic bombs could be made small enough to be dropped by airplanes, and that an all-out effort could produce a bomb in two years. All of this research was made available to the United States in the summer of 1941. It sent a tremor of alarm through the White House, the War Department and the navy. If the British had got this far it had to be assumed the Germans had done so too. Once the Nazis got the bomb fascism might never be defeated.

Pearl Harbor came just as the United States put its own atomic bomb project into top gear. It was a challenge to do on a heroic scale what it had been doing for decades: use its industrial might and engineering brilliance to make something workable out of Nobel Prize-winning ideas produced by the great research institutes and universities of Europe.

Military men had less than total faith in the potential result. The Joint Chiefs continued planning for the invasion of Japan. There were many scientists too who doubted that the A-bomb would detonate, or, if it did, that it would amount to anything more than an extra big bomb.

The first bomb for testing was not ready until two months after Germany's surrender. The successful atomic bomb test in New Mexico made certain that the weapon would be used. Marshall and many of the scientists who worked on the bomb thought the Japanese should be given a chance to avoid it. Eisenhower considered it "too horrible and destructive" to be used. Arnold remained convinced it was unnecessary. And Truman agonized. It seemed repugnant somehow to kill so many people so easily. Yet each week he received a summary of how the war was going from Marshall, just as Roosevelt had done. It always began with the previous week's casualty report in extra-large, colored figures. After Iwo Jima, after Okinawa, the estimated cost of invading Japan was 500,000 Americans killed and wounded. Japanese losses were put at a minimum of one million dead.

From Potsdam, Germany, where he went to confer with Churchill and Stalin in July, Truman made a declaration that he hoped would get him off the atomic hook, and circumvent the Casablanca demand of unconditional surrender. His statement left the future position of the emperor vague, promised to punish war criminals but spare the civilian population, foresaw the creation of a free and democratic Japanese government after a period of American occupation and strove earnestly to convince the Japanese that the United States would treat them fairly, not like a nation that deserved to be crushed once defeated. Truman was trying to offer Japan a way out without giving away the secret of the atomic bomb's existence. The response of the Japanese government was dismissive.

There remained only the question of picking the targets. Kyoto, the cultural and spiritual heart of Japan, was an obvious choice, because it had suffered little damage. Stimson, though, had visited it three times in the 1920s and struck it off the target list, apologizing as he did so for being "a sentimental old man." There were no objections to Hiroshima. It contained a garrison of 25,000 men plus the headquarters of one of the two field armies. Its factories produced artillery, machine tools and aircraft components. There were military supply depots in and on the outskirts of the town.

On August 6 a single uranium bomb, containing the explosive power of 150 B-29 bombloads. laid waste Hiroshima.

If a demonstration of the atomic bomb had possessed the power to make the Japanese to admit defeat this attack would have achieved that result. Instead, the Japanese army, which dominated the government, chose to fight on. With fifty divisions, twenty-nine independent brigades, large caches of weapons and ammunition, it continued to look to an American invasion as a realistic chance of winning the war on Japanese soil. It took a second bomb, of the more powerful plutonium variety, dropped on Nagasaki on August 9 to divide the Japanese cabinet down the middle. Split three–three for war and peace, the cabinet needed the emperor to use his casting vote to settle the issue. Even this was not enough for some army officers. They attempted a coup, but failed. Had they succeeded, another bomb would have been dropped, in September, after which there would be no more until 1946. The invasion would have gone ahead as planned, under MacArthur.

What September brought was the battleship *Missouri,* sailing into Tokyo Bay, bringing MacArthur and Nimitz to accept an almost unconditional surrender.

THE PRICE of victory was 325,000 American dead, nearly one million wounded; moderate losses given the ferocity of modern wars. Once begun, they tend to increase in tempo from start to finish, ending in killing and destruction on a scale that makes the initial phase seem mild and almost harmless. The intensity of close combat with modern weapons also meant that in time nearly everyone involved could expect to be killed or wounded.

Even so, the biggest problem American officers encountered in the field was getting their men to fire at other human beings. The infantryman did not have the psychological prop of the fighter pilot, who could tell himself he was only trying to bring down an enemy aircraft; or of the sailor, who could tell himself he was attacking another ship rather than the people aboard it; or the bomber crewman who was attacking a factory and not factory hands. The infantryman had to face the bleak reality that he was there to kill another human being, sometimes close enough to see his face. Only about one rifleman in four could bring himself to fire his weapon in combat. "The American soldier is willing to die," Patton discovered, "but not to kill."

Killing was something Americans preferred to hand over to machines. Time and again the country looked to its technology to save American lives by speeding the end of the war. They looked to the fast carriers to do it, to the strategic bombers, finally to the atomic bomb. There was no doctrine, no theory that covered the bomb, but it was used anyway in response to that overriding imperative.

It was in the air war that the traditional faith in technology and firepower was put to its severest test. The AAF had not, after all, been allowed to concentrate on strategic bombing. It had been pushed kicking and screaming into ground support, antisubmarine warfare and blockade missions. In doing so, however, it played a fuller, more valuable role in the war than Axis air forces, which had nothing like that scope.

The postwar Strategic Bombing Survey concluded that the victory-through-air-power theorists had been wrong. Strategic bombing had not been decisive. For every one million dollars' worth of damage done to the enemy the United States had been forced to spend one million dollars on bombers, bases, crews and bombs. It was just another form of attrition warfare, but in the air instead of trenches.

The victory-through-air-power theorists could argue in return, but wisely chose not to, that their ideas had *not* been pursued. One of the crucial elements in the thinking of pioneer air strategists such as Giulio Douhet was that civilian morale would be the real target and it would be attacked with the weapon guaranteed to break it—gas. By World War Two a range of nerve gases had been developed that were 1000 percent more dangerous than the crude poisons of the western front. They were incomparably more terrifying than high explosive, fire, and possibly the atomic bomb.

There were demands from some field commanders during the most intense fighting in the Pacific to use gas against Japanese caves and tunnels, but although the United States had never signed the Geneva Convention on gas warfare Roosevelt refused to countenance first use. Chemical and germ warfare *were* practiced: by the Germans against the Jews, and by the Japanese against the Chinese and in "experiments" on Allied prisoners. In all these cases it was employed against people who could not retaliate in kind. Large quantities of chemical weapons were shipped to Europe before D-Day in case Hitler, in desperation, was tempted. He never was. It marked a victory for deterrence, before deterrence theory existed.

The victorious American servicemen of 1945 were a new breed of conquerors. Immensely proud, they were also solicitous occupiers of the countries they had defeated. Occupation involved a kind of complicity among the parties. Early policies of nonfraternization simply failed in the face of the national character. By 1946 it was possible for American soldiers in Germany to spend all their energies in bed. At times it seemed the entire female population between fifteen and fifty was after them. "They consider four cigarettes good pay for all night," reported one soldier. "A can of corned beef means true love."

In Japan it was much the same. When the Americans arrived one large munitions factory shut down, tore out the machinery, partitioned the huge cavernous space created, and the 250 female employees who had worked there making munitions to kill Americans moved into the partitioned cubicles to welcome them with open arms.

At home the effects of the war exfoliated into the fissures of a divided, insecure nation and bound it together as nothing else could. The war experience was a social cement that created an America that haunts our dreams.

The most obvious result of the war was ending the Depression. The New Deal's brave, head-on, exciting attempt to wrestle it to the ground produced an awesome cloud of dust, but the beast would not stay down. A two-billion-dollar bonus paid to the doughboys in 1937 produced a brief upward jump in the economic indicators, followed by a fall in 1938.

From the moment Hitler's armies crossed the Polish frontier in August 1939 the Depression was doomed. Within weeks war orders from Britain and France relit furnaces in Pennsylvania and Ohio, reopened mines in West Virginia and Kentucky, put men back on the payroll in Detroit. From the spring days of 1940, when Congress began pouring money into national defense, the recovery took off like a rocket. By December 1941 there was virtually no unemployment and levels of prosperity were as high as they had ever been.

Once the country was fully in the war and the draft began taking all able-bodied males without an occupational exemption, job opportunities opened up for millions systematically denied them for generations past: for young women, for blacks, for the handicapped. The traditionally excluded finally broke into the Industrial Revolution. In doing so their life chances were transformed.

The problems of dependency and deprivation were so overwhelming in 1939 they shaped and embittered the whole of American life. The population stopped growing in the 1930s. Why bother to bring children into a life as stunted as this? Many spoke of hope but few really believed in it. Fear stalked even those with jobs and decent homes, and there was no abundance of those. More than half the housing stock was either substandard or simply unfit for human habitation. The war years aggravated this housing crisis but also produced the means to correct it.

It not only provided people with jobs, it provided savings. Wages were high but there was little on which to spend them. State and local governments too finished the war awash with money. The people went out and bought new houses, new clothes, new automobiles; and local government spent lavishly on new roads, parks and other improvements.

There was no war bonus for veterans this time. Instead, the GI Bill of Rights offered a wide range of benefits and economic help to remake your life if you wanted. It would help you buy a house, go to high school or college, learn a trade, start up in business. Of the seventeen million men and women who served in the armed forces half improved their education through the GI Bill. As in World War One, the people accepted by the armed forces were healthier, brighter, more ambitious than the average but now there were so many of them and they received so much help toward reaching their goals that the transition toward a prosperous, middle-class society was accelerated by decades. Without it American life in 1949, even 1959, would probably not have been greatly different from 1939.

Wartime military programs also created new, high-technology industries which were hungry for high school graduates or people with a year or two of college. The two-billion-dollar investment in radar provided the foundation for the postwar electronics industry. Computers were born out of code breaking and the construction of the atomic bomb. Arnold and the Army Air Forces took the small, almost experimental airline industry and created the Air Transport Command, which took the whole world as its place of business. While it lasted ATC—shipping men and military cargoes to wherever planes could put down—was the biggest airline ever. Out of it came the managers, the planes, the ideas, the experience that soon had Americans hopping on planes the way other people hopped aboard buses.

Intellectually too the war remade America. With Europe wrecked and impoverished it was no longer the scientific center of the world. Unable to count on importing basic science, the United States became the principal producer of scientific knowledge, while generously, wisely putting money into helping European science rise again from the ashes.

The war had come to a country riddled with class tensions, class anger. Since the end of the frontier the gap between the top one-fifth and the bottom one-fifth had been widening. For the only time in this century that gap narrowed as well-paid jobs became available to all willing to work.

As the war drew everyone into a historic shared experience it alleviated *the* American condition—loneliness. This heritage—from beginnings in vast spaces; reborn in the towering, impersonal cities of concrete and steel; sharpened by the misery of the Depression—was a psychological burden that drove millions to psychoanalysis or drink, knowing neither one was the true answer. The healing effects of the war on the nation's psyche, making a nation of individuals feel for a time as one, was a profound and priceless experience, easily as important as the material results.

17

WAR
WITHOUT
PARALLEL

THE BOMB concentrated minds everywhere. To some, including the president, it was the solution to the problem of defense after demobilization. To others, such as atomic scientists, it was less the solution than the problem. As Congress tried to make up its collective mind about how best to control atomic energy the scientists deserted their labs and their blackboards to lobby it. Congress was persuaded to deny the military direct control over atomic weapons. Public opinion meanwhile convinced the White House to seek ways of negotiating the Bomb out of existence.

Truman sent for Bernard Baruch, and a committee of wise men was duly formed. A plan for banning the Bomb was devised and in 1946 was duly rejected out of hand by the Russians. Nothing was likely to deter the Soviet Union from construction of an atomic bomb once the devastating genie was out of the bottle. Russian history might be written as a tale of failed treaties. No Soviet government would stake its existence on the risks of military disadvantage, least of all Stalin's.

The president was untroubled by the collapse of an effort he never really expected to succeed. Lieutenant General Leslie Groves, the army engineer who supervised the Manhattan Project, assured him it would take the backward Russians at least twenty years to build an atomic bomb. Groves was no scientist, yet his was the voice Truman heeded.

He ignored the predictions of the government's top scientific advisers, Vannevar Bush and James B. Conant, who forecast the Russians would have the Bomb in three or four years. On the mirage of an American atomic bomb monopoly lasting until 1965 Harry Truman proceeded to erect the postwar foreign and defense policies of the United States.

A bitterly disappointed Baruch returned to his estate in South Carolina, lamenting, "Today, we are in the midst of a cold war." The expression passed instantly into the language.

The Soviets had prepared for this unprecedented twilight struggle even before Roosevelt died. The postwar anti-American line was revealed to the Western party faithful in obscure theoretical journals such as *Cahiers du communisme* six months before the war ended. All the same, the mushrooming shadow of the Bomb made Stalin cautious. The postwar Red Army numbered three million men; battle-hardened, heavily armed, supported by tens of thousands of tanks and self-propelled guns. It could have gobbled up Eastern Europe within days and Western Europe within weeks. Stalin chose instead to expand the Soviet empire bit by bit, by stealth and subversion. The great military advantage the Soviets possessed in the Cold War would prove to be not their troops, their tanks, their air force or their navy, but their ability to keep the West guessing.

Early in 1947 George Kennan, one of the State Department's policy planners and an authority on the Soviet Union, proposed a policy of "containment" to check Stalin's ambitions. It was for the West, especially for the United States, he argued, to devise political counters to Moscow's policy of exploiting the weakness and instability of war-ravaged countries. The Soviet system itself was inherently volatile and alienating. Its claims to legitimacy at home and respect abroad were fragile. In time there would be profound changes within the Soviet Union. At some point in the future its leaders would turn away from the Cold War to concentrate instead on taming the monster that Lenin and Stalin had created. When that happened the Soviet system would "mellow" and cease to be a threat to other states.

The kind of containment he promoted was political and economic, such as the Marshall program of foreign aid that revived European economies, relieving the despair that Communism throve on. Military containment looked impossible. The vast landmass of the Soviet Union, deep into both Europe and Asia, seemed to rule that out. Events, however, soon gave containment a military dimension.

Early in 1947 the British government decided it could no longer afford to help the Greek government fight its civil war against Communist guerrillas. Truman and the Republican-controlled 80th Congress rushed aid to Greece and neighboring Turkey.

An American military advisory group under Lieutenant General James A. Van Fleet helped reorganize and revitalize the Greek army, modernized its tactics and logistics, and encouraged it to go onto the offensive. The end for the guerrillas came when Tito quarreled with Stalin. Demonstrating how strongly he disagreed with Moscow, he shut down the guerrilla base camps over the border in Yugoslavia. The Truman Doctrine that provided the justification for intervention in Greece appeared vindicated, but it left the United States committed to aiding countries that took up arms against Communist subversion.

In 1948 Stalin tested American resolve directly: he denied land access to Berlin. It was a blatant attempt to pressure the United States, Britain and France into abandoning the city. Had it succeeded it seems safe to assume that other unpleasant surprises would have followed.

Instead, the Soviet blockade was broken by an eleven-month Allied airlift that brought food, fuel and the other necessities of life to the two million inhabitants of the city. Taken by surprise at the airlift's success, the Russians could have stopped it only by shooting down Allied planes. To discourage any such thoughts a wing of B-29s was transferred in a blaze of publicity to bomber bases in England. The Berlin blockade set Western Europeans thinking hard about how vulnerable they were to Stalin's tank armies. They began moving toward collective defense, under American leadership.

The United States itself hardly looked like vigilance armed. By its assertive nature Truman's containment policy called for strong military forces to make it credible. Instead, he presided over a declining military establishment, one whose desuetude he actively encouraged. This bizarre state of affairs was the result of two seductive but dangerous ideas. The first was that the Bomb was so awesome it would keep the Russians under control. The second was that he, Harry S Truman, failed applicant to both West Point and Annapolis, knew more about war than professional soldiers and sailors.

His was the ambivalent stance that was almost a national tradition—fascination with the military combined with contempt for those who pursued military careers. As a member of the Missouri National

Guard, Truman had fought in the field artillery in World War One. He was active in the American Legion from its founding, read widely in military history and secretly fantasized like Walter Mitty that within him lay buried a greater general than Napoleon. Thinking thus, he was no more amenable to professional military advice than were all the generations of militia, volunteers and guardsmen before him. Above all he hated flamboyant generals, such as Custer, Patton and MacArthur.

His ideal professional military establishment was one that was small, unobtrusive and "unified." The unification idea became popular when interservice rivalries left the army and navy fighting what amounted to separate wars in the Pacific. Even so, a single uniformed service embracing land, sea and air was a pill too big for anyone to swallow. What emerged instead, in 1947, was a huge new coordinating body, the Department of Defense, under a secretary of defense.

Not surprisingly, the other major element in Truman's ideal military order was that old chestnut from before World War One, universal military training. It would have provided a reborn militia, in the atomic age. The aim was to give every youth a short spell of military training when he graduated from high school or reached the age of eighteen.

UMT was popular with the public, the press and most of Congress, but unpopular with Senator Robert Taft, the head of the Republican policy committee. The Republicans controlled the Senate, so Taft decided which bills reached the floor. This wasn't one of them.

In June 1948 the draft had to be reenacted, but the new law granted exemptions so generously that the army's strength fell 20 percent below the authorized limit of 700,000.

The legislation that created the Department of Defense made the air force an independent service, and the Bomb's supremacy in defense planning left the army and navy poor cousins to the airmen. Building on Truman's transfer of B-29s overseas during the Berlin airlift, the Strategic Air Command devised a strategy of air-atomic attack, to be launched from forward bases within reach of the Soviet heartland. It was a strategy sanctioned by the JCS in 1948 when it recommended using nuclear weapons early in any war with the Soviet Union to avoid a protracted conflict.

SAC planned to drop an average of two bombs on seventy Soviet cities and towns. The bombs, however, remained at Los Alamos, in an unassembled state, under the control of a civilian agency, the Atomic Energy Commission. To assemble them and ship them overseas meant a delay of at least three days between any order to use them and dropping them on a target.

There were also fewer than one hundred bombs available in 1948–49: not enough for SAC's strategy. Worse, an authoritative study concluded that SAC could not penetrate Soviet air defenses. Another equally authoritative study decided that if SAC did somehow get through and hit all seventy targets the Soviets would be hurt but not enough to make them sue for peace.

Truman had his own doubts about the Bomb. "This isn't a military weapon at all," he told his secretary of the army, Kenneth Royall, in 1948. "It is used to wipe out women and children and unarmed people, and not for military uses. . . ."

He saw its true function as deterring Soviet expansion, especially in discouraging any Soviet grab for Western Europe. Even before the creation of the North Atlantic Treaty Organization in 1949, America's European allies sheltered under SAC's nuclear umbrella. By forming NATO they committed themselves to rebuilding their armed forces and contributing heavily to their own defense. The United States, on the other hand, far from strengthening its armed forces, was cutting them back.

Truman's first secretary of defense, James V. Forrestal, found it all more than he could cope with. He resigned, entered hospital, but killed himself. His successor was Louis Johnson, a West Virginia lawyer who parlayed leadership of the American Legion into a spell as Roosevelt's assistant secretary of war in the late 1930s. Since then he had formed a close friendship with Truman.

Johnson saw the office of defense secretary as an anteroom to the wide-open Democratic presidential nomination in 1952. His bull-in-a-china-shop style and a total lack of self-control when dealing with people who disagreed with him made such aspirations risible. Nor did they help much in his new job. The Pentagon rumor mill claimed the man was crazy. Johnson's violent and erratic behavior passed into Washington legend while people wondered how on earth Harry Truman could have picked *him*.

As an aspiring presidential candidate Johnson was eager for name recognition. Taking his cue from the White House that what the people wanted was armed forces that were small, humble and cheap, Johnson bore down on the men who had won World War Two as if they were the nation's enemies.

The army was already suffering from a large dose of benign neglect, but it expected that in peacetime. Americans had such strongly mixed, conflicting feelings about war that gratitude soon wore thin. And no doubt it was better for the health of democracy that soldiers did not have their heads turned by excessive admiration.

Not even the glamorous air force was spared the chill winds blowing down the Pentagon corridors. It had finished the war with 75,000 propeller planes, and a clutch of experimental jets. Budget cuts repeatedly hampered the transition to the new technology despite the fact that the air-atomic strategy could never hope to succeed while it was tied to outmoded aircraft.

The navy felt even more aggrieved. Forrestal, who had been elevated from running the Navy Department to become secretary of defense, had given the go-ahead to a 58,000-ton supercarrier, the USS *United States*. These were anxious times for admirals. The air-atomic strategy made the navy seem quaint and the air force was demanding a monopoly on air power. Some admirals were driven in desperation to argue that the Bomb was unethical, when their problem was not ethics but the fact that the navy could not hit Moscow.

Yet even now the fleet was sidling into the nuclear future. On the eve of World War Two naval scientists had begun studying the possibilities of nuclear propulsion for submarines. Those studies continued during the war. By 1946 there were visionaries who foresaw nuclear submarines that carried long-range missiles armed with atomic warheads.

All of which seemed farfetched to the aviators. By the end of the war they had utterly supplanted the Gun Club. It was their navy now and what they wanted was not Jules Verne submarines but carriers. Above all, they wanted this one, the *United States.* * The keel was laid on April 18, 1949, just as Johnson succeeded Forrestal. Five days later Johnson ordered a halt to construction.

---

*It would have been the biggest warship up to that time, operating fifty-ton, four-engine jet bombers with a range of two thousand miles—capable of making air-atomic strikes deep into the U.S.S.R. Both the air force and the army were keen to see this carrier scrapped.

Navy brass threw something resembling a mass fit, provoking Congress to hold hearings. A long line of admirals worked out their frustrations in public, savaging the air-atomic strategy. They drew heavily on the secret studies that said SAC could not force Stalin to cry "Uncle Sam." Inflated by headline writers into "a mutiny" or "the revolt of the admirals," the navy's howl of protest could have come about only in a moment when the old rules were dead and the new ones were still inchoate.

Truman and Johnson were pressuring and manipulating the JCS into lying to Congress over the state of the armed forces and the adequacy of defense budgets. The "revolt" won the navy few friends. It was misinterpreted as resentment at civilian control. Military men were still innocents in the world of big-time public relations, but they learned quickly from experiences such as this. In time they would be able to play the game as well as most politicians. The navy's outspoken protest focused on its parochial interests, yet it lifted the veil on a defense policy that was expanding military commitments worldwide while simultaneously undermining the war-making capacity of the armed forces.

Hardly had the furor abated when, in September 1949, rainwater samples revealed a Soviet atomic explosion. Truman and Johnson refused to believe the Russians had the Bomb. Maybe it was simply an atomic accident triggered by a failed attempt to build one? The evidence was overwhelmingly against an accident.

The administration's reaction was to step up atomic bomb production and, in a bid to win back clear nuclear superiority, to authorize construction of the hydrogen bomb. The army was also given approval to secure its own entrance card to the new era, the development of tactical nuclear weapons.

The fallout from the Soviet atomic explosion included a report from Truman's national security adviser, Paul Nitze, in April 1950. Under the blank bureaucratic designation "NSC-68" it was a document that could prickle the hairs on the back of a sane man's neck. Nitze said that war with the Soviet Union was not far away. By 1954 the Soviets would have a sufficiently large arsenal of atomic bombs to make them feel strong enough to challenge America's air-atomic strategy. Under those circumstances, Soviet aggression or miscalculation would make war more likely than not.

NSC-68 called for American and European rearmament. Nitze put no numbers on it, but if fully implemented it meant increasing defense spending by as much as 300 percent.

Truman and Johnson would have burned NSC-68 gladly. It remained a closely guarded secret for years. Yet it was destined to shape American defense policy, and much of American life, throughout the 1950s, because only weeks after it reached the president's desk one of its warnings came true. Nitze forecast that war could come before 1954 (which he termed "the hour of maximum danger") if it were waged by a Soviet ally or proxy. In the early hours of June 25, 1950, seven North Korean divisions and an armored brigade spilled over the 38th parallel to seize South Korea by blitzkrieg.

THE PARALLEL meant nothing to anyone except cartographers until one night late in World War Two when the people at "Swink" (the State-War-Navy Coordinating Committee) noticed it. They were trying to organize the impending surrender of Japanese forces spread across 2,500 miles of Asia, from northern Manchuria to the jungles of Burma. There was a Japanese army in Korea. What would happen to that?

As the weary officers of Swink stared at the map someone noticed the 38th parallel. It ran across the center of the peninsula. Perfect. The Russians had a short (twelve-mile) border with Korea. They could come in and take the surrender north of the parallel, while Americans came in by sea and air to take it south of the line. No one intended to create an international boundary between antagonistic states locked in a civil war, which is what it turned into.

One third of Korea's 27 million people lived in the north and had nearly all of its industries and natural resources. The other two-thirds occupied most of the arable land, consisting mainly of paddies carved out among the mountains and able to bring a lump to the visitor's throat. South Korea reeked of human fertilizer.

Attempts by the United Nations to organize Korea-wide elections, as a prelude to unification, failed. North Korea's Communist dictator, Kim Il Sung, refused to let the United Nations in. Kim had spent much of his life in the Soviet Union and took Stalin as his role model. The South Korean leader, Syngman Rhee, had spent much of his life in the United States, but he too seemed to take Stalin as a role model.

Four years after the defeat of Japan there were no Russian or

American military units remaining in Korea, only a handful of advisers to provide guidance to the armies each had created. The North Korean People's Army, or Inmun Gun, was small but formidable. More than 30,000 Koreans who had fought in Mao Tse-tung's victorious armies came home after the creation of a Communist government in Peking in October 1949. These hardy veterans formed the steel backbone of the Inmun Gun. Seven infantry divisions were organized plus an armored brigade, equipped with 150 T-34 tanks. Two thousand artillery pieces, some of them self-propelled, provided tremendous firepower for an army this size. Including its paramilitary police units it could field 135,000 men. A combat air force of 110 planes provided close air support. The Inmun Gun was an Asiatic miniature of the mighty Red Army, with staff officers trained at the Frunze military academy and invasion plans written in Russian.

The Republic of Korea army was an afterthought, hurriedly thrown together as American military forces departed. In June 1950 it numbered 95,000 men. They had no tanks, 90 small artillery pieces and no air support. It was an army that was deliberately kept weak to discourage any ideas Rhee might have about attacking the North. It bore more resemblance to a paramilitary constabulary than a genuine army.

For three years the North Koreans tried to bring down Rhee's autocratic and unpopular government by guerrilla warfare, subversion and probing attacks across the border. Korea was a hot spot, with invasion scares every month. The secretary of state, Dean Acheson, nonetheless declared in January 1950 that Korea and Taiwan were both outside the "defense perimeter" of the United States. Which amounted to saying that the United States would not fight for either one. Mao wanted desperately to take Taiwan, to which Chiang Kai-shek had fled, but as he had trouble taking small islands close to the mainland distant Taiwan was in no serious danger. All that stood between Kim Il Sung and South Korea, however, was a line on the map.

The invasion came in the early hours of a Sunday morning, just like Pearl Harbor. One third of the ROK army was at home, on weekend leave. The Inmun Gun covered the forty miles from the parallel to the outskirts of Seoul in forty-eight hours, led by its armored spearheads. The Rhee government departed in haste. The panic-stricken evacuation of Seoul wrecked the ROK army. The bridges over the wide Han River, skirting the southern side of the city, were blown while half the army was on the other side. A few units fought briefly for Seoul but on June 28 the North Koreans entered the city in triumph. The Inmun Gun seemed unstoppable.

MacArthur, commander in chief of American forces in the Far East and master of the occupation of Japan, acted quickly. Within hours of the invasion he ordered a cargo ship be loaded with ammunition and sent to South Korea under American air and naval protection. Later that evening Truman authorized the use of air and sea power to secure the evacuation of American citizens from the Seoul area and in support of ROK forces. By these early decisions, taken in a period of extreme confusion and considerable ignorance, the United States was set on the slope that led to massive intervention.

As the North Korean army entered Seoul on June 28 its follow-on forces and logistical tail covered the roads and railroad lines all the way back to the parallel. For mile after mile there flowed an unbroken stream of tanks, trucks, self-propelled guns, towed artillery, ammunition trains, and chanting, excited infantry regiments, jubilant as only conquerors can be. Suddenly broad, weather-beaten faces turned upward to the sky. Twin-engine B-26 medium bombers swooped, followed by F-80 Shooting Star fighters. Bombing, strafing, rocketing, the American pilots could hardly miss. Wherever they attacked they left flames, explosions, scattered troops. They blew up ammo wagons, ignited fuel trucks, smashed locomotives into junk. A shaken Inmun Gun spent nearly a week in Seoul picking up the pieces before heading south again.

While Far Eastern Air Force was working over the North Koreans, MacArthur was making a command reconnaissance, viewing the smoke and dust rising above Seoul from south of the Han. The virtual destruction of the ROK army dismayed him. Returning to Tokyo, he concluded that only one thing could save South Korea—American troops. Truman, Johnson, Acheson and the Joint Chiefs of Staff agreed.

The issue was not South Korea, still less the fate of Rhee. The issue was armed aggression. To abandon South Korea to an army trained, supplied and advised by the Russians would have been the most dangerous brand of appeasement.

The invasion was originally scheduled for later in the year, but for reasons still obscure it was launched early. By striking when he did Kim Il Sung paid a high price. The Soviets had a habit of walking out when they could not get their way. After the United Nations refused to give the new Chinese Communist regime the Security Council seat held by the Nationalists on Taiwan, the Soviet delegation boycotted the Security Council. This fortuitous absence enabled the United States to win U.N. sanction for resisting one of the clearest cases of aggression this century and to fight in Korea under the blue-and-white U.N. flag.

It had to do so with an army that was a shadow of the force it had been only five years earlier. Reduced to ten divisions and nine independent regiments, the U.S. Army was a monument to the theory of defense on the cheap. Its regiments had been reduced from three battalions to two; a move akin to removing one leg from a three-legged stool. The triangular three-battalion structure had allowed regiments to attack with two while holding the third in reserve to exploit success. Under the present arrangement a regiment would have to fight with nothing in reserve or to attack (feebly) with only one battalion. During the war nearly every infantry division had its own tank battalion, providing a valuable addition of firepower and mobility. The divisions had been stripped of their tank battalions. A field artillery battalion normally consisted of three batteries of guns. Now it consisted of two. Here was an army short of those essentials of success: manpower and firepower.

This was especially true of the four divisions that comprised Eighth Army, based in Japan. All four were poorly trained and poorly motivated. That was ever the fate of the regular infantry in peacetime but the changes imposed by severe budget cuts reduced fighting ability still further. Eighth Army was commanded by Lieutenant General Walton H. Walker, a short, fat Texan whom MacArthur despised even though (possibly because) Walker had been a superb corps commander under Patton.

When the Inmun Gun started moving south after its enforced halt in Seoul, Walker began feeding ground units into South Korea piecemeal. Their task was not to win battles but time.

They suffered the predictable consequences of green troops put into battle in small packets against an aggressive army on the move. It was a story as old as warfare and characteristic of American troops in the early stages of conflict: Long Island 1776, Bladensburg, First Bull Run, Kasserine Pass. Like most peacetime armies it had too little combat experience at the lower levels and too much age at the top, leading right up to the seventy-year-old MacArthur.

The battalions and regiments sent into Korea that desperate July were also let down by their arms. Mortar ammunition had deteriorated in prolonged storage. Armor-piercing artillery shells were rationed. The 2.36-inch bazooka originally designed to stop the thin-skinned tanks the Germans used in North Africa was impotent against the T-34.* It should have been easy to slow the Inmun Gun's tanks by sowing mines in the few roads leading south from Seoul. There were no antitank mines in Korea when the war began. Eight hundred were shipped over but in the confusion of retreat no one bothered to teach people how to set them and bury them properly. So the Inmun Gun rolled on, heading for the port of Pusan, in southeastern Korea. If Pusan fell, the Americans would be forced back to Japan. Kim would have won.

Fortunately the Inmun Gun had limitations of its own. It was inexperienced at mechanized warfare. With weak opposition before it the North Korean army advanced at a rate of only six miles a day. It showed no ability to improvise. If an attack was held up the whole army halted. Infantry-armor coordination was poor; and when American troops began receiving 3.5-inch bazookas and large supplies of antitank artillery rounds, they paid heavily for their practice of sending tanks forward down unreconnoitered roads.

Its higher-level staff lacked strategic sense. They tried to do everything at once, even sending a division up into the high mountains that run along the east coast of Korea. In the mountains movement is slow and defense is cheap. Lightly armed ROK troops bled the division white. Two other divisions were diverted to the southwestern corner of Korea, contributing nothing to the main effort heading toward Pusan.

The Inmun Gun had no answer to the 600 combat planes of FEAF. On the other hand, neither did American or ROK ground troops. Much of the havoc FEAF wreaked was on friendly units, for want of proper communications with the ground, but the whole effort to slow the advance of the North Koreans was improvised and inelegant. Yet it worked.

---

*The Germans had improved on the bazooka by beefing it up, to produce a weapon that would knock out Russian tanks. Called the *Panzerfaust*, the German version of the bazooka fell by the thousands into American hands in late 1944 and was used widely to destroy German tanks in the Bulge.

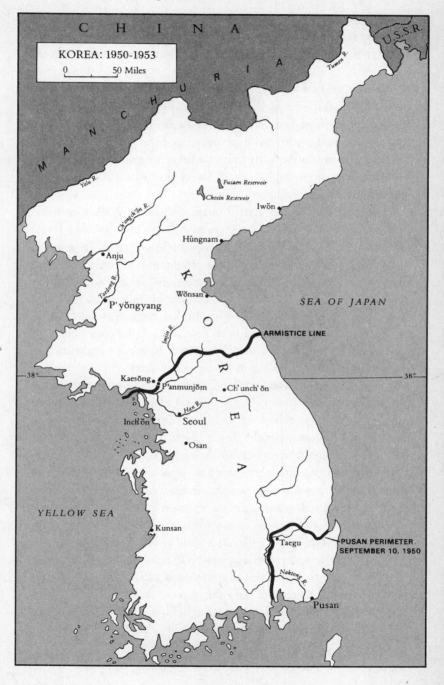

KOREA: 1950-1953

0   50 Miles

CHINA

U.S.S.R.

MANCHURIA

Tumen R.

Yalu R.

Ch'ongch'ŏn R.

Fusaen Reservoir

Chosin Reservoir

Iwŏn

Hŭngnam

Anju

Taedong R.

K

Wŏnsan

P'yŏngyang

SEA OF JAPAN

Imjin R.

ARMISTICE LINE

O

38°

Kaesŏng

P'anmunjŏm

Ch'unch'ŏn

38°

R

Han R.

Inch'ŏn

Seoul

E

Osan

A

YELLOW SEA

Kunsan

Taegu

PUSAN PERIMETER
SEPTEMBER 10, 1950

Naktong R.

Pusan

No one can say that the pilots bought so many days, the infantry so many more. What one can say is that American opposition when added to the efforts of Rhee's army bought just enough time to do the job.

During the first week in August, North Korean divisions reached the Naktong River, which encloses the southeastern corner of the peninsula. Securely based on the port of Pusan, Eighth Army prepared to make its stand—with twice as many troops as the North Koreans, six times as many tanks, vastly more artillery, complete air superiority, and possession of the high ground. Every ship that arrived in Pusan made Walker even stronger.

The river forms an inverted *L* shape. Within it Walker occupied an area fifty miles wide and eighty miles long. His divisions found themselves assigned immense frontages, of a length normally assigned to an army. Yet by holding on to the mountain tops overlooking the river they were able to dominate a vast area below and around them. Walker had all the usual advantages of interior lines, and a secret ace in the hole: his intelligence officers had broken the Inmun Gun's codes.

Toward the end of World War Two, Red Army code books fell into American and British hands. The North Koreans were trained to use Russian codes and coding machinery of wartime vintage, much as they used Russian tanks and artillery. Walker soon developed a reputation for having an uncanny ability to guess where the North Koreans would attack his 250-mile-long perimeter. Time and again the Inmun Gun walked into an ambush. Its one hope, surprise under cover of darkness, had been taken away by the code breakers.

At the start of September came the expected all-out offensive to break through the Pusan perimeter. Instead of concentrating their effort, the North Koreans scattered it, hoping to find a weak spot somewhere. On the few occasions when they did manage to seize ground, FEAF came in the morning to blow them off it.

MacArthur was meanwhile preparing to launch a deep strike in the enemy's rear, to make an amphibious assault at Inch'ŏn, halfway up the west coast of Korea and only thirty miles from Seoul. American marines had landed there eighty years earlier, on a punitive expedition against Korean pirates. The Japanese had invaded Korea by way of Inch'ŏn at the turn of the century. And army planners had drawn up contingency plans for an assault there only days before the North

Korean invasion. So logic pointed straight at Inch'ŏn. Everything else, though, was against it.

The tides were all wrong. The geography was all wrong. And it meant landing in a city of 250,000 people. The assault could turn into house-to-house fighting. That would throw away all the advantages of a landing—maneuver room, surprise, momentum. It took all the resources of MacArthur's melodramatic and manipulative personality to beat down the JCS's doubts and objections, getting his way without winning converts.

The instrument he needed to make the assault was 1st Marine Division. It no longer existed; another result of Truman's defense economies. The division had to be re-created from a variety of scattered battalions and recalled marine reserve units. Forty-seven rusting LSTs were found. A second command, X Corps, was created under MacArthur's chief of staff, Major General Edward M. Almond. There was no hope of keeping the planned operation secret. In Tokyo's bars and bathhouses it was known as Operation Common Knowledge. A deception operation was nonetheless mounted to make it appear the assault would come ninety miles farther south, at Kunsan.

On September 15 the marines hit the beach. The North Koreans had left Inch'ŏn lightly defended. The main shipping channel was clear of mines. By nightfall the port was in American hands. Inch'ŏn was one of the most brilliant amphibious assaults ever even though it had none of the high drama of Iwo Jima or Omaha Beach. Having won a dazzling victory, MacArthur proceeded to waste it. He told Almond to capture Seoul.

He wanted it liberated by September 25—three months to the day since the invasion. This symbolic date assumed a talismanic importance in his mind that had nothing to do with military strategy.

The promised result of the Inch'ŏn assault was not the speedy reconquest of Seoul but the destruction of the North Korean army. Once that was achieved the city would fall inevitably, without a fight. Success at Inch'ŏn should have doomed the Inmun Gun's divisions investing the perimeter two hundred miles away. For five days news of the landing was kept from them. Once word filtered through, they pulled out in a hurry, aggressively pursued by Eighth Army.

By September 20, X Corps had landed 70,000 soldiers and marines, 6,000 vehicles (including 250 tanks) and a mountain of ammunition. Strong blocking forces positioned north and south of Seoul could have isolated the city, while the bulk of X Corps pushed east, to cut all roads leading to North Korea. MacArthur's quixotic obsession with Seoul reenacted Clark's controversial breakout from Anzio, giving a retreating army a break for the sake of grabbing a prestige prize.

Tenth Corps concentrated its strength against Seoul and the 25,000 North Koreans rushed in to defend it. They were bright green troops in brand-new units, diverted to the city on their way to the perimeter. They stood no chance against X Corps's massive firepower, yet they denied MacArthur his talisman. It was September 29 before he could welcome a weeping Syngman Rhee back to his liberated capital.

THE DECISION to fight in Korea was a popular one. Truman's brisk, decisive action during the first week of the invasion raised his standing considerably in the opinion polls. The decision to intervene provided reassurance that despite setbacks such as the "loss" of China to Communism and the Soviet Union's entry into the atomic club the United States had not lost the will to hang tough in the Cold War.

Korea did not unleash a stampede to join up, however. People supported intervention without wishing to intervene personally. The country had not been attacked, nor had any of its European allies. Only a direct, unmistakable threat to American security produces long lines at the recruiting station.

The Pentagon faced a manpower crisis. Korea was generally seen in Washington as a diversionary attack, designed to tie down American forces on the far side of the world so that Stalin could invade Western Europe. There was a strong determination to deny him that opportunity or temptation.

As NATO came into being, American commitments to it grew dramatically. An American army was established in Germany and bomber bases built from Turkey to Thule. Eisenhower was called back from civilian life to become supreme allied commander, Europe. General Reserve forces, maintained in the United States for emergencies, were beefed up. At the same time, men had to be found for Korea.

Every source of manpower was tapped: draft calls were raised, 500,000 reservists were called back, recruiting was intensified, four National Guard divisions were federalized, and 200,000 civilians were hired to do clerical and maintenance work formerly done by military personnel.

MacArthur's ground forces rose from four divisions plus to eight divisions plus. Even so, he had trouble keeping his army units up to full strength. As a desperate expedient each infantry division was fleshed out with several thousand ROK conscripts, known as KATU-SAs (Korean Augmentation to the U.S. Army). Fifteen allied countries sent combat units to Korea, varying in size from a 5,000-man Turkish brigade to a 200-man company from Luxembourg, to underline the principle of mutual security.

With congressional elections due in November, Truman hoped to boost dismal Democratic fortunes by cashing in on the resounding acclaim from Inch'ŏn. He summoned MacArthur to meet him at Wake Island on October 15. Their discussion was disjointed, superficial and brief. The big post-Inch'ŏn decision had already been made—to cross the 38th parallel. Even as they mimed a pretense of "conferring," Eighth Army was sixty miles into North Korea.

The breakout from the perimeter had turned into a rout. American and ROK forces covered in ten days a distance it had taken the Inmun Gun five weeks to cover on its drive south. The failure to cut the roads east of Seoul nevertheless allowed 30,000 or more North Koreans to escape back across the parallel. Evading capture and refusing to surrender, these were the Inmun Gun's more resourceful and experienced troops, with a high proportion of officers and NCOs. Around such men the North Korean army could, surely would, rise again.

The decision to go after them was agreed to by Truman, Acheson, the JCS and the new secretary of defense, George Marshall. Truman had finally forced the erratic, difficult Johnson to resign. MacArthur was told to continue the pursuit and complete the destruction of the Inmun Gun. His secondary objective was the unification of Korea. A strict condition was imposed: he was to keep American forces away from the Yalu River. More to the point, he was to keep them out of northeastern Korea, where there was the twelve-mile border with the Soviet Union. Only ROK units were to go to the Yalu.

Even before American units crossed the parallel, the Chinese, using an Indian diplomat as an intermediary, warned that an American presence in North Korea would force them to intervene. At a Pentagon meeting while Truman was heading for Wake, the Joint Chiefs and their British counterparts considered the threat. "We all agree," summed up Bradley, the chairman of the JCS, "that if the Chinese Communists come into Korea, we get out." Given that the British embassy at the time contained two highly placed Soviet agents, Kim Philby and Donald Maclean, it would not be surprising if that news reached Peking.

MacArthur considered himself an expert on "the Oriental mind." The Chinese warnings were bluff, he maintained. And if for any reason China did attempt to intervene, its forces would be blasted into oblivion by FEAF.

His plan to trap the surviving elements of the North Korean army was a campaign of converging columns. He would reembark X Corps: the marines at Inch'ŏn, 7th Infantry Division at Pusan. Tenth Corps would assault Wŏnsan, the major port on the east coast of North Korea. From there it was to drive west, heading for P'yŏngyang, while Eighth Army advanced north from Seoul. The two columns would link up around Kim Il Sung's capital.

It meant breaking off the pursuit. The two major ports were tied up for ten days reembarking X Corps, during which time Eighth Army got no supplies through Inch'ŏn. Supply shortages had already slowed it to a crawl. The North Koreans used the hiatus to put three thousand mines into the waters off Wŏnsan, some of them going back to the Russo-Japanese War of 1905.

Wŏnsan fell on October 10, but to ROK troops advancing up the east coast. When the marine division arrived nine days later it was forced to steam around offshore for a week, waiting for the mines to be cleared. The Bob Hope USO show got into Wŏnsan before the marines did.

His campaign of converging columns having failed, MacArthur mounted a campaign of *di*verging columns. The Joint Chiefs looked on in bemusement, but after Inch'ŏn an aura of infallibility hedged MacArthur. No mere mortal dared break the spell.

Instead of merging X Corps with Eighth Army he continued to keep them separate. Almond, still MacArthur's chief of staff, assigned resources to himself that made his command virtually as big as Walker's. While Eighth Army advanced into northwestern Korea from P'yŏngyang, X Corps was to push into northeastern Korea from Wŏnsan. The farther north they went, the greater the distance separating Walker and Almond.

A strategy that scattered troops far and wide over hostile, mountainous terrain, with no good lateral roads and inadequate reconnaissance, held obvious risks. The mood of the men who had broken the

Inmun Gun was such, though, that few paused for thought. They pushed on, eager to finish the war quickly, victims in their time of victory disease. The conquest of North Korea was going to be a stroll, then home for Christmas.

Constitutionally cautious O. P. Smith, the lanky, white-haired commander of the marine division, did not like his assignment. If X Corps's drive into northeastern Korea really was necessary, it should be done the way it was taught in staff colleges: follow the coast, under the protective fifteen-mile arm of battleship guns, with marine air wings providing cover, with secure communications all the way and with naval resources on call to envelop enemy positions. Almond brushed such caution aside. The marines were told to plunge inland, heading for the Yalu by way of the Chosin reservoir. Smith moved slowly, as he usually did, and built an airstrip to evacuate his casualties. Almond was incredulous. "What casualties?"

All through October the Chinese warned publicly and privately they were about to come into the war. Intervention was a difficult decision for the new regime in Peking. Its hold on power was far from secure. A million Communist soldiers were still trying to pacify the countryside. A campaign had just begun to conquer Tibet. Fighting was still going on to seize islands offshore. Half the government's revenues went on defense.

While they warned, the Chinese also infiltrated. Marching by night, hiding by day, up to 60,000 Chinese troops entered North Korea; 240,000 more remained on the Manchurian side of the Yalu, in readiness to cross. Dressed in padded mustard jackets and canvas mustard shoes, armed mainly with light mortars, underpowered grenades and Japanese firearms, they were among the most battle-experienced soldiers on Earth. Veterans of China's Fourth Field Army, many of them were men who had been fighting for more than ten years, first against the Japanese, then against the Nationalists. Here were troops accustomed to hardship and victory. They saw themselves as idealists enlisted in a cause. Their only pay was cigarettes.

After taking P'yŏngyang, Walker's Eighth Army moved up to the Ch'ongch'ŏn River, fifty miles south of the Yalu. Walker pushed two divisions across, but the rest of his army marked time for want of supplies. By his control over MacArthur's logistics, Almond was assuring that X Corps would have the larger role in the conquest of North Korea. He spread his five divisions (three U.S., two ROK) far and

wide, in pursuit of real estate. By late October the marines had reached
the reservoir.

The Chinese attacked. By using the creek beds as roads they moved
by night deep into the flanks and rear of American and ROK units.
When they struck, they appeared to strike everywhere at once—from
in front, from the flanks, from the rear. They overran the ROK 6th
Division, on the right of Eighth Army. First Cavalry Division (infantry but proud all the same to wear the yellow cavalry scarf) shored
up the flank but one of its battalions was virtually destroyed.

Marine and ROK units around the Chosin reservoir were hit with
the same kind of night attacks. For a week the Chinese attacked both
Walker's and Almond's forces. Suddenly they stopped. These attacks
were, in effect, Peking's last warning. The troops involved were pulled
out, marching back to Manchuria.

The response to this tentative intervention was to decide that the
Chinese were not seriously committed. If this was all they intended
to do, it represented no real threat to American forces. MacArthur,
Almond, Walker, the White House and the Pentagon were for once
in complete agreement. There was resistance all the same to MacArthur's demand that FEAF attack the twelve bridges spanning the broad
Yalu and "isolate the battlefield" against further interference. He got
his way, but the attacks hit only the Korean end of the bridges. They
were not very effective.

Ignoring the restrictions placed on American forces, a task force
from 7th Infantry Division was sent all the way to the Yalu, reaching
it on November 21. The marines were far to the south, still close to
the reservoir. Eighth Army had just received the supplies it needed to
move in force beyond the Ch'ongch'ŏn. On November 23, Thanksgiving Day, hot turkey dinners with all the trimmings were served to
frontline troops across frozen North Korea. The Yalu was a sheet of
ice and the Chinese were back, this time to stay.

As many as 300,000 had crossed into North Korea. The Inmun
Gun's survivors plus militia and guerrillas gave Kim Il Sung a new
army of 100,000 men. The 118,000 soldiers under Walker and Almond's 102,000 were outnumbered overall by nearly two to one. That
made it easy in this rugged terrain for enemy forces to achieve a local
superiority of five to one or even ten to one against the leading
elements of both commands.

Around midnight on November 25 the Chinese hit the ROK II

Corps, on Eighth Army's right flank. By dawn three South Korean divisions were in flight down the roads leading south.

That left the U.S. 2nd Division out on Walker's broken right. That night its frontline units were hit hard. Some were overrun, but the division held. The Chinese struck again on the next three nights. Walker's units across the river also came under heavy pressure. The 2nd Division's front was beginning to buckle and the divisions on the other side of the Ch'ongch'ŏn were in danger of being trapped. He had little choice but to withdraw.

Every American division save one got away without heavy losses. For 2nd Division the pullback from the Ch'ongch'ŏn turned into catastrophe. Organized for a motor march and not for a fighting retreat, it was sent south down a road that the Chinese controlled for six miles. Machine-gun fire from both flanks turned all six miles into a murderous trap. In a single day the division suffered more than 3,000 killed and wounded. Thousands more were taken prisoner. It lost most of its heavy equipment, including its artillery.

The near-destruction of 2nd Division turned an orderly, limited withdrawal into a scramble. Bug-out fever ran through Eighth Army from Walker down.

It moved faster going backward than the Chinese could move going forward. To the British brigade, soldiers in an army with a long history of fighting retreats, it was a shameful panic, ruinous to morale and heartening to the enemy. Eighth Army left nothing behind on its race for the parallel but scorched earth. When it abandoned P'yŏngyang it even burned supplies of winter clothing.

Tenth Corps was meanwhile reeling back from the Yalu. In heavy snow and subzero temperatures the Chinese launched one of the most remarkable winter offensives in history. It is hard to move in such weather, let alone fight in it. Thousands of Chinese perished from the cold, thousands more lost fingers and toes to frostbite, yet they routed Almond's two ROK divisions and mauled the widely spread regiments of 7th Infantry Division.

Like Walker, Almond had to withdraw, but the marine division was virtually cut off. More than sixty miles from the sea it was tied to a narrow, winding mountain road. To get out, the marines would have to fight their way out. O. P. Smith announced, "We are attacking in a different direction."

The Western world looked on with breath suspended as the marines and 2,500 soldiers from 7th Division who came out along the same road clawed their way down to Hŭngnam, where the navy was waiting for them. There was a crisis a day, a drama every hour. A relieving force of soldiers, marines and British commandos fought their way up the road at sacrificial cost to keep it open. This epic struggle against terrible terrain, superior numbers and killing weather redeemed the shaken reputation of American arms.

The pilots of FEAF, the navy and two marine air wings flew themselves to exhaustion, and sometimes into the ground, in supporting the ground battle. Smith leapfrogged his battalions skillfully, sending them again and again onto the snow-covered heights overlooking the road to root out Chinese machine guns and mortars. It was a blessing in some ways that the weather was so cold: guns jammed easily and mortar tubes shrank so much they would not take the rounds. Men who would normally have bled to death often survived because the blood froze in their wounds.

After ten days of incessant fighting the defensive perimeter around Hŭngnam was reached. Naval gunfire, including sixteen-inch shells from the *Missouri,* raised a wall of steel that the Chinese were too cold, too hungry, too tired and too sick to penetrate. Half the 24,000 men of the marine division were killed, wounded or suffered frostbite, yet they came out with nearly all of their equipment, their wounded and their dead.

The first two weeks of December 1950 marked one of the lowest points in American history. Fear and paralysis gripped the upper ranks of national leadership as Chinese forces made American divisions retreat, something the Wehrmacht had never achieved.

Whatever had been said back in October, there could be no American pullout under these circumstances. At a short meeting in the Pentagon on December 1, Acheson, Marshall and the Joint Chiefs decided to advise the president that he should no longer seek victory in Korea. He should seek a truce, along a line both sides could live with, *then* pull out.

MacArthur too was badly shaken. "We face an entirely new war," he complained, as though someone had cheated him by changing the rules. In these trying days he was demoralized and defeatist.

Truman considered using nuclear weapons to help rescue X Corps and Eighth Army, and in his plain-man style blurted it out, scaring America's allies half to death. It was no bluff. Atomic bomb components were shipped to a navy carrier in Korean waters. From that time on the military gained control of nuclear weapons. B-29s began practicing an atomic bomb attack on P'yŏngyang.

By December 15 the evacuation from Hŭngnam was complete and most of Eighth Army had reached the parallel. The worst of the crisis was past but the situation remained dire. That day Truman declared a state of national emergency. This in effect gave him wartime powers to increase the size of the armed forces and to direct industry to shift over to military production. It was a signal to Americans, and the rest of the world, that the United States was settling in for the long haul. If there was not going to be a U.N. victory in Korea, neither was there going to be a defeat.

EVEN THOUGH he had broken contact with his pursuers Walker continued falling back. Shortly before Christmas he was killed when his jeep hit a wayward ROK army truck. He was replaced by Lieutenant General Matthew B. Ridgway, the vice-chief of staff. Ridgway had commanded 82nd Airborne Division during World War II, rising to command XVIII Airborne Corps. He was both a fighter and a thinker, but above all a natural leader—able to inspire a platoon, a division or an army. To the battered, scattered forces bundled out of North Korea such a man was what they needed most.

One of his first actions was to integrate X Corps into Eighth Army. He sacked five of the eight American division commanders. He got his road-bound troops out of their vehicles and onto their size nines. An ardent believer in command reconnaissance, he took it to hair-raising extremes. In a tiny L-17 spotter plane he scoured the Korean landscape, landing on roads that ran between the stinking paddies, even on city streets and squares, building up a vast collection of mental photographs. When he looked at an operations map he knew which way the streams ran, if the slopes were too steep for men to take heavy weapons, if a valley was likely to be flooded, if a road was suitable for tanks; above all, if this was a good place to attack or a better place to defend.

To avoid being outflanked when the Chinese armies poured over the parallel at the end of 1950 Ridgway evacuated Seoul. He organized a strong line of defense forty-five miles farther south, running unbroken across the peninsula from sea to sea.

The force he had taken over was still depressed and disorganized. To change that he had to trade space for time, but the day after his defense line was ruled secure, he launched a reconnaissance in force.

When it found no serious resistance halfway to Seoul, Ridgway set his entire army in motion. He was going back, but this time there would be a line without gaps. Two weeks later Eighth Army was just south of Seoul. On February 11 the Chinese counterattacked at midnight, aiming straight for the three ROK divisions in the center of the line. The ROKs broke, but American and French troops held the vital crossroads at Chipyŏng, which was the key to the U.N. position in this area.

In a striking facsimile of the Battle of Bastogne, they were surrounded. Ridgway supplied them by airdrop. The Chinese launched human wave assaults ("sea of the people" tactics, as the Chinese called them) for the first time in the war. Napalm drops turned the hills around Chipyŏng into an inferno. After three days the Chinese faltered. On the fourth, they broke away. Ridgway resumed his advance. Seoul fell once more to Eighth Army.

Ridgway was using Mao's tactics against Mao's armies: when the Chinese attacked in strength, he gave ground; when they paused, he attacked; when they withdrew, he went after them. And he could do all these things with superior firepower and mobility. He turned Eighth Army into a huge killing machine—"the Meat Grinder," he called it—and restored its self-confidence. By April 1 it was back on the parallel.

Ten days later the long-awaited showdown between MacArthur and the president came to a head. Ever since the Chinese onslaughts in late November MacArthur had been struggling to alter American strategy. The hope of a truce—and hope was all it was—seemed to him like no policy at all. He resisted and resented directives that exempted China from American air attacks.

Through his many admirers in Congress and sympathetic members of the press he mounted a one-man propaganda campaign to enlarge the war. Yet to men such as Bradley this was a snare and delusion. A bigger U.S.-China fight would be, he later testified, "the wrong war, in the wrong place, at the wrong time, with the wrong enemy." The real threat to American security did not come from Peking but from Moscow. To meet that challenge, the war in Korea had to be kept from growing any bigger.

MacArthur's outspokenness in a communication to the speaker of the House of Representatives gave Truman all the excuse he needed. The president, in his usual unguarded way, allowed word to leak out that he intended to dismiss MacArthur, before he was really ready to announce it. A White House press conference had to be hastily called for 1 A.M. so the president could retain the initiative. As Truman explained it to Bradley, "The son of a bitch isn't going to resign on me. I want him fired."

MacArthur heard of his dismissal from journalists. It still rankled more than a decade later, when he wrote his memoirs. "No servant would have been dismissed with such a callous disregard of the ordinary decencies."

Ridgway was moved up to replace MacArthur as commander-in-chief, Far East. Van Fleet was brought in to take over the reborn Eighth Army, just in time to meet an expected Chinese spring offensive. A vast killing ground was being prepared on the approaches to Seoul.

By a series of errors the British brigade was left holding high ground overlooking the Imjin River twenty miles northwest of the city. The British stood their ground and gutted the three divisions of the Chinese Sixty-third Army before being overrun. Other Chinese armies drove on, getting to within five miles of the city limits before being blown apart by massed artillery fires and a deluge of napalm.

Van Fleet resumed Eighth Army's advance, recrossing the parallel. The Chinese counterattacked in mid-May, this time striking hard at the right of the long U.N. line, composed mainly of ROK units. Once more artillery and air power covered Korean hillsides with mustard-clad corpses, but now Chinese stolidity broke. They began surrendering in their thousands.

To regain and retain the fighting spirit of their troops Chinese commanders had to assume the defensive. They had no appetite left for pushing their men into the open to be blasted and burned in doomed assaults. Van Fleet resumed his offensive but in June Peking hinted that it too was interested in a truce. One month later talks began at Kaesŏng.

When negotiations broke down later that summer Van Fleet went on the offensive again. North Korea is more rugged than South Korea. Eighth Army learned how bloody mountain warfare can be. No matter how much firepower was laid down every yard gained cost a fortune in lives. Nearly half of all American combat casualties in Korea were to occur after peace talks had opened. Names such as Heartbreak Ridge and Bloody Ridge given to terrain features told their own story. The rebuilt 2nd Infantry Division suffered 5,600 casualties in the fall of 1951 in seizing Bloody Ridge from the rebuilt Inmun Gun. The North Koreans then simply fell back to the next ridgeline.

When peace talks resumed again Ridgway, in Tokyo, ordered that no more attacks be launched above battalion size without his permission. U.N. forces dug in along the 150-mile main line of resistance, or MLR, that bisected the peninsula, mainly above the parallel. Across from the MLR the Chinese and North Koreans created a defense zone twenty-five miles deep, with line after line of tunnels, caves, bunkers, pillboxes and underground supply dumps.

To the Communists the truce talks were only the continuation of war by other means. From time to time they walked away from the table. Truman turned to air power to get them back and to negotiate seriously.

For the first few months of the war FEAF had enjoyed undisputed air superiority, blasting out of the sky the elderly propeller fighters flown by North Koreans. In November 1950 the first MiG-15s appeared, operating from bases in Manchuria.* Piloted by Chinese and a handful of Russians, these small, fast, air-superiority machines flew rings around FEAF's obsolescent Shooting Stars.

Within a month the latest American jet fighter, the F-86 Sabre jet, was on its way to Korea, dispatched like an aerial fire brigade. It had not been designed to win dogfights but to fly high and shoot down Soviet bombers. It had a big wing to make it stable in the thin air at 35,000 feet. By chance that made it more maneuverable at the lower altitudes where most dogfights occur than the MiG.† Its six heavy machine guns also pumped out a torrent of lead in the two seconds or less that a jet pilot had to make a kill. The MiG-15 with its three small and slow-firing cannon was outgunned. In the hands of well-trained American pilots the Sabre jet was awesome. Some 792 MiGs fell in aerial combat, for a loss of 78 F-86s. Of the 1,900

---

*It was not exactly a triumph of Soviet technology. The MiG-15 was the fruit of technical drawings and plane designers captured in Germany in 1945. The engine was an exact copy of a stolen Rolls Royce Nene.

†The F-86 also had a secret—a movable tail plane—that put it years in advance of other jet fighters.

U.N. aircraft shot down in the war, more than 90 percent were lost to ground fire.

Korea reopened all the old arguments about the proper use of air power. Soldiers complained bitterly all over again about air support and envied the marines their air wings; employed, in the words of an admiring army colonel, "like artillery."

FEAF was much more interested in strategic bombing. Almost from the beginning of American intervention, airmen such as LeMay argued for a fire-bombing campaign over North Korea, to wipe out the industrial base and break civilian morale. Truman turned it down flat. There was no chance of selling that to the United Nations.

Following Chinese intervention, FEAF mounted an intensive interdiction campaign called Strangle to choke off reinforcements and supplies. Besides bombing anything that moved it scattered millions of roofing nails on North Korean roads. Strangle hurt but did not strangle. China's 300,000 troops needed a mere fifty short tons of supplies per day. Porters could carry that, panting and bent double under A-frames, across the hills in the night.

In the summer of 1952, with patience running out at the peace talks (since moved to P'anmunjŏm), FEAF got its fire-bombing campaign. What was left of P'yŏngyang was burned to the ground. When this failed to produce the desired effect, FEAF turned its attention to North Korea's power stations. There was no evident change at the negotiating table.

In 1953 the strategic bombing effort was turned, with misgivings, against five of the twenty major irrigation dams. If successful, a dam-busting campaign could wipe out the rice crop. The Luftwaffe had done something similar in the Netherlands in 1944 by bombing the dikes. Up to 100,000 Dutch had died of starvation. At Nuremberg Luftwaffe officers involved were tried as war criminals and punished. The bombing of the North Korean dams was a measure of American frustration.

The ostensible issue that kept the two sides at P'anmunjŏm by turns arguing and sulking was the fate of their prisoners of war. The Communists overreached themselves by demanding that all POWs be screened and their wishes determined. Nearly 40 percent of the Chinese and North Koreans said they did not want to go home.

Enraged by this propaganda disaster, the Chinese turned to the great teacher, Stalin. In the 1930s he had justified the murder of three million Russian peasants who resisted the collectivization of agriculture by accusing them of germ warfare. The Chinese whipped up a propaganda campaign around dead flies and mice that they claimed were infected with just about every odious disease imaginable and liberally scattered over North Korea and China by American airmen. By torturing captured pilots long enough and hard enough they got a few to confess that, yes, it was all true, they had dropped plague-ridden lice on peace-loving people's republics.

Under the Geneva Convention there was no reason for prisoners of war to be an issue. Each nation had a right to recover its imprisoned men, but Truman wanted assurances that POWs were not being returned to China and North Korea against their will. Millions of Russians taken prisoner by the Germans in World War Two had been returned by Allied soldiers to Stalin's tender mercies. Some had gone over to the Nazis, but the crime of the majority was that having seen life outside Russia, they had seen through Soviet lies. They faced stony-faced interrogators who asked one chilling question: "Why are you alive?" Hundreds of thousands were murdered, hundreds of thousands more perished in the Gulag Archipelago.

What broke the deadlock at P'anmunjŏm was the threat by a new president, Dwight Eisenhower, to use the tactical nuclear weapons just coming into production, such as a two-kiloton atomic bomb that could be carried by fighter-bombers. Eisenhower's inaugural parade in January 1953 featured the army's latest artillery piece, the 280-millimeter atomic cannon. In the spring a battery of these guns was shipped to Korea. And much as the Chinese had used Indian intermediaries to warn the United States of what was about to happen in 1950, so the United States used Indian intermediaries to warn the Chinese of what was about to happen in 1953.

The death of Stalin in March probably contributed something to the breakthrough, but the Russians had always been reluctant supporters of the Communist regime in China. In the course of the war it became increasingly evident they had no intention of intervening to help the Chinese.

On May Day 1953 the United States exploded its first hydrogen bomb*—"no accident," as an old-fashioned Marxist might say. In the weeks that followed, progress at P'anmunjŏm moved inexorably to-

---

*A "device" that tested the components was exploded in October 1952.

ward settlement. On July 27 a truce was signed. No prisoner who did not want to return home was forced to do so. In all 45,000 of the Communist prisoners in U.N. hands refused repatriation, against 21 Americans and a Briton who, out of curiosity, conviction or fear of punishment for having collaborated with the enemy while in captivity, went to China. In time all but one—James Veneris—came home.

The war was over, but few outside the families of released prisoners rejoiced. Thirty thousand Americans had been killed, another 100,000 had been wounded, and for what? Americans don't cheer a tie. The men who returned from Korea were ignored.

They had served their country and the world better than they, or their fellow citizens, knew. NSC-68 was implemented. Defense spending rose from $11.5 billion a year to $45 billion a year between 1950 and 1952, closing the dangerous gap between a strong foreign policy and weak armed forces. The war had revived a flagging economy and launched seven years of prosperity.

Congress paid a tribute to the marines by putting the commandant on the JCS. Truman, who loathed the Marine Corps, had to bear it. If he did any grinning that went unrecorded.

Like America's first limited war, the War of 1812, this one was much misunderstood. To understand its importance the first question that had to be asked was what the results would have been had the United States abandoned South Korea to conquest. It would certainly have wrecked containment, at a time when great-power rivalry was at its most inflammable, something that could only have encouraged Communist adventurism. It would have sent a shock wave through a Japan that was only just recovering and in which left-wing political movements were strong. That country's present political stability and its commitment to the West were not decreed by fate: they had to be created.

Second, the decision to fight convinced European democracies to stake their existence on mutual security and American leadership. If America would bleed for South Korea it would assuredly do the same for them.

Third, the people of South Korea have justified the sacrifices made on their behalf, and the even greater sacrifices they made themselves, by their attempts to create a democratic government and a prosperous economy. While they still have some way to go by Western standards, they are decades ahead of the brutal tyranny of Kim Il Sung. Had it not been for the successful defense of South Korea tens of millions of South Koreans would, like the North Koreans, have been condemned to live in one of the most impoverished and backward societies on Earth. For all its novelty and shallow roots, there is hope for democracy in South Korea. In North Korea, that hope has long been dead.

Finally, the Cold War is as good as over. The West won. This economic, ideological and psychological struggle was unprecedented, but in time people everywhere came to realize that it was nuclear weapons alone that made the Soviet Union a world power. Not only did it fail in its appeal to hearts and minds, but in the 1980s Soviet living standards fell, the economy shrank, even life expectancy worsened.

It was a failure so comprehensive that a new generation of Soviet leaders, better educated than the old-time Stalinists, openly admitted the failure of communism. It was an admission that surprised no one, for by then the U.S.S.R. had been overtaken as a development role model for countries seeking to move toward greater freedom and prosperity by a country the Soviets would not recognize existed . . . South Korea.

18

NUCLEAR
ABUNDANCE

DURING his eighteen months as supreme allied commander, Europe, in 1950–51, Eisenhower wrestled with a problem to which he could find no solution. What would he do—what could he do—if the Soviets launched an all-out attack? He reckoned he needed at least 96 divisions and 9,000 combat aircraft to defend Western Europe against Stalin's tank armies. He did not have a half, or even a third, of the manpower and firepower necessary to stop the Red Army from reaching the English Channel.

When he became president in 1953 NATO's defenses suddenly looked so strong that the insoluble problem was solved. The line in Europe could now be held with a mere 26 divisions and 1,400 combat aircraft—plus hundreds of battlefield nuclear weapons. All that was needed was for NATO to be strong enough to force the Russians to mass their armies before they attacked. Those concentrations would then be wide open to devastating spoiling attacks with tactical nuclear weapons.

The United States had roughly 1,000 atomic bombs, hydrogen bombs and tactical nuclear weapons in its inventory in 1953, thanks to Truman's belated efforts to build up a large nuclear arsenal. In 1954, NSC-68's "hour of maximum danger," there would be nearly 2,000 nuclear weapons available. The rapid development of nuclear abundance revived the feeling of security that people had enjoyed during the years of American atomic monopoly. The return to nuclear superiority was so reassuring that there was no alarm when the Soviets exploded a thermonuclear device in August 1953, unlike the anguish four years earlier when the Russians acquired the A-bomb.

Nuclear abundance and the sense of security it generated made it possible for the president to cut military spending by 25 percent. This would not normally have seemed much of an achievement. The end of most wars brings a sharp drop in military spending. Eisenhower took office, however, at the height of the Cold War and at a time when the Soviets were making rapid advances in military technology. He entered the White House deeply afraid that he would not be able to cut the defense budget by more than a trifling amount. He counted that 25-percent cut among his major achievements.

The level of defense spending that he established ($35 billion in 1954) would be maintained, in real terms, until the 1980s. What he judged was adequate for national defense and the health of the economy was accepted, in effect, by the next five presidents.

Within the new Republican administration there was talk of "rolling back" the Soviet empire. It was encouraged not by Ike but by his secretary of state, John Foster Dulles, who was a strange character. Outwardly, he had excellent credentials for a secretary of state. In his college days he had participated at the first Hague peace conference, before World War One. For more than forty years he had written and lectured on international relations. As a lawyer he specialized in international law.

Even so, this overtly upright, devout Presbyterian had much of the character of a snake oil salesman. He had a fanciful imagination, boasting that he could speak French, which he couldn't, and that he was directly descended from Charlemagne, which he wasn't.

Over the years he had developed a penchant for the striking utterance, such as "roll back." With the new administration engaged in what it called a "New Look" overhaul of defense policy, Dulles was inspired by the abundance of nuclear weapons to declare that henceforth the United States would adopt a military stance of "massive retaliation."

Journalists, military men, diplomats and politicians demanded to know what it meant. To the world at large it created the impression that if the Communists dared step out of line, Armageddon would follow. Did massive retaliation mean that a Soviet conventional attack on Western Europe would unleash nuclear devastation on Moscow? What if North Korea attacked South Korea again, would that start a nuclear war? And so on. To questions such as this (and there were dozens of them) Dulles had no coherent answers to give. He backed away from massive retaliation, just as he was forced to back away from "roll back." This meaningless expression remained in people's minds all the same, even though it did not express the doctrine that governed the use of tactical nuclear weapons or describe the strategy for employing Strategic Air Command.

The basic foreign policy posture of the Eisenhower administration toward the Soviet Union and its satellites in the mid-1950s was the hard line. That had paid off for Truman in dealing with Tito. Forced to choose between closer ties with Stalin and closer ties with the West, Yugoslavia chose accommodation with the rich West, rejecting the smothering embrace of Stalin and the impoverished Russians. Under Eisenhower an equally tough line was taken with other socialist regimes, notably China, in the belief that the more they knew of the U.S.S.R. and life under communism, the less they would like it.

This hard-line approach to containment was made militarily credible by the rapidly expanding ring of SAC bases that put all parts of the Soviet Union and China within reach of American air power. A huge new jet bomber, the B-52, went into production in 1954. Powered by eight jet engines, it could fly higher and faster than a MiG-15; flew ten thousand miles without refueling; and carried four hydrogen bombs.

SAC devoted itself in the 1950s to creating a force capable of knocking out the Soviet Union with a single punch. The eventual aim was to be able to destroy more than 100 Soviet cities and towns, plus 645 military installations, in a single, crushing strike. It was an attack whose ferocity would equal that of World War Two many times over, but compressed into less than a day. A navy captain who was briefed on SAC's war plans was amazed. SAC intended, he told fellow sailors, to leave the entire Soviet Union "a smoking, radiating ruin at the end of two hours."

The awesome, growing might of the strategic bombers seemed to give credence to Dulles's claim that defense policy was being geared to massive retaliation. Civilian experts on defense, on the other hand, were claiming that SAC was vulnerable to a first strike; that a sneak

Soviet attack could wipe out the bombers before they got off the ground.

Such confusion over what SAC could or could not do, did or did not intend, entirely suited the purposes of Curtis LeMay, the SAC commander. The air force had a very clear idea of how it wanted to use its unprecedented powers of destruction, but wisely kept that idea to itself. What that idea was—and probably still is—will be explained later in this chapter.

By 1958 Strategic Air Command had 44 operational bases (29 of them overseas) from which to launch its 1,800 heavy and medium bombers. The Soviet long-range bomber force was barely one-tenth that size.

The primacy of SAC in deterring a Soviet attack meant that the air force took 46 percent of the defense budget, the navy and Marine Corps got 28 percent, leaving the army with 23 percent (the Coast Guard accounted for the remaining 3 percent) and outraged feelings.

Soldiers were haunted still by memories of those ghastly days in December 1950 when Eighth Army and X Corps flirted with annihilation. Had potential technologies such as helicopters been fully exploited in the late 1940s the disasters along the Ch'ongch'ŏn and the Chosin might never have happened. "Sky cavalry" would have flushed out the Chinese first.

To its fury and disgust the post-Korea army was denied the money needed to develop those technologies even after the war ended. It wanted to develop reconnaissance drones, long-range radar, very short takeoff and landing (VSTOL) aircraft and battlefield nuclear missiles, but could not. It got short shrift, it discovered, from the soldier-president.

Nor was Eisenhower prepared to risk any "revolt of the generals." He and his secretary of defense, Charles E. Wilson, slammed the lid firmly on the army's rising indignation. Matthew Ridgway was removed after only two years as army chief of staff, instead of serving the customary four, because he refused to go along with proposed cuts in combat unit strength.

His departure was a clear signal to his successor, Maxwell D. Taylor, and the other chiefs. Indeed, before he was appointed Taylor had to promise Wilson that he would not cause trouble.

From here on the Joint Chiefs of Staff were expected to support the administration line on defense, or they were out. This crude, high-pressure approach to controlling the armed forces marked a watershed in modern civil-military relations. The president's principal military advisers were reduced to the status of mere political appointees, whose function was to defend the administration's policies whether they agreed with them or not. That undercut their primary role, which was to provide authoritative advice on defense policy and the great issues of war and peace. This might have been just tolerable while Eisenhower was president, but there would not always be a career soldier in the White House.

While the military retained enormous respect for Eisenhower despite this downgrading of their functions, they had none for Wilson. Before coming to Washington he had been president of General Motors. His lack of manners, his irascibility and his complete ignorance of anything other than car making created a kind of tacit alliance between the press and the armed forces: both heartily despised him.

Wilson's violent temper was employed to cow the military. Year after year army generals and navy admirals testified to Congress on how much they agreed with the military budget, on what excellent defense they thought it provided, on how wonderful everything was. They did not believe a word of it. Officers who found it too demeaning resigned. Taylor fumed, but kept his word and made no criticism in public. The Ridgway example had a powerful effect on ambitious military men.

The army could only envy the air force's strategic mission of striking the Soviet Union. The navy too had a vital strategic mission to plan for, seizing command of the North Atlantic so that the sea-lanes to Western Europe remained open. The army's strategic mission was dull and defensive—helping to hold the line against Soviet tank armies when the Warsaw Pact forces attacked. Ground combat itself was thought by some commentators to be so old-fashioned its days were numbered. If so, the army had no future.

It sought to secure its place in modern warfare by pursuing the few opportunities left open to it to develop modern technologies. Airmen were so committed to strategic air-atomic attack they ignored air defenses. The army assumed the air defense role, claiming that surface-to-air missiles were really no more than an extension of antiaircraft artillery. It also began developing intermediate-range ballistic missiles (IRBMs), claiming that these were only a logical continuation of long-range artillery.

Such initiatives irritated the air force and the navy, who had their own interests in missiles to pursue. In December 1956 Wilson issued a directive that limited army missiles to a range of two hundred miles; it was reminiscent of the prewar navy's curb on Army Air Corps flights over the sea. Limits were also placed on the size of army light planes and helicopters, to keep the air force happy. Above all, Wilson ordered, the army must not use any of its IRBMs to launch a satellite; something army missile engineers were confident they would be able to do around April 1957.

The navy had a rocket called Vanguard under development to put a satellite into orbit at the end of 1957 or early in 1958 as a contribution to the International Geophysical Year. An army satellite would be too obviously a military leap forward. It would be better public relations, reasoned Eisenhower and Wilson, to make the satellite part of a civilian scientific project. In their obsession with public relations, combined with a determination to keep the army in its place, they squandered the opportunity to score the greatest propaganda coup since Wilson's Fourteen Points.

On October 4, 1957, the Russians put *Sputnik I* into orbit. Vanguard flopped, repeatedly blowing up on the launch pad or shortly after lift-off. Wilson rescinded his earlier order banning an army satellite launch. On January 31, 1958, the first American satellite was put into orbit by an army IRBM, the Jupiter C.

Instead of responding to *Sputnik* with a major increase in military spending—which was what Congress and the country expected—Eisenhower reverted instead to a military faith that was almost as old as the Republic. He poured federal money into science, into technology, into the colleges, and into the graduate schools. Hundreds of thousands of bright students were to profit from the National Defense Education Act of 1958. Professors did better out of the *Sputnik* scare than anyone else.

The Soviets' success shocked people almost as much as Pearl Harbor, yet it did nothing to change the balance of military power. The Soviet premier, Nikita Khrushchev, was well aware of that, for all his bombastic boasting. To his alarm he discovered that the Chinese leadership *did* believe the balance of military power had changed.

On a visit to Peking in 1958 he tried to explain to Mao Tse-tung that *Sputnik* really was great—but not that great. Mao didn't want to believe it, preferring to think that the historic moment had arrived to unleash the final, climactic war against American capitalists and imperialists. With superior Soviet technology and superior Chinese manpower, how could they lose?* Somewhat shaken by Mao's casual attitude to nuclear war, Khrushchev concluded that Mao was not mad but a fanatic—and a danger.

Soon thereafter all Soviet assistance to China's nuclear program came to a screeching halt. By 1960 all Soviet engineers and scientists had been withdrawn from China.

The White House and the Pentagon had been monitoring the Soviet missile program closely since mid-1956 by means of a high-flying reconnaissance aircraft, the U-2. An army missile expert warned in *The New York Times* a month before *Sputnik* went up that the Russians were about to put a satellite into orbit. The strongest motive for the first U-2 flights was to pick up any preliminary signs of an impending Soviet surprise attack on Western Europe or the United States. Soviet long-range missile developments were the prime target of regular flights over the launch pads under construction at Tyuratam, in Soviet Central Asia.

The real objective of Soviet missile research was not putting *Sputnik* into orbit but development of an intercontinental ballistic missile (ICBM) capable of striking the United States. As the Russians prepared to build their first operational ICBMs, there came an intelligence breakthrough. British intelligence was approached by a colonel on the the Red Army General Staff, Oleg Penkovskiy. He was, moreover, the son-in-law of the commander of Soviet Long-range Rocket Forces. His reports plus U-2 reconnaissance made Russian missile capabilities about as well known in Washington as in Moscow.

The final U-2 flight was authorized for May Day, 1960, to be flown by Gary Powers; taking one more look at Tyuratam and at the first ICBM site, about to become operational, at Plesetsk, two hundred miles northeast of Leningrad. His flight was scheduled to take him 3,800 miles, from Pakistan to Norway.

The Russians shot down his U-2, probably with a surface-to-air missile (SAM). Khrushchev demanded an apology from Eisenhower, did not get it and canceled a meeting the two were to have held in Paris. Ending the U-2 overflights was of little consequence, because something far better was about to go up—the first spy satellite.

---

*In a conversation with Nehru in 1959 Mao suggested that the deaths of half China's people was a price worth paying to win a nuclear war.

This project was one of the best-kept secrets of the Cold War. The first thirteen attempts to orbit the satellite and retrieve its film packets failed. In August 1960 there was complete success with Number 14. The chance of a Soviet surprise attack fell to zero.

American ICBMs were presently entering service. When the first four SS-6 Sapwood missiles were installed at Plesetsk in 1960, the air force had already won the race: it had twelve Atlases in operation before the first Sapwood reached its launch pad.

Shortly after World War Two ended, Chester Nimitz, succeeding Ernest King as chief of naval operations, committed the navy to constructing a nuclear submarine. Nuclear propulsion made a true submarine possible for the first time; a vessel, that is, able to spend most of the time underwater. All previous submarines were really torpedo boats that could dive. They spent up to 90 percent of the time on the surface.

The admiral in charge of the nuclear submarine program, Earle W. Mills, had an assistant, Captain Hyman G. Rickover, a naval engineering officer whose career up to that time had been nothing unusual. To keep the admiral up-to-date on the state of nuclear research, his assistant was made a member of the Atomic Energy Commission.

Rickover soon emerged as one of the most unusual figures in naval history. His behavior was eccentric, his aversion to uniforms almost a personal crusade and his outspokenness on every topic under the sun so pronounced that he seemed to come equipped with a soapbox. There were times when Rickover appeared to hate the navy, yet he never wanted to leave it.

In the early 1950s, with the nuclear submarine program well under way, he came up for promotion to admiral, and was passed over. After he was passed over for a second time he was, in the usual way, scheduled for retirement.

As a midshipman at the Naval Academy in the early 1920s his hero had been William Sims. He now reacted as Sims might have done, by making an appeal beyond the tradition-bound navy hierarchy. Rickover used the connections in Congress and with the press that he had developed as a member of the AEC to create a personal legend. He appeared on the cover of *Time*. A flattering biography was produced by a major publishing house. A legend was born of Rickover "the

Father of the Atomic Submarine." He had not invented it, or thought of it first, or worked out the major scientific and engineering problems involved. He was simply the project manager. Which was how the navy saw him: someone who could be replaced by another captain, another project manager. There would have been atomic submarines without Hyman G. Rickover.

The outcry in Congress and the press was so vehement, however, that the navy was forced to promote Rickover to admiral. In later years it was forced to keep on promoting him, to waive the rules on retirement age, and allow him to remain in harness almost to the day he died, at the age of eighty-four.

The atomic submarines Nimitz, Mills and navy scientists envisaged marked a great leap forward in antisubmarine warfare: ultra-quiet boats could track down and destroy other subs. The strategic mission the postwar navy established for itself was winning a third Battle of the Atlantic, this time against the huge Soviet submarine fleet of 350 to 400 boats. Sonar had been refined to a point where one sub could find another under the water, and sink it with a torpedo.

In January 1955 the first nuclear submarine, the *Nautilus,* steamed under her own power. Her propulsion system was based on a new type of nuclear reactor, the PWR (or pressurized water reactor), originally designed for nuclear-powered aircraft carriers. However, the first nuclear carrier, the *Enterprise,* would not be commissioned until 1961.

In the tradition of dual technologies, the navy's PWR created a whole new industry—nuclear power. Within a generation there would be more than one thousand PWRs in operation worldwide providing electricity. The navy provided the civil nuclear power industry with thousands of managers and engineers, trained at government expense on nuclear engineering programs that Rickover set up to provide trained manpower for his nuclear navy. They stepped straight from naval service into the new industry. In the 1980s more than half the managers and engineers in American nuclear power plants had a navy background.

With the *Nautilus* a resounding success, a handful of naval visionaries began pushing hard for a different kind of nuclear submarine, one armed with nuclear-tipped missiles. Targeting them accurately from underwater seemed impossible, though. Besides, the admirals who ran the navy were still in love with carriers. And then two important developments broke almost simultaneously. One was *Sputnik,* the other was the air force's success in developing a guidance system for the Atlas ICBM. *Sputnik* drew Eisenhower's attention to the merits of a fleet of nuclear submarines armed with long-range nuclear missiles, hiding where the Russians stood little chance of finding them, even with satellites. And the guidance system developed for the Atlas made submarine-launched ballistic missiles (SLBM) feasible—just accurate enough to hit major Soviet cities.

To the indignation of the carrier admirals, the Polaris submarine was pushed through like a peacetime Manhattan Project. Under the hard-driving leadership of Rear Admiral William F. Raborn, Polaris went from being a design concept to having a boat in the water in just two years. In 1960 the first Polaris submarine, the *George Washington,* was at sea. She was joined by a second boat before Eisenhower left office. Each Polaris boat carried sixteen missiles, with a range of 2,500 miles. Over the next seven years another Polaris boat would be finished on average every two months.

DURING HIS eight years in the White House, Eisenhower's views on nuclear weapons changed radically. In 1953 he considered them usable in a wide variety of conflicts. By 1961 he considered them practical in almost none. Their main role was that of a deterrent to Soviet nuclear weapons. Eisenhower had meanwhile become a strong believer in arms control and a nuclear test ban treaty.

The Soviets were interested in neither. They rejected every plea for arms control and when the United States and Great Britain declared a moratorium on nuclear testing in 1958 the Russians continued to set off nuclear explosions underground, underwater and in the atmosphere.

In his farewell address to the nation in January 1961 Eisenhower warned against two new dangers created by the Cold War. The first was "the conjunction of an immense military establishment and a large arms industry," which he termed "the military-industrial complex." The second was the federal government's domination of research, which threatened the future of free, disinterested intellectual inquiry. The country and the world were surprised, as if they had discovered a man they never knew existed. Eisenhower had spent much of his life concealing how intelligent he was, except from those who needed to know, such as Marshall.

His successor, John F. Kennedy, had campaigned on the theme that he was going to "get the country moving again." He peddled the myth of a "missile gap" hard, playing on the post-*Sputnik* feelings of insecurity, although in truth it was the Soviets who were on the losing side of whatever gap there was.

Defense and foreign policy were the strongest interests of the new administration. There was wide and deep anxiety when Kennedy became president that the United States was losing the Cold War. The Russians had a dynamic new leader in Khrushchev, a man who denounced Stalin, allowed greater openness in the Soviet Union, promised reform and freed hundreds of thousands of political prisoners. Kennedy rose to what he saw as a great historic challenge with a mixture of inspiring rhetoric and awesome inexperience.

His secretary of defense, Robert S. McNamara, had barely been installed as president of Ford Motor Company when Kennedy called him to Washington. Since his days as a statistician employed to improve management in the wartime Army Air Forces, McNamara had taken no interest in military affairs. Nor, he soon made clear, did he think much of military men. His passion was control—over men, over organizations, over events. It was control not by money, or political clout or promises or prizes, but control by the discipline of numbers: statistical control. Put everything in numbers and make sure the people below you keep producing the right figures.

His stated goal was to make the armed forces strong enough to fight "two and a half wars." What this meant, no one ever really knew. The result, though, was more ships for the navy, more planes for the air force, and three more divisions for the army, giving it sixteen.

The biggest increase of all was in strategic missiles. Eisenhower had planned a force of 1,100 ICBMs and SLBMs, split roughly 50–50 between the air force and the navy. To justify the Kennedy election claim of a dangerous missile gap the number of strategic nuclear missiles was raised to 1,710, even though both the president and the secretary of defense knew no such gap existed. Nor, as McNamara admitted after he left office, was this huge increase necessary for deterrence.

Defense was the essential issue in the election and the new administration professed to be horrified at the situation it inherited. It promised to bring a new rationality to defense, to make the country strong again. The truth, however, was that the United States was virtually invulnerable in 1961.

Nuclear abundance had imposed close coordination between the three components of the "Triad" of strategic forces Eisenhower had created; that is, the B-52s, the ICBMs and the SLBMs. In 1960 a single integrated operations plan (SIOP) was devised to share out targets among the forces of the Triad.

Few presidents and secretaries of defense have taken a close interest in the targeting of strategic nuclear weapons. For one thing, it is a complicated, technical subject. For another, they share the repugnance that most civilians have (and which military men are expected to overcome, much as they are expected to rise above the fear of physical danger) for weapons of mass destruction. Robert McNamara was different. He insisted on being briefed on the SIOP, shortly after he became secretary of defense.

What he saw astonished, shocked, ultimately unnerved him. As one transparent overlay flopped down on top of another, to be projected onto a large illuminated screen, McNamara appeared to quail, gripping the arms of his chair like a man in distress. On the screen the Soviet Union, Eastern Europe, China and North Korea were smothered under layer upon layer of glowing circles, triangles and dots: 2,500 targets, wiped out by 2,500 hydrogen and atomic bombs. The casualties from this onslaught were estimated at 360 million, plus.

This was what nuclear abundance meant; this was what it could do; and this was McNamara's inheritance. The briefing exposed more dramatically than anything else could just how ridiculous was the Kennedy claim that Eisenhower had left the nation militarily weak. As a stunned McNamara sat staring at that screen one afternoon in April 1961 the United States had the world at its mercy, with no fear of retaliation from anyone. For within the SIOP there was buried a secret. There was a plan within the plan. The military did not tell him what it was. He had to guess it.

The SIOP showed only what the United States could do—the targets it could strike, the power of the weapons that exploded, the estimated dead. What it did not show was intention, yet intention was—and is—the key to strategic planning: if they do such and such, here's what we'll do.

The assumption that was made by civilian strategists who argued that SAC was vulnerable to a first strike was that LeMay intended to strike second. All talk of retaliation, of deterrence, encouraged that idea. Certainly it was unthinkable that the United States would strike first, to launch a surprise attack.

What was generally overlooked was another possibility: the preemptive strike triggered solely by Soviet preparations for a nuclear attack. SAC was not planning to fight a nuclear war: it was planning to prevent one.

The first Soviet atomic explosion back in 1949 had led to the construction of a vast early-warning radar system across Canada. This was integrated with the most advanced computer systems money could buy, so that fighters and SAMs might bring down Soviet bombers long before they reached the densely populated cities of the East and Midwest.

Throughout the 1950s that early-warning network spread overseas, to protect SAC's forward bases. Soviet military radio traffic was intensively monitored by the National Security Agency for signs of unusual activity. The navy constructed sonar networks on the seabed, some running for hundreds of miles across underwater choke points, to track the Soviet submarine fleet.

The fear of a surprise attack by a nuclear-armed enemy produced a drive to collect information whatever it cost. The modern electronics industry was created largely as a result. Nearly all computers have their roots in military contracts of the 1950s and early 1960s, when data processing emerged as the central pillar of early warning. The advent of reconnaissance satellites, packed with sensors, cameras and communications gear, made surveillance of the Soviet military machine doubly effective.

Early warning, intelligence gathering and code breaking were integrated with control of the Triad. By 1961 American monitoring stood an almost certain chance of detecting any Soviet attempt to launch a surprise attack on the United States at least twelve hours in advance.

At that point the military would go to the president with the evidence they had gathered and say, as firmly as they knew how, "We must strike with everything we have, as quickly as we can, or else this country will die." Americans have seen it a thousand times—the man in the white hat waiting for the man in the black hat to go for his gun, and beating him to the draw.

If the director of the CIA and the head of the NSA agreed with the military's estimate of an impending Soviet strike, the pressure on the president to order a spoiling attack would be overwhelming. The SIOP would then be used, but not for retaliation, not for a second strike, not to fight a nuclear war. It would be used to eliminate the Soviet Union and its allies, and for reasons that were entirely justifiable. The Triad would be unleashed only if the Soviets moved first. Among American military men there was a kind of unspoken vow— "No more Pearl Harbors." Least of all a nuclear one.

McNamara appears to have guessed the secret behind the SIOP, the intention to strike the first blow, and that alarmed him. To his mind, that made more important than ever the need for tight control of the military. He advised Kennedy never, ever to use nuclear weapons. Even if nuclear explosions started wiping out American cities, he should keep his finger off the button until he knew what caused them and who was responsible.

With great fanfare McNamara informed the press and Congress— and, through them, the Soviet leadership—that he was changing the philosophy behind American strategic weapons. The new policy was to try to spare Soviet cities. The hope was that this would encourage the Soviets to plan to spare American ones. The new philosophy was termed "counterforce."

Soviet nuclear forces such as the Sapwood missiles went to the top of the target list. Hailed as an important advance in controlling nuclear war, counterforce overlooked the fact that the vast majority of important Soviet military installations are in or adjacent to the major cities and towns. Destroy the base with a one-megaton bomb and the town goes with it.

Nor could counterforce reassure the Soviet leadership of America's good intentions. What was the point in attacking empty missile silos in northern Russia after a Soviet attack had incinerated half the United States? The switch to counterforce and away from city-busting only served to improve the planning for a preemptive, disabling strike. So too did increasing American strategic nuclear forces by nearly 60 percent.

The more the Kennedy administration tried to move away from the first strike capability that was built into the SIOP, the more it ended up adding to its chances of success. Having boxed itself in on defense, this was the result.

Instead of bringing a new rationality to nuclear weapons McNamara and his assistants seemed bemused by them. They failed utterly to develop a doctrine for employment of battlefield nuclear weapons, for example, yet backed the development of new ones enthusiastically.

The initiative behind these weapons came mainly from the army. All through the 1950s it sought to fill the space between its nuclear cannon and the huge bombs carried by SAC's B-52s. The strategy it offered to cover the employment of a wide range of nuclear weapons was termed "flexible response." The idea was to provide the president with a host of options; as its proponents put it, to avoid having to choose between surrender and suicide.* The argument for flexible response was·at the heart of a best-selling book published by Maxwell Taylor in 1960, after he retired.

Taylor's book, *The Uncertain Trumpet,* made a deep impression on Kennedy. He brought Taylor out of retirement and gave the army the nuclear weapons it wanted, all the way down to a miniature atomic bomb that could be fired by two infantrymen equipped with a small rocket launcher.

The army's ability to fight conventional wars was improved. It got "sky cavalry," much expanded airlift and more men. The president took a strong personal interest in the development of the Special Forces, men who were trained to raise guerrillas and fight as guerrillas.

The army got all these things because Kennedy saw a military challenge almost wherever he looked. He responded to them with a bravura not seen in the White House since Teddy Roosevelt left it.

Cuba in particular affronted him. When Fidel Castro came to power on New Year's Day 1960, after overthrowing the odious Fulgencio Batista, there was much American goodwill toward him. This was alienated by the medieval barbarity with which Batista's henchmen, and then anyone who criticized the new regime, were tortured and killed. American investments in Cuba were seized by the revolutionaries, creating outrage in Congress and business circles. Like other pariah regimes of a left-wing persuasion, Cuba nonetheless found it had a good friend in the Soviet Union.

The installation of a Communist state only ninety miles from American territory seemed to Americans of the time almost a crime against nature. The bearded Castro was dangerous, evil, sinister. Some-

*SAC had not let the army in on the secret of the SIOP, any more than it let the civilian strategists the air force employed in on it.

thing had to be done. And John F. Kennedy, coming to the White House, found there was a plan available to do just that.

Miami was filled with middle-class Cuban refugees longing to go home again, with guns if necessary. Nearly 2,000 Cuban refugees were being trained in Nicaragua for an invasion of Cuba. The operation was organized and financed by the CIA. Kennedy was so determined to keep the plan secret it was not revealed to the JCS. He chose to dispense with expert military advice.

It was no secret from the Russians, though. Two weeks before the invasion, in April 1961, Khrushchev discussed it with the well-known American journalist and friend of presidents Walter Lippmann. There was going to be an invasion of Cuba, said Khrushchev, and it would fail. And fail it did. There were American ships and planes within range of the invasion beaches in the Bay of Pigs, but Kennedy, still hoping to deny American involvement, refused to let them intervene.

Nearly all of the Cubans involved were killed, wounded or captured. The 1,600 survivors were later ransomed for $62 million in spare parts and medical supplies. Kennedy had been forced to abandon the pretense of no American involvement, but he blamed it on the JCS, who had not learned of the plan until they had figured out that something was going on and demanded to know what it was, on the eve of the invasion. He attached no blame to the CIA, whose optimistic reports about the Cuban people being ready to rise up against Castro had made the plan seem realistic.

Two months after the Bay of Pigs fiasco Kennedy went to Vienna, to meet with Khrushchev. It was a disaster. For ninety minutes the two men sat on a couch and for most of those ninety minutes Khrushchev blustered and Kennedy tried to be reasonable. The Russian left Vienna convinced that the president was not only inexperienced, as the Bay of Pigs showed, but soft. He began squeezing Kennedy hard.

Twice he threatened to tear up the Four Power Agreement on Berlin. The first time, Kennedy sent an extra division to Germany and strengthened the Berlin garrison in a dramatic show of force. The second time, he called up 75,000 reservists. In September 1962 the East Germans raised tension still further by erecting the ultimate symbol of Communist failure, the Berlin Wall.

Khrushchev, like Russian leaders before and after him, was looking for the quick fix. In a slow-moving society there is always the tempting illusion of redressing a generation of stagnation by one day of inspired action. The czars were as addicted to it as their Communist successors. And so, in the fall of 1962, Khrushchev thought he might catch up overnight in the strategic arms race.

He decided to install Soviet IRBMs in Cuba. From there they might reach every important city along the East Coast up to New York. He was gambling on winning strategic parity on the quick and on the cheap.

In mid-October a U-2 photographed the unmistakable signs of a missile-launching area under construction at the western end of the island. It also picked up an IRBM being hoisted into firing position.

The swiftest way of eliminating the missiles was with an air strike, but Tactical Air Command advised that it could not guarantee to take out more than 90 percent. In the carnage and confusion following an attack there would be dead and dying Russians. It was possible that those Soviet officers who survived would be moved to avenge their dead comrades by using the few remaining missiles to wipe out an American city.

McNamara suggested another way—a naval blockade of the island, leading to air strikes if necessary, and an invasion as the ultimate resort. Here was a crisis, he argued, but it could be managed by the deliberate, gradual, controlled application of force.

Kennedy liked this crisis management approach. It suited his well-bred temperament, his longing to bring a higher order of rationality to international affairs. He could also afford to take a cool, high-minded stance—he held nearly all the picture cards: 112 Polaris missiles, 284 ICBMs, 105 IRBMs (stationed in Britain and Turkey and capable of reaching Moscow), plus the 659 B-52s of SAC.

Khrushchev had 150 long-range bombers of dubious worth and 35 ICBMs of proven unreliability. They were so inclined to blow up when ignited that one of them killed the commander of Soviet Rocket Forces and 300 other people. Soviet ICBM development was slowed down in the early 1960s, while a more reliable model was designed. Thanks to Penkovskiy, satellite photography and the code breaking of the NSA, Kennedy knew just how weak a hand Khrushchev held.

Cuba was quarantined. Every Soviet submarine in the Atlantic was picked up by the navy's sonar barrages and shadowed by attack submarines. Ships under Soviet charter bound for Cuba were boarded and searched. Soviet ships carrying missiles stopped short of the quarantine zone, then turned around.

A face-saving formula was devised to help Khrushchev end his dangerous game of bluff, but the episode left the Soviet leadership so shaken his hold on power was broken. Eighteen months later he was overthrown. He became a nonperson, doomed to die in disgrace.

THE DAY before his inauguration Kennedy called at the White House. Many on the incoming presidential team felt only an amused disdain for Eisenhower. He was a decent old sort, true enough, but forever on vacation, playing golf with other chairmen of the board, way past his prime and as capable of running the country as your beloved but doddering grampa.

That was the myth about Ike, and the Democrats had run hard against the myth. Kennedy knew better. Eisenhower was a tough-minded man who knew how to make a hard decision look easy, and how to get his way without starting a fight. For better or worse, he left the presidency stronger than he found it. So when Ike told him that he might soon find himself at war, Kennedy took him seriously.

The problem, said Eisenhower, was Laos. That landlocked country, once part of French Indochina, was on the verge of being conquered by Communist insurgents known as the Pathet Lao. The outgoing Republican secretaries of state and defense both considered Laos the key to Southeast Asia. Both recommended American intervention if nothing else would stave off victory by the Pathet Lao.

A month after that White House meeting the Royal Laotian Army was shattered on the Plaine des Jarres by lightly armed guerrillas. Kennedy asked the army if it could send in airborne troops to stop the descent of the Pathet Lao on the Laotian capital, Vientiane. The army could get its paratroopers there, was the reply—but it might take years to get them out again. The JCS put a price tag on Laotian intervention: 250,000 combat troops and possible use of nuclear weapons.

Kennedy began looking for a negotiated settlement. Enough assistance was provided covertly to the Vientiane government to prevent an immediate collapse. The Russians knew the Pathet Lao was a ragtag guerrilla force with not much more fighting spirit than the Royal Laotian Army. Khrushchev seems to have decided in mid-1961 that the insurgents had accomplished about all they could achieve on their own. The best thing would be to consolidate their gains. An agreement that "neutralized" Laos was reached, and an illusion instantly arose that peace had been brought to it. In fact, a secret war there was about to unfold, because impoverished, landlocked, remote Laos bordered on one of the major combat zones of modern history—Vietnam.

AFTER fighting an antiguerrilla war for twenty years France managed to rule all of Vietnam after 1887, but its hold on the country was never truly secure. Vichy's acquiescence in 1941 to Japanese demands for use of ports and airfields in the country only roused Vietnamese nationalism to a new pitch. The slackening grip of the French, moreover, was bound to stimulate sentiments of active opposition, which had never been dormant for long in Vietnam. A resistance organization, the Viet Minh, came into existence. Composed of Vietnamese Communists, such as Ho Chi Minh, non-Communist nationalists and some of the mountain tribes (who were composed mainly of nonethnic Vietnamese), it fought the Japanese occupation, with aid from Britain and the United States. The Viet Minh expected the defeat of Japan to prove the short, straight road to national independence.

Instead, the end of the war brought the return of the French, the reestablishment of French control—with help from Britain and the United States—and the continuation of the puppet emperor the Japanese had created, Bao Dai. Fat, amiable, inexhaustibly pliant, Bao Dai had a talent for being a puppet. He was in the rent-an-emperor business, only now the paychecks, like the mistresses, came from Paris.

The downside, the French discovered, was that Bao Dai's rule gave the outraged, frustrated Viet Minh a virtual monopoly on Vietnamese nationalism. He was simply too tainted by his former association with the Japanese. Guerrilla warfare flared up throughout the countryside. By 1950 the French were under strong military pressure from thousands of partisans.

That September a Military Assistance Advisory Group was established in Saigon to provide American logistical support to the French. American distaste for colonialism had been overtaken by hostility to communism and by this time there was little doubt that real power within the Viet Minh was in the hands of Ho and his Marxist-Leninist acolytes. Besides the aid that MAAG-Saigon provided, the United States effectively subsidized the French war effort through the arms it provided free or almost free to France as a member of NATO.

Even so, the 70,000 French troops and the 200,000-strong Vietnamese army that French officers created and led could not defeat the Viet Minh. In the spring of 1954 came *la catastrophe*. A powerful French garrison at Dien Bien Phu, on the Laotian border 160 miles west of Hanoi, was besieged. It was intended to be besieged. The French had set up this position as a well-prepared killing ground, as a magnet to draw their elusive enemy who refused to stand and fight.

The Viet Minh outsmarted the French. They seized the surrounding hilltops, portered the components of disassembled artillery pieces through the jungle and over the mountains, reassembled the artillery on the captured hills, brought the Dien Bien Phu airstrip—its lifeline—under direct fire, and thereby trapped 10,000 French and Vietnamese soldiers.

Ridgway, the army chief of staff, was following these events with grim foreboding. It seemed inevitable to him even before Dien Bien Phu's ordeal that the French were heading for defeat. And at some point, he was certain, they would seek American troops. On his own initiative and instinct, he began sending army experts to Vietnam, to report on what it would take to defeat the Viet Minh. During the last days of Dien Bien Phu, when the French asked for help and Ridgway was asked for advice by Eisenhower and Wilson, he was ready.

It would take up to one million American troops to defeat the Viet Minh, he said. Draft calls would have to be raised to 100,000 men a month. The reserves would have to be mobilized. The logistical infrastructure to support a large American army in Vietnam would have to be built almost from scratch. The war would be bigger than Korea and would last longer. The fighting would be like that in the Philippine Insurgency, but against a better-armed, better-led, better-organized foe. What Vietnam promised, Ridgway concluded, was one of the longest, bloodiest, hardest wars in American history.

The chairman of the JCS, Admiral Arthur W. Radford, was virtually alone in wanting to go to the rescue of the French, using air power and tactical nuclear weapons. Ridgway argued that in this kind of war only ground forces could prevail. Old soldier Ike agreed with him. There would be no U.S. cavalry sent to rescue the French.

Shortly after Dien Bien Phu fell, a powerful French armored and mechanized force, Groupement Mobile 100, was ambushed and destroyed on Route 19, the main east–west road through the Central Highlands of Vietnam. Such defeats and the absence of American intervention left France no choice but departure.

A peace conference at Geneva secured French withdrawal and created two statelets: one composing the northern half of Vietnam above the 17th parallel, to be ruled by the victorious Viet Minh; the other in the south, under a Saigon government created by the departing French.

Nationwide elections were scheduled for 1956. The result was a foregone conclusion: a unified state under Communist rule. North Vietnam contained 60 percent of the total population, even after nearly one million people moved south (many of them carried there by the U.S. Seventh Fleet). Washington and Saigon felt free, however, to block the scheduled elections. Neither had signed the Geneva Accords.

The French-created government of South Vietnam was in the hands of Ngo Dinh Diem and his family, Roman Catholics with powerful friends in the Church and in the United States. Shortly after Diem's accession to power Eisenhower pledged American support "in developing and maintaining a strong, viable state, capable of resisting attempted subversion or aggression through military means." There was a string attached: "The Government of the United States expects this aid will be met by performance on the part of the Government in Viet-Nam in undertaking needed reforms." If Ike ever wanted or needed an out, he had one.

The MAAG created an army for Diem, the Army of the Republic of Vietnam (or ARVN, pronounced "Arvin"). It was a miniature of the U.S. Army. Tens of thousands of diminutive Vietnamese were drafted to carry weapons that dwarfed them while they struggled half blind under heavy steel helmets that reached their narrow shoulders.

By the late 1950s the United States was paying 80 percent of the cost of running the Diem government, and 98 percent of the cost of its armed forces. Diem himself was lavishly paid in the coin of flattery. When he traveled to the United States in 1957 *Air Force One* was sent to collect him. He was acclaimed when he addressed both houses of Congress and New York welcomed him like one of the great statesmen of the age.

The countryside back home was meanwhile bursting into flames. Knowing they were going to be denied the unifying elections promised at Geneva, the Viet Minh had left thousands of veteran cadres in the South after partition. For several years they mounted nothing more than nuisance raids on such symbols of the Diem regime as police stations. The police were controlled by his feared and hated brother, Ngo Dinh Nhu. By 1960 former Viet Minh networks had been re-created, base areas securely established and political indoctrination was under way in countless hamlets and villages. A new struggle, born of the old one, was about to begin. The Viet Minh terminated its historic existence. From its self-extinction in December 1960 it was instantly reborn, as the National Liberation Front of Vietnam.

One month later, in January 1961, Khrushchev publicly declared Moscow's support for "wars of national liberation." And two weeks after that Kennedy was sworn in as president. Khrushchev's pledge sounded remarkably like a direct challenge; one that could not go unanswered.

Kennedy's emotions were already deeply engaged in Vietnam. Back in 1954, while a senator, he had been a founder-member of the American Friends of Vietnam. The main function of the AFV was to lobby the government for more aid to Diem. In 1957 Kennedy had hailed South Vietnam as "the cornerstone of the Free World in Southeast Asia," on which hung the security of countries as far away as Japan. One of his first foreign policy initiatives as president was to ask Congress for a big increase in aid to Saigon.

Whether or not Khrushchev had Vietnam in mind when he praised wars of national liberation, it weighed heavily on the consciousness of the new administration. In the midst of the Laotian crisis Robert Kennedy, the president's brother and his closest, most trusted adviser, asked at a meeting of top-level defense and foreign policy experts, "Where would be the best place to stand and fight in Southeast Asia?"

Their answer was unanimously "Vietnam."

The correct answer to the question was Thailand, but no one involved was able to muster the degree of objectivity required to see that. Vietnam was all that Kennedy and his advisers could think of. One powerful reason that their minds were so fixated was that the situation there was deteriorating with attention-grabbing speed.

Top military men were nonetheless as reluctant to get involved as Ridgway had been. "We cannot win a conventional war in Southeast Asia," advised Army Chief of Staff George Decker. If the United States did choose to fight there, said Decker, the only real pressure it could apply against China and North Vietnam was by using nuclear weapons. The chief of naval operations, Arleigh Burke, agreed with Decker.

This nukes-or-nothing approach irritated Kennedy. He made it plain in discussions with those close to him that he found the "can do" spirit sadly lacking in his military advisers. For that, he began looking to civilians such as McNamara and his national security adviser, McGeorge Bundy, the former dean of Harvard College.

To get a reliable measure of the state of the war and the character of the Diem regime, Kennedy sent to South Vietnam two people whose judgment he trusted, Walt Whitman Rostow and Maxwell Taylor. Rostow was a former professor of economics at the Massachusetts Institute of Technology, sometime target selector for Eighth Air Force, longtime heavyweight thinker about such matters as nation building. Kennedy had installed him as the head of State's policy planning staff.

Taylor had been called back from retirement. Not that he was ever unbusy. He had written *The Uncertain Trumpet* and assumed the presidency of the Lincoln Center for the Performing Arts. If ever there was a Kennedy-type general, a book-writing, arts-loving, decorated war hero of airborne operations had to be it. Taylor came back into uniform specifically to serve the president as a kind of military troubleshooter. In October 1961 his mission was to travel to Saigon with Rostow, appraise the war and come up with specific recommendations on what the United States ought to do about it.

They came, they saw, they concurred: only an injection of American combat troops could save the Diem regime. It was hated, ineffective, corrupt and brutal. Taylor called for 8,000 American combat troops just to stabilize the worsening battlefield situation. Unlike Ridgway's experts, he reported there would be no serious logistical problems to surmount. Nor, he went on, would the climate or the terrain impose unusual burdens on American troops.

McNamara supported Taylor's recommendation, but he added that he could see the 8,000 becoming as many as 205,000 if the Viet Cong (a term of disparagement coined by the Saigon regime for "Vietnamese Communists") were ever to be defeated, not merely held at bay.

The Taylor-Rostow-McNamara line was completely at odds with the advice coming from Decker and Burke. Confronted with that division, Kennedy shrank from committing American troops in a combat role. Instead of sending 8,000 men to fight he resorted to a little political legerdemain. He would send 16,000 soldiers instead—to "advise."

He seemed happily unaware that those 16,000 advisers would be hostages to fortune. They would have to be protected from the Viet Cong. The ARVN was never likely to be able to do that.

Shortly after Kennedy's decision, in February 1962 MAAG–Saigon became the Military Assistance Command, Vietnam (or MACV). This was no longer an outfit that did no more than give advice. It was a command that could, if necessary, direct operations.

The infusion of up to 1,000 new advisers each month meant an inevitable increase in military aid to Diem. The ARVN got more trucks, more artillery, more helicopters, armored personnel carriers, plenty of small arms and an abundance of advice. Throughout 1962 the situation seemed to stabilize, but in January 1963 at the Battle of Ap Bac a VC battalion of roughly 400 men showed what it could do: it shattered an ARVN brigade-strength attack of 4,000 men riding into battle in armored personnel carriers, supported by American helicopters and artillery. In this stand-up fight nine of the ten helicopters involved were shot down or badly damaged.

Meanwhile Decker's two-year term as army chief of staff had expired. He did not get a second term. Like Ridgway, who had refused to go along with Wilson's demands that he support policies he disagreed with, Decker was forced into an early retirement, a victim of his own integrity. His fate, like Ridgway's, was a warning.

His successor was the scholarly, mild-mannered Earle G. Wheeler. As director of the Joint Staff he had frequently briefed the president. Kennedy therefore knew Wheeler's unassertive personality; here was a general who would not create difficulties. He also kicked the chairman of the JCS, General Lyman Lemnitzer, upstairs by making him ambassador to NATO. The new JCS chairman was Maxwell Taylor. The commander of MACV was, moreover, Lieutenant General Paul D. Harkins, a Taylor protégé.

The critics, the doubters were being shut out. When Lieutenant Colonel John Paul Vann returned from Vietnam in 1963 he was scheduled to brief the JCS. Vann was known in the army as an awkward cuss but also the most perceptive, best-informed officer on Vietnamese affairs and the ARVN in MACV. At the last moment Taylor, recently installed as chairman, reached down and canceled the briefing, rather than expose his fellow chiefs to Vann's expert criticism of the Saigon regime and its army.

At the same time the torrent of optimistic assessments pouring out of Harkins's headquarters was widely circulated in the Pentagon and the White House.

Like a young man's sense of immortality, that optimism defied common sense and history.

In May 1963 Diem's brother, the archbishop of Hue (formerly the capital of Vietnam, before the French came and created a new one), ordered the Buddhists of the city not to fly Buddhist flags on the Buddha's birthday.

Protest demonstrations were organized. ARVN troops fired on the crowds. More than one hundred people were killed or wounded. Buddhist temples became centers of protest throughout South Vietnam, and a monk named Thich Quang Duc drew the attention of the world when he set himself ablaze with two gallons of gasoline on a street corner in downtown Saigon.

A score of monks followed his example. Diem's brother tried to stop the protests by having his paramilitary police force storm the biggest pagoda in Saigon. Thirty monks were shot, hundreds arrested. The telephone lines to the American embassy were cut in an attempt to prevent the U.S. government from learning what was happening in the capital of its ally.

With the Diem brothers as bent on self-destruction as Thich Quang Duc, Kennedy and McNamara signaled to the generals of the ARVN that a change of regime would not be unwelcome in Washington. The generals were not yet ready to move and Diem, virtually a prisoner in his palace, held on into the fall.

Incredible as it might seem in retrospect, Taylor and McNamara visited South Vietnam in October and reported back that the war was going so well that some of the 16,000 advisers could be withdrawn in the coming months. The Diem regime was, in fact, in its final days.

By now, however, no one around Kennedy felt able to advise him to pull out. Not even dyed-in-the wool liberals who thought that was the right thing to do could bring themselves to tell him so. They too went along. As one of them, John Kenneth Galbraith, reasoned, if he said what he really thought, "My effectiveness would be at an end."

Considering the excitement, the romance, the idealism of Kennedy's Camelot administration, it was understandable that no one wanted to leave the party early. Yet the "effectiveness" point of view assumed it was better to be inside the government giving the wrong advice than to be outside it speaking the truth, even on a life-and-death issue. If mental shutters were made of steel Washington in the Thousand Days would have resounded to metallic clanking.

On November 1, 1963, disgruntled ARVN generals overthrew Diem and his brother. Both were murdered next day. Within three weeks John Kennedy too would be dead.

He left an America that was more committed than ever to the war in South Vietnam, for although the United States was not directly involved in the coup it had promoted the downfall of Diem. That left Washington committed to supporting the coup makers and whatever government they created.

THE IDEA that anyone but Diem would be an improvement was soon proven false. Government in Saigon became a revolving door as a succession of ambitious but politically inept generals seized power from one old rival only to lose it to another. All the while the Viet Cong were conquering the countryside.

The NLF had created a three-tier military structure: local defense forces at village level, small guerrilla units of 25 to 30 men capable of mounting ambushes and raids, and main force battalions of 300 to 400 men able to defend VC bases. Such bases were located in border areas close to Laos, Cambodia and North Vietnam, or were buried in huge tunnel complexes only a day's march from Saigon.

In time main force units would grow to become 1,500-man regiments and 5,000-man divisions, less than half the size of their American equivalents yet formidable all the same. This war was both a guerrilla struggle and a conventional conflict; just as it was both a civil war and a political-social revolution.

The blurring of categories baffled American politicians and military men. Too late would they comprehend the complex nature of the struggle for South Vietnam. They preferred to portray it as an invasion from the north, much like the war in Korea. They sought to win South Vietnamese hearts and minds by promising to make the Saigon regime better. The Viet Cong had more success by promising to throw it out.

Lyndon Johnson found himself plunged into this bewildering, growing war without any real background in foreign or military affairs. His political hero was Franklin Roosevelt, the great political adventure of his life had been the New Deal. Johnson had his heart set on ending poverty in America, not on fighting a war ten thousand miles from home.

He wanted to put South Vietnam on hold until after the 1964

election. By then—who could say?—things might somehow improve. All the same, something had to be done to save the ARVN from the Viet Cong.

In February 1964 a secret air war was begun in Laos, run by the CIA and the American ambassador, William Sullivan. It was aimed at cutting the Ho Chi Minh Trail, which then consisted of a few narrow paths leading from North Vietnam down to Cambodia and South Vietnam by way of the Laotian Panhandle. The bombing was also aimed at neutralizing the Pathet Lao.

Covert operations that took South Vietnamese raiding parties by air and sea into North Vietnam had begun under Kennedy. Johnson provided a large increase in logistical support for these.

He also sent Harkins the army's fastest-rising star, William C. Westmoreland, to serve as deputy commander of MACV. Known as "Chief" to his friends ever since his days at West Point, as an expression of their conviction that he would rise to the top, Westmoreland did indeed cut an impressive figure, and knew it. To some who served with him his vanity at times seemed to undermine his judgment.

After becoming a very young chief of staff of the 9th Infantry Division in World War Two, he had risen to command Taylor's old outfit, the 101st Airborne Division. Westmoreland had also been secretary of the JCS under Taylor. Like Harkins, only more so, Westy was a Taylor protégé.

What he discovered when he arrived in Saigon early in 1964 amazed and depressed him. To an old friend from World War Two he confided, "There is no military solution to this problem of Vietnam." In an official report he described the war as "a bottomless pit." The abounding optimism of Harkins annoyed him.

Despite all of which, when he succeeded Harkins in July 1965 he too would find it impossible to tell the president that the war was unwinnable on any terms that the United States was ready to accept. "The armed services were not about to go to the Commander in Chief and say we were not up to carrying out his instructions," he told that same friend a decade later, "as a matter of service pride." To Decker to Ridgway, service pride had required saying exactly that, but look what happened to them.

When Westmoreland took over as commanding general, MACV, VC main force units were regularly engaging the ARVN in open warfare. They were receiving a new generation of Soviet and Chinese automatic weapons, notably the AK-47 assault rifle. It was a rugged arm with a high cyclic rate of fire, small enough for Vietnamese to handle easily and simple to keep clean. It gave the VC and North Vietnamese Army (or NVA) troops a firepower advantage over the ARVN, who carried World War Two–vintage carbines and rifles.

As Westmoreland pondered developments such as this, the war took a dramatic turn. On August 2, 1964, the U.S. Navy destroyer *Maddox* was nearly thirty miles off the North Vietnamese coast, in the Gulf of Tonkin, monitoring radar emissions. As the destroyer headed away from the coast, it was attacked by three North Vietnamese torpedo boats. Only thirty-six hours earlier South Vietnamese raiding parties had landed on North Vietnamese islands nearby and that operation was still under way. This may have explained the attack on the *Maddox,* which took evasive action. No damage was suffered and the attack was shrugged off as an accident or mistake.

Two days later the *Maddox* and another destroyer, the *Turner Joy,* reported they were the targets of a second torpedo boat attack, this time sixty miles off the North Vietnamese coast. Johnson ordered a reprisal air attack. Strikes were made against torpedo boat bases and an oil storage facility.

The president meanwhile asked Congress for authority to take further steps to protect American forces. On August 7 Congress overwhelmingly (88 to 2 in the Senate, 419 to 0 in the House) gave him what he wanted: a resolution that authorized him "as Commander in Chief, to take all necessary measures to repel any armed attack against the forces of the United States and to prevent further aggression . . . [and] to take all necessary steps, including the use of armed force" to aid members of the Southeast Asian Treaty Organization (SEATO) in defeating subversion and aggression. South Vietnam was a member of SEATO. If not carte blanche for Johnson, this was very close to it. He used the Gulf of Tonkin resolution to justify every escalatory step he took thereafter.

IN THE fall of 1964 Maxwell Taylor stepped down as chairman of the JCS to become American ambassador to South Vietnam, the better to help run the burgeoning war. Wheeler moved up to the chairmanship while Harold K. Johnson, a survivor of the Bataan death march, became army chief of staff.

In November the president won a landslide victory at the polls by pledging, "We seek no wider war ..." and by portraying his Republican opponent, Senator Barry Goldwater, as a war-loving air force reserve general who could hardly wait to expand the conflict.

Shortly after the election a long cable arrived from Taylor. He reported that the 16,000 advisers needed secure bases, bases that would have to be defended by American combat troops. A B-57 squadron sent to Bien Hoa as a boost to ARVN morale had just been attacked, leaving five Americans dead, 76 wounded, and half the squadron's aircraft destroyed or damaged. Events such as this left the ARVN demoralized. Something new was needed to revive its fighting spirit. The something new Taylor had in mind was bombing North Vietnam. Alarmed, Johnson sent Bundy to Saigon to see if things really were as bad as Taylor painted them.

While Bundy was touring South Vietnam, in February 1965, the VC attacked Camp Holloway, near a town in the Central Highlands called Pleiku. Three days later VC sappers blew up a hotel being used as an enlisted men's billet in the coastal town of Qui Nhon, killing 23 American soldiers. These attacks underlined Taylor's point about the vulnerability of the advisers. Bundy strongly recommended reprisal bombings of the North, which McNamara just as strongly endorsed. The bombing of North Vietnam, known as Operation Rolling Thunder, began, but under very severe constraints.

In March two battalions of a marine expeditionary brigade entered South Vietnam; one to guard the jet airfield at Danang, fifty miles from the Demilitarized Zone that straddled the 19th parallel; the other to seize and hold ground for a new jet airfield, at Chu Lai, sixty miles to the south of Danang.

Not even these measures did much for the ARVN. The conflict was ceasing to be a guerrilla struggle. It was turning into a conventional war. Up to 1,000 North Vietnamese regulars were entering South Vietnam each month, either down the ever-widening Ho Chi Minh Trail or brought by sea to the Cambodian port of Sihanoukville and then through the jungle and over the border. With this added muscle the Communists were destroying ARVN battalions at the rate of one a week; twice as fast as they could be replaced.

Westmoreland advised McNamara that only a huge, rapid infusion of American combat troops could save South Vietnam now. He recommended a force of 44 maneuver battalions (1,000-man units, that is, of infantry or armor) immediately, with a follow-on force of 27 maneuver battalions as soon as they became available. With support units and artillery he was calling, in effect, for a force of 300,000 men. This would allow him to take the offensive at the start of 1966.

More American ground troops were already entering South Vietnam to help save the ARVN. The 173rd Airborne Brigade and 1st Brigade of the 101st Airborne Division arrived in May 1965. Like the marines, they soon found themselves in bloody clashes with VC main force units and NVA regulars.

As he mulled over Westmoreland's request, Johnson asked Wheeler what he thought it would take to defeat the Viet Cong. Wheeler and the Marine Corps commandant, General Wallace M. Greene, had already agreed that it would take up to 1.2 million American troops fighting for seven years. And after that a sizable American army would have to remain for up to thirty years to make sure the VC did not reestablish themselves. Wheeler began to explain this to Johnson, but at the mention of a million men the president cut him short. That was ridiculous, impossible. He didn't want to listen to talk like that.

How Johnson knew that Wheeler's figures were wrong, he never said, and Wheeler was not going to argue with him. Making waves was not how he had become chairman of the JCS.

Having kept secret the air war in Laos, having kept secret the North Vietnamese Army's increasing infiltration of the South, having kept secret the impending destruction of the ARVN, Johnson went on television on July 28 to announce he was ordering 58,000 American combat troops to South Vietnam. This news burst on the country like a bombshell. Even now he did not dare to tell the American people the truth, for fear that they would turn against the war.

He had already altered the mission of American forces in South Vietnam from that of advisers to that of combatants. Yet when word of that leaked out in May, the White House had denied there had been any such change. And having accepted Westmoreland's request for up to 300,000 men, he kept that secret too. Those 300,000 were going to turn this into America's war.

19

WITHDRAWAL
PAINS

THE CRISIS atmosphere of the early 1960s, presidential attention and a larger share of the defense budget transformed the
unhappy post-Korea army. By 1965 it was prouder, better trained,
better equipped and more confident than at any time since the victory
parades of 1945.

Kennedy took a strong personal interest in the development of the
Special Forces. These elite units, lineal descendants of the Rangers of
World War Two, who had performed high-risk missions behind
enemy lines, were expected to set Eastern Europe ablaze. In time of
war with the Soviets, they were to operate in places such as Poland
and Hungary, stirring up partisan activity against Warsaw Pact forces,
threatening the Red Army's lines of communication.

Kennedy recast them as frontline warriors in wars of national
liberation, only instead of raising and leading guerrillas they were now
expected to stop them.

In 1962 he bestowed the distinctive emblem of the Special Forces,
the green beret, on these his favored troops. Such gestures riled the
normally phlegmatic George Decker. "Any good soldier can handle
guerrillas," he told the young president. That was the kind of dull
utterance that won no hearing in Camelot. It was doubly unwelcome,
because it cast doubt on the fashionable talk about counterinsurgency

being a unique kind of warfare, one that called for a different, Kennedyesque kind of soldier.

Besides being sold on the Special Forces, the president and McNamara were enthusiastic about the sky cavalry idea. Helicopters had made their combat debut in Korea, when they helped lift a company of marines into action in October 1951. Even before that war ended the army set a goal of twelve airmobile battalions, despite the fact that no suitable trooplift helicopter existed or was being designed.

In 1958 Bell Aviation unveiled a new aerial ambulance, the XH-40 utility helicopter. Sky cav believers immediately saw possibilities in it. With slight modifications this noncombat machine became the HU-1B, or Huey, an aircraft made with battle in mind. As it entered army service in the early 1960s so did another helicopter, the big, powerful Chinook. With fast, stripped-down Hueys (known as "Slicks") for airlifting infantry into battle, plus armed and armored Hueys (known as "Guns") serving as gunships, and Chinooks to move artillery around on the battlefield, true combat airmobility was possible.

A brigade-strength unit, the 11th Air Assault Division (Test) was created at Fort Benning, Georgia, to develop doctrine, equipment and organization. Its proposed missions were the classical cavalry roles: deep reconnaissance, screening the movements of friendly forces, and fighting delaying actions.

It was an exciting concept, but many senior army figures remained skeptical. The idea was both unproven and very expensive.

The decision to Americanize the war changed everything. McNamara outmaneuvered the doubters and imposed sky cavalry on the army. He merged the test division with the understrength 2nd Infantry Division to create the reborn 1st Cavalry Division and shipped it off to Vietnam in the summer of 1965, against the army's advice.

Sky cavalry and greatly expanded Special Forces (which had grown from roughly 1,000 men to more than 3,000 under Kennedy) had not remade the army. Nor had these innovations really prepared it to defeat wars of national liberation.

McNamara had revamped management in the Pentagon but he had not succeeded in getting the military to rethink their traditional doctrines. Kennedy had promoted counterinsurgency as the new way to fight yet neither he nor anyone close to him knew much about it. The army therefore ignored the military pontification offered by its political masters and stuck to what it knew and trusted.

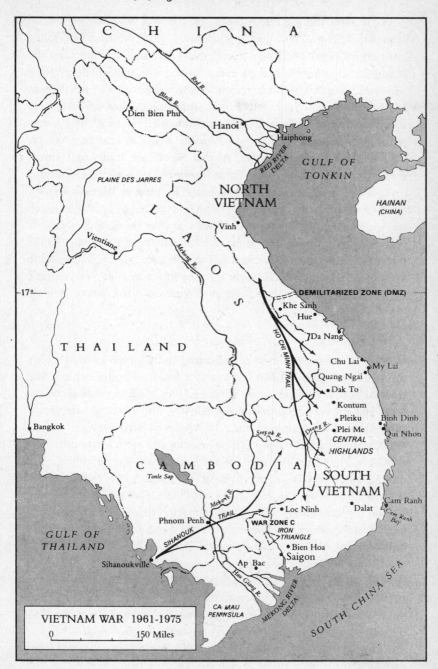

VIETNAM WAR 1961-1975

0   150 Miles

Not even the Americanization of the war in Vietnam would change that. Troops heading for Southeast Asia got hurried, half-baked instructions based on the successful counterinsurgency campaign the British had mounted in Malaya in the 1950s; a war, incidentally, fought and won by ordinary soldiers, most of them draftees. The situation in Malaya was so different in its fundamentals that it had little to teach about Vietnam. It was mainly a conflict in which the minority Chinese population tried to seize power from the Malayan Islamic majority. Counterinsurgency tactics based on that experience hardly represented a chance to rethink the U.S. Army's essential war-fighting doctrine.

That doctrine remained rooted in the fighting in Western Europe from Omaha Beach to the Elbe. The army expected to fight over much the same terrain, in much the same way, against the Red Army. That was its primary mission. Sky cav and Special Forces did not change that mission. In doctrine, training, organization and equipment the U.S. Army of 1965 was the right instrument for smashing Soviet tank armies attempting to thrust deep into West Germany but the wrong one for jungle warfare.

WHEN THE marines arrived at Danang and Chu Lai in March 1965 the general intention of MACV was to secure firm positions along the coast of South Vietnam. From these enclaves it could establish strong bases and provide support for the ARVN, and possibly offer some protection to the people of these heavily populated areas.

The marines were blooded in skirmishes and patrols, ambushes and accidents. The first major fight did not come until August, when a VC regiment of up to 1,000 men prepared to attack the airfield under construction at Chu Lai. A Marine Corps helicopter assault trapped the VC on a promontory, while another marine force made amphibious assaults in their rear. Naval gunfire crashed down from vessels steaming offshore. The VC regiment was virtually annihilated.

Events at Danang were less auspicious. The marines there had all the indications they could want that the VC were about to attack the airfield. They did nothing to frustrate the enemy's preparations. When the attack came, the VC broke through marine positions and got onto the main runway, destroying or damaging a dozen aircraft.

This was just the kind of enemy operation the marines had been sent to Danang to prevent, but complacency and contempt for the enemy proved too strong for that. After the shock and embarrassment at Danang, however, a change came over the aggressive, confident marines. They stopped mounting large-scale offensive operations.

The epitome of open, mobile, aggressive warfare, the marines hunkered down, assuming a static, defensive posture. Offensive operations hereafter were limited to patrols that went out a kilometer or so to help secure marine positions.

It was the army that waged the offensives. Westmoreland was unhappy with the strategy being urged on him by Taylor of remaining in enclaves along the coast. He was anxious too about the buildup of enemy strength in the Central Highlands of Vietnam.

This region, bordering on Cambodia, had for a generation past been under Communist control. He feared, or claimed to fear, an attempt to cut South Vietnam in two by an enemy drive from the Highlands to the coast. Considering that this would have committed the enemy to defending territory, he might have better viewed it as an opportunity rather than a threat.

In an assertion of his own strategic preferences, Westmoreland thrust the 1st Cavalry Division into the Central Highlands when it arrived in the summer of 1965. It was a bold, aggressive move, fraught with risks.

First Cav troopers called their role "on-the-job fighting." The final phase of the planned testing of the airmobility concept had been scheduled to take place in the swamps of Florida, against 101st Airborne Division. Instead it would take place in Vietnam, against a real enemy, on his home ground. The east–west road that ran through here was Route 19—the famous Street Without Joy—where the Viet Minh had ambushed dozens of French convoys and wiped out Groupement Mobile 100.

Special Forces units had entered the Highlands back in 1963, to work among the Montagnards, the nonethnic Vietnamese tribes who felt no loyalty to either Hanoi or Saigon. In the early fall of 1965 thousands of NVA troops crossed over from Cambodia and besieged the Special Forces-Montagnard base at Pleime, in the Ia Drang Valley, twenty miles from Cambodia. Reinforcements were rushed in by air. Intensive bombing forced the North Vietnamese to break off the siege. Best of all, a skirmish between 1st Cav troopers and an enemy patrol brought an intelligence windfall: a dead North Vietnamese officer whose pockets were stuffed with maps, on which were marked NVA bases and infiltration routes through the valley.

With that, 1st Cavalry Division loaded aboard its Hueys and went looking for the enemy; forcing him to fight by landing on his lines of retreat into Cambodia. All through November three NVA regiments slugged it out toe to toe as Slicks whirred in over the double and triple canopy jungle to disgorge troops who hit the gorund running.

No infantry had ever gone so light into battle. All they carried was ammo, rifles, hand grenades, canteens and grenade launchers that fired a 40-millimeter projectile. Everything else was brought in by the helicopters.

These troopers hit with the shock force of armor, took ground with the élan of hard-charging infantry, moved with the mobility of cavalry and in their gunships had airborne artillery. In the dozens of firefights that rang through the Ia Drang Valley the North Vietnamese stood no chance. All three regiments were chewed up. The Cav's losses were comparatively modest.

The Battle of the Ia Drang Valley made the division famous and adored. They had beaten the enemy in his lair and done it in style, with flashy modernity. In those heady, early days no soldier on Earth walked taller than a 1st Cav trooper.

Any threat there may have been of South Vietnam being bisected was banished. Westmoreland made the most of his victory in the Highlands—he asked for another 100,000 men, on top of the 300,000 already promised. He got all he asked for, and more. In a burst of generosity and optimism, and hoping it might speed the end of the war, the troop level set for Vietnam was raised to 470,000 men.

Westmoreland would have preferred to fight the whole war in the Highlands, but in 1966 the Viet Cong began launching main force attacks in the heavily populated coastal plain of Binh Dinh Province. If this was intended to draw 1st Cav away from the border areas where NVA divisions were entering South Vietnam, it worked. Throughout Binh Dinh the Cav used the air assault techniques it had perfected in the Ia Drang Valley, while warships out to sea thundered their support. Thousands of enemy troops were reported killed, wounded or captured. Yet ground taken was not held and some main force units proved impossible to engage. Binh Dinh remained insecure, only now 30 percent of its population of 900,000 had been made refugees.

During those summer months of 1966, 101st Airborne Division was up in the Central Highlands mounting a major offensive, Operation Hawthorne. After licking their wounds and drawing lessons from the battles of fall 1965, the NVA and VC emerged ready to fight again. They ambushed the paratroopers, they booby-trapped everything in sight, and when it suited them, they stood and fought. Then they pulled out, as effectively as if they'd vanished.

Westmoreland mounted several other major offensives in 1966 but they too ended in frustration and bemusement. The enemy fought with the infuriating elusiveness of the guerrilla, but the firepower and discipline of a conventional army.

While young Americans were bleeding and dying in these battles South Vietnam (unlike South Korea) seemed unwilling to save itself. The death of Diem stirred a vortex of coup making that sucked down every hope of national self-preservation.

After two years of political chaos a fragile partnership between General Nguyen Van Thieu and Air Vice Marshal Nguyen Cao Ky emerged and appeared to offer a chance of effective rule. In February 1966 Johnson and McNamara flew to Honolulu to meet with Thieu and Ky, more or less to bestow their blessing and send a signal to the South Vietnamese military that the coups had to stop.

May, however, brought yet another Buddhist crisis. This time a Buddhist nun burned herself to death in Hue's central pagoda. Rioting students from the university set fire to the U.S. Information Service library in the city. ARVN units revolted against the Thieu-Ky regime. Marines at Danang looked on in disgust and fascination as the South Vietnamese air force, loyal to Ky, strafed and rocketed ARVN units that supported the Buddhists. Washington firmly backed Thieu and Ky, which helped bring the waverers into line, and the revolt was crushed.

By this time the war was thoroughly Americanized. American troops did most of the fighting, American generals made most of the important decisions, Americans suffered most of the casualties, yet Westmoreland was still groping for a strategy. He got nothing one could seriously call guidance from the president or secretary of defense.

He found conferring with Johnson useless and exasperating. The commander in chief had no clear idea what he was doing in Vietnam or what he wanted his soldiers to do. Conversations between the courtly, imposing South Carolinian general whose very southernness helped win the president's trust and the Texan who had no experience of foreign policy or military affairs consisted of little more than small talk, a charade that on the evening television news could pass for discussions of strategy. Johnson was vacillating and anxious. His instructions to his main field commander consisted of orders such as "You get things bubblin', General."

The traditional custom and practice was for the president to provide a set of well-defined objectives for the senior American commanders overseas. While they fought the war he would devote his energies to securing from Congress the resources needed to attain those objectives. That had worked for Scott, for Shafter, for Pershing, for Eisenhower. Korea had weakened that proven system, mainly because of the mercurial MacArthur. Vietnam destroyed it absolutely.

Nor could Westmoreland expect the army itself to produce a clear, realistic strategy. The postwar military had abandoned thinking about strategy to civilians. Military men turned their intellectual powers to more pressing concerns—to weapons development, or new management methods, or relations with Congress. Thinking about strategy withered within the armed forces. It was contracted out instead to think tanks such as RAND in Santa Monica.

That left the army and Marine Corps in Vietnam in 1966 with no one in uniform able to offer thinking that matched the scale of the challenge. To be fair, the civilian strategists did not fare any better. The performance of even the brightest civilian strategists when they turned their thoughts to victory in Vietnam was no better than that provided by amateurs such as McNamara and Bundy.

By allowing thought on strategy to wither, however, the military had abdicated one of its essential functions. That abdication also left it in a weak position to challenge the Whiz Kids—the bright young lawyers and college professors whom McNamara brought in to help him run the Pentagon. Intellectually, the military had disarmed itself, and in Vietnam that meant paying a price.

The absence of a clear strategic objective left a vacuum at the heart of the war. Something had to fill it. What did was one of the most curious institutions in American military history, the Tuesday lunch bunch. Every Tuesday Johnson took lunch in the White House dining room with McNamara, Dean Rusk, Rostow (brought in to replace Bundy in 1966 as the national security adviser) and Richard Helms, director of the CIA.

They pored over maps of Indochina, deciding what should be attacked, which weapons were appropriate, even what flight paths should be used as planes approached assigned targets. The mind-set of these men had been fixed by the Cuban missile crisis, where carefully graduated escalation of military power had brought pressure to bear on a dangerous adversary yet all the while giving him a chance to back down. Besides that formative experience the lunchers were also moved by a profound distrust of the military. They did not seek military advice, and when it was offered it was ignored.

In 1967 the existence of the Tuesday lunch bunch became public knowledge, so for the sake of appearances it was decided to include Wheeler. He was so diffident around powerful civilians his presence had as much impact as that of the White House servants who brought in the meal. The war continued to be run by men who had little military experience, and that little was long out-of-date.

Their policy of graduated response had the seductive illusion of control yet it was also a thinly disguised excuse for timidity. North Vietnam had an army of 250,000 men, led by tough, battle-hardened NCOs, veterans of victory over the French. It also had an army reserve of 200,000 men. Yet the Tuesday lunchers in their innocence signaled to Hanoi, publicly and privately, that it had nothing much to fear: no matter what, there would be no American invasion of North Vietnam. It never occurred to them that what they were doing was freeing Ho Chi Minh to send his entire army south if he wished, plus all or part of his reserves. Up to 450,000 of the best infantry in the world were released for the journey down the Ho Chi Minh Trail. This was not the kind of issue that the Tuesday lunch bunch even discussed.

When, in the fall of 1965, it dawned on some of Westmoreland's intelligence officers that North Vietnam had a big army and was being given a free hand to commit nearly all of it to battle, that rocked them. "Jesus!" exclaimed a general on Westmoreland's staff. "If we tell the people in Washington that, we'll be out of the war tomorrow. We'll have to revise it downward."

IN HIS first year as commanding general, MACV, Westmoreland tried to get control of the pacification program. He launched an initiative of his own to create protected hamlets along the lines of those the British had built in Malaya. The corruption of the South Vietnamese government, all the way down to village level, and the disorganization of the ARVN doomed his project before it began.

Americans were also less than ideal, as a rule, for a "hearts and minds" contest in Southeast Asia. The overwhelming majority felt themselves to be infinitely superior to these "gooks" and "dinks." More than a few made it plain they despised the Vietnamese and loathed the country.

Westmoreland nonetheless believed the political nature of the war required the army to assume responsibility for protecting the rural population while fighting to secure the countryside. The State Department flatly refused to surrender its guiding role in pacification. That was one battle he lost.

It left Westmoreland little choice but to concentrate his energies on winning the war by bringing the enemy to battle. When he was forced to improvise a strategy, it was a measure of his desperation and the poverty of his thought that he tried to revive a French idea that had failed completely. They called it *quadrillage,* from the grid pattern commonly overprinted on military maps. The idea was to secure squares of territory, a few at a time, until one fine day they all linked up and the whole country was free of enemy forces. *Quadrillage* was the kind of notion that Francophiles might consider amusingly French: intellectual clarity and neatness achieved by ignoring murky, untidy realities, such as the political challenge of the Viet Minh.

Westmoreland called his version "the spreading oil spot." A flop by any other name is still a flop, but this one might pass in a poor light for a strategy provided it was not examined closely. In Phase 1, he was going to secure vital areas such as Saigon, Chu Lai, Danang, Hue and Binh Dinh. In Phase 2, his troops would move into the surrounding countryside, to clear it of enemy forces and uproot the VC's political structure. As towns, even entire provinces, were secured they would be entrusted to the protection of the ARVN, freeing American units for Phase 3: pursuit and destruction of enemy regiments and divisions, the elimination of his bases and sanctuaries.

The buildup of maneuver battalions by 1967 and the impressive creation of a large, modern logistical infrastructure in a Third World country meant that Westmoreland felt able to move to Phase 3. There were 1.3 million American, South Korean, Australian, Thai and South Vietnamese troops in the country at the end of 1966, with more on their way. Confidence in MACV was high. The time had come to crush the Viet Cong as a military force.

THE YEAR 1967 opened with one of the biggest operations of the war, code-named Cedar Falls, to clear the Iron Triangle. This was a sixty-square-mile area of woodland northeast of Saigon, at the confluence of two rivers. It had been a Communist stronghold for a generation. It was honeycombed with what amounted to an underground city. Thirty-five thousand American and ARVN troops burned, shot and blasted their way through the Iron Triangle. Hundreds of VC were killed, hundreds more captured. The villages were razed and their inhabitants moved out.

Combat engineers proceeded to demolish the woodland, using Rome plows: bulldozers that had a huge spike at one end of the dozer blade, capable of punching huge holes in even the hardest cedar tree and loosening the roots. Cedar fell all over the Triangle, but even with the earth stripped bare the tunnels remained, layer upon layer, complex after complex. The army lacked the manpower to try clearing or destroying them. An important enemy base had been found—and left almost untouched.

One month after Cedar Falls the army launched Operation Junction City, against War Zone C, an area near the Cambodian border, northwest of Saigon. This was another corps-size operation. As many as 2,000 VC were killed. Much of the area was devastated. During the action the 173rd Airborne Brigade made the only combat jump of the war. American troops performed superbly, but so did the VC. Their fighting spirit was never higher. During one firefight wounded Viet Cong were brought into combat by riding piggyback, both the rider and his bearer firing their AK-47s as they charged.

Shortly after Junction City, Westmoreland returned to plead in private with Johnson for another 200,000 men. In public, addressing a joint session of Congress, he promised victory. Everything was going so well, he declared, he expected American troops to be withdrawn starting in 1969. Johnson gave him an extra 55,000 men, raising the troop ceiling to 525,000. This was about as high as he could go without mobilizing the reserves, something the president was determined not to do.

The policy was still to lie about the war. The administration lied to Congress about it, lied to the public about it, even lied to the Treasury about it, fearing that if the truth were known about the size of it, the nature of it and the cost of it, the country would want to pull out. So far, public opinion supported the war, but there was a fragility to that support that Johnson wanted never to see tested. So although Westmoreland got more men he was told firmly that this was the limit.

In November 1967 the 4th Infantry Division and the 173rd Airborne Brigade fought a month-long Battle of the Highlands around Dak To in some of the hardest, costliest ground clashes of the war, almost destroying one of the NVA's finest divisions. The North Vietnamese survivors simply retreated over the border into Laos, to await reinforcements. The Highlands were still under threat, for all the casualties and courage of the American units, from an enemy whom MACV described to the world as being defeated.

Similarly, the net effect of Junction City had been to push the enemy over the border into Cambodia. From his sanctuaries there he was as much of a menace as before. The timidity of the policy of graduated response was so paralyzing that it not only kept American divisions out of North Vietnam, where there was a danger of Chinese intervention, it also kept them out of Laos and Cambodia, where there was no danger of Chinese intervention. Instead, the policy was to try to win the goodwill of Prince Sihanouk, the ruler of Cambodia. This included sending Jacqueline Kennedy to visit the temples of Angkor Wat in 1967 and to convey the president's good wishes to the prince. The policy also included not telling the American people that much of Cambodia was a sanctuary for the North Vietnamese Army.

While the army was engaged in major offensives such as Cedar Falls and Junction City, the strategy of the spreading oil spot dictated that the ARVN and various local militia and mercenary forces, such as the Montagnards, would be occupying the villages and uprooting the VC political structure. In this, as in much else, Westmoreland was doomed to disappointment. American troops were forced to conduct the holding operations and mount the dull yet dangerous patrols that the ARVN was reluctant—to the point of refusal—to undertake.

With much of the enemy's main force strength now pushed back into Laos and Cambodia, Westmoreland tried sitting on his infiltration routes. This soon tied down much of the army in remote areas. Static, positional warfare had many of his maneuver battalions virtually immobilized by 1968. The great sweeps had been a great letdown.

These "search and destroy" missions were often described in the press as though they were blood-crazed ventures in nihilism. They were, in fact, classic Clausewitzian tactics aimed at bringing the enemy to battle, then destroying him with superior numbers and superior firepower.

The pattern of operations was often reminiscent of that used for hunting pheasants or quail, with a line of beaters trying to flush the game from cover and drive it onto a waiting line of guns. In other countries, against a different enemy, it might have worked, but in their vegetation-festooned fiber helmets and camouflage capes VC and NVA troops who crouched among the foliage were as good as invisible so long as they remained still.

The undergrowth was so dense that ambushes were set up within fifty feet of the trail, sometimes less than half that, with the ambushers almost on top of their victims. In combat this close and armed with modern automatic weapons, a dozen VC could kill or disable one hundred men in less than a minute and escape more or less unscathed. As with their forerunners, the Viet Minh, ambush was their specialty. Roughly 90 percent of all firefights in Vietnam were initiated by the enemy. American troops fought on his terms.

Besides the danger of being bushwhacked, the whole country was littered with mines and booby traps. Weeks would pass in which a maneuver battalion suffered a remorseless, demoralizing stream of casualties without ever seeing the enemy who inflicted them. In 1967 the attrition rate in some battalions was about the same as that of British battalions in the trenches of the western front fifty years earlier.

On those occasions when the enemy was pinned down, whether by good luck or good intelligence, there was not much to choose between this and some other wars. In places like the Iron Triangle the fighting resembled that on Japanese-held islands in the Pacific, where another foe had burrowed deep and fought to the death. And for all the glamorous high-tech weaponry of this war many infantry actions came down in the end to highly personal killing, with axes, knives, machetes and entrenching tools.

To help reduce his casualties, Westmoreland encouraged his battalion commanders, "Use bullets, not bodies." (His version of an old army adage, "Send a bullet, not a man.") In South Vietnam this usually meant shooting up the jungle or plastering the rice paddies. Known as "harassment and interdiction" fire, or H&I, it was provided mainly by the artillery. Such fire was supposed to be directed against known or suspected enemy positions, infiltration routes, headquarters and supply dumps.

The chief victim of H&I was not the enemy but pacification. The Viet Cong's political base in the villages meant those same villages were also military installations, where arms were hidden, bunkers dug, supplies stored. That made it impossible for the army to secure the countryside without making war on the rural population. Search and destroy plus H&I meant that just a few rifle shots from a village were enough to bring its total destruction. Among the survivors, the able-bodied men were likely to join the VC. The other survivors became refugees. (And by 1968 there were at least one million refugees.) The razed village and the area around it became a free-fire zone, where anything that moved was presumed to be hostile and therefore a target for more H&I fire.

Instead of reducing casualties, this lavish application of firepower probably increased them. Thousands of tons of artillery shells, along with thousands of tons of bombs, were duds. These unexploded bombs and shells provided the VC with a bountiful harvest of matériel for creating mines and booby traps, which accounted for 20 percent of American casualties.

In fighting a foe who held the initiative, Westmoreland's manpower advantage was nullified. His superior firepower wrecked pacification and harmed his own troops. Even American mobility proved to be a lot more problematical than McNamara and the sky cav enthusiasts had imagined. More mobility was a long way short of ubiquity. Helicopters *were* great—during the day. This was a war fought mainly at night, against an enemy who moved mainly at night. Few helicopters flew in the darkness, and then with heart-thumping caution.

The very nature of the war undercut the army's mobility still further. By 1968 hard-charging infantry were rare. Mines, ambushes, booby traps—all had taken a toll. When soldiers or marines came under fire now even the best units went to ground quickly, and stayed there. This was no longer a fire-and-maneuver army (one that pinned down the enemy with fire, then moved to trap or outflank him) but a maneuver-and-fire army. Again and again units engaged in close combat would report they were pinned down and could not move, yet the VC main force unit they were fighting was not pinned down, because whenever they chose to, the VC were nearly always able to pull out.

The enemy had also learned by now that if they could close quickly with an American unit they could escape American bombs and artillery fire, because it was then impossible to hit them without hitting American troops. So it was increasingly the Americans who went to ground and the Viet Cong and North Vietnamese who did the charging.

The jungle itself sapped men's confidence. Its ovenlike heat and dense, tangled undergrowth slowed down men who had cheerfully marched thirty miles a day back home. Here a three-hour patrol would reduce them to listless, shuffling zombies. The terrain in much of South Vietnam was a man-killer.

So was the climate. It drove some men crazy, killed others. Blood temperatures rose as high as 109 degrees. At that level the blood, in effect, bubbled in the brain like boiling water, leaving those who survived brain-damaged for life.

This was the terrain, this the climate that Maxwell Taylor had reported from the comfort of hotels and headquarters would pose no unusual difficulties for American troops.

Even now the spirit of purblind optimism flourished. In the spring of 1967 Westmoreland reported to Washington that the "crossover point" had been reached. This was the point at which Hanoi would be losing troops faster than it could replace them. This report was as much a fantasy as anything that Harkins had ever produced. There were nearly two million men aged eighteen to thirty-four in North Vietnam. A further 120,000 reached the age of eighteen each year. Fewer than half these were being drafted by the North Vietnamese Army. If anything, the NVA was growing bigger from year to year. In his eagerness to win the war, Westmoreland had lost the objectivity he possessed when he arrived in 1964.

After the Battle of the Highlands he reported flatly, "The enemy's hopes are bankrupt," and at a top-secret briefing on New Year's Day 1968 he delivered the message in person to the president and the JCS: this would be the year America won in Vietnam. In the Highlands and in towns down in the Mekong Delta, VC units had come in, run up their flags, stood and fought, and been blasted to smithereens. Dozens of main force units had been mauled. The war was going his way at last.

Viet Cong strategy called for war in three acts. It began with revolutionary forces embedding themselves deep in the society, limiting themselves to lightning raids against the power structure. In the second act, guerrilla war would break out, with pitched battles that established the ascendancy of the revolutionaries. As the tempo of violence reached a crescendo the curtain would go up on Act Three—the mass of the people, strong in their wrath, would rise as one and with irresistible heroism seize power for themselves.

The general uprising, suffused with operatic melodrama, was a piece of romance that Vietnamese Communists had tacked onto Marxism-Leninism. And for reasons still unclear the Viet Cong decided in the fall of 1967 that the historic moment had arrived for Act Three.

That was why main force units stood and fought in the Battle of the Highlands; that was why forty towns in the delta were seized almost simultaneously despite the fact that they could not be held. The VC was holding its dress rehearsal. It was a venture that also had the effect of drawing American forces away from the cities and towns, which was where the general uprising was supposed to occur. The date set for the grand finale was the Vietnamese New Year, known as Tet, at the end of January 1968.

The force of the VC's Tet offensive struck an American public opinion that had been so deceived, so manipulated, so bamboozled so long it was as shocking and bewildering as being awoken in the middle of the night with a kick in the shins and a dazzling light shone in the eyes.

Viet Cong sappers blasted their way into the U.S. embassy in Saigon. The Saigon government's radio station was seized. Enemy troops fought their way onto the tarmac at Tan Son Nhut Air Base, one of the key military installations in the whole of Southeast Asia.

In Hue, the VC seized the heart of the city, the huge stone fortress known as the Citadel. Dozens of district capitals and provincial capitals fell to them all over South Vietnam. They were demonstrating in the most effective manner that two could escalate as easily as one. The NVA too was emboldened, employing tanks for the first time.

For an entire month the Viet Cong flag flew over Hue, while marines dug them out in an epic of street fighting. By April the offensive was spent and nearly everything the VC had captured had been recaptured. In May VC commanders tried to renew the offensive, throwing in the last of their reserves, believing as attacking generals often do that one final push will bring victory. Nearly fifty cities and towns came under intensive rocket and mortar fire, but the follow-up infantry thrusts lacked weight and were beaten off.

For the most part, the battles of the Tet offensive were fought between ARVN troops and the VC. This time the ARVN fought well. Located in or near their hometowns, having their families nearby, and fighting mainly on the defensive, they put up a fight that surprised and delighted their American advisers.

The psychological blow of Tet was double-edged. It turned American public opinion against the war, yet it also turned many South Vietnamese against their so-called liberators. There was no third-act uprising of the downtrodden urban masses. The proud, black-clad, armed peasants of the VC were scorned by city dwellers: the people who had shunned the countryside, shunned the war. They despised much that the VC were ready to die for.

Shamed, then enraged, the Communists took a barbaric revenge that besmirched every ideal they pretended to defend. In Hue up to three thousand unarmed and helpless people, many of them with no ties to the Saigon government or American forces—children, medical missionaries, Buddhist pilgrims—were murdered.

Lacking the active support of the urban masses, the Viet Cong would have to rely on victory by arms alone, yet that was beyond them now. Tet and the May offensive had wiped out the veteran cadres of the main force units. After the spring of 1968 the North Vietnamese Army would do nearly all of the fighting on the Communist side of the war.

WESTMORELAND considered the Tet offensive a massive diversion. The main effort, he proclaimed from the body-strewn grounds of the U.S. embassy, would be mounted elsewhere—against the marine base at Khe Sanh. He had pushed and pestered the marines to plunge deep inland, to make the same kind of large-scale search-and-destroy missions as the army. The marines resisted. Beaches and blue water were what they knew best, but in 1967 Westmoreland forced them into the kind of static, positional, defensive warfare they really loathed. He ordered them to reinforce the remote base known as Khe Sanh. It was located in the northwestern corner of South Vietnam, close to the DMZ and the Ho Chi Minh Trail. It was both a blocking position against enemy infiltration and a promising killing ground.

By January 1968 Khe Sanh was besieged by three NVA divisions. The 5,000 marines there dug furiously as they came under the heaviest bombardment endured by American forces since World War Two.

All through January and into February the president fretted. Suppose bad weather made air supply impossible? Suppose the marines were overrun? The White House in February 1968 resembled a command post under attack. A vast aerial mosaic dominated the Situation Room. Every yard of trench, every hole diligently excavated by the marines was there. The mosaic was updated twice a day, then three times a day. A tide of brightly colored markers for the encroaching enemy moved forward steadily, until it lapped against the trenches like waves breaking on a shore.

There was also the huge terrain model, looking like something made for a millionaire's son on which to set out his toy soldiers, built especially for the commander in chief. He would come down four or five times every day, call down several times in the night. The president was mentally in there, down in the trenches with his troops. From the JCS he wrung a paper, "signed in blood," as he put it, that Khe Sanh wouldn't fall. Not ever.

The NVA had hopes of another Dien Bien Phu, but unlike the French the marines made sure they held the high ground: they occupied the six hilltops around it. Despite fierce night attacks, they hung on, supported by some of the closest, most intensive air support in history.

Tet and Khe Sanh frayed Johnson's taut nerves, eroded his shaky self-confidence. And in the midst of this ordeal challengers arose within his own party to contest his bid for reelection in the fall. The success of these Democratic insurgents was an expression of the dramatic, irreversible shift in public support for the war.

The JCS meanwhile encouraged Westmoreland to request an additional 206,000 men. The seizure of a navy electronics intelligence vessel, the *Pueblo,* by the North Koreans in international waters in January had exposed the comparative military impotence of the United States. Everything it had seemed to be tied up in South Vietnam. There was no strategic reserve left to speak of. Combat units worldwide had been stripped to the bone, and even the marrow, to be fed into the maw of jungle warfare. Westmoreland was to get half of the new troops, if the president agreed to the request. The remainder would go to restoring the strategic reserve.

The demand for more men threw the administration into confusion. An extra infusion of men would not bring victory in Vietnam. Nor were they needed to sustain the war at its present level. McNamara was in the process of stepping down after seven years as secretary of defense, to be succeeded by Clark Clifford. Neither man could get from MACV or the JCS a clear explanation of what these extra troops would achieve. Clifford went to Vietnam, and returned to tell the president that the only thing to do with the war was to de-escalate; to wind it down to what it had been back in 1962, a guerrilla conflict. And once it was wound down, the United States might be able to pull out.

Johnson was bewildered, having mistakenly believed that Clifford was a hawk. He had one last card to play, though—his Wise Men. This was a body of twenty notables, men who had once exercised great power but were now out of government. They were elder statesmen, beyond the interests of this party or that, and the repository of much experience. The question they were asked to consider was simple: should Westmoreland get more troops?

After a full day of briefings on March 25 the Wise Men faced the president. They told him they could find no way of winning the war, even with extra troops. Nor could they think of a strategy for winning the peace. The best advice they could give was for him to look for a way out of South Vietnam. The astonishment he felt in that moment was written all over that expressive face. "He could hardly believe his ears," said Clifford.

Six days later Johnson went on television to announce that all bombing of North Vietnam above the 20th parallel would stop. He invited the Hanoi regime to enter into peace talks. Then he sprang the real surprise: he would not seek reelection in November.

That night bonfires crackled and church bells rang across the land. At midnight hundreds of people gripped the White House railings, singing lustily. There had been no spontaneous national celebration like this since the surrender of Japan.

A few weeks later, almost unnoticed, the North Vietnamese broke off the siege at Khe Sanh and the road to it from the coast was opened once more. In the summer Westmoreland came home, to succeed Harold K. Johnson as army chief of staff. He was not disgraced, just ignored. The road ahead in Vietnam led down, and out.

THE AIR WAR was as frustrating as the war on the ground. Early in 1965 the JCS developed a plan for massive air attacks that made a target of everything of military or economic importance in North Vietnam. Johnson and McNamara flatly rejected it.

They created instead Operation Rolling Thunder.* There was virtually no discussion of this plan, which envisaged on-again, off-again bombing, carefully limited in scope, tightly controlled means, gradually increasing in tempo. The targets consisted of a barracks here, a truck park there, maybe a small bridge or possibly an ammunition dump. When Rolling Thunder began in February 1965, however, the grandiose name and the way Johnson boasted about it ("I just cut Ho's pecker off") suggested a crushing aerial assault; on a par, say, with the big bomber raids of World War Two.

The reality was an average of three attacks per week, against two or three minor targets below the 19th parallel—thereby sparing Hanoi, the port of Haiphong and the major industrial areas of North Vietnam. Each raid was conducted by a handful of jet fighter-bombers, usually F-105s, a dozen of which had the payload equivalent of two B-29s. In 1965–66 that was what Rolling Thunder amounted to, sending two or three B-29s to attack unimportant targets several times a week.

Every bomb dropped amounted to a vote for Ho Chi Minh. Air attacks may have been the best thing that ever happened to him, from being Escoffier's *sous-chef* at the Paris Ritz to beating the French. Bombing pushed the weary, impoverished North Vietnamese into total support of the Communists and the war. It stirred up worldwide sympathy for little North Vietnam; brought in trainloads and shiploads of Soviet and Chinese weapons, East German medicines, Czech machinery and Swedish foreign aid; it fanned antiwar sentiment in the United States and alienated America's allies; and it brought in so much economic assistance that the gross national product actually increased.

One month after Rolling Thunder began, MiG-17s rose to chal-

*The name came from Stephen Crane's description of a cannonade in *The Red Badge of Courage:* "The battle roar settled to a rolling thunder. . . ."

lenge the fighter-bombers. Meanwhile surface-to-air missile sites were under construction, in full view of American aircraft. Nothing was done to interfere. Johnson and McNamara were afraid of Soviet engineers being killed if the sites were attacked. By the summer of 1965 a dozen SAM bases were operational, firing SA-2 Guideline missiles—the size of a telephone pole and detonated by a proximity fuse—up to sixty thousand feet.

The SAM sites had to be attacked then, but airfields remained off limits for two years. Attacking them would have been the quick and easy way to deal with the MiGs. Instead, air force pilots were forced to devise ruses to lure the MiGs into the air; such as making a formation of F-4 Phantom fighters appear on radar like a formation of slower, heavily laden F-105s heading in on a bombing run.

The air war evolved into a contest of electronic wizardry, aimed on the American side at destroying North Vietnamese radar sites and decoying Russian-made missiles. The enemy fought back tenaciously and skillfully, constantly developing new tactics and new pieces of equipment. And each time American techniques such as radar jamming gained the upper hand, they sent up the MiGs. These represented Hanoi's bottom line in its efforts to deny the air force and navy the kind of absolute air superiority they had enjoyed in the Korean War.

The MiG-17 and its successors, the MiG-19 and MiG-21, were pure fighters, designed for aerial combat and nothing else. Light, fast, highly maneuverable, they posed a serious threat to the heavier, less agile Phantoms, which were multirole aircraft, packed with missiles and modern electronics. American pilots emerging from narrowly won dogfights were heard to cry, "Oh, for an F-86!"

Even so, the Phantom had its advantages: better radar, the ability to kill at long range with its missiles, superior speed and huge fuel tanks. A historic dogfight between the best North Vietnamese pilot, known as Colonel Tomb (credited with downing thirteen American planes), and U.S. Navy pilot Lieutenant Randy "Duke" Cunningham in 1972 lasted fifteen minutes; one of the longest ever. When Tomb tried to break away, probably because he was running out of fuel, Cunningham downed him with a missile.

The war in the air resembled the struggle on the ground. Countless clashes involved big American planes with noisy, smoky engines being attacked from below and behind by small, fast fighters that zoomed up from out of the background clutter on radar screens. It was a scenario remarkably like a Viet Cong ambush.

Vectored to the target by North Vietnamese radar sites, MiG pilots climbed at 35,000 feet a minute. American pilots hardly had time to pick them up on their airborne radars before the MiGs were closing fast on their tails, firing Atoll air-to-air missiles or getting off a burst of 23-millimeter cannon fire, before flashing down and away, to be lost once more against the dark green foliage, the narrow roads and shining rice paddies far below. This was not aerial combat as USAF tactical doctrine taught it.

By the end of 1968 air force and navy pilots claimed 120 victories in dogfights, but at the cost of 55 planes lost. A success ratio of two to one gave no one much satisfaction, considering the success ratio in Korea.

The great danger was not enemy aircraft but intense ground fire. Of the 900 planes lost over North Vietnam roughly 700 were victims of antiaircraft artillery. The North Vietnamese had scads of antiaircraft guns, including 2,000 that were radar-controlled and capable of firing 100-millimeter shells as high as twenty thousand feet. Heavy cloud covers North Vietnam for half the year, and American planes were forced to fly many missions as low as five thousand feet. Some areas, moreover, were protected by so much firepower that AAA gunners did not bother to aim at attacking aircraft. They simply filled the sky above with flying lead.

The gradual buildup of the air offensive gave Hanoi time to learn how to cope with it. Periodic bombing halts (on average once every ten weeks, in a desperate attempt to coax Ho into peace talks) provided welcome respites for North Vietnam to rethink tactics, strengthen defenses and train new gunners and Guideline crews.

In the course of the war the bombing campaign was stepped up, so that most of the targets on the JCS's original list were eventually hit. After the airfields were attacked in the fall of 1967 North Vietnamese MiGs were pulled back to bases in southern China. The modest industrial infrastructure was obliterated by bombing. "Smart" bombs of astonishing accuracy were developed, guided by television cameras in the nose. Two huge smart bombs were flown in through the windows of the control room of the Hanoi thermal power plant, shutting it down in a stunning explosion.

A range of sensors was developed to increase the effectiveness of the air war. Some could detect the odor of human urine, thereby locating enemy troop concentrations. "People sniffers" played an important role in the demolition of the three NVA divisions that besieged Khe Sanh.

Despite such successes the results were disappointing in the air mission that mattered most. Air power proved almost useless in cutting the Ho Chi Minh Trail. By 1967 the trail had been expanded so that in places it consisted of four highways, each about twenty-five feet wide, down which trucks roared at night in a steady stream. Heavy AAA discouraged pilots from strafing runs and the steep mountains ruled out diving attacks. Few trucks were ever troubled by American planes.

The failure of the interdiction effort was epitomized by the present that Mao Tse-tung sent to Prince Sihanouk in 1966. The token of the Great Helmsman's esteem for the Cambodian leader was a sixty-foot yacht, gleaming white, on a forty-foot trailer. Hauled down the trail, it reached its berth at Sihanoukville without a scratch.

It was a foretaste of humiliations to come. In 1968 the NVA started sending the ultimate in big, slow, heavy weapons down the trail— tanks. The air force never even saw them.

The demoralizing realization that the bombing campaign had failed finally convinced McNamara that the war was hopeless. After he expressed that opinion to a Senate committee at the end of 1967, Johnson forced him out as secretary of defense.

A year later the president brought Rolling Thunder to a halt, days before the 1968 election. The destruction of VC main force units during Tet and the fighting that followed compelled the enemy to ask for talks and play for time. The United States accepted the offer of talks with almost pathetic eagerness. Discussions opened in Paris that summer, where the Communists did little more than argue about the proper size and shape of the negotiating table and who should sit where.

Despite these obvious stalling tactics, Johnson had lost all desire to prosecute the war. His main interest had become securing the election of his vice-president, Hubert Humphrey, and denying the White House to Humphrey's opponent, Richard Nixon. To help Humphrey, Johnson halted the bombing of North Vietnam above the DMZ, in exchange for no more than vague promises from Ho Chi Minh's successors.*

Taylor and Rostow, Bundy and McNamara, but Johnson above all had escalated the war confident that American air power was the trump in the game. And now Johnson had more or less tossed it away. It was the clearest signal short of writing it in fire across the sky that the United States was determined to get out of this war.

ONE OF THE FEW positive developments of the Vietnam debacle was the destruction of the myth that blacks could not or would not fight. Yet it was in keeping with the dismaying character of the conflict that this forward step had little impact.

There had been no doubting the courage of black soldiers and sailors in the nineteenth century. It took the rise of imperialism, and especially the Spanish-American War, to bring segregation to the military. A world view that exalted the supremacy of the white warrior had to deny or ignore the role of blacks in the Union's victory over the South, in the army's conquest of the Plains and in the lightning defeat of Spain.

During World War One black regiments had served with the French army, not Pershing's. Their officers, though American, were nearly all white, and those officers nearly always considered assignment to a black unit a setback to their careers. The resentments common to officers and men in these segregated regiments made impossible the kind of cohesion, the mutual trust and respect that produce effective combat performance.

Although there were more black officers and NCOs in the army in World War Two the same general pattern obtained: unhappy black troops forced into segregated units run by equally unhappy white officers. The records of the two black divisions, the 92nd and 93rd, were predictably poor.

Most blacks were kept away from the combat arms. They were relegated instead to such tasks as handling ammunition or driving supply trucks. The Army Air Forces had a few segregated flying units, but even when they performed well only the readers of black newspa-

*"Uncle Ho" died in 1969.

pers were aware of it. The navy and Marine Corps accepted very few blacks, and those few were kept in menial assignments.

The chance black troops were hoping for came during the Battle of the Bulge. Frontline units were so desperate for infantry replacements that Eisenhower agreed to a proposal that fresh infantry platoons be formed from volunteers whatever their training and whatever their color. Cooks, bakers, truck drivers—almost anyone who knew which way to point a rifle was accepted.

These integrated platoons fought well. No one ever denied that. Yet the army still refused to desegregate. Most of its major training bases were in the South. It was averse too to what Bradley and others considered "social engineering."

In 1948 Truman tried to improve his chances of election by issuing an executive order that directed an end to segregation in the military. With the exception of the 82nd Airborne Division, commanded by James Gavin, who had seen how well integration worked during the Bulge, the military ignored Truman's order.

In the Korean War black units' successes were slighted, their failings publicized, but in 1952 Ridgway became chief of staff. He imposed desegregation on the army. This time it worked.

Many battalions serving in Korea had been forced to take infantrymen wherever they could find them. Hundreds of white officers saw for themselves that black soldiers who were treated equally with whites fought just as well. That kind of experience did more than anything else to change the army. By the time Ridgway stepped down as chief of staff in 1955 it was fully integrated. So was the Marine Corps. The air force and navy, both devoted to operating complicated machines, wanted only the well educated, thereby excluding all but a handful of blacks.

The Kennedy administration's strong commitment to civil rights brought some reduction in those barriers, but it was the army that continued to offer the widest opportunities to young black men of all national institutions. This unfortunately did nothing to shield it from some of the most harrowing racial conflicts of the turbulent time ahead.

The Vietnam War tore at the bonds that create a society, whipping up the kind of tensions that historically formed the prelude to civil war or revolution. The 1960s were, for many people, a historic moment when love congealed into hatred, when those who should have been dear to them assumed the face of the enemy. In countless homes, in a thousand towns, brother turned against brother, children rejected their parents, pupils reviled their teachers, friend stopped speaking to friend, the young despised the old, and the citizen learned to hate his country. Traditional social divisions were sharpened. Ancient strife revived. White once more feared black.

This was a stunning turn of events, for the civil rights movement of the 1950s and early 1960s had raised high the hope that racial inequalities were going to be narrowed, racial prejudice overcome. The war blasted those hopes by killing off Lyndon Johnson's promised Great Society.

The centerpiece of this ambitious effort, a new New Deal, was to be the abolition of poverty in America. Freedom from poverty would have been the greatest possible advance for ordinary black people. Nothing would have so fully realized the aims of the civil rights movement. The hundreds of billions that were needed went instead into financing the war. Vietnam stopped the civil rights movement and the war on poverty dead in their tracks.

"Hope deferred maketh the heart sick." In this instance, hope deferred proceeded to turn the passions the movement had aroused into bloodshed and destruction (mostly self-destruction: black rioters of the 1960s did not burn down white neighborhoods but black ones). And by 1968 the fierce sense of outrage, of betrayal, of hopelessness that fueled the riots in the cities was affecting blacks in the armed forces.

Meanwhile, the presence of large numbers of blacks in combat units, either because they had volunteered for elite outfits such as the airborne or were assigned to the infantry because they lacked high school diplomas, meant that although they made up 10.5 percent of the army, in Vietnam they were taking 21 percent of the casualties. Figures such as this at a time such as this were meat and drink to black militants. And the murder by a white man of Dr. Martin Luther King, Jr., in April 1968 raised black anger to a terrible pitch. A horrifying cycle of violence took hold within the military.

There were race riots—some instigated by whites—at dozens of bases in the United States and overseas, leaving blacks and whites dead or mutilated for life. There were riots at air bases, marine barracks, even aboard warships at sea. The only salute some black servicemen would offer was the clenched fist of the Black Panthers.

It was possible to put down riots and to cope with minor breaches of discipline. The real horror story was "fragging." This murderous practice took its name from the disgruntled soldier's weapon of choice, the fragmentation grenade. Thrown into someone's tent under cover of darkness, it offered lethality with anonymity.* Fragging took the lives of nearly one hundred officers. Almost all the five hundred officially recorded instances of fragging were believed to be racially motivated. Nearly all the victims were white. And for every fragging incident many more were threatened, leaving thousands of officers and senior NCOs terrified of the men they supposedly commanded.

By 1970 black radicalism was hampering combat operations in the air force and navy. Army commanders were reluctant to issue weapons to black troops. Racial conflict undermined prosecution of the war.

And yet, ironically, nearly every racial clash in Vietnam occurred in rear areas. In the combat zone, where white and black had to trust each other, support each other in order to survive, they fought the real enemy, not one another.

THE ELECTION of Richard Nixon brought a new approach to the war: pursuit of victory in Vietnam while withdrawing ground troops from it. To do this he had to continue the dishonesty policy of his predecessor. As a result, his handling of the war was destined to generate nothing but distrust, to drive some elements of the antiwar movement into terrorism, and to degrade the nation's armed forces.

From early 1969 the commitment of American combat troops was reduced. Melvin Laird, Nixon's secretary of defense, read the election result as a mandate for withdrawal. His vigorous promotion of troop reductions exasperated the president and the national security adviser, Henry Kissinger, who saw withdrawals as a sop to public opinion while they tried out new approaches to winning the war. The JCS had its own doubts about rapid withdrawal, fearing it might offer the NVA a chance to inflict heavy losses on weakened American forces.

---

*Fragging was not a new phenomenon. During the Mexican War, for instance, an artillery shell was set off underneath the bed of that cantankerous character Braxton Bragg. He survived by sheer chance, while his tent was reduced to shreds.

Laird, however, had strong backing in Congress, where he had served for twenty-two years, and from the nation at large. He demanded daily reports on the progress of withdrawal. The aim of his policy was, in a term he coined, "Vietnamization."

Laird's popularity made it too costly for Nixon to fire him. The president resorted instead to bypassing his secretary of defense. On some occasions, when Nixon anticipated that Laird would object to decisions being taken to pursue the war more vigorously, orders went directly from the White House to the JCS, with instructions that the secretary of defense was not to be informed.

The three instruments on which Nixon and Kissinger relied most to turn the war around were air power, terror, and a stronger ARVN. To manipulate public opinion, which had come to regard bombing as a barometer of American intentions in Vietnam, the air war had to be stepped up by subterfuge. The ploy most commonly used was the "protective reaction strike." American aircraft loaded with bombs and rockets would fly over North Vietnam and Cambodia, escorted by fighters. At the first sign of hostile intent—detecting a radar being switched on, for example—the bombers unloaded their ordnance. The air war over ostensibly neutral Cambodia was considered especially sensitive, so intense pressure was placed on air force personnel to lie about the bombing of that country. They had to deny it was happening.

Much of South Vietnam was being bombed heavily too, mainly by the 650 combat planes based there. Efforts to bomb the Ho Chi Minh Trail more intensively were stepped up. And North Vietnam was regularly attacked for about fifty miles north of the DMZ. The tonnage of bombs dropped on Southeast Asia in 1969–72 far surpassed the American bombing effort in both major theaters in World War Two.

The inevitable result of so much destruction was a flood tide of refugees. Roughly two million South Vietnamese—20 percent of the population—were herded into refugee camps, where it was comparatively easy to control them. To control dissident elements among the remaining 80 percent there was a new instrument of terror, the Phoenix program.

Run mainly by the CIA, with help from the army, this was essentially a murder program, aimed at eliminating VC sympathizers. Phoenix hit squads were composed mainly of nonethnic Vietnamese mercenaries, VC defectors or former NVA soldiers hoping to start a new life in the South. Operating on rumor, suspicion, secret denunciations and names extracted under torture, the program claimed twenty thousand lives a year. It spread terror throughout South Vietnam.

The president's third card was a revamped ARVN. By 1970 it numbered 1.1 million men: roughly half the able-bodied male population aged eighteen to thirty-four. Its fighting power was increased by lavish reequipment with the M-16 assault rifle, with M-79 grenade launchers, with better machine guns, as well as heavier items such as armored personnel carriers, tanks, patrol boats and artillery. Tet had shaken the Thieu-Ky regime and seemed to have transformed the fighting spirit of its soldiers. With the ARVN at last enjoying firepower superiority over the enemy the obvious thing to do was to put it onto the offensive.

The opportunity came in the spring of 1970. While Prince Sihanouk was out of the country there was a coup d'état by Cambodian generals who resented his complaisance in the Communist occupation of the border areas. The new government invited these unwelcome guests to leave. The North Vietnamese Army's response was to attempt to seize a continuous strip of territory about ten miles wide along the Cambodian-South Vietnamese border. General Lon Nol, leader of the coup, asked for American help.

To the president this looked like the perfect chance to attack the sanctuaries. The army and air force advised him strongly that nothing would be achieved by plunging into Cambodia. The virtual destruction of the Viet Cong had robbed the sanctuaries of most of their importance. Swayed by fantasies that he might capture the secret enemy headquarters that directed operations in South Vietnam from the safety of Cambodia, Nixon brushed off their advice. Nearly 60,000 ARVN troops and 15,000 Americans crashed into Cambodia. Large supply caches were found and destroyed, but few enemy units were encountered. The fabled headquarters was never found.

This "incursion," as the president called it, shook the country more violently than Tet. In the frantic atmosphere it unleashed, bombs went off on university campuses. At Kent State University the Ohio National Guard shot dead four students who were peacefully protesting what appeared to them, and to many others, a reescalation of the war.

The White House was besieged, while in the basement were troops armed with machine guns. The ring of antiwar demonstrators around 1600 Pennsylvania Avenue was so dense that key aides such as Kissinger could not get out at night and were forced to sleep in the nuclear bomb shelter deep underground. Congress pressured Nixon into recognizing at last that the only thing the country would accept was rapid, large-scale troop withdrawals from South Vietnam.

He still had hopes for the ARVN. In February 1971 two ARVN divisions crossed the DMZ, heading for Laos and the Ho Chi Minh Trail. The thrust into Cambodia had encouraged the NVA to run down what remained of its base structure there and to concentrate instead on improving the trail, which it turned into an impressive highway system of all-weather roads. The ARVN's objective was to cut the trail, and keep it cut.

That was a threat Hanoi could not treat lightly. Four of the NVA's finest, most battle-hardened divisions swarmed to the attack, backed up with armor and heavy artillery. American aircraft devastated these large NVA formations, but the NVA devastated the ARVN, shattering eight battalions, shooting down 107 American helicopters, and inflicting 10,000 casualties on the South Vietnamese. The survivors pulled back across the DMZ.

It was a defeat that marked the end of Nixon's hopes of winning the war despite the rundown in American maneuver battalions. It was also an ominous harbinger of what would happen when the war became a straight fight between the ARVN and the NVA.

THE TROOPS sent to Vietnam after 1967 were mainly draftees. Of the 27 million men who reached draft age between 1964 and 1973 some 65 percent nevertheless avoided, evaded or were given exemption from selective service. As a result, the average draftee was much less educated, less ambitious, came from a poorer family and was in worse physical condition than the typical young American of the 1960s. Drafting men who were below average was a reversal of conscription policy in the three previous wars.

The draft was further degraded by the man who had presided over the Selective Service System for thirty years, Lieutenant General Lewis B. Hershey. Outraged by the behavior of antiwar protestors—some of them provocative figures who burned draft cards or poured blood on draft board records—he used the system to harry them. Protesters were assigned a high draft priority. This turned service in the armed forces from being a duty and a privilege into a punishment.

In a misguided gesture of support for the antipoverty goals of the Great Society, McNamara made his own contribution to the declining quality of military manpower by forcing the armed services to take 100,000 men each year whom it would rather have rejected: social misfits, people of low intelligence, men with serious personality disorders, those who were defeated by the routine demands of everyday life, men who were undersized or in poor health. He expected the military to save them from poverty, from despair, from themselves. Inevitably, almost all failed as soldiers and marines as spectacularly as they had failed as civilians, but now they possessed bad conduct or dishonorable discharges.

The World War Two U.S. Army had consisted, on average, of twenty-seven-year-old men with wives and jobs to return to. They considered beer a great treat, accepted the necessity of the war and had faith in their country's leaders. It was an army that Pershing, Grant, Scott, even Washington would have recognized. The troops in Vietnam were something else. On average, they were nineteen years old, unmarried, preferred Coke to beer, smoked dope, had faith in nothing much, least of all in men like Johnson and Nixon. Despite all of which they served their country a lot better than it served them, both then and later.

When he arrived "in country" the "fuckin' new guy" or FNG (as he was invariably called) knew exactly when he could expect to leave: he would be out in one year. The twelve-month tour was Westmoreland's idea. He said it would help morale by giving men a goal to aim it. He was right. The comforts of living at well-equipped bases and commuting to the war by helicopter, of periodic trips to Bangkok and other exotic places for "rest and recreation" (usually in the prone position), along with the one-year tour meant that for all the misery and danger in Vietnam morale remained remarkably high until late in the war. The goal that the one-year tour set, however, was survival, not success.

It also short-circuited institutional memory within fighting units. The war was not fought over a ten-year period (1962–72) with a steady growth in wisdom, experience and leadership. Instead, it was broken down into ten miniwars, each lasting a year, with little continuity among them. The moment troops learned to fight effectively and their officers learned how to handle them effectively under fire, they and their company officers were on their way home.

Just as crippling, though, was the absence of the educated, highly motivated people who had provided company-grade officers and NCOs in previous wars. To obtain officers and NCOs the army lowered standards drastically, and paid a high price. The result was epitomized by granting a commission to William Calley, Jr., a diminutive dropout from Palm Beach Junior College, where he had compiled a perfect record—straight Fs. In March 1968 Calley's company was sent on a search-and-destroy mission to a village complex called My Lai. The objective was a VC main force battalion hiding in one of the villages.

Calley misread the map and had the helicopters put his platoon down in the wrong place. Despised by his men, uncertain of what to do, he allowed the wanton shooting of an old man to degenerate into an orgy of killing. Losing his head completely, he decided to exterminate all of the Vietnamese his men rounded up. The result was a massacre that irreparably stained the army's reputation, and left more than 120 women, children and old men dead. The exact number will never be known. There were other atrocities in Vietnam due to weak leadership, poor training, contempt for the Vietnamese, but this was by far the worst.

When Lieutenant General Raymond Peers completed his inquiry into this unspeakable affair he compiled two reports. One was for publication, the other for Westmoreland, on the state of the officer corps. Peers considered the demoralization and declining quality of its officers more of a threat to the army's future than anything that happened at My Lai. Westmoreland agreed, and when he became chief of staff he tried to encourage reforms, but his conservative temperament made him a poor radical.

His successor in Vietnam, General Creighton Abrams, was meanwhile left to fight a ground war that was obviously running out of time, and with an army that saw less and less reason for running risks and taking casualties. Abrams's proclaimed strategy was the "One War" plan, which promised to integrate combat operations more closely with pacification. As a former tank commander under Patton, however, Abrams was a feisty, aggressive character. An endless succession of small patrols to secure villages and hamlets was not his idea of how to fight the enemy. In 1969 he launched large-scale search-and-destroy operations.

The most notorious was an offensive on the Laotian border that turned into a battle for an eminence that became known as Hamburger Hill in mock tribute to what happened to the men ordered to charge up it. This ten-day clash left 500 men of the 101st Airborne Division dead or wounded. After which the hill was abandoned to the enemy and the troops pulled out.

The clamor this operation aroused in Congress and the country could be heard all the way to Saigon. The time had passed when such tactics could be tolerated. They also encouraged fragging. An underground newspaper in the 101st began running advertisements that offered a ten-thousand-dollar reward for the death of any officer who again ordered frontal assaults.

The army in Vietnam settled down to "enclave security" and rotted away, just counting the days to withdrawal. In the early 1970s there were hundreds of instances of men refusing to obey orders they disliked. Few were ever punished. Even the vaunted 1st Cavalry Division was a sad imitation of what it had been only a few years before. There was dangerous slackness even in the combat zone. In the spring of 1971 a force of fewer than 100 North Vietnamese overran an artillery fire base called Mary Ann that was manned by 300 troops of the Americal Division. Thirty Americans were killed, 82 wounded. They were too drunk, too stoned, too lazy and too indisciplined to mount a proper perimeter defense. The enemy simply walked in and took the fire base.

The intention of Taylor and Harkins a decade before had been to turn the ARVN into a semblance of the superb U.S. Army. After ten years in the Nam it was the army that resembled the ARVN.

And what did that prove? Only the obvious, that even the best armies can be ruined by misuse. Napoleon created, then destroyed the *Grande Armée*. The Great General Staff wrecked the magnificent German army of 1914 by giving it too much to win too quickly. Hitler's vacillation over strategy doomed the unbeaten German army of 1941 by spreading it all over the Russian landscape instead of concentrating on the capture of Moscow and Leningrad. Even the strongest army can be broken.

The way in which three presidents pursued the war in Vietnam not only guaranteed failure but made the ruination of the U.S. Army as certain as tomorrow's sunrise. The damage spread, like a pandemic, around the globe. There were riots, breakdowns of discipline, even fragging at bases in the United States and Western Europe. Fighting ability crumbled as combat units worldwide were stripped of vital equipment, weapons, ammunition stocks and trained personnel to feed the war in Southeast Asia. Many of the most promising, most thoughtful officers left in despair, to write hand-wringing books with titles such as *Death of the Army.* By 1973 the once proud, confident Green Machine no longer existed. One day it would have to be created all over again, by a new generation of soldiers.

EARLY IN 1972 the last maneuver battalion was withdrawn. What remained was 90,000 troops who provided support and advice to the ARVN, and protection for American bases. There were 364 USAF combat planes in Thailand and South Vietnam, plus two aircraft carriers in the Gulf of Tonkin. There was enough American help available, it was hoped, to prevent the defeat of the ARVN when— not if—the NVA attacked. With 1972 being a presidential election year it was a safe bet that a fresh offensive would come sooner rather than later.

It began March 30, as 150,000 North Vietnamese troops surged across the DMZ and over the border with Laos, sweeping into the northern provinces and the Central Highlands, led by armor and backed up by self-propelled artillery.

In the early stages the offensive was unstoppable, but the NVA dispersed its strength too widely, frittering away men and momentum on minor objectives. The biggest battle of the war raged for possession of Hue. Thieu and Ky put their three best divisions into this fight—the Airborne Division, the Marine Division and 1st Infantry Division. The NVA kept feeding in troops, until eight of its divisions were tied down around Hue. American air power hammered them mercilessly.

Everything that could drop a bomb was pressed into service to stop this offensive and a new air campaign was begun over North Vietnam, called Linebacker. A furious President Nixon seized the opportunity to hit the enemy hard. Almost everything but the irrigation dams was an acceptable target. Haiphong harbor was shut down in an afternoon by seeding it with air-dropped mines. Even after the Easter offensive ran into the sands the bombing of North Vietnam continued until Hanoi signaled its willingness to resume peace talks.

After nearly two months of fresh haggling in Paris, the talks broke down again. On December 13 the North Vietnamese delegation walked out. To get them back, Nixon ordered yet another bombing campaign, but far bigger than anything attempted before. This time he okayed the kind of massive raids the JCS had urged on Lyndon Johnson back in 1965: he unleashed the B-52 force, in Operation Linebacker II.

For eleven days and nights in December 1972 Hanoi shook and exploded as wave after wave of B-52s dropped one-ton bombs. A remarkable change came over the troops holding American POWs: they stopped beating their prisoners. The guards became solicitous, and worried. They resembled the cowed Germans and Japanese in charge of Allied prisoners in the last days of World War Two. North Vietnam was hurting badly. Its people began thinking the unthinkable— they might still lose the war.

The SAM sites used up their entire stock of Guidelines, nearly 1,300 in all, bringing down a dozen B-52s, damaging a dozen more, but the bombers kept coming; up to 120 in a single attack. Flying high above the AAA, they dropped 15,000 tons of bombs, destroying the SAM sites, huge supplies of military stores, and almost all of North Vietnam's oil and gasoline stocks. Hanoi was more than willing to talk peace to get the bombing stopped.

On January 23, 1973, an agreement was signed in Paris. The United States agreed to remove all its remaining forces from South Vietnam within sixty days. American air and naval units would cease all attacks on North Vietnam and would no longer support South Vietnamese forces. The Saigon regime pledged not to expand its military power. In return Hanoi promised to remove all its forces from South Vietnam.

Only one of these promises was kept—the United States pulled out. In Vietnam, Laos and Cambodia it had suffered 47,000 killed and 10,000 dead from other causes. It was the fourth-costliest war in American history and by far the longest.

The ARVN grew in size and the NVA held on to its territorial gains from the Easter offensive of 1972. The war went on, but in a muted key. For two years the North Vietnamese either dared not or could not mount another offensive. Linebacker II had planted, amid the rubble of Hanoi, seeds that sprouted into caution.

The resignation of Richard Nixon in late 1974 revived enemy hopes spectacularly. The Watergate scandal came close to paralyzing American government. Nixon's successor, Gerald Ford, made clear his complete aversion to the war: in his January 1975 State of the Union address there was not a single mention of Vietnam. The subject was too painful to talk about, even to think about.

When spring came once more to South Vietnam, so did the NVA. It had learned much from its failure in 1972. This time it pushed inexorably down the major highways, concentrated its efforts on key objectives, bypassed much of the ARVN or brushed it aside, until at last armor-infantry teams maneuvered outside the presidential palace in Saigon, then crashed through the wrought-iron gates.

It fell to Ford's secretary of defense, James Schlesinger, to deliver the bad news one April night. "Mr. President, this war is all over," he told him. *"It is all over."*

Ford stared at him in stark disbelief. There must be some mistake.

20

TOMORROW BEGAN YESTERDAY

FOR at least one generation Vietnam cast a shadow over American life. It was as inescapable as the kind of curse laid on powerful families in Greek epic drama. Long after the war ended it gnawed at the national will, confused the traditional sense of mission, left festering wounds among the 2.5 million men who served in Vietnam, and undermined America's self-esteem. If anything good came out of the war, it's hard to see what it was. Although not defeated on the battlefield, the country had failed, and that felt much like defeat measured by previous American wars.

In a desperate bid to appease antiwar sentiment, Nixon decided to abolish the draft and create an all-volunteer army. The entire Cabinet was opposed to the move, Laird above all. The Paris Accords were signed before lunch on January 27, 1973. After lunch the end of conscription was announced.

Congress doubled the pay of enlisted men. Recruiting budgets more than tripled. Bonuses of three thousand dollars were offered to men who signed up for the combat arms. Almost all military jobs were opened up to women. Traditional irritants and disincentives were abolished, such as reveille, short hair, bed checks and Saturday inspections. Beer-vending machines were installed in the barracks. A five-day workweek was established, despite the obvious risks to combat readiness in places such as Germany and Korea. The military justice system was overhauled to make it more open and less arbitrary.

Recruiting picked up. Desertion and AWOL figures dropped. In all the services it became easier to retain people at the end of their first enlistment. Yet standards fell, especially in the army, and kept on falling.

In NATO competitions, involving everything from gunnery to maintenance, American teams invariably came last. The volunteer army was more skewed than it had been even during the war toward the poor, the uneducated and the unambitious. The draft at least had brought in a trickle of men with college degrees. The volunteer army brought in virtually none.

For a decade or so following the withdrawal from Vietnam all the services were troubled by poor morale, drug abuse and deteriorating discipline. At times they seemed almost unable to help themselves, having chosen to shun old-fashioned leadership, with all its demands on emotion and imagination, to surrender instead to the siren song of modern management, with its blandness, its safeness, its anonymity and its usefulness to those officers who decided to change careers. And yet, and yet . . . The dedication of the small band of reform-minded officers who stayed through thick and even thicker, aided by sympathetic figures in Congress and the executive branch, gradually helped to brake the decline. Since the mid-1980s there has been a general improvement in morale and training.

The world at large helped too. Never during the post-Vietnam slough of despond was there a prolonged period of quiescence when the armed forces could gently rot away without anyone noticing or caring. A succession of challenges to American power and interests exposed military inadequacies and strengthened the hand of the reformers and experimentalists.

In May 1975 a group of Khmer Rouge—the Communists who had seized control of Cambodia and who were diligently murdering half of its six million people—captured a U.S.-registered cargo ship, the *Mayaguez*. Determined not to be dragged into a hostage crisis over the fate of its crew, President Ford ordered a naval air strike against Cambodian targets and an assault on the captured ship. The air strike pressured the Khmer Rouge into freeing the ship's crew, although a marine assault on a nearby island led to a firefight in which 38 marines died.

Four and a half years later Ford's successor, Jimmy Carter, saw his presidency come to grief over 52 Americans seized when Iranian revolutionaries stormed the U.S. embassy in Teheran. An attempt to free the hostages in April 1980 failed completely. The raid that Carter and the JCS sanctioned was too complicated, too poorly thought-out and too poorly organized to have a realistic chance of success. The hostages were not released until the day Carter left office in January 1981.

His successor, Ronald Reagan, came to the White House determined to reassert the country's leading position in world affairs; by force, if necessary. His commitment of American combat troops to Lebanon in September 1982 in an attempt to stabilize a dangerously chaotic situation came to grief thirteen months later. An Islamic suicide driver rammed a truck loaded with explosives into the marine headquarters in Beirut, killing 237 marines. Shortly thereafter American troops pulled out, leaving the Lebanese to murder one another in the tradition of that blood-soaked place.

Only days after the destruction of the marine headquarters the president moved to defend American interests in the Caribbean by intervening in Grenada. The island was well on the way to becoming a Cuban fiefdom when the country's Marxist leader was murdered by a staunchly pro-Soviet, pro-Cuban rival. The hundreds of Americans on the island appeared to be in some danger and the head of state, ostensibly only a figurehead, appealed for American help. Five hundred marines and 5,500 paratroopers from the 82nd Airborne Division took control of Grenada after skirmishing with Cuban troops, sent to the island as construction workers for the airfield. For all its success the Grenada operation excited criticism of the poor planning involved and the failure of the services to communicate effectively with each other.

The growth of terrorism in the 1980s led in April 1986 to an air strike against military and government installations in Libya. The Reagan administration considered the Libyan leader, Colonel Muammar el-Khaddafi, a major actor in various terrorist outrages against Americans. The attack by F-111 aircraft based in Great Britain and by aircraft from the Sixth Fleet appeared in retrospect to have had the desired effect on Khaddafi and his sole ally in the Arab world, President Hafez al-Assad of Syria.

American intervention in the Persian Gulf in 1987–88 was undertaken to bolster the pro-Western states in the area but mainly to ensure that the Strait of Hormuz remained open to international shipping. The move was widely deplored as a risky and hopeless venture. The United States could hardly shrink from those risks. While it might dispense with the small amount of oil it took from the Gulf, its European allies and Japan were heavily dependent on the region. A shutdown of the Gulf would throw their societies into turmoil, wreck their economies and paralyze their governments. Acting as it did, the United States was protecting the alliances on which Western security depends. It was surely wiser to have a foot in the door to keep it from being shut than having to break down the door once it was closed.

LIKE John Kennedy, Ronald Reagan reached the White House on the theme of a militarily vulnerable America. "We are second to one," he intoned, "—to the Soviet Union." It was as untrue as Kennedy's vaunted missile gap. Carter, and Nixon before him, had added massively to the heritage of nuclear abundance. The 3,500 strategic nuclear weapons in the Triad when Johnson stepped down in 1969 had become 9,000 when Carter left office in January 1981.

The sharp fall in military manpower levels after the Vietnam War ended in 1975 had allowed lavish reequipping of the army and air force. It was badly needed. The war had seen the consumption of everything from spare parts to fighter-bombers without any attempt to replace them. That was part of the conflict's hidden costs. The navy missed out on the reequipment effort of the Carter years, mainly because ships take up to a decade to design and get into the water.

The Reagan administration was happy to step up the level of defense spending. For one thing, it had pledged during the campaign to do so. For another, it hoped to push the Soviet Union into trying to match those rising expenditures and thereby wreck its faltering economy. The Defense Department's share of the budget jumped from 23 percent to 28 percent.

The navy benefited from this largesse. Undermanned and short of ships, it had fallen in the late 1970s to pre–World War Two force levels. The Sixth Fleet was reduced to cruising slowly from port to port around the Mediterranean doing little more than showing the flag; it had too little fuel for exercises or full combat readiness. Under Reagan and his tough-minded, highly educated defense secretary, Caspar Weinberger, the navy was transformed. The number of carrier battle groups rose to fifteen, from twelve. Nearly one hundred new warships (many of them originating with Navy Academy graduate Jimmy Carter) were brought to completion by 1989.

So much money was poured into procurement that billions went unspent in some years, and billions more were wasted in every year. Procurement foolishness is a continuing thread through two centuries, from the first American frigates through buying the wrong machine guns on the eve of World War One, down to the failure of the Sheridan tank and the M-16 rifle in Vietnam.

The free-spending ways of Reagan and Weinberger nonetheless coincided with and helped advance one of the most important developments in the history of warfare, the "precision revolution." Since the Chinese invention of gunpowder in the twelfth century more than 90 percent of all the artillery rounds fired, bombs dropped and missiles launched have missed whatever they were aimed at. The rise of information technology in the 1980s has merged with the development of sensors, lasers and microwaves to reverse that figure in what amounts to a mere instant in the long sweep of history: in future wars waged by modern powers 90 percent of shells, bombs and missiles—unless jammed or decoyed—will strike their targets.

During the Vietnam War, Robert McNamara had asked defense scientists for ideas on how technology might win the war. They proposed to create "an electronic battlefield"—a high-tech no-man's-land between North and South Vietnam.* Thus began "the McNamara line" and so long as it was maintained it made a successful conventional attack by the North Vietnamese Army across the DMZ virtually impossible. Abandoned after the marines pulled out of Khe Sanh in July 1968, the line had a profound influence on the Pentagon's thinking about warfare in the year 2000.

Ten years after the war ended a true electronic battlefield was almost within reach; a battlefield, that is, where nothing could be hidden without being found, where nothing could move without being detected. And the precision revolution meant that whatever was located could almost certainly be destroyed.

---

*The original idea goes back at least as far as Mark Twain. In *A Connecticut Yankee at King Arthur's Court* the Yankee inventor Hank Morgan invents "an electric battlefield." Those who command it fight entirely with machines. Their less advanced enemies, attacking with flesh and blood soldiers, suffer appalling losses and are defeated.

Nor would it require nuclear weapons to attain that assurance of destruction. The power of modern explosives has more than doubled in the 1980s. A range of conventional weapons exists that are as devastating as tactical nuclear warheads, but without the radiation effects. Fuel air explosives, for example, create a cloud of vapor that ignites, making a huge fireball. The resulting explosion is five times more powerful than anything possible with a comparable weight of high explosive. The vapor covers an area that makes traditional artillery fire look modest. A conventional war fought in Europe in the 1990s could be as ruinous within weeks as World War Two was over six years.

Defense technologies in the 1990s will be shaped largely in response to the precision revolution, to make it possible to move and survive on the electronic battlefield. Jamming devices, decoys (such as the ten thousand dummy main battle tanks the army has bought) and robots will be lavishly employed. Radio frequency weapons are being developed to home in on enemy radars, computers and radios and blow out their microchip circuits. Microwave radiation is being researched in tunnels under the Nevada desert to explore its potential for scrambling enemy communications and wiping out electronic sensors.

The ancient struggle between offense and defense continues, although studies have shown that few general officers and admirals truly understand the effects of high-tech warfare on tactics. It may take until 2010 for enough teen-aged computer addicts of the 1980s to have joined the military and risen to high command before leadership meets microchip.

THE PRECISION revolution and the advent of conventional firepower that rivals the havoc of nuclear arms give obvious advantages to the defense. Paradoxically, they have been turned to revitalizing the spirit of the offensive.

On NATO's central front in West Germany, where Western armies have stood toe to toe with Communist forces since 1945, defense is never as simple as it seems. On the open, rolling tank country of the North German Plain are excellent British and West German units, plus some of the weakest divisions in the alliance, contributed by some of the less-enthusiastic members. "Penetrations waiting to happen," as some senior commanders refer to them.

Farther south are a West German corps and the U.S. Seventh Army, holding terrain that is heavily wooded, rugged, and where the main approaches from the east pass through narrow gaps. The United States is the mainstay of the alliance, yet its troops are in the wrong place: any major attack will almost surely come much farther north.

To this illogical disposition of forces (which reflects where the Allied armies concluded World War Two) the West Germans make a contribution of their own: they will not allow a defense in depth. That might imply a willingness to sacrifice territory. Just as adamantly, they refuse to allow defense based on a strong line of fixed positions (or electronic battlefields) along the border with East Germany: that might imply an acceptance of the permanent division of Germany.

The emergence of new weapons systems based on the microchip and the helicopter, plus the complexities of German defense, plus the fresh thinking of the radical reformers in the military after Vietnam, led in the 1980s to the remaking of conventional war-fighting doctrine. The result was AirLand Battle, a concept that restored the American tradition of mobile, aggressive warfare.

AirLand Battle relies heavily on the airmobility of Seventh Army in Germany and its reserve, III Corps, based in the United States. It calls on American forces to respond to a Warsaw Pact attack by launching powerful strikes against the flanks and rear of advancing tank armies, while other NATO forces try to hold the line.

For a long time the French complicated planning for the central front. They left the military command structure of NATO in 1962. French chauvinism made it intolerable that an American supreme commander should give orders to French officers. Yet there were three French armored divisions based in West Germany. What would they do if war broke out—go home?

The eagerness of French governments in the 1980s to reassure West Germany that their troops would join the battle led in 1987 to a simple, elegant solution. The French could, for reasons of domestic politics, continue to pretend they were in NATO but not of it. For military planning purposes, the French armored divisions, tactical air force and airborne were simply penciled in as NATO's frontline reserve if war broke out.

This freed Seventh Army to commit both its frontline corps plus III Corps to AirLand Battle counterattacks. In all, up to 350,000 men, 8,000 tanks and armored personnel carriers, plus 2,500 helicopters would carry the battle into East Germany and try to assure that the war was fought mainly on enemy territory. Meanwhile even deeper strikes would be launched by missiles and aircraft against bridges, tunnels and marshaling yards, to bottle up Soviet follow-on forces.

As the very name AirLand Battle suggests, the concept is one that sees the struggle for control of the air as integral to operations on the ground. It aims at a degree of interservice cooperation that was secured in World War Two only toward the end of the conflict.

The new spirit of the offensive, of blitzkrieg, animates the army field manual on tactics, *FM 100-5,* adopted in 1982. To augment the rapid striking power of airmobility, the army has created two light divisions, the 7th and 25th. With the other services it has helped form a rapid deployment force of 125,000 men for action outside the NATO area in an emergency. The emphasis is on speed, mobility and cooperation. It is to be hoped that the lessons learned from the botched Iranian rescue effort and the messy operation on Grenada have been absorbed.

The navy too has rejected the fundamentally defensive posture of the thirty years following World War Two. In the 1980s it shifted over to "forward deployment." No longer does the navy intend to fight the battle for command of the sea out in deep water. In time of crisis it advances toward Soviet ports, to mine them if the Soviet fleet appears about to come out with hostile intent. Its submarines and surface units stick close to Soviet ships, to beat them to the punch, if the word comes down. It is prepared, should the need arise, to sink the Soviet navy, and to do it quickly.

Forward deployment has obvious risks. The navy has been involved in more "incidents," more shows of force, more confrontations with hostile forces in peacetime than the other services combined. Even among navy officers there is a belief that if war with the Soviet Union ever starts by accident, it will probably begin at sea.

There is no denying that forward deployment is risky and expensive, as is AirLand Battle. Yet this change in military posture may be the only way of keeping the NATO allies from drifting into neutralism and defeatism, for it underlines America's commitment to paying the price, running the risks, of defending Western civilization.

Strictly defensive deployments carry other, less obvious dangers— low morale, poor discipline, a decline in fighting ability. Morale, discipline and fighting ability have instead revived in the nation's armed forces as the spirit of the offensive has been reborn. They should grow still more in the 1990s. As the long shadow of Vietnam lifts, its baleful influence dies.

F O R twenty-five years the attempt to control nuclear weapons by international agreement was a story of failure. In 1963 the Soviets finally agreed to a ban on nuclear testing in the atmosphere, but this was more an act of environmental protection than an arms control pact. Besides, two nuclear aspirants, China and France, refused to sign it. The Non-Proliferation Treaty of 1970 was similarly spurned by a half-dozen states with ambitions to acquire the Bomb, such as Israel, Pakistan and South Africa.

In the early 1970s Nixon reached two arms control agreements with the U.S.S.R.: a treaty that limited the deployment of antiballistic missiles to the protection of national capitals; and the Strategic Arms Limitation Treaty, or SALT. If nothing else, this marked an intellectual turning point. Nixon had campaigned in 1968 pledging to restore American nuclear superiority. He was kidding himself and the SALT agreement was an acknowledgment that parity or sufficiency was the most that was possible. SALT I put a limit on the number of ICBMs and SLBMs, but cut nothing from the strategic weapons arsenals.

Jimmy Carter, on the other hand, believed in truly radical arms reduction, leading eventually to the end of nuclear weapons. He proposed cuts of more than 95 percent, wanting each superpower to have no more than two hundred missiles, all of them based on submarines. Such modest forces would rule out preemptive strikes and impose strategies of minimal deterrence. Who was more scornful of this idea, the Soviets or his own armed forces, is not easy to say, but the Russians firmly rejected it. Even so, in the fall of 1979 a new arms control treaty, SALT II, was signed in Moscow. It called for substantial cuts in strategic systems. The promise of SALT II was never realized. The Soviets invaded Afghanistan in December 1979, making ratification of the treaty unthinkable.

The first nuclear arms control measure that might cut the number of nuclear weapons is the Intermediate Nuclear Force (or INF) Treaty of 1988. It represents the payoff on the decision made a decade earlier to match Soviet SS-20 missiles deployed in Europe with the air force's ground-launched cruise missiles (GLCMs) and the army's fast, highly accurate Pershing II, capable of reaching Moscow from West Germany in seven minutes.

While attempts to control strategic systems by mutual agreement failed, there was another possibility: control through doctrine and force structures.

McNamara was a pioneer in this effort. His first major success was in getting NATO to agree to the strategy of flexible response. Although this loudly trumpeted idea was not really very different from strategic thinking under Eisenhower, the West Europeans screamed blue murder. They preferred massive retaliation, with its comforting illusion that it threatened the Warsaw Pact with the Apocalypse if the Soviets made the wrong move. Flexible response seemed less reassuring, *too* rational, if anything.

The 1960s brought nuclear abundance to the Soviets. McNamara made the best of it, seeing in parity a chance to enhance stability. The aim for both superpowers, he argued, should be to ensure the survivability of enough strategic nuclear weapons that they could absorb a first strike and still launch a crushing retaliatory blow. He called this doctrine mutual assured destruction, or MAD, and in it thought he saw a glimmer of sanity.

Attempts at control through doctrine and force structures, like the effort to secure control by mutual agreement, also failed. For a year or so Carter thought he had achieved the breakthrough, but then the Soviets invaded Afghanistan. He ordered his national security adviser, Zbigniew Brzezinski, to undertake a wide-ranging security review in the wake of that shock. The result was Presidential Directive-59.

This document represented the final flowering of the hope—or illusion—that flexible response contained of controlling a nuclear war. McNamara had pushed it to a point at which he thought it possible to fine-tune the SIOP so that the Soviet and Chinese leadership might be spared and the damage to their communications minimized, in order for them to negotiate a cease-fire in the midst of a nuclear holocaust.

American military policy, spelled out by every president since (and including) Eisenhower, was that no one could win a nuclear war. This stood in stark contrast to Soviet doctrine, which claimed that those who prepared for it could fight and win one. PD-59, adopted as policy in 1980, accepted the Soviet view. It committed the United States to fighting and ultimately winning a protracted, controlled nuclear war.

A year later, when Reagan succeeded Carter, he issued National

Security Directive D-13, reaffirming the strategy of PD-59. Reagan explicitly declared his personal belief that victory in a nuclear war was possible. Toward the end of his second term he repudiated that view. Like Eisenhower, he spent eight years traveling from faith to doubt.

Public support for nuclear weapons fell sharply in the 1980s. Democratic governments throughout NATO were attempting to respond to that. The INF treaty was one such attempt. The adoption of AirLand Battle was another, for it held out the possibility of stopping a Warsaw Pact offensive without resorting to nuclear arms.

Denuclearization was encouraged by the president's Commission on Long-term Integrated Strategy, a body that included leading civilian strategists, military figures and former national security advisers. The thrust of their report, issued in 1988, was that ways must be found to avoid any use of nuclear weapons, because these could all too easily lead to the nation's own destruction.

There was a catch, though, to arms control. The story had a sting in its tail. The main result was to promote the technological imperative—the blind urge that technology seems to possess to inspire newer, smarter weapons. Scientists and engineers cannot stop thinking. Laboratories cannot stop exploring new ideas. The complexities of trying to control the Triad, whether by treaty or doctrine, lead to fresh efforts to protect it, to refine it, to make it more effective. Arms control produces better weapons.

During the SALT I negotiations the Soviets urged a ban on multiple, independently targeted reentry vehicles, or MIRVs. This mouthful of a name meant that the nuclear warheads fitted to ICBMs and SLBMs could be miniaturized, fitted with small rocket motors and made capable of flying to targets hundreds of miles apart as the missile reentered the earth's atmosphere. Up to five MIRVed warheads and decoys could be crammed into the nose cone of a Minuteman ICBM.

This was a technology that the United States possessed, but had not yet deployed, in 1970. The Soviets were still trying to steal or copy it. Nixon flatly rejected a ban on MIRVs. As they poured from the production line the number of targets in the SIOP shot up to 25,000. There was hardly a shabby little town hall or police barracks in the remotest part of the Soviet Union that was not assigned to a warhead as the SIOP planners began running out of targets.

The Soviets meanwhile developed the SS-18, a very big, very accurate ICBM, and MIRVed it. As the number of SS-18s grew, so did the threat it posed to the 1,000-missile force of Minuteman. When Reagan took office he spoke often and loudly of the "window of vulnerability" he inherited. He used it to justify the large increase in military spending.

Even before Reagan's election, SALT I had led to the decision to build a billion-dollar submarine, the Trident. It would ultimately be equipped with a new generation of missiles possessing a range of seven thousand miles and sufficient accuracy to destroy Soviet ICBMs in their silos. By tripling the range of SLBMs by a factor of two and a half the Trident fleet would be able to operate over so vast a space that there was little to fear from a Soviet breakthrough in antisubmarine warfare.

While the navy was acquiring Trident, the air force was trying to develop a new bomber, the B-1, to keep SAC flying after the B-52s wore out. The B-1 proved to be a grade-A dud; but a dud with a $28 billion price tag.

The air force wanted a new missile, the MX, to replace Minuteman. Powerful, accurate and fast, the MX was the ideal weapon for a preemptive strike against SS-18 silos. The air force. however, was not about to start talking publicly about wanting a first-strike capability. The debate over MX therefore degenerated into an irrelevant and turgid wrangle over where to put it, whether to make it mobile, and its vulnerability to a Soviet first strike. Forced to make a case for the MX that it did not believe—that it would make a good second-strike weapon—the air force lost the argument and Congress funded only fifty MX missiles, to explore the technologies involved.

The debate then moved on to Midgetman, a small one-warhead ICBM that could be placed on trucks. Its first-strike potential was low, its chances of surviving a Soviet first strike high, and its political prospects fairly promising.

The two great achievements of the technological imperative of the 1970s, spurred on in the 1980s by anxieties over arms control, were the cruise missile and the Stealth aircraft.

Cruise came about more or less by accident, as a by-product of several disparate technologies being brought together so that a computer flying through the air could read a map and make corrections to its course where necessary. By the late 1980s a range of cruise missiles was deployed, aboard ships and planes, submarines and trucks. Armed with nuclear or conventional warheads, they could fly up to two thousand miles, at heights as low as fifty feet, and land within one hundred feet of a target. They were comparatively slow, but flew under the coverage of ground radar.

The second major breakthrough was Stealth, which also promised to elude radar. Stealth aircraft were based on wing and fuselage shapes that were known to give a poor radar return. The aircraft was made out of a sandwich of plastics, ferrites and insulating materials that produced not one but two radar returns. These overlapped in such a way that they virtually canceled each other out.

Stealth fighters and reconnaissance aircraft were so successful that a four-engine Stealth bomber, the B-2, was designed to go into service in the early 1990s, along with "stealthy" cruise missiles of intercontinental range. Cruise, Trident and Stealth represented the future of the Triad, while older missiles, bombers and submarines became promising candidates for arms control treaties and the appeasement of public opinion.

Since the days of Robert McNamara, civilian strategists and politicians believed it was possible to fight a controlled, carefully escalated nuclear war. Military planners emphatically disagreed. To strike the Soviet Union with a few nuclear missiles, they insisted, would most likely provoke a full Soviet counterattack. If a nuclear strike had to be made, nothing but an attempt at a knockout blow was worth risking.

The way American command and control systems evolved, the hardware of American strategic forces and the design of the single integrated operations plan are all geared to the preemptive strike. Whatever scenarios of controlled nuclear war defense intellectuals elaborate, there is no intention among high-ranking officers to fight one. Nor do they intend their country to absorb a first strike.

Public incomprehension and anxiety over nuclear weapons make it almost impossible for the subject to be discussed openly and calmly. Common sense too makes it unwise for the military to spell out their true intentions for the benefit of potential foes. The result has been three decades of unrealistic public discussion, unwarranted fears and unfair criticism.

The system that has developed for the control and possible use of strategic nuclear weapons has worked, is working and will continue to work far into the future. It is stable, robust and sophisticated. Over the years it has accumulated institutional strength, so that the technological imperative regularly enhances it.

The preemption force consists of SAC's bombers and missiles, designed to have sufficient accuracy and striking power to take out military targets quickly. This force relies as heavily as ever on satellite reconnaissance, which improved spectacularly in the late 1970s. A rapid flow of high-resolution photographs only one hour old and showing Soviet missile activities could reach the president's desk. The conversations of Red Army platoon leaders over their walkie-talkies are bugged from space. The monitoring of Soviet military radio traffic is comprehensive. Even in the 1970s eavesdropping techniques were so sophisticated that the car phones of top Soviet leaders, including Leonid Brezhnev, were bugged by U.S. Army cryptographers from inside Moscow, and revealed Soviet cheating on the SALT I agreement.

Technical feats such as this when combined with code breaking and old-fashioned spying make a surprise attack on the United States practically impossible. They give the president sufficient time to order a preemptive strike. More than that, they give him the chance to get on the hotline to inform the Soviet leadership that he knows what they are doing, and advise them strongly to stop their preparations for a nuclear strike.

The 1990s will see the orbiting of satellites that will put what amounts to a television film of Soviet missile fields on the president's desk in thirty minutes or less. Satellite "antenna farms" of phased array radars will be developed.* These will ring the United States with what amounts to a radar fence, capable of picking up Soviet cruise missiles, stealth aircraft and anything else more than seven feet long. Like all of the early-warning hardware that preceded it for half a century, the new technologies will be essential elements in the command and control of strategic forces.

If by some unforeseeable chance Soviet military leaders were able to launch a first strike that destroyed SAC's bombers and missiles,

---

*Phased array radars do not revolve but are fixed to search one portion of the sky continuously. Hundreds of such radars linked by computer can provide effective coverage from ground level up to the fringe of space, and vice versa.

killed the president and the JCS and knocked out American military command and control facilities, they would be releasing the safety catch on the nuclear forces that survived. Half a dozen generals and admirals hold predelegated authority to use nuclear weapons in circumstances such as this. Nor would killing them achieve anything, for in that case the authority cascades downward, to dozens of colonels and navy captains. The navy above all provides the revenge force. Just two Trident submarines, hidden under the North Pole, could kill thirty million Russians. With up to fourteen Tridents continuously at sea half the entire Soviet population is within reach.

Under these circumstances it is hardly conceivable that the Soviet Politburo would ever sanction even a limited nuclear attack on American forces anywhere. Battlefield nuclear weapons are probably unusable, because any decision to use them would dictate bringing Soviet strategic forces to a high state of readiness, in case the United States responded by upping the ante and striking the Soviet Union. In bringing its strategic forces to such a state of readiness, however, its moves might easily be read in Washington as preparation to launch a first strike against the United States, thus triggering an American preemptive strike. No limited, short-term advantage that a tactical nuclear explosion might secure on the central front could remotely justify such a risk.

Finally, where does the Strategic Defense Initiative, the cause of so much sound and fury, fit into this scheme of things? To begin with, the hope that Ronald Reagan held out of a shield that would protect the United States from a first strike was misleading. All those who claimed that such a shield could be penetrated by swamping it with extra warheads and decoys were correct. The real value of the project was and is to offer defense against the comparative handful of Soviet missiles that might survive a preemptive strike. The SDI will help round out the SIOP nicely.

"Star Wars" is not going to go away. The technological imperative will keep it alive, perhaps under a different name, possibly at a slower pace than its enthusiasts hoped. By the end of the Reagan presidency some of the glitter had rubbed off the SDI, but a sizable industrial base had been created and a political constituency developed to ensure the research continued into the next century.

.   .   .

THE 1980s have seen no diminution in the fierce and probing criticism of the military. The dramatic rise in defense spending only added to it, but then, one expects more from a Cadillac than from a Chevrolet.

Far from seeming models of sacrifice, of idealism, of Spartan living, military men came to stand for self-indulgence. There were far more generals and admirals for every one thousand enlisted men in 1985 than there had been in 1945—at the height of World War Two. In the meantime the proportion of low-ranking officers had changed hardly at all.

Hand in hand with rank inflation went decoration inflation. In Vietnam there were 1.3 million army decorations for bravery, almost equal to the number of soldiers who served there. As the American role in the war dwindled, more and more medals were awarded. Colonels and generals did especially well, garnering so many decorations for valor one might have imagined they were leading platoons into fire-fights.

For Grenada, the army handed out 8,612 decorations, including 170 for valor. There were more medals awarded than troops on the island.

The lust for rank and decorations has been accompanied by a taste for comfort verging on luxury; no doubt encouraged by the growing trend toward management and identification not with the great soldiers, sailors and airmen of the past, who spent most of their lives in genteel poverty, but with the executives of modern business and their upwardly mobile lifestyles.

Nor has the shift from leadership to management proven itself in war. In Vietnam each service fought the war in its own way, whether the others liked it or not. Even within the services there was stiff competition for resources, missions, attention. All of which fragmented the impact of American military power, instead of concentrating it on the achievement of clear objectives. The management structure of the war was absurd. Its very absurdity seemed to Westmoreland to absolve him of any blame for the outcome and prevented him from resigning. Why should he? He had not created this mess; he was trying to fight despite it.

The management of operations such as the Iranian rescue mission and the landing on Grenada gave proof that matters had not improved much since Vietnam. The rundown in the combat arms will continue to deprive the military of the world's best school of leadership—the daily challenge of inspiring other people to do dirty and dangerous work. In World War Two nearly 40 percent of servicemen were in the combat arms. Forty years later the figure was down to 10 percent. The remaining 90 percent were clerks and technicians. The automated battlefield seeks to reduce the number of soldiers who actually handle weapons to less than 10 percent. The only infantry forces around the year 2000 will be elite formations—sky cavalry, airborne, marines, Special Forces, commandos and raiders. Line infantry will probably cease to exist in advanced twenty-first-century armies. Armored units may well go the same way, although armor officers are no more willing to believe in their demise than cavalry officers were in theirs.

Nothing will halt the trend from leadership to management. Truly enlightened management would assure that leadership was nonetheless preserved; not as a museum piece but because at the very top of the military and out in the field there is no substitute for the courage, moral and physical, of the handful of people who can inspire others to trust them with their very lives.

The rise and rise of the military manager has not spared the taxpayer the exasperating experience of seeing his money thrown away on designer gewgaws for the military yuppie, such as the air force's $7,600 coffee pot. Weapons procurement is, as it always has been, heavily politicized. To blame fiascoes such as the B-1 bomber program on that is to overlook or be unaware of the past. The problem is not going to be solved nor is it going to go away. It has to be contained.

It is also fair to say that while there is never a shortage of examples of procurement idiocy and profligacy, some weapons work very well. It is almost unheard-of for the military to be congratulated for getting things right, but in 1988 Congress spoke glowingly of the navy's management of the Trident program. No one doubts that Trident will work, and when it comes to national security the nuclear-powered ballistic missiles submarines are the nation's bottom line.

A Defense Department stuffed with managers in uniform has not brought a wholly rational force structure. This too is an insoluble problem. American armed forces have to be prepared to fight everywhere on the planet, and possibly in space by the year 2000. There is not a region of the globe, not a microclimate, that they can ignore. Yet more resources does not mean infinite resources, so choices have to be made and some of them are going to be wrong.

There is a tendency almost as old as the Republic to put the money into big-ticket items, such as major warships, and try saving on less imposing war materiel such as small arms. When the navy projected an impressive naval presence into the Persian Gulf in 1987 it was promptly embarrassed by its acute shortage of humble minesweepers. It will take a genius greater than Einstein to get the force structure right for all the contingencies American forces have to deal with in the 1990s.

A spate of books has poured something close to vitriol on the military in recent years. *Defeated, Death of the Army, The Pentagon and the Art of War, National Defense, The Straw Giant* and *Wild Blue Yonder* are only a small part of this output, yet together they provide some of the most dismal reading a paranoid, pacifist anarchist could hope to find. They provide irrefutable examples of military waste, stupidity, corruption and manipulation. The criticisms they make of the modern military are telling and for the most part undeniable.

The larger context in which the armed forces exist, however, is ignored. Without reference to that, the shortcomings of the military are themselves seriously flawed.

The crisis of the American armed forces was not simply a by-product of Vietnam. From 1961 to the late 1980s all the major American institutions were in serious trouble. From Eisenhower to Reagan there were four broken, failed or caretaker presidencies. Reagan's own last years in office were clouded with scandal. While the presidency declined, so did Congress. Its performance was less than inspiring. Nor was it free of the taint of dishonesty or greedy self-interest. Congress became a place to get rich.

The country's leading economic institutions meanwhile faltered as they tried to cope with the inflation unleashed by Vietnam, the 1973 oil shock, the 1979 oil shock, and soaring budget and trade deficits. American living standards in real terms hardly rose between 1968 and 1988. Big business failed to match the productivity and quality control of its foreign competitors. The volatility of finance led to a stock market crash even greater than the 1929 bust.

The forces of law and order continued to fail in stemming the tide of rising crime. By the late 1980s they had lost the drugs war. The streets were more dangerous than they had been thirty years before. Confidence in the courts was low.

The media on which people relied for news and information were looked on with suspicion. Belief in their honesty and fairness was unusual, not to say eccentric.

The nation's schools, colleges and universities had become places overwhelmingly associated with falling standards of performance. This was the most tragic of institutional failures, for none blighted brighter hopes.

It is too much to expect that the armed forces will hold out as models of excellence while the other pillars of society crumble around them. If that were somehow to happen, then democracy itself might be under threat, because that is the political milieu of most Third World countries, where the military alone come to stand for competence, honesty and patriotism.

What has happened is what any free people would prefer: as the major institutions have faltered, so have the armed forces. A democratic society and its military rise and fall together, like galley slaves chained to the same oar. In a free country the military cannot perform well, no matter how much is spent on it, when government, the banks, the big corporations, the schools, the colleges, the courts, the police and the media perform badly.

The declining effectiveness of the American military since the Korean War is no aberration. It is the inescapable result of institutional growth in an era of declining self-confidence and moral purpose. Growth that is not tamed and shaped by commitment to excellence and goodness dilutes the very qualities on which the best military forces have always depended. Being a soldier, a sailor, an airman or a marine is not just another job. At its best, it is a calling, a vocation. And much as the churches and monasteries found themselves in decline as the world around them became secularized, so the military went into decline when the world around them seemed to lose interest in anything but money and material possessions. One thing is certain: if American institutions fail to improve, so will the armed forces' ability to protect America's interests and preserve its security.

The strongest hope for the future is that there is still a clear thread with the past. The success of American arms was based, as this book has shown, on a trinity that is unique in the history of military forces.

There is, first of all, the remarkable faith in education as a factor in military affairs. The result was epitomized by the creation first of West Point, later of Annapolis, and still later of the Air Force Academy. These are not simply military institutions but degree-granting colleges; more so than ever with the introduction of women cadets. In European military academies matters were handled differently:

what they provided was simply instruction in the art of war and enough of the social graces for officers and their wives to ape the manners of the aristocracy. Intellectual development was not considered useful. Lord Wolseley, the commander of the British army in the late nineteenth century, turned down a proposal for tests of literacy among officers on the grounds that "It might soften their brains."

Even now, the American military is unique in the large number of officers with PhDs and MAs, and the fact that a large majority have at least a bachelor's degree. The United States has the most highly educated military in the world. And if education does not mean the ability to go on learning, it means nothing. A change in direction in American society would be felt more quickly and probably lead to reform more quickly in the military than in any other important institution.

The second leg of the trinity is the faith in firepower; something that at times seems to threaten the extinction of us all. It is not an easy development to live with, yet the American faith in firepower has saved this nation from defeat, succored its allies and helped secure it from attack in the course of two centuries.

The faith in firepower has spread out, become democratized. Half the population now owns at least one firearm. When tension rises Americans have learned to follow the military example—they arm themselves.

The faith in education combined with the faith in firepower has fashioned the third leg of the trinity, the dual technology. An educated, adaptable military has sought out weapons of increasing sophistication and power. The complexity and abundance of the machinery operated by American forces have never failed to impress foreign observers.

In many instances this machinery has been the product of new industries created to meet military needs. This was true of the machine tool industry of the nineteenth century. The "American System" of mass production and interchangeable parts was founded on arms contracts and the work of arms inventors such as Whitney, Hall and Colt. The benefits of these new industries were not reaped, however, simply by the military. They enriched and enlarged the entire economy, thereby creating more wealth than the armed forces consumed. In a growing country with little cash to spare, there could be no other way. Congress was traditionally parsimonious with the military and strongly influenced by the militia.

The tradition of dual technologies, serving both the needs of the military and the development of the economy, continues to flourish. There is not one civil jet airliner that does not trace its roots to military research and development. The modern electronics industry is based on military spending in World War Two and after. Digital sound is only one example of the result. Originally developed in the 1960s to help track Soviet submarines, by sorting the boat's noise from all the other sounds of the sea, it has led to a multibillion-dollar extension of the record industry. The idea that military spending is money poured down a hole is seductive, simplistic and false. Some of it's wasted, but a lot of it isn't.

The tripartite foundation of American defense is enduring. It is not infallible or invulnerable, but it is strong and adaptable. Because it represents the continuation of more than two hundred years of American military history it could survive even something as tragic and farcical as Johnson and McNamara's mismanagement of the Vietnam War.

The faith in education, firepower and dual technologies has provided an internal cohesion to the struggle for national defense, but military historians do not go in much for theories or abstractions. Like military men themselves they stick to numbers, topography, the clash of arms, the whiff of cordite, the sound of armies on the march, to battles lost and won. The only unifying, synoptic interpretation of American military history is the one developed by Emory Upton, more than a century ago.

After traveling around the world in the 1870s to study foreign armies this handsome and gifted soldier was deeply impressed by what he had seen. The small post–Civil War Army, occupied with chasing savages around the Plains, seemed a poor thing compared with the army of the new German empire, victorious in three lightning wars.

Peace itself seemed to play on Upton's nerves. For him, as for other men who had risen rapidly to high command in the Civil War, life itself appeared diminished when combat ceased. Upton wrote his masterwork, *The Military Policy of the United States,* while tormented by agonizing headaches and profound depression. It is not really a finished piece—he ends his narrative halfway through the Civil War. Upton had had enough and shortly afterward killed himself.

The thesis of his book was that the United States had been woefully unprepared for every war it had fought. The country had "no military policy worthy of the name." As a result, when conflict came victory was possible only at an exorbitant price in blood and treasure.

Emory Upton has held American military history in a viselike grip for more than one hundred years. What he offered was an analysis— and a solution: a large military staff and a strong standing army. His solution was rejected, but his analysis was accepted by military thinkers in his time and by military historians ever after. The unpreparedness thesis has become an article of faith, criticized in detail but accepted in its fundament.

The idea of perennial unreadiness is certainly seductive. For one thing, it fits the American self-image of a peace-loving people dragged reluctantly into war. Civilians and military men alike find that idea appealing. For another thing, it is the stuff of epic drama—the ultimate triumph, after near defeat, of good over evil, us over them.

No one can reasonably be expected to be wholly immune to something as appealing on emotional and dramatic grounds as the unpreparedness thesis. And war, with its inevitable risks, surprises and secrets, will always provide some comfort to those who share Upton's views.

The unpreparedness thesis nonetheless fails the first test of a general theory—how does it account for change, as well as continuity? There is no history without change, development, accommodation to new influences. The Uptonian approach is simply to ignore all that.

As a result it does not and cannot account for this country's unparalleled success in war over more than two centuries. Since 1775 no nation on Earth has had as much experience of war as the United States: nine major wars in nine generations. And in between the wars have come other armed conflicts such as the Philippine Insurgency and clashes in the Persian Gulf.

America's wars have been like the rungs on a ladder by which it rose to greatness. No other nation has triumphed so long, so consistently or on such a vast scale, through force of arms.

To describe any great power as being in some way "made" by war risks being dismissed as offering no more than a glimpse of the obvious. Yet is it not evident that the other five leading military powers of the past two hundred years—France, Germany, Britain, Japan and Russia—were *un*made by war?

The failure of French arms at Waterloo marked the end of Napoleon. Subsequent military disasters were to wreck French constitutions, excite contempt abroad and culminate in Nazi occupation. France represents comparative military decline over two hundred years, or near enough.

Germany represents the conscious attempt to create a great power by warfare, with the result that the country is divided, virtually occupied. Conquered twice in less than thirty years, Germany stands as powerful proof that armed might is not enough. The nation that yields to militarism builds its funeral pyre.

Britain, the country closest in political and military ethos to the United States, has also failed to grow stronger and richer through war. Every major conflict since Waterloo has seen it fall behind the other great powers of each era. Its military history has been largely one of pursuing military policies beyond its means. It has been militarily dependent on the United States since 1939, even to defeat a puny power such as Argentina.

Japan's intoxication with modern weaponry brought some early military successes over China and Russia. The rampant militarism this encouraged led in time to one of the most crushing defeats any nation has ever endured. Japan is now lightly armed, rich—and dependent on the United States to protect it, including the oil supplies on which its economy hangs by a thread.

Finally there is Russia. Under czars and Soviets alike it has never been at peace for long. Its territory has expanded through war. It is the last of the great empires, still clinging to its gains, yet its political system lacks deeply rooted stability and there is no real prosperity: only riches for the new ruling class, poverty for the rest.

World War One foisted communism on an exhausted, demoralized and hungry people. World War Two brought success for Russian arms after more than a century of failure, including two lost wars. The result of its one major victory since 1815 is a highly militarized society, in which the only well-made products are weapons, and whose status as a great power rests entirely on nuclear arms. Economically and politically it is a monumental failure.

The United States alone has risen to both riches and global power since 1775. The Uptonian explanation tends to account for this by dumb luck and Yankee ingenuity. The unpreparedness thesis runs roughly as follows: The United States came into existence through French aid, native courage and superior marksmanship; lost serious interest in fighting after that, succumbing to old superstitions about standing armies; thereby becoming overly dependent on the unreliable militia and becoming accustomed to bad, ultimately costly habits of unreadiness; stumbled like a sleepwalker into subsequent wars, usually with its trousers flopping around the knees; never had a real military policy at all; had to be pushed and dragged into achieving its destiny as a world power by toppling Spain in 1898; was manipulated into World War One; reverted blindly to the old dismal ways in the 1920s and 1930s; received a historic chastisement for its folly on December 7, 1941; only to flirt all over again with the same dangerous complacency. The Soviet A-bomb and the Korean War finally put paid to its tattered delusions.

After that the United States chose not to drop its guard very far, but the result has been a badly distorted economy and a permanently anxious society. Even Dwight Eisenhower, a career soldier, worried about where all this was tending and warned against it in his farewell address. Then came Vietnam and the country discovered it still had no workable military policy, the proof being that the United States failed to get a grip on that war and was forced to withdraw, bested by peasants in black pajamas.

There is no doubt that Americans have been emotionally unprepared for most of the nation's wars, and nothing could have prepared people for Pearl Harbor. The very idea of unreadiness has a certain appeal: Nice people are bound to be unready for war, or should be. The antimilitaristic side of the American character is forever on guard. Americans are so suspicious of military ambition that even when the armed forces win wars they are criticized as robustly as if they had lost them.

The military themselves keep the unpreparedness ax well ground. If things go wrong (and in war something always goes wrong) they can put it down to lack of political foresight and/or budget constraints on the armed forces before hostilities commenced.

Such sterile bickering takes preparedness as an absolute condition, when it is in fact a relative one. It is always relative to whom you fight, when you fight and where you fight.

Many of the most important elements, moreover, are intangible. Courage, willpower, imagination, leadership and cooperation are all crucial, yet they cannot be crated and stored like ammunition, numbered and distributed like spare parts, or be obtained by filling in the right forms.

Nor are superior numbers of the items that can be counted—troops, planes, ships, guns—any assurance of success. German armies destroyed superior Russian armies in both world wars. The German army of 1940 utterly crushed a bigger French army that enjoyed British support. The Imperial Japanese Army of World War Two was larger than the combined force of American soldiers and marines that defeated it.

True preparedness cannot be quantified. Trying to wrestle with the question of preparedness is like trying to hold on to mercury. Dextrous you may be, but it will eventually get away. And as this book has shown, the American record of military preparedness is not uniform, simple or clear, but for the most part the United States has been better prepared for what actually ensued than its enemies.

Half the country was agitating and preparing for the War of 1812 long before it began. Had it not been for the broken nerve of William Hull, Canada would have been dismembered. The superb small army that Scott led into Mexico fought one of the most brilliant military campaigns of all time and won a lasting peace. This was not an army created in a day.

As for emotional and psychological preparedness, at least half the country was ready for the Civil War when it came, welcoming it with an ardor that the final cost made painful to recall. It was American bellicosity that brought war with Spain in 1898, and within three months an "unprepared" army and navy had won for America an overseas empire. The Japanese and Germans were meanwhile taking decades with their highly prepared forces to achieve something similar.

Wilson certainly ensured a thorough lack of preparedness for the entry into World War One. At least a year of valuable time was wasted in pursuing the chimera of neutrality long after the mythical quality of the beast was obvious even to the president.

Franklin Roosevelt made no such mistake in World War Two. He began American rearmament in November 1938, with the decision to build ten thousand planes and start restocking military depots to support an expanded army. The whole history of the army, navy, air corps and marines between the world wars is one of purposeful preparation, with whatever means available, for a conflict that military leaders were certain was coming. As Chester Nimitz later remarked, almost nothing happened in the Pacific war that the navy had not practiced many times before Pearl Harbor. The ships, the planes, the submarines, the small arms, the landing craft, the tanks, which American forces employed in the war nearly all predated American entry into it—and were designed with this war in mind.

The result of such preparations was that Americans could fight and win two of the biggest wars in history in less than the span of a single presidential term. A single term is generally considered "a learning period" for someone entering the White House; four years in which to get ready for his major achievements, which will come during his second term.

Korea represents a mixed case: The United States had the means to drive the invader from South Korea and thereby achieve its original aim, but not to unify Korea by force of arms. Vietnam represents an example of political confusion and hubris triumphant over sound military advice. There is no form of military preparedness known to history that serves as the antidote to that. In such a case, all talk of preparedness is irrelevant.

Even so, neither in Korea nor Vietnam were there anything more than limited local defeats. There was nothing like Stalingrad, or even Bataan. No conquering enemy divisions marched down Fifth Avenue, no president had to surrender. There was no rationing, no hunger; none of the ordeals of the truly unprepared. For them, defeat gives unpreparedness a meaning that Americans have never known.

The illusion that American military history can be told as a story of eternal unreadiness will never die, but for those who might like to contemplate another view, this book has sought to offer one. It has placed the nation's military history as a constant factor in the evolution of American life. It is a factor as important as geography, immigration, the growth of business, the separation of powers, the inventiveness of its people, or anything else that contributes strongly to its unique identity among the nations of the Earth.

The result is that the average American cannot move without bumping into the country's military past. Take a man reading this book. If he is sitting down, he is probably sitting on a wallet, with greenbacks in it—a memento of the Civil War. If he smokes cigarettes or wears a mustache, they ought to remind him of the war with Mexico. The wristwatch he wears was popularized among American men by the army in World War One. The standardized tests he took in high school and college have the same provenance. The title deeds to his house and his car were issued by state governments whose authority is in every case traceable to victory by American forces in some war. If he has a computer, he has a direct link with World War Two. His home is likely to be filled with electronic equipment rooted in military contracts somewhere in the past. When he pays his taxes a large slice of what he hands over will go to defray the cost of wars long concluded.

At a thousand unnoticed points America's military past impinges on his daily life. Far from being separate and apart from it, that history helps make his life what it is, has been and will be.

The story continues.

NOTES

1. The Inaccurate Farmers

For Gage's last unhappy year in Boston the essential work is volume 2 of *The Correspondence of General Thomas Gage*, edited by Clarence E. Carter (New Haven, 1931). The evolution of the king's war policy may be traced in *The Correspondence of King George III*, edited by Sir John Fortescue (London, 1928).

The Letters of Hugh, Earl Percy, edited by Charles K. Bolton (Boston, 1902), provides an eyewitness account by a highly placed British officer of the opening stages of the war. Equally valuable is *The Diary of Frederick Mackenzie*, 2 volumes, edited by Allen French (Cambridge, Massachusetts, 1930). Mackenzie was a British infantry officer who served in America throughout the war, starting with the march on Concord.

Paul Revere's account of his famous ride is reproduced in facsimile in the first volume of Elbridge H. Goss, *The Life of Paul Revere* (Boston, 1891). The standard account of April 19 remains Allen French, *The Day of Lexington and Concord* (Boston, 1925).

The question of who fired the first shot has excited disagreement from the moment that shot was fired. The balance of probabilities suggests strongly that it was fired by one of the British platoons—but only powder. At least one militiaman standing on the Green was convinced that was what happened and the testimony of others hints at it. Compare the deposition of Sylvanus Ward reproduced in Henry B. Dawson, *Battles of the United States by Sea and Land*, volume 1 (New York, 1858).

There are two excellent works on the British army at this time: Sir John Fortescue, *The History of the British Army*, volume 3 (London, 1905), and

Edward P. Curtis, *The Organization of the British Army in the American Revolution* (New Haven, 1926). British supply problems have only recently received the attention they deserve. Both Norman Baker's *Government and Contractors* (London, 1971) and R. Arthur Bowler's *Logistics and the Failure of the British Army in America* (Princeton, 1975) are valuable.

W. Y. Carman, *A History of Firearms* (London, 1958), is authoritative on flintlock arms. On the effectiveness of eighteenth-century weapons, Dominique Larrey, *Mémoires de chirurgie militaire* (Paris, 1812), is gruesomely enlightening.

There are excellent accounts of the early clashes in volume 1 of Christopher Ward, *The War of the Revolution* (New York, 1952), and Allen French, *The First Year of the American Revolution* (Boston, 1939). There are two fine collections of eyewitness accounts: George F. Scheer and Hugh Rankin, *Rebels and Redcoats* (Cleveland, 1957), and Henry Steele Commager and Richard B. Morris, *The Spirit of '76* (Indianapolis, 1958).

Washington's view of the war's twists and turns may be followed almost from day to day in the John C. Fitzgerald edition of *The Writings of George Washington* (Washington, D.C., 1938). His period as commander of the Continental Army is the subject of volumes 3 and 4 of Douglas Southall Freeman, *George Washington* (New York, 1951). James Flexner's *George Washington and the American Revolution* (Boston, 1968) and Marcus Cunliffe's *Washington—Man and Monument* (Boston, 1958) are both filled with perceptive observations on Washington the soldier.

John Shy, *A People Numerous and Armed* (New York, 1976), offers a vivid sketch of Charles Lee and an important reappraisal of the militia.

There is a major reinterpretation of Jefferson's Declaration of Independence in Garry Wills, *Inventing America* (New York, 1978). Philip Davidson's *Propaganda and the American Revolution* (Chapel Hill, 1941) is useful.

There are two important articles on the riflemen: Horace Kephart, "The Rifle in Colonial Times," *Magazine of American History*, XXIV (1890), and John W. Wright, "The Rifle in the American Revolution," *American Historical Review*, XXIV (1924). Morgan is the subject of a fine biography: Don Higginbotham, *Daniel Morgan: Revolutionary Rifleman* (Chapel Hill, 1961).

2. Winter Patriots

Howe's account of his campaigns is to be found in *The Narrative of Lieutenant General Sir William Howe in a Committee of the House of Commons* (London, 1780). This needs to be read with a copy of Ira D. Gruber, *The Howe Brothers in the American Revolution* (New York, 1972), within reach.

Volume 2 of Ward offers an excellent general account of the Long Island fiasco and all subsequent battles in this war, especially when read in conjunction with the relevant volumes of the Freeman biography of Washington and the Fitzgerald edition of the *Writings*.

On Nathanael Greene, there is a biography by Theodore Thayer, *Nathan-*

ael Greene (New York, 1960). Also useful is M. F. Treacy, *Prelude to York-town: The Southern Campaigns of Nathanael Greene* (Chapel Hill, 1963). Greene, along with other leading Continental Army commanders, is briefly but perceptively described in a work edited by George Billias, *George Washington's Generals* (New York, 1964).

Burgoyne's account of the Saratoga campaign is set out in an inimitable rococo style in a report he made to Parliament, *A State of the Expedition from Canada as Laid before the House of Commons* (London, 1780). Clinton, by any measure a dull figure, gave rise to a sparkling biography: William B. Willcox, *Portrait of a General* (New York, 1964). The most gifted of the British generals gets his due in Franklin B. Wickwire and Mary Wickwire, *Cornwallis: The American Adventure* (New York, 1970).

On William Rogers Clarke and the campaigns against the Indians, there is Dale Van Every, *A Company of Heroes: The American Frontier 1775–1783* (New York, 1962).

There are two full-length appraisals of Washington's command ability and strategic vision, both highly adulatory: Thomas Frothingham, *George Washington: Commander in Chief* (Boston, 1930), and Dave R. Palmer, *The Way of the Fox* (Westport, Connecticut, 1975). His neglect of cavalry, however, comes in for serious criticism from a Civil War cavalry veteran, Charles F. Adams, *Studies Military and Diplomatic* (Boston, 1911).

The early days of the Continental Army are re-created through telling the story of an ordinary soldier: Arthur B. Tourtellot, *William Diamond's Drum* (Garden City, New York, 1959). The best memoir to come from the musket line is that of Joseph Martin Plumb, edited by George F. Scheer, *Private Yankee Doodle* (Boston, 1962). A well-illustrated guide to a Continental's life is Harold F. Petersen, *Book of the Continental Soldier* (Harrisburg, Pennsylvania, 1968).

Interest in men such as William Diamond and Joseph Martin has been keen in recent years, producing such advances in scholarship as Edward C. Papenfuse, "General Smallwood's Recruits," *William and Mary Quarterly*, XXX (1973), and John Sellers, "The Common Soldier in the American Revolution" in *Military History of the American Revolution*, edited by Stanley J. Underdall (Washington, D.C., 1976). There are also many personal details to be found in a work based on pension applications by aged veterans of the war: John C. Dann, *The Revolution Remembered* (Chicago, 1980).

Long-established general accounts such as Charles K. Bolton, *The Private Soldier Under Washington* (Boston, 1902), and Lynn Montross, *Rag, Tag and Bobtail* (New York, 1952), are still of value and interest.

Completely different in perspective and tone, however, is the ground-breaking work by Charles A. Royster, *A Revolutionary People at War* (Chapel Hill, 1979), which seeks to integrate the story of the Continental Army with the social context of the Revolution. That same approach also informs a fresh look at Washington's logistical problems, E. Wayne Carp, *To Starve the Army at Pleasure* (Chapel Hill, 1984).

More traditional is Erna Risch, *Supplying Washington's Army* (Washington, D.C., 1980), by a leading authority on the history of logistics. Louis C. Hatch's *The Administration of the American Revolutionary Army* (New York, 1904), though dated, has not been wholly supplanted. One crucial supply problem is considered by O. W. Stephenson, "The Supply of Gunpowder in 1776," *American Historical Review*, XXX (1925).

The privations inflicted by want of supplies and attention are graphically described in the war memoirs of a Continental Army surgeon, James Thacher, *A Military Journal of the American Revolutionary War* (Boston, 1827). The melancholy fate of those taken prisoner is narrated by Charles Metzger, *The Prisoner in the American Revolution* (Chicago, 1971), and Larry G. Bowman, *Captive Americans* (Athens, Ohio, 1976). It was by adding prisoner deaths in captivity to an exhaustive study of known combat losses that Howard H. Peckham, *The Toll of Independence* (Chicago, 1974), demonstrated that contrary to established belief this was a very costly war.

There are two indispensable firsthand accounts of fighting in the South: Henry Lee, *Memoirs of War in the Southern Department* (Philadelphia, 1812), and Banastre Tarleton, *A History of the Campaigns of 1780 and 1781 in the Southern Provinces of North America* (Dublin, 1787). These memoirs do not reveal the eventual fates of their authors: the victorious Lee went on to suffer bankruptcy, imprisonment and penury; the defeated Tarleton to marry an heiress and become Major General Sir Banastre Tarleton, Knight of the Bath, Member of Parliament.

John Pancake, *This Destructive War* (University, Alabama, 1985), offers a survey of the partisan struggle in the Southern states. Robert C. Pugh, "The Revolutionary Militia's Role in the Southern Campaign," *William and Mary Quarterly*, XIV (1957), is also helpful in clarifying the relationship between guerrilla and conventional warfare in the South.

There are two standard accounts of the naval war: Gardner Allen, *The Naval History of the American Revolution*, 2 volumes (Boston, 1913), and Alfred Thayer Mahan, *Major Operations of the Navies in the War of Independence* (Boston, 1913). There are two good popular accounts: William Fowler, *Rebels Under Sail* (New York, 1976), which takes a skeptical view, and Nathan Miller, *Sea of Glory* (New York, 1974), which is somewhat romantic. Jack Coggins's *Ships and Seamen of the American Revolution* (Harrisburg, Pennsylvania, 1964) is a useful, lavishly illustrated guide ideal for anyone who doesn't know a futtock from a taffrail.

3. Chrysalis

There are hundreds—possibly thousands—of histories of the Revolutionary War. Among the more valuable accounts, besides those already mentioned, must be included: John R. Alden, *The American Revolution* (New York, 1954); Don Higginbotham, *The War of American Independence* (New York, 1973); Robert Middlekauff, *The Glorious Cause* (New York, 1983);

John C. Miller, *The Triumph of Freedom* (Boston, 1948); Howard H. Peckham, *The War for Independence* (Chicago, 1958); Page Smith, *A New Age Now Begins,* 2 volumes (New York, 1976); and William M. Wallace, *Appeal to Arms* (New York, 1951).

There is also a recent collection of essays representing some of the best modern scholarship on the subject: Ronald Hoffman and Peter J. Albert, editors, *Arms and Independence* (Charlottesville, Virginia, 1984).

For British interpretations, there are three outstanding examples: George Otto Trevelyan, *The American Revolution,* 4 volumes (London, 1899–1907); Eric Robson, *The American Revolution in Its Political and Military Aspects* (London, 1955); and Piers Mackesy, *The War for America* (London, 1963).

Anyone interested in almost any aspect of the War of Independence will find highly useful a thoroughly reliable and dispassionate work of reference: Mark Boatner III, *Encyclopedia of the American Revolution,* revised edition (New York, 1974).

Robert R. Palmer, *The Age of the Democratic Revolution,* 2 volumes (Princeton, 1957–64), places the consequences of the war in their global setting. The first work to show just how revolutionary these consequences were for American life was the pioneering J. F. Jameson, *The American Revolution Considered as a Social Movement* (Princeton, 1926). This line of scholarship was advanced still further by Evarts B. Greene, *The Revolutionary Generation 1763–1790* (New York, 1943), and Jackson Turner Main, *The Social Structures of Revolutionary America* (Princeton, 1965). For a moderately dissenting view: F. B. Tolles, "The American Revolution Considered as a Social Movement: A re-evaluation," *American Historical Review,* LX (1954).

Interpretations of the Constitution as a plutocrat's charter distorted understanding of the document for the first half of the twentieth century. The "scholarly" foundations of such views have long since been exposed for what they were. The principal clash—between Federalists and Antifederalists, fighting over the fate of the militia and the future of the army—is revealed clearly in such works as Merrill Jensen, *The Making of the American Constitution* (Princeton, 1964); Leonard Levy, editor, *Essays on the Making of the Constitution* (New York, 1969); Forrest McDonald, *We the People* (Chicago, 1958); and Eric McKittrick, "The Founding Fathers: Young Men of the Revolution," *Political Science Quarterly,* LXXVI (June 1961). Carl Van Doren, *The Great Rehearsal* (Boston, 1944), provides a traditional, popular account.

4. Hammer and Anvil

The attempts to turn Indians into farmers and thereby resolve the military challenge of the frontier through assimilation is narrated in two distinguished works: Bernard Sheehan, *Seeds of Extinction* (Chapel Hill, 1973), and Anthony F. C. Wallace, *The Death and Rebirth of the Seneca* (New York, 1968).

The best account of the disasters befalling Harmar and St. Clair is contained in James Ripley Jacobs, *The Beginning of the US Army, 1783–1812* (Princeton, 1947). Wiley Sword, *President Washington's Indian War* (Norman, Oklahoma, 1985), offers a reliable, modern overview of this little-known, underestimated conflict.

On life at the forts built to advance the march of conquest there are two useful articles by Norman Caldwell: "The Frontier Army Officer 1794–1814" and "The Enlisted Soldier at the Frontier Post 1790–1814," both in *Mid-America*, XXVIII (1955). On Wayne, there is a good recent biography: Paul David Nelson, *Anthony Wayne* (Bloomington, Indiana, 1985). Dale Van Every, *Ark of Empire* (New York, 1963), offers a good popular account of the long struggle to secure the Old Northwest.

Leland Baldwin's *The Whiskey Rebellion,* revised edition (Pittsburgh, 1962), was for half a century the standard work on this bizarre episode; until the publication, that is, of Thomas P. Slaughter's *The Whiskey Rebellion* (New York, 1986). While Baldwin portrays the rebellion as a local uprising (and doesn't hide his sympathy for the rebels), Slaughter convincingly portrays it as an epochal national event, a major chapter in the long-running clash between the frontier and national government, itself one of the formative influences shaping the American character.

There is a good brief introduction to the Barbary Wars in Robert Albion and Jeanette C. Pope, *Sea Lanes in Wartime* (Princeton, 1942). Marshall Smelser, *The Congress Founds the Navy* (South Bend, Indiana, 1959), offers an authoritative reconstruction of the legislative struggle. William Fowler, *Jack Tars and Commodores* (Boston, 1984), offers a lively, readable account of naval affairs from the foundation through the War of 1812. Leonard F. Guttridge and Jay D. Smith's *The Commodores* (New York, 1969) is a minor classic, focused largely on the brief life and tragic death of Stephen Decatur.

On the Adams administration's handling of the quasi-war with France volume 2 of Page Smith, *John Adams* (Garden City, New York, 1962), is essential. So too is Leonard D. White, *The Jeffersonians* (New York, 1951), on the failed efforts of Jefferson and his followers to halt the growth in American military power.

The Barbary Wars provide the subject of the entertaining yet reliable Glenn Tucker, *Dawn Like Thunder* (Indianapolis, 1963).

The early days of the infant American arms infantry are described in various places: Roger Burlingame, *March of the Iron Men* (New York, 1938); Curtis P. Nettles, *The Emergence of a National Economy 1775–1815* (Indianapolis, 1959); Carl Russell, *Guns on the Early Frontier* (New York, 1957); Merritt Roe Smith, *Harper's Ferry and the New Technology* (Ithaca, New York, 1977); and John K. Winkler, *The Dupont Dynasty* (New York, 1935).

There are two standard works on Whitney: Constance Green, *Eli Whitney and the Birth of American Technology* (New York, 1952), and Jeanette Mirsky and Allen Nevins, *The World of Eli Whitney* (New York, 1958). For a more skeptical appraisal of Whitney's achievements: Robert S. Woodbury,

"The Legend of Eli Whitney and Interchangeable Parts," *Technology and Culture,* I (1960).

Robert Fulton's *Torpedo War and Submarine Explosions* (New York, 1810) contains not only descriptions of his experiments but his original drawings of his "torpedoes" and submarine. Wallace Hutcheon, Jr.'s, *Robert Fulton: Pioneer of Undersea Warfare* (Annapolis, 1981) is an essential, well-realized study.

For Jefferson's presidency: volumes 4 and 5 of Dumas Malone's magisterial *Jefferson in His Time* (Boston, 1960–64). The path by which Federalist military ambitions were achieved, ironically, by their political opponents is described in an important study: Richard H. Kohn, *The Eagle and the Sword* (New York, 1975).

The fundamental importance to the life of the new Republic of the ongoing struggle between regulars and militia is the subject of Lawrence Delbert Cress, *Citizens in Arms* (Chapel Hill, 1980), and John K. Mahon, *The American Militia: Decade of Decision* (Gainesville, Florida, 1960). On the early years of West Point, the best account is in Stephen Ambrose, *Duty, Honor, Country* (Baltimore, 1964).

The relevant volume of Irving Brant's biography of Madison is *James Madison: The President* (Indianapolis, 1959).

Nearly every account of Tecumseh fawns; a way of expunging white guilt, perhaps. Nearly all the anecdotes that prop up the legend may be traced back to Benjamin Drake, *Life of Tecumseh, and of His Brother the Prophet* (Cincinnati, 1841). Modern romantic interpretations include Alvin Josephy, *The Patriot Chiefs* (New York, 1961), and Glenn Tucker, *Tecumseh: Vision of Glory* (Indianapolis, 1956). Only recently, however, has the kind of imaginative, pioneering research been done that was needed to produce a reliable, if less flattering, version of the story: R. David Edmunds, *Tecumseh and the Quest for Indian Leadership* (Boston, 1984).

On Harrison, the standard work is Freeman Cleaves, *Old Tippecanoe* (New York, 1939). Harrison's *Messages and Letters,* 2 volumes, edited by Logan Esary (Indianapolis, 1922), offers some insights into political and military responses to the Indian presence on the Old Northwest frontier.

5. America's First Limited War

Irving Brant's *James Madison: Commander in Chief* (Indianapolis, 1961) is standard. There is a good recent account of the government's efforts to raise armies and find a workable strategy: J.C.A. Stagg, *Mr. Madison's War* (Princeton, 1983). Dense and not always easy to follow, it is nonetheless well worth the effort. There is still interest to be had in reading the classic account by Henry Adams, edited by Harvey A. De Weerd, *The War of 1812* (Washington, D.C., 1944).

There is a variety of good popular accounts available, such as Harry L. Coles, *The War of 1812* (Chicago, 1965); Reginald Horsman, *The War of 1812*

(New York, 1969); and Glenn Tucker, *Poltroons and Patriots*, 2 volumes, (Indianapolis, 1954).

All of these, like most other works on this war, depend to a considerable degree on a work of much idiosyncrasy and charm: Benson J. Lossing, *The Pictorial Field Book of the War of 1812* (New York, 1868).

A Canadian view is offered by Pierre Berton, *The Invasion of Canada* (Boston, 1980), and *Flames Across the Border* (Boston, 1981). This is human-interest history, heavily influenced it would appear by the best-selling *Paris, brûle-t-il?* A less flamboyant, more scholarly approach from the Canadian side is offered by J. McKay Hitsman, *The Incredible War of 1812* (Toronto, 1966).

The two best British works on the war are limited in scope: C. S. Forester, *The Age of Fighting Sail* (London, 1956); and Robin Reilly, *The British at the Gates* (London, 1974), the first detailed British account of the Battle of New Orleans. Sir John Fortescue's *History of the British Army*, volume 9 (London, 1911) is now very much out-of-date.

The navy's exploits attracted two distinguished chroniclers: Alfred Thayer Mahan, *Sea Power in Its Relation to the War of 1812*, 2 volumes (Boston, 1905); and Theodore Roosevelt, *The Naval War of 1812* (New York, 1888). On Perry, Charles J. Dutton's *Oliver Hazard Perry* (New York, 1935) remains the standard account. Also valuable are Max Rosenberg, *The Building of Perry's Fleet on Lake Erie* (Harrisburg, Pennsylvania, 1950), and an article by distinguished Canadian historian C. P. Stacy, "Another Look at the Battle of Lake Erie," *Canadian Historical Review*, XXXIX (1958), 41–51.

Nothing written about Scott quite compares with the charm of his unreliable *Memoirs of Lieut.-General Scott, LL.D., Written by Himself*, 2 volumes (New York, 1864). He was nonetheless fortunate in his biographer, Charles Winslow Elliott, who produced the superlative *Winfield Scott* (New York, 1937), which is a model of scholarship and a labor of love.

Walter Lord, *The Dawn's Early Light* (New York, 1971), offers a highly entertaining, well-researched account of the burning of Washington and the attack on Fort McHenry.

Jackson's campaigns, first against the Creeks, then against the British, are described by the general himself in John Spencer Bassett, editor, *The Correspondence of Andrew Jackson*, 2 volumes (Washington, D.C., 1926–27). There is also a fascinating, firsthand account by his chief engineer in New Orleans, Arsène Lacarrière Latour, *Historical Memoir of the War in West Florida and Louisiana* (Philadelphia, 1816).

The relevant volume of Robert Remini's pathbreaking, prize-winning biography is *Andrew Jackson and the Course of American Empire* (New York, 1977). Marquis James's *Andrew Jackson: The Border Captain* (New York, 1933) is still of value and interest.

On the relationship between the Creek campaign and the fight to save New Orleans there is an excellent study: Frank Owsley, Jr., *The Struggle for the Gulf Borderlands* (Gainesville, Florida, 1981). A marine major general, and veteran of the Pacific war, Wilburt S. Brown, offers an expert's analysis of the military problems met and overcome in *The Amphibious Campaign for West Florida and Louisiana in 1814–1815* (University, Alabama, 1969). Charles B. Brooks, *The Siege of New Orleans* (Seattle, 1961), provides a sparkling narrative account of Jackson's greatest battle.

The Treaty of Ghent and the negotiations that produced it are the subject of Fred Engleman, *The Peace of Christmas Eve* (New York, 1970).

6. Natural Frontiers

On the program of Indian removal the Remini biography of Jackson is essential. Michael Rogin's *Fathers and Children: Andrew Jackson and the American Indian* (New York, 1975) is an exercise in "psychohistory." More useful is Richard Slotkin's *The Fatal Environment: The Myth of the Frontier* (New York, 1985), an impassioned study of the destruction of the tribes. Dale Van Every's *The Final Challenge: The American Frontier 1804–1845* (New York, 1964) and Grant Foreman's *Indian Removal* (Norman, Oklahoma, 1932) are both reliable, well-written histories, the one popular, the other scholarly.

Perry B. Armstrong, *The Sauks and the Black Hawk War* (Springfield, Illinois, 1887), and Reuben G. Thwaites, *The Story of the Black Hawk War* (Madison, Wisconsin, 1892), provide good accounts of this tragicomic affair. Although of controversial authenticity, *Black Hawk: An Autobiography,* edited by Donald Jackson (Urbana, Illinois, 1964), is worth consulting for the broad outlines.

Francis Paul Prucha, *Sword of the Republic: The US Army on the Frontier 1783–1846* (New York, 1969), provides a valuable survey of this little-known phase in American military history. Prucha's earlier scholarly monograph, *Broadax and Bayonet: The Army in the Development of the Northwest 1815–1850* (Madison, Wisconsin, 1953), is authoritative. Edgar B. Wesley, *Guarding the Frontier* (St. Paul, 1935), is also useful on the challenge of providing enough security for these territories rapidly to become states of the Union.

C. P. Stacey, "The Myth of the Unguarded Frontier 1815–1871," *American Historical Review,* LVI (October 1950), takes a rewardingly iconoclastic look at the conventional view of U.S.-British-Canadian relations after 1815.

William H. Goetzmann's *Army Exploration of the American West 1803–1863* (New Haven, 1959) is the definitive account of the Topographical Engineers.

John Charles Frémont, *Memoirs of My Life* (Chicago, 1887), is of interest not only for his accounts of western exploration but for his version of events as one of the Union's least successful generals in the Civil War. Allan Nevins, *Frémont: Pathmaker of the West* (New York, 1939), does a fine job of explaining why Frémont was a major figure of his time.

On the pre–Civil War volunteer militia companies, Marcus Cunliffe's *Soldiers and Civilians: The Martial Spirit in America 1775–1865* (Boston, 1968) is simply wonderful. Cunliffe is also very good on the flowering of military schools in a country that despised militarism.

On West Point: Stephen Ambrose, *Duty, Honor, Country* (Baltimore, 1964), and James Morrison, *The Best School in the World: West Point 1833–1866* (Kent, Ohio, 1985).

T. R. Fehrenbach, *Lone Star* (New York, 1968), offers a useful synopsis of Texas's turbulent origins and early days. José Enrique de la Peña's *With Santa Anna in Texas* (College Station, Texas, 1975) is based on the diary of a Mexican army captain. It offers the best of the many eyewitness accounts of the fall of the Alamo. Walter Lord, *A Time to Stand* (New York, 1962), offers a meticulous reconstruction of the fight for the Alamo as seen by both sides. On the battle that decided the independence of Texas, Frank X. Tolbert's *The Day of San Jacinto* (New York, 1959) is the most complete account.

Antonio López de Santa Anna's *Mi Historia Militar y Politica* and *Las Guerras de Mexico con Tejas y los Estados Unidos* (both Mexico City, 1974) are essential sources. The first of these works is his autobiography, the second is a collection of letters and official documents. Together they offer a fascinating if less than reliable account of Santa Anna's amazing career, as well as a Mexican perspective on events.

The best biography remains Wilfrid Hardy Callcott, *Santa Anna* (Norman, Oklahoma, 1936), although Oaka L. Jones, Jr.'s, shorter *Santa Anna* (New York, 1968) also has its merits.

Allan Nevins, editor, *Diary of a President* (New York, 1949), offers an edited version of Polk's splenetic diaries. Justin H. Smith, *The Annexation of Texas* (New York, 1912), carefully traces the course of this inevitability.

The standard biography of Taylor is the somewhat plodding Holman Hamilton, *Zachary Taylor* (Indianapolis, 1941). Edward J. Nichols's *Zach Taylor's Little Army* (Garden City, New York, 1963) is a useful supplement to it.

By far the best firsthand account to emerge from Taylor's army is Samuel Chamberlain, *My Confession* (New York, 1956), a minor classic among war memoirs. Lost for nearly a century, it offers a narrative that contains memorable descriptions of Taylor and Wool, vivid accounts of the battles in northern Mexico, and bold watercolors painted by the author. Almost as good is John Kenly's *Memoirs of a Maryland Volunteer* (Philadelphia, 1873), by a man who raised one of the first companies of twelve-month volunteers. He served with Taylor from Matamoros to Victoria, before transferring to the invasion force under Scott.

A very different but rewarding account of Taylor's army and its battles comes from a Mexican artillery officer who fought at Monterrey and Buena Vista: Manuel Balbontin, *La Invasion Americana* (Mexico City, 1883).

Walter P. Webb, *The Texas Rangers* (New York, 1935), concentrates largely on their feats in the Mexican War. It was scouting for Taylor that brought them worldwide fame.

Fairfax Downey, "The Flying Batteries," *Army*, VII (1957), takes a close look at this battle winner. James K. Holland, "Diary of a Texas Volunteer in the Mexican War," *Southwest Historical Quarterly*, XXX (1926), provides a good account of a typical three-month volunteer's experiences. George B. Fisher, "Buena Vista: A Western Thermopylae," *Coast Artillery Journal*, LXXII (1930), offers a professional appraisal of this clash of arms.

Philip St. George Cooke's *The Conquest of New Mexico and California* (New York, 1878) is an essential account, along with Frémont's memoirs. Frank A. Golder's *The March of the Mormon Battalion* (New York, 1928) is based on the journal of Henry Standage, a young Mormon soldier who never doubted that the march to San Diego was an epic feat on a par with the anabasis of Xenophon's immortal band.

There is a fine biography of Kearny: Dwight L. Clarke, *Stephen Watts Kearny, Soldier of the West* (Norman, Oklahoma, 1961). Bernard DeVoto, *1846: The Year of Decision* (Boston, 1943), is good on events in California and New Mexico and the Doniphan expedition.

On the landing at Veracruz: Scott's memoirs, Elliott's biography of Scott, and the excellent *Surfboats and Horse Marines: US Naval Operations in the Mexican War* by K. Jack Bauer (Annapolis, 1969), which makes clear that the Gulf was an American lake.

There are some splendid memoirs from officers and men who campaigned from Veracruz to Mexico City: Robert Anderson, *An Artillery Officer in the Mexican War* (1911), combines doubts over the rightness of the war with a determination to do his duty; George Ballentine, *An English Soldier in the US Army* (New York, 1854), offers one of the best accounts of everyday life in Scott's army as experienced by a private in the regulars; Ulysses S. Grant, *Personal Memoirs of U. S. Grant*, 2 volumes (New York, 1885–86), condemns the war, praises the army, and is modest about his own role; George B. McClellan, *Mexican War Diary* (Princeton, 1917), is of interest for his observations on his fellow officers; J. J. Oswandel, *Notes on the Mexican War 1846-7-8* (Philadelphia, 1885), offers a good private's-eye view of the fighting.

James W. Pohl, "The Influence of Antoine Henri de Jomini on Winfield Scott's Campaign in the Mexican War," *Southwest Historical Quarterly*, LXXVII (1973), is instructive. One of the more intriguing minor dramas bearing on the composition and morale of Scott's army is the subject of Richard Blaine McCormack, "The San Patricio Deserters in the Mexican War," *Americas*, VIII (1951).

There are some excellent general accounts of the war, beginning with Justin H. Smith, *The War with Mexico*, 2 volumes (New York, 1920), a monument of historical scholarship. No subsequent account matches its thoroughness. Also noteworthy, however, are Alfred H. Bill, *Rehearsal for Conflict* (New York, 1947); Seymour V. Connor and Odie B. Faulk, *North America Divided* (New York, 1971); Robert Selph Henry, *The Story of the*

Mexican War (Indianapolis, 1950); and K. Jack Bauer, *The Mexican War* (New York, 1974).

There is a fine, pioneering biography of Grant as a junior officer: Lloyd Lewis's *Captain Sam Grant* (Boston, 1950), which covers extensively his service in Mexico, first under Taylor, later under Scott. George Winston Smith and Charles Judah, *Chronicles of the Gringos* (Albuquerque, 1968), provide a useful collection of eyewitness accounts, but one with a strongly held point of view—that the war was an immoral conflict forced on Mexico by the imperialistic United States.

Robert W. Johannsen's *To the Halls of the Montezumas* (New York, 1985) is a novel interpretation of the war's impact on the American imagination and popular culture.

7. Triple Revolution

William Goetzmann, *Army Exploration of the American West,* of course. Odie B. Faulk, *Destiny Road* (New York, 1973), traces the post-Mexican War development of the road the Mormon Battalion cut across the desert. Faulk's *Camel Corps* (New York, 1976) is a dryly humorous account of the army's unsuccessful attempt to conquer the vast spaces of the West by camel.

Percival Lowe, *Five Years a Dragoon* (Kansas City, 1906), portrays memorably a soldier's life on the Plains in the 1850s. Robert Utley's *Frontiersmen in Blue: The US Army and the Indian 1846–1866* (New York, 1967) is a work of considerable distinction.

On John Brown, the essential work is the biography by Stephen B. Oates, *To Purge This Land with Blood* (New York, 1970).

Carl Sandburg's *Abraham Lincoln: The War Years,* 4 volumes (New York, 1939), retains its power and readability after half a century. Benjamin P. Thomas's *Lincoln* (New York, 1952) is still the best one-volume life.

Jefferson Davis's *The Rise and Fall of the Confederate Government,* 2 volumes (New York, 1882), is essential. The impression it leaves of Confederate government is one of bad-tempered chaos. Clement Eaton's *Jefferson Davis* (New York, 1977) is a good biography that gives its subject the benefit of most doubts. Frank Vandiver, *Rebel Brass* (Baton Rouge, Louisiana, 1956), offers a valuable study of the Confederate high command.

On First Bull Run, as on nearly every battle in this war, there are two essential reference works: Robert C. Johnson and Clarence Buel, editors, *Battles and Leaders of the Civil War,* 4 volumes (New York, 1884–87), based entirely on accounts by eyewitnesses and participants, is one. The other is volume 1 of Vincent J. Esposito, *The West Point Atlas of American Wars,* 2 volumes (New York, 1959). Of value too is the *Atlas to Accompany the Official Records of the Union and Confederate Armies* (Washington, D.C., 1895), whose large format and full-color maps give a better idea of terrain features than *The West Point Atlas.*

It is a great loss that Lee never wrote a memoir of the war. The nearest to it, but not really a substitute, is Clifford Downey and Louis H. Manarin, editors, *The Wartime Papers of Robert E. Lee,* 4 volumes (Boston, 1961). Douglas Southall Freeman's *R. E. Lee: A Biography,* 4 volumes (New York, 1949), is a great work. Clifford Downey's *Lee* (Boston, 1967) is a solid, reliable one-volume life.

George B. McClellan produced a memoir: *McClellan's Own Story* (New York, 1887). Published after his death and edited by his friends, it has never been considered reliable. While it is useful and revealing in places, its pompous tone and provable inaccuracies helped bury the reputation this memoir was intended to rescue. William W. Hassler, *George B. McClellan* (Baton Rouge, Louisiana, 1957), strongly defends Little Mac against nearly a century of criticism.

By far the best account of a soldier's life in the Army of the Potomac is John D. Billings, *Hardtack and Coffee* (Boston, 1887). Bell I. Wiley's *The Life of Billy Yank* (Indianapolis, 1952) is simply splendid; based on extensive research into soldiers' diaries and letters.

Bruce Catton's famous three-volume *Army of the Potomac* (Garden City, New York, 1951–53) amounts to a well-deserved tribute to a splendid army. Michael C. C. Adams, *Our Masters, the Rebels* (Cambridge, Massachusetts, 1978), on the other hand, offers a theory that its troubles sprang from a deep-seated inferiority complex vis-à-vis Lee's smaller, less well-equipped forces.

Carleton McCarthy's *Detailed Minutiæ of Soldier Life in the Army of Northern Virginia* (Richmond, 1882) is filled with fascinating details that add up to a fine memoir. Sam R. Watkins's *"Co. Aytch"* (New York, 1962) is a classic of the war, written by a veteran of the First Tennessee. Fitzhugh Lee's *The Confederate Soldier in the Civil War* (Louisville, Kentucky, 1895) is a lavishly illustrated work that offers a text written entirely by soldiers who fought for the South and by officers who led them. Bell I. Wiley's *The Life of Johnny Reb* (Indianapolis, 1943) is the justly renowned predecessor to *Billy Yank.*

The economic and political problems that undermined Confederate armies continue to fascinate scholars, producing such excellent recent works as Richard Goff, *Confederate Supply* (Durham, North Carolina, 1969), which is a saga of shortages; Emory Thomas, *The Confederate Nation* (New York, 1979), which is a tale of mismanagement; and Frank Vandiver, *Their Tattered Flags* (New York, 1970), which paints Davis in a much more favorable light than he appears in *Rebel Brass,* perhaps because many of the problems he faced were simply insuperable.

John Hall is, in effect, the hero at the center of the pioneering study by Merritt Roe Smith, *Harper's Ferry and The New Technology* (Ithaca, New York, 1977). There are two short, colorful accounts of Colt's short and colorful life: Jack Rohan, *Yankee Arms Maker* (New York, 1935), and Bern Keating, *The Flamboyant Mr. Colt* (Garden City, New York, 1978). On the emergence of the Connecticut Valley as one of the earliest sites of technological convergence: Felicia Deyrup, *Arms Making in the Connecticut Valley 1789–1870* (York, Pennsylvania, 1970).

Robert V. Bruce, *Lincoln and the Tools of War* (Indianapolis, 1958), shows just how close an interest the president took in advanced weaponry. Carl Davis, *Arming the Union* (Port Washington, New York, 1973), demolishes many of the myths about the Ordnance Bureau and repeating arms; based on a close study of Ordnance Bureau records. And David A. Hounshell, *From the American System to Mass Production 1800–1932* (Baltimore, 1984), makes clear the vital role that Ordnance officers played in the evolution of new technologies.

8. General Abraham Lincoln

There is an excellent life of Lincoln's fiery secretary of war: Benjamin P. Thomas and Harold M. Hyman, *Stanton* (New York, 1962). Fred A. Shannon's *The Organization and Administration of the Union Army,* 2 volumes (Cleveland, 1928), is useful, but concerned largely with problems of recruiting and conscription.

Kenneth P. Williams's *Lincoln Finds a General,* 5 volumes (New York, 1956–64), was cut short by the author's death just as Lincoln did indeed find his general. So instead of being mainly about Grant, this unfinished masterpiece is, by a twist of fate, mainly about other men, notably McClellan. Williams's description and analysis of the Peninsular campaign are first-rate.

Douglas Southall Freeman, *Lee's Lieutenants,* 3 volumes (New York, 1942–44), offers a fine account of the eastern theater of war. George F. R. Henderson's *Stonewall Jackson and the American Civil War,* 2 volumes (New York, 1898), is an enthralling biography of this strange, gifted figure. Ezra J. Warner, *Generals in Gray* (Baton Rouge, Louisiana, 1959) and *Generals in Blue* (Baton Rouge, Louisiana, 1964), provides striking miniatures of some of the best, and some of the worst, on both sides.

T. Harry Williams, *Lincoln and His Generals* (New York, 1952), makes a persuasive case for Lincoln's superiority as a strategist. So too does an earlier work by a British general: Colin Ballard, *The Military Genius of Abraham Lincoln* (Cleveland, 1925).

David Homer Bates's *Lincoln in the Telegraph Office* (New York, 1906) is a memorable personal account from one of the cipher clerks at what amounted to the president's command post.

Stephen E. Ambrose's *Halleck* (Baton Rouge, Louisiana, 1962) is the standard biography of this learned soldier cursed with a timid soul.

Richard Harwell, editor, *Two Views of Gettysburg* (Chicago, 1964), offers, from the Union side, the recollections of Captain Frank Haskell, and from the opposite side of the field, those of Colonel Sir Arthur Fremantle, a British officer attached to Lee's army as an observer. George R. Stewart, *Pickett's Charge* (Boston, 1959), offers a short, trenchant account of these heroics. Longstreet's doubts about the Gettysburg venture (and much else) are set out at length in James Longstreet, *From Manassas to Appomattox* (Philadelphia, 1896). Meade's glum nature comes across in William S. Myers, editor, *The Life and Letters of George Gordon Meade* (New York, 1913).

Ulysses S. Grant's *Personal Memoirs of U.S. Grant,* 2 volumes (New York, 1885–86), are in a class of their own for lucidity and interest. Fascinating too for their frankness and acumen are Charles Dana's *Recollections of the Civil War* (New York, 1899). Sent by Stanton to spy on Grant, Dana became one of his greatest champions.

James Marshall-Cornwall's *Grant* (London, 1970) is a rewarding study of Grant's strengths and weaknesses as a commander. The earlier analysis by J.F.C. Fuller, *The Generalship of Ulysses S. Grant* (Philadelphia, 1929), is a landmark work that revealed Grant's profound contribution to modern warfare. William S. McFeely, *Grant: A Biography* (New York, 1979), is concerned mainly with his post-Civil War career. The judgments on Grant the soldier appear colored by a fundamental disgust at men who fight.

There is an excellent account of the Vicksburg campaign in *Lincoln Finds a General,* as well as Bruce Catton, *Grant Moves South* (Boston, 1960). Two essential sources are Joseph E. Johnston, *Narrative of Military Operations* (New York, 1874), by one of the ablest commanders the South possessed, and William T. Sherman, 2 volumes, *Memoirs of General William T. Sherman* (New York, 1875).

John W. DeForest's *A Volunteer's Adventures* (New Haven, 1946) is a wonderful memoir from the Union army serving in Louisiana. Jay Monaghan, *Civil War on the Western Border* (Boston, 1955), provides a fine account of the fighting beyond the Mississippi.

9. Modern Times

Charles Lee Lewis's *David Glasgow Farragut: Our First Admiral,* 2 volumes (Annapolis, 1943), is valuable not only for its splendid account of Farragut's key role in the Civil War but for its depiction of the navy in the decades before the conflict. Samuel B. Morison's *"Old Bruin": Commodore Matthew C. Perry* (Boston, 1967) is also an important addition to nineteenth-century naval history.

Gideon Welles, *The Diary of Gideon Welles* (Boston, 1903), sheds light from the top on naval operations, and provides some striking views of Lincoln as commander in chief. David Dixon Porter's *Incidents and Anecdotes of the Civil War* (New York, 1885) is an essential memoir of the naval war.

James Phinney Baxter III, *The Introduction of the Ironclad Warship* (Cambridge, Massachusetts, 1933), places the *Monitor-Merrimack* combat in the context of rapidly evolving naval technologies in modern states. William C. White and Ruth White, *Tin Can on a Shingle* (New York, 1957), tell an interesting tale well.

Virgil Carrington Jones, *The Civil War at Sea,* 3 volumes (New York, 1960–62), offers the most detailed general account, from a strong human-interest angle. H. Allen Gosnell's *Guns on the Western Waters: The Story of the River Gunboats* (Baton Rouge, Louisiana, 1949) makes fascinating reading. Rowena Reed, *Combined Operations in the Civil War* (Annapolis, 1978), is a valuable contribution to this underappreciated aspect of the war.

Raphael Semmes's *Memoirs of Service Afloat During the War Between the States* (Baltimore, 1869) is an engagingly indignant work.

There is an excellent account of Union artillery, focused mainly on the Army of the Potomac: L. VanLoan Naisawald, *Grape and Canister* (New York, 1960). The authoritative account of Lee's artillery is Jennings Cropper Wise, *The Long Arm of Lee*, 2 volumes (Richmond, 1915). Bad as things were for Lee's artillery, they were even worse out west, as is made clear by Larry J. Daniels, *Cannoneers in Gray: The Field Artillery of the Army of Tennessee 1861–1865* (University, Alabama, 1984). For the recollections of Lee's artillery commander: E. Porter Alexander, *Military Memoirs of a Confederate* (New York, 1907). Warren Ripley, *Artillery and Ammunition of the Civil War* (New York, 1970), provides a well-illustrated guide to the bewildering variety of shot, shell and artillery pieces employed by gunners on both sides.

Philip Sheridan, *Personal Memoirs*, 2 volumes (New York, 1888), portrays a man in love with his own legend. Jubal A. Early, *Autobiographical Sketch and Narrative of the War Between the States* (Philadelphia, 1912), is not exactly modest either. Burke Davis's *Jeb Stuart: The Last Cavalier* (New York, 1958) is a good popular account that brings out the charm and gallantry of the man. Robert Selph Henry's *"First with the Most" Forrest* (Indianapolis, 1944) does its talented subject justice.

Stephen Z. Starr, *Union Cavalry in the Civil War*, 3 volumes (Baton Rouge, Louisiana, 1979–85), is exhaustive and authoritative. Samuel E. Carter III, *The Last Cavaliers* (New York, 1979), offers a popular account of cavalry engagements great and small.

For Grant's descent into Virginia there is a splendid memoir, Horace Porter, *Campaigning with Grant* (New York, 1906); and another fine work by Bruce Catton, *Grant Takes Command* (Boston, 1967).

A useful recent account of the early clashes in The Wilderness is Robert Garth Scott, *Into the Wilderness with the Army of the Potomac* (Bloomington, Indiana, 1985). Gene Smith's *Grant and Lee* (New York, 1984) is a somewhat romantic double portrait, while the earlier J.F.C. Fuller, *Grant and Lee* (London, 1933), offers a professional soldier's appraisal that is decidedly pro-Grant.

On the gifted but tragic Upton, Stephen E. Ambrose's *Upton and the Army* (Baton Rouge, Louisiana, 1964) is the standard, indeed only biography.

Richard J. Sommers, *Richmond Redeemed* (New York, 1981), offers a densely detailed re-creation of the fighting—and for Grant the sheer frustration—outside Petersburg in the fall of 1864.

B. H. Liddell-Hart's *Sherman* (Philadelphia, 1929) is a work that did much to reveal the true nature of Sherman's genius. Lloyd Lewis's *Sherman: Fighting Prophet* (New York, 1932), added to that, while revealing more about the man. The troops he commanded were markedly different from the men who composed the Army of the Potomac. In many ways they might have passed for Confederates. That comes over very clearly from Joseph T. Glathaar, *The March to the Sea: Sherman's Troops in the Savannah and Carolinas Campaign* (New York, 1985).

On Thomas, the standard biography is Richard O'Connor, *Thomas: Rock of Chickamauga* (Englewood Cliffs, New Jersey, 1948). His young cavalry commander, James Wilson, left an excellent, outspoken memoir that provides fine descriptions of both the Army of the Cumberland and its brilliant commander: James H. Wilson, *Under the Old Flag,* 2 volumes (New York, 1912).

Of the many general accounts in recent years two of the best are undoubtedly Shelby Foote's *The Civil War: A Narrative,* 3 volumes (New York, 1958–74), which never allows the author's admittedly pro-Southern sympathies to unbalance the story, and James M. McPherson's *Ordeal by Fire* (New York, 1982), which embraces both the war and Reconstruction.

William C. Davis, editor, *The Image of War,* 6 volumes (New York, 1981–84), forms the best collection of Civil War photographs ever published, combining four thousand images—many never before available—and a text based on the best modern scholarship.

Analyses of grand strategy continue to flow. David Donald, editor, *Why the North Won the Civil War* (Baton Rouge, Louisiana, 1960), contains a variety of explanations which for the most part stress Confederate weakness. Herman Hattaway and Archer Jones, *How the North Won the Civil War* (Urbana, Illinois, 1983), attribute it mainly to superior Union logistics. Richard Beringer et al., *Why the South Lost the Civil War* (Athens, Georgia, 1986), disagree, blaming instead "the failure of Southern nationalism." Grady McWhinney and Perry D. Jameson's *Attack and Die!* (University, Alabama, 1982) puts down Confederate defeat to an age-old Celtic horde approach to combat that was racially and historically predestined in Southern armies. Archer Jones, *Confederate Strategy* (Baton Rouge, Louisiana, 1960), takes a close look at ten major strategic decisions, nearly every one a mistake.

The only full-scale biography of Mahan is Thomas E. Griess, *Dennis Hart Mahan,* PhD dissertation, Duke University, 1969. The full flowering of his thinking is to be found in Dennis Hart Mahan, *Advanced-Guard, Out-Post and Detachment Service of Troops, with the Essential Principles of Strategy, and Grand Tactics,* revised edition (New York, 1864). The magnum opus of his favorite pupil is H. Wager Halleck, *Elements of Military Art and Science* (New York, 1846).

Mark Boatner III, *The Civil War Dictionary* (New York, 1959), is a valuable reference tool. B. A. Botkin's *A Civil War Treasury of Tales, Legends and Folklore* (New York, 1960) is a delightful compendium of army gossip and military anecdotes from both sides.

Thomas L. Livermore's *Numbers and Losses in the Civil War* (Bloomington, Indiana, 1957) is the most thorough study ever made of this contentious subject and provides a statistical breakdown for every major battle.

Comparatively little attention has been paid to blacks in the Civil War. There is a classic memoir: Thomas Wentworth Higginson's *Army Life in a Black Regiment* (Boston, 1870), by a former Boston clergyman who commanded the 1st South Carolina Volunteers, the first regiment to be raised from former slaves. He found them cool and courageous under fire, and great fun to be with the rest of the time.

Benjamin Quarles, *The Negro in the Civil War* (Boston, 1953), and James M. McPherson, *The Negro's Civil War* (New York, 1965), make clear the considerable contribution blacks made to eventual Union victory.

The Civil War draft is covered by Eugene Murdock's *One Million Men* (Madison, Wisconsin, 1971), which concludes that the draft produced fewer than 50,000 conscripts—but a million volunteers.

Paul W. Gates's *Agriculture and the Civil War* (New York, 1965) is a valuable guide to the economic and social impact of the war on what was still a predominantly agricultural country.

Thomas C. Cochran, "Did the Civil War Retard Industrialization?" *Mississippi Valley Historical Review*, XLVIII (September 1961), raises serious doubts about many traditional assumptions on the economic legacy of the war.

10. Imperial Crumbs

James E. Sefton's *The United States Army and Reconstruction* (Baton Rouge, Louisiana, 1967) is the principal work on the subject, and a good one. Also useful is James M. McPherson's *Ordeal by Fire* (New York, 1982), which considers the Civil War and Reconstruction an integrated historical experience.

George Armstrong Custer, *My Life on the Plains* (New York, 1874), deals mainly with the Washita campaign. Elizabeth Bacon Custer's *Boots and Saddles* (New York, 1885) is good on army life but really a romanticized account of her *beau chevalier*. This work more than any other is the fountainhead of the Custer legend.

William A. Graham's *The Custer Myth* (Harrisburg, Pennsylvania, 1953) is a source book that contains most of the major eyewitness accounts from Custer's last campaign. Robert M. Utley, editor, *Life in Custer's Cavalry* (New Haven, Connecticut, 1977), contains contributions that are illuminating on the whole of the army's experience fighting the Plains Indians, not just the 7th Cavalry's. Evan S. Connell's *Son of the Morning Star* (Berkeley, California, 1984) is a brilliant history not only of Custer and the Battle of the Little Bighorn but of life in the post–Civil War army.

Martin F. Schmitt, editor, *General George Crook, His Autobiography* (Norman, Oklahoma, 1960), is an important account of Indian fighting by one of its greatest practitioners. Unfortunately, it ends with the Battle of the

Rosebud. John G. Bourke's *On the Border with Crook* (New York, 1891) is one of the most fascinating and valuable of all memoirs of life on the Plains and the campaigns against Apaches and Sioux. John J. Finerty's *War-Path and Bivouac* (New York, 1890) is filled with memorable incidents, by a journalist who traveled with Crook in 1876 and at times joined in the actions he wrote about.

Nelson A. Miles's *Personal Recollections and Observations* (Chicago and New York, 1896) is one of the essential works on Indian fighting and contains some of Remington's best illustrations. Ami Frank Mulford's *Fighting Indians! in the Seventh United States Cavalry, Custer's Favorite Regiment* (Fairfield, Washington, 1972), is a valuable memoir from one of the "Custer Avengers," recruited after the Little Bighorn fiasco. Charles King's *Campaigning with Crook* (Norman, Oklahoma, 1964), based on King's participation in Crook's campaign to avenge Custer, is, on the other hand, a work of "faction" and utterly unreliable.

George F. Price's *Across the Continent with the Fifth Cavalry* (New York, 1883) is a useful if pious regimental history. Don Rickey, Jr., *Forty Miles a Day on Beans and Hay* (Norman, Oklahoma, 1963), is a superb re-creation of life in the post–Civil War Indian-fighting army. Hershel V. Cashin's *Under Fire in the Tenth Cavalry* (New York, 1970) contains the reminiscences of black cavalrymen, who bore much of the burden of combat on the Plains.

The memoirs of both Sherman and Sheridan are primary sources. Also valuable is Paul A. Hutton, *Phil Sheridan and His Army* (Lincoln, Nebraska, 1985), the first in-depth study of Sheridan the manager of Indian campaigns.

Charles E. De Land's *The Sioux Wars* (Pierre, South Dakota, 1931–34) is one of the most thorough accounts of the destruction of the Sioux. Mari Sandoz's *Cheyenne Autumn* (New York, 1953) amounts to a powerful elegy. Ralph K. Andrist's *The Long Death: Last Days of the Plains Indians* (New York, 1964) is a survey of Indian wars that tells its sad tale effectively. Robert M. Utley's *Frontier Regulars: The US Army and the Indian 1866–1891* (New York, 1973) is the best general account; highly sympathetic to the Indians, less so to the army. An earlier survey, Fairfax Downey, *Indian-Fighting Army* (New York, 1941), has its merits but inclines strongly toward the melodramatic.

Martha Summerhays's *Vanished Arizona* (Salem, Massachusetts, 1911) provides an interesting account of life in the Old Army, in the Arizona desert and elsewhere, by an officer's wife.

Jay Monaghan's *Custer* (Boston, 1959) finds little to fault in its hero. Stephen Ambrose's *Crazy Horse and Custer* (New York, 1975) is an unusual double biography, highly admiring of both men. Valuable too for their insights are Edward S. Godfrey, "Cavalry Fire Discipline," *Journal of the Military Services Institution,* XIX, No. 83 (September 1896) and James S. Hutchins, "The Seventh Cavalry Campaign Outfit at the Little Bighorn," *Military Collector and Historian,* VII, No. 4 (Winter 1956).

Thomas B. Marquis's *A Warrior Who Fought Custer* (Minneapolis, 1931) is that rarity, a reliable Indian biography, based on a lifetime of working among Indians. This work tells the story of a Cheyenne brave. John G. Neihardt's *Black Elk Speaks* (New York, 1932) is a classic firsthand account of the 1876 campaigns from the Indian side. Merrill D. Beal, *"I Will Fight No More Forever": Chief Joseph and the Nez Perce* (Seattle, 1963), recounts one of the worst examples of injustice toward an Indian tribe. Dee Brown, *Bury My Heart at Wounded Knee* (New York, 1970), offers a similar uncompromisingly pro-Indian account of white versus Indian conflicts, but on a larger scale.

On army reforms in the post–Civil War era: Sherman's *Memoirs,* again; the Ambrose biography of Upton; Emory Upton, *The Military Policy of the United States* (Washington, D.C., 1904); Jack Foner, *The US Soldier Between Two Wars: Army Life and Reforms 1865–1898* (New York, 1970).

Robley D. Evans, *A Sailor's Log* (New York, 1901), puts an interesting deck-level perspective on the New Navy. Albert Gleaves's *The Life and Letters of Rear Admiral Stephen B. Luce* (New York, 1925) is the standard biography of the great naval reformer. Harold Sprout and Margaret Sprout's *The Rise of American Naval Power* (Princeton, 1939) is a now-famous study and in some respects is still unsurpassed. While the Sprouts stress the political pressures behind the rise of the navy, Benjamin Franklin Cooling, *Gray Steel and Blue Water Navy* (Greenwich, Connecticut, 1973), emphasizes the impetus provided by post–Civil War industrial development.

Alfred Thayer Mahan's *The Influence of Sea Power upon History* (New York, 1890) is essential to any understanding of the man and the age. Robert Seager's *Alfred Thayer Mahan* (Annapolis, 1977) is a lively, thorough biography; it will be a long time before anyone produces a better work on Mahan.

The same is true of Edmund Morris's *The Rise of Theodore Roosevelt* (New York, 1979), which follows its hero up to his accession to the presidency. TR's boss at the Navy Department left a memoir intended to set the record straight: E. B. Long, *The New American Navy* (New York, 1903).

Howard Beale, *Theodore Roosevelt and the Rise of America to World Power* (Baltimore, 1956), presents him as the driving force behind imperialism. Ernest R. May, *Imperial Democracy: The Emergence of America as a Great Power* (New York, 1961), places imperialistic impulses in a broader framework of American politics and culture. James A. Field, "American Imperialism: The Worst Chapter in Almost Any Book," *American Historical Review,* LXXXIII (1978), offers a well-merited rebuke to the liberal *angst* which distorts much of the literature on this subject.

The biography of McKinley is Margaret Leech's *In the Days of McKinley* (New York, 1959), which brings out his saintly character very effectively. The most reliable general account of the war is David F. Trask, *The War with Spain in 1898* (New York, 1981). Walter Millis's *The Martial Spirit* (Boston, 1931) is highly readable and demonstrates how popular the war was.

Frank Freidel's *The Splendid Little War* (Boston, 1958) is a profusely illustrated work, containing long extracts from eyewitness accounts. Gerald

Lindeman's *The Mirror of War* (Ann Arbor, 1974) is a critical study of the war's roots in popular culture and xenophobic prejudice. G.J.A. O'Toole's *The Spanish War* (New York, 1984) is a popular account that is useful not least for unearthing fresh material on the intelligence operations of all the interested parties.

Russell A. Alger, *The Spanish-American War* (New York, 1901), offers the viewpoint of the secretary of war. Nelson A. Miles, *Serving the Republic* (New York, 1911), casts little light on his misjudgments in this war. Virginia Johnson's *The Unregimented General* (Boston, 1962), the standard biography of Miles, is somewhat pedestrian.

George Dewey, *Autobiography of George Dewey* (New York, 1913), is quite frank about some controversial episodes, but guarded about others. There is a fine biography of the man: Ronald Spector, *Admiral of the New Empire* (Baton Rouge, Louisiana, 1974).

French Ensor Chadwick's *The Relations of the United States and Spain,* 3 volumes (New York, 1909–11), is written mainly from the navy's perspective. Chadwick was Samson's chief operations officer. Based largely on navy documents, this work amounts to a semiofficial history. Herbert H. Sargent, *The Campaign of Santiago de Cuba,* 3 volumes (Chicago, 1907), offers the most thorough and careful military analysis ever made of the land operation.

Graham Cosmas's *An Army for Empire* (Columbia, Missouri, 1972) is an excellent study of the army in the Spanish-American War. Theodore Roosevelt's *The Rough Riders* (New York, 1899) is of undeniable interest despite its unreliability. By far the best memoir, however, is Charles Johnson Post's *The Little War of Private Post* (Boston, 1960); engagingly written, it is of value not least for the author's illustrations, painted close to the events depicted.

11. Planetary Soldiers

After half a century William T. Sexton's *Soldiers in the Sun* (Harrisburg, Pennsylvania, 1939) remains the best general account of the Philippine Insurgency. Almost as good is John M. Gates's *Schoolbooks and Krags* (Westport, Connecticut, 1973).

Leon Wolff's *Little Brown Brother* (Garden City, New York, 1960), is scathingly critical and highly readable. Stuart Creighton Miller's *Benevolent Assimilation* (New Haven, 1982) is a work largely inspired by the Vietnam trauma. It depicts American suppression of the insurgency as little more than a criminal enterprise. Joseph L. Schott, *The Ordeal of Samar* (Indianapolis, 1964), on the other hand, casts Waller as a tragic hero, a scapegoat used to appease press hysteria and outraged public opinion.

Funston produced the most important memoir of the insurgency: Frederick Funston, *Memories of Two Wars* (New York, 1911).

For an excellent account from the field, see James Parker, "Some Random Notes on the Fighting in the Philippines," *Journal of the Military Service Institution,* XXVII (November 1900).

John K. Mahon, *History of the Militia and National Guard* (New York, 1983), provides a careful, scholarly account of this critical period in the Guard's history. Useful for its strongly pro-Guard perspective is Jim Dan Hill's *The Minute Man in Peace and War* (Harrisburg, Pennsylvania, 1964). The standard biography of Root is Philip Jessup's *Elihu Root,* 2 volumes (New York, 1938), a work of unalloyed admiration. There is a good article on this phase of Root's career: Elbridge Colby, "Elihu Root and the National Guard," *Military Affairs,* XXIII (Spring 1959).

On doctrine, see Dudley R. Knox, "The Role of Doctrine in Naval Warfare," *US Naval Institute Proceedings,* XLI, No. 2 (March–April 1915).

The story of the construction of the Panama Canal is brilliantly narrated in David McCulloch, *The Path Between the Seas* (New York, 1978). Theodore Roosevelt's naval program is really the centerpiece of the Sprouts' *Rise of American Naval Power.* It also figures largely in another minor classic, Bernard Brodie, *Sea Power in the Machine Age* (Princeton, 1943). Peter Karsten's *The Naval Aristocracy* (New York, 1972) is a study of Annapolis graduates in the Rooseveltian era. Much of the time the author treats them like defendants on trial. On the other hand James L. Abrahamson's *America Arms for a New Century* (New York, 1981) is a study of reformers in the army and navy that shows them as having much in common with political Progressives.

Among these reforming spirits was Bradley A. Fiske, whose memoir *From Midshipman to Rear Admiral* (New York, 1919) is delightful. Sims was immortalized in a superb biography: Elting E. Morison, *Admiral Sims and the Modern American Navy* (Boston, 1942). For Sims's famous demolition of Mahan's attachment to outmoded warships, see William S. Sims, "The Inherent Tactical Qualities of All-Big-Gun, One Calibre Battleships," *US Naval Institute Proceedings,* XXXIII, No. 4 (December 1906).

The most authoritative, most complete work on machine guns has to be G. M. Chinn, *The Machine Gun,* 4 volumes (Washington, D.C., 1951–53); well illustrated, well written and exhaustively researched. G. S. Hutchison's *Machine Guns: Their History and Tactical Employment* (New York, 1938) is a useful introduction. John Ellis's *The Social History of the Machine Gun* (London, 1975) is a good idea—with a catchy title—imperfectly realized. Curt Gentry's *John M. Browning: American Gunmaker* (Garden City, New York, 1964) is a competent, not overly technical biography of the greatest gun designer in history.

Hiram Maxim was his own public relations expert and tells his story very well in his autobiography, *My Life* (London, 1915).

John Patrick Finnegan's *Against the Specter of a Dragon* (Westport, Connecticut, 1974) is a valuable history of the preparedness movement. These activities are placed in their larger context in Frederick L. Paxson, *Pre-War Years 1914–1917* (Boston, 1936).

There is a good popular account of Pershing's pursuit of Villa: Clarence C. Clendenen, *Blood on the Border* (New York, 1969). It gives a telling view of the army on the eve of intervention.

Josephus Daniels, *The Wilson Era,* 2 volumes (Chapel Hill, 1944–46), provides an insider's account of the navy and the Cabinet, but better still is E. David Cronon, editor, *The Cabinet Diaries of Josephus Daniels* (Lincoln, Nebraska, 1963). The authorized biography of Baker, based on his papers and correspondence, is Frederick Palmer, *Newton Baker,* 2 volumes (New York, 1931).

Arthur S. Link's *Wilson: The Struggle for Neutrality, 1914–1915* (Princeton, 1960) and *Wilson: Campaigns for Progressivism and Peace* (Princeton, 1965) chart the president's tortuous path toward intervention most sympathetically, defending Wilson at every turn. These volumes are as much about the age, however, as the man. Arthur Walworth's *Woodrow Wilson,* 2 volumes (New York, 1965), is a prize-winning biography that never takes its eyes off its subject for long. Ernest R. May's *The World War and American Isolation 1914–1917* (Cambridge, Massachusetts, 1979) is an excellent study of the pressures on Wilson for intervention.

Walter Millis, *The Road to War* (Boston, 1935), attributes intervention to foreign loans, business investments overseas, and British propaganda. Charles C. Tansill, *America Goes to War* (Boston, 1938), places the blame on Wall Street as firmly as it has ever been put. Charles Seymour, *America's Diplomacy During the World War* (Baltimore, 1934), just as strongly places the onus on Germany's determination to win the war by means of the U-boat.

Modern scholars take a more nuanced, less impassioned view, as exemplified by the coolly reasoned Ross Gregory, *The Origins of American Intervention in the First World War* (New York, 1971).

12. A Learning Army

Frank Freidel's *Over There* (Boston, 1964) is a good introduction to America's role in the war; copiously illustrated. Edward M. Coffman, *The War to End All Wars* (New York, 1968), provides by far the best general account of the war as seen from Washington and Chaumont.

John J. Pershing's *My Experiences in the World War* (New York, 1931) is based on his wartime diaries. This has given the book a reputation for being difficult to read, yet it does give a good idea of how the war unfolded from Pershing's point of view. Donald Smythe's *Pershing: General of the Armies* (Bloomington, Indiana, 1986) is by the acknowledged authority on Black Jack. Its major revelation is Pershing's colorful private life.

Peyton C. March's *The Nation at War* (Garden City, New York, 1932) is the work of a man who served his country well but himself badly with this memoir filled, as it is, with spiteful envy of Pershing.

Daniel R. Beaver, *Newton D. Baker and the American War Effort* (Lincoln,

Nebraska, 1966) tells a story that is half the labors of Hercules, half the legend of Sisyphus.

Robert D. Cuff's *The War Industries Board* (Baltimore, 1973) is a highly critical account of the wartime alliance of business and government. Paul A. C. Koistinen, *The Military-Industrial Complex* (New York, 1980), places the rise of this phenomenon squarely in that alliance, and claims it has undermined military professionalism ever since.

Josephus Daniels, *Our Navy at War* (Washington, D.C., 1922), provides a view from the top of the scope and depth of the navy's achievements. William S. Sims and Burton J. Hendrick's *The Victory at Sea* (Garden City, New York, 1920) is devoted mainly to the war against the U-boats. So too is a firsthand account by Joseph K. Taussig, "Destroyer Experiences in the Great War," *US Naval Institute Proceedings* XLVIII, No. 12 (December 1922) and XLIX, Nos. 1–3 (January–March 1922).

William Mitchell's *Memoirs of World War I* (New York, 1960) is an essential source on the air war. The best biography of Mitchell is Alfred F. Hurley's *Billy Mitchell: Crusader for Air Power,* revised edition (Bloomington, Indiana, 1975), which lauds his vision but criticizes his methods. The Hurley biography completely supplants the hagiographic *Flying Crusader* by Isaac Don Levine (New York, 1943), a piece of patriotic mood music written in wartime.

Benjamin D. Foulois's *From the Wright Brothers to the Astronauts* (New York, 1968) is the memoir of a onetime chief of the Air Corps and deals mainly with World War One. It is a valuable corrective to some of Mitchell's flights of fancy. James J. Hudson's *Hostile Skies: A Combat History of the American Air Service in World War One* (Syracuse, New York, 1968) is a fine, scholarly account that is as reliable as it is readable.

Eddie V. Rickenbacker's *Fighting the Flying Circus* (Garden City, New York, 1965) is a splendid, down-to-earth memoir, utterly free of false heroics and false modesty.

James G. Harbord's *The American Army in France* (Boston, 1936) amounts to a semiofficial history of the AEF. Lawrence Stallings's *The Doughboys* (New York, 1963) is by a former marine officer seriously wounded at Belleau Wood. Written with tremendous verve, this is indisputably the best general account of the war as the footsloggers knew it.

The American Battlefields Monuments Commission's *American Armies and Battlefields in Europe* (Washington, D.C., 1938) was written, anonymously, in large part by Dwight Eisenhower. It contains reliable accounts of all the big battles, and many of the smaller engagements, involving American forces. Robert B. Asprey's *At Belleau Wood* (New York, 1965) is a careful reconstruction of this famous struggle. A German view is to be found in Ernst Otto, "The Battles for Belleau Wood," *US Naval Institute Proceedings,* LIV (1928), by a German officer who fought there.

It was long believed that because of the unpleasant Pershing-March feud fought out in their memoirs the fastidious George C. Marshall chose not to write of his own experiences in the war. Then, after resting forty years in an attic, a manuscript was found that proved the opposite was true: George C. Marshall, *Memoirs of My Service in the World War* (Boston, 1976). It contains no shattering revelations and attacks no one's reputation, but is valuable for all that. Forrest Pogue, *Marshall: The Education of a General 1880–1939* (New York, 1963), makes clear how important Marshall's role was within the AEF despite his modest rank of colonel.

Douglas MacArthur's *Reminiscences* (New York, 1964) contains some telling anecdotes of his experiences on the western front. For a thorough and objective account, however, the reader has to turn to D. Clayton James, *The Years of MacArthur,* volume 1 (Boston, 1970).

Hunter Liggett's *Commanding an American Army* (Boston, 1925) is written with characteristic forcefulness and perception. Robert Bullard, *Personalities and Reminiscences of the War* (Garden City, New York, 1925), is outspoken about everything that involved his command, including his fellow generals. He is also the subject of a good biography: Allen R. Millett, *The General: Robert L. Bullard and Officership in the US Army 1881–1925* (Westport, Connecticut, 1975).

Maury Maverick's *A Maverick American* (New York, 1937) is an autobiography that contains a vivid account of his time as an officer in the AEF.

Florette Henri, *The Unknown Soldiers: Black American Troops in World War I* (Philadelphia, 1974), fills a gap too long ignored.

George G. Bruntz's *Allied Propaganda and the Collapse of the German Empire in 1918* (Palo Alto, 1938) provides a valuable account of one of the more important but neglected elements in eventual German defeat.

Frederick L. Paxson's *America at War 1917–1918* (Boston, 1939) was long the standard narrative of life on the home front. It has been supplanted by David M. Kennedy, *Over Here* (New York, 1980), and Edward Ellis, *Echoes of a Distant Thunder* (New York, 1974).

John Dos Passos's *Mr. Wilson's War* (Garden City, New York, 1962) is a brightly colored account of both the home front and the western front, showing how events on the one profoundly affected events on the other.

Robert H. Ferrell, *Woodrow Wilson and World War I: 1917–1921* (New York, 1985), is concerned mainly with the consequences of the war, both at home and abroad. Ferrell portrays Wilson as a man overwhelmed by great events. Paul L. Murphy, *World War I and the Origin of Civil Liberties in the US* (New York, 1979), focuses on one of the least expected, more ironic legacies of the war.

13. Sun Day

The Washington Conference is examined in depth in Harold M. Sprout and Margaret Sprout, *Toward a New Order of Sea Power* (Princeton, 1943). Norman Polmar, *Aircraft Carriers* (London, 1968), provides the best—and best-illustrated—history of the development of the carrier. Walter Turnbull and Archibald Lord's *A History of Naval Aviation* (Princeton, 1950) is good as far as it goes, which is up to 1941.

There is a fine biography of Nimitz that offers some valuable insights into the interwar navy: E. B. Potter, *Nimitz* (Annapolis, 1976).

The Marine Corps's long and careful preparation for World War Two takes up much of Robert Debs Heinl, *Soldiers of the Sea* (Annapolis, 1962). Heinl, a marine officer, was one of those involved in this effort. John A. Lejeune's *Reminiscences of a Marine* (Philadelphia, 1930) is both a memoir of his war experiences in France and a cogent expression of how he was trying to prepare the Corps for a war he was certain was coming.

Burke Davis, *Marine! The Life of Chesty Puller* (Boston, 1962), narrates how officers such as Puller spent much of the interwar period fighting in the Caribbean and Nicaragua. Lester D. Langley's *The Banana Wars* (Lexington, Kentucky, 1985) is a useful general account of these struggles, showing that American soldiers, sailors and marines did all that was asked of them, but failed in one crucial respect: they were not cut out to rule foreigners.

William Mitchell, *Winged Defense* (New York, 1925), offers the Mitchellian vision in all its optimism. Volume 1 of R. Frank Futrell's *Ideas, Concepts, Doctrines: A History of Basic Thinking in the United States Air Force 1907–1971* (Maxwell Air Force Base, 1971) is the official history. It provides an excellent account of the development of air force doctrine at the Tactical School between the world wars. Burke Davis, *The Billy Mitchell Affair* (New York, 1967), effectively debunks many of the myths that sprang up around this unfortunate episode.

Benjamin Foulois's *From the Wright Brothers to the Astronauts* (New York, 1968) is the memoir of the first chief of the Air Corps. His successor is the subject of an excellent biography: Thomas M. Coffey, *HAP* (New York, 1982). The struggle to get a genuine heavy bomber for the new corps is considered in some detail in Robert Krauskopf, "The Army and the Heavy Bomber 1930–1939," *Military Affairs,* XXII (Summer 1958; Winter 1958–59).

On MacArthur, his powerful, eloquent but less than reliable memoir, *Reminiscences* (New York, 1964), must constantly be referred to D. Clayton James's magisterial *The Years of MacArthur,* 3 volumes (Boston 1970–84), for confirmation. The sorry tale of the failure to exploit an American breakthrough in tank technology is explained in George Hoffmann, "A Yankee Inventor and the Military Establishment" *Military Affairs,* XXXVII (Spring 1975).

The best biography of Eisenhower during his military career is Stephen Ambrose, *Eisenhower: The Soldier* (New York, 1983). There is also a massive oral biography: Merle Miller's *Ike the Soldier* (New York, 1986). On Marshall, Forrest Pogue, *George C. Marshall: The Education of a General* (New York, 1963), takes him up to his appointment as chief of staff. The subsequent volume, *George C. Marshall: Ordeal and Hope* (New York, 1966), covers the period up to the North African landings.

Henry L. Stimson, with McGeorge Bundy, *On Active Service in Peace and*

War (Boston, 1948), is an essential source on the War Department's struggle for preparedness after war began in Europe. The standard biography of this remarkable man is Elting B. Morrison, *Turmoil and Tradition: A Study of the Life and Times of Henry L. Stimson* (New York, 1960).

Of the many works that deal in one way or another with the conflicts between isolationists and interventionists, two that are reliable and dispassionate are Wayne S. Cole, *America First: The Battle Against Intervention* (Madison, Wisconsin, 1953), and Robert A. Divine, *The Reluctant Belligerent* (New York, 1965).

On the navy's preparations for war—as on everything else affecting the navy in World War Two—the most authoritative synoptic account is Samuel E. Morison's *The Two-Ocean War* (Boston, 1963), a work summarizing the 15-volume official history, which Morison wrote. The timely development of the fleet submarine is described by one of the men responsible for it: Charles A. Lockwood, *Down to the Sea in Subs* (New York, 1970). For the development of the other major naval weapon of the war, see Clark G. Reynolds, *The Fast Carriers* (New York, 1968). Thomas C. Hone, "Battleships v. Aircraft Carriers," *Military Affairs,* XLI (Fall 1977), effectively demolishes the myth that carriers were neglected for the sake of battlewagons on the run-up to war.

W. J. Holmes's *Double-Edged Secrets* (Annapolis, 1979) is an enthralling account of breaking Japanese codes, by someone who did it. Edwin T. Layton et al., *"And I Was There"* (New York, 1985), is another insider's account. Ronald W. Clark's *The Man Who Broke Purple* (New York, 1977) is a biography of one of the pioneers of American cryptography, William Friedman. Ronald Lewin's *The American Magic* (New York, 1982) is a clear, well-written overall account of this complicated business. Roberta Wohlstetter's *Pearl Harbor: Warning and Decision* (Palo Alto, 1962) is a subtle, creative study of why even superb signals intelligence is no guarantee against a disaster.

Paul S. Dull's *The Imperial Japanese Navy* (Annapolis, 1978) is based on a careful study of Japanese naval archives. It offers a good picture of the Imperial Japanese Navy, and its leaders, on the eve of war.

Gordon W. Prange et al., *At Dawn We Slept* (New York, 1981), is an absorbing, well-written and exhaustive account of the Pearl Harbor attack, from original conception to ultimate execution.

John Toland, *Infamy: Pearl Harbor and Its Aftermath* (New York, 1982), claims that Roosevelt, Stimson, Marshall and Knox knew Pearl Harbor was about to be attacked, and did nothing to prevent it. This is a work for those who believe in conspiracy rather than confusion, and in hearsay rather than evidence.

Walter Lord, *Day of Infamy* (New York, 1957), offers a vivid narrative of the attack as recollected by those on the ground. Yet here too Gordon W. Prange et al., *December 7, 1941* (New York, 1986), is the nearest thing to a definitive version.

14. The Best-Laid Plans

There is only one work in English on the Japanese army: Saburo Hayashi and Alvin D. Coox, *Kogun* (Westport, Connecticut, 1978). John Toland's *The Rising Sun* (New York, 1970) is an effective, prize-winning account of the war from the Japanese side, with some sharp sketches of leading generals and admirals.

Louis Morton's *The Fall of the Philippines* (Washington, D.C., 1953) is the official U.S. Army version. Rarely has a national humiliation been described so brilliantly.

MacArthur's *Reminiscences* are never more misleading than in dealing with this calamity. Volume 2 of D. Clayton James's *The Years of MacArthur* (Boston, 1975) contains a meticulous, lucid account. James H. Belote and William M. Belote's *Corregidor: Saga of a Fortress* (New York, 1967) is also valuable. Daniel Harrington's "A Careless Hope: American Air Power and Japan 1941," *Pacific Historical Review*, XLVIII (May 1979), is a useful study of the illusions about air power that only added to the problems of defending the Philippines.

E. B. Potter, *Nimitz* (Annapolis, 1976), portrays the admiral as the most engaging of men while being a talented manager of mighty—and mightily far-flung—naval forces.

The works by Holmes and Layton are essential accounts of the signals intelligence war in the Pacific. Valuable too is Ronald Lewin's *The Other Ultra* (New York, 1984).

Gordon W. Prange et al., *Miracle at Midway* (New York, 1982), is the most complete study of this epic battle, unearthing considerable new evidence. Valuable too is the account in Dull's *The Imperial Japanese Navy* for its insights into the effect of Japanese interservice rivalry on this, as on all other major, operations.

There is a competent telling of the tale by two Japanese participants in the battle: Mitsuo Fuchida and Masatake Okumiya, *Midway: The Battle That Doomed Japan* (Annapolis, 1956). Walter Lord, *Incredible Victory* (New York, 1967), provides a thrilling narrative based on extensive interviews.

Thomas B. Buell's *The Quiet Warrior* (Boston, 1974) is the standard biography of Spruance. It is a notably fine piece of work and makes it clear that it was Spruance's tactics that brought victory.

The official history of Marine Corps operations in 1942 is Frank E. Hough et al., *Pearl Harbor to Guadalcanal* (Washington, D.C., 1958). Jeter A. Isely and Philip Crowl, *US Marines and Amphibious War* (Princeton, 1950), cover Guadalcanal, and all other marine assaults, with a depth of analysis that makes this one of the quintessential works on the Pacific war.

There is an evocative account of what Guadalcanal was like to one ordinary marine in William Manchester's *Goodbye, Darkness* (New York, 1981).

On the carrier battles in the South Pacific, there is a good memoir from a man who commanded several famous carriers in the course of the war: Frederick C. Sherman, *Combat Command* (New York, 1950).

Morison's *The Two-Ocean War* is masterly, yet it has a blind spot—fast carrier operations. This is a lacuna more than adequately filled in by the superb *Fast Carriers* by Clarke G. Reynolds (New York, 1968), a thorough, well-balanced account of these ships and the men who commanded them. Polmar's *Aircraft Carriers* concentrates, inevitably, on U.S. Navy carriers in the Pacific war.

There is an interesting article on the capital ship they displaced: Malcolm Muir, Jr., "The Misuse of the Fast Battleship in World War II," *US Naval Institute Proceedings,* CV (February 1979). This amounts to a summary of fast battleship operations in the Pacific.

Eric Larrabee, *Commander in Chief* (New York, 1987), focuses on FDR's relationships with his senior military commanders, and emphasizes the president's role in the Torch decision. Forrest Pogue's meticulously researched *George C. Marshall: Ordeal and Hope, 1939–1942* (New York, 1966), charts the tortuous route to Torch and makes clear Marshall's misgivings about it.

Kent Roberts Greenfield, editor, *Command Decisions* (Washington, D.C., 1959), analyzes all the major strategic decisions made by the Allies. Useful too is Maurice Matloff's "The American Approach to War 1939–1945," in Michael Howard, editor, *The Theory and Practice of War* (London, 1965).

Patrick Beesly's *Very Special Intelligence* (London, 1977) is an authoritative personal account of the Admiralty's ultimately successful attack on German naval codes. One of Beesly's coworkers subsequently edited the British official history of Ultra and related intelligence operations: F. H. Hinsley, *British Intelligence in the Second World War,* 3 volumes (London, 1979–88).

William T. Y'Blood's *Hunter-Killer* (Annapolis, 1983) is the most complete accounts of the CVEs and a good general introduction to the antisubmarine campaign. On the development of radar and other high-tech devices: James Phinney Baxter III, *Scientists Against Time* (Boston, 1946); J. G. Crowther and R. Whiddington, *Science at War* (London, 1948); and Ralph Baldwin, *The Deadly Fuze* (London, 1985).

Ernest J. King and Walter Muir Whitehill's *Fleet Admiral King* (New York, 1952) is the authorized version of King's wartime activities. It is as austere and buttoned-up as its subject. To find out what King really did the reader has to turn to the biography by Thomas Buell, *Master of Sea Power* (Boston, 1980), which is sympathetic toward King without being admiring.

Stephen Ambrose's *The Supreme Commander: The War Years of General Dwight D. Eisenhower* (Baltimore, 1970) and *Eisenhower: The Soldier* (New York, 1983) are essential. Robert H. Ferrell, editor, *The Eisenhower Diaries* (New York, 1981) is so studiously unrevealing on contentious issues that Eisenhower seems to have anticipated eventual publication. Nor is there a great deal of enlightenment to be gleaned from Dwight D. Eisenhower's *At Ease* (Garden City, New York, 1967), Ike's episodic autobiography.

Ladislas Farago, *Patton: Ordeal and Triumph* (New York, 1964), offers some memorable glimpses of Patton. Martin Blumenson's *Patton* (New York, 1985) is a short biography that nonetheless does Patton much justice. Blumenson's biography of Clark, *Mark Clark* (New York, 1984), offers a fierce defense of Clark against his many critics.

Omar N. Bradley's *A Soldier's Story* (New York, 1951) was frank for its day, but better by far is his autobiography written with considerable assistance from Clay Blair, *A General's Life* (New York, 1985).

Charles B. MacDonald's *The Mighty Endeavor* (New York, 1969) is the most reliable, most readable general account of American ground forces from North Africa to Berlin. Ernie Pyle's *Here Is Your War* (New York, 1944) contains some wonderful incidents from the North African venture—the poignant, the funny, the unexpected, the illuminating.

15. A World of Sand

There is an authoritative, extended discussion of assault shipping in James A. Huston, *The Sinews of War* (Washington, D.C., 1966). The vital issues of priorities in construction and the constraints imposed by shortages of landing craft are made clear—along with much else—in Robert W. Coakley and Richard M. Leighton, *Global Logistics and Strategy, 1943–45* (Washington, D.C., 1969).

On Roosevelt's influence on strategy making at Casablanca, and elsewhere: James MacGregor Burns, *Roosevelt: The Soldier of Freedom* (New York, 1970), and Eric Larrabee, *Commander-in-Chief* (New York, 1987). On the part played by the JCS in these matters, see Grace Person Hayes's *The History of the Joint Chiefs of Staff in World War II* (Annapolis, 1982).

George S. Patton's *War as I Knew It* (Boston, 1947) is, for Patton, a somewhat anodyne account of his part in the war. A much better idea of what he really thought of his superiors and his allies can be found in Martin Blumenson, *The Patton Papers, 1940–45* (Boston, 1974). A sample of the general's style in front of his men is to be found in "Patton's Farewell Address to His Troops" in the August 1945 issue of *Politics*.

The essential account of Patton's great rival in Sicily, and later, is Nigel Hamilton, *Monty: Master of the Battlefield* (London, 1983), even though it is an extended act of veneration.

Mildred H. Gillie's *Forging the Thunderbolt* (Harrisburg, Pennsylvania, 1947) is the standard account of the development of American armored forces. Richard Ogorkiewicz's *Armoured Forces* (London, 1970) contains an excellent summary of the American contribution to armored warfare in World War Two.

Mark Clark's *Calculated Risk* (New York, 1950) is one of the best memoirs to emerge from the Mediterranean theater but is at times on the disingenuous side. Lucian K. Truscott's *Command Missions* (New York, 1954) is a franker, less defensive memoir of the fighting in Italy, by one of the ablest division and corps commanders in the army.

Fred Majdalany's *The Battle of Cassino* (London, 1957) is a splendid study of the campaign by a British officer who participated in it. John Ellis, *Cassino: Hollow Victory* (London, 1984), is scathing toward both Clark and Alexander. The most satisfying general account presenting these events from the perspectives of all the major participants is David Hapgood and David Richardson, *Monte Cassino* (New York, 1984).

To make sense of any of the important ground operations in Europe or the Pacific, volume 2 of Vincent J. Esposito, editor, *The West Point Atlas of American Wars* (New York, 1959), is an essential reference tool.

For the island-hopping push across the Pacific in 1943–44: Potter, Reynolds, Morison, Isely and Crowl, Dull, and the Marine Corps official histories; Henry I. Shaw et al., *The Isolation of Rabaul* (Washington, D.C., 1958) and *Central Pacific Drive* (Washington, D.C., 1966). There is also a fine, synoptic account that manages to say something significant about nearly every aspect of the Pacific war: Ronald Spector, *Eagle Against the Sun* (New York, 1985).

Howlin' Mad produced a characteristically outspoken memoir: Holland M. Smith, with Percy Finch, *Coral and Brass* (New York, 1949). The uneasy relationship of marines and soldiers in these campaigns is explored in Harry A. Gailey's *Howlin' Mad vs. The Army* (San Rafael, California, 1986), which centers on the relief of Ralph Smith.

Robert Sherrod's *A History of Marine Aviation in World War II* (Washington, D.C., 1952) is a semiofficial account of the marines' frustrating struggle to do things their own way. Gregory Boyington, a marine fighter pilot, produced one of the war's more remarkable memoirs, *Baa Baa Black Sheep* (New York, 1958), in which his shortcomings are mercilessly exposed. It is nonetheless an absorbing narrative of aerial combat. The Japanese equivalent is Masatake Okumiya and Jiro Horikoshi's *Zero!* (New York, 1956), a fascinating book on what it was like to fly against American pilots.

Arnold attempted to tell his own story in H. H. Arnold's *Global Mission* (New York, 1949), an unusually dull work coming from so colorful a figure. Better by far is the biography by Thomas Coffey, *HAP* (New York, 1982). Valuable too are a pair of articles by an Arnold protégé: Lawrence Kuter, "How Hap Arnold Built the AAF," *Air Force,* LVI (September 1973), and "The General vs the Establishment," *Aerospace Historian,* XXII (Winter 1974).

There is a workmanlike biography of Ira Eaker by his wartime aide and confidant James Parton: *"Air Force Spoken Here"* (Bethesda, Maryland, 1986).

John Comer's *Combat Crew* (New York, 1988) is a gripping personal account of the air war over Germany in 1943 as experienced by the crew of a B-17. John Muirhead's *Those Who Fall* (New York, 1986) is a memoir by a B-17 pilot flying missions from southern Italy in 1943–44; a remarkable work suffused with poetry and terror. Roger Freeman, editor, *Mustang at*

War (Garden City, New York, 1974) is an interesting, well-illustrated book written mainly by wartime Mustang pilots and ground crew.

Ronald Schaffer's *Wings of Judgment* (New York, 1985) is a study of strategic bombing in World War Two that is one of the best examples of the new approach to military history. Schaffer's work is sophisticated, lucid and objective. Similarly, R. J. Overy, *The Air War 1939–1945* (London, 1980), provides a trenchant comparative analysis of Allied and Axis handling of the air weapon.

Wesley F. Craven and James L. Cate's *The Army Air Forces in World War II,* 7 volumes (Chicago, 1950–51), is the official history and therefore an important source. Its defects, however, have been exposed by the researches of scholars such as Schaffer. Michael S. Sherry's *The Rise of American Air Power* (New Haven, 1987) is both a study of strategic bombing in World War Two and a strong protest against it.

On Marshall, the essential account for this period is Forrest C. Pogue's splendid, *George C. Marshall: Organizer of Victory 1943–45* (New York, 1973).

The official army history of D-Day, Gordon Harrison's *Cross-Channel Attack* (Washington, D.C., 1951), is excellent. It follows the fighting as far as the capture of Cherbourg. The crucial intelligence operations are described authoritatively in volume 3, part 2 of F. H. Hinsley's *British Intelligence in the Second World War: Its Influence on Strategy and Operations* (London, 1988).

Two reliable accounts of the signals intelligence success that played a key role in the European Theater are F. W. Witherbotham, *The Ultra Secret* (New York, 1974) and Ralph Bennett, *Ultra in the West* (London, 1979).

There is a good, best-selling account by Cornelius Ryan, *The Longest Day* (New York, 1959). S.L.A. Marshall's "First Wave at Omaha Beach," *Atlantic Monthly,* November 1960, offers a reminder of how a small number of brave men can produce a large measure of victory.

The airborne element of the D-Day operation is recalled in James M. Gavin, *On to Berlin* (New York, 1978) and Maxwell Taylor, *Swords and Plowshares* (New York, 1972). Gerard M. Devlin's *Paratrooper!* (New York, 1979) is a good history of the airborne. Clay Blair's *Ridgway's Paratroopers* (New York, 1985) focuses on the most impressive of the airborne generals, yet also serves as a first-rate narrative account of American airborne operations throughout the European theater.

The struggles in the *bocage* and marshes are analyzed with clarity and subtlety in John Keegan, *Six Armies in Normandy* (London, 1982). A valuable German point of view is provided by Hans Speidel, *Invasion 1944* (Chicago, 1950). Speidel was Rommel's chief of staff.

Russell F. Weigley's *Eisenhower's Lieutenants* (Bloomington, Indiana, 1981) is the work of a military historian at the height of his powers. Highly critical of American generalship, it follows the course of American armies from the Normandy beaches to the Elbe.

Other essential accounts of the breakout and pursuit include Bradley and Blair, Patton on Patton, Blumenson on Patton, Ambrose, Hamilton, and

Dwight D. Eisenhower's *Crusade in Europe* (Garden City, New York, 1948). A work by his grandson, David Eisenhower, *Eisenhower at War 1943–1945* (New York, 1986), is a massively detailed study of Ike as supreme commander. On his turbulent relationship with Monty: Nigel Hamilton's *Montgomery: The Field Marshall* (London, 1986), but any work that portrays Eisenhower as suffering from "insanity"—see page 269—has serious problems of its own.

For a pioneering analysis of SHAEF's logistical difficulties and the effects of these on Allied operations, see Martin Van Creveld, *Supplying War: Logistics from Wallenstein to Patton* (Westport, Connecticut, 1978).

16. Irresistible Force

On Market Garden: Eisenhower, Gavin, Bradley and Blair, Hamilton, Weigley; Blair, *Ridgway's Paratroopers;* Hinsley, volume 3, part 2; and a meticulous popular account, Cornelius Ryan, *A Bridge Too Far* (New York, 1974).

There are two near-definitive accounts of the Bulge: Hugh M. Cole, *The Ardennes: Battle of the Bulge* (Washington, D.C., 1965), the official army history; and Charles B. MacDonald, *A Time for Trumpets* (New York, 1984), by a former army historian, and company commander in the battle. Valuable for its interviews with many high-ranking officers involved on both sides is John S. D. Eisenhower's *The Bitter Woods* (New York, 1969).

The commander of the Pacific submarine force that wreaked so much devastation wrote a useful memoir: Charles A. Lockwood, *Down to the Sea in Subs* (New York, 1967). The most complete history of this underseas onslaught is Clay Blair's *Silent Victory* (Philadelphia, 1963), by a former enlisted submariner in the Pacific war.

The bitterness submarine commanders felt over their malfunctioning torpedoes is conveyed strongly in Edward L. Beach, "Culpable Negligence," *American Heritage,* XXXII, No. 1 (December 1980). The futility of Japanese efforts to find and destroy the fleet submarines is made clear by Atsushi Oi, a former Japanese naval officer, in "Why Japan's Anti-Submarine Warfare Failed," *US Naval Institute Proceedings,* LXXVIII (June 1952).

The unnecessary assault on Peleliu is described by Isely and Crowl, Holland Smith; Burke Davis, *Marine!;* and volume 4 of the official Marine Corps history of the Pacific campaigns, George W. Garland and Truman R. Strobridge's *Western Pacific Operations* (Washington, D.C., 1971). There is also a vivid personal account in Manchester, *Goodbye, Darkness* (New York, 1979).

On MacArthur's return to the Philippines: MacArthur, James, Toland's *Rising Sun,* and a good general account by Stanley Falk, *The Liberation of the Philippines* (New York, 1971).

Naval operations are described and analyzed by Potter, Morison, Reynolds, Sherman, Buell and Dull. For the recollections of an ordinary sailor, serving aboard a cruiser: James F. Fahey, *Pacific War Diary* (Boston, 1963).

C. Vann Woodward's *The Battle for Leyte Gulf* (New York, 1947) is a masterly account of this huge, complex battle.

Volume 4 of the official marine history covers Iwo Jima in depth. A thorough personal account is Bill D. Ross's *Iwo Jima* (New York, 1985), by a marine combat correspondent who was there from start to finish.

The two key works on Okinawa are Roy Appleman et al., *Okinawa: The Last Battle* (Washington, D.C., 1958), the official army history, and not one of the best; and James Belote and William Belote, *Typhoon of Steel* (New York, 1970), which is excellent.

Curtis E. LeMay, with MacKinlay Kantor, *Mission with LeMay* (Garden City, New York, 1965), is remarkably frank, and keen to counter the belief that LeMay had no conscience and little humanity. Thomas M. Coffey's *Iron Eagle* (New York, 1986) is based on many long interviews with LeMay. It is a major contribution to the history of the air war.

Paul Schaffer's *Wings of Judgment* (New York, 1985) and Michael S. Sherry's *The Rise of American Air Power* (New Haven, 1987) are important studies of the bombing of Japan. Both challenge long-established beliefs about how crucial decisions were made. There is also an interesting article, George Hopkins's "Bombing and the American Conscience in World War II," *Historian*, XXVII (May 1966), which charts the steps by which the unthinkable became the inevitable.

William H. Morrison's *Point of No Return* (New York, 1979) is a sound popular history of the brief life and spectacular deeds of the Twentieth Air Force.

The Manhattan Project has excited renewed interest in the 1980s; one manifestation of the rising concern over nuclear weapons. The result has been the publication of major reappraisals of the effort to build the Bomb and the decision to use it. Two outstanding examples are Peter Wyden's *Day One* (New York, 1984) and Richard Rhodes's *The Making of the Atomic Bomb* (New York, 1987). Both are strong on the human interest side.

The official history, written under the auspices of the AEC, takes a different approach, as might be expected, yet it is a model of its kind—well written, objective and thorough: Richard Hewlett and Oscar F. Anderson, Jr., *The New World, 1939–1946* (University Park, Pennsylvania, 1962). The memoirs of Leslie R. Groves, *Now It Can Be Told* (New York, 1962), give a decidedly partial version of events, but one that cannot be ignored.

There is a wonderfully subtle and penetrating biography of Groves's principal antagonist, the tormented Robert J. Oppenheimer: Nuel Pharr Davis, *Lawrence and Oppenheimer* (New York, 1968).

On the decision to use the Bomb and the selection of targets, Stimson's memoir is a primary source. Truman offered his own version in volume 1 of his presidential memoirs, *Year of Decisions* (Garden City, New York, 1956), and in Merle Miller's *Plain Speaking* (New York, 1973).

His daughter's gushy biography of her adored father also contains a leading account: Margaret Truman, *Harry S. Truman* (New York, 1973). Robert H. Ferrell, editor, *Off the Record: The Private Papers of Harry S. Truman* (New York, 1980), presents a Truman more doubtful, more anxious over the Bomb than he cared to admit.

All the official histories contain evaluations of how American servicemen and women performed under the stress of war, nowhere more so than in Ulysses Lee, *The Employment of Negro Troops* (Washington, D.C., 1966). Kent Roberts Greenfield, *The Historian and the Army* (New Brunswick, New Jersey, 1954), summarizes some of the more important conclusions of the 96-volume official army history.

S.L.A. Marshall's *Men Against Fire* (Washington, D.C., 1947) is one of the most influential works ever written on combat performance by American troops, claiming that no more than 20 percent or so actually fired their weapons at the enemy. Martin Van Creveld's *Fighting Power* (Westport, Connecticut, 1982) is a comparative study of the American army and the German army in World War Two which makes some cogent observations on how each managed the men it sent into battle.

The tools of the modern social scientist were applied in two pioneering studies of what motivated Americans to fight—or not to fight: Samuel A. Stouffer et al., *The American Soldier*, 2 volumes (Princeton, 1949), and Eli Ginzberg et al., *The Ineffective Soldier*, 3 volumes (New York, 1959).

J. Glenn Gray's *The Warriors: Reflections on Men in Battle* (New York, 1958) is a moving philosophical inquiry into motivation by a former ETO infantryman, based on his own experiences and those of the people he knew.

It is a lasting pity that the autobiographical account from the most highly decorated soldier of the war, Audie Murphy, *To Hell and Back* (New York, 1949), is a ghost-written exercise in mediocrity. Ernie Pyle's *Brave Men* (New York, 1945) captures the ordinary soldier, sailor, airman and marine as he was, in a parade of striking vignettes.

Harold P. Leinbaugh and John D. Campbell's *The Men of Company K* (New York, 1985) is an inspiring "autobiography" of a rifle company that portrays men overcoming terrible hardships and dangers mainly by their loyalty to one another.

Regarding the home front: Richard R. Lingeman's *Don't You Know There's a War On?* (New York, 1971), is a breezy exercise in nostalgia. John Morton Blum, *When V Was for Victory* (New York, 1978), considers the war's effects on politics and culture. My own *Days of Sadness, Years of Triumph* (New York, 1973) is a broadly based social history that seeks to re-create the period and offer an appraisal of it.

17. War Without Parallel

The role of the atomic bomb in Truman's foreign policy has been sharply criticized by some scholars. Gar Alperowitz, *Atomic Diplomacy* (New York,

1965), and Martin J. Sherwin, *A World Destroyed* (New York, 1975), contend that American efforts to wring political advantage from the monopoly of the Bomb were responsible for the Cold War. Such arguments minimize the part played by Stalin, whose official Soviet biographer in 1988 described him as "a madman and a criminal."

It was a long time before a well-balanced and objective assessment of the atomic bomb's part in the emergence of the Cold War was published, but the result was a work of distinction: Gregg Herken, *The Winning Weapon* (New York, 1985).

Bernard Baruch, *The Public Years* (New York, 1960), and David E. Lilienthal, *The Journals of David E. Lilienthal,* volume 2 (New York, 1964), describe their own roles in the effort to find ways of controlling the Bomb. The attempt made by scientists to keep nuclear arms under civilian control is narrated best by Alice Kimball Smith, *A Peril and a Hope* (Chicago, 1965). The effort to ban the Bomb by agreement is the subject of another distinguished work: Joseph T. Lieberman, *The Scorpion and the Tarantula* (Boston, 1970).

Truman accounts for himself in this period in the second volume of his presidential memoirs, titled *Years of Trial and Hope* (New York, 1956). The two volumes of Robert J. Donovan's *The Presidency of Harry S Truman* (New York, 1977–82) give a more complete account. The biographer's admiration for Truman is clear on nearly every page. A more critical, and in some respects still unsurpassed, portrait is contained in an earlier work, Cabell Phillips, *The Truman Presidency* (New York, 1966).

George F. Kennan, *Memoirs, 1925–1950* (Boston, 1967), describes his crucial role not only in the development of containment but in other important initiatives such as the Marshall Plan. Herbert Feis, *From Trust to Terror* (New York, 1970), describes the onset of the Cold War as seen from the State Department. Louis J. Halle's *The Cold War as History* (London, 1967) is one of the best surveys of this contentious subject, with a sharp eye for the bizarre, the unexpected and the telling detail.

The creation of the Department of Defense plays a large part in Richard Haynes, *The Awesome Power: Harry S Truman as Commander in Chief* (Baton Rouge, Louisiana, 1974). The doomed Forrestal's sense of being overwhelmed, as well of his high patriotism, informs Walter Millis and E. S. Duffield, editors, *The Forrestal Diaries* (New York, 1951).

There are some good glimpses of the DOD and the people who ran it in the early years in a book by the Pentagon correspondent of *The New York Times* in the period: Jack Raymond, *Power at the Pentagon* (New York, 1964).

Nearly forty years after NSC-68 was drafted it has not been made public, but there is little doubt about what it had to say. See John L. Gaddis and Paul Nitze, "NSC-68 and the Soviet Threat Reconsidered," *International Security,* Spring 1980.

Dean G. Acheson, *Present at the Creation* (New York, 1969), offers an important contribution to the literature on the Cold War, not least on the decision to fight in Korea. That decision is trenchantly analyzed in Glen D. Paige, *The Korean Decision June 24–30, 1950* (Glencoe, Illinois, 1968).

Volume 3 of D. Clayton James's *The Years of MacArthur* (Boston, 1984) covers the general's post–World War Two experiences, in which Korea inevitably predominates. James F. Schnabel's *Policy and Direction: The First Year* (Washington, D.C., 1972) is one of the official army histories of the Korean War. It offers an authoritative account of the first twelve months of the conflict as the fledgling DOD tried to get control of it. Omar N. Bradley was chairman of the JCS at the time. His recollections are to be found in Omar N. Bradley and Clay Blair, *A General's Life* (New York, 1983). Bradley's approach to Korea was, as he makes clear, strongly influenced by his distrust of MacArthur. These memoirs also contradict the myth that Bradley called Korea "the wrong war, in the wrong place, at the wrong time, against the wrong enemy." He believed as strongly as anyone that the North Korean invasion had to be checked. Lawrence J. Korb's *The Joint Chiefs of Staff* (Bloomington, Indiana, 1976) is an academic study that finds the JCS more or less impotent and vacillating throughout the Korean War.

Roy E. Appleman's *South to the Naktong, North to the Yalu* (Washington, D.C., 1961) is the splendidly lucid official history of ground combat in the first five months of the war. It is the starting point for nearly every major account published since 1961.

Donald Knox's *The Korean War* (New York, 1985) is an oral history of the first six months as experienced by infantrymen and marines. It offers a gripping account of the war as seen from a rifle pit.

Clay Blair's *The Forgotten War* (New York, 1988) is a combat history that is formidable in its grasp of detail, focusing closely on the personalities involved, down to battalion level. The result is an important study not only of the Korean War but of the U.S. Army in the early 1950s.

Russell A. Gugeler, *Combat Actions in Korea* (Washington, D.C., 1954), examines the actions of platoons and companies. This is one of the essential half-dozen works on what battle was like. Every engagement (there are twenty altogether) is clearly described, intelligently appraised, on the basis of interviews with survivors shortly after the events described.

Inch'ŏn is recounted and authoritatively analyzed in Robert D. Heinl, Jr., *Victory at High Tide* (Philadelphia, 1968). Eric Hammel, *Chosin: Heroic Ordeal of the Korean War* (New York, 1981), provides a clear, workmanlike account. The key role played by Chesty Puller in that successful disengagement is described in Burke Davis, *Marine!* (Boston, 1962).

Allen S. Whiting, *China Crosses the Yalu* (New York, 1960), attempts to fathom the reasons for Chinese intervention. Until Chinese archives are opened to genuine scholars, these have to be guessed at. The chief merit of Whiting's study is the evidence he marshals for Chinese reluctance to become involved.

S.L.A. Marshall's *The River and the Gauntlet* (New York, 1953) is an account of the defeat of the Eighth Army in November 1950 that concentrates on the near-destruction of the 2nd Infantry Division. This is one of the finest battle studies ever written.

Ridgway tells his own story in Matthew B. Ridgway with Hal B. Martin, *Soldier* (New York, 1956), with becoming modesty, characteristic forcefulness and more than a little style.

Arthur M. Schlesinger and Richard H. Rovere's *The General and the President* (New York, 1952) was written close to MacArthur's dramatic firing and exaggerates whatever "threat" he might have posed to the Constitution. John M. Spanier's *The Truman-MacArthur Controversy* (Cambridge, Massachusetts, 1959) is a more objective account, based on exhaustive research.

The part played by Marshall, however, only became clear with the recent publication of Forrest D. Pogue's *George C. Marshall: Statesman, 1945–1959* (New York, 1987), the fourth and concluding volume in this monumental biography.

Walter G. Hermes's *Truce Tent and Fighting Front* (Washington, D.C., 1965) is the official army history of the last two years of the war. It is a tale of one damned ridge after another.

The official history of the flyers' contribution is R. Frank Futrell's *The United States Air Force in Korea,* revised edition (Washington, D.C., 1983). It must be the most lavishly illustrated official history ever produced. It is a well-written work, even so. James T. Stewart, editor, *Airpower—The Decisive Force in Korea* (Chicago, 1957), is a popular account, written by USAF officers, covering all aspects of the air war.

James A. Field, Jr., *History of United States Naval Operations, Korea* (Washington, D.C., 1962), is the official navy history. It emphasizes that the navy's main contribution was air missions; as does an earlier semiofficial history, M. C. Cagle and J. A. Manson, *The Sea War in Korea* (Annapolis, 1957). Richard P. Hallion, *The Naval Air War in Korea* (Baltimore, 1986), concentrates on this in a well-written, well-researched work.

Prisoners of war, in particular Americans in captivity, were the subject of a sensational work that portrayed them as the weak-willed objects of Communist brainwashing: Eugene Kinkaid, *In Every War but One* (New York, 1959). A more level-headed treatment of the POW issue was written in rebuttal: Albert D. Biderman, *March to Calumny* (New York, 1963).

Exactly how the war was brought to a conclusion remains controversial, but there can be little doubt that the threat to use nuclear weapons played a part; possibly a decisive one. Dwight D. Eisenhower, *Mandate for Change, 1953–1956* (Garden City, New York, 1956), is understandably circumspect. Stephen E. Ambrose, *Eisenhower: The President* (New York, 1985), gives a somewhat fuller account. Rosemary Foot's *The Wrong War* (Ithaca, New York, 1985) is a scholarly study of high-level policy-making during the war that is especially interesting in its conclusions about the atomic threat.

For a conflict that is variously described as forgotten or unknown, Korea seems remarkably well provided with general accounts. These include Robert

Leckie, *Conflict* (New York, 1962), now somewhat dated; T. R. Fehrenbach, *This Kind of War* (New York, 1963), also dated, but valuable all the same as the work of an infantry officer who served there and for its vivid brief accounts of small unit actions; David Rees, *Korea: The Limited War* (New York, 1964), provides one of the best-balanced, stylish narratives of the high-level politics of the war; Edgar O'Ballance's *Korea 1950–1953* (London, 1969) is an excellent short history of the struggle by a distinguished war correspondent who saw it from beginning to end; Robert R. Simmons, *The Strained Alliance: Peking, Pyongyang, Moscow and the Korean War* (Glencoe, Illinois, 1975), presents it as a civil war, which is credible, but portrays the Inmun Gun as liberators, which is pushing credulity pretty hard; Joseph C. Goulden's *Korea: The Untold Story* (New York, 1982) rarely strays from Tokyo and Washington, portraying the war as it was fought at headquarters; Callum MacDonald's *Korea: The War Before Vietnam* (London, 1986) is the work of a British scholar who gives the Chinese and North Koreans the benefit of every doubt, the United States the benefit of none; Bevin Alexander's *Korea: The First War We Lost* (New York, 1986) is by a combat historian in Korea and offers mainly a straightforward narrative of army operations; Max Hastings's *The Korean War* (New York, 1987) is written from a British perspective but offers something new—interviews with Chinese veterans of the war.

18. Nuclear Abundance

The new alliance's daunting problems and the search for solutions are authoritatively narrated by one of Eisenhower's deputies, Hastings L. Ismay, in *NATO: The First Five Years, 1949–1954* (New York, 1955).

John Robinson Beal, *John Foster Dulles* (New York, 1957), is fairly evenhanded; Townsend Hoopes, *The Devil and John Foster Dulles* (Boston, 1973), is critical to the verge of being hostile. Beal is good on explaining the man, Hoopes on analyzing the policies. Samuel F. Wells, Jr., "The Origins of Massive Retaliation," *Political Science Quarterly*, XCVI (Spring 1981), is a sharp, iconoclastic and persuasive reinterpretation.

The development of SAC and its air-atomic strategy is set out with clarity and authority in volume 2 of the official air force history by R. Frank Futrell, *Ideas, Concepts, Doctrine: A History of Basic Thinking in the US Air Force, 1907–1964* (Maxwell Air Force Base, 1972). This is an essential source, but it has taken academic researchers using the Freedom of Information Act to unearth some of the details on targeting that the air force would have preferred to keep to itself. The most effective of these researchers has been David Rosenberg, who produced three key articles: "American Atomic Strategy and the H-Bomb Decision," *Journal of American History*, LXVI (June 1979); "A Smoking, Radiating Ruin at the End of Two Hours," *International Security*, VI (Winter 1981–82); and "The Origins of Overkill," *International Security*, VII (Spring 1982).

The creator and driving force behind SAC for more than a decade was Curtis LeMay. The biography of him by Thomas Coffey, *Iron Eagle* (New York, 1986), is based on extensive interviews and is essentially an inside account of this daunting organization.

There is a good, objective survey of the challenges facing the makers of strategy in the period between World War Two and Vietnam: Urs Schwarz, *American Strategy* (Garden City, New York, 1966).

The rise of the civilian strategist is traced in two superbly researched works, Fred Kaplan, *The Wizards of Armageddon* (New York, 1982), and Gregg Herken, *Counsels of War* (New York, 1985).

To understand the kind of thinking such strategists produced, the key texts include Henry Kissinger's *Nuclear Weapons and Foreign Policy* (New York, 1957) and Bernard Brodie's *Strategy in the Missile Age* (Princeton, 1959), which try to provide theories for using battlefield nuclear weapons, and Herman Kahn's *On Thermonuclear War* (Princeton, 1960), a massive tome that attempts to do the same for strategic weapons.

The army's hostility to the air-atomic strategy forms the bedrock of James M. Gavin, *War and Peace in the Space Age* (New York, 1958). The plea for more battlefield nuclear weapons for the army, to give it a share of nuclear abundance, is made forcefully in Maxwell D. Taylor, *The Uncertain Trumpet* (New York, 1960).

The uneasy relationship between senior military men and civilian superiors such as Wilson provides much of the human interest material in works such as Carl Borklund, *Men of the Pentagon: From Forrestal to McNamara* (New York, 1966); William R. Kintner, *Forging a New Sword: A Study of the Department of Defense* (New York, 1958); and Jack Raymond, *Power at the Pentagon* (New York, 1964).

The army's missile program—its problems and achievements—is described by the man who ran it in the 1950s, John B. Medaris, with Arthur Gordon, *Countdown for Decision* (New York, 1960).

Gary Powers provided an autobiographical account of the U-2 missions, including his own last flight, in a work written in collaboration with Curt Gentry, *Operation Overflight* (New York, 1970). Michael R. Beschloss, *Mayday* (New York, 1986), is the most thorough account but, as he remarks, there remains "a fog of doubt" about how Powers was brought down. The satellite program is described in a remarkable work of history and investigative journalism, William E. Burrows, *Deep Black* (New York, 1986).

Khrushchev's conversations with Mao, and Mao's hair-raising views on nuclear war, are to be found in Nikita S. Khrushchev, *Khrushchev Remembers,* translated by Strobe Talbot (Boston, 1971); and Stuart Schram, "The 'Military Deviation' of Mao-Tse-Tung," *Problems of Communism,* I, 1964.

The career of Hyman Rickover is described in detail in a work that seems torn between admiration for the man's achievements and profound distaste for his personality: Norman Polmar and Thomas B. Allen, *Rickover* (New York, 1982). A dispassionate general account of the rise of the nuclear navy is to be found in Paul B. Ryan, *First Line of Defense: The US Navy Since 1945* (Palo Alto, 1981).

Eisenhower's account of his second term is *Waging Peace, 1956–1961* (Garden City, New York, 1965). It has a somewhat bittersweet flavor. There are two excellent analytical accounts of Eisenhower as he struggled to create coherent defense and foreign policies at a time when nuclear weapons were making professional military men rethink national strategy. Both are by men who served the president: Emmet John Hughes, *Ordeal of Power* (New York, 1964), and Arthur Larson, *Eisenhower: The President Nobody Knew* (New York, 1969).

Henry L. Trewhitt's *McNamara: His Ordeal at the Pentagon* (New York, 1971) is, as the subtitle suggests, sympathetic. Not so is David Halberstam's *The Best and the Brightest* (New York, 1972), a massive study of the policymaking that got the United States to fight a major war in Vietnam. McNamara is the central figure in Halberstam's book, and described as "a liar" and "a fool." McNamara's memoir of his time in office, Robert S. McNamara's *The Essence of Security* (New York, 1968), is a curiously empty work, but in the later *Blundering into Disaster* (New York, 1986) he makes plain his profound repugnance at nuclear weapons and his enduring fear of a preemptive strike. He presses hard for a pledge of "no first use."

David K. Betts's *Soldiers, Statesmen and Cold War Crises* (Cambridge, Massachusetts, 1977) is a pioneering study of the effect of military advice on postwar policy makers such as McNamara and Kennedy. According to Lawrence J. Korb, *The Joint Chiefs of Staff: The First 25 Years* (Bloomington, Indiana, 1976), that advice has often been so mealymouthed as to be useless.

Desmond Ball, *The Politics of Force Levels* (Berkeley and Los Angeles, 1980), demonstrates convincingly that McNamara and Kennedy paid no attention to military advice in deciding to increase American strategic forces. Another key work in understanding how the Triad evolved is Paul Bracken's *The Command and Control of Nuclear Forces* (New Haven, 1983), which is concerned with the fragility of command and control to a degree that may not be wholly justified.

Roger Hilsman's *To Move a Nation* (Garden City, New York, 1967) is an insider's account of policy-making in the Kennedy administration. Its unreality and lack of perspective led to his departure. That shortage of realism and perspective is dissected in depth in Peter Wyden, *Bay of Pigs* (New York, 1979).

The two essential works on the Cuban missile crisis are Robert F. Kennedy, *Thirteen Days* (New York, 1969), and Elie Abel, *The Missile Crisis* (Philadelphia, 1966).

The slippery slope down which the United States slid into Vietnam is narrated in depth by Halberstam; by Robert Shaplen, *The Lost Revolution: The US in Vietnam, 1954–1966;* and by Bernard Fall, *The Two Viet-Nams* (New York, 1967). David Halberstam's *The Making of a Quagmire* (New

York, 1965) is a brilliant piece of reporting from the field in the early 1960s; one that accurately foretold disasters to come.

The nature of the struggle, as seen from the other side, is spelled out in Vo Nguyen Giap, *People's War, People's Army* (New York, 1962); Wilfred Burchett, *Vietnam: The Inside Story of the Vietnam War* (New York, 1965), the work of an Australian journalist sympathetic to the Viet Cong and well connected with Asian Communists; Fernand Gignon, *Les Américains face aux Vietcong* (Paris, 1965), by a perceptive French journalist familiar with Vietnam; and by Douglas Pike, *Viet Cong* (Cambridge, Massachusetts, 1966), by a leading American scholar working for the government.

Maxwell D. Taylor's *Swords and Plowshares* (New York, 1972) is largely a frank memoir of his time as Kennedy's chief military adviser and as ambassador to South Vietnam at a critical stage in the growing American commitment.

Arthur M. Schlesinger, Jr., *A Thousand Days* (Boston, 1965), and Theodore Sorenson's *Kennedy* (New York, 1966) are important biographical accounts that are good on nearly everything but Kennedy's handling of Vietnam. This was his hostage to fortune and they were aware of the vulnerability of his reputation if the war turned out badly. William J. Rust's *Kennedy in Vietnam* (New York, 1985) is an important work. It focuses on American involvement in Diem's overthrow.

Lyndon B. Johnson's *The Vantage Point: Perspective of the Presidency* (New York, 1971) is a memoir that is bland, sanitized, misleading and false. It is hard to see why he even bothered to write it; assuming he did.

William C. Westmoreland's *A Soldier Reports* (New York, 1976) is good, in parts. It amounts to a memorable self-portrait of a man who had all of the information he needed to know the war was hopeless, but so conditioned by patriotism, ambition and loyalty to the army that he simply refused to draw the obvious conclusion.

The most important single source of materials on decision-making on Vietnam under Kennedy and Johnson is undoubtedly the famous *Pentagon Papers,* of which the most complete version is *The Senator Gravel Edition— The Pentagon Papers,* 4 volumes (Boston, 1971). What is truly remarkable is that the bulk of these reports provides overwhelming evidence that the policy of Americanizing the war and escalating it was doomed to fail. It tells its own tale of good advice, sound reasoning and solid information persistently, almost willfully ignored.

19. Withdrawal Pains

There is really only one serious history of Kennedy's favorite troops: Shelby L. Stanton, *Green Berets at War: US Army Special Forces in Southeast Asia, 1956–1975* (San Rafael, California, 1986). Aaron Bank's *From OSS to Green Berets* (San Rafael, 1986) offers a uniquely personal and historical perspective. Robin Moore's *The Green Berets* (New York, 1965) is a work of fiction, based on incidents that occurred in Vietnam in the early 1960s.

Philip Caputo's *A Rumor of War* (New York, 1977) is an autobiographical account by one of the first marine officers to fight in Vietnam. It is a searing narrative of fear, frustration and failure. The perspective of the ablest marine general on the scene, a man Caputo admired greatly, is offered in Lewis Walt, *Strange War, Strange Strategy* (New York, 1970).

The sky cavalry story is told authoritatively by one of the officers who pioneered this innovation: John J. Tolson, *Airmobility 1961–1971* (Washington, D.C., 1973). This is one of the more important "Vietnam Studies" that, for the present, has to take the place of the long-awaited official army history of the war, projected to run to 20 volumes. To date, only one volume has appeared: Ronald Spector, *Advice and Support: The Early Years 1944–1960* (Washington, D.C., 1983). Largely an account of the Military Assistance Advisory Group, it also makes clear the army's resistance to intervention. There is a good academic study of the sky cavalry: Frederick A. Bergerson, *The Army Gets an Air Force* (Baltimore, 1980).

Robert C. Mason's *Chickenhawk* (New York, 1983) is more than a fine account of what it was like to fly a helicopter in air assaults in the Central Highlands in 1965–66. This is one of the best war memoirs of the twentieth century.

Westmoreland's attempts to formulate a strategy are described in *A Soldier Reports.* He makes it clear that what he got from the president and the secretary of defense was not guidance but what he saw as constant interference. Blair Clark, "Westmoreland Re-appraised," *Harper's,* November 1970, is based on two interviews, one given at the start of his assignment to Saigon, the other at the end. Clark and Westy were old friends and for once Westmoreland lowered his guard.

Harry Summers's *On Strategy* (Carlisle, Pennsylvania, 1981) is a semiofficial army critique of the bankruptcy of strategic thinking on Vietnam. Betts's *Soldiers, Statesmen and Cold War Crises* and Halberstam's *The Best and the Brightest* both contain some fascinating vignettes of powerful civilians and hand-wringing senior commanders trying to formulate strategy. Best of all, however, is Herbert Y. Schandler, *The Unmaking of a President* (Princeton, 1977). Based in part on interviews with Earle G. Wheeler, the picture it conveys of the Johnson White House as the Vietnam command post is devastating.

Shelby L. Stanton's *The Rise and Fall of an American Army* (San Rafael, California, 1985) is a superb battlefield history of the war. This is one of the essential works. Andrew F. Krepinevich, Jr., *The Army in Vietnam* (Baltimore, 1986), offers an excellent analysis of what went wrong and why.

Albert N. Garland's *Infantry in Vietnam,* revised edition (Nashville, 1982) is a collection of short studies of small unit actions in 1965–66; despite the title these are not limited to the infantry. Bernard Rogers's *Cedar Falls–Junction City: A Turning Point* (Washington, D.C., 1974) is an authoritative account of these major operations. S.L.A. Marshall's *Battles in the Monsoon* (New York, 1967) is a vivid narrative of some of the clashes in the Highlands in 1966.

The best account of the Tet offensive is undoubtedly Don Oberdorfer's *Tet!* (Garden City, New York, 1971), which combines excellent description with incisive appraisal. Kenneth William Nolan, *The Battle for Hue* (San Rafael, California, 1983), tells the story of the marines' hardest fight in Vietnam with astonishing sureness of touch and mastery of detail for a military historian aged nineteen!

Moyers S. Shore II, *The Battle for Khe Sanh* (Washington, D.C., 1969), and William Pearson, *War in the Northern Provinces 1966–1968* (Washington, D.C., 1975), provide a clear and complete account of the battles for this key position.

David Donovan's *Once a Warrior King* (New York, 1985) is a vivid, and sometimes moving, memoir of one man's war down in the Delta in 1969. Michael Lee Lanning, *The Only War We Had* (New York, 1987), recounts his experiences day by day that year leading an infantry platoon.

Carl Berger, editor, *The United States Air Force in Southeast Asia 1961–1973* (Washington, D.C., 1977), is a splendidly illustrated, semiofficial history of the air force's role in the war. Randy Cunningham and Jeff Ethel, *Fox Two* (Mesa, Arizona, 1984), tell what it was like to fly as a navy fighter pilot. John Trotti's *Phantom Over Vietnam* (San Rafael, California, 1984) is by a marine pilot flying ground support missions. Peter B. Mersky and Norman Polmar's *The Naval Air War in Vietnam* (Baltimore, 1986) provides a well-illustrated short history of the war as fought from carrier decks. There is a good introduction to everything involving the air war—missiles, electronics, men and planes—in Lon O. Nordeen, Jr., *Air Warfare in the Missile Age* (Washington, D.C., 1986).

John M. Van Dyke's *North Vietnam's Strategy for Survival* (Palo Alto, 1972) is a careful and impressive study of how North Vietnam learned to cope with the bombing. James Cameron's *Here is Your Enemy* (New York, 1968) is a protest against the campaign by a left-leaning British journalist, containing some telling descriptions of how the bombing appeared from ground level.

Seymour Hersh's "How We Ran the Secret Air War in Laos," *New York Times Magazine,* October 29, 1972, is a tragicomic account of the failure of air power to cut the Ho Chi Minh Trail.

Ulysses S. Grant Sharp's *Strategy for Defeat* (San Rafael, California, 1978) is the indignant memoir of the man who ran the air war, the commander in chief, Pacific, from a desk in Hawaii. Sharp bitterly protests against "graduated response," holding it responsible for increasing American casualties and leading to ultimate defeat.

Wallace Terry's *Bloods* (New York, 1984) is an impressive oral history of blacks in Vietnam, by a black war correspondent. Bernard C. Nalty's *Strength for the Fight* (New York, 1986) is a history of blacks in the armed forces, but concentrates largely on the period since 1945. Still valuable is Richard C. Dalfiume's *Desegregation in the US Armed Forces* (Columbia, Missouri, 1969) for the historical background to Vietnam.

Bill Gulley's *Breaking Cover* (New York, 1981) is an account of the little-known White House Military Office. Gulley has some good stories to tell about the Nixon White House and antiwar protestors. Henry Kissinger's *White House Years* (Boston, 1979) is a valuable work on his time as national security adviser in the first Nixon administration, when the war was the first order of business. The view Kissinger offers of political-military-bureaucratic relationships in modern America is probably the most revealing published to date.

The Nixon-Kissinger role in the destruction of Cambodia is the subject of a polemical history: William Shawcross, *Sideshow* (London, 1979).

Lawrence Baskir and William Strauss's *Chance and Circumstance* (New York, 1978) is an authoritative history of the Vietnam era draft, draftees, draft evaders and draft avoiders.

Seymour Hersh's *My Lai 4* (New York, 1970) is by the journalist who broke the story after the army spent a year trying to cover up, but good as Hersh's book is, the story is more effectively told by Richard Hammer, *One Morning in the War* (New York, 1970).

Edward L. King's *The Death of the Army* (New York, 1972) is a work in which there is more than a little personal anguish. William L. Hauser's *America's Army in Crisis* (Baltimore, 1973) is not exactly an elegy, but at times comes close to it. David Cortright's *Soldiers in Revolt* (Garden City, New York, 1975) is well researched, and its sympathies are clearly not with the army. Ward Just's *Military Men* (New York, 1970) is a brilliantly written portrait of the army during the withdrawal from Vietnam, as discipline and morale broke down.

Stuart Loory's *Defeated: Inside America's Military Machine* (New York, 1973) is a graphic view of the military as a whole at about the time it touched bottom.

No Quang Truong's *The Easter Offensive of 1972* (Washington, D.C., 1977), is a "Vietnam Study" that offers a broad outline of the North Vietnamese attack and the ARVN's fight back. William E. Le Gro, *Vietnam from Ceasefire to Capitulation* (Washington, D.C., 1981), tells the story of the last two years effectively.

Van Tien Dung's *Our Great Spring Victory* (New York, 1977) is a revealing North Vietnamese account of the final offensive. Alan Dawson's *55 Days: The Fall of South Vietnam* (New York, 1977) is a vivid, journalistic account. So too is David Butler's *The Fall of Saigon* (New York, 1985).

There is a wide variety of general works on the war; nearly all written from a strongly held view that the war was wicked or stupid, a mistake or a plot, a crime of capitalism and imperialism, or a worthy effort by idealists to save South Vietnam from Communist tyranny. A truly objective history of the Vietnam War has yet to be written, but it will no doubt appear one day.

Meanwhile, there are some impressive major histories to draw on. Frances Fitzgerald, *Fire in the Lake* (Boston, 1976), has a tendency to romanticize the NLF and Ho Chi Minh, but her depiction of Americans failing to comprehend the Vietnamese situation and thereby making a mess of everything they attempted is persuasive. Dave R. Palmer's *Summons of the Trumpet* (San Rafael, California, 1978) is a history of the war written by a general with many perceptive points to make on tactics and strategy, but clearly admiring of Westmoreland and the ARVN.

Guenter Lewy's *America in Vietnam* (New York, 1978) is the nearest there is to an objective work, but beneath the scholar's detachment runs an undercurrent of disdain for military men. Similar criticism can be leveled at Stanley Karnow's *Vietnam: A History* (New York, 1983), the work of a distinguished journalist.

Bruce Palmer, Jr.'s, *The 25-Year War* (Louisville, Kentucky, 1985) is by Westmoreland's deputy commander. It is remarkably evenhanded, written from deep immersion in the war, and the product of prolonged reflection upon it.

From a strictly human interest point of view, four outstanding accounts are Michael Herr, *Dispatches* (New York, 1977), a collection of stunning, impressionistic pieces; Ronald Glasser, *365 Days* (New York, 1971), the often harrowing recollections of an army doctor; Al Santoli, *Everything We Had* (New York, 1981), one of the first oral histories of the war, and still one of the best; and Truong Nhu Tang, *Journal of a Vietcong* (New York, 1986), by a dedicated VC cadre who was in on the foundation of the NFL and the ultimate victory in Saigon, only to discover that Communist rule meant oppression, corruption and the substitution of one brutal oligarchy for another.

20. Tomorrow Began Yesterday

The armed forces in the post-Vietnam era provoked fierce criticism. James Fallows's *National Defense* (New York, 1982) describes itself as "an introduction" to the modern military, but "indictment" would be more accurate. Edward M. Luttwak, *The Pentagon and the Art of War* (New York, 1985), excoriates the tendencies to self-indulgence and the exaltation of management over leadership. Arthur T. Hadley's *The Straw Giant* (New York, 1986) is an unremitting catalog of failures, by someone who cares deeply about the armed forces.

Jimmy Carter's *Keeping Faith* (New York, 1982) is unusual among presidential memoirs for the number of mistakes admitted to, but it shows a surprising lack of depth in military affairs for an Annapolis graduate. Zbigniew Brzezinski's *Power and Principle* (New York, 1983) is the memoirs of Carter's national security adviser and therefore an important source on the defense policy issues of the late 1970s.

Charlie A. Beckwith and Donald Knox's *Delta Force* (New York, 1983) is an authoritative account of the failed mission to rescue the hostages, but a better analysis of what went wrong and why is Paul B. Ryan's *The Iranian Hostage Mission* (Annapolis, 1985).

The creation and management of counterterrorist forces is vividly described in James Adams, *Secret Armies* (London, 1988), which also contains good accounts of Grenada and Lebanon.

The military buildup under Ronald Reagan is traced in accounts of the two most important weapons systems revived under his presidency: John Edwards, *Super Weapon: The Making of MX* (New York, 1982), and Nick Kotz, *Wild Blue Yonder: Money, Politics and the B-1 Bomber* (New York, 1988).

Frank Barnaby, *The Automated Battlefield* (New York, 1986), provides a valuable *tour d'horizon* of the precision revolution.

The emergence of AirLand Battle and Follow-On Forces Attack is authoritatively described, and analyzed, in Thomas B. Cardwell III, "Follow-On Forces Attack," *Military Review,* LXVI, No. 2 (February 1986); William R. Richardson, "FM 100-5: The AirLand Battle in 1986," *Military Review,* LXVI, No. 3 (March 1986); and John J. Romjue, "AirLand Battle: The Historical Background," *ibid.*

Continuing developments in AirLand Battle, FOFA and related doctrines and weapons systems can be followed by reference to a recent addition to defense publications: Joseph Kunzel, editor, *American Defense Annual,* volumes 1–4 (Columbus, Ohio, 1985–88). Useful too is Richard Simpkin's *Race to the Swift: Thoughts on 21st Century Warfare* (London, 1985), by a British armored division commander noted for his deep knowledge of military history and his mastery of leading-edge ideas.

James L. George, editor, *The United States Navy: The View from the Mid-1980s* (Boulder, Colorado, 1985), contains some remarkably informative contributions on what the navy is doing and intends to do.

The report of The Commission of Long-term Integrated Strategy, *Discriminate Deterrence* (Washington, D.C., 1988), contains some radical shifts in attitude and perception. It is a testament to nuclear anxieties.

Gerard Smith's *Doubletalk* (New York, 1980) is an interesting account of SALT I and the attempt by each side to outfinesse the other. Strobe Talbot, *Endgame* (New York, 1979), does much the same, but with a little more flair, for SALT II. Talbot also wrote a seminal work on the first Reagan administration's attempts to negotiate a strategic arms agreement, *Deadly Gambits* (New York, 1984), which can only have been written with considerable cooperation from the American negotiators, and some help from the Soviets.

Ralph Lapp's *Arms Beyond Doubt: The Tyranny of Weapons Technology* (New York, 1970) and Herbert York's *Race to Oblivion* (New York, 1970) were two of the first works to alert the public to the problems, and the dangers, posed by the technological imperative. Both Lapp and York were men with inside knowledge of the nuclear arms race. More recently, Robert S. McNamara, *Blundering Into Disaster* (New York, 1986), has put in a passionate plea for the country to renounce its faith in technology before it is too late.

Desmond Ball, "Can Nuclear War Be Controlled?" (Adelphi Paper 169) ISS (1981) doubts it. John D. Steinbruner, "Nuclear Decapitation," *Foreign Policy,* XLV (Winter 1981–82), considers the advantages of a certain type of first, or preemptive, strike to be so attractive as to be almost irresistible. William Arkin, "SIOP-6," *Bulletin of the Atomic Scientists,* XXXIV (November 1983), spells out the implications of MIRVed abundance for strategic targeting. So, in greater depth, does Ted Greenwood, *Making the MIRV* (New York, 1975).

On cruise missiles and stealth technology: every month since about 1985 *Aviation Week and Space Technology* and *Jane's Defense Weekly* have run at least one, often two or three articles on both these new technologies. Newspapers such as *The New York Times* and *Washington Post* also run features on them from time to time. And what goes for stealth and cruise missiles also goes for SDI.

Paul Bracken, *Command and Control* (New Haven, 1983), and Daniel Ford, *The Button* (New York, 1985), emphasize the fragility of existing arrangements as they apply to SAC and the ICBM force, but in doing so they tend to slight the bottom line—the SSBNs. Both, however, make clear the integration of the warning system with the control of the Triad. That warning system is elucidated in two brilliant examples of investigative journalism: William Burrows, *Deep Black* (New York, 1987), on satellite reconnaissance; and James Bamford, *The Puzzle Palace* (Boston, 1983), on the workings of the National Security Agency—ten times the size of the CIA and the real power in American intelligence.

General

Walter Millis's *Arms and Men: A Study in American Military History* (New York, 1956) is a pioneering attempt to bring out the connections linking America's wars and the evolution of American society. Critically acclaimed and still in print, it is unfortunately so concerned with the danger of nuclear weapons that it is inclined to read the present too readily into the past. Even so, Millis's attempt to explore new pathways into military history made a difference to modern ideas about it.

The most popular general account is Robert Leckie, *The Wars of America,* 2 volumes, revised edition (New York, 1981). This offers an exciting narrative, with plenty of color and striking anecdotes. To the extent that it has an interpretation it is Uptonian. Leckie's interest, though, is really in storytelling.

The best recent synoptic account was unfortunately cut short by the author's death. T. Harry Williams's *The History of American Wars* (New York, 1979) concludes abruptly with World War One. Had it been completed there can be little doubt that this major work from one of the country's premier military historians would have been an important contribution.

Russell Weigley, *Towards an American Army: American Military Thought from Washington to Marshall* (New York, 1962), outlines a conflict between professional military men and amateurs that was immortalized by Upton, and carries the story on to show how important it was right up to World War Two. Weigley's later volume, *The American Way of War* (New York, 1973), is a sharp critique of strategy in every American war. The approach taken is reminiscent to Millis's, and so is the conclusion—that war "has lost all useful purpose."

Warren Hassler's *With Shield and Sword* (Ames, Iowa, 1982) is strongly Uptonian, pushing the unpreparedness thesis vigorously. Allen Millet and Peter Maslowski's *For the Common Defense* (New York, 1984) is a long, dense, highly praised survey from 1607 to 1983. It offers no fundamental reinterpretation and makes little attempt to link American military history to that of the larger society. For reliability and thoroughness, though, it can hardly be faulted.

Samuel P. Huntington's *The Soldier and the State* (Cambridge, Massachusetts, 1957) is the work of a preeminent political scientist. It is both more limited and more ambitious than the usual survey of military history. More limited in that there is almost nothing about battles and wars, more ambitious in the depth of analysis. Huntington sees American military history revolving around the tension created on the one hand by the need for military security and on the other by the demands of a liberal democracy to be free of the burdens and constraints that military preparedness requires.

The generations of Americans who have gone to war are studied in an impressionistic work: Victor Hicken, *The American Fighting Man* (New York, 1969). It is a book that brings out the characteristics that over two centuries distinguished American servicemen from their allies and their foes.

There is a wonderful account of the return to civilian life of veterans of the Revolutionary War, the Civil War and World War One: Dixon Wecter, *When Johnny Comes Marching Home* (Boston, 1944).

Finally, there is the memoir of the doyen of American military historians, a man whose work not only enlightened the armchair strategist but influenced the way his countrymen fought: S.L.A. Marshall, *Bringing Up the Rear* (San Rafael, California, 1979). In the course of rising from being an eighteen-year-old private in World War One to wearing a general's star by the time he went to Vietnam, Marshall had a uniquely privileged view of American armed forces from the inside. The fact that the memoir was published posthumously (like McClellan's) means it needs to be read with care. Even so, it provides a unique overview of Americans at war in the twentieth century.

INDEX

ABOUT THE AUTHOR

After graduating from high school in Wheaton, Illinois, GEOFFREY PERRET joined the U.S. Army. He holds degrees from the University of Southern California and Harvard, and studied law at the University of California at Berkeley. His first book was a highly acclaimed account of the home front in World War Two, *Days of Sadness, Years of Triumph.*